A Textbook of
Human Resource Management

GEORGE THOMASON

George Thomason was born and brought up in the English Lake District. He read economics and management at the Universities of Sheffield and Toronto and obtained his doctorate from the University of Wales in 1963. He joined the staff of the Industrial Relations Department of University College Cardiff in 1953 and remained there (with an interlude in industrial management in the early 1960s) until his retirement in 1984. He held various research and teaching posts before being appointed Montague Burton Professor of Industrial Relations and head of the Department of Industrial Relations and Management Studies in 1969. He was Dean of the Faculty of Economic and Social Studies from 1971 to 1973 and Deputy Principal for the Humanities from 1974 to 1977. He was elected a Fellow of University College Cardiff in 1980.

He served for two periods as a member of the Management and Industrial Relations Committee of the Social Science Research Council. He has served as an industrial relations arbitrator and as a member of a number of Wages Councils and the two health service pay review bodies. He is an appointed person under the Employment Agencies Act, 1973. He has been actively associated with the Institute of Personnel Management and the British Institute of Management for many years. He is the author of a number of books on management and community development.

On retirement he was appointed Visiting Professor in the Department of Behaviour in Organisations at the University of Lancaster and has held part-time teaching appointments at the University of Wales Institute of Science and Technology and the West Glamorgan Institute of Higher Education.

Professor Thomason is married to a Cardiff solicitor and has two children.

A TEXTBOOK OF HUMAN RESOURCE MANAGEMENT

George F Thomason

Institute of Personnel Management

For my daughter, Sian Elizabeth.

First published 1988
Reprinted 1990

This book replaces the highly successful *A Textbook of Personnel Management* which was published in 1975 and subsequently appeared in four editions, the last in 1981.

Phototypeset by Action Typesetting Limited, Gloucester
and printed in Great Britain by
Short Run Press Ltd., Exeter.

British Library Cataloguing in Publication Data

Thomason, George F. (George Frederick), *1927–*
    A textbook of human resource management.
    1.   Great Britain. Personnel management
    I. Title
    658.3′00941

ISBN 0-85292-403-8

Contents

List of tables

List of figures

Abbreviations used

ACAS	Advisory, Conciliation and Arbitration Service
All ER	All England Law Reports
APEX	Association of Professional, Executive, Clerical and Computer Staffs
ASLEF	Associated Society of Locomotive Engineers and Firemen
ASTMS	Association of Scientific, Technical and Managerial Staffs
AUEW	Amalgamated Union of Engineering Workers
BACIE	British Association for Commercial and Industrial Education
BIM	British Institute of Management
BISAKTA	British Iron, Steel and Kindred Trades' Association
CAC	Central Arbitration Committee (formerly the Industrial Court and the Industrial Arbitration Board (1972–4))
CAWU	Clerical and Administrative Workers' Union, now APEX
CBI	Confederation of British Industry
CIR	Commission on Industrial Relations
C of E Act	Contracts of Employment Act
COHSE	Confederation of Health Service Employees
COIT	Central Office of Industrial Tribunals
DE	Department of Employment
D & HA	Docks and Harbours Act
DHSS	Department of Health and Social Security
EEF	Engineering Employers' Federation
EEPTU	Electrical, Electronics, Telecommunication and Plumbing Trade Union (formerly ETU: Electrical Trades Union)
EP Act	Employment Protection Act
EP (C) Act	Employment Protection (Consolidation) Act, 1978
EPEA	Electrical Power Engineers' Association
GMWU	General and Municipal Workers Union
H & SWA	Health and Safety at Work etc Act

HMSO	Her Majesty's Stationery Office
ICR	Industrial Court Reports
IPM	Institute of Personnel Management
IRLR	Industrial Relations Law Reports
IR Act	Industrial Relations Act 1971
IT	Industrial Tribunal
ITB	Industrial Training Board
ITR	Industrial Tribunal Reports
MBO	Management-by-Objectives
MCB	Management Centre, Bradford
NALGO	National and Local Government Officers' Association
NATSOPA	National Society of Operative Printers and Assistants
NEDO	National Economic Development Office
NGA	National Graphical Association
NIIP	National Institute of Industrial Psychology
NIRC	National Industrial Relations Court, 1972–4
NUBE	National Union of Bank Employees
NUPE	National Union of Public Employees
NUR	National Union of Railwaymen
OD	Organisational Development
PBR	Payment by Results
RCTUEA	Royal Commission on Trade Unions and Employers' Associations (the Donovan Commission)
RP Act	Redundancy Payments Act
SOGAT	Society of Graphical and Allied Trades
TASS	Technical and Supervisory Staffs Section of the AUEW
TGWU	Transport and General Workers Union
TUC	Trades Union Congress
TULR Act	Trade Union and Labour Relations Act, 1974; 1976
USDAW	Union of Shop, Distributive and Allied Workers

Preface

Personnel management as an activity has been with us now for almost 100 years. A century ago, welfare workers inside and outside the factory were still not distinguished from one another, but they did exist. The later emergence of specialist welfare workers in some factories put the occupation on the map. It is now part of the legend that personnel management developed from an original concern with human welfare at work.

Since then, the occupation has extended its activities in response to need and demand and has acquired additional activities by merger with other specialist groups. The demands of two major wars for increased co-operation in industry gave the occupation a boost, and by the 1970s changing social values helped it to acquire most of the attributes of a professional occupation, which was concerned to do well by workers in industry.

The 1980s have been characterised by a further shift in social values. Some see this change as a response to changed economic conditions on a world scale; others see it as a much more parochial response to the power structure which had by then emerged in British industry. Whatever the cause, the effect has been, broadly, to alter the core values accepted by industry in its dealings with workers. The easy assumptions of the preceding quarter-century have been challenged and replaced in many instances.

The change has taken the emphasis from equitable treatment and collective organisation and placed it on recognition of individual responsibility for improved work performance. This has had its implications for personnel management as well as for trade unions. Instead of being focused on equitable treatment of people at work as a basis for achieving improved performance, it is now aimed more often at securing improved performance from people which builds a foundation from which more equitable treatment may be developed.

So far, the movement has not all been in one direction and is in no sense 'complete'. In some instances, the function has been pressured away from a concern with welfare towards a concern with business results; in others, the older values have been sustained. In some instances, the function has been dispersed and pushed back to a concern with local problem-solving (firefighting), but in others, equally prominent, it has been assigned increased status and a broader policy-making role. In particular, in organisations operating at the frontiers of electronic or production technologies, 'personnel' has acquired a greater prominence, and those with relevant knowledge and a proven track record in the area have assumed more dominant roles.

This has led many to speculate on the possibility that organisations with different missions and different working environments may make disparate demands on their human resources − and consequently, on those who claim special expertise in the area. Organisations are seen to be spread through a continuum or a matrix, according to their mission/market position.

As a consequence, personnel management becomes less of a process which has a single, universally relevant focus and more one which is diffuse in its activities and objectives, changing according to its location on the spectrum. It has long flourished on the recognition that individuals are different and require differential treatment: it is now encouraged to recognise that organisations are systematically different from one another and require servicing in different ways.

It has also flourished on the basis of increasing specialisation, but this may also become more muted. The need for fairly mundane administrative activity may well continue but it is likely to become more divorced from policy making. It has long been suggested that the main task of personnel managers is to work themselves out of their jobs as everyone else in the organisation becomes a competent personnel manager. In some parts of the industrial universe, this objective comes close to being realised, and a gap appears to develop between personnel direction and personnel administration. In many organisations, managers other than the personnel specialists are increasingly expected to develop expertise in human resource management, because the necessary commitment of staff cannot be secured in any other way. At the same time, personnel specialists are increasingly expected to contribute to the solution of more general business or mission problems, and, as a consequence, find themselves required to spiral through other specialties during the course of their careers.

This totally new version of the *Textbook of Personnel Management* has been re-titled to take account of developments in human resource management as its main focus. Much of what it contains is familiar to the trained personnel specialist but it is not written exclusively for personnel managers. It is expected that many others, who in the course of achieving their professional qualifications are expected to develop an appreciation of human resource management, will find the contents of material value.

The theme is developed in a way that identifies the relevance of the many methods and techniques of personnel management with the different kinds of situation in which they have to be applied. Little space is devoted to the 'collective' aspects of human resource management, not because current social values tend to be more dismissive of trade unions and their contribution, but because it is intended that this Textbook should be read in conjunction with *The Textbook of Industrial Relations Management* (in which the 'collective' aspects are more fully discussed).

It is constructed in two parts, each with its own introduction – one dealing with the context and the other with the content of human resource management. The first section of the book is devoted to a discussion of the basic concepts which define the context of human resource management. This covers the manner in which work is defined and organised and the way in which human capacities and processes facilitate and limit the use of people as 'human resources' in work settings. Attention is then paid to the framework of cultural values within which industry operates and the ways in which these values are embodied in law and convention and how they are applicable to relationships in the work environment. (This aspect is more fully developed in the *Textbook of Industrial Relations Management*.)

This is followed by a discussion of the manner in which markets and technologies impinge on the definition of working relations, the aim here being to show how opportunities for and limits to managerial decisions and actions are established by the economic and technological circumstances of the particular organisation. This first section concludes with a consideration of the nature of policy as it impinges upon the utilisation and treatment of personnel.

The second part of the book is devoted to the identification of strategies and operations which have been shown to be relevant to the various kinds of work situation. The methods and techniques, which form the stock-in-trade of the personnel specialist, are then considered, starting with those associated with human resource planning, recruitment and selection and moving through those associated with communication, training, and remuneration, and concluding with a discussion of organisational and management development. As far as possible these are related to the strategic circumstances in which they are likely to prove most appropriate.

The concluding chapter highlights some of the main trends

and challenges in this area and gives a broad indication of the limits of any particular style or method of human resource management.

George F Thomason

Part A:
Human Resource Management in Context

'Industry' is a term used to identify that grand transformation process during which 'raw materials' or 'resources' are converted into the 'finished products' (whether goods or services) which people demand. Industry comprises all that purposive human activity which contributes to the production, distribution, and exchange of goods and services which people think they need or want. The term is defined so broadly as to include all those activities which are referred to as 'work' (more strictly, as 'employment work'). This is 'work' which people undertake (usually in association with others) for extrinsic reward or satisfaction, rather than for the sheer (intrinsic) pleasure of doing it.

Industry is an important institution in any society if only because it is a source of both material well-being (wealth and income) and co-operative activity for a large section of the population. Modern industry can only serve these ends of generating wealth and providing opportunities for co-operation by combining many different elements or factors (financial, material, and human) in the production (transformation) process. This process of combination turns all of these things into 'resources' – a term usually defined as anything which contributes to the achievement of an underlying purpose. This is usually carried out by some external agency which we identify as 'management'. Industry thus creates a demand for both human resources and management and associates both with employment work.

'Human resources' are simply 'people' cast in the role of contributors to the production of goods and services (Hayes Report, Department of Employment, 1972). They are essentially individuals or persons endowed and equipped with the usual range of human abilities and attributes. They become 'resources' by virtue of the roles they assume in employment work through which they contribute to the

1

achievement of the economic objectives. They thereby become caught up in a purposive or 'disciplined' activity designed to achieve objectives not necessarily of their own making.

'Management' is at once a group of people who manage and a process of co-ordinating resource contributions. Managers' roles involve organising production and trade activities to satisfy the demands of the citizen-consumer who, in our society, is the final arbiter of what is proper (Brech, 1975, p 5). It involves the combination and organisation of resources and their direction, co-ordination, and control in the interests of generating wealth. The necessary decisions depend upon management's identifying the client need to be served by the provision of products and services (which is how Ansoff (1975) defines the 'mission' of the enterprise). They are implemented through varying processes of coercion, utility manipulation, suggestion, and persuasion of the human resources involved.

Industry

The term industry is used here to include all kinds of work. This work is structured in many ways and is located in enterprises of greater or lesser complexity. It makes different demands for and on people, offering a satisfying challenge to some and dissatisfaction and strain to others. These demands in turn stem from the kind of relationship which the enterprise attempts to develop with its market and the complexity of means (technology) it employs to sustain and develop them.

It is usual to draw distinctions between enterprises according to the principles of their governance. This leads to the separation of private enterprise from public industry or service, and both from voluntary (such as community service bodies) and mutual benefit organisations (such as trade unions). The distinctions are usually associated with the form of control by private stockholders, the State (or government), or elected committees of representatives of interested parties. It is generally thought that these different forms will make systematically different demands upon the people who work within them, because, even if some are concerned directly with profit-making and others not, they are all caught up in the requirement to be efficient (over the longer term if not in the short run).

Similarly, it is common to divide organisations which provide services to identifiable clients or society generally from those which produce and distribute products. In the first category fall such apparently disparate enterprises as the public service, the health service, the hairdresser or the chiropodist. Included in the second

Table 1

*Distribution of the working population
(unadjusted figures)*
Great Britain, December, 1986.   Thousands

Category	Sex	SIC Nos	Number
Working population	All		27,308
of which			
Unemployed	All		3,100
Self-employed persons	All		2,618
HM Forces	All		320
Employed labour force	All		24,207
of which			
Employees in employment	All		21,270
	Male Full-time		11,658
	Male Part-time		866
	Female Full-time		9,612
	Female Part-time		4,227
Employees in Employment		0-9	21,269.7
Agriculture, forestry, fishing		0	312.9
Index of production and construction industries		1-5	6,672.7
of which manufacturing industries		2-4	5,152.1
Service industries		6-9	14,284.0
Agriculture, forestry and fishing		0	312.9
Energy and water supply		1	513.8
Other mineral and ore extraction, etc		2	777.4
Metal goods, engineering and vehicles		3	2,252.3
Other manufacturing industries		4	2,037.7
Construction		5	1,006.9
Distribution, hotels, catering, etc		6	4,318.8
Transport and communication		7	1,339.4
Banking, finance, insurance		8	2,166.3
Other services		9	6,459.5
of which			
* Public administration and defence		91	1,598.7
Sanitary Services		92	389.2
Education		93	1,669.6
Research and development		94	112.7
Medical and other health services		95	1,271.6
Other services		96	761.8
Recreational and cultural services		97	467.7
* Personal services		98	188.1

*excluding members of HM Forces and domestic servants.

Source: Department of Employment *Employment Gazette*, May, 1987, pp S9-S11.

are the workshop and factory industries in which anything from an egg-cup to a generator may be manufactured. The distribution enterprises (wholesalers or warehousers) may appear to fall in between these, being concerned with the distribution of goods as a service. It is not unusual, however, when all of these types are spoken of together, to use the metaphor of 'delivering' a product or service to give some cohesion to the idea that they can be treated alike.

Another common source of categorisation is that which relies upon size. Size can be measured by capital assets (the value of the plant and machinery employed), 'turnover' (the amount of revenue generated), or numbers employed. This last statistic is more relevant in the present context than the others because the extent to which human resources are aggregated is frequently demonstrated to influence behaviours and the impacts of work on people (Acton Society Trust, 1953 and 1957). Further examination of these influences may reveal size as a proxy for other variables such as extent of job fractionalisation or failure to match job design with human needs, but this does not prevent the proxy being used extensively as a shorthand expression. For the purposes of this book, the term 'industry' is used to refer to all of this 'employment work' which engages over 27 million people in Britain (Table 1) and subsumes public and private, manufacturing, and service undertakings.

HUMAN RESOURCES

Industry does not require human beings to exercise their full potential, but human resources which can and will perform work *roles*. Roles are inherently social in that they impute expectations to others. Work roles are defined and described in a manner intended to maximise particular people's contributions to particular wealth-creating objectives. A role is made up of the behaviour or the activity which a person is expected to engage in within some structure of action. Put more simply, it is what a person ought to do or is expected to do in a particular set of circumstances (Homans, 1951, pp 11 – 12). In industry, the role most often delimits a specialist area of activity within which the individual – the role occupier – will be expected to cope with whatever problems or tasks arise.

Role in this normative sense – the prescription of what ought to be done – is to be distinguished from role in the descriptive sense of *performance* – what the incumbent actually does (see Goffman, 1961, p 85), because people do not, for a variety of reasons, always do what they ought or are expected to do. In work, expectations of what the person, a worker, should do can be ascertained from a role prescription (which may or may not be formally expressed as a set of duties or as a 'job description'). Generally, the role prescription can be represented as a set of expectations that the individual will take certain kinds of decision, perform certain specified activities, and otherwise conduct himself or herself in accordance with the policies (or norms and rules) laid down by authority to govern behaviour and relations within the work situation.

The nature of the expectations will vary in a systematic fashion through the hierarchy of roles in the typical work organisation. Some will apply to manual workers at the bottom of the hierarchy and others to the managerial workers at the top of it. The general expectation of manual or routine office workers is that they will perform the work they are hired to do, obey the instructions which are given by those in authority, and help others in the performance of their work. The general expectation of managers is that they will decide what is to be done in the light of external and internal conditions and direct (or steer) subordinates' activities along the desired paths and monitor their progress along them.

It is the human beings' capacity for deciding and acting which makes them a potentially valuable resource to industry. They are normally equipped with a capacity to cope with their environment, material and otherwise, as they progress through life. This aptitude reveals itself most obviously and most generally in an ability to decide what to do in varying circumstances and to put that decision into effect. The first depends largely upon a mental or intellectual capacity and the second upon a motor or muscular capacity; and industry makes use of both to varying extents according to the role occupied.

The Individual

Anyone aspiring to manage human resources must not only understand the management process but also the opportunities and the limits set by these human capacities. This focuses attention on the individual who is to be regarded as a kind of clever computer. Individuals are, of course, much more than that, but use of the analogy of the computer helps to emphasise some fundamental points about human beings as resources.

One major difference is that where a computer needs to be 'operated' by somebody, human beings can operate themselves (even if they are sometimes manipulated by others). The important point to note in this connection is that, as Kelly expressed it, human beings are motivated (or moved to cope with the environment) simply because they are alive. Some such 'movement' can always be relied on, even though it may not be possible to rely upon it being directed towards the ends which someone else (management, for example) might desire.

Given a basic motivation of this highly generalised type, individuals may then be seen to be variously equipped with motor and mental capacities which enable them to cope with their environments. By analogy with the computer they possess:

(a)   a physical shape and structure which incorporates a number of sensory devices capable of taking in messages (whether information or experience) from the environment;

(b)   a built-in operating system, including a language and a memory storage capacity, which allows information and experience to be made sense of and recast or modified to provide operating instructions;

(c)   a built-in motor capacity which permits muscular and nervous activity to be directed at the environment in a controlled way.

Taken together, these provide the individual with a basic capacity for deciding about and acting upon the environment.

They enable individuals interacting with their environments to engage in activity which is similar to that of computers:

(a)   to recognise when a problem exists for them to deal with (using the sensors and capacity for measurement and judgement);

(b)   to search out appropriate solutions (courses of action) relying on both memory and on capacity for creativity;

(c)   to select, in accordance with some internalised scale of priorities or preferences, the most appropriate solution from the alternatives discovered (involving capacities for measurement and comparison); and

(c)   to put this selected course of action into effect (relying, *inter alia*, on muscular, motor, and mechanical capacities).

The Person

This way of thinking about the human being highlights the features in which industry has a main interest. The human being contains much more – for example, in the way of personality or creative capacity – than industry usually demands (although there are some exceptions to this and demand is variable between organisations). A good deal of the human being is therefore unwanted in the work context (see Miller and Form, 1951, Figure 118, p 757). Some of the impedimenta of personality will get in the way of using capacities in work, although the person cannot leave the unwanted bits at home in order to fit exactly the industrial mould.

The whole person, therefore, possesses certain 'passive' attributes (such as stature or personality) and a number of capacities and capabilities of a more 'active' kind (such as ability to drive a bus or to type), which can be usefully classified under four headings:

1   *Physique* refers to the physical shape and size of the individual which indicate something of what he or she is and what he or she may be capable of physically. Physique indicates how tall or short, weak or strong a person may be.

2   *Physical capability* refers to the things people can do using this 'physique'. The physical dimensions support or augment the physical 'health' (in its broadest sense) of the individual and the acquired muscular and sensory abilities and skills which vitally affect perception of the environment and ability to act upon it.

3   *Personality or Character* is the mental equivalent of the physique and indicates something of the kind of person he or she *is* intellectually and emotionally: either bright or dull, shy or out-going, good or bad, honest or dishonest, pleasant or unpleasant, aggressive or submissive, co-operative or awkward. It includes the variety of the individual's traits or attributes − his or her 'character, temperament, intellect and physique' (Eysenck, 1960, p 2) − which are capable of being deduced from examin-ation of and reflection on expressive behaviour (see Maslow, 1970, p 133; Mischel, 1971, p 4). Personality or character has some utility in the industrial context because it identifies the individual's 'unique adjustment to his environment' (Allport, 1957, p 48; Eysenck, 1960, p 2), permitting some prediction of 'what a person will do in a given situation' (Cattell, 1950, p 21).

4   *Capacity or Capability* has to do with the extent to which the individual is able to cope with his or her environment. It relates to what the individual *does* (is capable of doing) as distinct from what the individual *is*. It is typically revealed by 'instrumental' or 'coping' behaviours (*ibid*).

Any of these may function as either resources for or constraints on industry. Physique and physical capacities at once allow the individual to bend energies towards the performance of manual or mechanical work and limit what he or she is capable of achieving. The personal dispositions and motivations to think, feel, and act comparably affect what people *will* do, and their mental and emotional capacities and capabilities what they *can* do (although the two are not independent).

Individual Differences

People differ on all of these dimensions, partly because of genetic endowment and partly as a result of differences in experience and in opportunities and capacity for learning (where 'learning' is defined as that 'which enables [the person] to adapt to the changing demands of the environment (King, 1964, p 109)). Human beings are now thought to have relatively few instincts which produce automatic (or unthought-out) responses to environmental stimuli. As Maslow claims, both traits of character and coping behaviours are 'characteristically learned' (Maslow, 1970, p 136). Personality and capacity at any point in time are largely the product of what has previously been learned, either from experience or from formal or informal instruction (Bass and Vaughan, 1966, p 7).

This general learning process is referred to as 'socialisation'. It commences at birth and, although many of the traits and skills which the individual needs to cope with adult life are implanted during childhood, never ends. A distinction may be drawn between childhood socialisation and adult socialisation (Brim and Wheeler, 1966). Nevertheless, both depend upon the same learning processes (Gagne, 1970) and both serve to improve the capacity of the individual to relate to and operate on the physical and social environments.

Consequently, society has the opportunity to 'teach' relevant personality patterns and appropriate instrumental behaviours both prior to the individual's embarking upon employment work and simultaneously with his engagement in it (see Miller and Form, 1951, Part Four). In the most general sense, the stock of experience or wisdom is referred to as the 'culture' of the host society. Culture represents the embodiment of all those designs for living which have been developed and found useful or valuable in the past.

Their transmission to the succeeding generations through socialisation may be more or less efficient, and some differences between individuals may stem from these variations in success of transmission. This can be highly functional in a society exhibiting considerable stability between generations. But it can be highly dysfunctional in a changing, dynamic environment. Some individual differences may arise from differing perceptions of the relevance of what is transmitted, especially where these are traditional designs being passed on in a changing situation.

The Work Contract

The presence of variation on both sides of the supply and demand equation creates the need to attempt a matching of personal traits and capacities with industrial needs for role performance. This is sometimes expressed in terms of the need to secure a person-environment 'fit' (through the application of the methods of job design and selection). Mismatching stems from failure to fit one or other of the three elements in the difference, associated with role perceptions, abilities and traits of personality, and motivational level (see Steers and Porter, 1979), where:

(a) role perception depends partly upon how clearly the role expectations are specified and partly on the individual's capacity for perceiving and understanding them;

(b) abilities or skills refer to conceptions of *knowledge about* and *know-how* related to the role in question, and personality traits to those *behavioural predispositions* displayed by the individual and relevant to performance in the role;

(c) motivational level refers to the extent to which the individual *wants* to perform the role as specified or as he or she perceives it.

Given the probability of mismatching, it is a major task of those who 'manage' human resources to act in ways which will reduce its occurrence.

The problem can be resolved primarily through the definition of the work role itself. This is conceived as a contract between the enterprise (acting through management) and the individual. Thus, Torrington and Chapman argue that job design is 'the central feature of the contract for work' and amplify this by reference to the expectations which are thereby established:

> 'For the individual employee, the design of his job specifies the content and nature of his contribution to work activities and many of the conditions within which the work is carried out. For the organisation, job design determines the allocation of work, including supervision and integration between different job holders in the organisation. For both parties to the contract, job design is important for the utilisation of individual skills and abilities, satisfaction with mutual expectations about work, and the achievement of goals and objectives through work'
> (Torrington and Chapman, 1979, p 96).

This quotation sets out the antithetical expectations which have to be reconciled in the design of the job and the specification of the terms of the work contract, all of which have to be taken into account in activities such as selection and placement.

Selection and Placement

If the job design is taken as given (determined, for example, by the state of the production technology) the problem of securing a fit between person and job environment hinges on the selection process. If there is nothing to be done about the demands of the job upon the person, any solution to the problem must rest upon either selecting people who have the matching personalities and capacities, or moulding them by training and development activities to fit better the demands which are thought to be unchangeable. Because moulding people is both difficult and expensive, enterprises are predisposed to place the whole onus on selection and deselection.

Where the requirement is 'general' – a requirement to secure 'good workmen', for example – the approach to controlling selection may be equally general: management relies on a broad and general judgement of the character and capacity of the potential employee, encouraged by the possibility that services can be dispensed with if the assessment proves wrong.

Where the requirement is much more specific and precise – a requirement for a strong aptitude for hand-eye co-ordination or for analytical judgement, for example – reliance upon broad assessments, as in interviews, may prove insufficient for the purpose. The quiver of psychological tests is then raided to provide means for measuring more precisely the personality traits or aptitudes which are thought to be required in the employee.

A significant change in technology (such as those associated with automation or 'the chip') usually makes additional demands for much more sophisticated measuring activities – in relation to both the job and its demands and the person and the traits and aptitudes supplied. This was true of the period of rationalisation around the turn of the century (in which F W Taylor made his mark) and is true of the rationalisation taking place in the period since the 1960s (in which selection testing has played a prominent part). As a result, measurement operations and activities become a much more significant requirement of human resource management.

Thus, securing human resources depends upon making ever more sophisticated assessments of the complex human being and particularly of those attributes which contribute to the realisation of material and social ends. The demands made are on 'management', that group of people who occupy the crucial decision-taking and gatekeeper roles in industrial organisation. Although the concept of management (and particularly of management's rights and prerogatives) may itself be undergoing change at the present time, it is imperative to be clear about the role which managers carry out, both generally and particularly in relation to the coordination and control of human resources.

MANAGEMENT

The role of management, regardless of *who* actually performs it, is commonly regarded as crucial to the production of wealth. In the clinical language of the economist, management constitutes 'a factor of production ... similar to capital, labour or natural resources, [which] is combined with them in varying factor proportions in productive processes' (Harbison and Myers, 1959, p 19). Drucker argues that managers are the specifically 'economic organ' of an industrial society (Drucker, 1955, p 6) which turns resources of production into actual production. They do this by coordinating the contributions of physical (technology) and monetary resources (finance), with those of people (human resources) with the aim of producing the goods and services which people demand (Brech, 1975, pp 38–40).

Such definitions of management may help to mislead, in the sense of producing images, models, and theories which inhibit action (Argyris and Schon, 1978, p 10): managers, wherever they are or whenever they operate, are required to make choices or take decisions. But important though decision-taking may be to the definition, this aspect does not sufficiently define the requirement of management. An older but now less-frequently used concept of management more usefully distinguishes direction (involving the 'ultimate' authority to decide) from management in the narrow sense (in which it is not very different from administration) (Lewis and Stewart, 1958).

Direction, as performed by the board of directors, is essentially the function of setting the objectives, the criteria of success, the broad strategies and the policies for the undertaking of them, and of evaluating the undertaking's overall progress and development against the criteria. The directors must automatically look outwards from 'the organisation' as the success and health of the exercise will depend on their understanding of environmental demands and their ability to translate these into realisable objectives and strategies.

Non-directorial managers, by contrast, work within this framework and are concerned primarily with monitoring the performance of the system in relation to these objectives and criteria and with taking any remedial action necessary to maintain the system-as-is in a kind of equilibrium. The above definitions are essentially concerned with these processes. What is particularly important about them is that in their particular form they are subordinate to that system which sets and maintains objectives.

This distinction is not always maintained in the literature. When, for example, Drucker asserts that the management role developed comparatively recently (Drucker, 1961, p 1) he appears to be thinking of the two subsets together. But the subsequent development of his theme retains the classic textbook emphasis on an inward-looking, techniques-oriented approach to the managerial task.

The Classical Conception

In the classical conception, the antecedents of which go back to Moses's response to the advice of the first management consultant, Jethro (Exodus, 18, 13 – 27), 'management' is regarded as primarily concerned with internal affairs – that is, with methods of organising, directing, and controlling resources of production (whatever the form of words used to express this). The objectives of doing this are often taken as given (implicitly as having been determined by the owners or directors) and the focus of the role is upon realising them as economically as possible (see Haas, 1987).

This idea is embodied in Tannenbaum's statement based on a synthesis of the views of numerous writers on the subject:

> '. . . Managers are those who use formal authority to organize, direct or control responsible subordinates (and therefore indirectly, the groups or complexes which they may head) in order that all service contributions may be co-ordinated in the attainment of an enterprise purpose . . . '
> (Tannenbaum, 1948; Tannenbaum, Weschler, and Massarik, 1961, pp 263 – 4).

The person is otherwise not a manager and is not endowed with this kind of authority, nor expected to engage in this kind of decision-taking and coordinating activity. Managers are required to provide at least this coordinating function; should they fail to supply this, they either cease or fail to manage.

More recent expressions of the function may use different terminology but essentially make the same kind of point, even if 'control' is often given less prominence. Kotter (1982) defines the core tasks of the general manager as:

(a)   setting up the agendas (or tasks and procedures) for action;

(b)   setting up the social networks needed to work through them; and

(c)   persuading people (many of whom are not subject to the general manager's authority) to put the agendas into effect.

This plays down the function of control, but otherwise puts in more 'modern' terminology, the organisation and direction functions found in Tannenbaum.

This way of defining management means that in theory anyone can manage if they perform this broad function or role. Those who have the title are the ones who, by tradition, are allocated the authority and responsibility which 'goes with the role'. But this should not obscure the possibility that management is a role (or complex set of them) which could be allocated to anyone, appropriately titled or not, who possesses the capacity and motivation to manage.

The effect of this manner of construing management is to focus it on the mastery of error-detection and correction which are *internal* to the organisation. In Argyris's terminology, managers ('members of the organisation') are led to: 'respond to changes in the internal and external environments of the organisation by detecting errors which they then correct so as to maintain the central features of organisational theory-in-use' (or a theory of action constructed from observation of actual behaviour) (Argyris and Schon, 1978, pp 18 and 15).

The expectation is that managers will organise, direct, and control the various resources of production, including the human ones behind given objectives. The role involves some people, the managers, in work-flow relationships, in leadership, and in monitoring the actions of others (Sayles, 1964, p 49). It may be carried out in large or small undertakings, relate to specialised technologies, result in high or low added value, and prove easy or difficult in the event.

The Alternative Construction

The managerial role may be construed somewhat differently, following the theme of the entrepreneur in classical economics. This places prime emphasis on fundamental issues of resource *allocation* rather than utilisation which focuses greater attention, not only on

Figure 1

Control loops in the management process

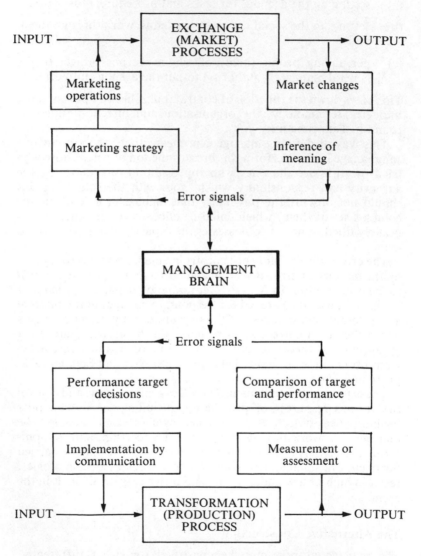

the need to choose or decide on allocations, but on the need for criteria to be used in deciding such issues and the related need to monitor what *external* effects any chosen allocation has. The emphasis in this construction is upon the need for an external view, which is logically prior to the internal one so firmly established by the exponents of 'scientific management'.

In this alternative construction, management is treated, by analogy with the human being and by developing F W Taylor's notion that management was responsible for the 'brainwork of production', as the 'brain' of the enterprise or organisation. Like the human brain, this one must determine how the unit is going to cope with its external environment and how it is going to maintain itself in a healthy and capable state. It is seen to be served by sensory devices which gather intelligence about the external (for example, market) environments and the internal (for example, production) environments, and by the equivalents of the servo-motors in simple systems — the methods, techniques and procedures through which decisions are implemented.

This model also relies on the construct of the control loop to identify the necessary elements in the decision-taking and action processes involved (Figure 1). This analogue has crept into the management and organisational literature as a useful heuristic with which to explain control in complex organisations (see Shone and Paterson, 1963; Boulding, 1956; Buckley, 1967). One of the simplest examples of such a closed loop control is supplied by the thermostatic control built into central heating systems. This relies on the setting of a target temperature, and the linkage of this to the heat source through a servo-motor and a means of measurement of the output (in terms of temperature in the room).

In Argyris's writings, this model has been developed to the point where it can be associated with conditions of both stable and dynamic equilibrium. In the former case, the external environmental pressures are either constant or readily predictable and can be taken as a given. Therefore the theories and norms to which members of the organisation are expected to subscribe emphasise the objective of maintaining a set of stable relationships within the total system. This maintains the focus of attention upon the internal system. Managers will be required to detect and correct any internal 'errors' which appear so that the whole remains stable and able to secure its success by internal improvements (as, for example, in efficiency of operations). This approach is depicted by the lower half of the diagram, below 'the management brain'.

The Dynamic Condition

Where and when the external environment of the enterprise or organisation is more volatile (less capable of being predicted) this classical construction may prove positively dangerous. Whether the volatility arises in the market or from protesting environmentalists, any such feature in the environment will force more attention on the need to subject the external situation to a similar kind of control to that which is usually developed internally. This, at base, calls for the development of at least one other control loop, extended outwards, and informing the management 'brain' of the nature of the condition it has to cope with. This is the essence of Argyris's approach to 'double-loop' learning (*ibid*, pp 18–26).

Given a high probability that no environment will actually remain stable for long, it normally becomes necessary to multiply the number of detection and correction loops to accommodate both external (for example, market, political, social or professional demands) and internal (for example, the supply of machine or labour performance, or product quality) pressures.

When put together, the model depicts a series of overlapping and interlocking control loops which form the basis for control of both internal and external environments. The system is held together by the norms and theories which are embodied in policies and held and applied by the actors (managers) in the situation. In each case, feedback links enable intelligence to be gathered and activities to be monitored (as in the links on the right-hand side of Figure 1). In each case, feed-out links are also set up to enable the management centre to exert influence on the exchange or transformation process involved.

In principle, one feedback link or other triggers perception of the need to decide and one of the feed-out links carries the decision into action, but this presupposes a human readiness to respond infinitely to changes indicated by the data fed back. Argyris argues that because of a human propensity to ignore or misread data in the interests of preserving the *status quo*, managers often miss the opportunities for addressing and resolving the inconsistencies and conflicts in theories and norms which form part of the taken-for-granted way of going about things. It is therefore necessary, he argues, to adopt a questioning approach to the existing 'theories-in-use' (or the objectives, strategies, practices, and policies which embody them) in order to produce the changes in them which will accommodate those revealed by the data from the external environment.

Specialisation in decision-taking may not be carried to the point where directors are concerned exclusively with the double loop concept and 'ordinary managers' with that of the single loop. The distinction does help to show the two main components of management decision-taking. What is more important is that effective management can be considered to exist only where both types of 'loop' are employed by 'management'.

Varying Circumstances

The decision-taking involved in the directorial or senior managerial role is highly contingent on the immediate context in which the decisions are taken. The decisions required are essentially *non-programmed*, being, as Simon defines them, 'novel, unstructured and consequential' (Simon, 1965, p 59) in the sense of having no direct precedent nor assured basis for assessing their correctness. What assures this variability are the differences in the nature of the objective pursued (expressed, for example, in terms of the market), the resources employable (expressed in terms of factors of production), and the methods available for use (expressed in terms of 'technology'). None of these is homogeneous in its nature, nor of universal incidence.

First, markets are defined not merely in terms of their size and buoyancy but also by the relationship of seller and buyer. The relationship of the tailor to his client is quite different from that of the car-manufacturing firm to its customers. The markets may also be very different in their 'size', measured in pounds sterling, and one may be looking up and the other turning down, a sellers' market or a buyers' market. Both the statics and the dynamics of markets may vary in these ways, and because they do, managers are presented with unstructured and relatively novel problems to be decided about. Whether the aims of managing are then expressed in terms of sales or profits may have less influence on the nature of the decision-problem than these other variables.

Secondly, employable resources vary in time and space. The plant (machines and tools) available at any one time is not capable of resolving every problem presented – computer assisted manufacturing (CAM) is, after all, a very recent concept and an even more recent reality. For market and financial reasons, not every undertaking is in a position to acquire even that which is technically feasible. Undertakings side by side may therefore have very different mixes of old and new physical/technical resources.

The human resources, as we have just noted, exhibit a considerable range of differences. People are not alike, and what people bring to their work roles is variable. Attempts to 'process' human beings into resources of production (or consumption) (McKinlay, 1975, pp vii-viii; Burns, in Welford, 1962) have some influence but are never so completely successful as to homogenise the resource (Anthony, 1977b). Non-conformity and deviance remain characteristic features of most societies, but they contribute little to the comfort of the resource allocator.

Thirdly, the methods and techniques, which human beings have devised and developed to enable them to cope more successfully with the physical environment and to bend it to human use, also vary. Some of this is subsumed in the artefacts of plant and machinery, which couple some of the techniques to inanimate power sources that do not rely on human muscles. But some of it is more concerned with ideas — for example, of how to organise men and machines into productive combinations, or of how to devise a more efficient measure of efficiency. As man by no means knows everything that he might find useful, and as some men do not know what other people may know, there is considerable scope for difference in the way in which particular men, such as managers, attempt to resolve their problems of method and technique.

Taken altogether, this suggests that the industrial situation, which any manager or any worker faces, is likely to display considerable variation from location to location and from time to time. Such variety is at once a factor in the creation of the kind of novelty which Simon notes, and a factor in maintaining a condition of uncertainty around the process of decision-taking and action. Against such a background, it should not be at all surprising that those who attempt to define and describe management as a process should find it full of ambiguities and conflicts of meaning.

HUMAN RESOURCE MANAGEMENT

The management of human resources is, in principle, not different from the management of any other resource. What makes it different, in practice, is the nature of the resource in question — human resources are human, not material — and the value which we as individuals and as a society place on human beings. Living beings are ultimately more valuable than inanimate things. These values constrain human resource management and make it more difficult. It may have a different significance from the management of other resources for these reasons, but the 'management' component of all of them remains concerned with processes of organisation, direction, and control.

The management of any resource, including human resources, is, in this sense, a part of any process of managing. It is, as Woodward characterised it, an 'element' function of managment: it is necessarily a part of any managing task and role. It differs from the task functions of managing, which is to say those acts of managing concerned with production, or marketing, or research and development. These latter functions can be assigned to separate individuals who need not, in the process of managing their specialty, become at all concerned with the other task functions. The element functions, on the other hand, are inescapable, no matter what task functions are being performed.

Human resource management is not, therefore, the exclusive concern of a *specialist* function or role of 'personnel management'. It inheres in any managerial role. The specialist function of personnel management has only slowly and intermittently become associated with human resource management and certainly did not invent it. In the earlier growth phases, characterised by a specialised involvement in welfare work, recruitment and selection, staff training and industrial relations, it was often only peripherally engaged in the formation of human resource strategy: this was dictated from elsewhere and the specialist personnel officer gathered up the crumbs from this larger table (Drucker, 1961; Crichton, 1968).

This is because, traditionally, labour coordination and control strategies have been determined by corporate management in the light of what were perceived to be the main conditions in the product/service and labour markets. Historically, such control has been sought and secured in one of three main ways, each of which, it is at least arguable, responded to the main dimensions of these two types of market. Broadly, industry (in both Britain and the USA, albeit on a slightly different time-scale) has moved from relying upon a strategy of selection, through dependence on a strategy of supervision, to embrace a strategy of bureaucratic control (although this last phase may now be giving way to a more open strategy).

Selection as a Labour Control Strategy

The strategy of selection was, historically, the first to be adopted in modern industry. This strategy demands that the worker shall warrant at the point of selection that he or she can and will perform work of the kind and to the standard required, for the wage or salary offered. It relies upon the selection of workers already possessed of appropriate skills and motivation to perform the work in line with accepted understandings and practices about what type and amount of work is required at what time and in what sequence. This strategy presupposes that such workers are available because they have been produced 'by the system', in much the fashion that the old guilds produced labour of this general type.

For so long as the employer could count upon securing skilled workers who were still committed to a uniform view of enterprise, he was able to select workers who could then be relied upon to carry out the necessary tasks, as it were autonomously. Management was not involved in people management, but often simply subcontracted the work. Many of the 'craft' industries originating in the last century, for example, relied on some variant of the 'ganger' or 'butty' system in which a craftsman or skilled worker undertook to perform a certain amount of work for a defined remuneration, and he it was who recruited other craftsmen and labourers to allow him to do this.

This early control strategy clearly depended upon the availability in the labour market of workers possessing values and norms, as well as capacities and skills, which would act – as it were automatically – to order their activities behind the realisation of the wider economic and organisational objectives. In early recruitment operations, it is common to find references to 'reliant' workmen, by which was meant workmen on whom the employer could depend to accomplish their tasks without it being necessary to resort to imposed discipline (Pollard, 1965, p 200). It was when this assumption no longer held that the rigour of the law against leaving work unfinished was invoked.

This method ceased to be effective with the growth in industrial scale, the increase in competition, and the development of physical technology and work specialisation. This kind of change occurred in Britain from the middle of the last century onwards (Hill, 1981, pp 24–35).

Supervision as a Labour Control Strategy

In its full development, this became the strategy of 'supervision'. In this phase, control was made to depend upon a close personal supervision of narrowly skilled workers by a good all-rounder or generalist (who, in the early stages, was probably a good broadly skilled workman). Supervision involved detailed instructions about what was required and when and *how* and by what methods it was to be accomplished. Symbolically, this strategy was associated with the 'bowler-hatted' foreman, a person of high status and consequence in the local community. The change was often effected by bringing the 'ganger' or 'butty' who had previously contracted to have the work performed for a fee into employment. He then became management's front-line organiser and disciplinarian, and acted as the agent of management directly and stood in a more distant relationship to the workers whom he controlled.

This strategy relied on the probability that workmen would more readily accept the leadership, or follow the orders, of one of their own group or class. This person would function as the embodiment (and reminder) of the principles of self-reliant workmanship which were handed down from the mediaeval guild organisation. Leadership, in this context, was either charismatic or traditional, or some mixture of both. This in turn implied the continued acceptance of a set of common work values and norms by the artisan population at large.

It was only when this consensus as to values and norms could no longer be counted on that a fundamental change occurred. This happened in the United States in association with the influx of immigrants (who often did not speak the language let alone share the artisan values) into the factories. It happened in Britain as a result of the rural-urban movement and the progressive rationalisation of industry towards the end of the century. The now absent norms had to be replaced by formal rules which were to be created, administered, and enforced by a special cadre of functionaries, and the condition for Weber's rational-legal authority was created.

Incentive as a Control Strategy

The strategy which gradually replaced this became associated with Taylorism and scientific management, and because of that connection has been referred to as the strategy of 'incentive' (but could be termed a strategy of bureaucratic control).

The effect of this change was to make control dependent on a complex process of defining work tasks and monitoring the workers' performance of them, carried out by specialist functionaries – work study engineers, progress chasers, bonus clerks, or personnel officers – facilitated by the offer of incentives for improved performance and ultimately enforced by the supervisors as disciplinarians.

In this phase, functionally specialised management defined very precisely the tasks to be performed by workers and secured the requisite performance by offering material incentives to them, so that an assumed self-interest is brought to serve the business interests of management. The bowler-hatted foreman is now eclipsed, as the control roles are taken over by the work study engineers, the production schedulers, the progress chasers, and the personnel specialists, and the supervisor becomes much more a general purpose worker at the front edge of the functionally specialised management bureaucracy.

With this change, leadership evolved from that associated with the small, local group (or workers) to that linked with the formal organisation of a rational-legal authority. Control on the basis of sentiments shared by employers and employees was now replaced by a system of rationally derived rules which were enforced in much the same way as was the law of the land. The qualification for leadership of the working group now became, not ties of sentiment, but certified competence in specialist functional areas of industrial concern which could be 'inspected' by those who were to be subject to it. The condition for the replacement of the natural system by the bureaucratic form of organisation (see below pp 188–98) was now in place.

Much of the evidence available at the present time suggests that this strategy may be giving way, in organisations with advanced technologies at least, to one which returns to dependence on worker autonomy – but in the context of the working group. This is essentially a corporatist strategy which relies upon the propagation within the organisation itself of the kind of labour required to accomplish its tasks.

This strategy rests on the belief that it is management's responsibility to select workers according to attitude and aptitude and to provide training and development to make them capable of performing the tasks to the standards demanded. It is for the management to establish the rules and procedures, including those which (as with remuneration schemes) determine the relationship between contribution and rewards. The worker forfeits discretion in carrying out his work, and the control passes into the hands of the corporate organisation as a whole (which is now likely to be a looser federation of roles than before). But the control is now effected through acceptance of subcultural values and norms developed within the enterprise itself and disseminated through the training and development processes. The generalist first line managers or supervisors, and the specialist management functionaries (like work study engineers and personnel managers) are, in consequence, no longer expected to develop the same kind of functional relationships with workers as before.

Reliance on distinct labour control strategies at different periods of time, and in different circumstances, makes the approach to the management of personnel variable. In the various contexts, the responsibility is assigned to line management or to specialist functionaries (personnel officers) according to the strategy and the way in which the organisation develops to deal with it. But the general responsibility of all managers (who necessarily work through other people) for the management of human resources, is inalienable, and all must therefore develop a familiarity with the problems, the methods, and the skills involved.

SUMMARY

The production of wealth calls for the purposive combination of financial, physical, and human resources. As this is not 'automatic', the necessary allocation decisions have to be taken by those who occupy managerial roles in complex organisations. Such decisions are constrained by the nature and form of the markets, the technologies, and the human resources available. These constraints determine the broad limits to the opportunities for defining 'work'.

Human resources are a particularly important resource, but because they vary in their composition and capacity, decision-takers have the basic task of matching the needs of both enterprise and labour.

This matching process may be facilitated either by designing work tasks to match human capacities and needs or by selecting or moulding the human resources to match the demands of the work tasks on offer. Historically, both have been attempted, and have been associated with distinct labour control strategies.

Reading:

Allen (1977; 1979).
Argyris and Schon (1978).
Barnard (1938).
McGregor (1960).
Porter (1985) pp 1–61.
Tannenbaum, Weschler, and Massarik (1961) pp 243–64.

1 The Work Context

Work and Jobs

Work is an activity which demands the expenditure of energy or effort to create from 'raw materials' those products or services which people value. In this sense, work is the prime energy source in a transformation or conversion process: something which is less valued in its current form is turned into something which is more valued. It is performed either by the direct use of brain or brawn or by machines invented by people to take over some of the tasks which are more highly demanding of human energy. It inevitably involves both a cost (of effort or energy) and a benefit (in the form of created or 'added' value).

Nowadays, work is normally associated with employment in complex organisations and the links between energy and added value may be tenuous. This has not always been the position nor is it exclusively so now. In 'subsistence' economies, work may be performed without benefit of much formal organisation, the value created being intended for the immediate gratification of those who create it. Even in the modern economy, the business executive who relaxes by digging the garden at the weekend performs work 'informally' and for immediate satisfactions.

The 'employment work' (as Jaques has termed it) with which we will be mainly concerned here is, however, that located in complex organisations which produce valued goods or services mainly for the gratification of others, and which remunerate the workers for their work contribution, usually in the form of cash derived from the 'sale' of the goods and services to others.

Such work is the source of demands for and on people and has been described as 'the key transaction' which relates workpeople to their working environment (Trist *et al*, 1963, p 20). It comes in many shapes and sizes, some being associated with 'big jobs' and some with 'little jobs'. Some of it is very demanding of physical energy, some more so of mental energy; some uses human energy alone, and some a combination of human and machine power. This variety of work hardly requires proof, as our experience testifies to its existence.

The variety is *created* by dividing work (using methods which form the subject matter of this chapter) into jobs, each of which becomes a set of tasks put together for somebody's (whether a worker's or the organisation's) convenience, and then allocated to people to perform as their own. This process of creating jobs has usually fallen outside the ambit of the specialist personnel officer, whose first involvement has usually been at the level of describing the jobs once they have been created. Nevertheless, the first element in the process of managing human resources in the wider sense focuses on the creation, definition, and organisation of work for people to perform as jobs in order that the wider objectives of the enterprise are served.

SCIENTIFIC MANAGEMENT

The process of dividing up and allocating work as jobs, entails the design of both the tasks and their inter-relationships, along with the standards expected to be attained in performing them. The process is one which is guided by well established principles. Two broad approaches, each carrying distinct principles, can be identified:

1. job simplification and standardisation based on work study; and

2. job enlargement and enrichment (or job redesign).

Which approach is used depends on and responds to both the production technology employed to serve organisational mission and the orientations (wants and expectations) of workers.

Standardisation and simplification of work tasks has proceeded farthest where the technology employed permits jobs to be fractionalised and spread through a number of specialist workers who each perform similar or comparable jobs. The more obvious examples are those associated with the manually controlled line operations of manufacturing industry; it is in this area that mechanisation has usually developed first and farthest.

Technology, however, does not always allow work activity to be reduced to this level or degree of specialisation. Traditionally, tasks in batch production technology and 'indirect' work (associated with stores or maintenance, for example) and administrative and managerial work within 'mass' production technology have escaped. This is because the jobs are insufficiently structured, have too little pattern, and are too dependent upon invisible sensory processes (as distinct from visible manual activities) for their performance.

The techniques of scientific management or organisation and methods are not the 'causes' of work fractionalisation; they are merely tools for improving definitions. The cause of fractionalisation lies in the application of the principles of 'division of labour', which, *inter alia*, link specialisation and simplification to increased performance efficiency.

Industrial Engineering

Much management effort has gone into breaking down complex work processes (simplification) into jobs with short cycle times (standardisation) with the intention of increasing efficiency and productivity by ensuring repetition (routinisation). The traditional approach to the streamlined definition of such jobs uses those methods and techniques of job analysis associated with industrial engineering or 'work study'. In the interests of improving efficiency, 'jobs' are made as simple and as standard as possible so that each comprises no more than a main task which is repeated. Any subsidiary or ancillary tasks are removed to ensure that they do not interfere with repetitive performance of the central task.

The origins of this approach to analysis and definition are to be found in 'scientific management'. This broad philosophy and approach developed in the era of industrial rationalisation around the turn of the century. It is associated with the work of Frederick W Taylor, Frank and Lillian Gilbreth, and Henry L Gantt. The perspective adopted by these practitioners was that efficiency would be increased if management carried out the thinking necessary to define work tasks so precisely that the workers need waste none of their time and energy on thinking out how to perform, but were left free to perform repetitively and unthinkingly in the manner defined.

The learning theory underlying this approach is known as 'conditioning'. By constant repetition of the same work 'problem', the worker would become more and more proficient in solving it, especially if he simultaneously received reinforcing rewards in the form of performance-related payment. A major consequence of applying this approach and theory has been that many jobs became simplified, routinised, and standardised to the point where the skill required to perform them and the worker's commitment to the work were both considerably reduced. Industrial engineering (or, more simply, work study) applications of this kind came to be seen as the cause of 'alienated labour'.

Methods and Procedures

'Industrial engineering', as the tool of job standardisation and simplification, may be defined as:

> 'the systematic procedure for subjecting all direct and indirect operations to close scrutiny to introduce improvements resulting in making work easier to perform and allowing work to be done in less time and with less investment per unit'
> (Niebel, 1972, p 6)

The object is to define work in such a way that less expert or less well trained workers can perform it with optimum efficiency, for the greater benefit of the economy, the enterprise, and the workers themselves, all of whom share in the increased product.

Industrial engineering tends to accept the fundamental technology of production as a 'given'. Its main focus is upon routine manual and clerical work tasks, particularly those in which the volume of work is high enough to permit individual workers repetitively to perform short cycle tasks by hand or by machine. These kinds of operations are most often found in manually controlled production and assembly operations, whether these are associated with making products (for example, car manufacturing) or delivering services (for example, health or life insurance). Here the maintenance of a flow of work from one work station to another is crucial to efficiency; consequently, in these systems, particular attention to 'line balancing' based upon precise definitions of tasks and performance standards is needed.

These methods are also applicable, but in a different and more limited way, to unit and small batch production. Here a number of workers usually address themselves to one focal product (for example, a house under construction) or a machine or piece of plant (for example, a furnace or distillation plant). Analysis of schedules, processes, and procedures, based on 'gang' or 'machine-loading' charts, form the main methods of application. These jobs usually involve more variety of task and allow more discretion to the worker, so that precise definition is less possible or necessary.

Methods study

The way in which work flows depends upon the particular *organisational* and *machine* technologies adopted; these limit the opportunities open to organise and define work tasks. Between the main production methods (unit, batch, line and line-flow) for example, there are major differences in the potential which exists for interruption in and delay to work activity. For this reason, the analyses of office or plant layout, office or manual work procedures, and work flows are necessary prerequisites of any attempt to define criteria and performance standards.

This is usually carried out with the aid of process charts, some of which are more relevant to some kinds of production technology than to others. The techniques of Organisation and Methods (O&M) are somewhat different from these (Millward, 1959), but their consequences for clerical and administrative work, as the title of Millward's first chapter, 'The Simplification of Office Work', makes clear, are similar.

Process charting

Comprises several methods for plotting and analysing the flows of materials and partly completed work through the various work stations at which work is performed. All are designed to allow analyses to be made of these flows and sequences to highlight inefficiencies. Most make use of the standardised symbols of methods analysis (McCormick, 1979, p 72; Millward, 1959, p 4). Five such process charts are often used in manufacturing operations to highlight particular kinds of inefficiency: *the operation process chart*; *the flow process chart*; *the man and machine process chart*; *the gang process chart* (used to plot the activities of a group of workers employed as a 'gang'); and the *operator process chart* (used in association with motion study).

The first four types of analysis enable the industrial engineer to identify and recommend changes in the way in which materials and parts flow through the work system. One effect is that the relationships of workers (particularly those based on transfer of work from one work station to another) are structured in a way which satisfies the underlying efficiency criteria. Another is to define the actual jobs which particular workers will be required to do in the sequence of work activity. This becomes a major source of the 'job fractionalisation' which receives much attention from those concerned with the quality of working life (QWL) (Niebel, 1972, p 61).

Motion study

Is more directly concerned with the question of *how* the worker carries out the work tasks assigned, and is usually used in combination with time study. Motion study is concerned with:

> 'The careful analysis of the various body motions employed in doing a job, to eliminate or reduce ineffective movements, and facilitate and speed effective movements'
> (Niebel, 1972, p 171).

Over time, two main approaches have been developed: visual motion study and micro-motion study. These are differentiated according to the depth of penetration of the analysis, the equipment needed to perform it, and the costs of application. The first entails analysis of the motions which are recognisable by ordinary visual senses. The second uses micro-motion cameras to identify much smaller elements of motion than can be seen with the naked eye. Both make use of the concept of the 17 'fundamental motions' developed by Frank Gilbreth (who termed them Therbligs, derived from a reversal of his surname) (Niebel, 1972, pp 172–80). Their value lies in providing a vocabulary of motion analysis (focused on such terms as search, reach, grasp, locate, hold, move, etc., which in micro-motion study are further refined by linking them to distances moved, weights carried, or tolerances required in, for example, locating a part).

The purpose of this type of analysis is to achieve economy of motion in performing work. 'Economy' is defined mainly by reference to the time taken to carry out the motion, but partly also by reference to the physical capacity of the human being. The analysis is based upon recognition and application of certain principles of motion economy, originally developed by the Gilbreths but subsequently added to over the years. These may not be applied simply for humane or humanitarian reasons: it is good economy to define work in ways appropriate to the physical functions of the person, and efficiency is increased in most cases if the effort required is reduced.

Time study
The process of defining work is usually completed by using the methods and techniques of time study to establish the standards of performance required of workers. These enable the 'best' method or pattern of work activities to be derived, where 'best' is defined as most economical of the worker's time.

'Time study' is a method of establishing an 'allowed time standard to perform a given task based upon measurement of work content of the prescribed method, with due allowance for fatigue, personal needs and unavoidable delays' (Niebel, 1972, p 6). It is used synchronously with methods and motion study to determine the 'best method'. But is is also used *after* the best method has been found through application of motion study to establish a standard of performance, based on the time taken by an appropriately skilled worker to perform the task without undue exertion.

This entails the exercise of human judgement to establish a normal or standard time for a 'standard' worker. Like many other techniques of modern management, time study has progressed from reliance upon simple and rather crude judgements, such as are involved in estimating, through rating judgements made in association with stop-watch studies, to a more highly systematised judgement, such as is associated with synthetic time study methods (such as Work Factor, Methods-Time Measurement (MTM), Basic Motion Time study (BMT), etc).

Visual time study
Entails disaggregation of the total job into component elements of movement and the timing of these to provide the basis for an overall time for the job. The base time for the job as a whole is calculated from the mean times for each element and applying a 'rating factor' to take account of how near-normal was the observed operator's performance at the time of the study. The standard time for any job is then produced by making additions for fatigue, tool change, personal needs, and any other factor which is likely to vary the performance of the operator from the measured base time over the course of the working shift. These allowances are often based on conventions applicable to certain industries or occupations.

This yields a standard time for the operation under study. In some plans this is expressed as so many minutes per cycle or per piece. In the Bedaux and Manit systems (and those developed from them) the standard time is based on a 60-point hour where each point is a measure of human effort plus allowances in variable proportions according to circumstances.

Synthetic time study
'Synthetic' times are those which have been calculated on the basis of either historical times for other jobs or times which have been standardised in laboratory studies using micro-motion cameras. This method allows study of more minute elements of motion (Therbligs) than are feasible with stop-watch methods and the production of times worked out on the basis of very large samples to reduce statistical errors.

In practice, synthetic time study places the onus on the time study engineer to identify the minute elements of motion which are combined in any real job. Once these motions are identified, however, the standard times applicable are simply 'read off' the predetermined times from the data sheet. The judgement of the industrial engineer is replaced by the standardised judgement built into the elemental motion times. A number of branded plans of this kind now exist, including Work Factor, Methods-Time Measurement and Basic Motion Time Study. Examples of the basic motions in MTM are reaches, grasps, releases, moves, and positions, all variable according to the 'degree of difficulty'. The times are expressed in Time Measurement Units, each being 1/100,000 of an hour. The smallest unit of time used in the BMT synthetic system is 2/10,000ths of a minute.

The Notion of a Normal Level of Performance

In whichever mode the industrial engineer is operating, there is still the concept of a normal capacity for expending effort (as implied in the principles of motion economy) and a normal level of performance (defined in terms of amount of effort associated with 'rating'). As Lockyer, for example, says of rating in association with time studies, the observer is:

'Required to have a very clear concept of the rate at which a worker who possesses the necessary mental and physical attributes, and the required skill, would satisfactorily carry out the task under observation, safely, accurately, at the correct speed and without undue strain'
(Lockyer, 1974, p 162).

This norm or standard is commonly expressed as a scale. On some scales, the norm for a day-wage worker working without incentive is fixed at 60 (based on the 60 minute hour) compared with 80 as the expected average performance of a worker operating under incentive conditions. On other scales, these norms may be expressed in percentages (as is usual in Britain), for example, 75 against 100, or 100 against 133 (Lockyer, 1974, p 163; British Standards Institution, BS 3138, 1969).

This notion of normal pace of working, however, is based on certain definable speeds of activity. The analogues used for arm movements are based on dealing a deck of 52 cards in a standard time of half a minute, and for body movements, on a walking pace of 3 miles per hour. In practice, these standards have to be transposed to the particular activities under observation. But the fact of there being a notional ideal pace of this kind lends weight to Behrend's suggestion (1957) that what is involved is a process of 'guessing' (or otherwise uncovering) the levels of effort which are institutionalised in the norms of both workers and management and which will therefore provide an acceptable standard on which to determine fairness (Baldamus, 1961, p 99).

The development of other social norms (such as those which relate to discrimination in work) has produced a situation in which the development of notional standards has become fraught with other difficulties. The need to comply with norms of discrimination makes the judgemental process involved here one which must seek out more accurate indicators or measures of comparability in standards – for example, between sexes or ethnic groups or, ultimately, between adult white males. According to Behrend, if there is no institutionalisation of the norms of effort, there is no sound basis for reaching an acceptable compromise by either guess-work or negotiation.

Consequences

Where job standardisation and simplification are feasible, and where work study methods can be and are applied, certain consequences are produced for the nature of both the work and the worker. Since Taylor's time, both the philosophy and methods of scientific management have been refined to give increased operating efficiency (Niebel, 1972), and although they have not found universal application, they have been increasingly often denounced as essentially dehumanising of work and the worker (Bravermann, 1974). These dehumanising effects have received considerable attention in the social scientific literature and have recently, in the face of enabling technological developments, begun to influence the approach to job structuring.

In so far as all manual and routine clerical work has been affected to some degree by the processes of standardisation and simplification, such jobs could be considered to be subject to these undesired influences. But because their major impact has been upon work in the 'mass-production' and 'mass-assembly' plants, it is there that the effects of these processes for labour have been most avidly researched. The results of this work may be summarised under three broad headings:

1 *Material benefits*
The simplification and standardisation of work in association with line-flow technologies has generally yielded higher productivity to

the organisation and higher material rewards to the workers than are found in similar workplaces which do not employ the same material and organisational technologies.

The effect is usually achieved by providing incentive bonus schemes of one type or another: on the assumptions of the industrial engineer, incentives are expected to produce up to a third more production and up to a third more remuneration (see below, pp 382 *et seq*). The mass production plant has some advantage over batch production operations in this respect because incentive plans tend to rely upon the feasibility of introducing work study and because batch-production technology is less amenable to these methods. Whether this advantage is the cause or the effect of simplification is something which cannot be demonstrated: the association of the two features, however, seems to be fairly clear (Goldthorpe *et al*, 1968).

Nevertheless, it has long been recognised that specialisation might be carried too far, in the sense that the advantages in productivity (and therefore in pay) might be dissipated if carried beyond certain limits. Early work (Vernon, Wyatt and Ogden, 1924; Wyatt, Fraser and Stock, 1928) carried out on light jobs with very short cycle times (of a minute or less) suggested that boredom was often shaken off by the workers introducing variety for themselves by shifting position or changing tasks, and demonstrated that deliberate rotation of tasks could increase productivity by up to 20 per cent. It was sufficient to establish that whilst individual differences affected workers' responses, and whilst workers with no choice might get to accept or even like their work, generally speaking, boredom could remove all the advantages which might otherwise be anticipated.

2   Emotional disbenefits

This same simplification and standardisation of work tends to be deficient in providing emotional benefits to the workers involved. The identification of boredom at work was an early recognition of the probability of such disbenefits. This conclusion has been amplified and added to in the plethora of studies of job satisfaction in mass-production and mass-assembly plants. These yield indications but the results do not lend themselves to simple generalised conclusions.

Job dissatisfaction, or a low level of job satisfaction, has been found in one or more studies to be correlated with work-related factors such as conditions of work (for example, health or safety hazards, lack of control of work pace, lack of clarity as to work tasks, and long or abnormal working hours), job content (where the job is fractionalised, possesses little variety or makes little use of skills), supervision (giving little feedback and allowing little participation in decisions), work group (whether ostracism or simple lack of opportunity to interact with others at work), and rewards (low rewards or rewards perceived as inequitable and lack of advancement or promotion). The underlying implication is that there are some disbenefits associated with low-skilled, routinised, and repetitive work tasks which are not compensated adequately by monetary or social rewards.

The links between the nature of the work tasks and satisfaction are, however, not clear-cut as Turner and Lawrence found in their attempt to measure the two. They devised a method of rating job content (scaling such factors as variety, autonomy, responsibility, learning time and opportunities for interaction) which they referred to as the Requisite Task Attribute (RTA). They used this to test the hypothesis that there was a connection between job content (measured in this way) and job satisfaction and absenteeism. A high score on the RTA was found to be associated with low absenteeism and *vice versa*. But no simple correlation was found between RTA score and job satisfaction; only when the workers in their sample were divided into 'urban' and 'rural' subsets were they able to show that urban workers were generally more satisfied with low rated jobs and rural workers with jobs with higher RTA scores. This suggested that subcultural factors intervened between satisfaction and the 'objective characteristics' of the job. People may come to like what they feel they cannot escape.

3 Pathological effects

Recently, researchers interested in the question of what work does *to* people have switched their attention from job satisfaction to strain or stress as relevant indicators. It is recognised that stress is something which depends not only on the job but also on the person (and his or her tolerance for stress). But studies of stress make more use of physiological, psychological, and behavioural indicators of mental health (such as blood pressure, somatic complaints, anxiety, depression, smoking and drinking habits) which avoid some of the methodological problems associated with asking people their opinions on something like work.

The results obtained in this kind of research suggest similar conclusions to those reached in the studies on job satisfaction. Mental health measures correlate with the range of factors listed in the previous paragraph, but the indications, here as before, are neither perfect nor unidirectional. A number of studies suggest that those performing machine paced work have poorer mental health (Kornhauser, 1965; Gardell, 1971) but others fail to find this relationship

(Roman and Trice, 1972). There is, perhaps, enough evidence to sustain the view that there is something unsatisfactory about routine and fractionalised work of a machine-paced kind, justifying the need to effect improvements where the technology permits this, if only to reduce the incidence of physical and mental health problems.

Such evidence as is available, therefore, leads us to the conclusion that the full-blooded application of the principles of division of labour may produce some benefits in the form of productivity and performance, but it may also produce some dissatisfaction among some workers and some pathological conditions in people which may require treatment. The price may be too high for the benefits obtained. The important practical question is whether changes can be made which will improve the position.

JOB REDESIGN

There have always been problems about extending the application of the methods of scientific management to work which had not already been simplified and specialised. This remains true, whether the attempted application was to work higher in the job hierarchy, or across the range to indirect work, such as that involving maintenance or service. In spite of the new possibilities opened up by developments associated with micro-motion cameras, whenever attempts at application moved away from the comparatively routine tasks of the shop and office floors they encountered difficulties. These stemmed from two sources:

1   The lower element of structuring or the greater amount of variation in work patterns in these kinds of job. Generally, those who perform these roles do not repeat the same short cycle of motions throughout the working period; even if some of the basic tasks are frequently repeated, they are usually punctuated by others which occur only intermittently or spasmodically.

2   The greater dependence of the work upon perceptual and other mental processes which are less 'visible' and thus less easy to measure and analyse with techniques developed in the manual area. Generally speaking, problem-solving activity relies heavily upon the handling of information in the mind, and this is much less open to observation and measurement than manual assembly operations.

These problems inhere in the work being done, and are not caused by the methods of scientific management which might be used to detect and measure them. Consequently, any attempt to 'control' these activities was associated with the exercise of authority or the development of responsibility, not with definition and measurement.

In the case of managerial work, for example, high levels of discretion must necessarily be allowed to the manager to respond to situations as they develop. How the manager should respond to emergent situations depends on the exercise of judgement and is incapable of precise specification. Managers are hired on the assumption that they are capable of making the judgements and taking the decisions within their specialist or generalist areas. They have the authority and the responsibility to act as appropriate. Control of their activities depends on there being a consensus about the values and norms which are to be applied, not on following preordained rules and procedures.

At lower levels in the organisation the development of physical technologies has removed many jobs of the routine kind and created many other jobs which require (as managerial jobs have always required) the exercise of greater discretion by the worker. This development has fused with moral challenges to 'soul-destroying' work and led to pressure to develop alternative approaches to job design.

Job Redesign

These alternative approaches have now been identified to distinguish them as 'job redesign', defined by Davis as the process of: 'specification of the contents, methods and relationships of jobs, in order to satisfy technological and organisational requirements as well as the social and personal requirements of the job holder' (Davis, 1967, p 21). Strictly, this definition could have been applied to the early design approaches, but it is different in that it relies on different models of man in its concern to take into account the social and personal requirements of the job holder. Where the one continues to emphasise its contribution to efficiency and profit, the other does so in terms of personal satisfaction and growth.

The general effect has been to move from the position where jobs were extended by job enlargement or job rotation to include more variety as the antidote to boredom, to that where jobs have been 'vertically loaded' or enriched by incorporating a requirement that higher level skills have to be exercised as a necessary method of securing worker commitment to the work. A degree of variation is often permitted to make the job more interesting and secure greater commitment. These experiments in job enlargement and job enrichment allow more attention to be paid to the problems of tapping human motivation to work than was possible with the earlier (industrial engineering) methods.

It is not, however, possible to redesign *individual* jobs in interdependent work systems without also influencing the relationships between the jobs and the people performing them. The relationships between people involved in work sequences are inevitably affected by such changes, even when those changes do not set out deliberately to alter the relationships. More recently, however, this inevitable consequence has been recognised in the design process and some variant on the theme of designing autonomous work groups has resulted. With this development, job redesign takes on a social as well as an individual connotation.

These new developments differ in the extent to which they accommodate individual differences in human motivation and in social contexts. But they share the one feature of making the job bigger in some way, just which way being crucial to the distinctions in their methods and approach. Walker and Guest defined job enlargement as:

'Simply the combining of two or more separate jobs into one ... [leading to] a lengthening of time cycles'
(Walker and Guest, 1952, p 151).

Job enrichment involves a similar 'combination' but this entails bringing together tasks which call for different and higher levels of skill from those associated with the unenriched job; from this develops the idea, advanced by Herzberg, that job enrichment crucially requires some element of 'vertical job loading'.

In practice, there is often not such a clear-cut distinction between the two techniques. Richardson and Walker's description of IBM's job enlargement programme in its Endicott plant implies that some 'vertical loading' was involved:

'Machine operators ... began ... to make their own "set-ups" and to do their own inspection ... their jobs were *enlarged* to include the skills and responsibilities of "set-up" men and of inspectors'
(Richardson and Walker, 1948, p 12).

Similarly, autonomous work groups (in which the group rather than the individual job holder assumes some responsibility for scheduling and work allocation) may involve horizontal or vertical job loading, although at the level of the group there is usually some element of vertical loading.

Consequently, all of these various methods go some way to restoring to the worker some part of the work planning activities which was previously (in the heyday of scientific management) transferred to management functionaries. In conjunction with modifications to the physical technology, the worker may at least assume more control (or simply more semblance of control) over the work and workpace. To this extent, job redesign implies a major change in the direction taken by methods of job design and definition.

Reasons for the Change of Direction

The reasons for this change of direction are numerous and it is impossible to establish which is the most significant. Four main reasons appear to have been influential in some cases.

1 *Market reasons:*   Companies have often found themselves in a competitive market situation in which they have to secure higher productivity and lower unit labour costs to survive. Some managements have responded to this by taking on board the idea that too great a fractionalisation of work roles is inimical to increased productivity from more independent workers, and have reversed the trend to simplification.

In his discussion of the developments in the Phillips Eindhoven plant, van Beek argues that traditional job analysis allows managers to divide

> 'jobs into short-cycle tasks which could be learned
> quickly and in which unskilled workers could reach a
> high level of proficiency, the assembly line promoting a
> regular flow of production and wage systems ensuring an
> equitable remuneration'
> (van Beek, 1964, p 161)

may no longer provide a solution to the economic problems faced by management. In his view, extensive specialisation renders the production system vulnerable, sophisticated wage systems prove ineffective, better education and changed attitudes work against rigorous division, so that study and reassessment of unskilled work becomes a continual necessity (ibid).

2 *Technological reasons:*   One response to the above kind of

market problem is to improve the physical technology of production. This in itself often destroys old work tasks and creates new ones. It often happens that this change calls for a very different role and a very different kind of work commitment from the worker. For the same reason as before, managements may make a virtue out of the necessity for changing the definitions of work.

Walsh, discussing the introduction of job enlargement into electricity board district offices, saw the stimulus to change in the introduction of a computer which required a different approach to the traditional consumer service tasks and eliminated some of the more routine and humdrum tasks of preparation. Without management necessarily or consciously intending that the new jobs should be 'enriched' in any way, this consequence was virtually forced upon them by the nature of the technological change itself (Walsh, 1969, p 43).

3 *Psychological reasons:* A great many studies have indicated that many workers receive little 'satisfaction' from their jobs, and some of more recent origin have demonstrated the incidence and associations of strain and stress in work (Cooper and Payne, 1978). It is difficult to associate satisfaction with either productivity or cost to the employer, but the studies of stress are more pointed in this respect. This is particularly true in the primary sector, where these findings have helped to focus management minds on the problem of job design in the interests of improving efficiency, if for no other reason.

In their account of the job enrichment experiments in Imperial Chemical Industries, Paul and Robertson present both their definition of the economic problem to be resolved and their view of the connection between the proposed solution and theories of motivation.

> 'At a time when there is a premium on individual effort, as labour becomes too costly to waste and concern about under-employment of people in industry mounts, theory suggests that more attention to the motivators, a more critical look at the jobs themselves ... would pay dividends'
> (Paul and Robertson, 1970, p 2).

This experiment owed much to Herzberg's theory of work motivation which states that what universally motivates people at work are the factors associated with the work itself — achievement, inherent interest, recognition, responsibility, advancement, and growth in competence. Where these contribute to satisfaction and psychological growth, the contextual factors such as pay and conditions do not do so, although they may contribute to feelings of *dis*satisfaction (Herzberg, 1966, pp 71 – 6). As the motivators are jobrelated (where the others are system-related) the solution of the motivational problem seems to lie with job design.

4 *Social reasons:* It is a recurrent theme in the literature on job design that changes in workers' attitudes towards authority and the work systems which that authority offers have reduced the benefit to be gained by continued fractionalisation. It is often asserted that with higher education and higher general levels of economic self-sufficiency on the part of the workers they are now less willing to accept old regimes, and there is at least the suggestion that this shows up in lower commitment to work tasks and lower productivity.

This is supported by the development of the 'cognitive' theories of learning and motivation by people like Vroom, Porter and Lawler and, in terms of its direct impact on management thinking, by the motivator-hygiene theories of work motivation advanced by Herzberg (1966). These imply that workers at any level in the hierarchy take a considered view of the work which they do and the effort or contribution they should make in the context of the rewards which are made available. It is this element of 'consideration' which implies that the older, simpler, stimulus-response theories on which the scientific management approach relied, are increasingly less relevant to job and work design.

5 *Moral reasons:* A good deal of argument in favour of rehumanising jobs has been advanced in recent years, some by social scientists and some by those who see in their research findings indications of debilitating conditions which ought to be rectified. Managers are not impervious to this kind of argument, and there is no doubt that in some cases of change managements have responded to the moral arguments advanced.

This usually shows up as an argument justifying change after the change has been decided on for other reasons. It cannot, however, be completely discounted for this reason. The presence of predisposing attitudes may be just as necessary in managers as in any one else faced with a problem and a need to change in some direction. There is, however, little in the descriptions of innovations made to suggest that the QWL arguments have triumphed over arguments for greater efficiency and productivity as justifying job redesign (Davis and Cherns, 1975).

Principles

The comparative novelty of these approaches to job redesign means that the principles which govern the process are still evolving from practice. Herzberg has advanced a number of principles, which, he argues, need to be applied when taking decisions about vertical job loading (Herzberg, 1968). These principles are concerned with the kind of action that needs to be taken to produce consequences which are in accordance with his theory of motivation. He suggests that it is necessary to:

1 remove some controls of the work behaviour of the worker, whilst still requiring him to remain accountable for his work, so that he can assume control over the resources necessary to the performance of the job;

2 increase, as a part of the process of increasing the worthwhileness of the job, the accountability of individual workers for their own work, so that they perceive themselves to be individually accountable;

3 provide the worker with a unit of work which in some sense and on some criterion or dimension is complete in itself, so that he can assume ownership of his job;

4 increase the worker's authority, freedom, or discretion to decide, so that the worker can take control of his own work and satisfy the requirements for performance;

5 make the worker the recipient of information and reports which do not necessarily 'go through' the supervisor, so that the individual has direct feedback and a basis for self-appraisal;

6 introduce the worker progressively to new and more difficult tasks as previously assigned ones are successfully completed and mastered, to establish the organisation as a learning institution;

7 allocate individual workers to specialised tasks, so that they have the opportunity to become uniquely expert on some aspect of the work of the undertaking;

8 change the nature of the relationship between the corporate organisation and the worker from one of boss-subordinate to one which is more clearly 'professional', in that it supports the independent practice of the worker (Herzberg, 1968, p 58; Davis and Taylor, 1972, p 119; Herzberg, 1974, pp 72–4).

These develop out of Herzberg's theory of motivation, which draws a distinction between 'motivators' – factors inherent in and directly linked with the job itself, which will motivate people to work – and 'hygiene factors', which are those that surround and provide the context to the job, which may create dissatisfaction but cannot motivate. As motivators are concerned with inherent job interest and responsibility and with opportunities which the job provides for challenge, achievement, and recognition, vertical job loading must, in Herzberg's scheme, enhance these factors.

This model underpins the sequence of steps, which, Herzberg suggests, have to be taken to introduce job enrichment. These adopt an uncompromising managerial orientation, being directed towards increased efficiency defined in traditional ways. Although it is based on a theory of human learning and motivation, and could incidentally increase worker satisfaction, it finds no place for any increased employee participation in the decision-processes involved. He advocates:

1 Selection for enrichment of those jobs in which
   (a) technical changes can be made with a minimum of expense;
   (b) job satisfaction is low;
   (c) hygiene (wages and support costs) is expensive;
   (d) improved motivation will affect performance.

2 Starting with the conviction that the content of these jobs can be changed, use of brainstorming methods to identify possible changes which could result in enrichment.

3 Avoidance of any form of employee participation in determining the changes to be made on the grounds that this will clutter the process with emotion-based resistances.

4 Elimination of propositions for change which are
   (a) concerned only with hygiene (contextual) factors;
   (b) concerned only with generalities;
   (c) concerned only with horizontal loading factors;
   and retention only of those which involve vertical loading and are directly, specifically, and solely related to motivators (concerned with the actual job).

5   Establishing a controlled experiment to examine the job enrich-
    ment effects which follow on from the proposed changes.

6   Preparation of the management team involved to expect anxiety
    and hostility from supervisors and poor results from the workers
    affected, at least initially, and until employees become accus-
    tomed to their new jobs (Herzberg, 1968, pp 61 – 2).

The warning to managements not to regard job enrichment as an
immediate solution or as a longer term panacea whose benefits will
prove obvious to all is well made. Even in contexts where job
enrichment is economically warranted and technologically feasible,
there is a human variable to consider.

As others have pointed out, individual and subcultural differences are likely to render job enrichment unsuitable and unacceptable to many workers. Shepard (1974) suggests that urban-reared
workers might never meet the condition of becoming accustomed to
the new jobs, and Little and Warr (1974) that it may never prove
applicable to instrumentally oriented blue-collar workers. Reif and
Luthans (1974) point to the probability that many workers will react
negatively and with increased anxiety when they are invited to accept
changes in their known work environment, learn new skills, rise to
new challenges, and make fewer demands on the system through
their supervisor for security.

The 'implementing principles' advanced by Hackman *et al* (1975,
p 62) are not really very different from Herzberg's vertical job
loading principles. They do not seek to advance a new approach to
job enrichment as a practical method of job design; rather, they
attempt a different explanation of the links between kinds of
redesign and kinds of worker response, in which greater prominence
is given to the requirement that some workers need to be given
greater discretion in the performance of their work tasks (Lawler,
Hackman and Kaufman, 1973; Cameron, Orchin and White, 1974;
Hackman, Oldham, Janson and Purdy, 1975; Janson, 1975).

Consequences

Studies of the effects of the process of enlarging or enriching jobs
have been made by a number of people, and it is therefore possible
to consider whether this development promises to remove the
grounds for criticism which the previous fractionalising approach
attracted (Alderfer, 1969; Evans, 1973; Ford, 1969; Hackman and
Lawler, 1971; Hulin and Blood, 1968; Janson, 1975; Vroom, 1969).

The findings of these studies support the general expectation that
enlargement or enrichment leads to increased job satisfaction. The

elements which are singled out as contributing to this are: use of skills and abilities; opportunity to learn new things; perception of work as meaningful; and amount of autonomy and responsibility.

Job enlargement is also shown to contribute to performance improvements and reductions in labour turnover and absenteeism – factors which often go with relatively high levels of job dissatisfaction. There is also a suggestion in these findings that personal variables may be significant in producing these results. Work by Hackman and Lawler (1971), Hulin and Blood (1968), and Turner and Lawrence (1968) supports the view that these results may obtain with small town (rather than city) workers and with workers who have stronger needs for growth, challenge, and variety. The failures of some initiatives in job enlargement to produce beneficial results might be accounted for in these terms.

Kasl concludes his review of this literature with the comment that the survey data available support the view that:

> 'Men on dull and monotonous jobs do not misperceive their work: they call their jobs dull and monotonous. The levels of job satisfaction, however, do not correspond to this description, since they are not much different from other blue collar workers. Yet when their jobs are changed (enlarged), they do respond with higher job satisfaction, though this is probably not true for all subgroups'
> (Kasl, 1976, p 30).

Strauss and Kornhauser in turn offer a possible explanation of this by recognising that workers can and do adjust to non-challenging work (Strauss, 1974b, p 78), and although as a result their lives may be comparatively empty and only half meaningful (Kornhauser, 1965, p 270), workers do not see this as distressing because to do so would destroy their self-respect.

SUMMARY

The design and definition of work tasks and standards of performance is a primary managerial responsibility. The methods used depend on the kind of production technology employed and, consequently, upon the extent to which discretion is required in the performance of work tasks.

Where the work is routinised and, *a fortiori*, where it remains machine paced, job design will employ some variant on the theme of work study and involve boss-subordinate negotiation of standards based on the application of time-study methods. These methods have limitations when applied to so-called 'indirect' work and to management.

The original approach of scientific management has been modified to meet the demands of new technologies and to accommodate changed worker attitudes and orientations to work. Experiments in job redesign (which to some degree accept modern theories of human motivation) are not yet extensive, nor are they so revolutionary that their effects cannot be measured against the traditional criteria of individual productivity.

The assessment of these approaches against criteria of satisfaction and psychological growth cast some doubt on the capacity of job fractionalisation to produce a satisfying work context: there is some persuasive evidence that workers find their work boring and make a response which is characterised as bare acceptance of what cannot be avoided.

New technologies appear to require a more responsible attitude on the part of the worker, and this seems to call, in turn, for some form of job enlargement/enrichment (or vertical job loading) which can in some circumstances change worker orientations. The evidence suggests that the necessary learning of new attitudes remains slow and partial. Successful change appears to be conditional (and contingent) on existing worker orientations learned in different conditions of work definition.

Reading:

Baldamus (1961).
Behrend (1957) pp 503 – 15.
Beynon and Blackburn (1972).
Blackler and Brown (1978).
Blair (1974).
Boydell (1970).
Buchanan (1979).
Cemach (1969).

Cooper and Payne (1978).
Hackman *et al* (1975).
Herzberg (1968) pp 53 – 62.
Kasl (1978).
Likert (1961).
Millward (1959).
Niebel (1972).
Roff and Watson (1961).

2 The Human Context

Employment work makes different demands *for* people to do it and has different effects *on* the people who do it. The differences stem from the fact that work does not present itself as a constant demand. It is divided into jobs with distinct demand and effect characteristics. Nevertheless, industry can be said to make two broad types of demand of its human resources:

1 a capacity or capability for decision and action (or more generally, for problem-solving and for mental and motor activity); and

2 a disposition to cooperate with others (fellow workers *and* management) in interdependent and interrelated tasks.

The first of these is commonly associated with skill or ability. The second with motivation (or willingness to contribute work). The demands made under these headings vary, however, according to the kind of work (job) and the nature of its environment.

Industry must necessarily and at base regard people as instruments in the production of wealth, as willing 'cogs in the industrial machine'. It must place prime emphasis on ways in which their specialised perceptual and motor aptitudes and abilities can be made to contribute to broader objectives, without, however, necessarily diminishing them. What is needed in work is (in the language associated with the concept of artificial intelligence) a rather superior computer, capable of taking in, storing, logically processing, and constructively utilising information in decision-making as a prelude to taking appropriate action (Spence, 1969, pp 50–54). Personality may come into the equation, but the main emphasis is on capacity, ability, and skill.

In general, the demands made use but a small part of the human being's total repertoire of abilities and a fraction of the range of attributes of the human personality (Miller and Form, 1951, p 757). Man is broadly capable of both doing and being more than industry can make use of. Nevertheless, 'people are different', partly because of their natural endowment, but mainly because of their differential experience and their varied opportunities for learning and developing. The fact of such differences in both personality and capability creates different wants and expectations ('orientations') in people and offers the possibility of these being matched to greater or lesser extents with what is being offered by industry in the way of job demand or challenge.

There may therefore be a gap between human potential and industrial demand for it, but there is also opportunity for increasing or reducing this in each particular case of employment. Although few may realise their *full* potential in work activities, much can be done to match individual capabilities and personalities with the requirements of jobs.

RELEVANT ATTRIBUTES

Individuals have a good deal in common at the level of physiological and mental structure, but they differ from one another to some extent on practically all dimensions of their dispositions and abilities. They have their basic physique and operating systems in common (although these differ on physical dimensions), features which owe much but not all to inheritance. They differ in their personalities, attitudes, motivations, aptitudes and abilities, features which they acquire by learning through 'experience' (including that of learning itself).

These have a general import for industry because they have a bearing on the manner in which people approach and perceive the work situation and the relevance of the demands which it makes on them. This is but a special case of the individual's general approach to his or her environment, which has been stated by Kiesler (1978) in four propositions:

1 people respond and act on their *views* of reality, not on its objective qualities;

2 people are influenced by the immediate (social) situation they perceive themselves to be in;

3 people act on motives that they bring to situations, as well as motives altered or created by situations; and

4 interpersonal actions are guided by values and beliefs which derive from the culture in which people live.

Because of this general human orientation to situation, including the situation of work, the personality attributes indicated by the concepts of 'frame of reference', 'perspective', 'attitude', 'orientation' and 'motivation' assume importance in any attempt to achieve a match between the demands of work and the personality and capacities of the human resource.

We can, however, identify with confidence only those individual attributes and differences which psychologists have been able to describe and measure. Everyday observations may well suggest that many such differences do exist, but our confidence in discussing them stems largely from our ability to measure them by using appropriate instruments. Some of these instruments are concerned with physical dimensions (such as height or weight) but most are concerned with personality and intellectual and emotional dimensions whose measurement depends on the application of appropriate tests.

A description of individual differences is therefore very largely confined to the differences that can be identified by applying various types of test. A description of the individual differences that are important for industrial work is similarly restricted, even though industry is not concerned with the full range of differences of interest to the psychologist.

'Physical' Attributes and Aptitudes

People obviously vary in their purely physical attributes: some are tall and some short, some strong and others not so strong. People's sensory capacities are also likely both to vary and to play important parts in the individual's ability to learn and to perform certain types of action. People also vary in the extent to which they have been able to develop their physique and their sensory systems; this is likely to be affected by their dietary and learning experience as they have grown up. In extreme cases, individuals may have some deficiency in their basic endowment (such as mental or physical handicap) and may, as a result of illness or accident, have acquired handicaps during their lifetime.

These features of the human animal are more amenable to measurement than their mental and emotional attributes. Physique is largely a matter of height and weight, and physical strength is measurable by simple muscular tests. The person's health record or history is a further indicator of the likely future capacity of the body to perform motor and mechanical acts. A medical examination (physical screening) can tell a good deal about the individual's capability. It can also indicate potential problems, such as those associated with under- or over-weight conditions. Sensory capacities — sight, hearing, etc — are sometimes directly measurable in the course of such an examination, and are more extensibly measurable in various aptitude tests of the kind listed below.

Purely physical (motor or mechanical) aptitudes are important if only because action cannot occur if it is beyond the capacity of the person concerned. But these abilities and aptitudes are closely associated with and dependent on cognitive and affective abilities (if only because physical action depends on prior decision). The motor and mechanical aptitudes and those aptitudes which focus on perceptual speed, such as is involved in clerical work, are particularly relevant and important for the industrial and occupational selection and placement of workers who are essentially 'doers' (as distinct from 'deciders').

The most general of these are the motor functions which focus on speed and accuracy, and on the individual's co-ordination, in performing physical actions. These have been made the subject of tests of manual dexterity particularly, but also of dexterity in movement of other limbs and of the whole body. Such tests are, however, often linked with perceptual, mechanical, and spatial aptitudes, reflecting the rather obvious links between these more general aptitudes and the special ones concerned with physical activity. These come together in attainment tests for those who have undergone some training. Tests for proficiency in secretarial work, for example, will cover vocabulary, grammar, spelling, punctuation, arithmetic, etc., each graded in order of difficulty, and show the person's level of attainment, speed, and accuracy.

Equally important in some contexts are the individual's motor and perceptual capacities. The distinct emphasis in the one set of aptitude tests is on speed and accuracy of mechanical reasoning and mechanical knowledge. Such tests, however, are closely linked with perceptual and spatial aptitudes as well as motor function. In clerical aptitudes, the same considerations of speed, accuracy, and coordination as in motor functions are discernible and the link between the general aptitudes is much clearer. The special emphasis is on perceptual speed, or the speed with which the individual can spot verbal and numeral mistakes by making comparisons between data presented in different forms.

This view underplays the importance of theoretical knowledge which necessarily lies behind these activities. This is usually transmitted formally through education and training in the form of theories. These are usually assessed in a similiar fashion — that is, through 'attainment tests' in the form of examinations. Although some of the above tests do throw some light on the theories which respondents may hold, the testing of theories is likely to be done through some form of 'examination'. In the educational context, this is done by setting and marking examinations at the end of a course, but may be employed on a shorter term basis to provide feedback to the tutor and to the student. In the industrial context, it is more often carried out as a part of the process of evaluating learning during the course of training, and in that context, may make more use of 'practical' tests in which the assessment is of 'theory in use'.

Intelligence and Aptitude

Intelligence and aptitude enable individuals to make sense and use of their environment. It is now thought that much of what the individual is and does depends on the meaning which he or she attaches to experience – whether that is past experience or situations newly encountered. Past experience helps to develop the person's *frame of reference* which serves to focus attention and interest and to direct thought and action towards his or her environment.

A frame of reference has been defined by Thelen and Whitnall (1949, p 159) as: 'a conceptual structure of generalisations or contexts' which give meaning to what is experienced and direction to individual action. They see it as made up of:

(a)   postulates about what is essential;

(b)   assumptions about what is valuable;

(c)   attitudes about what is possible; and

(d)   ideas about what will work effectively.

These component parts are identified with a number of concepts used by psychologists to describe and measure aspects of the person: interests, preferences, attitudes, and theories.

Both general intelligence and particular aptitudes are thought to be largely the product of learning, without which the innate capacity of the human mind and body would not be translated into effective decision and action. Although a distinction between personality and aptitude is often maintained, this is to be regarded as a distinction of convenience, not of reality (Anastasi, 1976, p 354).

'Intelligence' is a generalised intellectual capacity distinct from specific 'aptitudes', although the measurement of the one is usually based on an aggregation of scores obtained on tests of specific aptitudes. An 'intelligence test' is usually concerned with a variety of stimuli, with the various aptitude scores being aggregated to provide a single score, such as that of the 'intelligence quotient' (IQ). It is intended to provide a broad indication of the individual's general intellectual level, and is validated against very broad criteria.

An 'aptitude test' attempts to produce a measure of the individual's intellectual level in respect of only one aptitude, but may be combined into a battery – a multiple aptitude test – to provide, not a single score of the IQ type, but a profile of the individual's aptitudinal strengths and weaknesses.

The range of intellectual aptitudes involved may be illustrated by reference to the 'primary mental abilities' designated by Thurstone (1938) and corroborated by later researchers (such as French, 1951). Anastasi (1976, p 272–3) lists seven such aptitudes:

1 *Verbal Comprehension* The principal factor in such tests as reading comprehension, verbal analogies, disarranged sentence, verbal reasoning, and proverb matching. It is most adequately measured by vocabulary tests.

2 *Word Fluency* This is found in such tests as anagrams, rhyming, or naming words in a given category (for example, boys' names, or words beginning with the letter T).

3 *Number* This is most closely identified with speed and accuracy of arithmetic computation.

4 *Space* This factor may represent two distinct factors, one covering perception of fixed spatial or geometric relations, the other manipulatory visualisations, in which changed positions or transformations must be visualised.

5 *Associative Memory* This is found principally in tests demanding rote memory for paired associates. There is some evidence to suggest that this factor may reflect the extent to which memory crutches are utilised (Christal, 1958). The evidence is against the presence of a broader factor through all memory tests. Other restricted memory factors, such as memory for temporal sequences and for spatial position, have been suggested by some investigations.

6 *Perceptual Speed* Quick and accurate grasping of visual details, similarities, and differences. This factor may be the same as the speed factor identified by Kelley and other early investigators. This is one of several factors subsequently identified in perceptual tasks (Thurstone, 1944).

7 *Induction or General Reasoning* The identification of this factor was least clear. Thurstone originally proposed an inductive and a deductive factor. The latter was best measured by tests of syllogistic reasoning and the former by tests requiring the subject to find a rule, as in a number series completion test. Evidence for the deductive factor, however, was much weaker than for the inductive. Moreover, other investigators suggested a general reasoning factor, best measured by arithmetic reasoning tests (Anastasi, 1976, pp 372–3).

Relationships of Intelligence and Aptitude

The distinction between general and specific aptitudes is not easy to draw but some tests are designed to measure the one and some the other. The relationship between the general and the specific is commonly depicted in hierarchical terms, following the theory advanced by Vernon. This places general intelligence (Spearman's **g** factor) at the apex of the hierarchy and below it the subcategories of general intelligence. First, there are the two broad-based factors of verbal-educational (**v:ed**) and practical mechanical (**k:M**) aptitudes. Each of these is then subdivided into subordinate factors, such as verbal and number, or spatial and manual, respectively, for the two factors mentioned. Even more specific factors may then be identified below this subfactor level.

Figure 2

Organisation of general and specific aptitudes

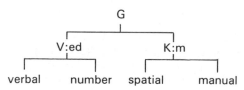

The whole hierarchy contributes to what we refer to as intelligence, but subordinate parts of it are related to broader or narrower components of this general aptitude.

Some multiple-test batteries are more directly concerned with the measurement of a limited range of specific aptitudes rather than general aptitude or general intelligence. One of the most widely used batteries is the Differential Aptitude Test (DAT) focused mainly on perceptual aptitudes. It was designed for use in educational and counselling meetings. It secures eight scores on: verbal reasoning;

abstract reasoning; mechanical reasoning; spelling; clerical speed and accuracy; numerical ability; space relations; language usage. The test has been extensively tested for validity and reliability. It used a standardised sample of 64,000 students in public and parochial schools in 33 states of the USA and the District of Columbia to establish the norms. As yet, however, the data on predictive validity against vocational criteria are not extensive.

What is 'measured' by such test batteries is primarily directed at what the individual might be expected or predicted to do in the sense of putting out behaviour or performance. Some tests, however, also look at the individual's capacity for 'taking in' or making sense of experience. This is obviously related to a wide range of aptitudes which are measured in many tests, but some make a specific point of attempting to measure capacity for learning or for taking in and making sense of experience. An example of this is provided by the General Aptitude Test Battery (GATB), developed in the USA for use by employment counsellors in the US Employment Service.

Relevant Aspects of the Personality

There remains an important relationship between general and specific aptitudes and other attributes of the personality (or the 'being' aspects of the human being). This concerns questions about the relationship between an individual's aptitudes and his or her frames of reference and motivation.

Only some aspects of personality are particularly relevant to work behaviour, and then more so in respect of some jobs but not others. That special aspect of personality which is associated with 'character' − focused on qualities of honesty and integrity, and associated with 'principled' behaviour − are of some importance, the more so where the work tasks demand trustworthiness in the performer or where they expose the individual to greater temptations. The traditional way of securing information on this aspect is the one which focuses on the reference or the testimonial. In former years, the 'character reference' was often an important factor in securing employment; nowadays, it has much less significance, except for certain highly specific types of work.

The other aspects of personality − those associated with attributes such as sociability, emotional stability, objectivity, or leadership quality − have a general importance for all jobs in so far as they (or some of them) are relevant to the question of whether a worker can tolerate and cope with such stresses or strains as the job may engender. Stress and strain are not thought to be 'caused' by either the personality characteristics or the job characteristics in isolation, but by a juxtaposition of the two in some combination. The assessment and measurement of tolerance for stress may be attempted by using personality tests, but cannot be completed unless some assessment is made of the jobs themselves, regarded as criteria.

These other aspects of personality also have a differential significance for particular jobs. Some such attributes are vital in some jobs, some are considered to be totally irrelevant in others. A salesperson may need to possess certain traits – thought of in terms of an outward-going personality, friendliness or sociability – but a semi-skilled machine operator may need none of these to do the job (and may indeed be less proficient in performing it if he or she has a personality characterised in these ways). Where, however, they are relevant or important, they can be identified and assessed by using personality tests.

This cannot, however, occur unless steps are taken to ensure that the tests are valid and reliable in themselves and have been validated for the kind of population to which they are to be applied. The obvious example of this problem is provided by the intelligence test; a test validated for a school population is unlikely to take one very far in assessing the intelligence of a population of 40 year old workers. The same principles apply in the application of personality tests.

Types of Personality Test

There are several hundred personality tests, using inventory or projective methods of measurement, practically all of them based on a definition of personality which emphasises the emotional, motivational, attitudinal and interpersonal aspects (rather than the intellectual ones which are usually considered under the heading of 'intelligence' tests).

One which attempts to identify and classify personality traits, using factor analysis and consequently illustrative of the kinds of factor or personality trait distinguished is the *Guilford-Zimmerman Temperament Survey* (GZTS). This is based on uncovering inter-correlations among individual items on a multiplicity of personality inventories. It has been used to yield separate scores based on 30 different items in each 10 traits, defined as follows:

G. *General Activity:* Hurrying, liking for speed, liveliness, vitality, production, efficiency, *v* slow and deliberate, easily fatigued, inefficient.

R. *Restraint:* Serious minded, deliberate, persistent *v* carefree, impulsive, excitement-loving.

A. *Ascendance:* Self-defence, leadership, speaking in public, bluffing *v* submissiveness, hesitation, avoiding conspicuousness.

S. *Sociability:* Having many friends, seeking social contacts and limelight *v* few friends and shyness.

E. *Emotional Stability:* Evenness of moods, optimistic, composure, *v* fluctuation of moods, pessimism, day-dreaming, excitability, feelings of guilt, worry, loneliness, and ill-health.

O. *Objectivity:* Thick-skinned *v* hypersensitive, self-centred, suspicious, having ideas of reference, getting into trouble.

F. *Friendliness:* Toleration of hostile action, acceptance of domination, respect for others *v* belligerence, hostility, resentment, desire to dominate, and contempt for others.

T. *Thoughtfulness:* Reflective, observing of self and others, mental poise *v* interest in overt activity and mental disconcertedness.

P. *Personal Relations:* Tolerance of people, faith in social institutions *v* critical of institutions, fault-finding, suspicious, self-pitying.

M. *Masculinity:* Interest in masculine activities, not easily disgusted, hard-boiled, inhibited emotional expression, little interest in clothes and style *v* interest in feminine activities and vocations, easily disgusted, fearful, romantic, emotionally expressive (Anastasi, 1976, pp 506–7).

These are used to yield *profiles* rather than single-trait scores, which are then used as the basis for diagnosis or prediction of the kind of personality being considered. Where there exists an awareness of what 'kind of personality' is best suited to a particular job, it can be used to inform placement decisions.

The *Minnesota Multiphasic Personality Inventory* (MMPI), can be used to identify, in advance, possible human malfunctions and is probably the most widely used test of its kind. It provides 550 affirmative statements about 'personality' to which the respondent is invited to indicate whether they are true or false or whether the individual is unable to say. These items range widely in content covering such areas as:

(a) health, psychosomatic symptoms, neurological disorders, and motor disturbances;

(b) sexual, religious, political, and social attitudes;

(c) educational, occupational, marital and family questions;

(d) a range of well known neurotic or psychotic behaviour manifestations, such as obsessive and compulsive states, delusions, hallucinations, phobias, and sadistic or masochistic trends (Anastasi, 1976, p 497).

From this list it will be clear that one very prominent use to which the test is put is the uncovering of evidence of abnormality, and a number of 'clinical scales' have been produced for use in this context. One very popular test for use in this fashion is Cattell's 16PF test, which invites subjects to record their personalities on 16 separate dimensions (primary traits). These are then aggregated to give second and third level scores, which can be used to screen candidates. Others based on measurements within normal populations and unrelated to pathology have been developed (Anastasi, 1976, p 499) and can be used to compare a test population with a normal distribution.

Predicting Motivation

Where these kinds of personality test have some value in indicating how well a person is likely to perform a given type of job, industry is at least as much interested in predicting whether the person will *want* to perform the job. This aspect is normally considered under the separate heading of *motivation*. This is a central concept in explanations of human action because it has an immediate relationship to action. Its greater immediacy is established by the definition of motivation as dependent on body energy being mobilised to act in a particular fashion or direction.

For example, 'motive' has been defined as 'a state of the organism in which bodily energy is mobilised and selectively directed towards parts of the environment' (Newcomb, 1952, p 80). By necessary implication, the 'state' does not exist (and therefore cannot be either recognised or measured) before the energies are aroused. It is in this sense that motivation is comparatively immediate. This does not deny motivation importance in determining what the individual will do, but it exists as an intermediate level concept between the more stable attitudes and the actual behaviour.

This immediacy makes the concept less useful than it might otherwise be in predicting behaviour in advance of its being called for.

Consequently, modern theories of motivation attempt to utilise measures of the deeper seated and more stable personality factors (such as interests, values, attitudes and orientations) to predict motivation.

Views taken of motivation can, however, be divided into two groups, with the alternative view to the one identified above, stressing general and on-going motivation.

Spence illustrates this view with his suggestion that: 'the one thing ... which the human being has in full measure is motivation, [which is] linked to instinctive and emotional impulses which arise from the simple fact of animal consciousness' (Spence, 1969, p 50). Motivation in this most *general* sense of 'movement', may, in other words, call for no other explanation than that the human being must move or act because he or she is alive (as is also argued by Kelly, 1963, p 37). This view can then be linked to the need and drive theories of specific motivation (Maslow, 1954).

This same idea that the human being cannot escape interaction with the environment also occurs in Hayes's (1962) suggestion that the individual is necessarily 'driven' to produce experience for himself or herself by manipulating the situation. This is done to increase learning and thus increase his or her intelligence (defined by Hayes as a collection of learned abilities). In this theory, these experience-producing drives are genetically determined and: 'represent the only hereditary basis of individual differences in intelligence' (Anastasi, 1976, p 355). This view is more directly linked with the 'reinforcement' theories of motivation (Skinner, 1965; Kenney and Reid, 1986, pp 117–21).

These views, taken together, suggest that the individual can be expected *and* predicted to act in ways which will enable the individual to survive in the environment in a manner which meets both the person's animal needs and accords with his or her self-perception. They do not, however, predict what he or she will eat, or when, or whether he or she is motivated to make more money by working harder.

Interests and Values

The 'longer term' perspective of motivation is, however, more amenable to prediction from the application of those personality tests which concentrate on particular facets of personality, such as interests, values, and attitudes. These tests, being more highly focused, are generally easier to handle than the broad based personality tests. They also have a greater relevance to the question of securing a basic (that is, long-term) fit between person and occupation or career and have been used extensively in occupational and career counselling and industrial placement.

The rationale of this approach is that people will be more highly motivated to do those things which they are interested in, those things which relate to whatever they consider to be valuable, and those things towards which they hold positive attitudes. If, therefore, any of these can be measured in advance of the requirement to do anything, these measures will have some predictive value at this level.

'Interests' serve to direct attention in some directions rather than others (Steers and Porter, 1979, p 21). Interests represent the outcomes of choice because people cannot be interested in everything in their environment. Attaching priority to some aspects over others because they are considered to be more valuable or important permits the individual to act both consistently and with economy of effort. A person who is 'particularly interested in money' is likely to be turned on by offers of it. A person who is uninterested in his power will tend not to attach weight to this when assessing alternative job opportunities. Differences of this kind provide the foundation for the development of scales of preference which are used by people as a basis for comparing and evaluating alternative courses of action open to them, in work or out of it.

People also attach value or importance to different things as being either essential to or desirable for life. How they distribute their values may reflect, to some degree, the values absorbed during socialisation, but each person's values will be unique to that individual. It is nevertheless possible to recognise some broad classes of value among people. For example, Riesman (1952) identified three distinct personality types, tradition-directed, inner-directed, and other-directed, which respectively attach importance to traditional values, inner (moral) feelings of rightness, and the opinions of others. Similarly, McClelland (1951) categorises human beings according to whether they value affection, achievement, or power. These classifications are established on the basis of observations of the stable features of behaviour, which in turn provide the basis for prediction.

Situations (such as those associated with work) may attract particular kinds of interest. Most individuals' primary interest in employment work (whether they are managers or workers) is likely to be in the returns of income and other satisfactions it offers. In addition to material rewards, some individuals will value the opportunity which working provides to use modern technology. But they may not (as Dubin's researches suggested) have much interest in work as a source of affective relationships because these are more easily found in the home and family (Dubin, 1956). Work is valued in ways which for most people may be different from the ways in which they value other institutions.

Measurement of Interests and Values

The identification and measurement of interests through personality tests (Anastasi, 1976, pp 541 – 3) are carried out 'indirectly'. In these tests, people are not simply asked what their interests (particularly their occupational interests) are, because they often have insufficient information on which to form views and their perceptions are, consequently, likely to be significantly influenced by occupational stereotypes.

How the measures are made may be illustrated by reference to the *Strong Vocational Interest Blank* (SVIB), now standardised as the **Strong-Campbell Interest Inventory** (SCII), which is based on:

a items concerned with the individual's liking or disliking for a wide variety of specific activities, objects, or types of person that he or she has encountered in the course of daily life;

b keying the responses for different occupations, treated as criteria.

In the SCII, 325 items are grouped into seven parts. The first five parts are concerned with occupations, school subjects, activities (such as repairing a clock, making a speech), amusements, and day-to-day contact with various types of people. Respondents are asked to indicate their preferences by marking L (for liking), D (for disliking), or I (for indifference).

The remaining two parts require the respondent to express his or her preference between two items in a contrasted pair (dealing with things or dealing with people, for example) and to make (with Y (yes), N (no) or ? (unsure)) a set of self-descriptive statements. The inventory produced by each respondent is scored for all occupational scales, and standard scores are given for the two sexes for each occupation, where such standard scores have been produced by testing appropriate occupational criterion groups (Anastasi, 1976, pp 528 – 36).

Tests of values (and also of attitudes) may be made to predict, when coupled with some assessment of the intensity with which the individual will pursue them, something of the person's general motivation (Anastasi, 1976, p 354). The instruments used to measure values vary in approach, but have a good deal in common with measures of interests (and attitudes).

One widely used test, the *Study of Values*, developed by Allport, Vernon and Lindzey (1960), is designed to measure the strength of six basic interests or evaluative attitudes:

1 *Theoretical:* Characterised by a dominant interest in the discovery of truth andd by an empirical, critical, rational, 'intellectual' approach.

2 *Economic:* Emphasising useful and practical values; conforming closely to the prevailing stereotype of the 'average American businessman'.

3 *Aesthetic:* Placing the highest value on form and harmony; judging and enjoying each unique experience from the standpoint of its grace, symmetry, and fitness.

4 *Social:* Originally defined as love of people, this category has now been modified and confined to altruism and philanthropy.

5 *Political:* Primarily interested in personal power, influence and renown; not necessarily limited to the field of politics.

6 *Religious:* Mystical, concerned with the unity of all experience, and seeking to comprehend the cosmos as a whole.

Each of these is approached via a scattered set of items, each of which the individual has to rate in an order of preference in the context of either two or four alternatives which fall within the different value categories. The raw scores are used to provide a profile, and although normative scores are given for comparative purposes, statistical parameters are not used to provide a basis for diagnosis or prediction.

Super's *Work Values Inventory*, designed for use in vocational guidance and personnel selection, explores the sources of satisfaction which the individual seeks from work. The respondent is asked to rate each of 45 work values on a five-point scale of importance for him or her. Fifteen scores are produced on such dimensions as creativity, economic return, intellectual stimulation, security, and prestige. Percentile norms for a sample of 10,000 college students are provided, and norms for occupations are being accumulated. These permit comparisons of a test population with an assumed standard, provided a comparable test population is involved.

Attitudes and their Measurement

Attitudes can be linked with motivation to the extent that they reveal the probable response of the individual to any category of stimulus in the environment. An *attitude* has been defined as a broad and general 'predisposition to perform, perceive, think and feel' in relation to some object (or issue) (Newcomb, 1952, pp 118 – 19). The notion of 'predisposition' is central to the definition and the predictive value of the concept, although it is to be distinguished from the more immediate 'predisposition' to act, which is associated with the concept of 'motivation'.

Attitude admits the possibility of predicting the individual's likely direction-set for perceiving, thinking, feeling or acting in advance of any specific motive being aroused in the individual by the situation. It may, therefore, indicate possible (even probable) motivation in advance of any mobilisation of energy (Steers and Porter, 1979, p 22), and it is in this sense that attitude has predictive value in relation to future motivation. Measurement may therefore be undertaken to provide an indication of the individual's likely predisposition to act in relation to that type of stimulus – whether object, social group, or event.

'Attitude' is sometimes used interchangeably with 'opinion'. Opinion surveys are widely used by both researchers and management to ascertain what people think about different aspects of their work and work environment. Opinions are sought as replies to specific questions about a named stimulus – a foreman, working overtime, work tasks, etc, and the replies are taken at their face value. The findings are then used as part of the evidential base for decisions about them.

Attitude surveys may have a similar form and purpose, but as developed by psychologists, attitudes are often scaled to 'provide a quantitative measure of the individual's relative position along a uni-dimensional attitude continuum'. Perhaps the best known of these attitude scales is the *Likert-type Scale*. This kind of scale asks respondents to make a graded response to each of a series of statements, selected for their relevance and internal consistency. The grading is controlled by presenting five categories: strongly agree (SA); agree (A); undecided (U); disagree (D); and strongly disagree (SD). These are scored 5, 4, 3, 2, and 1, respectively, and scores are derived by summation.

The results then have to be interpreted in terms of empirically established norms. This need is best illustrated by the use of such scales in surveys of job satisfaction, where, for example, a situation in which 100 per cent of respondents who indicated a degree of positive satisfaction would be extremely unlikely, but a result which placed about 80 per cent in this category might be taken as 'more normal'. These scales are, however, mostly used for research purposes, and are generally not sufficiently developed for application outside this context (as, for example, in connection with selection or vocational guidance).

The general profile of human personalities treated as resources which emerges from all this is one which focuses on what has been identified as human 'orientations' (Goldthorpe, *et al*, 1968). Orientations are usually defined in terms of two broad variables: wants and expectations. 'Wants' bring together the individual's interests, values, and emotions; expectations bring together the perspectives developed as a result of their experience, which depend on their evaluation of that experience and manifest themselves most readily in attitudes and opinions. An *orientation* thus relates to the individual's likely direction-set. It therefore has some predictive value in that it indicates what the individual 'wants' to acquire or achieve, qualified by what expectations he or she has that these wants will be satisfied by action in a given situation.

SUMMARY

Industry has a need of human resources, but because the form of the need and the character of the offers which people make to reduce it both vary over a range, there exists a problem of matching work to people and people to work. The one is attempted through job design and the other through selection and placement activities. These in turn depend on being able to identify and measure the differences between people, first, in terms of their (motor-mechanical and mental-perceptual) capacities and capabilities and, secondly, in terms of those aspects of their personalities which are related to their capacity to perform the work or to tolerate the demands (and stresses) of that work. The major problem presented by the need to match people to work is that of predicting in advance, either what the individual will be capable of doing, or of learning to do successfully (frequently based on the results of applying attainment and aptitude tests), or what the person will be best fitted to do and most highly motivated to do (based on scores obtained on general or specific personality tests).

HUMAN MOTIVATION

Motivation in the sense of movement in a more specific or focused direction is necessarily of more immediate interest to those (like managers) who are concerned to align behaviours behind organisational purposes. Indications of what interests a person has, what the person values, and what the person has positive attitudes towards, offer general guidance. Such indications are likely to serve long-term purposes, such as those associated with career selection or occupational placement. They do not appear to answer the more immediate questions about what will, in day-to-day terms, turn workers on and encourage them to act in particular ways or with particular intensities.

This purpose might be better served by concentrating on the individual's orientations, on his or her wants and expectations. It seems that if we know what an individual wants, we might make the satisfaction of that want conditional on a particular kind and level of performance. It also seems that if we have some understanding of the individual's expectations, we might be able to meet those advantageously, in terms of return of cooperation, loyalty, trust, etc.

If, for example, we know that an individual wants to secure an income adequate to meet his or her family needs, the offer of such an income on condition that a certain kind and amount of work is performed in a working week, may succeed in satisfying him or her and in securing the desired performance. This, after all, is the basis of the theory of the wage incentive. If, on the other hand, the person has, as a result of experience in the labour market, only a limited expectation that such income will be forthcoming on a regular basis, the provision of 'regular employment' might, in satisfying the underlying want, change the expectation and result in greater trust. This, it is argued, is at least the rationale of the offer of 'life-time employment' in Japanese industry (Ouchi, 1981, p 15)

There are very real differences in human values, wants, preferences and expectations, both between people and in the same people at different points in time, as has been demonstrated in many pieces of research. McDougall's survey of the values and motivations of middle and senior level managers in one large British company revealed six 'clear cut groups of executive in terms of their personal motivation' (based on what they said they wanted out of their jobs).

The six types she identified (with percentages in each category) were oriented towards material reward (25 per cent), opportunity to lead others (6 per cent), variety and challenge in the job (10 per cent), a job matching intellectual interest (or vocation) (15 per cent), a comfortable life among friends (18 per cent), and status and prestige on and off the job (19 per cent) (McDougall, 1973, pp 42−3). Each group also had ideas about how managers ought to be remunerated to satisfy their wants, some preferring straight salaries (with no fringe benefits), some fringe benefits, and some performance related pay.

Comparison of the expressed preferences of the six groups with the respondents' assessments of the satisfaction received, suggested that only those looking for match of job and intellectual needs and those seeking a comfortable working group were being satisfied by the company's policies and practices, and the materialists and leaders considered themselves particularly unsatisfied by them. Introduction of the related idea of (realistic) expectations allows the 'want' to be sharpened by association with the perceived probability that it could be satisfied in all the circumstances by any reasonable course of action.

Similarly, Goldthorpe *et al* were able to show from their Luton studies that the orientations of highly mobile car workers were towards high monetary rewards for their work. High rewards were seen as available for those willing to move to work in the car industry. These workers were said to have a strong 'instrumental orientation' to their work and the workplace. Other wage-workers, in other industries making different offers, might display possibly less strong instrumental orientations, but exhibit stronger orientations towards developing meaningful social relations (a solidarist orientation) at work or towards pursuing upwardly mobile careers (a bureaucratic orientation) – again, a suggestion of a similar difference between people.

This concept, expressed in a somewhat different form and language, also figures in modern ('expectancy') theories of motivation, which set out to demonstrate the process by which people arrive at decisions to act in particular ways in response to their conceptions of what is valuable and their expectancies of what is feasible.

Most of these categories of orientation found in McDougall's study were associated with specific occupations and age groups. The first correlation suggests something similar to that which emerges from Goldthorpe's study. The second, however, suggests (although of course it cannot by itself prove) that workers may develop different wants, expectations, or orientations as they move through life. Possibly the different home and family circumstances might be regarded as causal in this respect, with want of monetary return reflecting the position reached in the family's poverty cycle – which increases the demand for money at different stages in a family's development.

Variable Wants

This idea of variable wants – where what is wanted is varied according to circumstances – lies behind many of the theories of specific motivation. In the different theories or models of motivation, these may be spoken of as needs, wants, drives, or desired goal-objects. There are two sets of theories which vary from one another according to whether they regard the 'cause' of the motive as something internal to the person – such as hunger, which might be satisfied by any variety of food – or as something external – such as an iced cake, which may be desired for itself.

The one set of theories is referred to as 'push' theories in so far as the individual is seen to be 'pushed' by some inner condition of drive or need. The other set is referred to as 'pull' theories because the individual is seen to be drawn towards some valued object in the external environment. The push theories tend to start with a reflexive perception of the human animal and develop from this base. The pull theories tend to recognise the more 'human' level of consciousness and imply the involvement of a more rational thought process (even if it is not completely divorced from emotional influences).

Push Theories

The push theories of motivation, associated particularly with Maslow and Alderfer, are widely accepted in management thinking, largely because they offer a hierarchical conception of motivation. They regard people as having needs, wants, or drives which drive or push them to pursue objectives or goals which can be calculated to reduce some inner state of tension. Some of these stimuli may be animal in nature (the need to eat, drink, etc., or for safety and security) and required to 'keep body and soul together'. Some are more distinctly human or social in nature (esteem, respect, status, etc) and possibly expected to do more for the soul than the body.

The individual may order these wants or needs in some fashion, so that it is possible to give them some kind of priority ranking; this is the essence of Maslow's contribution to motivation theory (Maslow, 1943; Steers and Porter, 1981). Such a ranking permits prediction of the broad kind of action which might be expected to follow from a knowledge of where the individual stands in this rank order: if we know which need is 'prepotent' (the highest one in the hierarchy which is not yet satisfied), we can predict that the individual will act in a way which is most likely to satisfy that need. Attempts to test this theory have suggested that it is only among higher level managers that higher levels of need, particularly the need for 'self-actualisation', are prepotent.

In Alderfer's model, however, the essentially similar kinds of need (for existence, relatedness, and growth) are not ordered hierarchically. The individual is regarded as selecting which want to attempt to satisfy at a particular time according to his or her reading of the total situation. This alignment of the want with a calculation of what is possible of achievement in the circumstances moves this kind of theory in the direction of a more 'human' (and less animal) conception of motivation.

The push theories by themselves do not indicate what specifically the individual will do; they merely point to a broad area of possibly congruent action. A feeling of hunger may indicate that the individual will eat, but not what he or she will eat, if there is a choice to be made. It is here that the way is opened for considering the way in which the individual reaches his or her decisions about specific action.

This choice process is thought to depend on the individual's possessing (or acquiring) and using a scale of preferences or a frame of reference. This enables the individual to make calculations based on some ordering of the possible solutions to the problem of hunger and thus to decide on the form his or her action will take. The order of preferences may, in turn, be largely the product of socialisation in a particular culture (Kluckhohn, 1953, pp 88–9), but this does not leave the individual in the position simply of reacting to a situation without positive thought. At this point, where culturally influenced preferences enter the model, the push and pull theories come together.

Pull Theories

The pull theories are associated with Vroom (1964), who suggests that behaviour will tend to respond to the relative attractiveness (valence) of different outcomes of behaviour. This implies, first, that the individual simply takes any particular tension state as a signal that some action might be required, and secondly, acts only because he or she places a differential value on external objects or solutions. The rank order of value will then help him or her to decide which action is likely to be most rewarding and thus to mobilise his or her energies. In this sense, the individual is pulled towards certain valued objects or solutions to problems, according to the relative valence of the range of outcomes which can be anticipated to follow from acting in any particular manner.

This theory helps to establish the idea that behaviour might reflect the individual's 'considered responses' to stimuli located in the environment, rather than his or her blind reaction to internal drives, wants, or needs. This places more emphasis on the distinctly choice-making attributes of the human being and less on the purely animal reactions which inform the earlier theories. But the individual's preferences for the external objects are likely to be influenced by socialisation; people learn their preferences as they learn their multiplication tables.

Herzberg's treatment of motivation also uses this broad animal/ human distinction (1966, p 56). For him, it is made to distinguish between the 'lower order' factors (which he refers to as 'hygiene' factors) and 'higher order' motivators.

The hygiene factors are associated with environmental conditions – the policies applied, the supervision provided, the procedures adopted, the remuneration offered and the working conditions experienced – in respect of which the individual will have clear expectations that they be provided in certain forms and to certain standards, and will be dissatisfied if these are not met.

The motivators are associated with the work itself – its inherent interest, challenge, and responsibility and the opportunities which it affords for achievement, advancement (growth), and recognition – and need to be present in jobs before the individual will be turned on (or motivated to perform well). It is clear that in this approach expectations have a very real place in the scheme of things.

The idea that man is capable of discriminating thought about his behaviour is most fully developed in the 'instrumentality-valence-expectancy' theory of motivation (or 'expectancy' theory for short). This 'comprehensive framework for dealing with complex industrial behaviour' (Landy and Trumbo, 1976, p 309) is a process theory where the ones mentioned above are essentially content theories. This one places emphasis on the processes of choosing and deciding. It attempts to explain these choices and decisions on the basis of desired external rewards and internal frames of reference (Porter and Lawler, 1968).

Satisfaction and Reward Values

In the process theories of motivation the question of whether individuals are pulled by external objects or pushed by inner drives is avoided by making the end of the process a concern with satisfaction and the (perceived) value of the reward available. Just what the individual 'wants' is not the main concern of this theory: for explanations of variety in 'wants' it is necessary to turn to the 'content' theorists (Maslow, 1954; Herzberg, 1966). Nor do the process theorists regard it as necessary to develop any equilibrium theory about how the individual deals with these processes of pushing or pulling.

What the person regards as valuable can be ascertained either by questioning or by inference from behaviour where a choice is available. A questionnaire could well reveal a more 'honest' position, but this may be expressed in the abstract and be unrelated to the realities: the individual might abstractly prefer one outcome over others but be well aware that the possibility of realising it in real life is very small. Inference from behaviour is likely to reveal a more realistic position but will indicate little of what the 'real' or underlying preferences of the individual are.

Nevertheless, for present purposes, the satisfaction expected or experienced subjectively by the individual is simply regarded as depending on the value which the individual subjectively places on the available reward and the perception he or she has of how equitable that reward is in comparison with what others, similarly placed, receive.

It is envisaged that any one of a large number of objects could conceivably serve as rewards. They acquire valence (attractiveness) to the individual as a function of their ability to satisfy the person concerned. Their attractiveness as a reward thus depends on the nature of the individual and on the cognitive and affective processes that the individual goes through.

This view of the attractiveness of the object is not, therefore, inconsistent with the views advanced by the drive theorists. What is seen as important is the preference for action which results from any calculation of comparative valence. The theory postulates, simply, that whatever rewards are found attractive by the individual will be influential in directing that individual's efforts.

As Hackman (1969) makes clear, however, in his development of Herzberg's views on the nature of those who seek motivators and hygiene factors, it is necessary to find some place in the model for individual differences – why some want and find attractiveness in some objects and others want and find it in quite different ones. People obviously do differ in what they regard as attractive rewards and may also differ in the way in which they derive the criteria of judgement of attractiveness.

This is dealt with by treating these rewards as attractive, not for themselves, but for the subjectively assessed satisfaction that they provide to the individual.

> 'Satisfaction is determined by the difference between the amount of some valued outcome that a person receives and the amount of that outcome he feels he *should* receive. The larger the discrepancy, the greater the dissatisfaction. Moreover, the amount a person feels he should receive has been found to be strongly

influenced by what he perceives others like himself are receiving' (Lawler, 1971).

'People seem to balance what they are putting into a work situation against what they feel they are getting out of it, and then compare their own balance with that of other people. If this comparison reveals that their outcomes are inequitable in comparison with those of others, then dissatisfaction results'
(Porter, Lawler and Hackman, 1975, pp 53−4).

In line with this, McClelland's three drives towards affect, achievement, and power are likely to be associated with different perceptions of what is an attractive reward and what is not (McClelland, 1951). Riesman's tradition-, inner- and other-directed personality types could be expected to run different kinds of template over any particular object to assess its attractiveness (Riesman, 1952).

Satisfaction by this definition is then regarded as having some influence on the perceived value of the reward and on its valence (or attractiveness) for the person concerned. Without trying to explain why outcomes have this value or this valence, the theory simply states that whatever satisfies will have high valence. But this can only hold if the individual wants this form or kind of satisfaction: a person who wants a cup of tea might not place high value (or valence) on a cup of coffee.

The Decision-taking Model

In the expectancy model, the individual is regarded as 'deciding' to act − that is, to expend effort in order to realise some outcome − from which he or she will derive *satisfaction*, which depends on the perceived value of the rewards available to that individual for the performance he or she achieves by expending effort.

'Expectancies' are defined as a special category of belief about the nature of the environment and the way one thing is expected to cause another. 'Expectancies specify the relationships between what a person does and what outcomes he obtains in the organisational environment'. How expectancies influence the voluntary behaviour of individuals in organisations then forms the problem to be explained with the aid of expectancy theory (Porter, Lawler and Hackman, 1975, p 52).

The use of the term 'voluntary' is meant to deny the validity of the concept of 'drive' when applied to motivated behaviour. Instead the emphasis is placed on individual choice among alternative ways of expending effort in that situation, and, therefore, on an interactive response linking the individual and his or her environment. Nevertheless, this theory does not eliminate all concern with the content of motivation.

In its simplest form, the theory states that the individual's decision to expend effort (in order to realise some outcome) will depend on three kinds of perception or belief about the way the situation 'works':

1   the belief that there are both intrinsic and extrinsic rewards which have value and attractiveness for the individual and which are available to the individual for successful achievement.

2   the belief that the successful expenditure of effort (in the sense of realising the outcome expected) will secure these rewards for the individual.

3   the belief that the expenditure of effort will result in successful achievement, in the above sense.

In addition, the presence or absence of a belief in the relative equity of the available rewards is also expected to influence the individual's decision to behave in this way.

It is also recognised that actual 'performance' (behaviour) will depend not only on the decision to expend effort, but also on the individual's skills and abilities possessed by the individual. These set a boundary to the potential achievement, and the healthy individual will have a reasonable perception of where that boundary will lie. Actual performance will also depend on the individual's perception of his or her role and in particular on his or her perceptions of the standards or norms which apply to the individual in that situation.

Along with general models of decision-taking, this one can be depicted in the form of a complex feedback control loop (Figure 3). The decision to expend effort is linked to the derivation of satisfaction via a complex of information feed-out and feedback loops which serve to inform the individual about the extent to which he or she is on target at each intermediate stage in the process of choosing or deciding on action. This allows the model to be used in association with reinforcement theories as easily as with traditional theories of incentive.

The Necessary Conditions

What, exactly, expectancy theory addresses itself to is the question of how, given some pattern of 'want', the individual comes to decide

Figure 3

The structure of expectancies

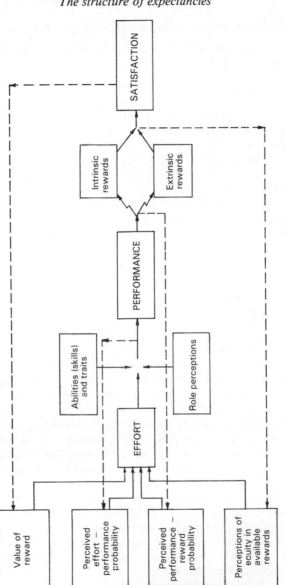

Modified from L W Porter and E E Lawler, *Managerial Attitudes and Performance* (Irwin-Dorsey, 1968)

on the expenditure of effort and the giving of a performance. The theory concentrates on answering three main questions:

1   whether outcomes exist as potential objects of value or valence?
2   what comparisons the individual is likely to make in order to attach that value or valence?
3   why different objects are associated with different satisfactions?

These are considered in terms of two basic conditions which are seen to be necessary to permit the individual to take a decision to act at all, and of two types of 'expectancy' which shape the nature of the decision made in these conditions.

1   *The Primary Condition*
The first condition postulated for motivated behaviour is that the individual believes that there are attractive rewards available for the actor as a result of the action taken. This implies two subconditions:

(a)   that the individual believes that some such rewards are available for distribution to those who take appropriate action;

(b)   that the individual trusts the system to ensure that they will be distributed fairly.

The first of these can be represented as an 'expectancy', or 'belief' that the environment is benign enough to make satisfying rewards available. In Maslow's terminology, the emphasis is on the availability of objects which can be used to reduce a hierarchy of needs. The second can be construed as an expectancy that the environment can be 'trusted' to distribute these satisfying rewards, the only condition to be met being that individuals shall act appropriately. In Maslow's terms, this puts the emphasis on a kind of security. The criteria of judgement in this context are essentially 'technical' ones; put simply, they are criteria derived from theories about how the 'system' actually operates.

This focuses attention on what rewards are available in work situations. This is likely to vary between different kinds of organisation, where difference is associated with the currency in which the organisation trades: money in the case of business organisations, a sense of public service in the case of commonwealth organisations, and personal respect and esteem in service organisations (Blau and Scott, 1963). Of these, the business type is, in general, most likely to have cash available for the purchase of different types of benefit, although the Boston Consulting Group's categorisation suggests that within the subset there are important differences (see below, p 163).

On the other hand, cash-deficient organisations may be able to provide cheaper incentives in the form of kudos, self-esteem, public acclaim, or status symbols, which might prove attractive to some, who recognise their superior value compared with mere money (Woodward, 1958; Orth, Bailey and Wolek, 1964; Scott Committee Report, 1981; Megaw Committee Report, 1982).

Because people's ideas of what valuable objects are may vary (even if everyone seeks money to some extent), there is scope for different organisations to provide a kind of 'incentive-mix' which will attract people with such different wants and expectations. This accords with McDougall's conclusion (see pp 63−4, above) that:

> 'attempts to apply a standardised, across-the-board system of remuneration, on the assumption of homogeneity of values and motives among those it is intended to reward, are unlikely to meet the needs of many of them'
> (McDougall, 1973, pp 42−3).

The idea that there might be a match or a fit between individual demand for and organisational supply of valued objects is an appealing one, but one which is unlikely to be found often because of restrictions on choice (Miller and Form, 1951, p 757). Consequently, both parties are likely to have to experiment with different combinations of incentives.

2   The Secondary Condition

The other basic condition to be met is that the rewards which are likely to be both attractive and available should also be equitable in their distribution among people. If one person puts out an amount of effort or gives a performance of a given quality, the amount of reward that person receives for it should be comparable with that received by any other who contributes or produces to the same standards. A reward therefore has both a direct and personal value, as perceived by the individual, which influences its attractiveness, *and* it also has an indirect and comparative value of comparable influence.

The secondary condition thus highlights the perceptions of equity and fairness as factors which influence the decision to act. Where, for example, the primary condition might focus attention on the availability and security of a wage rate for a given effort or performance, the secondary condition transfers attention to the wage structure. Another way of expressing this same point is to envisage the one looking towards the intrinsic rewards of achievement or self-esteem and the other towards the extrinsic rewards of recognition or social esteem. The criteria of judgement here are more clearly moral (as distinct from technical), appealing essentially to notions of fairness (Hyman and Brough, 1975, p 1). This, as Behrend (1957) has argued, provides the focus of informal and formal negotiations about the dimensions of the two factors in the wage-effort bargain: guessing, or otherwise arriving at the amounts of each which will be accepted as fair, takes up a considerable amount of working time.

The Expectations

The 'expectancies' referred to in this theory are essentially beliefs or theories which, in each case, link two variables to one another. Two pairs are singled out as especially significant for the determination of how the individual will act, given a condition in which equitable rewards are available and secure.

Type I Expectancy

Links together effort and achievement. As the individual perceives it, it must be possible to say (as Stinchcombe expresses the thought in another context entirely) that:

> 'it is possible to achieve certain purposes by carrying out certain [effort-requiring] activities and in order to carry out the activities, we must have such and such resources' (Stinchcombe, 1967, p 157).

The 'expectancy' becomes the belief that the expenditure of effort in activity (which calls for the individual's resources of personality, knowledge, and skill) will result in a certain achievement. The negative aspect of this is the belief that, 'no matter what we do, we can't crack this particular problem (that is, no achievement is possible)'.

Type II Expectancy

Links together performance (or achievement) and rewards. Performance is seen to be the result of 'the combined effects of effort expenditure, role perceptions, and ability and trait patterns' (Landy and Trumbo, 1976, p 307). Where such performance is given, there must be a security that rewards will flow back to the giver; only if this expectancy is present can the individual be expected to decide to act in the appropriate way. There must be a belief in the direct association of the amount of reward with the amount of achievement, and a belief that the production of the one will result in the other (Stinchcombe, 1967, p 159).

The theory can therefore be restated in the following terms:

> where the two conditions − guaranteeing reward availability and guaranteeing their equitable distribution − are met, and where the two expectancies or beliefs − that effort and performance and performance and reward are linked in some rational or calculable fashion − are present, the individual will be led to decide to mobilise energies and to expend effort to perform in a manner calculated to secure satisfaction from the proffered rewards.

What satisfactions the individual might draw from different rewards available remains a matter which will be influenced by the person's conceptions of what is valuable. What methods the individual considers likely to prove fruitful remains something that will be influenced by the perspectives adopted as a result of experience. What the theory attempts to show is the *process* by which energies become mobilised in the person.

SUMMARY

Work, as we noted in the preceding chapter, makes variable demands for human skills and dispositions, and some of the demands might prove to be undesirable in their consequences for the people who meet the demands. Although industry does not need to involve the 'whole person' in work activity, this cannot be avoided, nor can work involvement avoid having some influence, for better or worse, on the human personality.

People, as we see in the present chapter, also vary among themselves in the abilities and capacities for work which they offer to industry, and in the personalities which they necessarily bring into the work situation. The possibility of matching the offers and the demands in employment is an ideal which is usually thwarted by the existence of limited choices for either party.

Nevertheless, the ideal is pursued, both for its own sake and because the matching of people and work demands leads to lower costs of poor work output and poor application. In the extreme forms, mismatching produces a total inability to perform and/or serious stress in the worker. In less extreme forms, it is more commonly associated with barely adequate performance and/or general lack of 'motivation', either of which might be seriously damaging in the high technology work situation.

Some of the instruments which have been developed by psychologists to measure human abilities, aptitudes, and personality traits can assist in selecting those who most nearly match the requirements of work (taken, for this purpose, as given).

Selection does not, however, provide the complete answer to the problem, because motivation as strongly influences human performance. This is more difficult to predict, the measures of specific aspects of personality (such as interests, values and attitudes) having predictive value only in the broadest terms.

Motivation, being more immediately related to action, is more amenable to influence through the immediate situation. The importance of motivation theory lies in its ability to order thought about the aspects of the immediate situation which might be modified to affect motivation itself.

This theory simultaneously focuses on the more stable 'wants' and more immediate processes of calculation in the person faced with the necessity of making choices or decisions about action. Appreciation of the individual's likely wants and expectations facilitates management's consideration of the types and forms of 'incentive' or behavioural 'reinforcement' to be offered.

Motivation is perceived as entailing the mobilisation of energies to accomplish some act and to achieve some satisfying outcome simultaneously. It is seen to depend on:

(a)   the person's existing frames of reference and scales of preferences, implanted as a consequence of socialisation;

(b)   the person's capacity to calculate the likely returns of satisfaction from any course of action which might be open; and

(c)   the person's personality, abilities, and comprehension of the relationships between effort, performance, reward and satisfaction.

The number of factors affecting motivation makes it unlikely that simple effort-reward relationships can be supported. The possibility, for example, that the offer of more money might produce more performance might be countered by the alternative possibility that higher performance might be secured by providing intrinsic rewards from work.

Consequently, more complex strategies for securing performance from human resources than might have served in the past may be necessary to meet future challenges where work is redesigned to give greater discretion to the performer.

LEARNING PROCESSES

Expectancy theory does not attempt to answer the question about how the individual comes to have the wants and the expectations which he or she may rely on in making choices. This, as Maslow indicates in another context, is something which is likely to depend on what the individuals have learned to want and to expect as a result of their learning from experience. This process is likely to be crucial to any explanation of why people are motivated in the way they are, just as it is crucial to many other processes involved in human resource management, particularly training.

This is but a part of a more general perspective which regards human beings as the product of what they have learned. They have to learn how to cope with their environment in order to live (or to live better, as their motivation leads them) because they are born with few instincts for coping. Coping depends on the acquisition and application of abstract ideas (strategies and theories of coping), instruments (or tools designed to facilitate it), and skills (which enable these to be applied effectively). Because these have to be learned, people become, in effect, the creatures of their learning history.

As some of the individual's purposes in living are beyond his or her biological capacities, cooperation in this coping process must be learnt (Andrews, 1968). The process of acquiring the wherewithal to live is mediated by institutions and organisations – economic, political, and social – intended to facilitate and regulate the process. Coping therefore comes to involve both coping in co-operation with a hierarchy of institutions as well as with immediate tasks. Work has always involved instrumental behaviour, but modern industry embroils the individual worker in a hierarchy of instrumentalism regulated by a matching hierarchy of institutions. The existence of such institutions ensures that individuals cannot really avoid social interaction in the process of satisfying their other needs, wants, or desires (Dubin, 1956).

Much of what the person learns about ways of presenting the self and solving the problems likely to be encountered in life (and work) is embodied in what is commonly referred to as the culture of the society (or of the class or social group within it). From this point of view, this can be regarded as a stock of prescriptions and proscriptions, intended to facilitate human adjustment to the worlds of life and work, which the individual is expected to learn. It is also embodied in the institutions and the artefacts of the society, so that as and when the individual encounters them, they will tend to 'reinforce' any lessons he or she has learned through assimilation of other kinds of experiential messages communicated in other contexts.

Gatekeepers

Much of what has to be learned is in the possession of other people. Their knowledge of values, strategies, theories, and techniques has, therefore, to be tapped to facilitate learning. Some people, in fact, become specialists in providing the opportunities for learning in this way. They form a social context in which learning occurs, and in a society which honours separation and specialisation these tend to be specialist contexts. In recent times, the gravity of the economic situation has led industry to question what contribution the specialist contexts do make to socialisation.

Experience acquired during both childhood and adult life can never, therefore, be regarded as 'raw experience' from which people are free to draw whatever lessons or inferences they wish. Many people, from the mother serving meals to the school-teacher following a specific curriculum, act as gatekeepers of experience. In adult life, managers stand in similar gatekeeper roles, filtering out some kinds of experience and allowing others through, so that the individual's selection of experience is itself 'structured' to suggest that some kinds of experience are to be expected and others not.

This experience is further guided by a general educational or socialisation process designed to ensure that people grow up 'wanting' what is available and expecting only what it is reasonable to expect in the circumstances. Some of this 'training' comes through the family and some of it through school; but most of the institutions of society are themselves structured in such a way that they – as it were, impersonally – reinforce these verbal messages. Ideas are implanted in childhood which, in the most general terms, suggest what inferences should be drawn about any 'bit' of experience, and these include the inferences about whether the consequences of that experience are to be regarded as good or bad, proper or improper, and about whether they are to be expected as its normal consequences. All kinds of similar messages are passed to the individual during adult life – in the family, in work, or through the media – which are similarly intended to be opinion forming or attitude forming.

Consequently, people's frames of reference (comprising both

perspectives and expectations) and their scales of preference (embracing their interests, values, and attitudes) are not entirely their own. They are the product of a socialisation process designed to facilitate human adjustment to the circumstances in which people are likely to find themselves. They may break out of the intended mould, and might as a result do very well or very badly, but, in the event of either conforming or disconforming, people still tend to orient themselves to the values and perspectives that they have experienced during this 'learning process'. For this reason, the explanation of why people want and expect what they do want and expect is to be found in their childhood and adult socialisation processes.

At any point in time, individuals will possess frames of reference and orientations which they can and do use to order their action. Process theories of motivation are primarily concerned to establish the way in which they do so, not why they do it in ways which vary from individual to individual, which reflects their different frames of reference and orientations.

Learning Processes

Learning processes, therefore, focus on two kinds of attainment. First, the ability to do things (or make things happen) — lift weights, shape a piece of metal or wood, read a book, add a column of figures, etc., etc. Secondly, the capacity to live as an accepted member of a group or organisation. The first is usually thought of as concerned with the acquisition of skill — providing the individual with some capability — and the second with socialisation — making the individual 'social'. The content of the learning may be different, but the processes may be similar.

The theories of skill acquisition attempt to explain how it is that the individual learns the mental and muscular behaviour appropriate to the production of some concrete or tangible result. This means learning how to use and to control his or her mental processes and muscular activities to produce a concrete result which he or she desires. The outcome of such learning is a 'relatively permanent change in behaviour that occurs as a result of practice or experience' (Bass and Vaughan, 1966, p 8).

The theories of socialisation attempt to explain how it comes about that 'the individual learns the behaviour appropriate to his position in a group through interaction with others who hold normative beliefs about what his role should be and who reward or punish him for correct or incorrect actions' (Brim and Wheeler, 1966, p 9). This is a more restricted meaning than is required in the present context, but 'acculturisation', which comes closer to meeting the need, is a cumbersome concept. What is referred to here, however, is the process of passing on to succeeding generations the 'designs' or solutions to problems which are embodied in the culture (see below, pp 89–91).

The *child* learns both types of lesson in a number of different contexts, some of which are deliberate creations of the society intended to facilitate learning of an appropriate kind. The family obviously plays a significant part in the development of basic competencies and in socialisation. Because of differences in the capacity of the family to provide learning opportunities, this agency may produce a variety of products of diverse standards. The same may be said of the informal peer and play groups in which the child moves. The brunt of the problem of transmitting universal values of the culture and standardised capabilities is, however, borne by the educational system. This has recently been most strongly criticised, both for disseminating the wrong things or for doing it badly, or both, simultaneously.

The influence of other institutions (themselves embodying normative beliefs of the culture) which are not particularly aimed at learning cannot be discounted. People can and do *infer* meanings from the likelihood that most work is provided by large-scale organisations in private industry and in government, that work is usually highly specialised and fragmented, and that it imposes a kind of discipline on the doer. These inferences may reinforce or counteract the lessons learned in the family or school, although this process is often perceived as 'impersonal', stemming simply from 'the ways things are'.

Conditioning

There must be some tendency for these different agencies within a single culture to present the learner with similar messages, whether these take the form of language or of 'experience'. This consistency admits the possibility that the way people learn is by a process of *conditioning*: the fact that the individual encounters the same messages and the same experience, almost regardless of the context, suggests, as we say, that he or she will 'get the message', if he or she thinks about it at all.

Both of the two main types of conditioning theory rest on the assumption that man is fundamentally 'motivated', simply because he is alive, and that he is sufficiently motivated to learn how to cope with whatever has to be coped with to stay alive. This necessarily brings him into interaction with the environment, and the way he is treated by that environment will provide him with opportunities for learning.

Classic conditioning is based on the observation that some naturally occurring stimuli produce automatic responses (such as salivation when the individual is confronted with a tasty dish). If, therefore, a second stimulus (such as a bell ringing) is repeatedly presented in parallel with the first (naturally occurring) one, so that the two become associated, the removal of the first (the sight or smell of food) and continuation of the second (the bell) may well, after a period of time, produce the salivation response. This gives rise to a near law, to the effect that:

'The repeated presentation of a conditioned stimulus in a controlled relationship to an unconditioned stimulus (the 'natural' one) which can be demonstrated to produce a particular automatic response, will tend to form an association of a similar kind between the conditioned stimulus and that response'
(Bass and Vaughan, 1966, p 15).

Some 'animal' behaviours in the human being may well be learned in this way.

Instrumental conditioning develops this theory by giving the individual organism a more active part to play in the process: instead of behavioural responses being automatic, the individual's behaviour is instrumental in obtaining a valued reward which crucially reinforces the behaviour in question (Bass and Vaughan, 1966, p 19). In classical conditioning, the response is already part of the individual's repertoire of action; in instrumental conditioning it has to be learned. The 'conditioned instrumental response' (such as the dog sitting up to beg) has to be learned *and* produced in response to a 'conditioned stimulus' (a command) and this is facilitated by offering a reward (food) as a reinforcing stimulus.

Obviously, this all depends on food being a valued reward to the organism in question and consumption of food, therefore, being an unconditioned response. It then acts as a stimulus *by anticipation*, which is a mental state created in and by the organism. It is a more active, and to an extent more human, kind of process. But the importance of feedback (of information on what has been successful in the way of behaviours) in this should not be underestimated; unless a person has some way of knowing that he or she has been successful in whatever behaviour has been gone through, no lesson is likely to be learned from it.

Nevertheless, it is likely that only very basic learning in the human is at all fully explained by these processes: they may lead to the acquisition of basic responses of an intellectual, emotional, or behavioural kind in the small child. The observation that the human being can apparently produce much more complex and precise responses than the ones referred to above may suggest that the human being is able to build complex edifices of thought, emotion, and action on such simple beginnings, provided that there is reinforcement of the kind identified with instrumental conditioning.

Personality

Nevertheless, the personal attributes which we associate with the concept of personality are likely to be strongly influenced by a special kind of conditioning. These refer to such traits as tastes and preferences, perspectives and attitudes, frames of reference, and modes of self-presentation. Many of these simply 'develop' as people respond to the experiences they have. Personality becomes a kind of learned response to the situation as it is experienced.

People learn their tastes and preferences, not because their physiology dictates them, but as responses to the experience they have. The repeated presentation of a range of food dishes by mother, often in direct response to the child's reactions to them, sets up patterns of taste in food. The repeated presentation of other 'rewards' for certain valued types of behaviour has a similar influence on the development of scales of preference. What turns a person on is therefore often something which is responded to in the course of socialisation in the family, the school, the peer group, and so on.

But the response is never a simple reaction. It is often learned by emulation of others, using their personalities as exemplars to be followed when the situation seems to be similar. The fact that a person likes another, for whatever reason, may, for example, set up a desire to be like that person, either generally or in respect of certain character or personality traits. People may adopt macho postures or introspective characteristics in this way.

Learning from experience occurs at any time and in any context, and is not confined to those situations which have been formally structured or designated as training. The individual selects from experience of whatever kind to increase his or her own capacity. Even if the others involved have no intention of providing learning opportunity, individuals may still draw on it to learn something new.

Intention, as Cartwright has pointed out (in March, 1965, pp 10–11), is not a necessary ingredient of successful interpersonal

influence. McGregor sets this same observation in a more specifically industrial context.

> 'Every encounter between a superior and a subordinate
> involves learning of some kind for the subordinate (and
> should for the superior too). The attitudes, habits, and
> expectations of the subordinate will be reinforced or
> modified to some degree as a result of every encounter
> with the boss. ... Day-by-day experience is so much
> more powerful that it tends to overshadow what the
> individual may learn in other settings'
> (McGregor, 1960, p 199–200).

Individuals cannot be forced to learn, but neither can they be
prevented from learning if experience presents stimuli which attach
to their interests, meet their motivational requirements, and promise
to add to their repertoire of useful values, information, or skills.

Basic Intellectual Competence

Basic competences are likely to be acquired when the individual
masters two processes, one 'intellectual' which enables the person to
think through any problem to its abstract solution, and one 'motor/
mechanical' which permits the individual to carry out a creative
action successfully. These form the basic human capacities which
make the human being a potential 'resource' to industry. The one,
concerned with thinking and choice-making, is generally thought to
precede (or at least to be logically prior to) motor/mechanical action
directed to some concrete end.

Gagne has suggested that the early process of learning basic
intellectual and problem-solving skills can be thought of as involving eight elements:

1   recognition of signals and response to them in a diffuse way,
    rather as Pavlov's dogs recognised signals and responded by
    salivating.

2   linking stimulus and response in a more precise fashion, such as
    reaching for the phone when a particular ring of a bell is heard,
    so that in Skinner's words what is learned is a discriminant
    operant (Skinner, 1938).

3   making connections between two or more stimulus-response
    connections, which is referred to as chaining.

4   making verbal associations, an element that depends on the

existence of a repertoire of language, and which entails coping with chains that are verbal, allowing abstract learning to occur.

5 discrimination between signals in the sense of recognising which signals call for which kind of response — which names to give to persons or things.

6 conceptualisation, which is the opposite process, involving the allocation of different stimuli to categories or classes — males, plants, animals, colours, friends, enemies, etc.

7 learning rules, which link together different concepts in a 'chaining' process, so that relationships can be recognised — if a person is an enemy, then he will offer aggression.

8 solving problems, using all the previous elements by combining rules in novel and appropriate ways to yield a solution to the perceived problem — because there is a relationship between a light switch and the ceiling light, if I press the switch I will no longer be in darkness.

All of these, taken together, provide the individual with the basic intellectual tools required to make sense of and to develop broad strategies and tactics for coping generally with the environment.

Muscular Control and Motor Ability

Whether the individual will act constructively in the sense of taking effective action within the surrounding physical and social world will depend on learning how to control his or her muscular, motor, and mechanical aptitudes.

The process of 'control' may be instituted early in the family, when it can also be ascribed a wider 'meaning' as a part of character training. Gorer's exploration of English character suggested a broad measure of agreement among his respondents that children ought to receive very early training in cleanliness (potty-training), and that discipline ought to be imposed on them in support of this, so that undesirable innate tendencies could be nipped in the bud and 'good character' developed (Gorer, 1955, p 163). A desire to condition the child to control muscular activity to serve a 'social' end becomes associated with a desire to instill basic conceptions of right and wrong, good and bad, so that the child's personality and character become correctly shaped.

This is, however, only the beginning of control and discipline. Coping requires further abstract learning of how to recognise and interpret signals, how to understand concepts and rules etc., and how to apply them to real situations to produce more specific responses to the environment. But successful coping also requires the development of perceptual, motor, and mechanical skills or abilities, if tangible concrete results are to be achieved.

Learning Motor Skills

Learning muscular/motor/mechanical skills requires much greater precision in the control of muscles than is implied in the example given above. One view of the way in which the individual deals with this aspect is that in which the process is seen as one of structured 'trial and error'. Miller, Gallanter, and Pribam (1960) advance the acronym of TOTE (*T*est, *O*perate, *T*est, *E*xit) to suggest how this occurs. In a continuing activity, such as driving a nail into wood, these would typically occur in the sequence $T_1, O_1, T_2, O_2, \ldots\ldots$ T_n, E. In effect, the person performing this operation will first compare the actual state (a nail standing proud of a piece of wood) with the desired state (a nail fully driven into the wood) (T_1), and given the difference, the gap or the 'error' perceived, will hit the nail with the hammer (O_1). This is then repeated: if the comparison T_2 shows the nail still proud, the person will hit the nail again (O_2); if still the comparison shows ... (T_3) and so on, until finally, the final comparison T_n will show the nail fully driven in and so the individual can stop (E), having completed the task, solved the problem, and secured whatever satisfaction he or she was seeking from doing so.

This is recognisable as a simple systems model, involving decision, action, and feedback as a basis for further decision. It provides the individual with a way of approaching the problem, of coping with it, and of learning from it. This centres on the notion of a 'plan' as:

> 'any hierarchical process in the organisation that can control the order in which the sequence of operations is to be performed'
> (Miller, Gallanter and Pribam, 1960, p 16).

In effect, this allows a strategy to be followed in the performance of any complex set of operations, with a series of 'operations' succeeded by a series of 'tests' being contained within a broader conception of operation-and-test until the hierarchically superordinate 'test' reveals that the sequence of lower order operations is complete.

It is thought that this process of learning may require a similar build up from independent elements to a final integrated ability. Stammers and Patrick make the point that, 'the acquisition of skill may be viewed as the progressive organisation of units of activity into a hierarchical structure' (Stammers and Patrick, 1975, p 43). Similarly, Annett and Duncan's hierarchical task analysis is based on this kind of assumption, and proceeds to break down any task into component elements or operations, where 'operation' is defined as 'any unit of behaviour, no matter how long or short its duration and no matter how simple or complex its structure, which can be defined in terms of its objective' (Annett and Duncan, 1967, p 218).

In learning *how* to write, for example, some (but not all) of us were taught 'pothooks' and 'loops' on the way to producing 'joined writing'. This was an application of the belief about the way people learn such manual skills. But the fact that many of us were not taught in this way suggests that there are other theories which emphasise the 'gestalt' approach, in which the individual perceives and replicates the total image of the word as written.

Adult Socialisation

That 'education does not end on leaving school' is a statement frequently made, but much less frequently acted on in any very positive manner. If it does not end at that point, it is continued very largely through 'learning by and from experience'. This process can be very 'educational', provided that the individuals concerned have already learned how to learn from experience — and that is often in doubt. But industry might be said to have done very little deliberately to structure this process of continued learning, and it is probably not without its significance that the movement for continuous management and professional learning appeared only in the 1980s.

Recently, Sir Douglas Hague argued that the existing educational and industrial institutions provide too little opportunity for adult socialisation or resocialisation, because education and training are too often regarded as 'optional extras' rather than 'fundamental prerequisites' (speech to the City University Business School, 10 September, 1986; *Financial Times*, 11 September, 1986).

Examination of industry's record of formal training and informal structuring of learning experience suggests that it has badly botched adult training for the current work situation and continues to do so. The result is that traditional values and practices become entrenched in various (management or worker) ghettos, cut off from environmental influences which might effect new perspectives and new adjustments. For example, the assumption that a firm can acquire the 'labour' it requires (fully equipped with skills, attitudes, motivations, etc.) from 'the market' and does not need to participate in its development, may well ossify traditional working practices and attitudes when the need is for new and more flexible ones.

SUMMARY

Human beings are thought to learn both what kind of person they should be and the skills and competences they need to cope with living and working.

Learning is essentially a matter of making sense of (or giving meaning to) experience, whether that experience is seemingly idiosyncratic and circumstantial or deliberately formulated and presented (as in education and training).

Psychologists have suggested that the basic learning process is one in which people move from the simple to the complex and from the reactive to the intellectual response. Facilitation of the growth of basic competences occurs generally in the family and in a more specialised way through the institutions of education and training. Education, on the one hand, is usually concerned with the fundamental development of the individual to equip him or her to cope in the very general, long-run sense. Although it becomes involved in the development of 'practical' skills of reading, writing, and 'doing' arithmetic, it is more acutely concerned with rendering the individual capable of thinking to some purpose or of solving problems. Another way of expressing this is to treat it as concerned with teaching the individual to go on learning from any kind of experience.

This presupposes that a stock or fund of designs for being and doing, commonly identified as the 'culture' of a society is available for dissemination and learning. This is not, however, automatically available, so that it is necessary for others in the society to mould relevant personalities and to teach appropriately instrumental behaviours before and during the individual's employment in modern industry (Miller and Form, 1951). This process of transmitting the values and instruments of the culture becomes the means of 'processing' people to fit the opportunities which the society affords (McKinlay, 1974; Burns, 1962). This then constitutes a major part of the individual's learning environment: it comprises a cultural stock and an active mechanism for transmitting values and theories from that stock.

A constant jet of criticism has also been directed at the institutions through which such designs as we have are passed on. Proposals to have industry or the Manpower Services Commission more closely associated with the educational institutions at all levels are intended to produce improvements on both counts. Similarly, the role of industry in adult socialisation through training and retraining has been the subject of debate and coercive action by government as a further reflection of the growing belief that Britain fails to provide a learning environment which is appropriate to modern needs and circumstances.

Reading:

Alderfer (1972).
Allport (1937).
Anastasi (1976).
Brim and Wheeler (1966).
Gardner and Taylor (1975).
Goldthorpe *et al* (1968).
Hackman *et al* (1977).
Hall and Nougain (1968).
Harris and Moran (1983).

Herzberg (1966; 1968).
Levine (1973).
Maslow (1943).
McClelland (1951).
McDougall (1973).
Miner and Miner (1977) pp 61–87.
Opsahl and Dunnette (1966).
Steers and Porter (1979).

3 Culture and Subculture

The concept of 'culture' has appeared in British and American management literature in recent years with increasing frequency. The immediate reason for this is that other societies, particularly those of Germany and Japan, appear to have mastered the arts of producing and distributing goods and services with greater efficiency and profitability than either Britain or the USA. Sometimes this is taken as an affront to national pride and sometimes it is considered to be economically dangerous for the home society – especially when that society has large-scale unemployment. The question arises as to how this situation of comparative competitive advantage is to be explained.

At a relatively superficial level it can be dismissed as reflecting no more than a policy of subsidisation by a benevolent government. This is a superficial explanation because it does not, in turn, explain how it arises that a government, however benevolent, can find the wherewithal to provide the subsidies, especially where the levels of taxation and the costs of living are not markedly higher (and can be regarded as lower, in some cases at least). A more penetrating analysis and explanation is therefore sought and found in the catch-all construct of culture.

Culture is a term that is used to refer to the 'way of life' of a society. This is a deceptively simple way of characterising the taken for granted but complex assumptions of the society. The way of life includes the dominant values which pervade a society and by which people live; the norms and rules which the society imposes on itself to ensure that life is ordered and comfortable; the structures within which cooperative activites may be successfully carried on; the technologies through which it realises its aspirations for wealth creation or cooperation in a civilised society; the various artefacts which embody both the values and the achievements of that society; the whole adding up to a set of explicit and implicit designs for living which have evolved through time and which are considered to be still valuable and functional for that society (Kluckhohn and Kelly, in Linton, 1945).

The tendency of culture to be made up of solutions to past problems encountered by the society or its members, lulls everyone into a false sense of security: the old and tried remedies are considered best because everyone 'knows where they stand' in relation to them. But this same characteristic of culture places an immediate limit on its value as a design for living when conditions change. The existence of this repertoire of cultural designs for living has two major implications for both institutions (including that of industry) and people (including those who work within it):

1 it offers a set of 'solutions' to the problems of living and working in a complex social system, these taking the form of traditional ways of organising and running things, and traditional patterns of expected behaviour associated with types of activity;

2 it imposes a tradition-based constraint on what people may do, lawfully and legitimately, so that it serves as a source of control over people in the society.

Accordingly, it is expected that people will learn the cultural lessons about both how to cope with the problems of living and how to co-operate supportively with other members of the society. Once learned, they serve to *predispose* members of the society to think, feel, and act in certain ways. It is through the learned values, attitudes, perspectives and modes of action that the 'culture' (itself a construct in the mind of man) acquires any meaning.

Because men found that certain structures of rational-legal authority (which we now call bureaucracy) proved efficient in getting strangers to work together, bureaucracy became a valued part of the culture: as long as the conditions which allowed it to operate efficiently continue to be present, it will probably go on serving men's purposes, but as and when the conditions change, problems may well arise.

Similarly, because Henry Ford (and others after him) found it sensible, when confronted with a largely illiterate immigrant peasantry unused to industry and its ways, to construct an assembly line which reduced work tasks to fragments of a whole job, the assembly line passed into the industrial culture as a proven 'design'. As long as the condition continued it remained useful. But when, much later, the Swedish car industry confronted a problem of work motivation among immigrant workers, it was found just as sensible to overturn the principles of the assembly line and introduce auto-nomous groups engaging in batched work.

The 'consequences' of such cultural prescriptions and proscriptions for individuals and collectives are the source of the view that culture may have some bearing on the 'success' which any particular society may experience:

1 the 'solutions' which people learn during their socialisation may be inadequate to deal with their situational requirements – and may therefore need to be changed; and

2 the 'constraints' imposed by traditions may place burdens on people, individually or collectively, which restrict their freedom of action in meeting new conditions.

It is not uncommon to see or hear, on the one hand, references to British industry's failure to create ways of organising work which will encourage performance, and, on the other, criticisms of the burden imposed by tradition-oriented trade unions, or, indeed, managements.

CULTURE AND CULTURAL VALUES

The tasks which confront 'industry', or managers and workers individually and jointly, involve coping with situations as these may present themselves. Sometimes the situations may have traditional features, sometimes they may be largely novel. The manager is required to accommodate the vicissitudes of consumer behaviours in ways which will secure an adequate return. The worker is expected to solve the day-to-day problems of working (for example) with metal, plastic or wood, or of coping with particularly awkward customers. The situation which each confronts may or may not be 'covered' by the prescriptions of the culture.

Where they are not covered in this way, the individual must find a pragmatic solution. In a volatile environment – and there is some suggestion that all economic and social environments are becoming more and more volatile – the demand for this kind of solution is likely to increase. In recent years, novel problems associated with recession have led some managements to adopt styles of managing associated with alien cultures as a pragmatic solution to them. Pascale and Athos argue that the demands of the situation are such that managers, wherever they are located, have to bend their actions to meet them, even when this means going against the expectations of the culture (Pascale and Athos, 1981, p 118).

As international competition has threatened British industry's dominance in the home market, employee security of employment has been sacrificed. As trade unions have succeeded in securing a reduction in the length of the working week, the traditional concept of a fixed working week with overtime work attracting premium payments was abandoned, and management copied flexible working arrangements from elsewhere to meet the immediate requirements of the new situation (Connock, 1985, pp 36–8).

This kind of development illustrates the age-old conflict between the pragmatic approach to the solution of problems and the approach based on accepted principles and practices. The pragmatic approach is one which has traditionally been associated with the classical entrepreneur – the businessman who could see opportunities for gain and pounced on them. Recently, this image has been resurrected and held up as an exemplar, although in the context of privatising the formerly nationalised industries, some curbs had to be placed on the enthusiasm of some of these pouncers.

The more principled approach is one which draws more strongly on traditions and culture as the source of accepted norms. These, whether they are embodied in social conventions or in laws, are in themselves curbs on the more outlandish forms of behaviour. An approach which takes them into account is likely to be more measured and more closely associated with planning than with pouncing.

Cultural Values and Ideas

The values and ideas that make up a culture are pervasive, reaching down into the everyday behaviours which respond to them, although not necessarily in a conscious manner. In the words of Kroeber and Kluckholn, 'the essential core of the culture consists of traditional ideas, and especially their attached values' (Kroeber and Kluckholn, 1952, quoted in Mitchell, 1969, p 47). These inevitably influence all activity. They become embodied in artefacts (such as tools) and institutions (such as firms) and give a particular 'shape' or character to that society. They also become inculcated in the frames of reference of individuals socialised within the culture, and ever afterwards affect their success in coping with their environment.

Culture and its various manifestations in concrete artefacts and behaviours may be thought of as having a hierarchical form, with cultural values near the apex, related ideas below this, and behavioural practices applying these ideas, at the base. A number of ideas may support a single central value and a number of practices may derive from a single idea.

Figure 4

A hierarchy of influential cultural needs

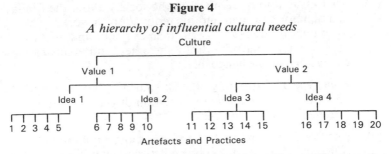

Change in a single practice is unlikely to be without effect on the ideas and values from which it derives.

The values serve as facilitators to the extent that they help to sustain the ideas and practices which either improve the standard of living or the way of life of the members of the society. They provide a basis for effective coping when the circumstances remain favourable, but in other circumstances, they provide the basis for calculated 'resistance to change' (Spicer, 1952). They serve as constraints to the extent that they aim to preserve the existing institution from attack as decisions are taken (pragmatically) about the best courses of action to adopt in all the circumstances. They do this partly by being associated with penalties or punishments for departing from the cultural norms and partly by becoming internalised by individuals as their own guides to conduct or action.

Fundamental Cultural Values

The basic values of the culture are likely to influence the way in which management defines its approach to managing. They may do so because the managers have themselves internalised them, treating them as their own for purposes of determining their style (Argyris, 1953). They may do so also because some of them are embodied in law or convention, and the law imposes punishments or penalties for breach while conventions attract sanctions of social disapproval.

Florence Kluckhohn (1953, p 91) suggested that all societies have to determine what value they place on certain alternative modes and methods of action at a very fundamental level. Her questions may be posed in a form which relates them to the concerns of industry (rather than of society in a more abstract sense):

(a) what relationship between man and the physical environment (or 'nature') is to receive most emphasis? (The main choices are between man over nature, man in nature, or man subordinated to nature.)

(b)   what assumptions are made in the society about the funda-
       mental nature of man and his motivation to work? (The
       main options are man as evil, man as good, and man as
       neither wholly one nor wholly the other, and in any case as
       changeable or unchangeable.)

(c)   what type of personality is most valued? (The main options
       might be those of Riesman: tradition-directed, inner-
       directed, or other-directed.)

(d)   what kind of human relationship is most emphasised?
       (There is a fundamental choice between individualised
       relationships, collective or peer-group relationships, and
       hierarchical relationships.)

(e)   what sources of authority and legitimacy are most stressed?
       (Some of the main variants are tradition, position in a social
       structure, charisma (special gifts), or certified competence.)

These are answered in different ways in different societies, and it has
become a favourite pastime of many management writers in recent
years to imply (although they usually say that it is not possible to
'take over' cultural values and ideas from another society) that a
change in the answers that a society provides to these may be
desirable for greater economic progress.

Cultural Values and Management

Harris and Moran have shown that the way in which a particular
society answers Kluckhohn's questions is likely to affect the kinds of
managerial response to any given set of circumstances. Their
comparison of identifiable American social values with some of the
major alternatives is used to show:

> 'how the cultural system or differences in attitude,
> values, assumptions, personal beliefs, interpersonal
> relationships, social and organisational structures,
> affect the traditional management functions of decision-
> making, promotion, recruitment and development,
> organising, planning and motivation'
> (Harris and Moran, 1983, p 48).

Where, for example, man is regarded as naturally evil, management
can justify the imposition of strict behavioural controls; if man is
seen as neither good nor evil, then management's task is to avoid the
presentation of temptations to the worker to behave badly; and if

the assumption is that man is good, then management's function is to ensure that the information necessary to decisions is collected and made available to mobilise good behaviours (Harris and Moran, 1983, pp 74–5). They go on to show that other fundamental assumptions will affect the way in which management sets about the tasks of selecting, organising, motivating, and treating workers for industry.

A number of such comparisons, which are critical (at least by implication) of British or American industry, have recently been made with Japan. That society is seen to give more respect to tradition and seniority (reflecting both a valued time dimension and a worthy type of relationship), to show respect for people as contributors and for the value of their agreement to action (reflecting a view of the nature of man and a low value on their exploitation), and to place more emphasis on collective responsibility for action (indicating something of the valued relationship type) (Ouchi, 1981; Pascale and Athos, 1981).

Ouchi also suggests, by juxtaposing organisational practices in American and Japanese industry, that the two cultures spawn models of industrial organisation which are 'different in every important respect' (Table 2). The implication is that the better performer might have the better model (Ouchi, 1981, pp 48–9).

Table 2

Contrast of cultures

Japanese Organisations	v	American Organisations
Life-time employment		Short-term employment
Slow evaluation and promotion		Rapid evaluation and promotion
Non-specialised career paths		Specialised career paths
Implicit control mechanisms		Explicit control mechanisms
Collective decision-making		Individual decision-making
Collective responsibility		Individual responsibility
Holistic concern		Segmented concern

He avers that the point of making the contrast is not to advocate that one ought to copy the other, but to increase understanding of the American model by using a strongly contrasting one. But the implication is that only if changes are made in particular directions is American industry likely to complete effectively with that of Japan. Dunning has, however, suggested that Japanese personnel practices can be transferred to the UK but only where a greenfield site is involved and recruitment is confined largely to school leavers (Dunning, 1986, pp 165–7).

The Culturally Defined Enterprise

It is possible to erect a model of industrial organisation based on the answers which have traditionally been given to these questions in British society. This will not describe a real organisation, but it will highlight possibilities which may be seen as tendencies in actual organisations. It is not, however, simply at the level of the cultural value that efficiency is determined, and so the model must be treated as an abstract ideal.

1 The enterprise will exploit material 'nature'

Western society emphasises the value of taming nature and subordinating it to the will of man. This puts value on the generation of wealth through human exploitation of the earth's natural resources. This in turn emphasises discovery (of materials) and invention (of improved means of exploitation) as processes through which the taming or subordination of nature can occur. Indeed, this is usually held up as the distinctive achievement of Western society, one which has given the world a generally higher standard of living than would have been possible without it. The alternative value of developing a symbiotic relationship with nature does have its adherents, although they may still be few in number.

This basic value of securing control over nature carries implications and justifications for the manner in which the other social values are interpreted in the industrial context. The generation of wealth becomes, for many Western societies, the dominant economic value which transcends other social values.

2 Industrial enterprises will be disciplined organisations

The Protestant work ethic (which regards man as basically evil but perfectible through hard work (and prayer)) remains influential. Work could be an instrument of human salvation if it was disciplined: without the discipline of work, man had little or no hope of redemption, whether in Christian or Marxist terms. This value has been used to justify the exercise of a strong disciplinary authority by the employer. It supported the approach of scientific management and it lingers in current theories of motivation which see work as a source of 'self-actualisation', itself a secular form of salvation. Where workers accept this value, they are more likely to accept the necessity of harsh work, discipline, and external authority (Hulin and Blood, 1968; Turner and Lawrence, 1965).

This carries over, as McGregor (1960) argued, into beliefs or theories about human motivation. He contrasted the traditional (Theory X) assumptions (that man is lazy and needs to be directed and controlled) with the emergent (Theory Y) assumptions (that man is capable of self-direction and self-control under appropriate circumstances). The traditional assumptions implied that man would only work if forced (coerced) or if it was made worth his while (through the offer of more money for more work). Both of these contrast with the assumptions in Ouchi's Theory Z, which emphasises that the nature of man is not to be defined in the abstract or in a vacuum, but is something which will develop in a social context (Ouchi, 1981).

3 The dominant relationship will be one of subordination
The dominant relationship with which Britain began the industrial revolution was that which emphasised individualism and relationships developed between individuals, who were assumed to be equal. The strength of this fundamental value is still considerable and influences many institutions and practices.

The aggregation of labour into larger factory organisations demanded firm control and this was achieved by developing hierarchical relationships based on ownership as the source of monocratic authority, protected by law. It carried over the kind of relationship which had previously been upheld by the institution of monarchy in Britain, but it had the effect of dividing the superordinates from the subordinates and thus of creating a basis for applying different values to the two classes so formed.

In recent years, the emphasis has meandered somewhat to emphasise more strongly the social or lateral relationship at one period and the individualised relationship at another, reflecting an ambivalence with respect to the role of subordination in inhibiting cooperation and industrial progress. The new element in this focuses on the peer group or partnership between different stakeholders.

Workers, however, had learned to value the peer relationship as a means of avoiding the harsher features of working life, and, in the face of opposition from practically every institution, sustained this value through the trade union association. In contrast to some other societies, the trade union's primary focus is not therefore upon developing cooperation with the employer to increase wealth, but rather on securing a more equitable distribution of it.

4 The preferred personality type is that which is inner-directed but aggressive in managers and compliant in workers
Those most directly concerned with the exploitation of nature, the entrepreneurs and managers, are seen to need active, achieving, even aggressive personalities. The early heroes of the industrial revolution were of this type. Such personalities fit the philosophy of

individualism and support the notion of the 'self' as a distinct and separate entity and as the source of all thoughts, feelings, and actions. This 'inner-directed' personality is not too tied to traditions nor too dependent upon the opinions of others.

Recent studies (Pascale and Athos, 1981; Ouchi, 1981) suggest that this is one significant dimension on which the Japanese industrial culture differs from that of the West. Pascale and Athos also argue:

> 'American executives traditionally have been taught to become independent of others, separate, self-sufficient. Japanese executives traditionally have been taught to become interdependent with others, integral parts of a larger human unit, exchanging dependencies with others'
> (Pascale and Athos, 1981, p 118).

Workers are also expected, in line with this same cultural value, to be individualistic and comparably inner-directed. The industrial revolution hero here was the self-reliant artisan or workman. In practice, however, the worker is also required to be compliant with the norms and rules of the organisation, where it is run by those entrepreneurs and managers who are engaged in the generation of wealth. This does not necessarily mean to take away their individuality, only that their inner-direction ought to be animated by similar values as the managers.

5 *The source of authority is position, supported by certified competence, and the source of legitimacy is the rationally derived rule given the force of law*

In Western society, property ownership (and control) provides the legally supported basis for exercising authority. The alternative basis is position in direct line of devolution or descent from property ownership. Where, however, this alternative is relied on, it is (slowly) becoming important to be able to demonstrate competence, and this may be certified in some fashion (such as by possession of a diploma or degree). Emphasis on these sources denies the validity of charisma (special personal gift) or tradition as adequate bases for authority.

With the growth of industrial scale the bureaucracy emerged as the dominant form of work organisation, and with it came the notion that the only source of legitimacy for any action taken was the rule which had been worked out in accordance with the 'objective' requirements of the situation. This bureaucratic basis of 'rational-legal' authority became pretty pervasive, and if few industrial organisations are 'true' or full bureaucracies, the value of the rationally evolved rule is strongly supported in the culture. In spite of this growth of bureaucracy (or perhaps because of it), the principle of *individualism* continues to dominate, preventing emphasis being put on the managed group as a whole, as a source of authority. This is more clearly discernible in the process of allocating authority in primary sector Japanese firms (Ouchi, 1981, pp 40–53).

An Alternative Model

An alternative model of enterprise, based on the application of such values as are found in strongly contrasting cultures, such as that of Japan (or at least partially in some of the deviant cultural values of Western society), can be described. This is no more real than the model just outlined, but does indicate how greater de-emphasis of an exploitative individualism might change the face of industry. This would involve emphasising the value of a symbiotic relationship with nature, man as essentially good, other-directed personalities, collectivised relationships, and authority stemming from the group rather than from property and hierarchical position. The effect of this kind of change might be to produce industrial organisations which were:

1 less openly exploitative and more conservation-minded.

2 less directed towards short-run profit gains and more concerned with longer-term stability and growth.

3 less reliant on limited purposive contracts and more willing to develop broader status contracts.

4 less keen to direct and evaluate individual performance from a position in a hierarchy and more eager to encourage self-direction and self-reliance.

5 less dependent on long hierarchies of specialist functionaries and more reliant on consensus achieved in loosely supportive groups in which 'social distance' is reduced.

6 less reliant on the making and application of rules and more concerned with the inculcation of social norms as guides to conduct.

7 less reliant on the incorporation of individuals within hierarchical structures and more concerned to evolve loose federations of working groups as occasion demands.

8   less interested in finding individually qualified and ambitious personnel and more desirous of securing the services of workers with a strong orientation towards cooperation in work activities.

9   less impatient of mistakes made by individuals and more tolerant of mistakes made in the course of honest attempts to try out new solutions to problems, within working groups.

10 less dependent on communication in hierarchical chains of command and more supportive of open communication through working groups.

An organisation with such characteristics would be somewhat different from many typical organisations, both in its appearance to outsiders and in the working experience which it offered to those within it. It might be expected to create a context for more creative action to deal with market and other external demands, a more satisfying working environment for employees, and a more efficient enterprise. It would not be easy to create or sustain, however, without important changes in the educational, political, legal, and social parameters within which industry currently operates.

Cultural Constraints on Management

Adaptations of this kind are remote because the rest of the cultural infrustructure works to prevent them. Cultural values and ideas embodied in other institutions and practices are likely to limit development more than they facilitate changes of this kind, however functional they may seem to be.

Farmer and Richman (1968) examined the question of why the universal functions of management are discharged in different ways, and with different degrees of success, in different societies and situations (see also Ouchi, 1981, p 12). This is to be explained, they suggest, by differences of an 'objective' (observable) kind in the cultural values and practices. Figure 5 illustrates the relationship of culture to managerial functions and efficiency that they describe.

This suggests that cultural values are associated with the major institutions of society, each of which impinges (in the sense of helping or hindering) to some degree on the work of management. It is at this level that ideas about effective action and the biggest cultural impact on management may be found.

Figure 5

Culture and managerial efficiency

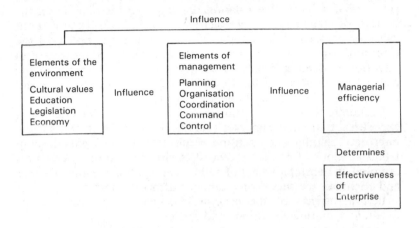

Source: Farmer R N and Richman B M: *Comparative Management and Economic Progress* (Richard D Irwin, 1968).

Institutional Influences

Farmer and Richman consider the culturally imposed sociological, political, legal, economic, and educational institutions and practices as restrictive, by virtue of their being either inescapable with impunity or internalised as valuable. One way or another, what management can and will do in various areas will be constrained by the consequences of organising these areas of life in specific ways.

Their list of sociological constraints includes the values placed by the society on such matters as business and its management; authority and subordination; wealth and material gain; scientific method; risk taking; and change. If business and its management are regarded as significantly less valuable than religion or education, for example, the brighter people will be encouraged to enter these careers rather than those offered in industry. If wealth is denigrated, obstacles are likely to be put in the way of its accumulation. If traditional ways of living are highly valued, attempts to introduce change may well be met with organised resistance.

Similarly, the political system limits action. The extent to which a government is prepared to subsidise industry varies between countries and affects industry's capacity to tender for business in both home and overseas markets. The imposition of an incomes policy restricts the opportunities available to firms to develop an appropriately skilled and motivated workforce.

The impact of legislation is more obvious. In Britain, in the period since 1963, a spate of legislation has imposed restrictions on the exercise of management's prerogatives in hiring and firing without cause or compensation; another set of statutes has restricted the traditional immunities of trade unions and compelled more careful attention to their internal democratic processes. Nor should the continuing influence of the Companies Acts on the structure and powers of public companies be discounted.

Economic constraints are those imposed by the size and degree of exposure of the home market and the way in which the society interprets legitimate competition. Educational constraints develop from the kinds of courses provided to citizens and the restrictions imposed on the employment of children and young persons. Farmer and Richman see these constraints as affecting both the static or structural aspects of the general management process and its dynamic operating conditions and processes.

In the first category they place the methodologies, techniques, and tools used in planning, the types of performance and control standards used, the degree of centralisation or decentralisation, the degree of work specialisation, or the distribution of participative as distinct from authoritarian management.

In the second, they place such aspects as the ease or difficulty of motivating both managers and workers to perform their jobs effectively and efficiently and to improve their performance; the degree of identification that tends to exist between the interests and objectives of individuals, departments, and the enterprise; and the amount of organisational flexibility in changing or adapting to surrounding conditions. All of these are likely to be similarly affected (Farmer and Richman, 1964, pp 55–68).

Changes in Practice

Culture is, of course, something which is made by man: it is not something somehow handed down from outside the social system. It is, in consequence, open to change by the same means. In fact, it is always in process of change. The rate of change may be too great for some and too slow for others, but it is always amenable to modification by the innovators, provided they can secure a power base on which to operate. Managers, in fact, are often in a position to make changes because they are permitted a strong power base within the culture and the discretion to make such changes as will serve the greater good of the society by increasing its wealth. Their remit, however, tends to run in respect of individual practices within the industrial organisations themselves.

Changing particular practices is, however, likely to prove easier than changing fundamental cultural values − for managers or any-one else. Changes at this level are less threatening to social stability than would be any attempt to change the underlying cultural values themselves. No doubt, if enough practices are changed, a major change in cultural values will result in time. If enough trade union 'restrictive practices' are bought out, it may become difficult to recognise the trade union idea of protecting and defending members' interests; if the law enforces more changes in employment practice it may become difficult to sustain the argument that British industrial relations subscribe to voluntarism in such matters. Never-theless, cultural values are likely to be changed, where they are changed at all, by this piecemeal alteration of practices at the bottom of the hierarchy.

Similar observations may be made about attempts to change institutions. If the values of a society are difficult to change by any deliberate action, so too are the ideas or designs for living − because of their hierarchical association. Values pin together extremely large numbers of practices, and cultural ideas almost as many. Tackling the problem of change at these levels is therefore difficult, if only because of the many likely ramifications. These are likely to be used as a basis for opposition and therefore need to be accommodated before any agreement to change can be reached.

The examples of cultural ideas or designs which Farmer and Richman consider (educational, political, legal, etc.) are probably more amenable to change than the underlying values, but probably more difficult to alter than specific practices (such as school leaving age, voting practices, or specific legislation). A proposal to change the way the educational system impinges on the perceived needs of industry is difficult because the system is usually so firmly linked to deep-seated values concerning the proper approach to individual development. These deep-seated anchorages have been seen in the debate between the British Secretary of State for Education and the teaching profession.

In any event, many of these, where they are regarded as being *imposed* on industry and its management, call for political action: industry may lobby for change but is usually not in a position to bring it about without the support of the political system. This is, however, less true at the level of change in particular practices.

Even the specific patterns of behaviour, from which the core elements of the culture can be inferred, are tenacious and difficult enough to change because they, too, are rooted in deep-seated cultural values. It is not that the practices (such as wash-up time, working with a mate, having an individual office, wearing individualised clothing at work) are valued simply because they are traditional, or that it has always been done this way; it is rather that they are associated with the maintenance of central values of the society or the class. Changing particular ways of going about things to meet one set of conditions (say, a rush job) could permanently affect some other aspect of life or living to which the people concerned prefer to cling.

Organisational Culture and Character

Industry is usually endowed with authority to make changes at this level of practice, and in so doing it may ultimately bring about more fundamental changes. Within modern society, industry is allowed appreciable discretion to adopt deviant values from those of the dominant traditional culture, if it confronts situations to which the traditional values and solutions patently cannot apply. It has frequently been argued in the context of 'industrialisation' at least that there remains much observational evidence of established industry's freedom to act in this way in its own interests. National cultures do normally bend to industry's supposedly universal or specific requirements.

It may often prove to be the case that the only culturally induced limitations on managerial activities are those which arise out of management's own predispositions to construe and act on situations in traditional ways. The organisations concerned may therefore need to work harder at producing change in management's values, attitudes, and dispositions generally, in order to produce their own, home-grown, accommodations of new situations. This is tantamount to suggesting that the organisation should bring about a change in its own culture (or 'subculture') to break out of its situation. The object would be not to break out of the broader enveloping cultural mould completely, but to provide more appropriate values, ideas, and practices.

In recent years, this concept of 'subculture' has been introduced into management literature to identify working philosophies, designs, and practices peculiar to the individual organisation. Its origins lie in Selznick's concept of 'organisational character' with which he associates the notion of an organisation's 'distinctive competence', where:

'The terms institution, organisational character, and distinctive competence all refer to the same basic process

  − the transformation of an engineered, technical
arrangement of building blocks into a social organism'
(Selznick, 1957, p 135).

The effect of this process is to generate autonomously values, ideas,
and practices, at the level of and appropriate to the particular
circumstances of the particular organisation.

This notion of philosophy is concerned with abstract values and
ideas, not directly with concrete methods and techniques. It offers
little that solves immediate and pressing problems, although it will
serve to guide and structure concrete action. It is, to use Lessem's
terminology, a 'soil' in which relevant ideas for methods and
techniques may grow or not, depending on its fertility (Lessem,
1985, p 11). The philosophy can be linked with the more usual
industrial concept of 'policy', which contains and reflects the fundamental values by which the organisation proposes to operate.
Similarly, at the level of ideas for strategy or tactics, there may be a
need for innovation. The historically derived designs for working
cooperatively may cease to be useful guides to current action when
circumstances change. Human resource management in a high-tech
situation sometimes attempts to continue in traditional moulds,
but may need to be rethought against the real demands of both the
technology and the social system in the new situation.

Traditions of organising and controlling work activities are slow to
change when markets and technologies do so because they continue to
command respect and to influence the ways people think, feel, and
behave. What at any moment in time we regard as normal starting and
finishing times for employment work are largely a matter of
tradition; they are what we have become used to, although they have
changed from one long period to another. They affect thinking to the
extent that when a reduction is made it is assumed that, for example,
the cut will be averaged over the days of the working week.

Differentials in pay are also difficult to explain except in terms of
traditions that have been established as workable solutions to past
problems of recruitment, retention, and motivation. Even when a
massive move is made to introduce equal pay for men and women,
tradition-dominated judgements still place the pay of the woman
doing women's work lower than that of a man doing men's work.

Traditional job demarcations, traditional allocations of authority
to control, traditional assumptions about the value of trade etc.,
may offer little current guidance as to the kinds of action needed in
British industry. But so strong is the force of tradition, and so ill
developed are the mechanisms for effective dialogue and discussion
that the alternatives never seem to materialise.

Effecting Change

Industrial institutions, no less than society at large, confront the problem of maintaining stability of practices and, at the same time, of bringing about changes which accommodate changes in the environment. It is common to argue that 'people resist change', although there is probably as much evidence to support the opposite proposition that 'people accept change'. Nevertheless, it is to be expected that people resist (or simply do not accept) changes which they do not understand, changes which threaten their basic securities, and changes which they are forced to make against their will or better judgement (Spicer, 1952).

The immediate problem about making changes in practices arises from the pervasive influence of wider culture and cultural values in conditioning the individual who is brought up within the society. Because the individual is repeatedly confronted with experience which is structured or given meaning by a central core of cultural values, the effect is that the individual will most probably 'orient', his or her behaviour to them. The individual's self-conception and personal security will become bound up in and with them; to change them is to confront the individual with a need to make some quite fundamental changes. In everyday language, the individual who resists such changes is likely to express the reason as one of lack of understanding: the change does not fit in with any existing structure of meaning and therefore cannot be assimilated.

This is not confined simply to 'workers'. A similar process of socialisation, albeit one which may inculcate different values and solutions to problems, helps to predispose managers to respond in some traditional ways rather than others. Cultural conditioning is not necessarily fully effective but it is no respecter of class or status.

This is a major part of the problem about adopting 'foreign' solutions to problems. These may be integrated with their respective (foreign) cultures but they have not figured as part of the acculturation process of the home population. The mechanisms of socialisation are, consequently, unable to transmit the values and perspectives which would provide fertile soil for their propagation here. Only if comparable and compatible values have been disseminated in that way is the problem likely to be eased.

This appears to be borne out by experience of attempting to introduce imported devices such as Quality Circles (QCs). These frequently swim into the consciousness of British management as a result of conferences attended or articles read. The attempt is then made to apply them as specific techniques for improving communication or increasing attention to quality, with no concern for their cultural or philosophical context, either there or here. But practically every discussion of such methods and techniques emphasises that they are integrated within a 'philosophy' – without which they become no more than stranded whales on an alien shore. Quality circles in Japan, for example, form an integral part of the philosophy and style of management and are not merely stuck on like limpets (Collard, 1981).

This kind of observation is by no means new. F W Taylor uttered a similar cry many years ago to the effect that both British and American industry were adopting his stop-watch methods but ignoring the philosophical underpinning which he thought necessary to their successful integration into a personnel strategy and policy (Urwick and Brech, 1945). Perhaps managements have not learned a great deal in the interim.

An alternative strategy that can be attempted in these circumstances is that which aims to provide 'adult socialisation' to make up for the deficiency in earlier socialisation. This means that the organisation introducing the novel ideas has both to find a way of integrating them with experience and to transmit information in the form of supportive and integrative messages about it. This requires a total immersion of affected personnel in structured experience and in both formal and information communications. It is unlikely to prove effective if the mechanisms for doing it are not already well established and familiar to those who it is intended will be influenced through them.

Frustration as a Stimulus to Change

Frustration is, on the other hand, likely to provide a stimulus to change and its acceptance. This may be brought about because continuance with traditional practices in support of some traditional value threatens the basic securities of the people involved in them. Where a problem is recognised but no new solution has been found (or if found, it has not been accepted as legitimate), frustration may be the most likely outcome. The two features – the persistence of outworn traditions and the non-appearance of innovative designs for living and working – are characteristic of Britain and many of its industrial organisations at the present time.

Society and its members are ill served when traditional solutions are continued simply because everyone is familiar and comfortable with them, even though they no longer fit, and because no more appropriate solution has been found. But it by no means follows that solutions will be found just because they are needed. It is increasingly unlikely in these circumstances that any individual is going to be in a position to hand down a new and more apposite design for working. Consequently, the 'problem' becomes one of establishing adequate intelligence-gathering, debating, and influencing institutions, from which new ideas can emerge and through which they might become acceptable and accepted. Blocking off contributions from some section of the population may simply serve to reinforce the others in a blinkered approach to the problem.

As problems of this kind mount, the theory that such new solutions are more likely to occur where the culture (or sub-culture) is thrown open to new ideas from any and all members of the society – another of the lessons drawn from the experience of Japanese industry – becomes more widely supported.

Rejection of existing cultural values and designs may be expected to occur more readily when people find and adopt new ways of coping with a changing environment, provided that the new practices promise to maintain or improve the standard of living or way of life of the people involved. People do, however, need time to work out the cost-benefit calculations involved in any such programme of change. Ensuring that social and institutional responses can match up to the environmental changes (over which no identifiable 'persons' may have any real control) is a process which requires time to work through.

It can, of course, be argued that time is not in plentiful supply. Against this, however, it can be countered that it is necessary to take time to ensure that not only are new solutions found, but that they are accepted by those who will have to work with them. There is enough evidence to suggest that changes which are imposed, or which are rushed through because of time pressure, are unlikely to be accepted to the extent that will ensure that they 'work'. There is also evidence to suggest that changes which are put in before people have assimilated their meaning (*for them*) are unlikely to command the human commitment required for success.

Recent experiences with the introduction of change do suggest that many people, including the workers who are often considered to be potentially the most resistant to it, are ready to embrace and welcome it, possibly as a way out of the frustration which they currently experience.

Divergent Values as an Aid to Change

The fact that not everyone in a modern society subscribes to the same set of cultural values can also facilitate effective change of this kind. At very least, those holding deviant values or different ideas about how to proceed in some area may form allies in a movement to bring change about.

In a complex modern society, which has been subjected to massive change over a significant period of time, it is not to be expected that the culture will exist as a simple, homogenous set of designs and instruments, about which there is broad consensus. At the level of fundamental values there may be some common elements; at the 'applied' level, there are likely to be few. As Gorer says, 'in a society as complex and diversified as contemporary England, there are relatively few areas in which two-thirds or more of the population share the same attitudes and practices' (Gorer, 1955, p 162).

In such a society a variety of values, ascribed meanings, beliefs, and theories exist side by side. Gorer's own questionnaire study revealed differences between regions in England, between religious groups, and between classes (Gorer, 1955, pp 297–303). Growing up within any one of these is likely to confront the learner with a different repertoire of designs from which to learn, and if the educational processes were equally efficient in communicating these, the result would be a range of different perceptions, values, and frames of reference.

Turner and Lawrence's (1965) generally unsuccessful attempt to link job characteristics with satisfaction revealed that predominantly Protestant workers living and working in rural and small town settings, whose jobs were rated highly in terms of variety, autonomy, knowledge, skill and responsibility required, were generally satisfied; while those on lowly rated jobs were generally dissatisfied and more prone to absenteeism. Predominantly Catholic workers in urban setings, on the other hand, were likely to show higher satisfaction with and lower absenteeism from jobs with relatively low scores on these dimensions. Turner and Lawrence's explanation of the differences emphasised the mediating effect of these underlying 'cultural' values, stressing ambition for the Protestant rural workers and alienation and absence of norms for the urban workers. The fact of the differences existing, however, carries implications for what is transmitted in socialisation.

Hulin and Blood (1968) hypothesised that people's attitudes towards their work would be influenced by the extent to which they held middle class values which support occupational achievement, responsibility, and hard work. Their studies to test this hypothesis revealed that those workers who showed little alienation from these middle class values tended to value demanding and creative jobs, those who revealed strong alienation from these values were more satisfied with less demanding jobs. To the extent that adults pass on their values to their children through the family, these are the different kinds of values which might be expected to be perpetuated unless interrupted by conflicting values inculcated in schools.

Other pieces of research have demonstrated that views of human nature and motivation are often associated with different classes and different cultural origins. Bailey's criticisms (1983) of Herzberg's findings on motivation (1959), for example, show that he saw them as inherent in the nature of the original samples drawn exclusively from professional and technical occupations; they necessarily reflect the cultural values of this middle class group. Schein (1980) also doubts the relevance of Herzberg's hygiene factors to low-status employees who do not usually seek 'meaning' in their work, but sees the growth in white-collar employment as a factor making them generally more compelling for industry.

Similarly, Porter's empirical testing (1961; 1962; 1963a and 1963b) of Maslow's concept of the hierarchy of prepotency of human needs (1943), reveals that the self-actualisation apex is to be found in association with senior management positions, but not among workers lower in the industrial/occupational hierarchy, suggesting that this, too, is status-linked if not exactly class-linked. The Luton studies of Goldthorpe and his colleagues suggest that the variety of orientations to work did not derive from the work situation as such, but from the workers' class, community, and family backgrounds (Goldthorpe *et al*, 1968, p 144).

The fact that such differences abound in society makes it likely that changes which threaten dominant cultural values may still appeal to groups holding different subcultural values. The future may lie in an explosive fragmentation of cultural values in the face of economic and industrial change. This presupposes, however, that there will be some way in which innovations can be communicated widely throughout the society to enable people to adopt such designs for living and working as fit the new circumstances. It may prove to be the case, however, that the very traditions which no longer fit the circumstances include the one which inhibits the development of the 'open society'. Nevertheless, it has been a persistent thesis in recent years that a more open social structure is a necessary precursor of fragmented cultures associated with individual economic institutions (Peters and Waterman, 1982, pp 97 *et seq*; Pascale and Athos, 1981; Ouchi, 1981).

SUMMARY

The feeling that culture (a shorthand expression to include a society's preferred mode of operating) plays a significant part in predisposing people to perform well or poorly seems to be growing. The underlying thought is that culture inevitably imposes some constraint on both individual behaviour (by inculcating traditional values and ideas which influence individuals' predispositions to act) and on organised action (by embodying them in artefacts and institutions).

The values and ideas embodied in the culture are derived from historical solutions to problems previously encountered; in a rapidly changing environment, uncontrollable by the society in question, these historical solutions may have little to offer as solutions to current problems.

A mild change in the values supported by such structures and processes as industry develops can be shown to have important implications for creativity, efficiency, and satisfaction. Whether such a change will occur, however, depends on responses from a wide range of institutions within the culture.

Even when the need for change can be demonstrated, the opportunities open to, say, industry to effect changes by itself tend to be limited because traditions tend to be upheld by other surrounding institutions over which industry has no control (and possibly little influence).

Industry's capacity for bringing about change may be restricted to effecting changes in practice within its own domain, by changing its own values, styles, ideas and practices, for which it is allowed considerable discretion.

Currently, action is being taken in some organisations to change structures of work experience and to multiply the opportunities which workers *and* managers have for developing new perspectives, attitudes, and ideas for operating. Frequently, this leads to the deliberate development of an 'organisation-culture' which is consciously sustained by experiments in adult socialisation within the individual organisation.

Such developments are unlikely to be sensible for or feasible in all industrial situations, but where they are introduced as appropriate, they indicate how the structures and processes of the wider society may be modified by new localised experiences.

Reading:

Ajiferuke and Boddewyn (1970).
Brim and Wheeler (1966).
Farmer and Richman (1968).
Frost *et al* (1985).
Kluckhohn (C) (1962).
Kluckhohn (F) (1953).
Lessem (1985).

Ouchi (1981).

Pascale and Athos (1981).

Peters and Waterman (1982).

Sorge and Warner (1980a and b).

Weinshall (1977).

4 Employment Law

Many of society's main cultural values and imperatives for action are embodied in law. These cultural values, clearly, come before specific legal requirements, whether embodied in legislation or common law. Because society places a high value on both the generation of wealth through industry and its distribution through the employment relationship, the law closely structures the relationships by defining rights in or ownership of real or personal property and in labour.

'Law', in this context, is a combination of *common law* and *statute law*. The one is 'judge-made' in the form of court decisions made in the past but binding on the present through established doctrines and precedents. Many of the legal rights and duties of employers and employees have been established in this way. The other is law enacted by parliament to express society's requirements with respect to conduct, and, in some cases, to overturn decisions made by judges (for example, the Trade Disputes Act, 1906, was passed to remove some of the disabilities imposed on trade unions by the Taff Vale Railway Company decision of 1902). Together both constitute 'the law'.

Because most people orient their behaviours to the law, it generally serves to direct and constrain their conduct in the interests of preserving those institutions and processes which are considered to be important to the welfare of society at large.

The law relevant to human resource management is that concerned with individual employment and association for economic purposes. These structure the fundamental relationships involved in employment by establishing the terms and conditions under and the contexts in which people either cooperate in the process of creating wealth or engage in exchange transactions in the course of distributing it.

In this chapter we look at the law as it relates to the employment contract and in the next we examine aspects of the law pertaining to

113

work-related associations. We will consider the law relating to employment contracts, in two parts:

(a) the nature of the contract itself as this is established in law as an instrument of control of exchange relationships, and as a vehicle for upholding rights and obligations drawn from a diversity of sources; and

(b) the content of the contract in so far as this establishes the rights and obligations which people enjoy or suffer, and thus determines what they can count on in developing their work relationships (Armstrong *et al*, 1981, p 7).

In recent years, however, the growth in self-employment, with its consequences for subcontracting, has made the 'contract for services' a more common feature of the employment scene. This type of contract is more akin to the commercial contract than to the employment contract, and as yet, it has not been subject to the same degree of regulation as applies to the contract of employment. Consequently, not all of the restrictions on the employer's prerogative power in relation to employment are applied to the contract for services.

The Contract of Employment

A contract, in its simplest form, provides the basis for the single act of exchange of goods or services for an amount of money, the usual basis of a commercial contract. In its more complex forms, it may serve as the basis for a relationship of cooperation extending into an indefinite future, as usually happens when an *employment* contract is established.

Contract is based on the voluntary acceptance of obligations to another – for example, an obligation to perform work and an obligation to pay for the work done. Contractual obligations differ from other legal obligations (such as those imposed by the criminal law or in the law of tort) in that they are based on the agreement of the contracting parties. But the courts supervise the discharge of these obligations because they are of sufficient importance to warrant enforcement in the public as well as the individual's interest.

The definition of contract, particularly as applied to employment, is essentially a legal one, focused on rights and obligations associated with the offer and exchange of labour for money. To be enforceable in law, such a contract must comply with certain legal rules governing who may enter into contracts, with what purposes and intentions, and how they shall do so, if they want the under-takings given and accepted to be recognised and enforced in a court of law:

1   the persons entering into the agreement must have capacity to contract. They must be of full (legal) age, mentally competent, and not in a dependency relationship to another who is responsible for them.

2   the objects of the contract must themselves be legal. The courts will not enforce contracts which intend breach of the law − for example, by avoiding liability for income tax − and a contract with such an object would prevent the parties enforcing any other rights or duties contained in it.

3   the parties must intend the mutual undertakings to be legally binding and enforceable through the courts, as is usually the case with business contracts but not with 'social' contracts (which, in Britain, include collective agreements).

4   what one party offers must be accepted by the other party *in the same terms* as the offer before there is a basis for an enforceable contract. If the employer offers a job of typist at £180 per week, and an applicant says he or she will work as clerk for that amount, this is not acceptance in the same terms.

5   some valuable consideration must pass between the parties. What is valuable consideration varies, but in the employment context work services usually pass from the employee and remuneration from the employer.

These indicate the clear interests of the law in the matter of contracting, but offers and acceptances about 'consideration' are but narrow definitions of the content of these agreements.

The Wider Concerns of Contract

Mumford has argued that there are five distinct aspects of the offers and demands of the parties to an employment contract, and not all of these are explicitly and fully acknowledged in the legal definition. Her five elements are:

1   *The element of knowledge*   The undertaking establishes what it requires in its employees by way of knowledge and skill and the means (for example, whether by recruitment or training) it will employ to meet these requirements; the worker establishes what he or she is prepared to offer to meet his or her requirements for income, security, etc.

2 *The element of motivation* The undertaking establishes what psychological contribution it will demand of its employees (for example, loyalty or commitment) and what incentives it will offer to secure this; the employee establishes how much contribution he or she is prepared to make for the incentives offered.

3 *The element of efficiency* The undertaking sets up standards of performance which it will expect of employees and rules governing their achievement; the workers form their own perspectives of what criteria are relevant to the wage-effort bargain struck.

4 *The element of commitment (ethics)* The undertaking must determine how much of the human personality it wants or is prepared to engage in the pursuit of its corporate ends; the workers must comparably determine how far they are prepared to commit themselves in this way.

5 *The element of interest (task structure)* The work which the undertaking offers may be interesting or boring, routine or challenging, and the workers' expectations of work may accord with what is on offer or conflict with it.

These do not necessarily stand in isolation from one another, but they do provide a basis for checking whether the different aspects of the offers and the demands involved in contracting are congruent with one another (which was the original purpose of this piece of categorisation) (Mumford, 1972).

The law emphasises the 'consideration' involved in contract (that is, the third of the above elements) but pays little regard to the others. Legal definitions are not, therefore, to be regarded as complete definitions of what is involved in this relationship, although they have obvious and crucial importance. Past experience suggests that some of these (for example, the wage-effort bargain or training) have been given much thought and effort, whereas the others have been largely ignored or assumed to be dealt with adequately under the other headings (Gowler, 1974, p 5).

Contract Terms and Conditions

What each party undertakes to do for the other under an employment contract is largely a matter for the parties concerned. They are regarded in law as free to undertake what suits them, and (the Wages Council trades apart) assumed to be equal in their power to secure their own terms. Provided certain conditions are met, the courts will generally accept that the parties went into a contract with their eyes open, and will be reluctant to overturn anything to which the parties have expressly agreed. What the parties voluntarily establish as terms of the contract is thus of paramount importance.

This contract may be established – that is, put in being – very simply. This is possible because it is such a well known institution supported by a great deal of law and convention, which can be relied on to fill in what may not have been made explicit. It may also be established in more complex ways and be put in writing to try to define the real intentions of the parties.

A formal written contract, detailing the terms and conditions, may be drawn up in some cases in advance of the employee joining, but this is not very common practice. In some cases, particularly those relating to white-collar jobs, there may be a formal written statement (say, in the form of a letter), which puts the main terms and conditions in writing before the person starts the job. In any event, the legislation now requires that the individual must receive a statement of the main terms within thirteen weeks of starting work (Table 3). Strictly, this is not a contract, although it is good evidence of its terms.

A contract may be established, either orally or by conduct (although the thirteen week statement is still required). Many are established *orally*: the employer says an applicant can have a named job at a certain rate of pay and this is accepted without further discussion. This establishes a contract whose detailed terms may be filled in later. Sometimes, so little may be said that the contract is established *by conduct*: the potential employee starts to do a job and the employer's representative (say, a foreman) does not stop him doing so, even though nothing may have been said about what the job entails or the money to be paid for it. The details of the terms and conditions remain to be established later.

It is impossible to write down *all* the terms and conditions of employment of any employee. This is because they are both infinitely numerous in their fine detail and subject to change with the exigencies of the employer's business and the employee's capacity to work. Most of them are therefore worked out and reworked 'on the job' in interactions with supervisors as management's first line representatives, and as 'understandings' rather than written agreements. Only the main terms and conditions, which someone has established as the more important ones, appear in written form.

The *express terms* are important because they are relied on, in the event of any dispute, to establish what the parties intended. The courts will enforce them, however, only if the terms and conditions are clear and unambiguous. In the event of dispute between the parties about intentions or meaning, where the express terms are not

Table 3

*Information on main terms and conditions of employment
(required by Employment Protection (Consolidation) Act, ss 1–7)*

---

1. Identity of the parties to the employment contract

2 The date on which the employment began

3 A statement on whether 'any employment with a previous employer counts as part of the employee's continuous period of employment' with the present employer, and if so, the date on which the continuous period commenced

4 The title of the job which the employee is employed to do

5 The terms of the contract applicable at a date to be specified which is not more than one week before the date on which the statement is given to the employee. The terms which have to be specified (or whose source has to be indicated) are:

  (a) the scale or rate of remuneration or the method used to calculate it;

  (b) the intervals at which the remuneration is paid (whether, for example, weekly or monthly);

  (c) any terms and conditions relating to hours of work (including any defining normal working hours);

  (d) any terms and conditions relating to
    – entitlement to public and other holidays and to holiday pay (the information given must enable the recipient to work out entitlements to holiday pay and accrued holiday pay (in the event of termination)
    – incapacity for work due to sickness or injury, and any entitlement to sick pay
    – pensions and pension schemes (if not provided for in an Act of Parliament), and whether there is a contracting out certificate in force;

  (e) the length of notice which the employee is obliged to give and entitled to receive to determine the contract of employment. (If the contract is for a fixed term, the date on which it is due to end must be stated.)

6. The employee must also be issued with a note which specifies:
  (a) any disciplinary rules applicable to the employee (or refers the employee to a readily accessible document which contains them);
  (b) the person or committee to whom the employee can apply if dissatisfied with any disciplinary decision relating to him or her, and what further steps beyond this appeal are open to him or her;
  (c) the person (or position) to whom an employee can take a complaint or grievance about his or her employment in order to secure redress, and the manner in which the application has to be made;
  (d) whether there are steps beyond that indicated in (c) and if so what they are (or refers the employee to a readily-accessible document which contains them (EP(C) Act, s 1 (4)).

clear, the courts may imply the terms of the contract on the basis of certain other common law principles and rules. This process relates in the so-called implied terms, which form part of the taken for granted aspect of the institution of contract.

Implied Terms

Where the express terms of the contract are silent, or unclear, or disputed on particular obligations, the courts may resolve the matter by implying terms to such contracts as may exist. The general rule about implied terms is that it should be normal for the parties to intend that the unexpressed terms should be incorporated in the contract. Implied terms affecting the employment contract may be derived from one or more of three sources.

1 *What is customary in the undertaking, trade, or industry*
To be enforced as an implied term, customs must pass two types of test:

(a) they must reflect the intentional acceptance of an obligation by one of the parties. The *ex gratia* payment is an obvious attempt to permit money to be paid without creating any kind of customary precedent of this kind. But the employer may even pay gratuities or bonuses over many years, and claim to do so out of a sense of philanthropy not of obligation. It would be pointless trying to persuade a court that these should be regarded as customary terms and conditions of employment. In the process of collective bargaining, however, such arguments may well be used and may succeed and thus allow custom to be read into the contract by implication.

(b) they must also be reasonable (according to the lawyer's usual tests of what a reasonable man would expect in the circumstances), certain (precisely defined and not capable of differing interpretations), and notorious (well established and well known to everybody in the factory, trade, or industry concerned).

2 *What has been established in understandings or agreements made between the employer and representatives of recognised trade unions*

A collective agreement is a charter of (procedural) rules governing the relationships between the employer (or the employer's association) and the employees' association (usually a trade union in the normal meaning of that term) and an expression of the agreed substantive terms and conditions under which employee-members will work for the employer (for a fuller treatment, see Thomason, 1984, pp 340–71). An understanding intends the same consequence without usually being committed to writing.

What is agreed or understood may concern the substantive terms of the individual contracts of members' employment or the procedures to be followed by the parties to the collective agreement.

Most of the procedural terms will not be enforceable in law as a term of the individual contract and are excluded from direct enforcement by specific legislation (Trade Union and Labour Relations Act, 1974, s 18, which reiterates the principle first established in the Trade Union Act, 1871; see also Monterosso Shipping Co Ltd *v* International Transport Workers' Federation [1982] IRLR, 468).

The substantive terms of the collective agreement may, provided they are clear and unambiguous, be read into the individual contract under certain circumstances defined by legal rules. Those governing express incorporation are to the effect that:

(a)   Both the collective agreement and the individual contract must make explicit provision for incorporation (see National Coal Board *v* Galley [1958] 1 All E R, 91).

(b)   The representatives were explicitly (by, for example, individual authorisation or union rule) in an agency relationship to their principals (the members or directors, as the case may be).

(c)   The terms of the collective agreement must also be capable of being translated into the individual's contract as relevant to individual conduct. This excludes many of the procedural clauses.

(d)   There must also be an absence of conflict as between different collective agreements which may conceivably be relevant. O'Higgins makes this point by saying: 'so far the (court) decisions suggest that the courts will only allow the worker to get the benefit of those terms in conflicting collective agreements which are least advantageous' (O'Higgins, 1976, p 35).

The rules governing implied incorporation – that is where there is nothing explicit on the matter, as in the case of an understanding – are similar to those applied in connection with custom:

(a)   It must be reasonable to assume that the parties intended that the terms were so vital as to necessitate incorporation in the employment contract.

Table 4

Common law duties of the parties to the employment contract

A.   The employee will be assumed, in the absence of contrary statement, to have agreed to:

1.   be ready and willing to work;

2.   provide personal service;

3.   avoid wilful disruption of the employer's undertaking or, put more simply, to cooperate with the employer and facilitate the execution of the contract;

4.   obey reasonable or lawful orders;

5.   work only for the employer in the period during which he is being paid by him to work;

6.   account for any profits received;

7.   respect the employer's trade secrets;

8.   take reasonable care of the employer's property when it is entrusted to him;

9.   take reasonable care when engaged in the employer's service.

B.   The employer, in similar circumstances, is assumed to have agreed to:

1.   pay for work done or service rendered under the contract;

2.   provide opportunity to earn remuneration and to provide work in some circumstances, for example where 'practice' is important to maintain the value of the service;

3.   take reasonable care for the safety and well-being of the employee whilst at work;

4.   indemnify the employee for any loss sustained in the performance of his or her duties;

5.   'treat the employee with appropriate courtesy' (Rideout, 1979, p 35) in order to sustain mutual trust and confidence.

(b)   Such incorporation has been taking place in the trade or industry for so long that it could be regarded as established practice for this to happen, or the terms may have stood for so long that they have become part of the custom and practice of the trade or industry.

(c)   What the law itself requires to be read into a contract which is otherwise silent. This is, effectively, in two parts: what the common law considers to be either commercially convenient

for the running of business, or universal standards of
conduct which must be assumed to apply in the absence of
agreement to do otherwise (Treitel, 1975, pp 1–2), and what
legislation has been established as individual rights.

In common law it is assumed that those who freely establish
contracts of employment intend to accept certain duties which are
consistent with commercial convenience and proper conduct. Where
these are not stated, the courts will imply these as terms of the
contract. These duties have been summarised by different
authorities in different ways: Table 4 shows one such summary.
People will normally order their behaviour (for example, in dispute
conditions) in accordance with these doctrines simply because they
know that the courts will be prepared to enforce them as 'implied
terms of the employment contract' if they are asked to arbitrate.

Legislation establishes rights for specific categories of employee
(for example, young persons and women) and in respect of certain
conditions (for example, in connection with health and safety at
work). Initially, these rights stemmed from the imposition of
'statutory duties' on the employer; this way of conferring rights
continues in the Race Relations and Sex Discrimination Acts, 1976
and 1975; the Wages Act, 1986; the Health and Safety at Work Act,
1974 (Table 5).

Table 5

Statutory rights and duties

1.	not to be discriminated against on grounds of sex, marital status, or race, whether in recruitment, or at engagement or termination, or during employment (SDA; RRA);
2.	in some trades, to be paid as an adult worker, at a statutory minimum rate for work done (Wages Act, 1986);
3.	to be provided with a healthy and safe working environment and with instruction in appropriate methods of safe working (Health and Safety at Work Act).

More recent legislation – Contracts of Employment Acts, 1963
and 1972; Redundancy Payments Act, 1965; Industrial Relations
Act, 1971; Trade Union and Labour Relations Acts, 1974–76;
Employment Protection Act, 1975; Employment Protection (Consolidation) Act, 1978 (as amended) – has established rights which
are deemed to be terms agreed between the employer and employee,
regardless of what their agreements actually state on these matters:

> 'The parties to the contract of employment are, by a statutory fiction, deemed to make the contract on the basis of the statutory terms ... The terms of the statute can be contracted out only for the benefit of the worker and if the parties purport to agree on terms less favourable to him, they are nevertheless deemed to have contracted for the minimum, and the worker's claim for the difference is accordingly (by fiction) a contractual claim.'

The fiction is: 'that the content of the statute was contractually intended by the employer' (Kahn-Freund, 1977, p 31). The effect is that the new rights are enforceable in contract, rather than in tort actions.

The main rights which employees have acquired in this way are shown in Table 6. The employee may need to have a certain minimum amount of service with the employer and to be within a certain age range to qualify for some (but not all) of these rights. Their enforcement is usually within the jurisdiction of the Industrial Tribunals (Thomason, 1984, pp 198–209).

Thus the general effect of this recent legislation has been to assure the employee of certain minimum rights in employment, and to modify certain of the implied terms derived from the common law. These constitute a floor of enforceable rights on which his or her trade union in negotiation may build a cooperating relationship (Thomason, 1984, pp 107–33).

Restricting the Employer's Freedom

In principle, everyone who has legal capacity to enter into lawful contracts is free to do so. Individuals are free to enter into such undertakings with one another, or not, as they choose. In the same sense, they are also free to withdraw from the contract on giving due notice – that is, the amount of notice provided for in, or customary for, that type of contract. This is the fundamental principle of freedom of contract.

The law also assumes that each party to an employment contract was equal in his or her power to secure the other's agreement to their preferred terms. It is assumed that neither was in a position to take undue advantage of the other in reaching agreement as to terms. This is a question which is widely discussed by social scientists in their analysis of the employment relationship. But the Denning doctrine of 'inequality of bargaining power' has not been applied to the establishment of employment contracts (see D and C Builders

Table 6

Qualifying periods for main individual rights under statute

Minimum Period	Nature of the right	Source of right
1. No period	Not to be dismissed for trade union membership or activities	EPCA s 58
2. "	Not to be dismissed on grounds of sex, marital status, or race	SDA ss RRA s
3. "	Not to have action short of dismissal taken against him or her for trade union membership or activities	EPCA s 23
4. "	To time off with pay for industrial relations activities or training thereof, in the case of lay officials	EPCA s 27
5. "	To time off without pay to take part in trade union activities in the case of members	EPCA s 28
6. "	To time off without pay to undertake public duties	EPCA s 29
7. "	To payments due in the event of employer insolvency	EPCA s 122
8. "	To receive an itemised pay statement	EPCA s 8
9. 4 weeks	To guarantee payments for lay-off	EPCA s 12
10. "	To payments in the event of a medical suspension	EPCA s 19
11. "	Not to be dismissed because of a medical suspension	EPCA s 64
12. "	To receive the (variable) notice provided for in statute as a minimum	EPCA s 49
13. Within 13 weeks	To receive written statement of main terms of contract (if changed, within four weeks)	EPCA s 1
14. 104 weeks	Not to be unfairly dismissed for a reason not given above	EPCA s 54
15. 104 weeks	To request and receive a written statement of reason(s) for dismissal	EPCA s 53
16. 104 weeks after age 18 years	To redundancy payment in event of dismissal for this reason	EPCA s 81
17. 104 weeks	To time off to look for work or to arrange training	EPCA s 31
18. 104 weeks prior to 11th week of confinement	To maternity pay in event of pregnancy	EPCA s 34
19. "	To return to work after pregnancy	EPCA s 45
20. To have the Industrial Tribunal or the courts review the conduct of his employer in respect of any aspect of relationship which is governed by Statute.		

v Rees [1966] 2 QB, 617; Lloyds Bank *v* Bundy [1974] 3 All ER 757).

Recent legislation has, however, restricted the employer's freedom in this respect, and in so doing has redressed some of the inequality suffered by certain categories of person seeking to contract in employment. This relates to the area of discrimination in offering or denying employment on grounds of marital status, sex, and race. The justification for this departure from the long-standing principle is that citizens shall not be disadvantaged simply because they fall into particular categories of this kind. The effect has been to provide penalties for discriminating in any of these ways (on methods of enforcement: Thomason, 1984, pp 194–222).

The effect, particularly of recent legislation, is to place some constraints on the employer's freedom to contract in terms which may not be resisted by employees, whether as individuals or as collectivities (such as trade unions). Where the common law, by and large, implies reciprocal duties on both parties on the assumption that they are equally powerful in trying to secure their own terms in the contract, legislation has imposed duties on the employer to redress a perceived imbalance of power favouring the employer.

The restriction on the employer's power to contract in his or her own terms affects a number of decisions:

1   He or she is restricted in his/her freedom to contract with anyone he/she chooses, particularly where this is exercised so as to discriminate against a person because of:
    (a)   colour, race, nationality or ethnic or national origin;
    (b)   gender;
    (c)   single status in preference to married status; or
    (d)   disability.

The Race Relations Act, 1976, aims to outlaw preferment on the basis of colour, race, nationality or ethnic or national origin, as a basis for selection for employment (and for promotion, advancement, training or any other choice-based decision). A ban is placed on *direct discrimination* (where choice is made against a person on these grounds), and for the longer term, provision is made to remove *indirect discrimination* (where, without the direct kind being practised, the proportions of persons of different colour, race, etc employed, do not reflect the mixture in the relevant population).

The Sex Discrimination Act, 1975, aims to outlaw preferment of one sex over the other as a basis for these same kinds of decision. It applies to all actual or potential employees, with a few exceptions (confined to such occupations as modelling or acting), and to all employers with six or more employees (including those in associated employers' establishments), and to trade unions, employers' associations, educational, training and qualifying bodies, advertisers, employment agencies and labour contractors. The Act applies to similar types of decision as the Race Relations Act and also makes provision in respect of both direct and indirect discrimination.

The Sex Discrimination Act also outlaws discrimination on the basis of married status, and in this case, specifically provides that it shall be lawful for an employer to treat married persons *more* favourably than unmarried ones.

In the area of disablement, the Disabled Persons Employment Act, 1944, imposed a duty on employers with 20 or more employees to employ a percentage of registered disabled persons. The current percentage (which is fixed by order after consultation) is 3 per cent. Provision is made in the Act for the registration of the disabled but not all of them do so, permitting the argument that employers do employ the disabled, but not necessarily the registered disabled.

It is thought that a high proportion of both private firms and public sector undertakings (which are not bound by the Act, but have agreed to observe its terms) do not meet their quotas. Failure to comply could lead to a fine or imprisonment, or both, but only after review and report by the relevant District Advisory Committee and court action instigated in the name of the Secretary of State. This procedure is so cumbersome that it is little used.

2   He (or she) is restricted in his freedom to pay different basic rates of pay and different levels of bonus related to performance to members of the two sexes: provided that the work of men and women is alike, equivalently rated, or of equal value, the same remuneration has to be paid.

Under the Equal Pay Act, 1970, and the Equal Pay (Amendment) Regulations made under it in 1983, all contracts of employment are deemed to contain an equality clause, guaranteeing men and women equal pay and conditions for:

(a)   like work;

(b)   work rated as equivalent by job evaluation; and

(c)   work of equal value in terms of its demands on the performer.

Pay levels may still differ if the employer can show that the difference is due to a 'genuine material factor' − that is, 'genuinely due to a material factor which is not the difference of sex ...' (s 1 (3) as amended).

3 He (or she) is restricted in his freedom to avoid payment to employees:

   (a) for temporary lay-off, when the cause of that lay-off is not industrial action and not the fault of the employees concerned; and

   (b) for medical suspension, provided the employee is fit for work.

4 He (or she) is restricted in his freedom to exercise his authority to fine workers for poor workmanship, to recover shortages in monies received by the employee on behalf of the employer, and otherwise to make deductions from their pay without specific authorisation.

The fining of workers and deducting of till shortages from wages are both restricted by the Wages Act, 1986. It is legal for an employer to make such deductions from pay only if the written contract specifically provides for this and if the employee has signified his or her consent to the deductions being made (Suter and Long, 1987).

5 He (or she) is restricted in his freedom to prevent employees interrupting the performance of their contracts where the interruptions are for purposes specified in legislation.

   (a) A woman may interrupt her employment in the event of pregnancy. Her rights are to:

> six weeks' maternity pay to be paid at the beginning of the 11th week prior to the expected confinement or weekly during the six weeks of absence, the amount being recoverable by the employer from the Maternity Fund

> forty weeks' maternity leave (extensible to 44 weeks, with postponement)

> to return to work with her original (or successor) employer in her original job or one substantially similar, at any time before the end of the period of 29 weeks (calculated from the beginning of the week in which the confinement falls), unless redundancy intervenes or it is not reasonably practical for her to do so.

There are complex requirements relating to the giving and receiving of notice of intentions and to the conditions under which the employer may avoid a claim of unfair dismissal if he does not permit the woman to return to the original or a substantially similar job.

(b) Employees may claim a reasonable amount of time off work (with pay, unless otherwise indicated):

> to take part in industrial relations activities, including training, provided they are officials of a recognised trade union

> to take part in trade union activities or representation, but not necessarily with pay

> to perform public duties, such as membership of a local authority, statutory tribunal or authority, without pay

> to receive antenatal care if professionally advised to do so

> to seek alternative employment or to make arrangements for training, where they are under notice of redundancy, with pay at their hourly rate.

The effect of these provisions is to avoid breach or suspension of the employment contract when employees take time out from work for these purposes. The Act itself offers guidance on the criteria of reasonableness in the context of time off for public duties and the Advisory Conciliation and Arbitration Service (ACAS) *Code of Practice* (1978) offers guidance on dealing with time off for lay officials and members of trade unions.

6 He (or she) is restricted in his authority to discipline and dismiss employees by requiring him to establish good cause in each case, and to avoid acting unfairly (as unfairly is defined by the legislation) (Thomason, 1984, pp 113–33).

The power of the employer *vis á vis* his (or her) employees has always rested on his freedom to determine individual contracts of employment with due notice. Because he is more likely to be in a position where he can find another employee more readily than the employee can find another employer, this has underpinned the authority of the employer to secure compliance.

Recent legislation has restricted this power, without taking away the fundamental right to discipline and dismiss. It has always been the case that if the employer dismissed an employee in breach of the terms of the contract itself (usually by failing to give the due notice, but sometimes by basing the dismissal on a reason which is excluded by the terms of the contract itself) he (or she) is open to a claim for 'wrongful dismissal'. The new enactments have introduced the additional concept of 'unfair dismissal' which recognises that the dismissal may not be based on the employer having a 'socially' good or acceptable reason for an action, in either disciplining or dismissing.

From the time of the Industrial Relations Act, 1971, dismissal qualifies as 'fair' where it meets the requirements stipulated in the Act (now contained in s 57 of the Employment Protection (Consolidation) Act), namely:

1   That the main or only reason for dismissal was a fair one by virtue of its being:

(a)   related to the capability or qualifications of the employee for performing work of a kind which he or she was employed by the employer to do; or

(b)   related to the conduct of the employee; or

(c)   that the employee was redundant; or

(d)   that the employee could not continue in work without causing either the employer or the employee to contravene a legal duty or restriction.

2   That he or she (the employer) had acted reasonably in treating that reason as sufficient to justify dismissal.

3   That the decision to dismiss was taken on the substantial merits of the case and was equitable in its consequences.

Where these requirements are not met, the employee has a claim for unfair dismissal and may secure from a tribunal (which finds his or her claim substantiated) compensation which varies in amount according to the circumstances.

An additional concept of 'inadmissable reason' (for dismissal) was introduced by the Trade Union and Labour Relations Act, 1974 (now continued in EPCA, 1978, s 58(5)). An inadmissable reason is defined as being that an employee acted or proposed to act on behalf of an independent trade union, either by becoming a member or by taking part in its activities, or alternatively that an employee refused to take membership or part in a trade union which was not independent. Into this category also falls the reason for dismissal which relies on the race or sex of the employee (SDA, s 65 (1) (b); RRA, s 58; EPCA, ss 75 and 76). In all of these cases, the amount of compensation which a tribunal may award on a finding of unfair dismissal is higher than in the previous cases.

Any employee dismissed also has the right to demand from the employer a statement of the reason(s) for his or her dismissal (EPCA, s 53). This is intended to help the employee decide whether the reason for the dismissal was 'fair'.

To qualify to bring a claim before a tribunal, the employee must not be in certain excluded categories and must have the required length of service. The excluded categories include dock workers engaged in dock work (EPCA, s 145), workers engaged in the shipping fleets on a profit-sharing contract (EPCA, s 144), members of the police and defence forces, and those who, not being merchant seamen, normally work under contract outside Great Britain (EPCA, s 141).

If these are cast in terms of restrictions, the more positive implications of the legislation may be expressed as:

(a)   the encouragement of employers to take their selection decisions solely on the basis of predicted capacity to do the job(s) in question and on demonstrated performance of the job(s) requirements;

(b)   the encouragement of employers to avoid purely arbitrary decisions and actions in meeting their obligations to provide consideration in the terms of the employment contract; and

(c)   the encouragement of employers to exercise their legally supported authority to discipline, demote, and dismiss employees in a manner which reflects application of the principles of natural justice.

SUMMARY

The contract of employment is a fundamental instrument in structuring the behaviour and the relationships of those at work. It is intended to influence the kinds of relationship which those in employment (both employer and employee) can establish. Although the contract does not determine the whole of the worker's status, it is an important influence on it; by defining rights and duties, it helps to shape both the nature of the work role and of the basic relationships in work.

The Common Law, for the most part, establishes those rights and obligations which would accord with the old individualistic or liberal principles which were applied in the first part of the industrial revolution. It imposes duties on both the employer and the employee, and it is largely with the discharge of the duty assumed under contract that the other party secures certain rights or benefits. The effect of recent legislation has been to establish positive rights or benefits for one party or the other, these remaining contractual in nature. In spite of these changes legislation has neither attempted to reform the employment contract as an instrument of cooperation, nor addressed the basic problem of inequality of bargaining power in establishing terms. The disparities may be smaller than they once were, but the dependent position of the worker in the employment relationship is upheld as a necessary support for control.

This same legislation also establishes for the employee rights which give protection to the individual during the course of his or her employment — that is, between the point of establishing a contract and the point at which it is determined. These rights relate to certain kinds of payment, to time off, lay-off and to treatment while at work.

Taken together, they give the individual employee some protection, but also restrict the authority of the employer to impose his or her will on employees. A knowledge of the prescriptions and proscriptions of legislation and judicial decisions becomes more important to the bargaining process as organisations more frequently seek to contract with employees directly and without the mediation of employee associations.

Reading:

ACAS (1977a).
Angel (1980).
Clayton (1967).
CIR (1974).
EOC (undated).
Fox (1974a), pp 152–206.
Gowler (1974).
Hepple and O'Higgins (1979), pp 52–75.
Kahn-Freund (1977), pp 1–47.
Rideout (1979), pp 3–66.
Treitel (1975), pp 1–7.

5 Associations: Law and Convention

Associations are groups of people who come (and may remain) together to realise some purpose which is of some (but not necessarily identical) interest to all of them. The basis for association is not necessarily that people are 'inherently gregarious': often they want to achieve some end which is either beyond their biological capacities or too costly for the individual. Association is one way of increasing human capacity to achieve something, whether ability to produce goods and services, or power to bargain with a superior adversary.

Cultural values and the law which embodies them might be expected to support such cooperative activity, but they do not always do so. The preferences of nineteenth century society for individualism, liberalism, and freedom in all trading relationships (including those embodied in the employment contract) inhibited the development of associations and virtually guaranteed that the achievement of cooperation in economic activities would become a problem as the scale of markets and enterprises increased. Attempts by the State to control the development both of company forms of enterprise and of professional association and trade union forms of stakeholder association were (and indeed largely remain) reluctantly accepted by virtue of their necessity and not encouraged.

The institutional structure supported by cultural values and law does not necessarily meet the changing circumstances of a society. The idea that the unitary State is both paramount and inviolate has helped to encourage the belief that the associations which the State does allow to exist should be modelled on it: there should be a central fount of all wisdom and legitimacy and this source of prerogative power should be protected against all assaults. This idea is still fervently upheld in those areas of employment which come directly 'under the Crown' (in the phrase which expresses this monocratic principle): the organisations concerned have Crown privilege (the right, for example, to dismiss employees at will) and 'Crown immunity' (a device for allowing them not to be bound by specific legislation unless the legislation states otherwise. These bodies (whether departments of state or creatures such as the National Health Service), in clinging tenaciously to their 'managerial' prerogatives, offer a role model which lesser associations might envy and seek to emulate.

Whether this is an apposite model for either industrial organisations or trade unions to adopt in the late twentieth century is debateable. Lessem has asserted that it still inhibits attempts to secure a competitive advantage for British industry (Lessem, 1985; see also Porter, 1985, pp 33–61) and may need to be changed. Recent legislation concerned with balloting has been challenged on the grounds that it seeks to deny trade unions the right to operate as monocratic bodies while simultaneously bolstering the prerogative power of the employer. Proposals, emanating largely from the EC, to increase the rights of workers to participate in business decisions, have, on the other hand, receded into the realm of abstract ideas with no immediate practical relevance. The question of whether we have yet evolved adequate forms of organisation for enterprise remains.

Industrial Associations

Industry (in the broad sense in which it is employed here) comprises two distinct sectors, one associated with 'public service' and one with trading activities (whether this trade is in services or goods). Industry involved in trade comprises two distinct types of formal 'association', where 'type' is defined by reference to the distribution of identifiable interests within them:

1 The commercial or public service enterprise taking the form of the partnership, company, nationalised industry, State (created) body, or in some cases, Department of State in which distinct interest groups (stakeholders, investors, managers, workers, suppliers, creditors, customers, etc.) must cooperate, at least minimally, to achieve the central purposes and objectives.

2 The association confined to one category of stakeholder, whether that category comprises employers, employees, stockholders, or customers, in which the aim is to try to aggregate power to regulate the stakeholders' relationship with the organisation as an entity. The extent to which the different categories of stakeholder are organised varies considerably.

The first type depends for its existence on securing the cooperation of people with different interests in the object and outcome of the cooperation. The second develops out of the differences in interest that are present in the first type and involves the making of a common cause in pursuit of that interest. This second type of association is also to be found in the assumedly unitarist State system, but its treatment tends to be different in some significant respects from that accorded – as it were, voluntarily – within the trading sector.

Cultural Value and Association Purpose

British society (in common with many other Western societies) places a high value upon 'trade', and anything which promises or purports to increase it is likely to find favour and receive support; anything which threatens or attempts to 'restrain' it is likely to be disfavoured and penalised. This explains the different treatment accorded in law to business enterprises and workers' associations. The value simultaneously placed on individualism acted against the facilitation of the enterprise as an association (particularly the company form of it) and strengthened the disfavour with which the association of workers was visited.

In principle, it is possible for industry and trade to be developed by individuals producing and trading alone in the market. In practice, however, the costs to the individual trader of carrying out all the buying and selling transactions are likely to make this form of organising them inefficient, unprofitable, and unworkable, except in markets of very limited scale. Corporate forms of organisation, based on the modes of organising government services and military organisations, seemed to offer a model which could be adapted to a new use. The growth of markets indicated the economic advantage of such individuals associating in companies or corporations which would be able to replace many of these transactions by less costly management decisions. The Bubble Act, 1720, denied company promoters an easy route to this form of association, and not until the first Companies Act, 1844, were they enabled to form companies by the simpler expedient of registering and complying with a limited number of requirements.

Companies formed under the Companies Acts (now, the Companies Act, 1985) must be concerned with the 'development of trade' (or in the case of non-trading companies usually limited by guarantee, with some acceptable charitable purpose). It is also possible to use the term 'company' rather loosely to refer to any group of persons associating for a common purpose (including the partnership form which is not included within this framework). This business 'company' (or enterprise) constitutes a unit of ownership of property (assets) which pursues profit through trading. In this respect it is made to simulate, at an associational level, the individual trader.

The attempt to model the company or corporation on the individual trader or businessman has produced 'a precise and limited conception of the company as a means through which capital may be invested in commercial enterprise' (Hadden, 1977). The shareholders (contributing the capital) are, by law, guaranteed a certain method of organisation and limited rights of supervision and control. The undertaking's creditors are given a degree of protection by requiring public disclosure of information about the company and its accounts. The growth in scale and the tendency for the number of suppliers to reduce (Allen, 1979) has, however, given more market power to 'the firm' (in the economist's term) and its Board of Directors, and reduced the practical relevance of the 'perfect market' assumptions of the economist.

Some 'trading' is conducted by nationalised industries and similar creations of the State (like the BBC), which are usually accorded monopoly or near monopoly positions in their 'markets'. These, although created by specific Acts of Parliament, are otherwise in the same general position in law as registered companies, but being incorporated by enactment, they do not need to register to secure this status. They may be differentiated from companies in that their requirement to pursue profit from trading activity may be muted by government policy or decree, but otherwise they are very similar.

The Directorate

The key figures whose positions, roles, and functions are most strongly upheld by law, are the directors. These are the people who most closely resemble the classical entrepreneur. They are the ones who determine what action is justified as being in the Company's interest. With the advent of the 'managed firm' (as distinct from an owner-managed business), the possibility arises that managerial (as distinct from 'company') objectives could replace or substitute shareholder objectives, although company law places restrictions on the purely self-interested actions which the directors can take with impunity.

They are enjoined, by law and convention, to give first consideration in their decisions to what is in the interest of the company, and therefore in the interest of the shareholders as the beneficial owners of it. Their *behaviour* cannot, however, be regarded as dictated, either by 'the market' or by the objective of maximising some single outcome (whether market share, market growth, or profit). That behaviour may sensibly respond to the need to protect their source of capital, by maintaining profits, but there could be circumstances in which they might (even if only in the short run) give preference to the interests of some other stakeholder group.

It remains open to the general meeting or the Board of Directors (according to which is given authority to act by the Memorandum and Articles of Association) to take into account the interests of employees, when to do so would, in their opinion, be in the interests and to the benefit of the company. This is not often done directly, although in the view of either Board or general meeting, that which is in the company's interest could be regarded as automatically in the interests of employees as well. It also remains open to them, in defence of their monocratic position, to deny recognition to any association of employees, as the recognition of such bodies has never been enjoined by law on them.

Trade Unions and Professional Associations

The main contrast with this type of association is provided by the trade union, an association of workers which aims to protect, maintain, and, where possible, enhance the interests and well-being of its members (Blackburn, 1967, pp 9–48; Thomason, 1984, pp 134–64). In its nature it is an association of one category of stakeholder in enterprise, and the pursuit of that stakeholder's interest involves pursuit of a 'sectional' interest, not, by definition, the interest of the whole. Society reacted to this by declaring trade unions unlawful because their 'sectional' purposes were necessarily and inevitably 'in restraint of trade'. This remains the position at Common Law, and the trade union has legality only because specific legislation exempts it from the consequences of its basic illegality (TULR Act, 1974, s 2 (5)).

At the present time, the trade union's legal position may be characterised as follows:

(a) it is accorded legality in spite of the fact that its purposes are still regarded as unlawful by being in restraint of trade (TULR Act, s 2 (5)); it is not, however, a unit of ownership and must hold real property through trustees;

(b) its members have certain immunities in criminal and civil law (TULR Act, s 13) which protect them from legal action or suit when they act within the context of a trade dispute which is duly authorised after a ballot of members (as defined by the Employment Act of 1982, s 15(1)).

(c) its members are protected in this way in respect of specific actions concerned with

Table 7

The legal parameters of a trade dispute

A trade dispute is defined in law as a dispute between workers and their employer which relates wholly or mainly to one or more of the following matters:

(a) terms and conditions of employment, or the physical conditions in which any workers are required to work;

(b) engagement or non-engagement, or termination, or suspension of employment or the duties of employment of one or more workers;

(c) allocation of work or the duties of employment as between workers or groups of workers;

(d) matters of discipline;

(e) the membership or non-membership of a trade union on the part of a worker;

(f) facilities for officials of trade unions; and

(g) machinery for negotiation or consultation, and other procedures, relating to any of the foregoing matters, including the recognition by employers or employers' associations of the right of a trade union to represent workers in any such negotiation or consultation or in the carrying out of such procedures (TULR Act, 1974, s 29, as amended).

Also included are disputes between workers and a Minister of the Crown (who is not their employer) where the dispute relates to matters which have been referred under enactment for consideration of a joint body on which the Minister is represented, or matters which cannot be settled without the Minister exercising a statutory power.

Where a matter is resolved by agreement, but would have led to a dispute if it had been resisted, any act, threat, or demand done or made in the course of its presentation and resolution is treated for legal purposes as having been done or made in contemplation of a trade dispute (TULR Act, 1974, s 29(5)).

Disputes relating to matters arising outside the UK are included within the definition only if members in the UK are likely to be affected by the outcome. Disputes between workers and workers (for example, jurisdictional and demarcation disputes) are now excluded (Employment Act, 1982, s 18), as are those related to acts to compel trade union membership (Employment Act, 1980, s 18).

Disputes may not extend beyond the situation domestic to the workers and their employer, and the situations of the employer's immediate suppliers and customers (Employment Act, 1980, s 17).

Table 8

Trade union immunities

Strikes, concerted withdrawals of labour, rely for their legality on persons being immune from actions in tort (that is, from actions leading to injunction or damages) for acts (committed *in contemplation or furtherance of trade disputes*) intended to:

(a)   induce another person to break his or her contract of employment or interfere with its performance, or threaten to do so (TULR Act, s 13); or

(b)   interfere with the trade, business, or employment of another person, or with the right of another person to dispose of his capital or his labour as he wills;

(c)   would not be actionable in tort if done by the individual alone without any agreement or combination.

These immunities are limited to those circumstances where employee-members have a trade dispute with *their own* employer (or employers' association) and the dispute is concerned essentially with *their* terms and conditions of employment and industrial relations matters. The boundaries of lawful industrial action are set with the employer's immediate suppliers and customers.

Outside these limits, trade unions (by virtue of the Employment Act, 1982, s 12) and their officers and members (as persons) are now exposed to the risk of actions in tort at the suit of any aggrieved party.

Unions and their members are, however, liable if they take action which has not been authorised by the relevant members in a properly conducted ballot, or which is intended to induce anyone to enter into or to break a commercial contract to discriminate between unionised and non-unionised labour or in order to compel recognition or non-recognition of a trade union (Employment Act, 1982, ss 12 and 13).

Picketing, in the context of a trade dispute (including permitted secondary actions), is lawful if it confines itself to attendance by an individual member of a union:

(a)   at or near his own place of work (with special provision for those who are mobile in their work or have been dismissed); or

(b)   if he is an official of a trade union at or near the place of work of a member of that union (but only such members) whom he is accompanying and whom he represents,

for the purpose only of peacefully obtaining or communicating information, or peacefully persuading any person to work or abstain from working (TULR Act, 1974, s 15, as substituted by Employment Act, 1980, s 16(1); see also SI, 1980/1957).

(i) striking work (as defined by TULR Act, s 29, amended by the Employment Act, 1982, s 15), and

(ii) picketing (TULR Act, s 15 as amended by Employment Act, 1980, s 16(10)).

The main elements in these immunities are listed in Tables 7 and 8. They are achieved largely by allowing the trade union the status of an unincorporated body (which makes it largely immune from suit in its own name) and giving the officers and members immunity from criminal and civil actions which might otherwise lie: these ensure that the union can rely upon members' willingness to take such action, by freeing them from the fear of the legal consequences.

The position of the trade union in law contrasts with that of the professional association. This is an association of workers which attempts to organise, qualify, and either maintain or improve their standards of performance in order to maintain or improve their status (including pay-status) in society (Millerson, 1964). The initial emphasis on improving work performance (and thus on improving trade and industry in line with the basic cultural value) is held to differentiate the professional association from the trade union.

Consequently, from the early years of the industrial revolution, professional corporations have been encouraged and facilitated to develop 'for the public good' (Carr-Saunders and Wilson, 1933, p 327). They were given and still retain legal status as corporations, and rights (not immunities), together with the valuable privilege of monopoly control over their services in the market, simply because their objectives accorded with dominant social values. They faced no necessity for struggle because none cast doubt on their purposes.

Associational Status: incorporation

These basic categories differ in their status in law (which affects their capacity to act in their own interests). Both law and convention allow associations to be either incorporated or unincorporated bodies. These differ from one another largely in respect of their legal status and the acts which they are legally allowed to perform.

An incorporated association, *as an association:*

1 acquires a legal personality so that it has perpetual succession as an entity regardless of its membership, and the association's common seal often symbolises this;

2 can, in its corporate name, enter into contracts with others, acquire and hold property, sue and be sued, and therefore 'do all other acts as natural persons do' (Blackstone's Commentaries);

3   can make its own rules and regulations (provided always that they are lawful) for the governance and ordering of its internal affairs.

This amounts to a grant of substantial autonomy in deciding on action and in ordering its own affairs, subject only to the general supervision of the law.

Incorporation is now most commonly secured by registering under the Companies Acts. These require the promoters to draw up a Memorandum of Association which forms the company's constitution and which is alterable only in ways permitted by these Acts. The Articles of Association provide for the administration of the company, and it is freer to alter these to suit its circumstances and wishes.

Most workers in Britain are employed by an incorporated body. The industrial company, the nationalised industry, and the State body have such incorporation. The partnership is similar, but is denied perpetual succession in its own name (terminating with the death or withdrawal of individual partners). Only the individual trader stands completely apart from these forms of organisation, being unincorporated largely because he or she has no need of a fictional legal 'personality'. The State has comparable corporate standing to that of the company, but for other reasons, and also has certain protections and prerogatives which facilitate securing worker compliance.

Some (but not all) employers' associations are also incorporated bodies, but these have the option of remaining unincorporated in the manner of trade unions. The qualifying or protective association to which many workers belong may also be incorporated. Many professional associations are incorporated, but their incorporation may be secured either by charter or by registration (like private companies) under the Companies Acts (Thomason, 1984, pp 135 – 9).

Associational Status: unincorporation

The law allows unincorporated bodies to operate but denies them legal personality as associations (apart from their members) as a collectivity. The members are held, in law, to have contracted, not with a separate associational entity with a specific name, but with one another as individuals to pursue certain objects. Significantly, an unincorporated association is not a unit of ownership and must therefore hold property through trustees, not in its own name. A trade union cannot, for this reason as well as for others, operate as a labour cartel, which would imply ownership of members' labour, nor can it easily replace the myriad of labour market decisions in which its members are involved by centralised 'management' decisions about terms and conditions to be accepted from individual employers.

The unincorporated body cannot hold property in its own name because there is no separate 'body' to hold it, so that any property must be held through 'trustees'. It can neither sue nor be sued nor be made the subject of proceedings in a court in its own name. In civil actions, it is possible to proceed only against the members, or against some of them as leaders or representatives of the membership. This exposes the individual members to personal liability for any actions taken on behalf of the association, and this may impede progress towards associational objectives.

Like any other association, the unincorporated body is legally bound (in the actions it can take) by its constitution and rules. Changing these could prove difficult or impossible unless there was unanimous agreement of all the members, or unless the rules provide for some simpler way of making changes.

The major advantage of remaining unincorporated is that the association thereby avoids the kind of supervision and control by the State which is inherent in incorporation. This does not, in practice, amount to complete avoidance for two reasons: first, because there are common law rules 'governing the right of individuals to associate for the promotion of a common purpose' (Carr-Saunders and Wilson, 1933, p 327) which can be applied to them; and secondly, because parliament from time to time extends the controls imposed by specific legislation to cover unincorporated bodies which do not conform to some convention or other.

Some unincorporated bodies, and particularly the trade unions within the present field of interest, may also be made subject to stricter legislative controls in the interests of 'public policy' (as was done most graphically in the Industrial Relations Act, 1971, the Employment Acts, 1980 and 1982, and the Trade Union Act, 1984). Consequently, although they remain unincorporated bodies, trade unions have effectively been made a 'third thing', something between the corporation and the unincorporated association.

Hybrid Forms

Most *trade unions* and some employers' associations fall into this general category of unincorporated association. The trade unions have traditionally preferred to avoid not merely formal legal incorporation but the concomitant degree of legal regulation associated with it. Attempts have been made by governments and the courts to impose incorporation on them, for example, in the Taff Vale Railway Company case, and in the Industrial Relations Act, 1971, but these have been resisted by the union movement. At the present time, trade unions are declared not to be, nor to be treated as, bodies corporate (TULR Act, s 2(1)), but this stipulation is now hedged about by other requirements imposed by legislation.

Since 1871, legislation has provided the trade unions with some of the specific benefits of incorporation without incorporation itself. They can therefore hold property and sue and be sued in property, through trustees. They are made capable of making contracts, suing and being sued, and having proceedings brought against them in their own names in matters of property and personal injury. They can protect themselves from fraudulent action by members (such as treasurers). By registering with the Certification Officer, they can also secure certain exemptions from taxation in connection with friendly society benefits, and certain benefits in connection with the protection and transference of property.

The effect of the Employment Acts, 1980 and 1982, has been to expose the unions to a wider range of possible actions for damages initiated by aggrieved parties because of the removal of the blanket immunity in tort and the redefinition of the limits of a trade dispute. Unions are now liable in their own names, in respect of a new class of torts (unless the action complained of was unauthorised by a committee or person with authority to do so under the union's rules) (Employment Act, 1982, s 15). Actions for injunction or damages may now be begun in more circumstances than before, both against the union in its own name and against officers and members. This does not change the union's legal status because it already had this kind of hybrid legal status.

An employers' association, although defined as a trade union from 1871 to 1971, may now be either incorporated or unincorporated. When it is incorporated it enjoys the advantages and suffers the obligations of any other corporation. When it is unincorporated it continues to enjoy the same status and, *mutatis mutandis*, the same immunities as the trade union (TULR Act, s 3). The new restrictions of the Employment Act, 1982, on trade unions' immunity in tort do not apply to the employers' association.

Before the Industrial Relations Act, 1971, blurred the long-standing distinction between companies and trade unions, cross-stipulations in the Trade Union Act, 1871, (now under s 2 (2) of TULR Act, 1974) and the Companies Act (1985) prevented any association whose objects would make it a trade union from registering under the Companies Acts and any registered Company from securing the kinds of immunities granted to trade unions as defined in the Trade Union Acts, 1871–76. Any association of workers therefore had to make a choice as to the kind of body it was going to be.

This also applied to the professional association. If incorporated as a chartered body, its charter probably prevents it from also being a trade union. If it was registered under the Companies Acts, it was not permitted to acquire both sets of advantages. The establishment of a special register in the Industrial Relations Act, 1971, and thereby the creation of a class of 'special register bodies', which were often associations of professionals who nevertheless wished to protect members' terms and conditions of employment by negotiation, also blurred this distinction.

Administrative Controls

The introduction of a simpler method of incorporation of commercial companies in the Companies Act, 1844, was based on registration and compliance with a limited number of administrative requirements. The first subscribers, or the company promoters, file a proposed company name (incorporating an indication of the extent of shareholders' liability, in the form of plc or Ltd), the memorandum and the articles of association, and comply with some other financial and administrative requirements.

The memorandum of association outlines the nature of the company and the relationship which it proposes to develop with the outside world. It states the company's name and country in which the registered office is situated; its objects and powers; the basis of liability for debts; the initial share capital and the number of shares into which this is divided; and whether it is a public or a private company. The memorandum is signed by the original subscribers who each affix their names, addresses, and number of shares subscribed.

The company's articles of association form the constitution or standing orders applicable to its operation. They deal with questions such as the classes of shares, the rights of each class of shareholder, transfer and transmission of shares, dividends, and procedures to be followed in annual and special general meetings and in meetings of directors. If the subscribers do not either provide a statement of this kind, or if it is incomplete, there is provision for Table A of the Companies Acts (issued in the form of regulations under s 8 of the Companies Act, 1985) to be used in place of the company's own articles. Thereafter, these two documents form the basis for determining whether any action taken is in conformity with the company's intentions.

The role of the Registrar of Companies is essentially administrative. He has powers to reject an application for registration if the objects proposed are unlawful, and to reject a name which is offensive or likely to mislead (for example, because it is the same as that of another registered company). Once the Registrar has issued a certification of incorporation and published it in the Official Gazette, the company is constituted and free to pursue its lawful objectives by any lawful means.

Controls on Company Operations

The obligations assumed on incorporation are few, but important in their protection of the interests of stakeholders and creditors. The company is obliged to keep proper books and records at its registered office and to file an annual return containing up-to-date information on the company, including, for example, any changes in its memorandum and articles, or in its office location or directing staff, resolutions passed at meetings, and changes in auditors, and accounts. For the rest, the company and its agents are required to conform to the constitution of the company and the law of the land in respect of such matters as fair dealing and fraud.

Companies are required to conduct their affairs in an open and ordered manner, and if arrangements for so doing are not included in the articles, those provided in Table A of the Companies Acts are assumed to be incorporated in them. The basic requirements relate to meetings and voting at them.

Public companies must hold an annual general meeting and give shareholders three weeks' notice of it. If the Articles provide, an extraordinary general meeting may be held if the directors think it necessary, and one must be held if requested by the holders of up to one tenth of the paid-up capital with voting rights, with (usually) fourteen days' notice. Every member must receive notice at his or her registered address. The notice must indicate the general nature of the business to be conducted at general meetings and give the exact wording of any proposed resolution to be put to an extraordinary meeting. Members also have rights (if enough are of a mind) in relation to proposing resolutions to annual or special meetings.

Meetings cannot conduct business unless they are quorate (only a small number have to be present to ensure a quorum). Articles usually provide that voting in meetings shall, in the first instance, be by show of hands of those members present in person and entitled to vote. Although members can appoint proxies to vote on their behalf, proxies are not counted in a show of hands. A poll can, however, be demanded by five persons entitled to vote (or holding one-tenth voting rights) either before or after such a show of hands; when a poll is held, each member has a vote for each of his or her voting shares (and proxies can now be counted in the voting figures).

Resolutions are considered to have been carried at ordinary meetings if a simple majority of the votes of those present is secured, or where proxy votes are allowed, by a simple majority of such votes. An extraordinary or a special resolution requires a majority of three quarters of those voting (defined as in the former case), but unless a poll is demanded, the chairman is entitled to rule on whether the resolution is carried without having to present proof of votes for or against. In fact, the chairman has wide powers in this respect at any meetings.

Provisions of this kind are normally built into the articles as a way of protecting interests. The law tries to interfere as little as possible in this matter, on the assumption that stockholders will be sufficiently assiduous in defending their interests to prevent directors or any one else abusing their power.

Administrative Control of Trade Unions

Over the history of legally recognised trade unionism in Britain, registration has been voluntary: even during the currency of the Industrial Relations Act, 1971, when it was required if the union was to qualify for its traditional immunities, it remained so. Registration imposed some obligations to keep the Registrar informed of the union's name, registered office, and rule book, and to provide some rules to cover aspects of the internal relationships (although the content of them was a matter for the union). The Donovan Commission regarded these as neither onerous nor vexatious, and as not going 'beyond what any well-run trade union would do in any event' (Donovan Report, 1968, pp 211–16).

The TULR Act, 1974, codified these requirements in respect of applications to be placed on the list of trade unions to be maintained by the Certification Officer (s 8). The requirement here is similar to that imposed by the Companies Acts on registering companies. An application to be placed on the list has to be accompanied by a statement of the name of the union, the address of its main or head office, a list of its officers and a copy of the rules of the union, together with a fee. The Certification Officer has a similar power to refuse to enter a name if it is the same as that of another organisation or is likely (because of similarity) to deceive, and to refuse listing if he is not convinced that the association in question is a trade union (or an employers' association).

The same Act (s 10) imposes duties on employers' associations and trade unions to keep proper accounting records and to establish adequate means of controlling their financial records. The following section also requires the union to submit annual returns to the Certification Officer, to appoint qualified auditors, and to ensure proper control of any superannuation schemes maintained by the union. It is made an offence, punishable by a fine on responsible officers, to fail to carry out these duties.

Once the trade union had acquired legality (and with it the freedom to make and enforce lawful rules and agreements in much the way that companies are permitted to determine their own Articles), the possibility was created that the Courts would now be able to supervise the union's internal affairs (including the rules it adopted). The unions did not want this and the early legislators did not intend it. The Trade Union Act, 1871 (s 4) therefore declared that, 'nothing in this Act shall enable any court to *enforce directly*' the agreements which trade unionists might enter into amongst themselves or with employers. They were thus to remain enforceable only by 'voluntary means' and to be binding in honour, not law. This did not prevent the courts *indirectly* enforcing some of them (Donovan Commission Report, 1968, paras 809–15) under the common law (Wedderburn, 1971, pp 314–5).

Control of Internal Processes

Trade unions have recently been required to conform to the requirements of legislation on elections and balloting on a number of issues material to their purposes. This means that the *content* of some of the unions' rules has had to be overturned to conform to a general requirement that the 'democratic' control of the union by the members shall be increased, to allow the union to qualify for the traditional immunities which protect members during industrial action.

1 *Strike ballots*
Trade unions are required to hold a properly conducted ballot of all members likely to be involved before calling, authorising, endorsing or actually starting any industrial action (whether a strike or concerted action short of a strike). They risk losing their immunity from civil actions in contract and tort if the strike commences without one (Trade Union Act, 1984, s 10). The requirements which have to be met if the ballots are to qualify as restoring the immunity are detailed in s 11. The majority of those voting in the ballot must answer affirmatively before the industrial action can acquire legal protection.

2   Closed Shop Ballots

The enforcement of a closed shop agreement (or Union Membership Agreement (UMA)) by means of disadvantaging, disciplining, or dismissing an employee who refuses to become a union member, becomes unlawful unless a valid ballot has been held within the preceding five years and has resulted in endorsement by 80 per cent of those falling within its proposed domain (for new proposals) or by 85 per cent of those actually voting (for renewals of existing UMAs). Even then, certain listed categories of employee are protected by one of the statutory exemptions from the UMA requirements, so that they cannot be lawfully acted against in the ways mentioned above (EP(C) Act, 1978, ss 58 (establishing the rights of unionists and non-unionists) and 58A (setting out the requirements in respect of a ballot) as amended by the Employment Acts, 1980 and 1982).

3   Political Fund Ballots

The Certification Officer may not accept as valid a union's rules in respect of political objects and political funds unless a valid ballot has been held within the previous ten years and a majority of those voting in it have done so affirmatively.

4   Executive Committee Elections

Every *member* of the union's 'principal executive committee' (PEC) (by whatever name it is known) and *any other official who has a right to vote* on any matter at that committee must be directly elected at least every five years in a ballot which conforms to the Act's requirements. Where a PEC exists at both a national union and an area/district level, both are affected. The Act makes no stipulation as to who should sit, or have a vote on, this committee, this being left to the union to determine for itself, excepting only that co-opting of voting members is outlawed (Trade Union Act, 1984, s 1).

5   Votes on Amalgamation and Merger

The Trade Union (Amalgamations, etc) Act, 1964, limits the opportunity for two unions to amalgamate (or for one union to transfer its engagements to another) to the situations in which the two unions (or the transferor union) have passed a resolution approving the instrument of amalgamation (or the transferor union has passed a resolution approving the instrument of transfer) − both have to be approved by the Certification Officer − on a vote which meets the requirements of the Act. Unions may conduct the 'vote' entirely under their own rules (provided that these have been

Table 9

Ballot arrangements

The legislation lays down six requirements in respect of ballots in connection with industrial action (Trade Union Act, 1984, s 11). These are intended to ensure that the ballot is 'properly' conducted, and although in the cases of ballots for other purposes, the requirements are less numerous and less stringent, this list indicates the broad thrust of the thinking behind the Act.

1. Entitlement to vote must be accorded equally to all those members of the union whom the union believes at the time are reasonably likely to be called on to take the action, and to no others (although overseas members may be ignored for this purpose provided they are *all* ignored)

2. The method of voting must be by *marking* a ballot paper by the person voting (where 'person' includes a person voting for someone else who is, for example, disabled)

3. The person entitled to vote must be allowed to vote in secret and without interference from, or constraint imposed by, the union or any of its members, officials, or employees, and in so far as is reasonably practicable without incurring any direct cost to himself or herself.

4. Everyone entitled to vote must have a voting paper made available to him or her, or be supplied with one at his or her place of work either immediately before or immediately after, or during his working hours, or at a place which is more convenient to him or her (for example, the home address)

5. Voting shall be either by post, exclusively, or at his or her place of work (or other convenient place) immediately before or after or during his or her working hours, exclusively, or by either of these methods as alternatives provided the individual can make use of only one of them

6. After the ballot the union must ensure that the voting papers are fairly counted and that all entitled to vote are informed of the numbers voting, answering 'yes', answering 'no', and spoiling their ballot papers (together with the numbers of overseas members in each category).

approved by the Certification Officer, and make reasonable provision with respect to majority voting).

These amount to a change in the manner in which these associations are regarded by society. On the face of them, they mainly compel an improvement in democratic practice within the unions, but (purely party political objectives apart) they also push the trade unions in the direction of greater incorporation. This could (although it is probably not the intention behind the moves) pave the way for incorporation of trade unions in a new conception of enterprise which might be more in keeping with the diffuse underlying values of the society with respect to associational forms and the requirements of their emergent external market environments.

These do not require any steps to be taken by the employer, but there are certain points at which the trade union's activities in compliance with the law will impinge on the employer. The employer will also want to establish for his own protection whether the trade union's activities are sufficient to restore the immunities, or are so deficient as to provide him with a cause of legal action against the trade union in the event of unlawful and unprotected industrial action.

The Concept of Enterprise

The concept of enterprise in these limited 'company' terms is now more often being seen as a barrier to progress in developing more cooperative enterprises capable of dealing with challenges from other economies whose enterprises are more broadly conceived. The concept of a company as 'a combination of three interest groups, the management as the directing brain of the enterprise, the shareholders as the providers of capital, and the employees as the providers of labour' finds no place in this limited concept of enterprise (Schmitthoff, 1975, p 266). Savage has pointed to the restrictions which this company law concept places on developing 'an institution with desirable social and economic responsibilities to groups other than shareholders' (Savage, 1980, p 5).

Gower, writing before the minor changes introduced into company law in 1980, argued that:

> 'In so far as there is any true association in the modern public company, it is between management and workers rather than between shareholders *inter se*, or between them and management.'

Nevertheless, he goes on to say that this 'fact that workers form an integral part of the Company is ignored by the law' (Gower, 4th ed, 1979).

The workers' position in enterprise is still defined by the employer's prerogative power to dismiss in the interests of 'the company' or of its beneficial owners. However charitable or far-sighted management may be in providing benefits designed to retain employees in the employment of the enterprise, and however much management may seek to regard employees as 'assets', the final

arbiter of the workers' status is the law which upholds the managerial prerogative (even if it also curbs it in the interests of equity and
natural justice).

The changes introduced in 1980 did not interfere with this basic
disadvantage. They required that directors 'shall' include employees' interests among those which they take into account in
carrying out their (directorial) functions, but upheld the directors'
basic duty *to the Company* rather than any interest group or section
of the members (Companies Act, 1980, s 46).

The problem about the change instituted in the legislation is that
it is unlikely to be enforceable as the initiation of the action would
lie with either the directors, or the 'Company' (shareholders in
general meeting), or by means of a derivative action, itself difficult
to mount in any circumstances. Any test applied would probably
continue to be whether the decision taken by the directors was in the
best interests of the 'company'.

The other amendment introduced in the same Act (s 74) allows the
company (regardless of its Articles) to make provision for the
benefit of employees or former employees in the event of cessation
or transfer of the undertaking. But in this case, it is not necessary to
justify the action on the basis that the action is in the best interests
of the company.

In the normal situation, however, the directors will tend,
(responding to the general expectations of them) to take into
account the interests of the property owners in preference to those of
the contributors of labour. With the divorce of ownership from
direct control and the entry of the manager who does not necessarily
own any of the assets or the equity, however, the interests of the
'controlling' group itself may also loom large in their decisions.

A Trade Union Bill of Rights

The manner in which British society has approached trade unions is
complementary to its treatment of companies: trade unions have been
accorded no very positive rights (in the sense of rights which are
reciprocated in another's duties) on which they might develop a more
collaborative or cooperative posture in relation to enterprise. Such
rights as 'workers' have obtained in their relationship with their
employers have often had effect as legal or conventional norms which
mitigate the severity of the employer's exercise of his or her prerogative, not as rights which could be legally enforced against another's
failure to discharge an obligation. The trade unions have had few of
either kind but have depended largely on the freedoms and immunities
granted to workers to win recognition and negotiating rights.

It is difficult to accord rights without first according corporate status (as was attempted in 1971). Only when this exists can positive rights and obligations (as distinct from freedoms and immunities) be established on a firm basis. There is also no guarantee that were trade unions to be granted a bill of (positive) rights, along with their current quasi-corporate status, they would cease to be competitive or conflictual, but to continue to treat them in simple 'immunity' terms is likely to offer even less of a guarantee. While this approach continues to be adopted, there is unlikely to be a legal foundation for any real extension of formal participation above the level of the job itself.

In recent years, however, some positive rights have been given by law (and some have been given only to be removed with a change of government). Most of these are connected with the trade union's access to information and the right to consultation. Significantly, these have not moved very far in the direction of increasing trade union 'security'.

Public policy has never compelled the employer to recognise the trade union (or to deal with a professional association). This reflects a dedication to the principles of a *voluntary* approach to the question. There has, over the years, been a growing moral pressure to recognise unions for purposes of collective bargaining, and recession conditions apart, more workers have joined trade unions, and more employers have recognised them. The role of the State in this has been to supervise and from time to time to facilitate this process without compelling against the exercise of the company's prerogative power.

Similarly, the right of the union to prefer to have union members rather than non-unionists in employment has been hard won (and then only partially) by negotiation. The law has never gone far in providing the union as such with this kind of security, usually referred to as 'the closed shop' (McCarthy, 1964; Szakats, 1972; Hanson *et al*, 1973; Gennard *et al*, 1980; Daniel and Millward, 1983). The right to maintain a closed shop on a voluntary basis remains, but the right to enforce this by dismissing or otherwise discriminating against non-unionists with impunity is now compromised with ballot requirements (see, EP(C) Act, s 58A as amended and SI, 1758/1980), and even this degree of tolerance may shortly be removed.

Nevertheless, the *recognised* and *independent* union has some rights to *information* for purposes of improving industrial relations or collective bargaining, and information and *consultation* on redundancy, transfer of undertakings, and health and safety matters.

1 Information for Collective Bargaining Purposes

The recognised independent union has a right to request information for purposes of facilitating collective bargaining and to receive it, provided that it is relevant, readily available, not confidential and not threatening to national security, and provided also that it complies with a procedure laid down in the Act (Employment Protection Act, 1975, ss 17 – 18). The qualifications which are built into the legislation to protect national and commercial interests are such that the employer has many grounds on which he can refuse and secure approval for so doing. Securing the right is likely, in spite of the enforcement provisions in the Act, to depend on the employer's voluntary assumption of an obligation.

2 The Right to Consultation about Proposed Redundancy

The recognised independent trade union has the right to be informed and consulted about a proposal to dismiss employees as redundant. The employer's duty in respect of redundancy is to inform and consult 'at the earliest opportunity' and in any event at least 30 days in advance of the proposed redundancy, where it involves the dismissal of 10 or more employees, and at least 90 days, where it involves 100 or more to be discharged within a period of 90 days (EP Act, 1975, s 99; and SI, 1979/958).

3 Consultation about Transfer of Undertakings

The recognised independent trade union also has a right to be given information (and consulted) about any proposed transfer of an undertaking (in the UK) in which that union has members (under the Transfer of Undertakings (Protection of Employment) Regulations, SI, 1981/1794). The main purpose of these regulations is to ensure the continuity of individual contracts of employment and any collective agreements in force in the undertaking which it is proposed shall be transferred by one means or another.

4 Consultation about Health and Safety

The recognised independent trade union has the right to appoint or elect safety representatives from among the employees, to consult with the employer, and carry out such other functions as may from time to time be prescribed by regulation (HASAW Act, 1974, s 2 (4); SI, 500/1977, Regulation 3). No stimulation as to numbers is made, although the representatives must have a minimum amount of service, but the Code of Practice indicates the factors which might be taken into account (see Health and Safety Commission, 1978b; Abell, 1979). Any two safety representatives may request in writing that a safety committee be established, and the employer is under a duty to create one, after consultation and within three months of the request being made.

5   *Rights of Trade Union Officers and Members*

These are supported by the legal requirement that employers provide certain facilities to trade union officers and members to enable them to carry out their industrial relations and trade union duties, or to participate in its legitimate activities, or both. The officer of a recognised independent trade union now has a right to *reasonable* (see ACAS Code No 3) time off work with pay to carry out his or her official duties or to undergo training for them. A *member* of such a union has a similar right to reasonable time off (but without any right to payment) to take part in any trade union activities (including acting as a union representative). Health and safety representatives also have rights to time off for training (H&S Commission, 1978a; see also TUC, 1978). These rights are supplemented by rights to other (for example, office) facilities.

Significant though these rights are, they have been granted in a piecemeal fashion (often responding to particular events which rouse the conscience of society) and, in total, stop far short of those granted to workers (and, in some cases, to their trade unions) in other countries within the EEC.

Participation

They stop short of granting workers or the trade union any legal right to participate in the important decisions taken about the enterprise. Such rights are accorded, in various forms, in other EEC countries, sometimes involving the trade unions directly but sometimes not. The attempt (by the Bullock Committee, 1976) to produce a way in which participation in decisions could be structured in accordance with British industrial values and practice, foundered − it might be said − on the shoals of the company concept of enterprise and the unincorporated status of the trade union. The one ensures confrontation with the values of monocracy based on property rights and the other with the pragmatic concern at the lack of any legitimate foundation for trust.

In the British context the prevalence of certain values (hinged on concepts of what really constitutes freedom) helps to ensure that participation will be acceptable only if it takes into account the plural interests gathered together in enterprise. It is usual to recognise a range of modes of establishing legitimacy in this context, focusing on the distinctions between company and enterprise concepts of enterprise, residual and trusteeship theories of power sharing, individualist and collectivist organising principles, or unitarist to pluralist frames of reference. In any of these concepts, the broad consequence is that approaches to participation are seen to range from complete management autonomy to work self-management, through intermediate stages that are characterised by information giving by management after decisions have been taken, consultation by management before decisions are taken, delegation of job-centred control to the workers involved, recognition of trade unions for purposes of collective bargaining over a narrower or broader range of issues, joint control (or co-decision) over some range of practices or administrative processes, and donation of control to a governing body elected by the workers themselves.

Examples of approaches at the ends of this continuum are few, but a number of experiments have been made in recent years within it. For convenience these can be grouped under the headings of unitarist and pluralist concepts to indicate where the source of originating power is located (Figure 6).

Figure 6

Forms of participation

Unitary Concept	Level	Pluralist Concept
	(High)	
Employee directors (elected from workforce)	Planning	Industrial democracy (with syndicalist implications)
Works councils	Administration	Full collective bargaining
Joint consultation	Administration	Joint decision-taking on specific matters
Briefing groups		Representative meetings
Vertical job loading Autonomous working groups	Action	Grievance bargaining
	(Low)	

The hierarchy on the left represents attempts by industry to find mechanisms for giving workers more 'voice' in the conditions of their working lives within the framework of existing law and convention. That on the right provides examples of the ways in which the workers, through the medium of trade union organisation, have secured recognition from (a sometimes reluctant) management of their right to represent the values, views, and aspirations of workers. Since many of these have been won long ago, some of them have also passed into the realm of accepted law and convention, but they rest on a foundation of duality which unitarists would find it impossible to accept fully as a way of securing commitment.

SUMMARY

The form of enterprise which is supported by law and convention in British culture is that of the incorporated 'company'. This ensures that the association receives certain advantages which allow it to deal effectively with the external world. It also imposes a basic disadvantage in securing cooperation from stakeholders, particularly the workers, who have interests which are partly separate from those of the prime beneficiaries, the shareholders.

The way in which the workers' trade unions, established to protect those interests which are antithetical to those of the shareholders, are treated in law and convention is different. They are, at best, tolerated as unincorporated bodies, and given support only through the grant of immunity in law from consequences arising from their basic illegality. The few positive rights donated to trade unions (mainly to information and consultation on certain defined matters) are intended to support voluntary negotiation, but not to coerce the employer to negotiate or to agree terms.

Professional associations have been accorded a different status from trade unions, being treated more like companies, largely because society (and the courts) took a very different view of their purposes and objects, as these related to the growth of trade.

The recent attempts to control the internal affairs of the trade union are modelled on, but extended from, the method adopted in the company form of organisation. This extension may contain some of the more dramatic manifestations of conflict demonstrated in recent years, but it does not by itself provide a remedy.

The lack of attention to the needs of enterprise for a legal basis of cooperation may disadvantage British private industry in its attempt to meet international competition. The problem in this is currently focused on the way in which some form of participation might be achieved in organisations, participation being thought to be a necessary fillip to increases in employment commitment to the ends of enterprise.

Reading:

On the nature of professional associations and trade unions:
Blackburn (1967), pp 9–43;
Millerson (1964), pp 26–46,
Poole (1986).
Prandy (1965), pp 30–47.
Turner (1962), pp 233–51; and in McCarthy: (1972), pp 89–108.

On the legal aspects:
Hepple (1979), pp 3–51.
Howells and Barrett (1982), pp 102–16.
Lewis, in Bain (1983), pp 361–92.
Steele *et al* (1986).
Wedderburn (1971), pp 160–221 and pp 304–409.
Weekes *et al* (1975), pp 193–7.

6 Product and Labour Markets

Enterprises and organisations, like persons (in this one respect at least), must cope with the situations in which they find themselves, as they attempt to achieve their goals. 'Decisions' have to be taken about *what* values, beliefs, and norms ought to apply to the situation and *how* (following what principles) they should be applied. Somebody, usually management, has to 'read the situation' to ascertain what 'demands' for action are being made (a perception associated with Mary Parker Follett). This is followed by consideration of the possible solutions that could be applied to the problem as defined by these demands, and by choice of a course of action as being an effective and acceptable way of dealing with it.

In principle, some of the cultural 'designs for living and working' are intended to facilitate this process, but environments are heterogeneous and do not always conform to the culture's inherent assumptions. While it is true that the general principles of law and convention both require application to situations and allow a certain amount of discretion to those who must do the applying, they do not always best fit the circumstances to which they have to be applied. This lack of fit is likely to become greater as situations are subject to change — as from international competition, changes in technology, or changes in models of how best to proceed in any set of circumstances.

The situation within which an enterprise operates, because its features are material to such decisions, is a distinct source of influence on human behaviour, imposing its own imperatives for action, which are different from those associated with laws and conventions, norms and rules, or structures and institutions. 'Situation' may be considered under two distinct headings (which form the bases for the next two chapters):

(a) the economic situation, composed of the market opportunities and limitations which constrain the ends of industrial activity in a private enterprise system

(b)   the technological situation, which is to be contrued in terms of both physical and organisational mechanisms for achieving economic ends.

The fact that differences exist under each of these headings means, *inter alia*, that anyone involved in the application of cultural (or specifically legal) prescriptions faces considerable uncertainty. When decisions about what to do have to be made, the decision-maker is called on to exercise judgement about the most appropriate course of action, given that there is no certainty that any one of them will succeed in solving the problem.

PRODUCT MARKETS

The economic situation is best considered in relation to the concept of the 'market', whether it is one for goods or services for money, or one for the exchange of 'factors' (land, labour, or capital treated as commodities) for return, remuneration, or reward.

The term 'market' is one of convenience used to identify the arena in which buyers and sellers come together to decide and implement the terms of an exchange of something valuable to them. Whatever its nature and form, a market serves to bring together buyers and sellers with fundamentally antithetical interests in the outcomes, within a framework of rules governing the transacting or 'bargaining' processes involved (Roncaglia, 1985, pp 72–6). The parties' 'power' to influence the outcomes of market transactions varies, and this aspect of the market is crucial to the definition of the constraint under which management operates.

The product market provides private enterprise with its basic raison d'être: private enterprise is a market system. But the market presents the private enterprise undertaking with both opportunities and limitations, which show up in the content of management decision-taking. The market is, in principle, the only provider of the cash (revenue) that is needed to finance all the necessary transactions with its various stakeholders (Brown, 1951). Because the availability of cash is fundamental to all other transactional activity, and because this is in turn dependent on the market relationship of the undertaking, that relationship is demonstrably crucial to behaviour.

The 'problem' manifests itself in concerns about ability to pay, or ability to afford courses of action which may be strategically desirable. An individual entrepreneur considering whether to start a business, or a board of directors giving thought to their firm's survival, are likely to survey the product market for opportunities to secure a cash return which will cover all costs of production, distribution, and exchange and yield a surplus (or profit).

The opportunities and limits set by cash availability are universal in that they apply to any manager who accepts the dominant values of the agency role or occupation. These values emphasise efficiency and profit-making to some degree, even if they also permit concern for growth, market share, and survival. In the non-profit-making public sector, the relevant values are those of efficiency, measured in terms of costs related to benefits. Such considerations must influence the manager's allocation decisions, provided that he or she approaches decision-taking within one of the frameworks postulated for the manager (Thomason, 1984, pp 50−60).

Competition in the Market

The economist's models of decision-taking provide managers with little direct help in decision-taking in conditions of market uncertainty (Nolan, 1983, p 292), but the managerial analysts' models of decision-taking tend to impose a conformity on behaviour which produces behavioural uniformities.

The economist's initial assumptions of perfect competition have led economic theory to aim at producing universal generalisations about the market behaviour of 'firms' or of 'people' in their economic roles. Such generalisations serve, as do the cultural values already explored, to indicate a single acceptable course of action for those participating in market transactions. That course of action is the one which is indicated in the concept of individualism: within this framework, the entrepreneur becomes the cultural hero. But this serves to deny legitimacy to alternative (divergent) courses of action which may appear more appropriate to the situation and circumstances and thus to create insecurity and uncertainty.

These assumptions enable the economist to develop, for example, a model of market operation in which market forces will *compel* a particular allocation of resources. On these assumptions, the price will vary in response to the levels of supply and demand, and at that price the market will be cleared. Factors of production will then be used in a way which equates the cost of an extra unit of the factor with the revenue that its employment will produce (which is the same as the price obtained for its product). This will give the firm (or the entrepreneur) the greatest return possible in these market conditions, thus indicating the level at which it (or he) will most likely operate. Market price becomes the key to the pricing of the

factors of production, and for this reason, it becomes the deter-
minant of the allocation of factors (Bridge, 1981, pp 24–51). This
seems, therefore, to deny any role for the human decision-taker.

It is only in conditions of perfect competition that all markets will
yield the same level of return on either assets employed or
expenditure incurred. Imperfect knowledge, immobilities, and
heterogeneities work against the realisation of the equilibrium condition. Different elasticities of demand for the product lead to
different consequences when changes occur in income availability.
The activities of competitors will affect the degree of stability of
return from the market and thus increase the uncertainty faced by
any one. This variability of both level and security of the return are
likely to influence the undertaking's structure and mode of
operating, without necessarily and immediately affecting allocation
and investment decisions. In reality, there are, therefore, many
impediments to the creation of the conditions in the model of perfect
competition.

Market Control

The reality is therefore more complex than simple competition
theory suggests, for five main reasons:

(a)   products are not homogeneous (varying in style or quality or
        brand);

(b)   people taking decisions do not have perfect knowledge of the
        alternatives;

(c)   people do not act so rationally as the assumptions of utility or
        profit maximisation imply;

(d)   people are not so mobile that they can move in or out of
        markets in response to changes in returns; and

(e)   it cannot be assumed that no buyer or seller has power to
        manipulate the market to his own advantage (Cohen and
        Cyert, 1965, pp 50–7)

Part of the reason for this is the natural human dislike of uncertainty and the consequent attempts by those who face it to reduce
it. Such attempts involve deliberately controlling the market so that
what is found there are varying degrees of:

1   monopoly (single seller) or oligopoly (a few sellers) who
        restrict the supply available as a way of holding up the price
        beyond the level which 'perfect competition' would permit;
        and

2   monopsony (single buyer) or oligopsony (a few buyers) who restrict the demand to reduce the price of materials or factors required.

These do not completely eliminate, but they do reduce the market uncertainty facing the manager. Consequently, managerial decisions about the control of the market are crucial to the success of the enterprise. It places the manager in the position of having to read the situation aright, to pursue objectives which will lead to greater control of the situation, and to keep performance under constant review.

Management analysts, rather than economists, can offer some guidance to the embattled manager attempting to read the situation correctly (Bridge, 1981, p 2). They have taken up the idea that undertakings, whether private or public, necessarily develop varying relationships with their 'market' environments and have sought the correlations between these and successful managerial strategies. They have then attempted to identify the successful strategies associated with different types of market relationship.

Their conclusions focus on strategic choices made by managers as they seek to shape their markets and to affect the size and stability of the return obtained from it. This implies that managers in different situations might need to adopt quite distinct strategies, although this does not imply that some are necessarily or absolutely better (or worse) than others.

Strategic Choice

The more dynamic theories of business direction suggest that enterprises in different circumstances may often demand diametrically opposed actions (Porter, 1985). Porter suggests that in corporate strategy formation, corporate (directoral) management must *decide* on its *generic strategy* in the light of circumstances. It faces the choice of aiming to be a low cost producer of a standardised product (as was the case with Toyota cars) or the producer of a higher value custom-made product, which (like the Rolls Royce car) taps the vanities of the affluent customer. In either case, management might aim to be the market leader or to be a major supplier. Any one strategy (of the four) could result in competitive advantage. Failure to segment and attack the market in this way, he suggests, is likely to provide no great competitive advantage: supplying anything and all things to all segments of the market is likely to prove costly and insufficiently rewarding because the enterprise is left vulnerable to all four types of competitor.

He also suggests that success does not arise out of the general state of health of the corporate organisation. Rather, he says, it stems from some part or parts of what he calls the 'value chain' – the various *activities* which range from development through to marketing and include production or human resource management on the way. In one case, the purchasing activity could give a competitive advantage; in another, the same result could stem from the quality of the human resource management. Management must, again, make a strategic choice if it is to be successful in the market.

Any or all of these elements in the value chain could be improved by investment of resources, but it is only by reference to the generic strategy that sensible choices can be made as to which part to develop to increase success. A low-cost producer is not likely to invest in human resource management which focuses on a large and bureaucratic personnel department, but is more likely to seek favourable buying in terms of both raw materials/components and labour. A high priced, differentiated-product manufacturer is more likely to be able and willing to invest resources in policies for retaining skilled and long-serving labour.

Porter's analysis emphasises that success depends on correct diagnosis and response to circumstances. It does not arise automatically from a juxtaposition of a given market type and/or a technology. This was the kind of inference often drawn from the early excursions into contingency approaches: the new realism in management serves to destroy this thought. Nevertheless, the position reached by such enterprises as a result of taking these decisions does provide a useful predictor of the likely response of the management to demands for internal investment.

The Market Relationship

The relationships of the product or the establishment with the market cover a range from dominating (in the case of the monopoly) to being dominated (in the case of near perfect or atomised markets). In the one case, in effect, the firm dictates the price (becoming a price-maker) and in the other, it accepts the price as given (becoming a price-taker). Different products (and thereby, in the case of the single product undertaking, the firm) may fall into one or other category, or tend more towards one than towards the other. The resultant categorisations allow inferences to be drawn about the likely effects of the specific type of market relationship on internal strategies and policies.

There are obvious advantages to the firm in having products in the position where price can be dictated: in this way at least some of the uncertainty surrounding decisions can be removed. In addition, the undertaking may facilitate the development of its production and personnel strategies by moving to this more favourable position. A market leader in a growing market will probably face a very different set of opportunities and restrictions from those faced by a price-taker, relying on a product which is reaching the end of its profitable life. In particular, what these two different undertakings can 'afford' in the way of internal strategies is likely to vary significantly.

The Boston Consulting Group's matrix of product-market relationships (Hambrick, MacMillan and Day, 1982, pp 512–513) offers one basis for speculating about the likely effects of different market relationships on internal (including human resource) strategies.

This matrix is based on the notion of a product-life cycle* and uses Levitt's four stage approach to derive measures of overall market growth and individual market share. The results are then presented in a 2×2 matrix (Figure 7). The four cells are identified as 'question mark' (or wildcat), star, cash-cow, or dog products, according to the size of the market share and the direction of total market growth. The distinction between high share and low share products, assuming that it could be translated to the level of the undertaking, produces a consequence which has much in common with that found between primary (corporate) and secondary (entrepreneurial) sectors of the economy (see below, pp 171 *et seq*).

Products in these market positions differ particularly in:

(a)   the amount of cash which they generate in the form of revenue from the market, and

(b)   the sources and extent of uncertainty surrounding its continued acquisition.

The first of these clearly affects the extent to which management can meet the demands of the various stakeholders. The second, however, carries less clear implications of the same type: where uncertainty is

---

*This concept highlights the sequential processes of demand creation, growth, stabilisation, and decline, through which a product will pass during its long or short life (Levitt, 1965, p 81). Both the returns and their security can be expected to vary from one stage to the next. This is because the ratio of the cost of accessing the market to the cash return to be obtained from it will vary in the different phases. As a result, both opportunities for, and constraints on, any action which bears a cost would vary from one part of the cycle to another. A management team would need to forecast the likely time-span of each of these phases in deciding to introduce a new product and to plan its actions in accordance with that forecast if it was to maximise and stabilise its return from this product.

Figure 7

The BCG Matrix

		High < Market Share > Low	
Market Growth	High	Star (Demand growth)	Wildcat (Demand creation)
	Low	Cash-Cow (Demand stabilisation)	Dog (Demand decline)

associated – for example, with product design, market develop-ment, or production methods – improvements in these will constitute a demand on such cash as is available, which will tend to be met before the demands of, say, purchasing or human resource development are met.

Each of the two major discriminations (between market trend and market share) can, therefore, be expected to influence manage-ment's consequential decisions. They have comparatively obvious implications for investment decisions: a high and stable return is likely, other things being equal, to attract inward flows of invest-ment, while a low and fluctuating one will have the opposite effect. The effects on the climate of relationships within the undertaking may be less obvious, but nevertheless very real. The cash return will have an important influence on the way in which management responds to the labour market, and orders the staffing processes.

Availability of cash is thus crucial in determining the limits and opportunities open to each management. The categorisation helps to identify products, and, on the above assumptions, establishments which fall into these different market positions. The star and cash-cow are better endowed with cash returns than the wildcat or dog. Such cash as is available to the wildcat is likely to be required to finance market growth and product development. What is available to the dog will probably be deployed to satisfy the stockholders. Cash in the hands of the cash-cow may be deployed to assist product and market development elsewhere, but some will be required to develop technology. Cash available to the star will probably be used to maintain customer and stakeholder commitment in order to maintain stability.

Investment analysts do not necessarily agree that particular strategies are restricted to classes of enterprise. First, this type of analysis is based on 'products', not firms. It is the product which penetrates the market and in so doing establishes a relationship. It is only where it is possible to identify the single product firm that generalisations can be carried over to the firm. Many firms, especially the big and internationally known ones, are not in this position, being conglomerates; any generalisations about product-market relationships do not carry over to indicate firm-market relationships. For this reason, it is more useful to look at establishments which, even within conglomerate firms, are more closely identified with single products than are firms (Doyle, 1969).

Secondly, firms may deliberately swim against the tide and in some cases win. But it is presumed that each class will tend to demonstrate a statistically normal distribution of strategies with most falling withing the median or interquartile ranges. The options open to the star are not as readily available to the dog. The dog's attempt to emulate the star would be to get it wrong, and the star's attempt to act like a dog would be to miss the most advantageous options available to it.

Thirdly, management has the opportunity to vary the cash return by changing the business 'strategy' (a term used to comprise all managerial activity which responds to the perceived situation and its uncertainties (Hofer, 1975, p 784). Management can, for example, improve the undertaking's cash position by expanding (adding new lines by invention or acquisition, or finding new uses for existing lines), or by retrenching (dropping old lines, selling off capacity, or curtailing product development), according to the 'position' of the product in the market. Each of these can be further divided to give a number of sub-strategies and to allow finer tuning (Glueck and Jauch, 1984, p 210).

Amplification

The single product undertakings (or the autonomous divisions of them where there are multiple product/service undertakings) falling into each of these cells, could be expected to exhibit the following typical features.

(a) The wildcat is often an innovatory enterprise, frequently small, and aiming to generate a market for a new product. Many of the recent small electronics companies, such as Sinclair, would probably fall into this category. The cash return will be comparatively small and precarious. The priority in dealing with uncertainty concerns the market and its development; all else is subordinate to this 'need' to develop and stabilise the market demand.

(b)   The star is more often the firm which has successfully developed a market for its product and which has grown in size as a result. This kind of enterprise may be exemplified by IBM which has market dominance in the electronic business machine field. Cash is comparatively plentiful and the uncertainties surrounding it are comparatively small and fairly evenly distributed through the various functional areas. Management is likely to have considerable discretion to dispose cash at the margin to deal with this wide range of relatively small uncertainties.

(c)   The cash-cow is more often the undertaking whose products have passed the peak demand point in the product life-cycle, but can be expected to continue to generate cash for some time into the future. Cash is plentiful but needs to be secured for the future by technological developments (of both products and processes) which is where the main uncertainties are likely to lie. This kind of undertaking can be exemplified by (at least certain major parts of) the GEC, which retains a high market share in many of its traditional markets and is able to draw comparatively high revenues from these although the traditional markets may now be falling away.

(d)   The dog is the undertaking which has passed its peak demand and moved into a declining market situation from which it is unlikely to continue to draw significant cash revenue with its present range of products. Maintenence of a viable economic position in the short run will require significant cost reductions which have to be achieved without unaffordable capital investment. This kind of undertaking is readily identifiable with some of the nineteenth century smoke-stack industries which have passed their heyday. Where they have been nationalised and restricted as to the product range they may offer, they have little discretion but to secure cost savings from improvements in per capita labour productivity. Private firms, which have not yet found a new product portfolio that would enable them to move out of their traditional markets, are similarly placed.

Many undertakings are, of course, multi-product firms, and this easy assumption cannot be applied to them. In these cases, the firm's management can use transfer-pricing and cross-subsidisation to avoid some of the characteristic problems of individual products. This, however, can only occur where there are products in the star or cash-cow phases of their life cycles. Thus, at the level of the enterprise as a whole, the dominant ethos will be determined by the mix of high and low share products and the revenue position established by it: cross-subsidisation can only occur where there is sufficient revenue from high share products to provide the necessary subsidy.

The position in the public, non-trading sector of the economy is obviously different from that in the private enterprise sector. This difference is, however, more of form and process than of consequence. The amount of a society's resources which people are willing to give up for public services varies over time, and indeed, may appear to respond to fashions as well as political ideologies. Ministers and their teams compete with one another for 'shares' of the public vote, and their success will determine how much cash will be available to provide a return to factors used in the provision of a public service. The time-lags may be much greater, but there is a sense in which the extent the service department can mobilise public confidence in its value will influence the department's cash position.

A management team may make quite different forecasts to reach decisions about what to do in these circumstances. A product-market relationship is by no means fixed nor does it come with its own specifications for action to be taken, but reasonably standard responses and consequences might be expected to follow from appreciation of the stage reached in the product-life cycle. The distribution of responses by managements to these kinds of situations is therefore likely to be normal in the statistical sense.

LABOUR MARKETS

In a private enterprise economy, the labour market, like other factor markets, is a dependent one. It depends on the supply and demand position in the product market. Given a supply of labour that is fixed in the short run, demand for labour, and therefore its price, depend on the demand, supply, and prices established (even if mediated by tastes and preferences) in the product markets. They are nevertheless markets in their own right. By regarding labour (or labour power) as a commodity which can be traded in the market, what can be said about the operation of product markets might be applied to the market for this factor of production.

One strongly held view is that the forces of supply and demand can (and will, if allowed to operate without artificial restraint) determine the wage rates at which the market will be cleared (with all those seeking employment being offered employment at that wage). It is often a part of this view that the function of trade unions in maintaining wage levels higher than might otherwise obtain acts against the interest of the unemployed worker *and* the economy as a whole. Empirical testing of the theory of competitive equilibrium in the labour market (Nolan, 1983, p 294) suggests that there is very little evidence that wage rates will tend to equalise (ibid p 296). Furthermore, not only is the evidence weak but the employer appears to have discretion to fix the wage rate he is prepared to pay (ibid p 298 and p 299).

Another firmly held view is that pay differentials are established independently of their absolute level in accordance with traditional conceptions of what a right ordering of rewards ought to be. These accomplish an ordering of rates through the informal operation of accepted 'distribution rules'. This has the effect of restoring traditional differentials whenever something temporarily upsets them. Consequently, if a shortage of labour in an occupation, or a windfall bargain secured in negotiations, results in an out-of-line differential for a time, this will be 'corrected' in due course as these rules are subsequently applied.

They are applied, consciously or not, by those who take pay decisions, and it is now widely believed that wage (and salary) rates, far from being determined by the operation of the forces of the market, are *decided* by someone (Pen, 1959). This 'someone' may be the employer, the worker, or the two acting in concert (as in the case of collective bargaining). The occasions when the worker determines the wage rate are few, however, and are confined to special types of worker − for example, pop stars − and to the short run. More often, wage rates are determined either by collective bargaining, or unilaterally by management.

Consequently, the labour market is unlikely to function as 'perfectly' as the classical economists implied. Both worker and management behaviours create 'frictions' which distort the equilibrium associated with the perfect competition assumptions, but these behaviours are not necessarily congruent with one another.

Market Imperfections

The tendency for pay rates not to find an equilibrium level in local or national labour markets could also be explained in terms of imperfections. These might be brought about by the employer's comparatively greater bargaining power than that of the individual worker. As Adam Smith remarked, this could be accounted for by the fact that the employer is usually in a better position to wait (and live off capital, if need be) until the worker is forced to accept his terms.

The imperfections might also be explained by actions initiated by workers themselves.

1   Workers may not adopt the simple criterion of maximising economic advantage in deciding their labour market behaviour. Psychological and social rewards may be as desirable, although they may also be traded off against economic benefits. Managers are more likely to develop a calculative approach to their labour market behaviour, because their employment security depends on adopting a maximising approach.

2   Workers tend to be relatively immobile, more particularly in the short term, because of the householders' commitment to particular houses and communities, and because of the impossibility of securing enough information about available opportunities in a wider geographical area to reduce the risks of moving to an acceptable level. By contrast, the employer usually has a greater capacity to secure more and more adequate information about conditions in the labour market.

3   The worker's endowment (of skill and aptitude) tends to become fixed, both by initial training and later experience, and protection of the fixed asset becomes a necessary defence against change in the environment. As Cairns (1874) recognised, workers' skills are layered and all workers do not compete with all other workers, so that they form 'non-competing groups' as they attempt to protect their positions in the labour market. The unskilled do not directly compete with skilled workers, and professional workers do not directly compete with either. Whether this is accidental or deliberate, it can increase the bargaining power of workers concerned by representing to the buyer that the labour is in some way special and worthy of higher remuneration.

4   With the growth of industrial scale, the number of opportunities for employment are limited. In effect, the individual worker's range of choice is reduced and he confronts a situation which is either monopsonistic (the one industry town or the one employer of a given type of labour) or oligopsonistic (a few employers in the relevant labour market). As no one, not even trade unions, sells labour, these conditions are not matched by labour monopoly.

The behaviour of trade unions could be added to this list of factors inhibiting the operation of 'market forces' as they attempt to replace individual competition with collective challenge to the employer's monopoly power. The unions' influence, however, was in the opposite direction to these factors because they attempt to distort the price of labour upwards.

Labour Control Strategies

The employer also segments the labour market as a consequence of the labour control strategies he decides are appropriate to the organisation's trading conditions. As we have already noted, these tend to vary between organisations and between products, and the labour control strategies which emerge are also likely to vary.

Some organisations consider that they need generally skilled personnel such as are available in the external labour market for at least some of the jobs they have on offer. The skills needed are those associated with broad occupational categories such as fitters, carpenters, brick-layers or yard labourers. Labour is recruited by general occupational or skill categories of this kind, and at the time of recruitment the worker guarantees that he or she is able to perform the work tasks associated with the particular occupational title.

For at least some of their labour force other organisations perceive their needs to be defined in terms of the potential for developing organisation-specific abilities and skills. This demand is not expressed simply in terms of 'fitters', for example, but in terms of people who can use specific skills in association with particular technologies to shape and fit particular kinds of metal in complex and varying ways. Such skills are unlikely to be available in the external labour market, and whoever is recruited may therefore have to be trained or retrained to use the specific methods to perform the particular kinds of work. As a result the organisation is likely to adopt a different approach to the mobilisation of skills – one that entails more in-house training and development, and which, therefore, further fragments the labour market.

Currently, examples of each strategy may be found. The cause of the switch is, however, likely to be found in the development of new market relationships (and particularly in the assumption by the firm that it exercises greater control of its own markets through branding, merger, and growth of manufacturing scale) and of new technologies to support these relationships. The different human resource strategies broadly correspond to the location of undertakings in the phases of the product life-cycle concept. There appears to be a broad association between the internal labour market and the cash-replete categories of the BCG matrix and the external labour market and the cash-starved categories.

Labour Market Segmentation

Modern theories of labour market segmentation suggest that there are two broadly distinct types of labour market – the internal and external – which are associated with primary and secondary sector organisations. Each operates according to different rules which establish whether recruitment is to be of labour already possessed of demonstrable skills, or of labour with potential for development on the basis of aptitudes.

The application of these rules yields different levels and forms of remuneration and provides distinctly different degrees of employment security for an otherwise homogeneous class of labour (Doeringer and Piore, 1971: Berger and Piore, 1980). Consequently, a difference is created between primary sector jobs which have relatively high earnings, good fringe benefits, good working conditions, a high degree of job security and good opportunities for advancement and secondary sector jobs which have relatively low earnings, poor working conditions, and negligible opportunities for advancement and a low degree of job security (Barron and Morris, 1976).

This simple dichotomy has been developed by Loveridge and Mok (1981) to take account of two other perspectives of modern occupations and (particularly high technology) organisations. This recognises that there has probably always been a distinction between 'cosmopolitan' and 'local' occupations (or jobs). The accountant, the engineer, and the doctor – to take three examples – have traditionally pursued occupational careers independently of specific organisations or localities, relying on an ability to apply a cosmopolitan knowledge to any situation or demand. The semi-skilled machine operator or the clerical worker has traded on applying more specific perceptual and motor skills and was often as mobile as the professional worker, although now within a local labour market. These 'types' of labour continue to be found, say Loveridge and Mok, within the 'external labour market' and in association with the secondary sector organisations.

The model takes account also of the emergent view of modern high technology organisations. It sees them drawing a distinction between 'core' workers and 'peripheral' workers. Core workers tend, increasingly, to be multi-skilled and flexible (at any level in the occupational or job hierarchy) and are bound to specific

Figure 8

Labour market segmentation

PRIMARY SECTOR ORGANISATIONS	
CORE	COSMOPOLITAN
Functional flexibility Job security Lifetime commitment to firm High rewards Regular retraining Skills specific to the firm	Highly specific tasks High demand in labour market Commitment to occupation High rewards High responsibility No retraining by firm Skills not specific to firm
INTERNAL ————————	———————— EXTERNAL
Numerical flexibility Little security Low material rewards Little responsibility Lack of career prospects Little skill requirement	Numerical flexibility No job security Low material rewards Little responsibility No training
FIRST PERIPHERAL	SECOND PERIPHERAL
SECONDARY SECTOR ORGANISATIONS	

Source: Loveridge R and Mok A: *Theories of Labour Market Segmentation* (Academic Press, 1981).

organisations by a range of benefits which do not apply to the peripheral workers. The latter tend, on the other hand, to be skilled in specific activities and engaged on more specialised tasks, but are less directly and firmly tied to the specific organisation, being part-time, seasonal, or subcontracted workers rather than full-time employees. These types of labour are to be found in association with primary sector organisations which adopt 'internal labour market strategy' in respect of the core workers.

Figure 8 shows how Loveridge and Mok depict the segments of the labour market.

The External Labour Market

The 'external' labour market retains many of the features of the neoclassical conception of a market and is associated with 'second-ary sector' undertakings. Both employer and worker compete with others of the same class for the available workers and employment, respectively, with each attempting to maximise advantage in the employment transaction. The employer will attempt to hold wage costs to a minimum and the workers will try to obtain the highest wages they can, given their basic endowment. Both are in the position of 'price-takers' because the labour price is seen to be determined by the market, not by any action of the two parties.

The employment contract will be regarded by the employer and accepted by the worker as being essentially purposive (Fox, 1974, p 153) entered into for a limited period of time and for specific purposes. Neither party sees itself as being in a position to secure a fundamentally better deal or a status contract, because these options are nowhere on offer in this kind of market.

This external market is associated with particular kinds of undertaking (at least in respect of some parts of its labour force) and particular types of labour (or particular segments of what would otherwise be a homogeneous grade of labour). This secondary sector of the economy is seen to comprise a large number of usually small, technologically backward firms, which operate in relatively volatile and uncertain markets (Nolan, in Bain, 1983; Craig, Gamsey and Rubery, Department of Employment Research Paper No. 48, 1984).

Their dominant concern is to remain free of long-term expensive commitments and to this end they rely on subcontracting many of their requirements, including those of labour. One manifestation of this is the use of outworkers which may not be confined to small firms in volatile markets, but which is strongly represented there (Nolan, 1983, p 309).

Where labour must be hired on a full-time basis, the contract is kept as simple as possible and the rates of pay as low as possible. These devices are intended to provide both a competitive production cost and sufficient flexibility to allow speedy responses to changes in market demand. Productivity is secured through 'supervision', a strategy of control which relies on a hierarchical structure of authority and the threat of dismissal to maintain discipline.

The workers in this kind of market are usually either broadly trained in some skill or occupation or untrained in any. In either case, the site of employment is largely incidental to the skills possessed.

In the first category are the professional workers and the skilled craftsmen, both trading on their cosmopolitan knowledge. They contribute to the organisation of their expertise (Burns and Stalker, 1961). They usually find they have considerable autonomy, reflecting the carry-over of the values associated with the strategy of selection, but their security depends on their actually performing to the standards applied in their occupation.

In the second are the semi-skilled and unskilled workers who frequently belong to minority and disadvantaged groups, such as immigrants, women, handicapped persons or illiterates. This group commonly finds itself in routinised and often boring jobs which have a limited life as sources of employment, and it receives relatively low remuneration for performing them. Such knowledge and skill as these people have and as they trade on may be limited, but like professional or craft workers, they are largely independent of the particular organisation in which they may be employed.

The first group can be expected to join professional associations or (in Turner's sense) closed trade unions whose main function is to protect the members' interests by maintaining the standards of performance. The employer may well encourage these workers to belong to such associations, where they do serve to protect standards, because this tends to be the main guarantee that the employer has that the workers will perform in the way and at the level which the employer demands.

The second group may need to join open unions to protect its interests by replacing individual dispensability with collective indispensability, but the employer operating with an external labour market is unlikely to encourage them to do so. If they do join, their unions will probably be denied recognition for purposes of bargaining over pay. Management's main concern will be to retain freedom to decide unilaterally and speedily in response to changes in the product market.

The Internal Labour Market

By contrast, the internal labour market is that which is developed within complex (usually bureaucratic) organisations (identified, for this purpose, as 'primary sector' organisations). In these organisations labour is recruited through several distinct 'ports of entry', and recruitment through these is restricted to those with aptitude or general capacity to develop with training the precise skills which the organisation requires. It is only at these 'ports of entry' that the traditional notion of an external labour market remains relevant. Otherwise, the labour force can be regarded as an employed pool of labour from which, with appropriate training and development, the organisation can draw workers to fill specific vacancies.

Once labour is recruited at the bottom of the various job hierarchies, the organisation will, by job rotation and specific training courses, develop the skills of the labour force to match those which are needed to accomplish the work as it has been defined by the management. These skills will usually be specific to the undertaking and are not easily transferred to other employments at the same rates of pay as may be obtained in their first employment. The labour force will then be advanced and progressed through differentially rewarded jobs so that a kind of career is offered. The actual remuneration will be augmented by other kinds of benefits which tend to accrue with length of service, so that the individual tends to be bound to the employer who has invested a good deal in his or her training and development. The comparatively high wages and the good career prospects tend to encourage both stability of employment and the development of work commitment.

There are obvious limits (particularly those imposed by the availability of cash) to the extent to which organisations can engage in this strategy, and the links to the product life-cycle analysis are thus likely to be strong. This kind of labour market is seen to be associated with organisations in the primary sector of the economy, comprising those firms, which by virtue of their product/profit position or their complex technologies, need and seek a highly stable and committed labour force. These firms are usually large and organised as complex bureaucracies through which multiple and complex rules of work are developed and imposed on the workforce in the interests of securing the amount and quality of production deemed to be required to stay profitable in the specific product market. Instead of a simple hierarchical structure of authority, such firms rely on a more complex structure of incentive (including many non-financial ones) to secure commitment. Enforcement of the rules relies much more on the threat of loss of privileges and benefits than on straightforward dismissal.

As in the case of the secondary sector, however, this strategy may be adopted for only part of the labour force — that part which is crucial to the achievement of profitable production and exchange. Other parts of the workforce may be relegated to the external labour market conditions, although moves towards status harmonisation in the primary sector undertakings suggest that with the reduction of the significance of manual labour cost in many technologically advanced firms, this segmentation may be disappearing.

The workers who become involved in these markets are more likely (than those in the external labour market) to be recruited on the basis of their personalities and aptitudes rather than their demonstrable skills. It has been suggested that such workers are recruited because they can demonstrate that they have the capacity to fit the modes of control used in the employer's undertaking rather than specific skills which fit the particular job requirements (Edwards and Harper, 1975; Blackburn and Mann, 1979). With the passage of time, therefore, they will tend to develop skills highly specific to the undertaking in which they are employed. They are rewarded for this commitment with a contract which more strongly resembles a status contract.

SUMMARY

The idea of 'a market' (generated by Petty) has remained pervasive. It is a construct which serves to organise thinking about economic processes, and particularly thinking about influences on prices or wages. It cannot, however, be used very constructively by corporate management unless the so-called 'market imperfections' are fully comprehended and acknowledged.

Both product and labour markets vary in the demands they make on those who operate within them, and both are themselves shaped by the decisions which are taken by the various sellers and buyers.

Corporate management is constantly faced with the need to decide to which parts or segments of the product market their organisations are to relate. In taking such decisions, they 'create' a market construct for their organisations, and this is both influenced by them and influences their subsequent decisions. A decision, for example, to go for low cost leadership in a product market, immediately creates a need for certain promotional and advertising tactics and imposes some restrictions on the opportunities available to design work tasks and work organisation.

Once such decisions have been taken, it becomes possible to categorise undertakings according to their product 'market relationships', as is done in the BCG matrix. The analysis tends to distinguish the new, thrusting dynamic enterprise (which is often small because it has as yet a low market share) from the well established and comparatively bureaucratic organisation (which is usually relatively large because of its attainment of a comparatively high market share) in the growing market situation. It also distinguishes the established enterprise with a high market share in a stagnating market from the declining (falling market share) enterprise in a declining market.

Location of undertakings on some such map offers a basis for predicting the probability that they will possess particular types of internal organisation and policy. In particular, the kind of labour control strategy followed, while not determined by stage or position in relation to the product life-cycle, is likely to be strongly influenced by it. This kind of analysis therefore provides some basis for prediction of the likely priorities for subsequent action, by highlighting the nature of the uncertainties which beset undertakings at different stages in their development of market relationships.

One such action is that which establishes the kind of relationship which the undertaking will develop with the labour market. This focuses on the broad distinction between internal and external labour market strategies, resulting in a division of the labour force into favoured and disfavoured subsets.

1   A strategy which depends on labour of the skill type required being available in the external labour market; relies on recruiting and selecting workers of the kind and number required when it is needed; and discharges or deselects the skill to that labour market when it is no longer required or no longer performs to required standards.

2   A strategy which stresses the need for the organisation to train and develop the types of labour required for its purposes for itself (and which therefore recruits untrained labour at the bottom of the various job families or hierarchies); selects on the basis of aptitude or training potential (rather than skill); and aims to retain that labour for as long as possible to secure a return on the investment in its development.

Each of these strategies carries distinct implications for the level and structure of rewards offered to labour, so that the fundamental division in strategy becomes linked with a fundamental division between workers, which is based on comparative affluence and employment security.

This distinction between internal and external servicing is much wider in its application than to human resourcing alone (and can also be applied, for example, to financing, or purchasing, or marketing). The general aim in all such organisations is to secure the degree of resource commitment appropriate to position (and therefore 'need'). The spectrum may be depicted as ranging from a requirement of temporary finance or casual labour to one of permanent investment and committed labour force. Personnel (or human resource) strategies will range from those emphasising 'external' provision of resources (such as recruitment of people with required skills and use of an employers' association to negotiate terms and conditions of employment) to those which stress 'internal' skill and commitment generation (through training and development of staff recruited at the lowest port of entry) and the development of undertaking-wide negotiating and agreeing processes designed to secure necessary commitment.

Reading:

Baldamus (1961).
Barron and Morris (1976).
BCG (1970).
Behrend (1959).
Bridge (1981).
Burkitt and Bowers (1979).
Craig, Garnsey and Rubery (1984).
Davenport (1926), pp 52–81.
Doeringer and Piore (1971).
Loveridge and Mok (1981).
Nolan, in Bain (1983).
Porter (1980; 1985).
Raimon (1956), pp 180–94.
Reynolds (1946), pp 366–75.

7 Technologies

The market of an undertaking provides the basis for its objectives, along with opportunities for and limits to action. The market is not the only such influence on goals because the organisation must also go some way to accommodating the political, legal, educational and social environments. This is even more the case with non-economic enterprises. But the market remains important for the industrial organisation's goals, just as the needs of the client system remain important for the definition of objectives of other kinds of organisation.

Realisation of the objectives depends, however, on finding appropriate means of coping with both the opportunities and limitations of the material, market, logistical or human environments. Such means come in a variety of forms – material, technical, organisational, etc. – but may be encompassed by the term 'technology' (Korach, 1964). This really identifies the modes, means, methods and techniques which enable man to realise definable objectives, although it is one of those terms which has narrowed its meaning to the point where it refers to no more than a small part of what it originally embraced.

The term 'technology' is now commonly used to refer to the physical plant and equipment which is employed in the production of goods or services. It relates to the chemical plant, the machines and tools of the workshop or factory, the mechanical and electronic equipment in the office, and so on. These artefacts of an industrial civilisation are instruments which embody ideas about how to cope efficiently with the material world, but they are not the only ones which do so.

Many remain abstract ideas. Some are theories or beliefs about what will *cause* what to happen, or about what needs to be done to create some product or service. Some are, for example, ideas about how to organise people and their activities for maximum effect. The techniques of industrial engineering or the methods of organising workers in autonomous work groups have as much claim to be included in the meaning as the machine systems already referred to. The way in which work is divided into discrete jobs, allocated to individuals as a set of duties, and coordinated into an ultimate whole, is itself a part of technology (as the term will be used here).

The trend towards separation of the two meanings of technology has created a situation in which it became necessary to put the two elements together again. This has been attempted in the development of the construct of the socio-technical system. This approach owes much to two lines of conceptualisation: general systems theory (von Bertalanffy, 1950, 1968; Boulding, 1956) and socio-technical systems theory (Trist and Bamforth, 1951; Emery, 1959; Emery and Trist, 1964; Hill, 1971). It brings together the social and mechanical system elements, both of which are considered in this chapter.

MECHANICAL TECHNOLOGY

The economic history of man is one of developing and powering tools which can be used to bend the natural world to his ends with the least expenditure of physical or mental effort. In the early stages of his development his tools extended his capacity but remained dependent on his physical strength and prowess. Subsequently, water, fire, and wind were drawn in to supplement this, and man ceased to be the main source of power (or the prime mover). With the development of steam power in the early years of the industrial revolution (Pollard, 1965), this became a prime mover of greater power and flexibility until it was replaced by electric motor and the internal combustion engine which permitted ever greater flexibility.

The steam engine virtually created what we now refer to as the industrial system because it provided new opportunities for powering machines to enable them to perform work previously powered by human energy. Once Watt had adapted the steam engine so that it was capable of rotary motion, it became possible to produce interchangeable parts (the foundation for 'mass production') which was the significant advance made at this time. But it also imposed its own requirements on the way work was organised because high losses of power in transmission demanded that work should be performed in close proximity to the prime mover (steam engine) itself. The complex linkages of shafting and belting between prime mover and machines ensured that the workshop or factory would replace the 'domestic' organisation.

The later development of electric power, applied through the electric motor, had a similar significance, but in the direction of allowing greater organisational flexibility. Electric power could be generated and transmitted over long distances with comparatively little loss of power in the transmission process. Electric motors could be (and were) attached to the machines themselves in whatever location those machines happened to be. The actual manufacture of products, components, or parts could therefore be located without reference to the location of the source of power. The need to bring parts together for final assembly and the cost of transporting them might still justify a factory organisation, but the degree of flexibility in location was considerably greater than in the earlier situation.

Contemporaneously, ever more sophisticated machines and tools were developed to take advantage of the capabilities of the new prime movers. Some of these were more significant in their impact than others. The harnessing of hydraulics and pneumatics to the transport of heavy components over short distances and the development of the internal combustion engine for transporting them over longer distances gave additional organisational and locational flexibility. All of these developments, however, were primarily concerned with reducing the need for human effort to move materials.

Electrical and Electronic Technology

The utilisation of electricity, in the form of a current which was capable of flowing, and of the electronic pulse with a similar capability, opened up new possibilities for control — not only of mechanical but also of logical (and therefore seemingly intellectual) activities. The harnessing of electronics, initially through the thermionic valve and later through the silicon chip, facilitated the development of more precise control of movements and locations, as well as of numerical values. Not only was the worker's strength thereby supplemented and eventually supplanted, but so also was the judgement necessary to decide about which actions to take.

Recent advances have made their main impact on the information processes associated with the control of production activities, where the earlier ones more particularly affected the physical or motor activities involved in work. This development focuses on the capacity of the computer to process vast amounts of data quickly — in fact, more quickly than the human brain — and to make routine comparisons with keyed-in standards to throw up any errors or gaps. In effect, therefore, this development facilitates (and even supplants) the 'brainwork of production' and makes its main impact on office workers concerned with information-processing rather than on manual workers.

These developments have in turn brought about two major changes in the worker's relationship to his or her work:

1 The progressive take-over by the machine of the physical effort required to perform work – in the sense that, for example, a hydraulic press enables much more physical pressure to be applied than human beings could muster on their own.

2 The assumption by the machine itself of responsibility for much of the precision in location of, and action on, materials and components which had previously been supplied by the skilled worker, so that the machine now supplies much of the perceptual and judgemental skill previously supplied by people.

The reduction in both the mental and physical demands which work makes on the worker as a result of these developments in physical technology has resulted in both a lowering of demand for labour to perform these tasks and a potential increase in the worker's freedom to engage in work of a more superior kind. Greater flexibility of location is possible, for example, through working at home, using an electronic computer linked by cable to some distantly located activity. More precise control of physical work activity is possible through linking the computer to mechanical, hydraulic, and pneumatic servo-systems, as occurs with Computer Assisted Design (CAD), Computer Assisted Manufacture (CAM), or Flexible Manufacturing Systems(FMS).

The fully automatic factory, operating without human labour of any kind, remains a pipe-dream, but the near-automatic factory (in which, say, two or three people control a whole factory's transformation process) is a present reality. This is the case because, as yet, no machine has the capacity for broad-spectrum control that the human being possesses.

These are the more concrete and dramatic aspects of the development of technology; they catch the eye just because statements that, for example, Anderson Strathclyde's FMS employs only two persons per shift to produce what previously would have required thirty persons with conventional machines, or that Rolls Royce's new automated production line in Derby requires only three persons in place of the previous thirty, are dramatic. In fact, the actual reductions in labour cost are rarely as dramatic as the staffing figures suggest, but they are impressive (of the order, for example, of 20 per cent in the case of Rolls Royce).

The Development of Production Technology

The industrial history of modern times is also one of increasing individual and organisational specialisation. As the *domestic system* gave way to the *factory system*, as new power sources were tapped, most of the attempts by the family to supply its own general needs from within its own resources were abandoned – although some residuals were found well into the present century among, for example, quarrymen and miners who continued to work their smallholdings as a source of food.

Many more individuals became specialists in some trade or occupation, and increasingly in some more highly fractionalised 'job', from which they hoped to draw enough remuneration to enable them to purchase their general requirements for living. Simultaneously, the factories themselves began to specialise, becoming cotton factories, engineering factories, chemical plants, and so on. More recent conglomerations have not destroyed this essential character of industry, as they have usually combined a number of different specialist plants under one unit of government or control.

The main justification for this embrace of specialisation lay with the theory that specialisation results in greater economy of both effort and cost. At the level of the individual worker, two main benefits of it are postulated.

1   Either labour with lower intelligence or fewer aptitudes can be recruited at lower cost to perform the tasks, or the worker can be trained more quickly (which itself reduces expenditure) to perform them.

2   The worker becomes more skilled or expert in the limited operations and is able to produce more in a given time with fewer errors, thus giving more quantity and quality per unit of cost.

It is assumed in all of this that the extension of the process of subdivision will produce no ill-effects in terms of motivation and commitment. Recent research suggests that this assumption is ill founded (Kasl, 1976). Even in situations where considerable fractionalisation is technically possible, the effect of further fractionalisation may be to reduce worker commitment to and motivation for the task to an extent which proves unacceptable from the standpoint of achieving necessary coordination and control.

At the level of the factory, concentration on a limited range of products fostered a growth of similar expertise on a group basis and produced similar results in terms of cost. This approach and these outcomes were not confined to the new manufacturers of the first industrial revolution. Albeit more slowly and with less spectacular results in terms of cost-savings, these same principles came to be embraced by the public service (Fulton Committee on the Civil Service *Report*, 1968) and other service organisations such as the schools and colleges and hospitals. Modern, industrialised society became a society of specialist individuals and specialist organisations.

Not every person and organisation attained the same degree of specialisation because variations in demand precluded this. In the case of individuals, demand for a complete personal service allowed professionals to continue as 'generalists'. Other work proved technically difficult to subdivide so that the workers doing it were able to continue in a similar generalist mould. But the growth in the numbers of semi-skilled workers over the past century attested to the success of management in subdividing very many work tasks.

The size of the market for a particular product was largely instrumental in determining the size of, and the extent of specialisation in, the workplace, and coincidentally, the basic production technology employed. Short runs in the manufacture of the product limited the scope for individual and machine specialisation and imposed the discipline of a batch-production technology; long runs increased the scope for both kinds of specialisation and allowed a mass (line-flow) production technology to be developed. In time, both the batch and the line-flow systems were facilitated by the growth of physical technology (as with Computer Assisted Manufacture or automated chemical processes).

Autonomous developments in markets and the impact of merger and marketing operations by undertakings have themselves served to create a technological structure over industry in which a variety of distinct situations can be identified. These are to be defined by the extent to which specialisation is facilitated by the market position of the undertaking and by the extent to which control of actual work processes is in the hands of persons or of machines. The resultant 2×2 matrix finds a place for the different categories which Woodward (1958) used in her South-East Essex study:

	Human Control	Machine Control
Batch production (short runs)	*Jobbing shop Bespoke tailor*	*CAM*
Line-flow production (long runs)	*Traditional car assembly line*	*Petro-chemical plant*

Job simplification, when applied to employment work has limits set by the market (scale), the available physical technology, and its potential for alienating the worker if carried to extremes. Specialisation also imposes the necessity for coordination and, therefore, for organisation itself as part of the technology of coping with the material environment.

The Development of Control Technology

Coordination and control of the specialised activities of specialist workers is a first justification of organisation. What is divided has to be put back together again at the level of the working group as a whole. The amounts of specialised activity have to be balanced around a standard derived from the output of finished good or service required. The interdependence of the different jobs (and the people performing them) imposes the necessity for a kind of discipline, established through 'organisational' rules and procedures intended to bind the individuals concerned.

The strategies of management control, associated with selection, supervision, and incentive (discussed above, pp 18–23) and adopted in different circumstances of time and space, rest on distinct principles and make quite different demands on those who are caught up in them.

The strategy which relies on being able to secure fully trained workers at the point of selection and on their responsible exercise of occupational autonomy during the period of employment, emphasises the possibility and desirability of achieving spontaneous consensus within the working group on the questions of what to do, how, and when. A model derived from mediaeval guild (or professional) organisations and carried into the industrial era by the craftsmen associated with the early trade unions, it has now secured a new vogue from the concept of the 'autonomous working group'. In its modern form it attempts to increase the significance of work for the worker by restoring to the working group some of the decisions which in the interim period have been abrogated first by supervisors and subsequently by management functionaries.

The quickened pace of technological change in the industrial period spelled the doom of this recruited-consensus strategy. It was most generally replaced by one which emphasised 'supervision'. The main decisions about what, when, and how to work now became the province of the formal working group leader, the foreman or supervisor, and he or she in turn became management's first line representative and a filter-amplifier in the communication between management and worker. Dependent on external circumstances (for example, the state of the labour market), the supervisor's responsibility would be discharged by relying on threats (of dismissal) or promises (of reward) – the origin of the stick-and-carrot approach to the control of the labour process.

Increases in scale of production, size of work organisation, and complexities of the man-machine relationship might account for the demise of this system of control. By the end of last century, all of these things occurred together, and a new strategy of control based on precise definition of tasks and measurement of performance by specialist management functionaries emerged. This was the era of 'scientific management' in which industrial engineers, following the precepts of F W Taylor, Frank and Lillian Gilbreth, and F Gantt, took over the functions of defining and measuring activities previously in the hands of the generalist foremen. These were the people who produced the rules and procedures to be followed in work activity; they were quickly joined by others who produced rules of discipline or conduct all designed to control the behaviour of employees, now that consensus and the personal authority of the supervisor could no longer be relied on to achieve the desired ends.

The Concept of a Control System

Behind these developments in control technology, which led to the utilisation of CAD, CAM, and FMS, lies the development and application of the notion of a 'system'. This concept has shown itself to be widely applicable as a basis for developing understanding as well as control of phenomena. It underpins developments in electrical, electronic, and mechanical engineering and has provided significant insights into the working of complex organisations (regarded as systems). Its usefulness for management lies in its ability to increase understanding of the boundary control function in which leaders and managers engage. In early characterisations of systems, this function was associated with 'controllers' (Shone and Paterson, 1963), but more recently it has come to be associated with the notion of a managerial 'brain' in complex organisations (Argyris and Schon, 1978).

As early as 1956, Boulding demonstrated that systems differ significantly in their capacity for control and consequently in their complexity. Some are simple closed-loop systems and some are complex open systems, some capable of controlling only limited parts of the environment and some able to control a wide range of variables (see also Buckley, 1967). All systems, however, have parts set in relationships with other parts, and depend on an exchange of matter or energy with their environment, regulate themselves, and have a capacity for equifinality (achieving an end from a variety of initial configurations).

The nature of a closed system of control is illustrated by the time-related control built into a street light. This allows the light to come on and go off at certain times of the day (when it is most probable that it will be darker than is desirable). But darkening caused by a thunderstorm at other times of the day will produce no response because the initial configuration does not allow for this.

The principles of thermostatic control of the temperature of a room are, in themselves, simple and straightforward, but they allow control to be exercised over temperature in response to temperature changes (not simply to time, as in the previous example). These depend on a means of sensing and measuring quantities (in this case, of heat), a communication process (feeding out and feeding back relevant information), and a servo-mechanism linked to the sensors and the source of heat. The essential ingredients are a target temperature (end) linked to an instrument for measuring actual temperature in the room and a means of comparison of the two, which generates a signal to activate a servo-mechanism which, in turn, will either switch on or switch off the heat supply. This is a simple control system because while it effectively controls the temperature within the set (temperature) tolerance limits, it does so only (or simply) in response to the system's initial configuration of parts and linkages.

Essentially similar elements and principles are applied within much more complex arrangements in computer controlled machine tools (where the speed of operation of the computer allows them to be applied swiftly and repeatedly to effect control over a much more complex set of variables). The effect of this built-in capacity to review extremely large numbers of 'either-or' choices, is to give the machine the appearance of being able to think, or to work out rational solutions to logical problems.

SUMMARY

The industrial revolution reveals many examples of beneficial changes made in mechanical technology and of responsive changes in production and control technologies. New sources of power to drive machines and take away the necessity for people to use their own energies to produce goods and services, allied with new specialist machines and tools, attracted innovations in ways of organising production activities and in controlling the remaining labour contribution to production.

These developments had the effect of making more detailed the control of the human contribution to work. This, in turn, was achieved through developments in organisational technology which left a legacy of elaborate models of organisation intended as responses to these changes in market size and supportive mechanical technology.

ORGANISATIONAL TECHNOLOGY

Many authors have found it helpful to employ system models to increase our understanding of organisations as instruments of control. Parsons and Selznick, in particular, took up the notion of 'system', treating human enterprises as if they were *open* systems (where 'open' implies that the system is capable of realising a single end from a much greater variety of initial configurations of roles and relationships). This view of organisations contrasts somewhat with that which treats them as purely rational or mechanical instruments which happen to use human beings as tools; it finds some place within the organisation as a system for independent human action.

Most organisation theories can be condensed to three essential ingredients: people, structure, and process, which are also the three ingredients recognised by general system theorists (Baskin and Aronoff, 1980, p 1; Roethlisberger, 1968, p 304). The differences between them lie in the manner in which each is defined and related to the other two elements.

The natural system theories of organisation perceive it as composed of a number of interrelated and interdependent roles (or parts) which perform different acts in pursuit of both common and distinct (though not necessarily incompatible) goals and accept some common and some specific norms as governing their behaviour. The spontaneous actions of the parts are then seen to produce a kind of equilibrium, an adjustment to, and an accommodation of the environment at any moment in time. This places emphasis on the 'whole' (not merely the rational features considered in Weber's model of bureaucracy) and on the *spontaneous* nature of action (in place of the action which is compelled or coerced by functionaries).

Parsons' main contribution to thinking about organisational technology lay in his identification of the four main types of problem which such a system had to deal with − through the roles of the organisation's members. Two of these, adaptation and goal attainment, he saw as related to the external environment, and the other two, integration and latency, as related to the internal environment (or to the maintenance of the instrument in a healthy condition so that it could deal effectively with the external environment, as expressed by Selznick, 1948). These, under various labels, have become the common currency of discussions of organisational and management development and figure in many of the programmes advanced to assist in these processes.

Adaptation is the process whereby the human and material resources relate to the external environment in a realistic manner and whereby they can work on that environment in the interests of achieving the organisation's objectives. Market intelligence and advertising are examples of these processes in operation in private industry.

Goal attainment is concerned with the general process of co-ordination of the activities of all concerned, with the particular processes which contribute to this of identifying and applying relevant principles and norms, and with taking and implementing the necessary decisions as to action.

Integration is the process of bringing about sufficient solidarity or consensus of value and norms to enable it to function in a sufficiently unified manner to prevent disruption (and thus inability to pursue goals).

Latency (or pattern maintenance and tension management) is concerned, on the one hand, with developing sufficient harmony or compatibility between the member's organisational role and the obligations on the incumbent from outside the organisation, and, on the other, with the development in the individual of sufficient motivation or commitment to enable him or her to cope with the organisational task set.

It is part of Parsons' theory that each of these may achieve prominence in different circumstances of time and space. Economic organisations tend to be oriented primarily to the first, governmental organisations to the second, political parties and hospitals to the third, and schools and similar bodies to the fourth. It is also part of the theory that any organisation will be required to give some weight to all four if it is to survive; consequently, the weight may be varied in response to changes in pressures stemming from either inside or outside the organisation (either 'spontaneously' or as a result of *dictat*).

Selznick's main contribution lies in his identification of five imperatives for reducing uncertainties for organisational members and for maintaining the system in a healthy operating condition:

1   the security of the organisation as a whole in relation to the social forces in the environment;

2   the stability of the lines of authority and communications;

3   the stability of informal relations within the organisation;

4   the continuity of policy and of the sources of its determination;

5   a homogeneity of outlook with respect to the meaning and role of the organisation (Selznick, 1948, p 34).

Some of these have a clear affinity with some of the points emphasised by Parsons, but together they focus attention on aspects of organisation which, while they may be attended to 'spontaneously', may also be regarded as a specific responsibility of those, like managers, who claim a special mandate to act in the name of the organisation as a whole. For example, managers might respond to pressures to achieve greater competitiveness and efficiency by creating a division between the brainwork and the execution of production and by developing a more rational model of the 'administration' of the 'brainwork' (which is one interpretation of F W Taylor's contribution).

Extensions of the Natural System Construct

Later thinking about organisational forms related them more directly to the situations in which they operated. This led to attempts to demonstrate the likelihood of a stage-phase progression of organisational forms being relevant to different stages of the undertaking's life cycle. This approach was based on the proposition that it is possible to treat the undertaking as if it had a life of its own and that, more than this, this life progressed through a cycle not unlike that of the human being. This may be no more than a useful heuristic and should not be taken to mean literally that the organisation can be personified in this way.

Lippitt (1969) makes use of this biological model in his suggestions that organisations can be regarded as passing through a series of life phases (such as childhood, youth, adulthood (or maturity) and senile decline) each of which has its defining characteristics, and that these phases can be seen as separated by 'crises' (birth, puberty, maturation and death).

Using these as labels rather than exact analogues, childhood is characterised by the tentative solutions which are relevant to coping with the consequences of creation; these solutions will focus on a longer or shorter period of learning how to cope with the internal and external environments. During this phase, the organisation may be characterised in its external relations by an aggressive and challenging attack on the market, and internally by volatility of roles and relationships, probably in what will be seen as a highly personalised working environment.

In time, the basic processes of learning (Brim and Wheeler, 1966) and adjustment are completed, and a more stable relationship with the market will have been established. The organisation may then find itself at a (puberty) threshold, where it has to determine whether it can move towards a more secure and stable set of relationships with the external and internal environments. The volatility and highly personalised approach of the earlier phase needs to be replaced by appropriate procedures and systems which will reduce some of the inherent uncertainty for the members of the organisation and equip it to maintain and develop its market position.

Success during this phase of youth may be brought to an end with a succession crisis, where the need to secure new talent at different levels may produce tensions. The need may now appear for a stable organisation to capitalise on the undertaking's market position and to ensure that the position is at least maintained. The organisation will also need to determine what kind of image it will seek to generate in the market place and in society, and once these questions have been answered, staff may need to be recruited and/or trained to implement the decisions.

The likelihood that this 'comfortable and secure' phase will continue for ever is small, and at some stage the organisation will become aware of the need for change — in its product portfolio and its market relationships. This middle life crisis may also prove traumatic, but it will lead to strategy, policy, and staffing changes as the organisation attempts to adjust to the situation as it is perceived. At this point, the analogy with the life cycle may break down, as it may be possible (as well as desirable) for the firm to move into a rejuvenated phase and relive a part or parts of the cycle.

If it does not succeed in doing this, it is likely to move into a phase of frustrating decline; both the market relationship and the internal relationships may become more tense and difficult to handle. Without rejuvenation, the outcome of this process is death by take-over or liquidation.

Each of the traditional crisis points is characterised by tensions that may be stimulated by changes which are either internal or external to the organisation, such as:

(a) when the external (market) demands move out of phase with the capacity of the organisation to deal with them in a rational and relevant way;

(b) when the internal (member) demands move out of phase with the capacity of the market to meet them (for example, with excessive demands for income or career development);

(c) when the phase of development reached in one part of the organisation is incompatible with the phases reached in others, leading to intradivisional tensions and traumas;

(d) when the environmental demands made on one part of the system take away resources which ought to be devoted to resolving problems in other parts of the undertaking.

It is to be supposed that each of these states of tension will stimulate coping behaviour and the possible development of rational solutions to the problems which give rise to them. Because these solutions will be different according to the phase reached, each of the phases identified can be characterised by the kinds of solution which are appropriate to them.

One insight which this mode of theorising offers is that which suggests that at different stages in the development process the type of organisation required to meet the surrounding conditions may be different. 'Youth', for example, may have more to gain from a spontaneous form of organisation which responds to normative controls, and 'maturity' more from a rule-constrained structure of the kind associated with bureaucracy.

The Bureaucracy

The 'bureaucracy' is a concept which we owe to Weber, who coined the term and described the main characteristics associated with it. What interested him is material to the argument being advanced here.

Weber noted that past systems of human cooperation had depended almost exclusively for their success on sentimental ties between the cooperators. The obvious example is provided by the family in the domestic system, where kinship ties complemented and even cemented work relationships; similar binding sentiments cemented relationships as different as those of the local community and the royal court. These were held together by norms of behaviour which everyone knew and accepted as guides to action.

What appeared during the last century – and what raised an interesting question in Weber's mind – was the organisation made up of specialists who were also strangers to one another (that is, without any prior or existing ties of sentiment). It seemed to be working efficiently enough, so on what did it rely to ensure this efficiency based on a necessary cooperation? Weber's answer to this was that it relied on control by either imposed or agreed rules of conduct, which were rationally derived from the requirements of the work being done and assigned the function and force of 'laws': it was an arrangement of 'rational-legal authority' through which the activities of workers were coordinated and controlled.

In its predominant modern form, this arrangement gives prominence to the specialist roles of those who were called on to administer the work, those for whom F W Taylor provided a function (the brainwork of production) and a philosophy (the absolute necessity for some small number of managers to define work tasks for the less capable masses of unskilled workers). These specialist roles Weber identified as administrative 'offices', and the rule (or government) by these office holders as 'bureaucracy'.

The model of bureaucracy that Weber advanced was one in which the spontaneity of cooperative activity in the natural system is replaced by a formalistic rationality and in which cognitive processes supersede sentimental ones. Fundamentally, the unwritten norms of the (natural) familial and communal systems are replaced by formal rules which are rationally derived (or created) to serve the ends of the cooperative activity and which assume the function of 'law' in that they bind those subject to them whether they internalise them or not.

This system of rational-legal authority possesses five distinct characteristics, which Weber saw as contributing to the observable efficiency of the administrative system in securing cooperation among people who were not bound by sentiment to their fellow workers:

1   The division of the total task of the organisation into specialist tasks which are then assigned as duties to individuals to create **offices** which they then hold as their own.

2   The arrangement of these offices into a **hierarchy**, usually on a monocratic principle, so that one person (office-holder) will assume responsibility for the control of the work of a number of subordinates who then report and respond only to this one superordinate.

3   The governance of the behaviour of the members of this whole edifice through a code of **abstract rules and procedures** which serve to discipline and control the members and which are accepted because they are rationally established.

4   The adoption of the principle that members of the bureaucracy will act totally **impersonally** in their dealings with one another and with clients or customers.

5   The provision of the prospect of a **career** for members, with the opportunity to move through the hierarchy of offices, providing the necessary incentive to participants to accept the principles on which the structure is based and to act in accordance with the underlying values and rules (Burns and Stalker, 1961, pp 105−6).

Although Weber saw this kind of organisation as much more efficient than the earlier forms, others have pointed to the actual or potential limitations of this type of organisation.

The term bureaucracy can be used derogatively and as a way of poking fun at the modern form of organisation, particularly in the public service sector. In so far as this is justified, it is because all of these distinguishing characteristics can, in appropriate circumstances, contribute to inefficiency − office being used to avoid other than narrowly conceived responsibility (Friedman, 1955), hierarchy permitting buck passing, rules becoming red tape (Merton, 1949), formalistic impersonality being associated with lack of interest or concern (Blau, 1956) and career becoming an end in itself (Burns, 1977).

In other words, bureaucracy can just as easily operate 'dysfunctionally' as 'functionally'. It is no universal remedy or panacea, although it may be more appropriate at some stages of development than at others. If the pure bureaucracy were ever to be established, however, it would probably as readily demonstrate debilitating maladies as it would healthy efficiency.

Tendencies in Rational Organisation

For this reason, rational organisation or bureaucracy should be seen as an abstraction, an indication of the direction towards which impersonal organisations incline (Burns and Stalker, 1961, pp 96-125). All modern organisations have features of the kind which Weber identified to some degree, some being 'more bureaucratic' and others 'less bureaucratic' (without ever ceasing to be based on rational-legal authority and without becoming familial or communal organisations). Bureaucracy becomes a tendency in all modern organisations, and bureaucratisation the process by which it is increased.

There remains considerable scope for variation among all the main dimensions singled out by Weber. These differences may prove crucial to the definition of organisational character and the manner of organisational operation and functioning. Burns provides two polar models of this kind of rational organisation which he sees as related to the degrees of stability and instability found in the organisations' environments. He refers to these as **mechanistic and organic systems** of administration.

The 'mechanistic' system is a rather rigid form of Weber's ideal-type bureaucracy, with closely defined tasks (or offices) which demarcate work territory, strict hierarchies of authority, communication and status, highly developed systems of rules and procedures covering all eventualities, compartmentalised activities, and carefully defined promotion routes, all of which have to be defended from marauders. Many of these are only possible if the 'organisation' has been operating for a considerable time in a stable environment; for as long as the environment continues in that form, they then serve their purpose. It describes a form of organisation which, if it has market location at all, might be found in the BCG's star situation.

The 'organic' system remains a rational organisation, but it functions as an altogether looser network of offices and less rigid hierarchy, in which rules function more like norms, being meant to guide but not enslave, and in which there is less concern to defend occupational/job territory and more willingness to contribute generally to the accomplishment of the organisation's main tasks. In this case, the looser arrangement may exist because it never had the chance to become rigid (as with the wildcat undertaking in the BCG classification) or because management recognises that it has to cope with a changed environment to which the old rules can no longer apply (as with cash-cow or, more probably, dog undertakings).

Organisational Variety

The fact that it is possible to identify variants of this kind suggests that the forms of control which Weber associated with the preceding systems are not completely dead. On the one hand, the model is regarded as applicable to the 'informal' organisations of workers; this was recognised by Roethlisberger and Dickson in their distinction between the managerial logic of efficiency and the workers' logic of sentiment which they found in the Hawthorne plant of the Western Electric Company in Chicago (Roethlisberger and Dickson, 1939).

On the other hand, it was thought to be found, albeit in imperfect form, in certain kinds of organisation where environmental conditions conspired to re-establish the normative controls of earlier structures. Burns's identification of an 'organic' system in the volatile conditions of the Scottish electronics industry after the Second World War offers one illustration of the idea that something more than a mere formalistic rationality was important to these organisations' operation. Selznick's experience with the Tennessee Valley Authority (TVA) suggested to him that something similar was animating that structure. The more diffuse experience of many managers with small undertakings has helped to keep alive the idea that there was something more available to ensure order and control at work than the rationally derived rules of bureaucracy.

This idea is also supported by the findings of such surveys as that made by Woodward (1958). She found that firms pursuing different objectives, and using distinct mechanical and production technologies to do so, were also organising and managing on different principles. She used two categories of objective: those of satisfying the demands of individual or small groups of them and those of meeting the demands of the mass market; and three categories of technology: unit and small batch production, mechanised line production, and process production. Using a number of measures (span of control of top and first line managers, of levels in the management hierarchy, and of the relative numbers of line and staff managers) and assessing the approach to relationships, she suggested that there were three distinct sets of 'rules' in evidence and that those of scientific management were followed only in the firm which aimed to supply a mass market and used a mechanised line technology to enable it to do so (Woodward, 1958).

The determination of which form of rational organisation is most appropriate is likely to reflect either or both of two perceptions:

1   The source of the greatest threat to the stability of the operating system – which may, for example, lie with customers, stockholders, workers or suppliers and seem to call for more or less centralisation of control in order to deal with it effectively.

2   The location of the problem which is most amenable to solution by application of available technology – whether this is perceived (along the lines suggested by Porter's value chain) as a problem of product development, market, production, motivation, or human capability, and amenable to R & D, take-over, marketing, retooling or rescheduling, disciplinary or training solutions.

Where the perceptions of the nature of the main pressures seem to demand an immediate and uniform response, the monocratic bureaucracy appears to be appropriate; where they are relatively un-structured and diffuse in their demands and seem to require measured consideration and 'innovative' solutions, the more organic or natural system model appears to be more appropriate. These show up in pressures towards centralisation and decentralis-ation (Kruisinga, 1954).

The pressure towards centralisation is created by the need or desire for unity or integrity in overall performance to meet certain standards: these may be set, for example, by the customer, or they may be set up by the undertaking as a matter of policy. Where product quality and delivery dates are established as sacrosanct, and where the working groups are regarded as untrustworthy, co-ordination of production activity may be drawn to the centre in a monocratic structure. This is no inevitable tendency: the develop-ment of quality circles implies that there is a decentralised solution to the quality problem, but it still depends on sufficient trust being present or being created.

The pressure towards decentralisation responds to the need to allow sufficient discretion to the executants of any action to facilitate their getting the required action right. Handling complex tasks (where complexity derives from the unstructured nature of the problem being handled or the uncertainty surrounding the efficacy of any given solution) will tend to stimulate a devolved structure of decision-taking, and thus to deny the relevance of monocratic control.

In reality, these pressures are likely to be present together, but affecting different issues and strategies. The effect is likely to be that some problems are tackled on a centralised basis while others are dealt with in a devolved fashion, according to both the perceived source of the problem and the perceived availability and applic-ability of the solution. As Peters and Waterman (1982) have suggested, the successful organisation is likely to be one which displays tight and loose controls simultaneously.

Organisation as Technology

'Organisation' is what results from attempts to define work tasks and work relationships in the interests of integrating what is other-wise divided and to protect the system of norm- or rule-making which produces the guides for human action from internal and external challenges. It is, however, no more a single 'thing' than a machine is a single 'thing'.

A variety of ways of organising exist, ranging from the natural and spontaneous to the formal and contrived forms to which different labels have been applied. These, it seems, may demonstrate greater relevance to certain types of situation than others, and a deliberate choice has usually to be made to ensure successful adaptation to the environmental pressures. They may also demonstrate a greater or lesser relevance to the handling of specific problems: marketing activities may lend themselves to one form of organisation and production activities to quite another. As the pursuit of the 'one best way' falls off in the face of a realisation that no such holy grail exists, more managers are coming to recognise that organisational technology confronts managers with choices.

Whether the human enterprise 'gets right' this mix of approaches to organisation and control, will depend on the availability of people with appropriate diagnostic skills and motivations who have the authority to take and implement the appropriate decisions.

SOCIO-TECHNICAL SYSTEMS

The tendency to regard machine technology and organisational technology as quite distinct phenomena responding to different rules has been challenged in work carried out by the Tavistock Institute of Human Relations. This has demonstrated that maintenance of the dichotomy is likely to cause management to miss solutions to the problems associated with means of production. The classic study in this context was that carried out in the Durham coalfield by Trist and Bamforth (1951). This showed how the social organisation of workers at work was influenced by the requirements of the machine technology used, and how a change in the machine technology could lead to considerable inefficiencies if it did not permit a supportive social organisation to develop.

This, at a micro-level, identifies similar considerations to those which, at a macro-level, support the observation that the development of rotary motion in the steam engine created the condition in which the factory mode of organisation and operation was likely. The rigidity of the shafting and belting associated with the steam engine as prime mover virtually dictated that economy in use could be achieved only by bringing a large number of machines and their operatives into close proximity. Similarly, the greater flexibility associated with the electric motor permitted greater decentralisation in the organisation of manual work, just as the microcomputer allows greater decentralisation of routine administrative work.

The realisation developed from this insight that the machine and social systems might best be considered together when decisions were being taken about possible changes in either one. This was justified on the grounds that to consider them together enables total (as distinct from partial) solutions to problems of control to be found. A change in machine technology might carry 'obvious' benefits in terms of productivity and might be favoured as a consequence. As the Trist and Bamforth studies showed, however, these benefits might be lost by failing to take the social consequences of the change into account simultaneously.

In an early paper, Emery put forward the basic proposition to the effect that:

> 'There is considerable agreement amongst specialists that ... problems are inter-related: beyond a certain point the solution of one kind of problem depends upon solving some of the others [because] there is some apparent order in the way that these problems depend upon each other'
> (Emery, 1959, p 1).

Earlier, Williams had suggested that the solution of this kind of problem required that economic and political systems ought to be brought within the analytical framework. The ultimate position could, in line with this, involve recognising that the system concept may be thought of as a psychological, economic, social and technical one, and all separate specialist facets might need to be considered in interaction with one another.

Emery rejects this on the grounds that the social (or human) and the technical are real (or substantial) whereas the others are concerned with 'analytical abstractions':

> 'This confuses the concrete or substantial referents with analytical abstractions. Substantially, an enterprise is a body of men and material means: analytically one may and should abstract from the concrete social relations existing between these things aspects concerning the allocation of limited resources for consumption or production, power and responsibility, etc'
> (Emery, 1959, p 5f).

This emphasises the fundamental relationship of man to tools (or machines), which is arguably of a quite different order from the relationship of man to systems of authority, power, or economy.

This more fundamental (or more concrete) relationship presents itself in a hierarchical form, beginning with that between the man and his hand-tools, moving through levels of man-machine and gang-machine systems, and reaching the level of the man in the context of a complex manufacturing or processing plant. Depending on which type is pertinent in the particular case, the potential for influence by either element (social or mechanical) on the other can be expected to vary systematically. The craftsman using handtools is in command of them; the more complex processing plant is more likely to be in command of the person monitoring its operation at a console.

Defining Socio-Technical Systems

The definition of the socio-technical system depends on the identification of similar fundamental elements to those found in any general systems theory. Emery suggests that the solution of the problem of definition begins with 'the three main stages in the analysis of an enterprise' (Emery, 1959, p 7):

1   'The analysis of the component parts to establish the nature of each in so far as it contributes to the performance of the enterprise and creates or responds to requirements of the other parts. The first components to be distinguished for purposes of analysis are:
    (a)   the technological; and
    (b)   the "work relationship structure" and its constituent occupational roles.

2   The analysis of the interrelations of these parts with particular reference to the problems of internal coordination and control which the definition of the constituent parts creates for the enterprise.

3   The detection and analysis of the relevant external environment of the enterprise, and the manner in which the enterprise manages its relations to it' (Emery, 1959, p 7).

For Emery, this provides the basic frame of reference of the socio-technical system. On this basis, the second function of developing and utilising an adequate set of descriptive concepts can be developed. In his illustration of the dynamics of building up the socio-technical system model, he relies heavily upon the work of Trist and Bamforth (1951) and Rice (1958).

   The parts and relationships in the Emery-Trist conception of a socio-technical system are defined by linking them with their contribution to the realisation of task-objectives. If a firm exists to produce Mini cars for a mass market, this objective colours the task-objectives of all the roles within it. If a firm exists to build power stations for a single customer, this objective will influence the task-objectives to the extent that they must be defined quite differently. The way in which the enterprise 'manages its relationships with its (market or any other) environment' is a prime influencer of the form the definition will take.

The original Trist conception and the later refinement by Emery of the socio-technical system model are both linked to a static or quasi-stationary concept of equilibrium. Trist makes the simple distinction between the 'technological system' and the 'social structure consisting of the occupational roles that have been institutionalised in its use' (Trist, 1951, p 5).

The use of this term 'institutionalised' implies that there is some relatively stable pattern which has greater value than any other pattern which might be applied. Within this framework, Trist is concerned to depict the characteristics of both the social and the technological systems and, more specifically, of the modes of inter-action between them. In line with this latter objective, only those features of, say, an engineering system which carry over to influence the social system need to be distinguished; while the actual mechanical functioning of a machine may be important to an engineer, this can be ignored where it does not carry over to influence the role of its human operator.

Technological Components

Emery suggests that although any particular technology will inevitably throw up its unique components and modes of inter-relationship with the social system, there are classes of technological components which will have general import and which can therefore function as a check-list for purpose of analysis.

1   *The natural characteristics of the material being worked with:* its hardness, variability, cleanliness, etc., any of which can have an impact on the form of work roles and (for example) the strain associated with them. One illustration of this is the differential impact on the role of producing 'teeth' for zip fasteners from metal (comparatively hard and dirty but capable of being worked to close tolerances) or nylon (comparatively soft and clean, but difficult to work to close tolerances).

2   *The immediate physical work setting*, including such features as the temperature, dustiness, wetness or smelliness of the workplace, which may be associated with the materials worked on or with exogenous factors (such as the weather in cases of outdoor working). Any of these can affect role

perceptions and role strain, and sometimes they are recognised either in the payment of abnormal condition money or by being given some weight in a job evaluation plan.

3 *The spatio-temporal setting of work*, involving such dimensions as geographical spread of operations through a factory or distribution through the working day or working week. Interest in this usually focuses on the implications of variations on these dimensions for interaction, communication, and supervisory control, as is illustrated in Scott's study of the changeover from handmill to stripmill technology in North Wales (Scott et al,1957), or in Trist and Bamforth's study of changeover in the mining industry from bord and pillar to longwall methods of coal getting in Durham (Trist and Bamforth, 1951).

4 *The level of mechanisation or automation*, which is frequently singled out for special attention as a technological influence on control of work roles. This aspect has been studied frequently, for example, in respect of assembly lines in the car industry (Walker and Guest, 1952) or in more general terms in Woodward's survey of industry in South East Essex (Woodward, 1958; 1965; 1970).

5 *The Unit Operations* or those operations which have to be performed in units because of the way the technology impinges on production. The kind of difference which is identified here is that which would appear on a engineer's flow process diagrams of, for example, the traditional assembly line and the kind of autonomous working group structure created in the Saab and Volvo car plants: the transportation operations required and the buffer stocks which may have to be held carry the implications for relationships there.

6 *The degree of centrality of the technical operation involved*, including the degree of precision with which the operation has to be performed to meet the requirements of other operations (which may themselves vary in number). This has clear implications for the skill of the operative but it is also likely to influence the position of the operation in the status hierarchy surrounding the work and thereby the prestige of the operative. In a traditional steelworks, the technical operations associated with first-hand melters, rollermen, or furnacemen helped, by their importance (centrality), to place them high in a prestige hierarchy.

7   *The boundary conditions of maintenance and supply*, both of which link the internal operations with the environment and cause, at least potentially, fluctuations in pressures on the inside roles. In some cases, the maintenance and supply operations are in the same hands and in some cases in different ones. As mechanisation increases, all three functions may be brought together within the one set of roles, thus reducing the degree of specialisation associated with their previous handling.

Analysis of these dimensions is regarded as necessary to the analysis of roles and relationships. As Emery argues:

'Sufficient empirical work has been done to indicate that it is the rule, not the exception, for these different technological facts to exert a significant influence on the social system. The failure to consider these facts makes it difficult to assess the validity of the findings of so many of the social scientific studies done in this field, including many done on the effects of automation. Their generalis- ations, in ignoring the technological variable, run the risk of attributing causal effects to factors that are merely concomitant'
(Emery, 1959, p 15).

But, it would be wrong to proceed from this point on the assumption that there is a direct, one-for-one relationship between the tasks and task relationships outlined here and the roles and role relationships of the social system itself. It is possible to make a distinction between the technological and the social, and between the external and the internal systems (Homans, 1951), but not possible to describe the relationship between them except in terms of mutual interdependence.

This is because, within each system, there are possibilities for variation which are contained in the system itself, as well as those arising from the interaction between them. For instance, tasks vary on a number of dimensions because of the technological options which remain open within that system; and roles vary on a number of dimensions because of those left open within that system. Con- sideration of interdependence between the two systems must there- fore permit each range of variability to have different implications for the tasks or roles of the other system.

Socio-Technical System Analysis

Once the validity of the fundamental proposition had been demonstrated in a variety of contexts, it was then but a short step to present a mode of analysis which allowed both social and material considerations to be analysed together. In 1966, Herbst put forward his nine-step 'critical specification design', related to process industry, and Hill offered a similar seven-step procedure related to service and advisory departments in 1971. These take up the approach of the industrial engineer and apply it not merely to the analysis of individual work tasks and flows but also to the human or social context within which it is to be carried out.

Herbst's 'critical specification design' takes the form of a sequence of nine steps to be followed in establishing a devolved organisational system (Hill, 1971, Appendix 5, pp 230-43). It indicates the broad design issues which need to be dealt with to create an appropriate socio-technical system for a continuous process technology but does not specify the dimensions of every variable.

1   *Initial Scanning* This involves identifying the main characteristics of the production system and its environment and the location of the main problems found in it. It examines layout, organisation structure, system inputs and outputs, the transformation process, the main 'variances' and their sources, the relationship betweeen the production system and the department in which it exists and production and system objectives.

2   *Identification of Unit Operations* The main purpose here is to identify the transformations effected by activities in the production process. The purpose of each relatively self-contained unit operation is described by reference to its inputs of men and machines, its transformations, and its outputs.

3   *Identification of key process variances and their inter-relationships* This step involves the analysis of the variances (defined as deviations from standard or from specification) which stem from raw material or from the nature of the production process itself (those arising from breakdowns, plant faults, and human factors being ignored at this stage) and which significantly affect system performance. A key variance is determined on four criteria: effects on output quality, quantity, operating costs, and social costs (such as stress, effort, and hazard).

4 *Analysis of the Social System* At this stage the organisational structure is reviewed to identify the major formal and informal groupings in the social system and their inter-relationships. A 'table of variance control' is then drawn up to 'show the extent to which the key variances are at present controlled by the social system' (Hill, 1971, p 233). This table lists each key variance, and against each records where in the process it occurs, where it is observed, where and by whom it is controlled, what tasks are necessary to control it, and the nature and source of the information necessary for the control activities to be carried out (Hill, 1971, p 235).

Analysis is also made of ancillary activities, layout, and dispersion of workers in time and space, workers' knowledge of each others' roles, the payment system, the extent to which roles meet a list of psychological needs and areas of frequent breakdown. Suggestions for job redesign which occur to the analyst during the course of this and later activities are recorded in a final column on the chart.

5 *Perceptions of roles* This continues the analysis of the social system. The workers' psychological requirements are worked out in interviews at step 4 and further job design proposals are developed from the results. This step completes the analysis of the production sytstem.

6-9 These subsequent steps are concerned with examining how and to what extent the maintenance (step six) and the supply and user systems (step seven) impinge on and affect the production system. This is followed by an examination of the manner in which the wider environment impinges on the achievement of objectives in the production system, and any proposals for change in strategy or policy are noted (step eight). A programme of action for redesigning the system to effect improvement in it is then drawn up (step nine).

This exercise was carried out in a refinery using process technology. The method developed was specific to that situation. Other situations are amenable to similar treatment, but differences in the production technology (batch production or cyclical working patterns through shifts, for example) might call for modifications of the actual programme adopted here.

Hill (1971, p 244) drew up a method of role analysis which he initially applied to a personnel and a catering department where no 'production' system as such was involved. This kind of situation he found amenable to a similar approach adopted by Herbst, but demanding fewer analytical steps. His seven-step model requires

1   General scanning to obtain a general overview

2   Identification of the departmental system objectives to provide a basis for later assessment of performance

3   Analysis of the system's roles and role objectives using a method similar to that involved in step 2

4   Measurement of roles against psychological needs assessed on the basis of interviews

5   Identifying interactions on the job to indicate groupings of roles

6   Production of change proposals in the form of an action programme

7   Establishing a framework for managing the department concerned by objectives (Hill, 1971, p 130).

This type of analysis, Hill suggests, can best be carried out by a small action group provided that it is focused on a small and not very complex unit of the 'production' system. It provides a form of training for learners in which an important element of system and control is introduced into the work programme.

Socio-Technical System Design

The design of socio-technical systems has usually been attempted in the context of the autonomous working group at the shop floor level, or the product team at managerial levels. Where these have been established, it is claimed (as, for example, by Hill) that they effect achievements in four main areas:

1   organisation and procedures, reflected in wider dissemination of company or departmental objectives at one level or abolition of clocking in favour of an honour system at another;

2   job redesign, resulting in an amount of job enlargement;

3   responsibility and commitment, shown in some improved attitudes towards work and in some relaxation of demarcation restrictions;

4   improved performance, shown in cuts in the incidence of overtime and some improvements in productivity.

Such improvements are usually found in *some* areas *some* of the time, not in all of them all of the time. This should be taken to indicate that what is attempted here is no panacea, and to suggest that situational factors are, here as elsewhere, important influences on achievement.

Reading:

Blau and Scott (1963).
Burns and Stalker (1961).
Daniel (1987).
Dunkerley (1975).
Emery (1959; 1969).
Emery and Trist (1969).

Herbst (1966).
Hill (1971).
Korach (1966).
Miller and Rice (1967).
Toffler (1985).
Woodward (1958).

8 Personnel Policy

Three features, objectives, strategies and policies, define the 'character' or 'personality' of an undertaking. The objectives point to what it is attempting to achieve. The strategies indicate the methods it proposes to adopt in achieving them. The policies reveal the consideration it desires to show in pursuing the objectives through these strategies. These, different in themselves, will combine in ways that are unique to the particular undertaking.

Policy, by analogy with personality in the individual, tells us something about the kind of undertaking it is, and by analogy with culture at the level of the society, indicates something of its preferred design for living in its chosen environment. Recently, Peters and Waterman (1982) drew on their experience of American industry to present a statement of the nature of the successful company, and in so doing, created an image of the main 'principles' of policy adopted in the successful undertaking (Table 10).

The substance of an undertaking's policy is usually drawn from a number of different sources, some of them broadly cultural and some of them essentially empirical. The first source contributes values (to influence objectives), ideas (which influence strategies) and practices which form part of the 'designs for living' established in the culture. The second contributes more immediate values, ideas, and methods which may or may not accord with the moral and technical imperatives of the culture.

Policies usually express a keenness to conform with the stipulations of the law of the land as the embodiment of the major cultural imperatives in order to avoid, at bare minimum, being 'outlawed' as a result of conduct. The undertaking will aim to conform with the requirements of the Companies Act and with legislation on discrimination, but frequently finds a way of interpreting these requirements in a manner which is both lawful and more consistent with the 'law of the situation'. For example, Peters and Waterman's principles relating specifically to treatment of employees represent

Table 10

Attributes of successful companies

Peters and Waterman's survey (1982) of successful, continuously innovative companies in the USA suggested to them that such companies displayed eight attributes:

1. *A Bias for Action.* They paid great attention to analysis and to the need to think out courses of action, but were not inhibited from acting by pandering to this need. Action was expected to follow analysis – and quickly.

2. *A Closeness to Customers.* They provide quality, service, and reliability, but they also listen to their customers and often receive ideas for new and improved products from them.

3. *Autonomy and Entrepreneurship.* They foster many 'leaders' at all levels of the organisation, encouraging people to innovate and see their innovations through. Staff are not kept on a short rein, which inhibits them, but held together in loose networks of relationship.

4. *Productivity through People.* They treat rank and file staff as the source of quality and productivity gain: this implies a policy or style which respects the individual as a person.

5. *Hands-on, value-driven.* They maintain close contacts between the members of the organisation, to foster the growth of a 'culture', whose values all members of staff share.

6. *Stick to the Knitting.* These companies stick close to the business they know: they do not usually seek to become conglomerates in which units are disparate and non-complementary.

7. *Simple form, lean staff.* The structure of these organisations is generally elegantly simple, and their headquarters staff is kept small in size. Matrix organisations are generally avoided.

8. *Simultaneous loose-tight properties.* These companies display apparent paradoxes: they are centralised and decentralised; they have central controls and divisional autonomy; the norms of the culture are relied on to hold the whole together.

These companies showed themselves committed to people (whether customers or employees) and to action (to improve productivity, quality, or service). They expected a professional approach from everyone concerned and respected and rewarded those who provided it. They rejected the idea that any problem needed long investigation and a report before any action could be contemplated; they looked for rapid action, accepting that this would produce mistakes which could nevertheless be tolerated.

one such response to circumstances which can be contained within broad cultural prescriptions and institutional constraints on the employment relationship.

But policies also express objectives and indicate strategies which may open up a potential conflict of values. This is most likely to occur where a policy statement indicates multiple objectives linked to the varying interests of the different stakeholders. As these are not always consistent with one another, any attempt to satisfy the aspirations of the stockholders may conflict with any simultaneous attempt to satisfy those of the employees. In Peters and Waterman's model (1982), this is contained by recognising an overarching principle of disciplining where one must create opportunities where one can – the principle behind their 'tight-loose' element.

These potentially conflicting stipulations are consequently permitted differential influence on the establishment of an undertaking's character and conduct. Certain principles of the culture, particularly those embedded in law, are acknowledged to be paramount and may actually influence choices. Others, particularly those associated with 'conventions' which do not have the force of law, may be verbally acknowledged but disregarded in practice, especially when they conflict with empirically derived indications of appropriate actions.

Similarly, some of the 'practical' or 'situational' pressures will receive more support than others. Where market trends indicate a likely loss of profitability unless certain remedial action is taken, that action is likely to be treated as more imperative than the action indicated by trends in public esteem needed to resurrect an image of the undertaking as a 'good employer'. These distinctions can be justified by appeal to the dominant values of the culture itself – such as the high value placed on 'trade' or 'productivity' *versus* the lower value place on 'satisfaction in work' – but any conflicts can be resolved at a purely pragmatic level, by the application of 'judgement' (see below, pp 242 et seq).

A higher order imperative in the one area will also take precedence over a lower order imperative in the other. Market-induced actions frequently oust considerations based on social conventions, and legally enforceable requirements will tend to take precedence over empirical solutions to problems.

THE NATURE OF POLICY

These statements assume a particular meaning for the term 'policy' chosen from several different ones available. Originally, policy referred to a course of action adopted by a government (Pen, 1959, p 9). This definition reflected the view that governments were not concerned to achieve specific tangible results, but rather to maintain order at home and abroad, both as a support for others engaged in decision-taking and as a desirable end in itself. In this context, policy indicated the way in which people would be expected to conduct themselves in their dealings and relations with others. Policy related, in the Aristotelian sense, to the morally practical aspects of life in the civilised society.

It has subsequently come to mean 'a systematic puposeful course of action in general' (Pen, 1959, p 9), particularly when applied to organisations. In this form, it embraces not merely the 'prudent conduct' (which the dictionary gives as one of the meanings of the word) but also the 'course of action', or the 'plan, method or series of manoeuvres for obtaining a specific goal or objective' (Brandt, 1973, p 11). Aristotle distinguished this more strategic aspect as being concerned with the technically practical acts of human creativity or production.

Currently, the two meanings are melded together in the post-Baconian mode, and 'policy' now embraces *both* civilised conduct *and* strategies for realising concrete objectives (Thomas, 1977, pp 79–93). Brech also defines it as embracing both 'the modes of thought and the body of principles laid down to underlie and to guide the activities of the firm (or other organisation) towards declared or known objectives' (Brech, 1975, p 37). Spence (1969, p 20) declares it to be the 'animating concept of management' revealed in 'a statement of company intention, purpose or objective' which is 'generally expressed in the broadest possible way'.

This historical distinction is not, however, universally drawn. Ouchi asserts that objectives in Japanese companies are usually defined by reference to the morally practical and American company objectives by reference to the technically practical, and concludes that in the Japanese setting, 'those who grasp the essence of the philosophy of values and beliefs (or ends and means) can deduce from the general statements an almost limitless number of specific rules or targets to suit changing conditions' (Ouchi, 1981, pp 34–5).

Strategy and Policy

There remains some point, however, in continuing with a distinction between 'strategy' (as concerned with the technically practical means to the realisation of concrete ends) and 'policy' (as having to do with the morally practical means to the realisation of more abstract social and political ends).

An organisation's strategy is normally embodied in a corporate plan. This usually identifies the concrete or material ends to be achieved by various courses of action and indicates broadly what that course of action is to be. The end here is to be recognised by its tangibility, and the means (increasingly in our 'scientific' culture) by its association with a theory of causality. The 'steps' to be taken are specific, tangible, and mandatory.

Policy statements frequently acknowledge the existence of such concrete objectives but say little about the economic strategies for realising them. Where strategies are referenced in them, they usually relate to organisational or social questions which need to be resolved so that the economic ends may be realised. For example, one statement in the Standard Telephones and Cables' policy document says that, 'For the foreseeable future, the Company will continue to operate as an organisation with centrally established strategies for performance and growth, and with the maximum possible auto-nomy devolved to its constituent operating companies'. This reflects the belief or theory that in the company's circumstances, this form of organisation will best contribute to the realisation of the business objectives.

In another example, the Standard Telephones and Cables' booklet includes as an objective the intention 'to make jobs as satisfying as possible and allow scope for the individual to develop and utilise skills'. There may be a theory behind this that satisfying jobs and personal development make for higher productivity, but this need not be so. It may deal with purely moral issues expressed (or expressible) in terms of cooperation and conflict, high and low trust, congeniality and uncongeniality. This is a much more abstract and intangible end of the kind found in such concepts as 'the good life' or civilised conduct.

Such statements commonly state the ends to be sought, but, being statements of policy rather than of strategy, they do not usually indicate the detailed steps which any member of the organisation will be expected to take to realise them. Standard Telephones and Cables, for example, state certain of the company's objectives as to 'enable people to share in the company's success; to recognise their individual achievements; to help them to attain satisfaction and a sense of accomplishment from their work . . .'. How, by what precise steps, these will be attained is likely to vary with changes in the society's approach to practices such as profit-sharing and in the company's own circumstances. The 'objectives' listed are intended to function as principles and as broad guidance to conduct.

In this sense policies remain statements about the principles intended to guide conduct (as distinct from concrete steps to be taken). This is clear in Shackle's definition of 'policy':

'A list or system of principles by appeal to which we can answer the question, what to do in this or that set of circumstances'.
(Shackle, 1970, p 20).

The IBM's statement of 'core values' and its *Managers' Manual* support this view. It makes clear that it is intended to be 'every man-manager's first source of guidance, when he or any employee of his is unsure what to do or say in any situation related in some way to IBM'. It becomes a fundamental and universal source of reference for reducing uncertainties surrounding conduct.

Espoused Policy

Not all undertakings have expressions of policy of this type. Spence argues that policy formation requires a deliberate act of commitment because it rarely happens automatically or as a matter of course. This does not imply that undertakings do not otherwise possess policies: all undertakings 'follow' some policy, but this, as with culture, need not be formally expressed in writing. It is the production of an express policy that requires the deliberate act.

The absence of a written expression does not necessarily mean that there is no consensus about how people should be treated or conduct themselves, nor that principled uniformities of conduct are not discernible. In such circumstances, policy can only be inferred from the consistent elements of conduct among those who supposedly act in the name of the organisation. This may be referred to as the undertaking's espoused policy.

Brown's suggestion that policy is made up of 'any statement adopted by a Council or laid down by a manager, or any established practice or custom, which specifies the behaviour required of members in any given situation' (Brown, 1960, p 79), allows for this process of 'espousal' by admitting established practices and customs. In some cases, agreements negotiated with the trade unions may serve a similar purpose, and the *Employee Handbook* may indicate policy by simply referring to the terms of such agreements.

Many organisations prefer to continue with implicit policies (or in the terms used by Brewster, Gill and Richbell (1977), with espoused policies) which have to be inferred only from conduct. They may avoid formal written statements for either or both of two main reasons:

(a)   an espoused policy is thought to be more easily and more quickly changed in the light of circumstances (including those of criticism);

(b)   an explicit written policy is seen as likely to create criteria or norms, or a floor of rights against which actual conduct may be judged, and, for this reason, to provide another foundation on which complaints or grievances might be developed.

Nevertheless, these may be given as rationalisations justifying disregard of the need to develop policy. In the area of industrial relations, for example, Flanders argued that development occurred, 'not as a deliberate policy but haphazardly and as the result of the pressures of the moment' as trade unions found vulnerable areas to challenge (Flanders, 1967, p 30). Clegg also suggested that managements could have done more to structure industrial relations if they had adopted more positive policies with respect to issues like trade union recognition (Clegg, 1972, p 66).

In recent years much effort has been devoted to persuading organisations to adopt explicit industrial relations or personnel policies. The Donovan Commission suggested that what was needed to reduce the county's industrial relations 'problem' was the centralisation of control within undertakings and the association of this with a central industrial relations policy. The commission felt that such a policy, in the hands of the personnel manager (as Flanders, 1967, p 31, had suggested) or of the Board of Directors (the Donovan Report's preferred solution, 1968, p 41) offered the obvious answer. Such advocacy has not been matched, so far as one can judge from the evidence, by the development of explicit policies, although some movement in this direction, particularly among larger and primary sector organisations, is discernible.

Explicit Policy

If a policy is not in written form it exerts influence only very generally and bluntly by relying on members' emulating superordinates or peers who are assumed to have the 'right approach'. Emulation is, however, a mode of influence with limited relevance and efficiency. The need to secure consistency leads pretty inevitably to the production of a written statement to which reference can be made continuously. Commitment of the principles governing conduct to writing may be largely unavoidable in large organisations or multi-establishment undertakings. For example, larger multi-establishment organisations may find it convenient to express their policies in writing so as to remove doubts in the minds of employees (and particularly in those of managers) located on different sites, in order to establish a basis for equitable treatment.

A written policy may take one of three main forms:

1   *A short statement of certain general principles which will govern the whole range of managerial conduct in dealings with employees* The intention here is to keep the principles as broad and general as possible, alluding to principles of fairness and equity but not relating these to any or every category of issue which might be identified.

2   *A comprehensive statement of policy which details the guidance with which managers will need to answer questions* This may shade into the presentation of decisional rules which managers will be expected to follow, provided that the circumstances permit this. The IBM *Managers' Manual* is of this type, and deals with many of the issues which might conceivably develop within a complex organisation.

3   *One or a number of policy statements on specific issues as the need for guidance in relation to them is perceived to be necessary.* Often these are negotiations with the trade unions as occasion demands, and may have the force of 'rule' in that they expressly or implicitly provide for some form of sanction in the event of breach. Cadbury-Schweppes plc, for example, have negotiated a comprehensive policy on demanning and redundancy with their unions which might affect junior managers, quoted in Incomes Data Service's *Guide to Redundancy,* (1980, pp 95 – 103).

These are not absolutely exclusive categories, and which form the particular undertaking will adopt is likely to reflect its labour market orientation and its policy with respect to trade union recognition. Each of these elements in the definition can yield its own problems and imperfections, even in a situation which might properly be described as static or stable, and more certainly in a volatile or dynamic situation.

The Purposes of Policy

A policy, whether espoused or explicit, establishes both the moral and social ends and principles which members of the undertaking will be expected to pursue. A policy:

(a)   aims to indicate what 'kind' of social and moral entity it is desired to create around the process of realising more concrete and tangible ends;

(b)   must be generally applicable throughout its domain (whether undertaking or establishment) and be communicated sufficiently effectively to influence the thinking, feeling, and behaviour of those within its range;

(c)   may be expressed in writing (explicit policy) or left unwritten to be inferred from the patterns of conduct of the principal actors (espoused policy), many undertakings preferring not to make it explicit in the interests of preserving flexibility and preventing the generation of complaints.

Whether it is explicit or simply espoused, it indicates to those outside the organisation what 'kind' of organisation it is. For example, potential employees may learn in advance of applying for a job of the kind of treatment they might reasonably expect should they secure employment. For those employed within the undertaking, it serves as a source of information on what ought to be done by various actors and as a basis for evaluation of their conduct. Even if these are not intended, they are likely to be the passive consequences.

There are more pro-active expressions of the purposes of policy which the undertaking can make, and some of them embrace considerations of strategy — that is, of actions to be taken to achieve concrete results. This idea appears in Hawkins's statement that the purposes of policy are to:

(a)   lay down the principles or settled rules of action to which operating management is subject; and

(b)   to define objectives (Hawkins, 1971, p 205; see also Cowan in BMC, 1970, pp 18 – 19).

The 'objectives' in this context, however, are often the moral and social goals or states which the organisation might hope to realise by following these 'principles'; usually they are not the goals of making a profit or meeting a market demand.

Decisions and Rules

Policy refers to something distinct both from decisions which may be taken by management and issued as 'instructions', and from rules which are established to direct human action and backed up by sanctions for failure to conform.

Spence (1969, p 21) draws the distinction between decisions and policy, suggesting that a decision is a 'settled resolution on a course of action selected from other possible courses of action, and in a management context is mandatory', where 'making or formulating a policy is an act of construction which consists of fitting together a number of acts drawn from widely disparate fields into a pattern or several patterns of executive thinking upon which subsequent decisions have to be based'.

Making policy therefore calls for a special determination and skill on the part of top management to develop two-way communication to ensure that policies are based on real facts and interests in the operating system, and relevant and acceptable as foundations for action within the enterprise.

A distinction can also be drawn between policy and rules. Policy aims to offer general guidance, but not mandatory requirements which, if not met, will attract penalty or punishment. Failure to conform to policies may attract expressions of disapproval but this will reflect on the individual's judgement rather than on his or her motivation or willingness to comply. Because they are not specific in the actions they require of individuals, they cannot readily attract punishment for breach.

Policies may well be backed up by rules and procedures to be followed in some defined circumstances. Where policies are not made explicit, on the other hand, such rules may well form the main sources of inference as to what the undertaking's policy would be if only it were to be written down. Where such rules exist they become the instrument through which sanctions can be brought to bear against those who do not conform to either the rules themselves or the broad principles established in explicit policies. But the rules remain a separate concept and usually serve a distinct purpose.

The Criteria of Policy

The criteria by which policies may be judged are those derived from its two contributory elements, the morally and the technically practical considerations that permeate all human activity. Once the distinctions between these became blurred, the criteria themselves became fuzzier and more difficult to link with either strategy or policy.

The first consideration is that all economic organisations have two categories of objective, one related to the efficient creation of wealth and the other to the satisfying involvement of people in the process. This distinction is recognised, for example, in the IPM's Jubilee *Statement on Personnel Management and Personnel Policies*, where it is asserted, *inter alia*, that:

'Personnel management is a responsibility of all those

who manage people, as well as being a description of the work of those who are employed as specialists ... Personnel management aims to achieve both efficiency and justice, neither of which can be pursued successfully without the other'
(*Personnel Management*, March 1963, p 11).

The statement also, by implication, recognises that policy is to be construed as embracing both strategic and moral considerations.

The two distinct objectives are associated with separate criteria and criterion measures, by reference to which 'success' may be established. Where, however, the IPM's statement refers to justice (equated with fairness and equity in other comments on this aspect), others prefer to identify this aspect with human satisfaction (on the assumption that what is unjust or unfair will not contribute to this objective and will show up in any measures that might be made). These are then treated as categories of criteria which carry their own measures.

1   The objective of efficiency can ultimately be measured only by comparing the value added with the cost of adding it. This can be expressed in various terms, although it is obviously an easier sum if everything is reduced to the measuring rod of money. It is, however, never easy in an absolute sense as the difficulties encountered in attempts to structure incentive plans on value added concepts demonstrate.

2   The measurement of human satisfaction with work (as distinct from satisfaction with its product) is more difficult to measure. The criteria can be identified with satisfaction, stress, or morale, and measurement made after a fashion by conducting a morale survey (where 'morale' is defined as 'the total satisfactions a person derives from his job, his work group, his boss, the organisation, and his environment'), or by establishing indices of physical or mental health (although recognising that both morale and stress are 'also affected by his personality structure') (Beach, 1975, p 472).

Both of these are of significance in the evaluation of the success of human resource management and some attention will therefore be given to them, although, because we are primarily interested in human aspects of policies and practices, less attention will be devoted to the first of them.

Efficiency, apparently more relevant to strategy, remains a criterion relevant to policy as well, if only because it is usually necessary in our material civilisation to justify any course of action in terms of its actual or probable contribution to wealth creation and profitability. The history of personnel management, for example, is strewn with attempts to persuade general management to adopt some approach or method, itself justified on criteria other than those of efficiency, by arguments that it will contribute to material ends. Human relations, improved communications, worker involvement and participation have all been advanced as potential or actual contributors to efficiency, even though their real origins lay in social research or social theory. It is therefore most unlikely that policy will be justified *simply* and exclusively in terms of its relationship to morality.

There is also a sense in which policies that contribute to morality often contribute to efficiency. This is not always the case, and it is always possible to challenge a statement of this kind by adopting divergent values. Nevertheless, it is possible to see in statements of successful company practice, such as that advanced by Peters and Waterman (1982), that many morally good practices are associated with success in efficiency terms (Table 10).

Fairness and equity of treatment are more problematical, although they have become salient criteria in the development of personnel management. They differ from the others advanced in that they are usually expressed as principles which will be followed by the organisation's representatives in dealings with any others with whom they come in contact. Criteria of fairness are complex in themselves, and whether they are met in the particular case can only be assessed as a matter of judgement. Measurement of fairness is therefore largely a matter of acknowledging the 'weight of opinion' in the matter. The other criteria mentioned are, however, usually accepted and spelled out in formal statements of undertaking policy.

CONTENT OF PERSONNEL POLICY

A personnel policy, whether expressed or implied, will concern itself with all the main aspects of conduct which affect people as employees. It will aim to indicate how both the employer and the people employed will be expected to conduct themselves in their relations with others. But 'conduct' covers a wide area of functional activity within modern organisations, and the guidance required could therefore be extensive. Organisations make selections from the total range to suit their predilections and circumstances.

Many find it difficult to separate personnel policy completely from the undertaking's policy with respect to any other set of people, such as customers, stockholders, suppliers, community, or society at large. This is not suprising, given that stakeholders do have different interests and in consequence make different demands on the organisation. Consequently, most explicit statements of policy attempt to define how those acting in the name of the organisation will be expected to behave in relation to any or all of these categories of stakeholder. It is in this context that organisations give expression to their 'core values', or those values which identify the specific organisational culture.

A good example of a comprehensive explicit statement is that advanced by Standard Telephones and Cables plc. This deals not only with personnel policy *per se*, but also with general policies with respect to other stakeholders, to which the former is related in a broad expression of company philosophy.

The statement of 'Overall Objectives' places particular emphasis on the Company's attitude towards customers and 'the market' generally, and some of its statements (such as that on 'fair contracts') could also apply to other commercial trading relations. These objectives also indicate the way in which the Company proposes that its agents will be expected to conduct themselves within the organisational context. These points are made under the headings of 'People', 'Management', 'Style', and 'Standards', with the last of these indicating the nature of the moral imperatives to which the Company subscribes.

Other organisations have, from time to time, advanced even more comprehensive 'credos' in which the separate stakeholder relations are specifically alluded to. One of the more famous is that put forward by Johnson and Johnson. Others have appeared in the context of those experiments in control structure associated with organisations like the Scot-Bader Commonwealth (Blum, 1968).

Types of Content

Whether policies are espoused or explicit, they have content, although it may be difficult to be categorical about what the content is in the case of the espoused policy. Content could be categorised by using the range of distinct contracts identified by Mumford (1972, p 51) — the psychological, knowledge, efficiency, ethical and task structure contracts. This would help to identify the respects in which undertakings show consideration for the person's 'possessions' (personality, intellect, skills, and the rest) which are brought to bear in work.

An alternative approach employs the more common characterisation of the range of activities contained within the 'personnel function'. There are policies on selection and deselection, training and development, placement and promotion, remuneration and benefits, health and safety, industrial relations and participation.

This has the merit of linking policy considerations with the major elements which normally enter into a personnel or human resource strategy. It is also one which tends to be followed by companies which develop explicit policies. For example, *The Best Company Book* (published by Standard Telephones and Cables plc) provides an example of a statement that deals with many of these, listing specific objectives and policies under the headings of 'Organisation and Jobs', 'Jobs and People', 'Personal Development', 'Growth and Learning', 'Pay and Benefits', 'Industrial Relations', 'Communication and Involvement', and 'Working Environment'.

Illustrations of the content of personnel policies can be given on this basis.

Selection and Deselection

Selection and deselection constitutes an area of personnel policy and practice that is closely constrained by legislation, and policy statements frequently but not exclusively acknowledge this. IBM's statement of broad policy with respect to recruitment (amplified in the *Managers' Manual*) is expressed in the form that:

> 'In the selection of candidates for appointment the one determining consideration is their suitability measured against the standards of IBM, the requirements of the job and future needs.'

Other companies also expand on this to state that they are equal opportunity employers, making no discrimination on grounds of race, ethnic origin, religion or sex, but confining discrimination to capacity to perform the job in question.

Policy with respect to demanning and dismissal is usually more reluctantly expressed because it is thought that raising the issue could reduce morale. In recent years, however, sometimes at the insistence of trade unions, many organisations have been led to negotiate new technology or redundancy agreements which serve as policy. Some of these may be little more than agreements by management to consult the unions in the event of the redundancy arising. Some are much more comprehensive, covering broad intentions, consultation, methods of selection for redundancy, assistance with finding new work, and severance payments and entitlements (IDS, 1980, pp 92–105).

Dismissal is, in law, unfair under certain circumstances, by virtue of either inadequate cause or inadequate procedure, and statements of policy therefore try to ensure that conduct is such that unwanted legal consequences do not follow from it. This may be tackled in either or both of two ways:

(a)   emphasis may be placed on the desirability of employees so conducting themselves that dismissal is not normally warranted and that other expedients (such as training or work flexibility) will be adopted wherever feasible to obviate any necessity for it; and/or

(b)   emphasis is placed on the need for supervision and management to handle any necessary disciplinary process strictly in accordance with principles and procedures, established to reduce the likelihood of any adverse verdict being given.

The first can be described as a more positive type of policy – being concerned to remove the causes of the problem – than the second – which is mainly concerned to reduce the consequential damage.

Remuneration and Benefits

It is not unusual for organisations in the primary sector to declare their policy in respect of benefits and rewards in terms which suggest that they have an ambition to remain high in the relevant league tables. Thus, Avdel Ltd. states that it, 'endeavours at all times to provide terms and conditions of employment of the highest standards which are at least equal to the leaders in the industry and can be compared favourably with the best in the area'. Similarly, IBM state their policy in terms of the objective of maintaining, 'an average level of pay that exceeds the average for similar work in other leading companies and competitors with which IBM competes for employees and/or business in the UK'. Although not every company can be at the head of the league table, many in the primary sector declare their policy objectives in these terms.

The Standard Telephones and Cables' document already quoted is explicit about the desirability of promoting people to vacancies from within the organisation, both as a desirable end in itself and as a means to wider ends. Under the heading 'Jobs and People', it is proposed that: 'Managers will, as far as possible, pursue a realistic policy of promotion from within. To this end they will:

aim that those recruited will normally have the potential for future successful performance in a job at least one

level above that at which they enter the Company and, in the case of staff who join below the age of 30, at two levels higher;
make available to existing employees, in an easily accessible form, information about vacancies for which candidates are being sought;
maintain systematic procedures to review the progress of promotable people and to take steps to encourage their development and promotion.'

Avdel Ltd also declares it to be a matter of policy that 'Wherever our existing employees show the necessary qualifications and experience, vacancies are filled internally'. The same company's document goes on to indicate that, 'opportunites are provided to train, both within the Company and on external courses, so as to assist them in attaining promotion, etc.'

Training and Development

Not untypical of explicit policies on training in the primary sector is that put out by A G Barr, plc., in their *Personnel Policies and Procedures: Management Guide*. This indicates that it is the 'policy of the Company to:

(a) ensure that all employees receive proper and adequate induction training and basic job training to enable them to achieve and maintain an acceptable standard of performance in their current job;

(b) develop employees with the potential to take on positions of greater responsibility;

(c) review Company and individual training needs on a regular basis and the arrangements for meeting these needs;

(d) ensure that all training is carried out by trained and competent personnel;

(e) ensure that training is directed towards the achievement of the business objective;

(f) maintain adequate records of training.'

Similarly, the South Glamorgan County Council, in a lengthy statement on training and development policy, declares that,

'The Council will provide facilities, financial support,

advice and opportunities to enable employees ... to acquire the attitudes, skills and knowledge (with related qualifications) needed to perform effectively the duties and tasks for which they are employed; to develop their potential to meet the future manpower needs of the Council and, in exceptional cases, to develop individuals beyond the Council's immediate and foreseeable needs, in order to meet the needs of the Local Government Service, as encouraged by the National Joint Council.'

This demonstrates a concern, which is also expressed elsewhere in the document, for the development of programmes of training and development which serve objectives other than those particular to the local authority organisation itself.

Health and Safety

On health and safety, companies often feel free to express their objectives and policies in absolute terms, capitalising on the tendency for this subject to be one on which the industrial relations parties usually agree. IBM, for example, says of this aspect:

'IBM's commitment to safety is every bit as important as our commitment to excellence, to outstanding service, and respect of the individual. There can be no compromise with safety.'

A similar effect is achieved in other companies by making breach of health and safety regulations a cause for summary dismissal, thus indicating the importance attached to the issue by the organisation.

Industrial Relations

The Donovan Commission recommended the adoption of explicit policies in the industrial relations and personnel area, and, whether in response to the recommendation or not, many organisations have since adopted this course of action. Its recommendations included one which urged that, 'the boards of companies review industrial relations within their undertakings' with six objectives in mind:

1　to develop, together with trade unions representative of their employees, comprehensive and authoritative collective bargaining machinery to deal at company and/or factory level with the terms and conditions of employment which are settled at these levels;

2   to develop, together with unions representative of their employees, joint procedures for the rapid and equitable settlement of grievances in a manner consistent with the relevant collective agreements;

3   to conclude with unions representative of their employees, agreements regulating the position of shop stewards in such matters as facilities for holding elections, numbers and constituencies, recognition of credentials, facilities to consult and report back to their members, facilities to meet with other stewards, the responsibilities of the chief shop steward (if any), pay while functioning as a steward in working hours, day release with pay for training;

4   to conclude agreements covering the handling of redundancy;

5   to adopt effective rules and procedures governing disciplinary matters, including dismissal, with provision for appeals;

6   to ensure regular joint discussion of measures to promote safety at work (Donovan Commission Report, 1968, p 45).

The criteria advanced by this provide a statement of the principles which guide the 'voluntary' system of industrial relations in Britain. They admit the degree of workers' participation (through representatives) in the running of enterprises which has been sanctioned by the growth of convention in this area. They do not, however, take the undertaking far along the road to significant participation in important decisions affecting the working lives of the workers concerned (Hawkins, 1971, p 205).

Correlates of Policy Content

We have noted that aspects of the culture are likely to influence the content of organisational policies. This influence on the actual content of the policy may be strong or weak just as the influence of the policy prescriptions on actual conduct may be strong or weak. We have also noted briefly that if a policy is to be accepted as a guide to conduct, it needs to bear a close relationship to what already occurs in practice.

It is also not unreasonable, however, to suggest (although specific research evidence is not available to demonstrate the truth of the proposition) that three sets of circumstances are likely to influence the content of policy statements:

1   The objectives pursued in the product/service market;

2   The labour market relationship which the undertaking
     develops; and

3   The ideological position adopted by the controlling elite.

These may indicate, possibly dictate, a content of policy statements
which run counter to the general values of the surrounding society,
as management pursues a pragmatic approach.

1   The product/service market position of the undertaking is
     likely to produce uncertainties in a number of areas, but which
     areas in which cases will tend to vary. This is the general infer-
     ence to be drawn from the various models of organisation-
     market relationships which depend on the idea of a product or
     an organisational life-cycle.
         At each stage/phase identified in these models, different
     kinds of threat to the continued stability of the undertaking
     and uncertainties about the solutions to be adopted to
     emergent problems impinge on the recognition and security
     that can be given to the workforce in distinct ways. The effect
     of these is not unlike the consequence which follows from
     Porter's recognition that different organisations have differ-
     ently distributed strengths and weaknesses all along the value
     chain; here too the implications for the remuneration and
     continuity of the workforce are likely to vary in ways that are
     associated with the strategic decision adopted.
         Consequently, we should expect to find the BCG star and
     cash-cow organisations (the mature organisations in Lippitt's
     model) and the undertakings enjoying competitive advantage
     in Porter's categorisation – adopting policies which empha-
     sise high reward, extensive fringe benefits, high security,
     strong opportunities for development, and high levels of in-
     volvement. Organisations without these advantages of secure
     returns would not then be expected to match these; their
     policies would tend to emphasise much more what is often
     referred to as a 'hard-nosed' approach to labour.

2   The labour market relationship developed by the undertaking
     is likely to carry very similar implications. This is not
     surprising, given that undertakings at different stages in their
     organisational life-cycle, or products at different stages in
     their life-cycle, would be expected to develop distinct varieties
     of relationship with the labour market.
         A watertight association of primary sector organisations
     with explicit personnel policies, and secondary sector under-

takings with espoused or externally dictated human resource policies, is unlikely to be found in practice. Nevertheless, where undertakings operate with an internal labour market, there is probably a greater pressure to commit the principles to writing in the interests of decreasing uncertainty and achieving equity and fairness. This is seen as a means of securing the loyalty and commitment which such undertakings regard as imperative to the meeting of their business objectives. In the secondary sector undertaking, on the other hand, the pressure for flexibility may lead management away from such explicit commitment to labour policies which their more volatile product-market relationship might be expected to force them to change suddenly or rapidly.

3   Management's ideology is likely to provide a third influence on human resource policy. Any statement of policy, and particularly any statement of personnel policy, exposes beliefs and assumptions about management's position and that of other stakeholders in relation to them. The conceptions and definition of the objectives, the means to their realisation, and the sources of legitimacy in respect of authority may all vary. Whether it can be assumed that there is some kind of shake-out which ensures that organisations secure the management ideologies that most closely align with product or labour market positions is a moot point, although there are those who think there is something in the idea.

Policies do, however, vary between those which emphasise unitary and pluralist ideologies (Fox, 1966) and residual and trusteeship conceptions of the management function (Hill and Hook, 1945). Policies rooted in either polar position are likely to be significantly different from one another. At the unitary-residual end of the continuum, the thrust of the policy is likely to be on preservation of management prerogatives and the development of a hierarchical team of individuals. At the pluralist-trusteeship end, greater emphasis on elaborate consultation, participation, and negotiation processes and practices, and on management by agreement, could be expected to occur.

SUMMARY

Policy refers to the 'way of life' of a particular organisation and usually includes statements of the objectives to be realised through conduct and of the principles which people will be expected to adopt and follow in pursuing them.

In its simplest terms, policy is 'a statement of company intention, purpose or objective and is generally expressed in the broadest possible way' (Spence, 1969, p 20), although the 'statement' might have to be inferred where it is not actually produced in written form. The purpose of 'policy' is to provide guidance to all those brought together within a society (or organisation) as to the conduct expected of them in defined circumstances.

It usually has to satisfy criteria of efficiency, satisfaction, fairness and equity of treatment, although the first two, being distinct ends in themselves, may be associated equally with strategy. Justice, fairness, and equity are more abstract qualities which can only be assessed by application of human judgement.

The conditions which must be met, if policies are to succeed in guiding conduct, are that they must:

(a)   have an accepted or actual relationship, more or less rationally derived, to objectives or goals, at least in so far as this is consistent with strategies and practices, but without having a simple identity with these other features of any course of action;

(b)   be cast in such terms as will enable the principles to be applied in a wide range of situations and circumstances;

(c)   be intended to have the status and function of a kind of rule or norm in so far as it is intended to guide others' conduct, but without the association with explicit penalties for breach usually found in association with these;

(d)   be created by someone or some body within the scope of that person's or body's legitimate authority or proper discretion to commit the totality to courses of action (the chief executive on the managerial side and the central negotiating body on the union side in cases where union commitment is sought and secured);

(e)   be recognised to be of variable relevance in its application according to the circumstances or situations encountered, although as a statement of guidance it is to be regarded as inviolate unless modified by following a defined procedure for its modification.

The contents of human resource policies include consideration of the various aspects of the 'personnel function' as this is normally defined — recruitment, discipline, and dismissal, remuneration and other aspects of treatment, working conditions, including health and safety, industrial relations and participation.

These contents, it can be speculatively suggested may vary fairly systematically with the position of the undertaking in the product and labour markets and with the ideological positions taken by those who have influence on the shape of the undertaking's policy. In recent years, the removal of some of the legislative constraints on human resource management and the development of new product and labour market relationships have led to a significant switch in policy in many undertakings. Although this modification is by no means universal, where it does occur, it usually places greater emphasis on dividing the labour force between employed and self-employed, reducing the importance of trade unions as bargaining partners, and linking remuneration and other aspects of treatment more closely with performance and potential performance.

Considered as a whole, policy becomes, as Spence puts it, the 'animating concept of management' (Spence, 1969, p 20) which influences the approach or style adopted in the course of realising substantive objectives by pursuing the strategies designed to achieve this end. The fact that policies have been reoriented in many undertakings in recent times shows that there is a growing acceptance of a 'new realism' in 'human resource management'.

Reading:

Brewster and Connock (1985).
Cowan (1970).

Peters and Waterman (1982).
Spence (1969).

Part B:
The Content of Human Resource Management

Human resource management is that general function of management concerned with people as resources — in their capacity to produce and deliver goods and/or services (Miner and Miner, 1977, p 4). As a former head of the American Management Association is reported to have said:

> 'If management means getting results through people, then management is nothing more than personnel administration'
> (L Appley, quoted in Odiorne, 1963, and Megginson, 1972, p 51).

A 'responsibility of line management' (Pigors and Myers, 1973b, p 3), it is implemented 'primarily through direct supervision and the development of official policies' (Sayles and Strauss, 1967, p 1).

The management of human resources is not, however, the whole function of management (or even of line managers and supervisors). Nor is it necessarily the prime or priority function. The basic purpose of industry is to add to the society's wealth, and, having done so, to play some part in its distribution through the 'profit system' and the 'wage system'. This way of characterising the priorities does no more than recognise that industry has a variety of stakeholders who are willing to cooperate for the material gain they can secure from so doing. Law and convention accord priority to the interests of the stockholders, not the workers, and management must respect this priority.

Management's function and role is therefore directed only secondarily at the satisfaction of the different stakeholder interests and aspirations. But management cannot escape the need to satisfy the various stakeholders, at least in a manner sufficient to secure and maintain their cooperation with the enterprise. This applies to both shareholders and workers, but usually not equally, because shareholders have more opportunities to withhold cooperation (by investing elsewhere) than have workers (who usually have fewer employment options). This distinction carries important implications for organisational maintenance, and therefore for human resource management.

As Sayles has indicated (1964, p 49), management performs necessary leadership and monitoring roles, but only within a framework of value which is imposed on the roles by the institutional structure within which they operate. The manner in which this institutional overburden constrains the leadership functions of guiding and conserving the human resources is arguably one of the major disadvantages confronting British industry. It has justified the hiving off of human resource management to personnel specialists, as a way of freeing line management to deal with the equally complex problems of creating wealth.

Management as Leadership

Leadership is variously defined as a personal quality, or as a process of helping people to achieve results, or of achieving results 'through people'. It may be associated with any person in relation to any group, where leadership is usually seen as one of many specialist roles assumed or assigned to group members: other members may specialise as information-givers, counsellors, clowns, or actors, and for the limited purposes indicated by their role designations, they may 'take the lead'. The term 'leader' assumes a more general connotation as a distinct status and role and thus attracts greater attention. The question remains whether those who assume these roles are 'natural' leaders.

The concept of leadership has developed through a number of phases which have emphasised the relevance of individual traits and the extent of norm-conformity as relevant criteria. In these terms, the leader is either a natural one or a conformist to the values and norms (or rules) of his or her group. The current view emphasises the leader's capacity to perform 'those acts which help the group achieve its objectives', including the objective of maintaining itself in a healthy and congenial condition (Cartwright and Zander, 1953, p 538). The actions required are likely to vary according to the objectives and the tasks before the group, as Carter's experimental studies suggest (Carter *et al*, 1950, pp 589–95; and Cartwright and Zander, 1953, pp 551–60; 1960, pp 511–20).

The important tasks of maintaining the health of the group are also likely to be different, and, on occasion, competitive with those required to achieve substantive effects.

> 'The leadership and other processes of the organisation must be such as to ensure a maximum probability that in all interactions and all relationships with the organis-ation each member will, in the light of his background, values and expectations, view the experience as sup-portive and one which builds and maintains his sense of personal worth and importance'
> (Likert, 1961, p 103; and 1967, p 47).

By caring for the members' needs and aspirations and the internal relationships, the aim is to ensure that even when any particular task is successfully accomplished, the group remains viable and capable of coping successfully with future tasks.

The activities involved are many and varied, reflecting and re-sponding to the needs, objectives, and character of the particular group. They may be categorised as those activities which contribute to:

Goal achievement	Group maintenance
Setting the goals	Increasing the cohesiveness/
Helping the group to move	attractiveness of the group
Securing necessary	Improving relationships
resources	between members

Should one person play a dominant part in performing these various activities, that person is likely to be identified as 'the leader'. Other members will tend to defer to him or her in the performance of these tasks. But leadership actions 'may be performed by one or many members of the group' (Cartwright and Zander, 1953, p 538) de-pending on the task requirements and the availability of resources within the group. More than one person may be involved in these activities and assume partial leadership to the extent that others defer to him or her in the performing of them.

This structure of leadership in groups is a function of their two main purposes: to realise certain material, intellectual, and emotional ends; and to maintain the group itself as a healthy and congenial context for their accomplishment. These same two cate-gories are to be found in work organisations, and some of the insights which small-group studies of leadership provide are applicable.

The Objective of Managerial Action

The functions of management are usually expressed in more formalised terms, and the relevance of the distinction between goal achievement and group maintenance activities identified in small *informal* group studies is often missed.

Managerial work is primarily oriented to the achievement of some surplus of output value over input costs (Koontz and O'Donnell, 1976, p 8). This is so, whether the management is concerned with private sector production or service 'for profit', or with public sector service provision for the equitable benefit of the citizen (Brech, 1975, p 6). That managerial work which is mainly concerned with reconciling this kind of problem is to be distinguished from non-managerial (including administrative) which is constrained by this same requirement, but not directly concerned with it.

The paramount need to pursue this surplus (or, more simply, to pursue efficiency) is made more complex by the institutional structure, which gives priority to the interests of the shareholders in securing the highest and quickest returns on their investments. Unlike some other major competitor nations, Britain has few effective institutionalised intermediaries able to concert the multitude of individual shareholder decisions in the interest of securing the longer term health of the enterprise. Individual shareholders are able to respond instantaneously to changes of enterprise fortune and without regard to long-term consequences, in order to preserve their immediate returns on investment. They are free to take up advantageous take-over offers for the sake of immediate gain, regardless of the longer-term prospects or needs of the undertaking.

Managers are therefore led inescapably into a mode of operation in which they must constantly measure their performances and those of their units against objectives or targets which derive from their fundamental purpose, *as mediated by the institutional structure*. In consequence, the longer-term health and security of the enterprise in Britain tends to be at a discount because this institutional structure, through which management's priorities for action and attention are communicated, tends to focus its attention on short-term gains to the investors. This diverts management's attention from conservation of the undertaking's human resources, and leaves the organisational maintenance function under-served.

In the circumstances, it is not surprising that senior management should be exclusively concerned with the economic *and political* problems which surround the undertaking, and uninvolved in the 'internal' social and organisational problems (Donovan Commission Report, 1968; Winkler, 1974). Nor is it perhaps surprising that the handling of these problems should be handed over to a specialised personnel function, acting as a kind of surrogate for the corporate management.

Historical Evolution

It is at least arguable that industry created a specialist personnel function to free senior management from the traumas of coping with human resource issues and problems, to allow them to deal with the equally complex political problems of creating wealth within this institutional context.

The evolution of the distinct control strategies identified above (pp 18−23) has over time allocated prime responsibility for the policies and practices of human resource management to different positions. In particular, the later phases of the development which have focused on 'incentive' and 'incorporation' strategies, have been allocated to 'personnel specialist' positions and roles within what are usually large-scale enterprises capable of maintaining an adequate cash return on sales by constantly ringing the changes on products offered. Where these conditions are not present, the specialist personnel officer is still not common.

The occupation of personnel management has, in fact, been extremely effective in picking up and handling those *consequences* of the various labour control strategies, which might otherwise have led to a more massive popular protest than that produced by trade unionism. But reflection on the evolution of the specialist function against the evolution of labour control strategies gives a somewhat different meaning to Drucker's quip that 'personnel management puts together and calls personnel management all those things that do not deal with people and that are not management' (Drucker, 1961, p 243).

Origins

The generally assumed origins of personnel management in the welfare movement of the later years of last century (Niven, 1967, pp 15−29) could, in this vein, be interpreted as an attempt to re-place a more personalised relationship and concern for workers at a time when the first major change of strategy − from selection to supervision − had reduced it within their immediate task groups. Its fuller development then occurred as the depersonalisation continued with the advent of scientific management. This need not impute unworthy motives to the main, especially Quaker, employers associated with such welfare policies; it merely presents one view of why such a development was perceived necessary or desirable.

At about the same period, the new unionism was taking hold amongst semi-skilled and unskilled workers — that new breed whose importance to industry was at this time rising above that of the craftsman. These unions also had a concern for the well-being of workers caught up in the wave of industrial rationalisation, and it was not at all surprising that:

(a) welfare officers had to decide whether they were on the side of the employer or the unionised workers; and

(b) many founding fathers of what became personnel management at a later date were at this period concerned with dealing with the consequences of the new unionism.

These developments initiated a double-headed spurt of occupational growth. The welfare origins allowed personnel officers to develop their roles along the path of the unitarist concept of management prerogative: they demonstrated an ability to deal better with issues of recruitment and selection, remuneration and reward, and the general administration of the individual employment contract than others. The union resistance origins provided the foundations for developing skills in the area of handling union claims, negotiation with the unions, administering agreements (and the rules associated with them), and eventually of involvement and participation as devices for securing improved worker commitment and loyalty. This led to an acceptance of a pluralist ideology as preferable to and more functional than a simple unitarist philosophy.

Extensions of the Role

The first major incursion of personnel management beyond welfare was that which was initially concerned simply with recruitment and selection. This same industrial rationalisation significantly increased the scale of production establishments (measured by numbers employed) and the extent of job factionalisation. In consequence, large numbers of essentially semi-skilled workers were needed to staff them, and because industry was no longer looking for all-round craftsmen with certified competence, recruitment and selection took on a new meaning. Procurement of labour of appropriate kinds and in appropriate quantity was a task which industry needed to have carried out, and early personnel officers performed it (Bloomfield and Willetts, 1916).

By the 1930s, it was already possible for Elbourne (1934) to identify six categories of personnel activities associated with:

1 Personal relationships, including mutual consultation and individual guidance, where required, on employees' problems.

2 Organisational relationships, including definition of responsibilities and duties, the notification of appointments, transfers, etc, and organised mechanisms for joint consultation and the dissemination of information.

3 Employment procedures, including labour supply and the determination of conditions and regulations of employment.

4 Education and training – operative staff (both factory and administrative), supervisors and executives.

5 Physical working conditions, including matters of health, convenience, and safety.

6 Social services and amenities, internal and external to the firm – physical, educational, social or recreational.

Moxon's slightly later description of the typical personnel department was similar in its coverage of employment, wages, joint consultation, health and safety, welfare (employee services) and education and training, each organised into separate 'divisions' of the broad function (Moxon, 1946, pp 9–47).

Growth of a Profession

By the Second World War, specialist personnel management had developed sufficiently to become described as a professional function, with a significant advisory and service role. Northcott's description of it stated that:

1 'Personnel management is an extension of general managment' concerned with management's 'second responsibility' of 'prompting and stimulating every employee to make his fullest contribution to the purpose of the business . . .'

2 'It is an advisory service . . . and a staff activity' carrying 'no obvious authority except that which arises from its terms of reference and the knowledge and skill of the adviser'

3 'It becomes organised as a function, that is, a body of duties brought together as the responsibilities of one person and carried out wherever they occur in the establishment' (Northcott, 3rd ed, 1955, p 12).

Other commentators, including Niven (1967, pp 135–63) and Crichton (1968, pp 293–300), recognised the emergent 'professional'

standing of this new group of functionaries. Others were less flatter-
ing, seeing the role as composed of remnants and unconsidered
trifles which other managers were too preoccupied, or too
contemptuous, to take up themselves (Drucker, 1955; 1961 ed, pp
241 – 54).

These descriptions are expressed in terms which reflect the conditions of their time, and in particular, the opportunity which
management faced to determine the issues involved in human
resource managment with little serious challenge. Later developments were stimulated by new and more serious challenges (for
example, from customers, competitors, and labour) and new efforts
to contain them (for example, through new labour control strategies
within industry and legislative prescription from outside). During
this period, some switch of emphasis occurred, putting the function
more firmly back in the laps of line management. This was heralded
by a readier use of the concept of 'human resource management', as
for example, by the Hayes Committee, which saw it as concerned
with:

> 'The optimum deployment and development of people
> within an organisation in order that the objectives of the
> organisation may be met and effectively adapted to
> changing circumstances'
> (Department of Employment, 1972).

Price recognised that this implied that 'the personnel function' was
being broadened to embrace much more holistic people concerns
within organisations (Price, 1975, pp 555 – 6).

On such bases, industrial relations and personnel-administrative
functions were able to develop, so that by the 1960s, the occupation
was able to claim professional status on a foundation of understandings and techniques related to the organisation, direction, and
control of labour in the processes of production and service-delivery
(Figure 9). Although the IPM's *Jubilee Statement*, 1963, acknowledged that personnel specialists were not the only managers to be
concerned with human resource management, it does associate
specialist function with the realisation of both efficiency and justice
in the processes of securing labour resources for industry and looking after employees in the course of their employment.

This development produced two consequences which come
together in some organisations in a rather uneasy relationship
(although the 'unease' may be no more than a reflection of the
'tight-loose' requirement of modern industrial organisation). On
the one hand, the specialist personnel department now embraces a

Figure 9

A hierarchy of personnel management activities

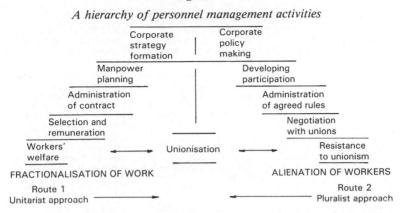

wide range of functions (policy-making, method-defining, and implementation; Table 11) in the hierarchical chain, and an extensive range of methods and techniques across the spectrum of people concerns (embracing the methods and techniques associated with such concerns as Elbourne and Moxon describe). On the other hand, the specialist personnel department is becoming more of a supportive service to line management as it takes back and more closely integrates with other concerns the human resource policy-making, method-developing, and implementation processes (Table 11).

Nevertheless, generalisations of this kind must be taken as applying to the profession itself, not to 'industry' in its generic meaning. Specialist personnel management remains more appropriate to some types of enterprise, and less appropriate and less frequently found in others. This is not to suggest that the management of human resources is necessarily and consistently better or worse in either category; the methods and techniques are not secrets of the professional association and its members.

The Custodian of Methods and Techniques

In the course of this occupational growth and development, the personnel specialists revealed themselves to be adept at both developing methods and techniques of human resource management (even if this term did not surface before the Hayes Committee reported in 1972) and at bringing these to bear on people problems in a variety of circumstances. It was as if personnel specialists, having no safe and assured function in management, secured their

Table 11

Personnel management activities

The textbook usually includes the following activities of personnel management	The enterprise usually requires action to provide the following	The individual usually demands action to create the following
1 Personnel policy formation (general)	A statement of objectives and standards to be followed by all acting in the name of the organisation.	A perception of the organisation's 'care' for its members, including a notion of justice and fairness.
1a Manpower policy and planning (dealing with the interface between enterprise and labour market)	A statement of how the enterprise projects itself into the future as an appropriately manned enterprise.	A perception of the organisation's concern to maintain efficiency in manning consistent with security of those who have invested their working lives in it.
1b Policy and planning in respect of the work environment (welfare amenities, health and safety and services)	A costed statement of the conditions under which employment is offered in order to secure contributions required of employees at all levels.	A perception of the treatment offered by the employer to employees, including opportunities for personal development and growth.
2 Organisation design (job analysis, communications, procedures, recognition)	An organisation equipped with adequately defined roles and adequate communications channels to permit optimisation of contribution.	An organisation equipped with adequate structures and procedures to allow individual and sectional goals to be given due consideration.
2a Communications (disclosure, counselling and consultation)	A solution to the top-down and lateral communications problems of organisations.	A reasonable opportunity for all employees to be informed of problems, policies and projections.
2b Mutual influence (joint negotiating, disciplinary committees)	A bargaining structure which meets the demand consistently with time and money, costs of securing acceptance of policies etc.	An adequate opportunity to employees to exert their influence upon policies, practices, and projects.
3 Control of labour	Informed action on activities intended to secure appropriate labour: (i) recruitment and selection (ii) performance appraisal (iii) promotion etc (iv) training (v) reward package (vi) environmental climate	Fair and consistent actions intended to ensure the dignity of labour: (i) job opportunities (ii) recognition of worth (iii) development of person (iv) learning opportunity (v) fair rewards (vi) good treatment
4 Control of power	Definition of authority or discretion to decide, usually by tacit or open agreement manifest in: (i) job definitions (ii) rule books (iii) collective agreements	Acceptance of fair definitions of authority and discretion preferably by open discussion and joint agreement manifest in: (i) collective agreements (ii) union rule books (iii) joint decisions

value to the employer by becoming custodians of methods and techniques which could be offered whenever human resource problems surfaced.

At the present time, therefore, it could be said of personnel management (if not necessarily of all individual personnel managers) that it is equipped with a range of methods and techniques of recruitment and selection, training and development, remuneration and reward, persuasion and negotiation, applicable to any and all levels of organisation and staff. Behind these techniques stand those of planning and policy making, and monitoring and evaluation, which are required for the sustenance of an occupational role which focuses on such immediate techniques as those listed above (Table 11).

It is, however, necessary that such methods and techniques should be applied only after adequate diagnosis of the problem and the likely consequences of treating it in specific ways. It is in this respect that, no matter how deliberately or how accidentally, personnel managers have demonstrated an ability to serve the basic labour control strategy pursued by the organisation. Thus in each of the strategies identified above (pp 18−23), remuneration has a place and function which is different from those in the others.

In the context of selection, remuneration is focused on the rate for the job (sometimes referred to as the 'market rate' or the 'going rate'), and establishing that rate has much occupied personnel people.

In the context of a supervision strategy, this basic rate is often supplemented by merit pay, given at the discretion of the supervisor, and finding ways of validating his judgements also occupies the time and attention of the personnel specialists.

In the context of incentive management, personnel specialists spend considerable time and effort in both establishing incentive levels and in dealing with the bargaining consequences which follow from the attempt to remunerate on the basis of measurable 'results' achieved.

In the phase of corporatist strategy, the personnel specialist's ingenuity is employed to put together ever more complex remuneration packages which will bind employees to the organisation with hoops of steel.

A similar kind of relationship is discernible in the area of formulating and securing acceptance of rules governing work in their various manifestations (Gouldner, 1955b).

In the first case, the rules are inculcated during training in the occupation and are thereafter 'carried' by the worker from job to job. These rules are largely independent of the workplace organisation and are more in the nature of occupational norms. The organisation buys a knowledge of the rules along with the labour.

In the second, the rules are more likely to appear to be highly personalised and idiosyncratic, established by the supervisor for his or her own purposes, and often for reasons which may seem to the worker to be irrational. In this case, the personnel specialist has no immediate role until he or she begins to take over this rule-making function from the supervisor in the interests of fairness or justice or of avoiding grievances.

In the third and fourth cases, the rules are likely to be more rationally developed by organisational representatives or functionaries, but difficult to associate with any identifiable person, although the personnel officer (as just such a functionary) usually plays a major part in both formulating and monitoring adherence to them. In the fourth case, however, the rules are more likely to be perceived as norms which emerge or evolve from an open organisational structure (although not 'by accident').

These different conditions and processes help to define distinct functions for those charged with human resource management. All of them, however, call for skilled performance in discharge of the function and in performance of the tasks.

THE SKILLS OF PERSONNEL MANAGEMENT

The identification of what constitutes managerial skills must start with an appreciation of the work which managers are expected to do. It may be divided into:

(a) its substantively creative aspects, which derive from the specific content of the objectives and the situation in which they are to be realised; and

(b) its processual aspects, which are associated with the means, methods, procedures, techniques and practices through whose application it is thought that the realisation of the substantive objectives may be facilitated.

The first of these emphasises the 'what' of managing and therefore the 'organisationally functional' nature of the managerial role: it may be concerned with the management of a petrochemical complex or a district health organisation, and in each situation will have its own established objectives and its unique physical and social dimensions. The second emphasises the 'how' of managing, and will form a unique combination of means, methods, etc., related to the realisation of objectives in that situation.

Each aspect makes its own distinct demands on the person performing the managerial role. The first demands a *knowledge* and *understanding* of the objectives and the principles which are to be applied in their realisation (Koontz *et al*, 1980, pp 8–14). The second demands a knowledge of the methods, techniques, etc., but more pertinently an ability to apply that knowledge constructively and effectively. In the process of application, the manager will necessarily confront the need to communicate with and influence the conduct of others, and interpersonal skills become a major requirement. It is the ability to apply effectively which highlights the 'skills' of management, although the objectives provide the criteria against which the success of the manager in exercising those skills is measured.

The Knowledge Requirement

In order to operate effectively in this framework, managers require a volume of knowledge. This knowledge is of two broad types: knowledge *about* their situation and *know-how* which is concerned with usable methods and techniques.

The first requirement of knowledge is concerned with two things:

(a) information about the product, its properties and its market, or about the service, its nature and its clientele;

(b) information about the people who will be involved in its production and distribution, including knowledge of their requisite skills and abilities.

This knowledge cannot be conceived simply as bits of information or 'facts'. It must also be thought of as 'organised' or 'integrated' information – that is, it must be held in the manager's mind in a manner that allows him or her to understand the referents and the way in which they relate to one another.

The second element of knowledge is concerned with know-how rather than purely factual knowledge. This focuses more clearly on the methods and techniques which may be employed to realise objectives, and on their properties and their potentials. In this case, too, it is not sufficient merely to know that a method or technique exists, or to be able to identify and describe it as a thing. It is also necessary to understand the way and the circumstances in which it might operate to bring about some desired result. In essence, this calls for an understanding of the processes of causality associated with any given method or technique. This is not the place for considering the purely local factual information which managers need to enable them to do their work, but some attempt is made in the following chapters to identify the main methods and techniques in the human resource management area, and some of the main considerations which arise in connection with their application.

Diagnostic Skills

Such knowledge is not to be confused with ability or skill: a person may know about a method or technique but be unable to apply it in a constructive way. The concept of know-how, however, is usually defined in such a way that it includes a skill. Koontz *et al* (1980) define management know-how as composed of both management principles and management techniques. Management principles are defined as the characteristic duties of a manager as expressed in basic concepts, such as those of organisation, direction, and control.

Management techniques are those methods which may be employed to put these principles into practice in a given situation. A manager needs a knowledge of both of these to be effective, and know-how involves the effective application of this knowledge. Know-how becomes a composition of both knowledge about a technique and skill in actually applying it. Nevertheless, skill may still be recognised separately.

The diagnostic role of the manager is associated with the skill of making judgements of the reality (or reality testing) and of what to do about it. Such judgements have to be made, not only of impersonal 'situations' but also of people in the work situation, and examples are provided in the following chapters of attempts to control this exercise of judgement in the human relations areas in relation to selection and performance appraisal. The exercise of judgement is a skill, in the sense that people can improve their ability by guided practice, although it also follows that not everyone is 'good at it'.

The most useful approach to categorising the judgement involved in management is that provided by Vickers (1965) in the course of the sixth Elbourne Memorial Lecture. His opening definition of judgement associates it with:

> 'The power of reaching "right" decisions (whatever that may mean) when the apparent criteria are so complex, inadequate, doubtful or conflicting as to defeat the ordinary man'
> (Vickers, 1967, pp 45—6).

He goes on to identify three types of judgement which he associates with the three stages of the decision process (as described above): reality judgements, action judgements, and value judgements.

Reality judgements are judgements of the nature of the world or of the environment. They establish what that world is like, or how it appears to the judging mind (and thus help to define any 'problem'). They depend, initially, on 'facts' about that world, but facts are themselves interpretations of the reality created by the judging mind. This intervention of 'judgement' to establish what *is* the state of reality makes the judgemental process hazardous. Information on market trends or individual performance trends may be gathered, but what is produced is what someone somewhere judges to be the material or desirable attributes of the situation which ought to be recorded or noted. The perception of that situation which emerges from a 'reading' of those facts is, consequently, a biased or 'slanted' one.

Action judgements are those made about what can be done about the reality, or about the 'problems' which a reading of its state throws up. They are applied to those potential actions or solutions which might be found by search or memory, and be expected, with some degree of probability, to 'pay off'. This does not mean that *all* potential solutions have to be reviewed: clearly, this is never possible as man's memory and capacity to search are limited. Nor does it mean that precise probabilities can be attached to those which are recognised; rough estimates of probability are frequently all that can be made. Nor does it mean that some actions are necessarily right and some wrong: the question of whether they are one or the other is itself often a matter of judgement.

Value judgements are those assessments which result in choice or decision. They do not necessarily respond to maximising or optimising criteria because they may be designed to produce no more than a satisfactory outcome, but they do depend on an assessment of value in relation to some scale of value or preference. They might satisfy one criterion, but be criticised or invalidated by someone else adopting a different one, or by the same person in other circumstances (Vickers, 1967, pp 47–9). It is the fact that a value judgement can only be evaluated by another value judgement that gives this type of judgement its special quality and its difficulty.

Vickers's own summary of his position on the subject states that:

1　Judgement is a fundamental, continuous process, integral with our thinking.

2　It has three aspects – for simplicity, three kinds of judgement – value judgement, reality judgement, action judgement. The first two are more fundamental and important. Action judgement is only called for by the interaction of value judgement and reality judgement, and is only selected by further use of the same criteria.

3 The aspects of the situation which are appreciated (reality judgement) and evaluated (value judgement) are determined by the interests of the judging mind (Vickers, 1967, p 52).

Mental Processes in Judgement

The exercise of these kinds of judgement is inescapable in all exercises of leadership, including those of management. Such judgements require the application of qualities of character and mental abilities to the ephemera of the situation. The nature of these requirements has been developed by Vickers, and some of the work of psychologists is also material to the issue.

Reality judgement must be continuously applied to the situation in which a manager operates: he or she is required to monitor events and trends in that situation to ascertain whether problems are developing and, if so, what their nature is. This calls for continuous analysis and synthesis, in fact, for the constant application of the 'problem-solving' processes which Gagne recognises in the human being's basic educational process (recognition, linking, connection, association, discrimination, conceptualisation, rule learning, and problem-solving) (see above, pp 83–4).

This application does not, however, provide a boundary to the problem: the limits are, in Vickers's words, established by the 'interests' of the judging mind. But the requirement that managers work to some defined objectives or in some identifiable interest (such as that of the shareholders) represents an attempt to place a boundary around the problem. Only those events and trends which operate against that defined interest are to be regarded as creating 'problems' which the manager is to recognise. Even when a restriction of this kind is entered, however, the decision-maker has to develop a sense of what is relevant to the undertaking. Furthermore, the maker of reality judgements must necessarily be open enough to recognition of unpalatable facts or trends and courageous enough to define undesirable problems (Vickers, 1967, p 60).

The action judgement also involves mental processes of analysis and synthesis, but the demand on its maker is less fraught than in either of the other cases considered. The need here is to be aware of what might solve the identified problem, or, where awareness is not present, to search (or research) for possible solutions. In some cases, what is required is a memory of what has succeeded in the same problem situation before, but in others, what is required is high level ingenuity in applying the 'rules' in a new way to produce a solution. This task is bounded by the definition of the problem on the one hand and the values to be applied to its solution on the other, but it still calls, on occasion, for qualities of imagination and creativity. It is also often capable of being handled experimentally and iteratively: as one step is defined, the next one takes shape, and so on.

This kind of judgement depends most directly on knowledge of models, theories, methods and techniques. These form the repertoire of solutions to past problems, which are thought to have value as solutions to possible future problems. Their sheer volume dictates that they be passed on to successive generations in ever more specialised packages – those forming the bodies of knowledge of the academic disciplines or the crafts. Once learned, they equip the individual with a specialised repertoire which can be drawn on when he or she is confronted with the need to find a way of solving some problem. But the tendency to focus learning on limited sets of such tools also helps to blinker the trained professional or craftsman, preventing really creative activity.

The processes involved have been widely researched, and it is clear that different people approach the exercise in different ways. There are those who tackle the problem of what might work in a piecemeal fashion, and others who attempt to deal with the broad principles before tackling the intermediate steps (Johnson, 1972; Raudsepp, 1963). There are those with a flair for being 'creative' and others whose painstaking approach eventually produces solutions. Nevertheless, most people faced with the need to make this kind of judgement will tend to review the known and familiar (the traditional solutions) before moving to consider totally new concepts (Vickers, 1967, p 59).

The value judgement is usually more difficult to make because it involves the application of 'values' (or preferences) which are always subject to evaluation by other value judgements, based on different values. Values, as we saw above, provide the basis of motivation: what is valuable provides the foundation for decisions about the action to be taken, and if that action is unlikely to produce a value, there is little incentive to take action. But values also enable people to organise their actions (and therefore their lives), but when value judgements are challenged the challenge occurs, consequently, at a fundamental level: the challenge can shake not only the judgement or decision, but the basis on which life is organised.

What helps in the process of making value judgements is the

existence of given values or given standards. Where the undertaking subscribes to certain 'core values' (such as those adopted by IBM — excellence in relations with customers, respect for the person, and excellence in all that IBM employees do), these provide a basis for appeal in the event of challenge, and thus provide a modicum of security in what is otherwise an uncertain area. It therefore helps the person to make such judgements if he or she has 'firmly held' values (ones which are 'unshakeable'), whether they are 'personal' or derived from incorporating the undertaking's values as the individual's own.

Implementation and Interaction

Managerial work also depends on either coercing or persuading others to perform their work more efficiently, sometimes referred to as 'doing their work by getting others to do theirs' or as the 'management of the labour process'. It is necessarily concerned with working through other people (managers or workers). Research into managerial *behaviour* tends to confirm that managers spend more than half of their time in some form of communication about work; just how much more apparently depends on the dynamics of the relationship between system and its environments (Dubin, 1962; Thomason, 1966). Because the achievement of managerial objectives depends on purposive and structured interaction, managers also need to possess interpersonal communications skills, identified as 'human relations skills' by Mann (1965).

Even judgemental activities are, in the context of management, usually related to the performances of others. The manager may define the objective to be attained and thus provide the criteria against which performance may be measured or assessed. But it is usually not the efforts of the manager alone which produce the results: these normally stem from the efforts of those who are employed in his establishment, department, or section, and they are what has to be assessed and compared. The measurement operations in which a manager engages are therefore measurements of the performance of other people, singly or collectively.

This provides the manager's role with its second distinguishing feature: its inter-relationship with and interdependence upon the roles of others. In one view of management, its function of making effective use of human capacities and capabilities is stressed above all else (Mann, 1965; Likert, 1961). These inescapable links make it equally inevitable that the manager must interact with other people in the work situation. Whatever his or her particular task functions (as Woodward (1958) calls them), working through other people or managing other people is a necessary element function of every managerial job. It accounts for some of the other distinguishing features, such as the high rate of interruption and the high levels of variation in activities.

The particular feature of this element in the managerial role is, however, that it gives the manager the singular task of determining the actions which these others are to take in order to realise the organisation's objectives. The manager takes the decisions, makes the choices of action, removes the discretion from the subordinates, and reduces for them the uncertainty as to the action required of them with which they would otherwise be beset. This personally satisfying feature of the role demands its price: the manager must know and understand the people through whom he or she must work.

The implementation of decisions calls for the exercise of two connected kinds of skill: the skill of communicating ideas and the skill of influencing others to modify their thinking, feeling, or behaviour. Because many decisions in organisational settings are intended to remove the choices which others might face, they must be communicated in such a way that the people intended to be affected are led to make the necessary changes.

Interpersonal communication can therefore be appreciated at three distinct levels – the technical, the semantic, and the impactual (Shannon and Weaver, 1949, pp 95–6) for each of which different kinds of managerial ability are called for: the ability to access channels of communication; the ability to construct messages capable of being comprehended; and the ability to effect influence.

The occasions for such communication are many. They assume different forms. Simple instructions from a supervisor to a worker is one form which relies on a predisposition on the part of the receptor to accept them. Training processes are similar but are usually intended to provide the individual with the understanding and skills necessary to perform tasks without the necessity for constant instruction. Counselling and other forms of advice-giving provide yet another setting in which there may be no presumption that the advice will be accepted as a basis for changing behaviour, and greater persuasiveness on the part of the communicator may be required.

The ability of the manager to influence is not merely a question of choosing the appropriate means of communication for transmitting decision-based messages to generally receptive receivers. In many circumstances, perhaps all, the meaning of the message transmitted may be unacceptable to the intended receptor, and the influence attempt must be conceived as being made against his or her wishes, or against opposition. This type of influence situation is often identified with negotiation or bargaining and is seen to require at least marginally different skills by virtue of the presence of opposition.

This resistance to attempts at influence may occur in a number of different settings, ranging from the settled primary group to the institutionalised trade union. The small group may form for a variety of reasons, but once it has done so, it tends to equip itself with its own frames of reference and norms of conduct, and thus present to the outside world an insulated cocoon of values, attitudes, etc., into which penetration of new ideas is often difficult. The institutionalised group, such as the trade union, presents a similar problem to the communicator and is able to back up the resistance to new ideas with recourse to more formalised sanctions than are available to the small voluntary group.

Organisation and Self-organisation

The other main type of skill required involves an ability to organise the relationships which contain the interactions of others (the organisation function) and the approach which the individual makes to the performance of his or her role (self-organisation).

The need for the first of these stems from the fact that management involves working through other people; the manager cannot, and is not expected, to take action directly to realise the ends being pursued by the enterprise. The requirement is not just that he or she should persuade others to do certain things in certain ways, as is most directly involved in supervision, but also to ensure that those who need to interact in their work will be helped to do so. This involves the design of the containing organisational structure, but it also entails putting in touch with one another those who need to meet and converse. This facilitator role applied at the local small group level is often under-recognised in practice.

The need for the second stems from the usual lack of an in-built structure for managerial work tasks. General objectives and key tasks may be identified, but this does little to reduce the interruption levels or prevent the development of unforeseen problems. It therefore becomes easy for the manager to become overwhelmed by immediate problems, so that the major tasks − particularly those which demand the development of plans and procedures, or the exercise of influence − become neglected. This tends to result in the momentum of the operation being lost. It also forces the manager to be concerned with choices of action to be taken, priorities to be allocated to tasks, and allocations of time to be allowed, and therefore with problems (and associated) skills of self-organisation and time management.

Reading:

Lawrence (1975).
Northcott (1955).
Price (1975).
Taft (1962).

Torrington and Hall (1977).
Torrington and McKay (1986).
Vickers (1965; 1967).

9 Human Resource Planning

Human resource planning (or manpower planning) may be defined as a process whereby courses of action are determined in advance and continually updated, with the aim of ensuring that:

(a)   the organisation's demand for labour to meet its projected needs is as accurately predicted as the adoption of modern forecasting techniques allows, and

(b)   the supply of labour to the enterprise is maintained by deliberate and systematic action to mobilise it in reasonable balance with these demands.

This remains an adequate description, regardless of the degree of sophistication with which the process is carried out. The small, secondary sector organisation goes through this process, even if it is done 'on the back of an envelope'. The larger, primary sector organisation may adopt some of the more complex approaches mentioned below, but it is attempting to achieve the same kind of end by so doing.

Human resource planning comprises three main types of activity, carrying out an analysis of human resource requirements, making forecasts of future states, and developing plans of action. In Bell's words, it requires,

> 'The systematic analysis of the company's resources, the construction of a forecast of its future manpower requirements from this base, with special concentration on the efficient use of manpower at both these stages, and the planning necessary to ensure that the manpower supply will match the forecast requirements'
> (Bell, 1974, pp 9–10).

The prior analysis is necessary to ensure that sufficient standardisation is introduced into both supply and demand side factors to permit forecasting and planning to take place, without having to rely on unsupported judgements (hunches or guess-work). Identifying trends in demand and supply (along with idiosyncratic developments which might introduce a quantum change in those trends) is needed to indicate whether some action is likely to be required to bring supply and demand into line with one another. Creating plans of action is a necessary basis for effective action (although they remain sterile without the subsequent action upon them).

It is by no means axiomatic that all organisations will carry out exercises of this kind. Nor does it follow that those which do not are necessarily inefficient or hide-bound. The extent to which a sophisticated approach to analysis, forecasting, and planning is necessary is likely to depend on the kind of relationship which the enterprise develops with its environments, and particularly its market environments. Consistent with the implications of the models advanced in the Introduction to this book, some primary sector organisations working with an internal labour market strategy will probably be drawn into these activities; most secondary sector organisations are likely to avoid them and rely on broad intuitive judgements unsupported by data.

ANALYSIS FOR HUMAN RESOURCE PLANNING

Human resource planning starts with an analysis of the demands which the job makes upon those performing it, and a consideration of the capacities and capabilities of people which might enable them to meet these demands. This focuses on job and skills analyses. The definition and description of the work demand is usually built into a set of job descriptions. These are then extended to identify the kind of person, by quality and qualification and by aptitude and skill, thought to be needed to perform the work as defined. Together, these constitute the database from which projections can be made (by modifying job descriptions to accommodate changes brought about by changes in mechanical technology, for example) and to provide a basis for future action.

The Job Description

The job description attempts to describe in relevant but not great detail what is involved, what kind of demands on the worker are made by it, and how it fits in with the other jobs which surround it (see below, pp 255–7). Sometimes it is prepared for a standardised job and sometimes for an individual job. Where work study analyses have been made, the descriptions prepared for this purpose may be used in compiling a job description, although they are usually not relied on because they deal only with the more mechanical features of work. Descriptions prepared in the course of exercises of job redesign may also be used in the same manner. Whatever analytical method is used, however, the aim is to state, in writing, just what is required by way of accomplishment and methods and how it is to link with other jobs in the work sequence.

This description should, in principle, be capable of serving a number of purposes — namely, those of:

1 human resource utilisation, based on the information about the nature of the tasks which will readily allow further division and/ or recombination in the interests of improving production and productivity;

2 performance evaluation (sometimes linked to schemes of incentive or measured day work), for which purpose the description must contain information on the standards of performance which are expected of the person performing the job;

3 recruitment, in that it provides the information necessary to infer the kind of person — defined by qualities and qualifications — needed to perform the work;

4 training, in that it will indicate what demands are made which are either not currently being met by personnel performing the jobs or not likely to be capable of performance by recruits without specific training;

5 job evaluation, in so far as the demands on the performer are identified in a sufficiently rigorous fashion to allow judgements to be made about the relative worth or value of the jobs in a job family or organisation.

In practice, very rarely does a single job description contain the information needed for all major control purposes. Separate job descriptions are often prepared for the purposes of training and job evaluation, which require information on skills and job demands, respectively.

Even if it is not complete in all of these respects, it serves two important purposes.

1 It serves as a basic instrument of control — which can be used for purposes of employee selection, induction and training, human resource utilisation, job evaluation, and employee development.

2 It provides a means of communicating what is required to those from whom it is required. It has its limitations as a 'static' record of something which is necessarily dynamic, but it also has advantages in offering some guidance to workers.

It also provides the foundation for specifications of the kinds of skill and person required in and for the job.

The Content of a Job Description

Typically, the job description has the form of an increasingly detailed statement of the nature and content of the job. It contains:

1 An identifying title, along with information locating the job in the horizontal sequence of work flow (for example, division or section) and in the vertical hierarchy (for example, whom the worker reports to and whom he or she is responsible for), and such cross references as enable further information on the job to be found (for example, to work study sheets).

2 A brief description of the nature of the job with the intention of identifying the kind of work it is, and indicating how it differs from other jobs (which may be superficially similar or be identified by the same generic title). Some reference is also made to the supervision received and given, and to the scope of the person's authority and responsibility for materials, tools, machines, people, finance and safety.

3 A more detailed description of the job responsibilities and content, detailing the tasks to be performed and the manner in which these both relate to overall purposes and differ from other jobs in the system. For each major component of the job, the section will then state:

(a) *What the worker does* This describes the physical and mental activities in which the worker is engaged (for example, checks figures, files letters and documents, assembles wooden structures, tends patients, repairs fences) and the periodicity with which he/she does so, so that main and subsidiary tasks can be distinguished.

(b) *How the worker does it* This identifies the things and people through or with whom the worker must work, describes the tools and equipment which the worker will use in the performance of the tasks, and indicates which physical and mental aptitudes will be applied in so doing.

(c)　*Why the worker does it*　This is intended to relate the tasks to the other jobs with which this one is associated, indicating the way this set of activities contributes to the completion of the total task and linking the work to the objectives of the organisation, department, or section.

(d)　*What standard of performance will be expected as normal*　This rarely appears in manual worker job descriptions but does so more often in managerial job descriptions in the guise of key results expected. There is, however, always an implicit conception of normal 'skilled performance', and where this can be defined on the basis of analysis and measurement, it is worth including as a basis for control.

(e)　*In what conditions the work has to be carried out*　This depicts the physical working conditions to which the worker must be exposed, and may include any of the following aspects: dirt, heat or cold, need for protective clothing, monotony, noise or vibration, other disagreeable conditions (such as smells), height of working (relevant to hazard), space limitations, wetness, dust, fume, or gases, exposure to weather.

Not all of these will be included in any one job description. (For an example, see Plumbley, 1985, pp 28–9).

The different nature of managerial work is often reflected in the manner in which the position requirements are summarised. The central section of the description will tend to be more explicit on the major areas of continuing accountability and responsibility and indicate the key areas requiring special short-run attention. It will also indicate the scope of the individual's authority for people, things, and territory, and the range of contacts outside this area which have to be maintained (Figure 10).

Specification of Skill and Aptitude

It is axiomatic that employment work can only be done by human beings, and it is well established that such work usually makes only limited demands on their personalities (but considerable demands in some types of job) and capacities. The next step is the process of analysis which involves working out just what requirements of these kinds are entailed in the work.

Figure 10

Position specification

Position Title . . . . Location . . . . Reports to . . . .
MAJOR RESPONSIBILITIES (What is to be done?) A statement of the major areas of activity for which the individual is to be held accountable, and an indication of the latitude the individual has to take decisions in those areas. Any limits to that discretion are stated. An indication of the levels or standards of performance which will be expected in each of the areas.
ORGANISATION TO BE MANAGED (Works through?) The people (identified by role), things, and territory which are to be supervised by the individual.
CONTACTS (Works with?) An indication of the individuals (by position) and groups with whom contact is to be maintained in order to facilitate the accomplishment of the work of the unit under his control.
PURPOSES/RESULTS SOUGHT (Works towards?) A statement of the reasons why the job exists and what overall purposes or results are intended to be served by the performance required.

Certain basic attributes of personality (pleasing disposition, cooperativeness) may be vaguely desirable in most jobs, but they are crucial to performance in relatively few. In specific instances, such as in the roles of receptionist, salesman, bank-teller, nurse or public relations executive, more demands may be placed on personality traits than are made in many other jobs, and where this is the case, special attention has to be drawn to the requirement, usually in a person specification (see p 262).

Capacities and capabilities are more universally required, although they take different forms, according to the type of work involved. These are capable of being represented in either of two ways. Capacity may be potential, when it is often identified as an aptitude, or actual and demonstrable, when it is normally referred to as a skill. Which form is used will depend very much on the kind of labour market strategy adopted.

Where industry relies on the recruitment of persons already possessed of fairly broad skills, such as those contained in job titles like carpenter, fitter, bookkeeper, nurse, teacher, or works manager, the emphasis will be placed on demonstrable skill. This implies that the underlying aptitudes have already been translated by training and experience into types (defined by their occupational titles) and levels of skill (skilled, semi-skilled or unskilled). Aptitudes figure mainly at the point at which career or occupational guidance is being offered on entry into the labour market: subsequently, skill is assessed by tests of attainment, and less attention needs to be paid to aptitude unless a change of occupational direction is contemplated.

Where, as a consequence of technological development or job-redesign, industry becomes dependent on workers who carry organisationally specific job titles (rather than the familiar occupational titles of the past), enterprises become more interested in workers' 'trainability' rather than demonstrable skill. Consequently, the specification of the human resource requirement will more probably emphasise the underlying aptitude of the person to perform certain types of work after the necessary training has been given.

Job Analysis

Some form of job analysis has to be used to identify the categories of skill or aptitude required. This term is used to mean many different things, but here it is used to refer to a process of analysing the demands which a job makes on the person performing it and the (demand-creating) conditions in which it is to be performed (Plumbley, 1985, pp 16–23).

Used in this way, it takes as given the definition of the tasks to be performed and the methods to be used in doing so, developed through application of the methods of the industrial engineer. Job analysis then becomes focused on the demands which these defined jobs make on the person performing them. In the context of selection and training, it aims to provide a specification of the kinds of skills and aptitudes which the person performing the job will require. In the context of job evaluation, it broadens this concept of demand as it seeks to uncover which demands differentiate the value to be attached to the different jobs.

Some of the charts produced by the industrial engineer (see above pp 27–8) in establishing the basic rationality of the job, can be employed in this other context. Many of the main applications of this kind of analysis, however, have been to work which has not been subjected to analysis by industrial engineering methods (for example, craft or managerial work), largely on the grounds that these are transferable skills which do not need to be developed inside the employer's undertaking. For this reason, job and skills analysis has often developed separately from work study analysis.

Job analysis undertaken to inform selection and training cannot, therefore, be divorced from 'skills analysis', which is sometimes put forward as a different method. Both aim to identify what is required by way of capability or skill if a 'skilled performance' is to be attained in any job. Skills analysis has been defined as:

'the identification and recording of the psycho-physiological characteristics of skilled performance and the determination of effector, receptor, and decision-making functions involved'
(Department of Employment, *Glossary of Training Terms*, 1971).

The product of this analysis is the person specification which may be used in selection processes and which may be employed to determine the approach and form of training most appropriate to the development of skilled performance.

The origins of the kind of job analysis which is focused primarily on selection and training, lie in the early work of Viteles (1932) and its application by Tiffin and Rogers (1943). The method was developed in the context of Training Within Industry (TWI), first in the USA (Dodd and Rice, 1942) and later in Britain (Ministry of Labour, 1962). The techniques of skills analysis, as a preparation for the development of a training programme, has grown up in Britain in recent years as a means of making the training process more systematic and more efficient (Seymour, 1949).

Approach and Method

Both approaches are principally concerned with the identification of the distinct skills required to perform a job. Any one job may call for a number of these distinct capabilities – motor, sensory, perceptual, interactive, etc – which may be applied to different parts or to the job as a whole. Both methods therefore proceed by breaking down the total job into 'tasks' or 'suboperations'. The aim of the breakdown is to identify the parts or sections of the job that are associated with a specific skill. This sets this approach apart from that of the industrial engineers whose aim in breaking down the job is quite different.

The criteria for break-down derive from the belief that separate parts of a job may call for the learning and application of similar or different skills, there being no necessary correlation of skill with specific tasks or suboperations. What is then identified as a distinct part is determined by answering the question whether it is associated with 'a new skill', which 'can be an uncommon manual motion with one or both hands, an unusual combination of controlling senses, a combination of foot-and-hand motions, or some necessary perceptual skill' (Singer and Ramsden, 1969, p 37). The analysis will then be employed to develop an appreciation of the job (and associated skills) as a whole, putting back together the separated parts, but now on the basis of a fuller appreciation of the job's demands for sensory aptitude and skill.

The necessary information about jobs and skills is obtained by using a variety of methods. The main one is that of observation by a trained analyst, but in any event this may require supplementation from other sources, and for some jobs, more specialist methods may be necessary from the outset. The supplementary methods are:

1 Interview (usually structured) by the job analyst at the work station or away from it.

2 Questionnaire about the job and its constituent tasks to be completed by the job-holders.

3 Conference with the supervisor, usually to establish that information obtained by observation, interview, or questionnaire has not omitted matters of significance.

4 Perusal of technical information about tools and equipment and data sheets used in work study.

More specialist methods which are applied to some special or unusual jobs are:

1 Film cameras used to record the detail of activity.

2 Diaries, in which a continuous record is kept of non-routine activities over a period of time.

3 Critical incident recording, often by the supervisor, to highlight particularly good or bad performances.

4 Group interview.

5 Group discussion.

Whichever method is used, the object is to assemble sufficient information to demonstrate that the description of the job that results from it is both accurate and recognisable by those who perform the work.

This information may now be added to the statements of duties and responsibilities, tasks, and relationships, which are produced in the form of a job description as a result of work study analyses. This information appears in two forms:

(a)   The abilities which the worker will need to be able to demonstrate in giving skilled performance. Some of these may, in appropriate circumstances, be regarded as being included in occupational titles (such as fitter or bookkeeper) or certified by some qualification acquired as a result of prior training and experience. Others may have to be assimilated in special *ad hoc* training, to be provided by the undertaking itself.

(b)   The capacities which the worker will need to perform this work in the conditions within which it is nested. The work may call for concentration on detail in a situation characterised by frequent interruptions so that in addition to sheer skill, the individual may need to display a particular kind of temperament in order to succeed in the job.

These may be identified with the Aptitude/Skill Specification which attempts to identify one or other of these aspects of the job demand.

It deals on the one hand with the established and familiar categories of skill, considered appropriate to the operation of the undertaking. At the manual level, this will identify broad categories of skilled, semi-skilled, and unskilled, and at the administrative level, a similar approach may be adopted, but with more attempt to identify the functional specialisms applicable. These categories are likely to link fairly closely with types and levels of training undertaken and are often identifiable from a biographical statement of the individual's attainments.

On the other hand, it seeks to uncover what aptitudes the person is required to have where the employment organisation is recruiting those whom it considers to be trainable. Instead of specifying the 'end-skills' which the trainee will be expected to acquire, the aptitude specification places the emphasis on those aptitudes which figure in the usual multiple-aptitude test — verbal fluency, verbal reasoning, spatial perception etc., where these have been demonstrated to be relevant to the training task.

The Person Specification and Planning

These conclusions from the analysis can then be written into the person specification. *The person specification* is built up after considering the demands made by the job as defined for personality traits and capacities and capabilities. These may be categorised as the person's physical, intellectual, or aptitudinal and personality or dispositional attributes (Miner and Miner, 1977, p 67), or by reference to the interview guides prepared by, for example, Rodger (1952) and Fraser (1978) (see also below, p 290). These check-lists, which have been provided for the guidance of selectors, serve equally well as guides to the preparation of the person specification, where one is required instead of a skill specification.

Not all specifications use the framework provided by interviewing plans. Sometimes professional groups develop broad general statements of aptitude and disposition. Niebel asserts that in order to 'achieve and maintain good human relations, the following personal requirements can be considered essential for the successful time study man' (Niebel, 1972, p 272): (i) honesty; (ii) tact, human understanding; (iii) resourcefulness; (iv) self-confidence; (v) good judgement, analytical ability; (vi) pleasing, persuasive personality, supplemented with optimism; (vii) patience with self-control; (viii) bountiful energy tempered with a cooperative attitude; (ix) well-groomed neat appearance; (x) enthusiasm for the job. This could serve as the basis of a person specification to be used for selection purposes.

Using the interview plan headings, such as general and specific aptitude, interests, and dispositions, however, helps to ensure that the questions which the interviewer needs answering about the personal requirements of any job are covered in the specification. The 'examples' given in Table 12 (see page 280) indicate the kinds of answers which might be supplied.

This person specification becomes important in the selection process, in so far as it provides a guide to selectors as to what they are looking for. But it also becomes important in the manpower planning process in so far as it indicates the type of 'manpower' which may be required and available.

The person specification will indicate in very broad terms whether the kind of labour thought to be required is likely to be already available in the labour market. If the required labour is thought to be in plentiful supply in the form indicated by the person specification, this indicates the relevance of a hiring strategy focused on advertising and selection. If, however, the required labour is considered not to be available in the required form, a hiring strategy based on selection by aptitude for training is indicated.

Where, as traditionally, or currently in some small-batch production situations, the demand is for conventionally defined and trained labour, the difficulties associated with the advertising and selection strategy are usually ones of coping with unexpected shortages in the labour market. Where, as in high technology undertakings, the demand is for non-traditional dispositions and unconventional skills, the difficulties are associated with trainability, not basic skill shortages in the external labour market. It is a function of manpower forecasting to attempt to predict and control these kinds of problem, although, it is repeated, not all undertakings will have the same need to engage in it.

Management succession planning is sometimes singled out for special consideration — usually because it seems to be insurmountably associated with performance appraisal (see below, pp 328 *et seq*). This particular form of manpower planning does not, however, demand the application of different principles from any other variety. If, in the appraisal process, judgements have to be made of the qualities and qualifications of the persons being assessed, these should reflect the same work requirements and the same derived qualities which would be developed to guide selection activities. If 'back-up charts' are prepared, indicating who might step into more senior positions should vacancies arise, these are not in principle different from what is aimed at in all exercises based on internal supply forecasting: one difference, however, is that such back-up charts are frequently ignored in the event of a vacancy arising.

FORECASTING

Forecasting is necessarily difficult because no one can 'know' the future but some statistical methods have been developed to reduce the inherent difficulties. There are, however, two very real dangers in all human resource planning:

1 That the outcomes will be dismissed because no one can know the future. This is to mistake the nature of systematic forecasting.

As Brech has argued, 'Forecasting is the use of a numerate and logical system, incorporating judgement values, to evaluate the probabilities of future occurrences or outcomes. It is not a scientific method of prophecy, which implies knowing the future with certainty ... It identifies possible outcomes and assigns them their relative probabilities. The logical structure is based on the known relationships and past experience ... and ... incorporates an assessment of how people or events are likely to react as judged from that experience, after allowing for known or probable changes in the environment' (Brech, 1975, p 28).

2 That forecasts will be treated as prophecies cast in tablets of stone and therefore unalterable and completely binding on all future actions. On the one hand, forecasts are as good as they can be made, but not perfect. On the other, they can be (and therefore must be) continually updated as new data become available and plans must then be altered in response. It is not unusual, therefore, for a *firm* plan to be adopted for the next year, with tentative plans for the next few years to be made as a back-up.

Human resource planning requires four sets of forecasts to be made of business objectives (or mission); of demand for resources stemming from the mission; of the supply of resources from within the organisation; and of the supply likely to be available only from outside it (Bryant, 1972, pp 14–15). The ease with which these can be forecast varies. Figure 11 shows the three main areas in which *resource* forecasts are required, and the factors which can, in the typical situation, be expected to influence the amounts and types required in the future.

Business/Mission Forecasts

Demand forecasts are based on 'the formulation of the organisation's overall objectives' for a longer or shorter period into the future. The length of this projection will reflect the amount of uncertainty which is perceived to surround its activities, but will usually be quite short for many business undertakings (Lawrence, 1973, p 15). In the context of recession, the horizon is likely to be brought much closer to the present.

By no means all organisations attempt to forecast how they will cope with their external (product markets or clients) environments in the future. Those which do not, preferring to operate as 'pouncers' rather than as 'planners', are in no position to make forecasts of demand for labour. Their human resource 'plans' will rest on the hope that whenever they need extra labour in future, they will be able to recruit it from outside sources; similarly if demand falls away, they expect to be able to discharge any surplus labour. This approach may not qualify as 'planning', but it is common and efficient enough where it fits the strategy dictated by the undertaking's market position.

Figure 11

Components of human resource forecasting

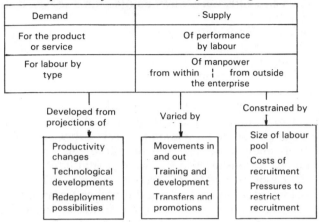

Demand	Supply
For the product or service	Of performance by labour
For labour by type	Of manpower from within ¦ from outside the enterprise

Developed from projections of	Varied by	Constrained by
Productivity changes Technological developments Redeployment possibilities	Movements in and out Training and development Transfers and promotions	Size of labour pool Costs of recruitment Pressures to restrict recruitment

Based on: D J Bell, *Planning and Corporate Manpower* (Longman, 1974, pp 10 and 12)

The many organisations which do have to make forecasts of where they will be operating in the future, do generate data which can be used in making forecasts of demand for labour. Even in this case, however, the translation of corporate plans into human resource plans is by no means easy, and many organisations may see little benefit in using them to project likely future demands for labour because of the inherent difficulties and the costs involved (Smith, 1971, p 49). If the corporate plan aims to achieve a particular return on capital, this by itself will not translate easily. If it is expressed in terms of sales of product units, it might prove somewhat easier. Nevertheless, the tighter the external labour market and the greater the organisation's perceived need for stabilising its supplies to its product market, the higher will be the probability that the undertaking will attempt to use its market/mission data to inform its human resource forecasts.

For many organisations, the forecasts of the future demand position for products or services will involve fairly straightforward extrapolations from the past. They will involve projections of past trends in the markets and the undertaking's market share, or in the need levels which service organisations attempt to reduce. Deliberate decisions about product mix or which markets to enter or develop and which to withdraw from, however, will clearly make such trends poor predictors of the future. This means that this area of forecasting is one in which deliberate changes can be expected and in which as a consequence accommodation must be made for non-trend data.

Such accommodation requires the running together of product/ service planning and human resource planning. But the gathering and manipulation of the data in respect of these processes are often carried out at different levels and in different departments within organisations. This leads to difficulties in reconciling data so that they are amenable to ready decision-making. Decisions to container-ise general seaborne cargoes during the 1970's were, for example, often taken for good economic reasons but in isolation from decisions about personnel and industrial relations: the early de-manning decisions in the docks were based on the proposition that the change-over could be effected by relying on voluntary severance of dockworkers, but in the event this proved too slow and led to the complete removal of container traffic from London and Liverpool. The two projections were clearly out of line with one another.

Labour Demand Forecasting

The forecasting of probable levels of demand for labour in the future requires that the 'work' requirement of the business/mission plan be translated into units of labour. This in turn depends on two translation exercises: the conversion of work into labour units; and the conversion of labour units into skill categories. Much of the first type of activity will, in line with what has been said above, involve the managment service specialists. Much of the second falls to the lot of the personnel specialists.

The particular contribution of the industrial engineers in this area lies in their ability to translate product/service demand data into *units of human resource*. This may be done by fairly simple forward projections from past data if the future is assessed to look very much like the immediate past (with perhaps some small percentage addition or subtraction). Whatever method is normally used to derive standards (from the range discussed in chapter 1), will serve here to support the forecasts. Where new products or services are to be introduced in the future, the work study procedures for reducing these to a set of labour standards will need to be applied. Similarly, where productivity changes are planned, new standards will need to be worked out in advance to allow forward projection.

Personnel specialists tend to have a more limited role in forecast-ing human resource demand. Many of the basic data on manual labour requirements are provided by line management and industrial engineers. The manpower planner's role is to read these into a demand forecast on the basis of appropriate job titles (usually of the skilled, semi-skilled, unskilled variety) with comparatively little modification.

Outside this area, labour tends to be regarded as possessing greater task flexibility, so that the one-for-one relationship implicit in highly standardised and routinised operations does not hold with the same force. Identification of job titles to be fitted into the forecast involves recognition that some, at least, are capable of performing very different tasks from the ones immediately demanded, so that there are more options for 'using' any particular unit of labour for different work should circumstances change.

The development of actual forecasts most commonly employs one of two main statistical techniques, depending on the structure of the workforce and the market circumstances within which it operates.

1 *Single-cell techniques, used to extrapolate employment in a particular skill (such as fitter or secretary) in a particular sector (such as a single industry or local labour market) on the basis of (possibly quite long) time series.* The method can be used to forecast what could be expected to happen to a single skill if the (forecast) trend in production or technological development is of a given order (Stainer, 1971, chapter 6). This method is most suitable for comparatively stable situations and relatively short-run forecasts.

2 *Matrix techniques, used to indicate how the numbers in a family of skill categories which influence one another might be expected to change over time as changes occur in substitution or productivity.* The emphasis in this technique is on showing how the job family as a whole is affected over time, given assumptions about changes in demand for work activities contained within the family (Lawrence, 1973, p 19; and Bosworth and Evans, 1973). This technique is more apposite to the situation in which jobs are less likely to stand on their own, and more likely to be linked to one another through promotions and transfers, as, for example, in white collar 'career' departments or organisations.

Whichever technique is used, what will emerge from the exercise is an indication of how many people in different age-skill-experience categories will be required to meet the work demands generated by the corporate plan.

Internal Supply Forecasting

Forecasting supply is more directly the province of the personnel specialist. It aims to answer whether the organisation can count on having labour available to it in the categories required when it wants it. Supply forecasts are of two types, internal and external supply. Because different organisations operate with different dependencies on internal and external labour markets, these two types of forecast have differential importance to different undertakings.

Internal supply forecasting tends to be easier to carry out than external supply forecasting, because the projection of how much of the present labour force will remain to the firm after labour turnover has been taken into account, is fairly readily established by using fairly straightforward statistical methods. This depends, however, on the collation and extrapolation of labour force trend data, but as these data are often assembled for other purposes, the recording and reporting activities may have to be restructured to support this kind of forecasting. When computers are introduced into the human resource recording process, it is usually sensible to rethink the whole process, including what data are to be collected and stored.

The organisation either has, or can obtain, the basic demographic data on its current 'stock' of employees (such as age, sex, skill, length of service, experience gained, capability and potentiality). It also has or can accumulate data on the flows of labour in and out (recruitment and wastage) and between similar or different status jobs within the organisation (transfer and promotion) (Smith, 1976, p 54). It can therefore project the future stock by modifying the present one according to the predicted flows over the intervening period. In effect, this uses an actuarial (life-expectancy) method to provide a picture or profile of what the workforce of the organisation can be expected to look like in x years' time. The opportunity to use computer technology in this process makes the whole exercise less of a burden than once it was.

The organisation that is comparatively small and without the services of highly skilled statisticians will usually be content with projections made on the basis of such simple actuarial models. In very large organisations, such as the civil service, producing internal supply forecasts to set against future project demand profiles, is thought to require greater sophistication in the application of statistical methods.

The three main techniques which have been developed to improve this kind of forecasting are based on the alternative views that either employees will be *pushed* through the system (for example, when being promoted), *or* they will be *pulled* through it (as a consequence of ageing) *or* they will move as a result of both sets of forces acting together. There is little doubt that these give more accurate forecasts (when the assumptions hold). The data can be run through a computer to give speedy output and allow the 'what if ...' questions to be asked and answered. 'Unfortunately, these models suffer from being computationally inconvenient and mathematically obscure to the non-technical person' (Lawrence, 1973, p 14), and tend not to be taken up by many organisations (Bell, 1974, pp 57–62; Bartholomew, 1976).

The extent to which sophisticated modelling of this type forces closer attention to be paid to the data being input does, however, tend to show where existing data are deficient in providing the kind of information needed to make decisions. Personnel departments frequently collect data on lateness, absence, labour turnover and the rest, but often in a form which will not inform decisions. In addition, the data that are collected are frequently subjected to no more complex statistical operations than averaging over a whole population, and even those subcategories may display quite different tendencies and propensities which are then lost sight of in the overall, average, figures. More sophisticated modelling and the need to input data to the computer frequently shows up these shortcomings (Lawrence, 1973, p 14).

External Supply Forecasting

Every organisation is, at least in the long run, dependent on the availability of labour from external sources. Even the organisation which operates as an internal labour market depends on external supply at the bottom end of each promotional ladder. The organisation that relies on the external labour market almost entirely, is, by definition, constantly dependent on its vicissitudes.

The NHS provides an example of this kind of problem, as it currently projects a major problem of nurse recruitment for the next ten year period. The manpower demand forecast, based on current figures and trends, is that the NHS needs to recruit about 30,000 additional nursing staff each year, of which currently about 70 per cent are drawn from education and training and about 30 per cent from the large pool of trained staff who return from other activities. Almost 50 per cent of recruits are females with between two and five 'O' levels. About 21 per cent of those entering training drop out before completing the three year training programme; wastage of trained staff runs at about 10 per cent per annum.

The projections of the numbers of people entering the labour market with these qualifications over the period suggest that there is likely to be a decline betwen 1983 and 1995 in line with the basic

Figure 12

Sources of labour to the undertaking

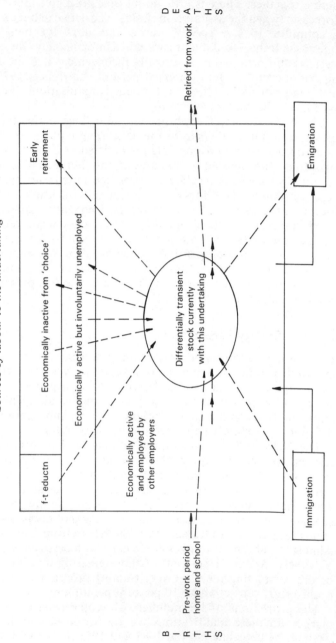

demographic trends (see Labour Force Outlook for Great Britain in *Employment Gazette*, May, 1987, pp 253–63). The UK Central Council for Nursing, Midwifery and Health Visiting has estimated that the numbers likely to enter nurse training in 1995 would be no more than about 16,000, against a projected demand for 32,000. These simple projections thus indicate a need for action to be taken now to ensure that this shortfall of 16,000 persons is avoided.

It is relatively simply to model the flows of human resources into and out of the country's employed labour force (or the economically active population) and to indicate the sources and routes taken by labour to the individual organisation (Figure 12). At any moment in time, the 'pool' of available labour is that part of the population which is either in employment or seeking it. This is variable in size and dependent on customs and attitudes to employment, the state of the economy, and the relative attractiveness of employment and non-employment. The amount of 'skill' available within it will reflect the amount of education and training which is provided and taken up by individuals, and this stock is also subject to variation as a result of actions by governments and government agencies (such as the Manpower Services Commission), as well as by organisations that make training available. Decisions by external agencies are, however, more likely to influence the amounts available than are those of the individual organisation.

Forecasting external supply is a task which is undertaken mainly by the national planners (see *Employment Gazette*), not by those within organisations. National forecasts are usually made of industrial and occupational categories of labour, and more rarely of specific skill categories. Shortage areas may attract *ad hoc* national studies and surveys, as has happened with scientists and engineers and skilled engineering craftsmen in the shortage conditions of the post-war period. For the rest, the generally large numbers included in any industrial or occupational classification render projections by extrapolation less prone to error than those of smaller and more local groups, and little further statistical sophistication seems to be called for.

The problems of forecasting external labour supply are less concerned with finding and applying appropriate statistical techniques (Patten, 1971, p 47) than with the availability of the data itself. Organisations should ideally integrate their demand and supply forecasting with external forecasts, but are often thwarted in this by data being unavailable for relevant categories. As Bell has suggested, 'the company manpower planner must make do with what information he can get' (Bell, 1974, p 75) from such general sources as the *Department of Employment Gazette,* the *Monthly*

Abstracts of Statistics, the data offered by industrial training boards, and special *ad hoc* studies.

Except for those categories of labour (such as managers and professional people) which are linked to regional or national labour markets, the human resource planner inside the organisation is likely to secure more useful information on likely availability of labour from close contact with fellow planners in other organisations in the same local labour market. This is less likely to produce data than to produce information on probable changes in the supply and demand position because of proposed actions by labour market competitors.

The Human Resource Plan

These forecasts do not in themselves indicate what has to be done to assure a balance of demand and supply. They merely inform the judgements and decisions which have to be made. As the quotation from Bell suggests, being informed in this manner is likely to result in better decisions. But the decisions still have to be taken and a statement prepared to indicate what would need to be done to achieve the balance if the assumptions of the forecasts remain valid.

A first and fundamental decision concerns the kind of relationship which the organisation wants to develop with the labour market. The choice is between developing an internal labour market and working with the external labour market. This choice (as has been considered above, pp 170–76) is likely to be influenced strongly by the market position occupied by the enterprise, or alternatively, by the position with respect to the cash available for competing uses within it. Thus the position of the star and cash-cow undertakings will probably dispose them to seek the stability of production given by developing an internal labour market, while that of the wildcat or dog is likely to dispose enterprises to work with the external labour market in order to gain greater labour cost flexibility.

The statement of intent – the human resource plan if one is developed at all – in the second category is likely to indicate the following:

1   What quantities of what categories of labour will be aimed for during any future period of time, with an indication of whether these are higher or lower than the quantities employed in the period prior to this.

    The plan will also need to indicate whether the work contribution required of these people will be the same as or different from that looked for in the immediately preceding period.

The preamble will also need to indicate whether what is being sought is a general capacity and skill which can be hired on the market, or an organisation-specific skill which can only be acquired by training and experience within the enterprise.

These indications are needed because they affect the range of responses which are open to the employer to deal with the problem.

2   Whether this adjustment will be effected by hiring the category in from, or discharging the category out to, the labour market, or alternatively, by internal development and promotion or demotion and transfer.

This will, in all probability, require diverse indications to be given for different categories of labour. For those in decline, indications will be required as to whether they will be allowed to leave or retire voluntarily without replacement, or whether they will be discharged as redundant. For those expected to grow, indications will be required as to whether they will be sought by training and development internally or recruited from outside the organisation.

3   Whether, in either set of circumstances, the pay plus the rest of the remuneration and benefit package offered by the employer will be sufficient − but no more than sufficient − to secure and retain the number of employees required in the various categories.

What constitutes the total remuneration package will be considered below (pp 358−99). It is likely to be a major influence on employee decisions to apply to join or not, and to stay or leave. Consequently, the employer must make some forecast, given the reading of the labour markets in which he chooses to operate, of the levels that will yield the kind of response required (which could be a response of not applying or quitting in decline situations, or one of application to join or decision to stay in growth conditions). He must also make some judgement about what parts of the total package are likely to secure his particular objectives at least cost. A hiring and firing employer is more likely to be forced to pay over market rates in full employment conditions than an internally developing employer who might secure loyalty and commitment by various deferred benefit schemes, whether profit-sharing or pension plans.

4   At what time action needs to be commenced under any and all of these heads to ensure that solutions are found on time to any of

the adjustment problems identified. This is largely a matter of calculating the lead times for any particular action and working back from the date when solutions are required.

The action dates will vary according to the methods which it is proposed to adopt. If new manual skills are to be bought in from a labour market replete with them, the lead time is likely to be shorter than in the case where the decision is to provide training and retraining of present employees who might otherwise be redundant. On the other hand, developing management potential to avoid going out to headhunters would require a longer programme of action.

5   Who is to be responsible for taking the action necessary to ensure that the adjustment of demand and supply is made by the time it is required.

It may be the case that the personnel specialist will have a major role in bringing about this end, but others will also have parts to play in the process. The role of each needs to be identified along with the dates when their action is needed. Where, for example, new products are to be introduced, it is for the development and production departments to indicate in reasonable time when they are likely to require new labour or new skills, and for the recruitment or training staffs to respond; without the initiation, there can be no warrant for action.

A plan that deals with each of these issues becomes the basis for guiding actions in the future. It cannot do this, of course, unless it is well conceived, effectively communicated, and fully accepted as a sensible foundation for action to ensure the matching of human resource supply with human resource need within the undertaking.

SUMMARY

The definition of work tasks and standards of performance remains very largely a managerial responsibility and task. Depending on the kind of production technology employed and consequently on the extent to which discretion is required for the performance of the work, their definition will require some form of job analysis, no matter how crude.

Extended forms of job analysis will permit the identification of the work tasks themselves, the skills and aptitudes associated with them, and, ultimately, the kind of person (defined by reference to capacities and capabilities, qualifications and qualities) needed to perform them successfully and without undue stress.

The results of these analyses, in the form of job, skill, and person descriptions, provide the basis for manpower planning and selection, training and evaluation (although they may need extension or modification when used for some of these specific purposes).

On the basis of the demand indicated by these analyses, it is possible to control the process of taking a view of the future, by adopting (mainly statistical) techniques evolved to handle forecasting problems. The data to which these techniques are applied are capable of being acquired by specialist personnel managers from within and from outside their organisations, although their quality is extremely variable.

The forecasts required are of four kinds; the forecasts of relationship to be developed with the market or the clients, those of the consequential labour demand, those of internal labour supply, and those of external labour supply. These are not all easy to make because of the quality of the data available, but the personnel department has some control over the quality of at least some of those data.

Forecasts of these variables offer guidance to those charged with planning action to maintain a balanced relationship between demand and supply positions; they do not, and are not intended to replace judgement, or to enslave the decision-makers. In practice, they need updating as improved data become available.

Human resource plans need to be drawn up systematically, answering the basic interrogatives (what, why, when, where, how and who?) as applied to manpower. They should not be cast in such detailed terms in the first place that updating produces major modifications to action with such regularity that those affected become disillusioned with the whole process.

Such plans form the basis for human resource management activities of the kind discussed below.

Reading:

ACAS (1987).
Bartholomew (1976).
Bartholomew and Smith (1971).
Behrend (1974–5).
Bell (1974).
BIM (1959; 1961).
Browning (1963).
Connock (1985).
Cooper and Payne (1978).
Hill (1951).
Smith (1976; 1980).
Stainer (1971).

10 Recruitment and Selection

'Selection' of workers with appropriate aptitudes, skills, attitudes and motivations constitutes one of three main methods of control of the labour process. Historically, it rested on the assumption that such workers (already possessed of such trained capacities) would be available to the enterprise from the external labour market. In the secondary sector organisation, this assumption and associated strategy continue to apply. More recently, selection, particularly in the primary sector organisation, has developed to the point where it is assumed that only workers with capacity to benefit from *training after selection* will be available from this source.

The two substrategies of recruitment, generally found in the two sectors of industry, call for different approaches to, and methods of, selection. The secondary sector strategy demands that decisions be made about the kind of labour required and the means of securing it, but this can often be done by using blunt concepts such as occupational training, and broad judgements based on 'experience'. The primary sector undertaking is likely to give more attention to the three sets of activity which form the basis of selection (and the subject matter of this chapter).

1   The identification, by means of job and skills analysis, of the personality and capacity (skill) demands which the job makes on the person performing it.

2   The attraction of enough applicants for the job to enable the organisation's management to select, at minimum cost, a sufficient number of people with the relevant capacities.

3   The selection, by application of judgement which is highly structured and controlled in its exercise, of the most appropriate candidates for employment.

The two substrategies are usually implemented by two distinct types of manager. Where the demand is for control through hiring and firing, the process can be and often is in the hands of the line supervisors and managers: the preparatory analysis and type of judgement required to secure the objective are such that it can be handled by them without overburdening them — unless very large numbers are to be recruited at any one time.

Where the demand is for control through in-house development of workers with no more, initially, than aptitude for training, the process moves into the hands of the specialists, particularly those of the personnel officers: this is because the preparatory analysis and planning requires more attention and this in turn makes implementation more complex and time-consuming. Indeed, dealing with these more complex processes was historically one of the justifications for introducing labour officers into industrial organisations.

The Person-Work Fit

The purpose (which accords with the interests of both parties) of this process is that of securing a fit of person and work tasks. The variable requirements of the different jobs available in industry and the variable capacities and dispositions of human beings pose a general problem of aligning people with jobs appropriate to their personalities and abilities, and that in turn poses for both parties a problem of measuring the differences on each side of the equation. The worker cannot find the job with the characteristics he or she demands (or considers appropriate). Industry, on the other hand, cannot find people with the required skills or dispositions and attitudes considered to be necessary to sustain an efficient and stress-free cooperative relationship.

In principle, these problems can be reduced if both parties, individual and industry, are dedicated to producing a more accurate fit between their several demands and offers. From the standpoint of industry, the need is one of either redesigning jobs to match the demands of people or selecting people who match the demands of the jobs available. From the standpoint of the individual, the need is one of finding the employment which most closely accords with their abilities and taps their motivations. In practice, they are frequently not resolved (and some form and degree of strain or stress results) because the range of offers on one or both sides of the equation are inadequate to meet the demands made by the other. The use of tests (such as 16PF when used, for example, by Informed Choice Limited) can help to screen out those most likely to experience unacceptable levels of stress in the circumstances of the job on offer (Stewart, in Harper, 1987, pp 252-74).

Both parties have some opportunity (but not necessarily equal power) to improve the position. Industry can improve human capacity through training but is likely to have little effect on dispositions in the short run. Only where the market and the machine technology are favourable can it redesign jobs. Individuals *can* (but may not want to) change either their attitudes or their abilities, to make themselves more 'presentable' and 'acceptable', but their opportunities to alter the shape of work are almost non-existent. Improvements are thus more likely to occur as a result of shifts in 'policy'.

Both the definition of the problem and the characterisation of its possible solutions depend on the ability to measure its main dimensions. Successful measurement of individual and job differences relies very heavily on testing instruments, mostly developed by psychologists to assist understanding of either th. numan being or human work. These aim to produce valid and reliable measures or indicators of individual differences or job differences. Industrial users are able to make use of these (where they have been validated) for purposes of predicting either the kind of person needed in particular jobs or the kind of performance a person might be expected to give on available jobs. Because the need for precision in this area is often not very high, however, assessments based on human judgement are often used instead of tests for this purpose.

PREPARATORY PLANNING

The preparatory planning for recruitment and selection relies initially on either:

(a) the managers and supervisors concerned having sufficient familiarity with the jobs, the demands they make on workers, and the kinds of workers able to perform them, to enable them to make adequate judgements in recruitment and selection;

(b) where this familiarity no longer exists, the production, following methods of job and skills analysis already considered (see above, pp 258–63), of two foundation instruments, the job description and the person specification, which will serve to focus and control judgements in the course of selection (see below, pp 289–94).

It scarcely needs repeating that these are likely to be found in association with different approaches to the control of labour.

Preparatory planning is not, however, complete when these matters have been dealt with and either the occupational title or the person specification has been produced. Two other issues have to be resolved, although again the extent to which elaborate procedures will be involved will reflect the fundamental labour-market orientation of the enterprise. These are:

(a) a specification of the terms and conditions of employment applicable to any job for which a vacancy exists, determined on the basis of what terms are necessary to mobilise people in the external labour market; and

(b) an evaluation of the media through which intimation of the existence of job vacancies will be communicated, where the criterion to be applied is that of return in respect of both quantity and quality of applicants.

These are likely to vary from situation to situation and cannot be taken as 'automatically' decided. The rates of pay may appear to be established by reference to a market or a going rate for the particular skill category, but this in itself is a decision as other options are usually open. As we have noted (pp 222–3) in connection with policy, some organisations take deliberate decisions to compete at different levels within the range of rates for particular categories of labour. The appropriate media are not defined automatically by the existence of the most obvious newspaper or journal in the particular labour market. We shall see that different media have very real differences in potential for delivery of applicants.

Over time, systems and procedures for resolving these kinds of question have been developed and are now widely used both by personnel specialists and recruitment and selection agencies who offer their services to employers on a subcontract basis.

Deciding Terms and Conditions

The job description and person specification, together, help to define the aptitudes and skills and the desired predispositions of the workers required. As has already been noted, these are likely to vary between sectors and between enterprises. Increasingly, it seems, a broad distinction is developing between the sectors not only on these dimensions, but also on the dimension of the package of demands (aptitudes, dispositions, and motivations) and returns (remuneration, security, and fringe benefits) which are associated with each.

In the past, it was often necessary in dealing with this question to do little more than consider how undertakings might determine the rate of pay which they needed to offer to mobilise labour. This was frequently accomplished by either informally exchanging information

Table 12

Human attributes required to perform specified work tasks

1. *Physical Attributes and Appearance*

   What does the job require in the way of general health, strength, agility, appearance, manner, and voice?

   It may demand a minimum or a maximum stature, absence of allergies, ability to work in confined spaces, pleasing appearance and manner (for contacts with the public) and absence of accent in speech.

   Examples: minimum height of 5'4" (to cope with reaching down), agility (to cope with crawling in confined spaces), pleasant appearance (to attract clients).

2. *General Intelligence*

   What level of general intelligence is required to do the job (a) satisfactorily and (b) well?

   It may make no particular demand in this area beyond 'ordinary intelligence', or it may require higher levels of generalised aptitude or 'book-learning' which may be measured by appropriate tests.

   Examples: IQ above 120, accurate memory.

3. *Special Aptitudes*

   Does the job require any special aptitudes, for example, motor, manual dexterity, verbal, musical, mechanical, spatial, or perceptual aptitudes?

   Manual work often calls for mechanical and spatial aptitudes and office work for perceptual and verbal aptitudes, for the measurement of which special tests are available.

   Examples: Neat writing and figuring, mechanical aptitude.

4. *Attainments*

   What does the job demand by way of general education, specialised training, and previous experience?

   One broad approach to identifying skills and aptitudes is to look at attainments which other successful job holders have had and to associate them with the kind of information to be found on the usual application form or curriculum vitae.

   Examples: Completed apprenticeship, four 'O' levels, five years' experience in toolroom work.

5. *Interests*

   Does the job require the holder to have special interests in, for example, outdoor pursuits, being with other people, artistic activity, or would performance be improved if the person had such interests?

   Although for many jobs such interests might be totally irrelevant, others, such as the jobs of farmworker, supervisor, advertising executive, might well benefit from their presence.

   Examples: interest in music, interest in public speaking.

6. *Disposition*

   Does the job call for special qualities such as those of leadership, reliability, sense of responsibility, self-reliance, acceptability to others?

   Personality and temperament clearly play a more important part in the successful performance of some jobs than of others.

   Examples: forthright, friendly, caring, not obviously reserved.

about rates paid in particular undertakings or by more formal surveys conducted whether by employer or by professional bodies. (Ways in which this problem might be tackled are reviewed below, pp 363-5.)

Although such a consideration remains relevant in all undertakings, it needs to be supplemented by reflection on the kind of remuneration package which has to be offered if the undertaking is to remain competitive for labour in highly volatile markets. In recent times, the 'big bang' in the City provided an example of the way in which reward packages can become, not only large, but extremely complex in their structures.

The increasing complexity of the package of returns offered to employees in certain labour markets makes it likely that these will be put together in response to what is interpreted as the current fashion. This is not meant to imply derogation: it recognises that the contribution of consultant organisations apart – undertakings are often put in the position where they can determine the contents of any offer only on the basis of what their managers hear or read of as having been offered by other undertakings competing with them in particular labour markets. Consultant organisations with wide contacts in a particular market may be able to produce conclusions based on larger and more controlled samples, but few other undertakings are able to do so where conditions are changing rapidly.

Whatever method is adopted to produce the result, the outcome is an indication of the rate to be paid or the reward package to be offered to attract and retain the labour needed. This forms the basis of the 'particulars' of the job which will be made available to potential applicants. These will also need to indicate some of the novel demands which the job will make of those engaged in it, if only because some newly designed jobs call for very different dispositions, attitudes, and skills from many of the traditionally defined ones.

Evaluation of Advertising Media

Recruitment of labour depends on the organisation that is offering the employment being able to communicate with and attract workers. The different categories of labour are, however, located in different markets, and attempts are usually made to identify that 'pool' of labour (for example, graduates, 16–18 year olds, upwardly mobile 25–35 year olds) within which the type of labour required (qualified or not) is most likely to be found. The basic question is which medium to use to reach potential applicants within this pool. A further question relates to the capacity of various media to deliver applicants in sufficient numbers and of sufficient quality to provide the organisation with a reasonable choice. It is desirable to answer these questions before the urgent need to fill a vacancy arises, and a number of techniques are available to assist in this process.

1   *Establish the location of the potential applicants*:
Potential applicants are located by geography (within a local, regional, national, or international market), age category (young, middle-aged, or older), educational attainment category (university or college graduates, school leavers, professionally or industrially trained, untrained), employment category (management, administrative, professional, clerical, skilled, semi-skilled, unskilled), and socioeconomic class (as defined by the Registrar-General, and identified as I, II, III, IV and V). These have different habits (for example, of reading or watching television or films) which affect their receptivity to messages of any kind, including those relating to job vacancies.

2   *Establish the range of media reaching the labour category:*
There are a number of different types of media (communication by existing employees by word of mouth to their contacts outside, written notices placed at the front entrance to the undertaking, posters in libraries, launderettes or cornershops, freesheets, local, regional, and national newspapers, newsletters and bulletins (often of occupational groups), professional and trade magazines and journals, local radio and television, and films). These have variable relevance for advertising to categories of labour in which the undertaking may be interested, but they also vary in their costs and in their capacity to deliver applicants. Each needs to be reviewed for its implications for encouraging or denying equal opportunities in employment (word of mouth by existing employees may lead, for example, to perpetuation of a particular ethnic or gender mix).

3   *Assess the readership or audience size in each case:*
The size of the network in which existing employees are involved may be small or large and, as with the effect of a notice at the gate, the use of this medium is likely to be assessable only on the basis of experience. The size of newspaper readership, often broken down into socioeconomic classes, and of radio and television audiences, is published by JICTAR.

4   *Assess the match between the labour market aimed at and the readership or audience coverage of the media:*
The decision about which medium to use must establish which medium is likely to 'tap' a large enough group of potential applicants to produce a sufficiently large group to allow a choice to be made. This rests on an assessment of where the bulk of the required labour is located (for example, locally or nationally) and is set against a measurement of the spread of the readership or audience of the medium in question. Ray suggests that the decision about where to locate a notice or an advertisement is best structured by using a decision chart which captures the main characteristics of both the labour requirement and the media (see Figure 13).

Figure 13

Decision chart: media selection

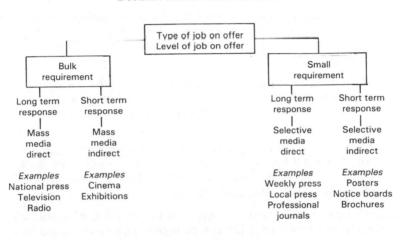

Based on M E Ray: *Practical Job Advertising* (IPM, 1971) p 27).

5   *Assess the response obtained from using any medium:*
Once a medium is used for a recruitment purpose, the employer can evaluate the experience to supplement any more general indications obtained from published sources.

One way out of the difficulty of carrying out this kind of survey is to engage the services of an agency specialising in recruitment. This may appeal to the organisation which does not have the personnel resources to carry out the surveys within the organisation. But useful though this solution is in the particular circumstance, it does not by itself render the method of assessment redundant (it still has to be done by the agency), and it faces the organisation with the task of making assessments of the agencies themselves.

RECRUITMENT

'Recruitment' (or 'employee resourcing') is the process by which an organisation secures the required labour (human resources). It involves four main types of action intended to persuade workers to take employment with the particular undertaking.

1   The trawl of the labour market to attract applications from sufficient numbers of workers of the required types, which may be identified as 'recruitment'.

2   The assessment, by one of more of a variety of methods, of those who do apply for employment as to their suitability for engagement, and the choice of the most suitable, identified as 'selection'.

3   The allocation of those selected to jobs within the organisation, their induction into the work tasks and the organisation, and their follow-up to encourage retention, which may be identified as 'placement'.

4   The evaluation of the performance of those selected, against the criteria established by job analysis and the predictions of the selectors, to provide a basis for review of the approach to staff planning, recruitment, and selection.

Recruitment, in the narrower sense, is the creation of a pool of labour from which a selection can be made. This has been a major function of the specialist personnel department for most of its history (see Niven, 1967; Renold, 1950a; Northcott, 1955, p 226). The preparation of a staffing plan and the recruitment and selection of personnel in accordance with it, still constitute a major part of the role of personnel specialists, although it cannot be carried out without reference to line management. The process is usually initiated by line management and administered by the personnel specialists, with, however, the line managers having the final decision as to who is selected.

It comprises a number of distinct steps, each of which involves its own methods and techniques.

1   *Initiation*   The line manager or supervisor usually initiates

recruitment activity. He or she requests the process to be set in train to secure the services of one or more employees. The stimulus may be:

(a) the termination of the employment of an existing employee for any one of a variety of reasons (replacement);

(b) the movement of an existing employee to a new position on promotion or transfer (substitution);

(c) the staffing of a new operation or process (expansion).

The justification for the initiation will be found in agreed staffing levels or (in the language of public sector undertakings) in agreed 'establishments'. Where a formal human resource plan exists, the request should be reviewed against it.

The initiation is usually effected by simple oral request or completion of a staff requisition form (specially designed for the purpose). The request (in whatever form) should contain sufficient information to enable the nature of the job to be identified and linked with other relevant information about the kind of person required and the terms and conditions of employment relevant to it. Essentially, this is met by bringing together the job description and the person specification where such exist; where they do not, the salient information must be assembled in discussion.

2 *Use of Agencies* Where an undertaking has the appropriate resources for the purpose, the whole recruitment and selection process may be carried out 'in-house'. Otherwise, it may be necessary or desirable to use one form of agency or another on a subcontract basis. This may also be done in respect of special categories of labour.

A number of different types of agency exist to facilitate recruitment and selection for such undertakings or occupational types:

(a) Employment agencies, which will find temporary or permanent employees from among those who register with them, in exchange for a fee charged to the employer.

(b) Candidate registers, sometimes offered by employment agencies, which will circulate lists to employers and in which those seeking other employment are listed according to qualification and interest.

(c) Advertising agencies, which will carry out the recruitment process of producing a field of candidates for a discount from the journals in which the advertisements are placed.

(d) Assessment centres, which use multiple evaluation techniques for evaluating the future potential of mainly managerial and supervisory personnel and thus obviate the need for an organisation to have to apply tests for selection purposes.

(e)   Selection consultants, who will carry out the whole recruitment and selection process to the point of final choice (reserved to the employer) for a fee, acting essentially as a personnel department engaged *ad hoc* on a subcontracted basis.

Employers with limited personnel resources and specialised requirements may find delegation of the recruitment, advertising, and short-listing processes in this way advantageous.

3   *Preparing Information*   Where the request for labour conforms with broad human resource strategies and policies, and it is not intended to use an agency, it is necessary to prepare for the first information exchange between (potential) applicant and the employer. Where it is decided to use an agency, this information may be put together jointly.

(a)   The first kind of information needed is that which is to be given by way of advertisement or 'further particulars', which may be made available on request. This may indicate little more than the occupational title and pay rate, but in other cases it may describe what is wanted by way of capacity and what is offered in the way of remuneration and other benefits. This may be undertaken coincidentally with the design of the advertisement.

(b)   The other side of the exchange relies on the application form (Plumbley, 1985, pp 110–11), which seeks biographical information for administrative purposes and contingent information (which may subsequently be used in the screening and selection processes). Where one is used, it also requires preparation. It ought to ask for that information about the applicant which (as indicated in the person specification) is pertinent to the decisions to shortlist and select for the position advertised. Recent court decisions have laid down some strict requirements in this respect to avoid discrimination; it may be necessary, for example, to show that literacy is a requirement of the job in order to make use of a written application form at all. Assessment information may be asked for (indications of strengths and weaknesses, for example) but this is done more rarely.

4   *Advertising*   If the decision is to carry through the process internally steps will then be taken to advertise the vacancy. This entails:

(a)   assessment of the nature of the appropriate labour market for this type of vacancy – internal, local external, district, national or international;

(b)   identification of the appropriate media to use in advertising the vacancy – internal notice boards, house journal, word of mouth by present employees, advertisement in local or national newspapers or trade journals – with selection based on comparative (past) assessment of efficacy (Ray, 1971; Braithwaite and Pollock, 1974);

(c) preparation of the advertisement in conformity with legal requirements and presenting the necessary information in the most attractive manner consistent with truth, decency, etc., and its publication in the chosen medium (Plumbley, 1985, pp 33 – 49).

The preparation of the actual advertisments can be subcontracted to copy-writers (particularly where large scale recruitment or very senior positions are involved). Where it is done in-house, it is necessary to consider the nature of its potential audience/readership and the nature of the medium through which the message is to be transmitted. It should also consciously aim to arouse attention (usually through the headline), build and hold the reader's interest (frequently by an informative and attractive sub-heading), give information about the advertiser (unless it is put out by a household-name company) and about the job which is on offer (written in terms which avoid clichés and pompous phrases and tap the language which the receptors normally use), and should tell the interested reader what he or she can do to secure information about, and consideration for, the job.

The information about the job will be shorter or longer according to whether the advertisement is for a familiar or an unfamiliar job. Attracting and holding interest in readers who might come across the advertisement only casually requires that the information given should indicate any unusual features – whether challenging or demanding work or highly paid or linked to fringe benefits. In a tight labour market, it might also be necessary to induce action to apply by indicating any incentives being offered for movement (such as the payment of relocation expenses).

5 *Screening* The receipt of applications for consideration initiates the process of screening of applications, using the biographical information supplied on the application form. This is usually done by specialist personnel staff, and increasingly (where large numbers of applicants are involved) with the aid of micro-computers (Lewis, 1984, p 14). This has two objectives:

(a) the elimination of those who, in spite of requirements stated in the advertisement or further particulars, do not have the basic qualifications asked for; and

(b) the categorisation of the remainder into probables and reserves, or the production on the basis of the 'paper' information, of an apparent rank order of suitability as a basis for shortlisting for interview or further action of a similar kind.

In this area, too, the availability of electronic assistance means that application forms can be 'scored' on the basis of selected criteria, and while this does not allow 'decision by computer' it can greatly assist in the reduction of time necessary to shortlist candidates where a large field of applicants is attracted.

This screening process may sometimes be assisted by taking up references before the shortlist is prepared. For example, Makin and Robertson's survey suggested that two thirds of their respondent organisations made use of references for all managerial vacancies (Makin and Robertson, 1986, p 39), a frequency exceeded only by the use of the interview as a selection aid.

References may be sought in the form of a letter expressing an opinion as to suitability, or of a completed questionnaire which asks for specific information or opinion on the applicant. These are usually of limited value because of vagueness in the one case or of misunderstanding in the second. Practice varies in this respect, and sometimes references are not taken up until after a selection has been made and a job offered 'subject to satisfactory references'. In this case, the reference is used to ensure that there are no contra-indications associated with honesty or integrity.

The opportunity to produce a shortlist of candidates who will ostensibly fit the requirements of the job indicates a degree of success in this part of the recruitment process. It indicates that enough candidates are available to allow a choice to be made from among a number of potentially satisfactory candidates. This is not the only criterion of success. In addition, some account must be taken of the cost of achieving this result, and that may be inordinate if a careful control is not maintained over the recruitment process.

Hasty judgements, however, should not be made about success or failure in this area. Many extraneous factors can influence the response obtained, such as the day of the week or the time of year, the coincidence of competitive advertisements appearing at the same time, the state of the economy, and the influence of government taxation proposals or policies. It is likely that the medium used and the form of the message communicated, the image of the employer and the reputation of the business will have some bearing on response, but in a world of competing messages, these endogenous factors may be overturned by exogenous ones.

SELECTION

Once a 'field' of candidates has been produced for the posts under consideration, it is necessary to make a selection from among the candidates. A number of methods of doing this exist, ranging from occasional reliance on the biographical information given on the application form, through the very common use of the interview, to the use of tests as a supplement to other methods.

1 *Planning Selection* Once a shortlist has been drawn up and (possibly) approved by the line manager concerned, it is necessary to plan the exercise in which a selection will be attempted. This usually requires attention to:
   (a) who will be engaged in the task;
   (b) what methods will be employed to inform their judgement in making the choice;
   (c) when the applicants are to be informed of the choice (at the interview or later), by whom (line manager or personnel specialist), and through what medium (for example, orally or by letter).

The first usually turns on which combination of line management and personnel specialists will be used in what numbers, ranging from a one-manager interview (possibly with personnel specialists carrying out some initial screening or tests) to an interview panel of half a dozen drawn from line and staff functions, assisted by specialists administering batteries of tests. The main problem with this is one of ensuring that the interviewers are competent. Most people think that they are good interviewers, and are reluctant to learn the methods necessary to give valid and reliable results and to avoid biases and prejudices (Plumbley, 1985, p 122–4).

The second usually resolves itself into a question of whether the basic selection interview is to be supplemented by any form of test or examination. The interviewer usually has some information on the application form or letter, and this may require supplementation in face-to-face communication. The main criterion determining whether tests are also required is whether the information required for selection must be derived from more precise measures of aptitudes, abilities or personality traits.

2 *Selection by Interview* The main purpose of the selection interview is to secure information on which a managerial judgement can be made and to provide information on which the applicant can make an informed decision as to whether to accept the job. It is necessarily a medium of two-way communication which supplements the information in the application form and

Table 13

An outline of the seven-point interviewing plan

Rodger's seven-point plan lists the following factors as being ascertainable by the interview method. Fraser's five-point plan is similar to this, although it uses different check headings: impact on other people (6), qualifications (1 and 2), brains and abilities (3 and 4), motivation (5), and adjustment (7).

1. *Physical Make-up:* referring to the job's requirements for general health, strength, appearance, manner, and voice, and stimulating the interviewer to ascertain that there are no defects or deficiencies in the candidate under these heads.

2. *Attainments:* referring to the job demand for general education, specialised training, and previous experience, and inviting the interviewer to discover both what experience the interviewee has had under each heading, and what levels of attainment or performance were achieved.

3. *General Intelligence:* referring to the levels of general intelligence required to give both a satisfactory performance and a good performance, and suggesting that the interviewer can ascertain how much intelligence the individual can and does normally display.

4. *Special Aptitudes:* referring to the requirements of the job for such aptitudes as manual dexterity and verbal, mechanical, spatial, or perceptual aptitudes, and inviting the interviewer to uncover these by questioning.

5. *Interests:* referring to the requirements of the job for special interests in different areas of human activity and general interests in work and income, and inviting the interviewer to explore whether interests in intellectual, practical, social, or artistic (etc) matters exist.

6. *Disposition:* referring to the demands of the job for qualities such as leadership, reliability, sense of responsibility, self-reliance, acceptability to others, and inviting the interviewer to find out how the individual rates on these dimensions either by questioning or offering opportunities to display them.

7. *Circumstances:* referring to the position of the inverviewee and the possibility that the pay, prestige, status, and demands of the job (such as hours of work or need to travel) are likely to affect the interviewee's self-conception and private life.

the further particulars, respectively, to help two people take decisions (Torrington, 1972a, p 3). For the selector, the interview 'can provide some provisional evidence and clues concerning the applicant's biographical data and personal circumstances, career pattern and attainments, powers of self-expression, range and depth of interests, intelligence and special aptitudes, behavioural patterns and preferences' (Plumbley, 1985, p 113).

The five- and seven-point plans (Table 13) have been constructed as control instruments, aiming to introduce a systematic element and a degree of standardisation into the interviewing process. The problem is to persuade interviewers to use one or other of them in a coherent manner to secure the information necessary to the making of judgements. There is reason to suppose that were this to be accomplished, the validity and reliability of the interview might be increased.

The interview remains an extremely popular method of selection; Makin and Robertson's survey showed that only 1 per cent of respondents never used it for managerial vacancies, while over 80 per cent used it in one form or another for all their vacancies in this class (Makin and Robertson, 1986, p 39). This is so in spite of the fact that it is costly of staff time, of doubtful validity and reliability (when used alone), and commonly regarded as unsatisfactory by the interviewees. Ulrich and Trumbo (1965, p 114) suggest that this popularity may be due to the fact that it serves a number of different purposes – as a tool of selection, a public relations medium, a recruiting device, and a means of disseminating information.

It has received surprisingly little attention from personnel management researchers (Dunnette and Bass, 1963; Ulrich and Trumbo, 1965; Monohan and Muchinsky, 1983) in spite of the doubts cast on its validity and its reliability (Wagner, 1949; Mayfield, 1964; Ulrich and Trumbo, 1965). Such work as has been done on it suggests:

(a)   that it has low validity and reliability when used on its own, but both may be increased by using it in association with bio-graphical information (from the application form), references and test findings;

(b)   that validity and reliability are higher where the jobs or the candidates concerned are in some sense 'standard' (well defined or very familiar jobs – candidates who can be classi-fied as, for example, craftsmen);

(c)   that the information obtained in interview is more accurate where it relates to the candidate's recent experience, but that accuracy declines with distance back from the present.

Both Wagner and Ulrich and Trumbo conclude that validity and reliability would be improved by securing:

(a)   greater standardisation of purposes and procedures;
(b)   more extensive use of alternative sources of data;
(c)   an interview limited to finding answers to questions about

the candidate's motivation to work and his or her potential for adjusting to the social context of the job (potential compatibility).

With this can be associated a need for provision of training in both values and processes involved.

3   *Use of Tests*   Tests can increase the validity and reliability of the interview method and may be necessary or desirable in their own right where the measures required to support selection decisions must be relatively precise. 'Tests' are of different types.

(a)   Tests of attainment or ability, where the candidate may be given a test of typing speed, skill in shaping a piece of wood or metal, addressing an audience, revealing knowledge and skill already possessed.

(b)   Tests of aptitude or potential for learning some skill, where the candidate is given a number of tests to indicate the extent of manual dexterity, hand-eye coordination, perceptual ability, etc., any of which might be crucial to learning how to perform a range of jobs.

(c)   The so-called personality tests, intended to reveal traits of the individual's personality, attitudes, interests, etc., and used to screen out those with characteristics which have been shown to be inappropriate (Stewart, in Harper, 1987, pp 252–74).

The use of tests to reveal attainments or typical performance may be superfluous, if adequate information is available on the application form and in references. In the ordinary case, tests are unlikely to be used for candidates above the age of 40 years, as their 'track record' is likely to give more indication of capacity and attainment than tests do. Attainments in some areas may be certified by educational diplomas or evidence of completion of apprenticeships, and written or oral evidence of *recent* attainments is likely to be valid and reliable. *Typical* performance is usually more difficult to appreciate without some test, and it is not uncommon to devise and use simple performance tests in reference to simple motor, mechanical, manual or perceptual skills (a short typing test, etc). Although, however,

> 'The unqualified can devise attainment tests they are ill-advised to do so, unless they have a thorough understanding of the statistical concepts involved'
> (Plumbley, 1985, p 138–9).

The layman's self-designed tests will usually be a much cruder affair giving much less validity and reliability.

As undertakings increasingly often recruit workers for their 'trainability' rather than for their demonstrated attainment, more emphasis is placed on the use of general (the old style 'intelligence' test) and special aptitude tests. There are now many of these in existence, but care has to be taken to ensure that they are validated for the kind of population in which the undertaking is interested. Where tests of this kind are available, their application to a cohort of candidates enables aptitudes of the candidates to be compared with those of a much larger relevant population.

The use of tests designed and validated by psychologists (often for research purposes) presents other problems because they are often not validated for the kind of population to which managers will want to apply them. Such plans may therefore present a picture of sophistication and precision, but the layman without knowledge of the underlying psychological and statistical concepts and models is in danger of drawing unwarranted inferences from the results obtained in his or her local application. It is sensible to avoid their use unless trained testers are available to administer and interpret them and to cope with any candidate resistance to this kind of procedure. The alternative approach is to use assessment centres to carry out the testing on a subcontract basis where it is imperative that this kind of information is obtained.

4 *Assessment Centres* Assessment centres represent one rather special kind of 'test' but because they are time-consuming and expensive they tend to be used mainly for managerial and supervisory selection, and where enough candidates are available (usually six as a minimum) to make the exercise worthwhile (Makin and Robertson, 1986, p 39).

Byham defines an assessment centre as:

'a formal system of evaluating individuals (for recruitment or promotion to managerial, supervisory, or sales positions) using multiple evaluation techniques, including various types of job-related simulations and, sometimes, interviews and psychological tests. Common job simulations include "in-tray" exercises, group discussions, simulated interviews with subordinates or clients and exercises in fact-finding, oral presentation, and written communication' (Byham, 1984, p 56).

In order that they can 'work' effectively, these require that the critical dimensions of the jobs in question, and the behaviours most directly associated with them, are identified in advance and used as the basis for the design of the simulations. Necessarily, they demand 'group work' and consensus assessments by a number of senior assessors (the source of time-consumption and cost). A decision to use such centres requires some assessment of their capacity to deliver. Byham has recently put forward suggestions for using assessment centres on an 'in-house' basis. This relies on highly structured interviews or video-tape technology, or both together, to reduce the time assessors spend observing (Byham, 1984, pp 56−57).

5   *Collating and Using the Information*   The various instruments used in the selection process generate both data and information, and these need to be put together in a logical fashion to provide a basis for informed choice. This is a skilled process, involving the assemblage of the information in a way which displays both the indications and the contra-indications of what has been gleaned from these various sources.

Plumbley suggests adopting a system of recording the information gleaned by these various methods:

(a)   assemble the biographical information in chronological order;

(b)   attach to it indications given of attitudes and explanations of reasons for changes in direction during this period.

On this basis the interviewer can make certain assessments:

(a)   what trends and typical behaviour patterns are discernible;

(b)   what progress has the individual made in his or her career; and

(c)   how do these compare with what is being looked for and with other people either in the job or generally?

Effectively, what the selector is attempting to do here is to make an assessment of whether the person under consideration can be 'seen' in the job in question and if so, what is the typical performance he or she likely to give (see Plumbley, 1985, p 113). This is a claimed advantage of the assessment centre which can project the candidate into simulated situations and observe behavioural responses to them, and this might be preferable to attempting to draw inferences from behaviour in other jobs which might not provide the same kinds of challenges and opportunities.

Where panel interviews are conducted, it usually falls to the lot of the chairman to organise these processes. The psychology of choice-making in groups is complex, and requires careful handling to avoid over-dependence on 'superior' and biased judgements. It is obviously much simpler, but not necessarily more valid and reliable, to have judgements of this kind made by the single individual.

Table 14(a):

Evaluation of selection

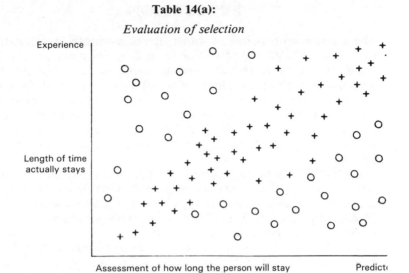

Table 14(b):

Expectation and experience

		Numbers predicted at selection to be:	
		In the better half	In the worse half
Those whose performance is measured as	In the better half	a	b
	In the worse half	c	d

Table 14 (c):

Table of coefficients

Index	Equivalent Coefficient
35.0	0.9
15.5	0.8
8.9	0.7
5.8	0.6
4.0	0.5
2.9	0.4
2.2	0.3
1.7	0.2
1.3	0.1

EVALUATION

The selection process, like any other, can be monitored or evaluated to feed back data on performance and achievement to inform judgements as to whether the methods being used are effective. At its simplest, the process admits of two types of successful decision (where success is evaluated in terms of subsequent performance): the decision to accept the suitable and the decision to reject the unsuitable. It also permits two kinds of unsuccessful decision: allowing the suitable candidate to be rejected and the unsuitable to be selected.

It is virtually impossible to compare the success of those selected with that of those who were not because the latter are not available for subsequent assessment. Some assessment is possible where a sufficiently large cohort is available. This involves comparing either rankings of candidates or their division into the better and worse halves on the score of predicted subsequent performance to indicate whether the method of deciding better and worse proved valid and reliable. As this method will be the same as that used to select or reject it gives some indication of the validity of the whole approach.

The method requires the selectors' predictions of the successful candidates' likely performance, made at the point of selection, to be ranked and set alongside the subsequent levels of performance, as these may be measured against the same criteria. If the assessments at the two points are plotted on a graph, containing the two variables on the two axes, a 'good' or effective approach to selection would be indicated if the plot revealed a long thin sausage-shaped spread. An example is provided in Table 14(a), using the criterion of (predicted and measured) length of stay with the organisation. The spread of ' + 's reveals an effective procedure, that of 'o's a poorer one.

An alternative is to split the selected population into better and worse halves at both prediction and performance stages, and to present this information on a 2×2 matrix, as shown in Table 14(b). If each cell contains the same numbers, the selection procedure is producing a result which would be obtained if chance alone were to determine outcomes. If the population is appropriately divided between cells a and d, the selection method is extremely effective in selecting 'the best candidates'. Intermediate points can be established by using the formula:

$$\frac{a \times d}{b \times c}$$

to establish an index and reading off the correlation coefficient from Table 14(c).

Although relatively simple, both of these methods provide a way of making some evaluation of a central process used in the management of human resources and prevent continuation in blissful unawareness of its shortcomings.

Reading:

Alderfer and McCord (1970).
Arvey and Campion (1982).
Braithwaite and Schofield (1979).
Bridges (1984).
Byham (1984) pp 56–7.
Keenan (1977; 1983).
Lewis (1984).

Makin and Robertson (1986).
McCormick (1979), Pt Two, pp 15–151.
Plumbley (1985).
Ray (1971).
Stewart in Harper (1987), pp 252–74.
Ulrich and Trumbo (1965).
Wright (1969).

11 Training and Development

Training is a process through which experiences are deliberately offered to trainees to enable them to absorb some new perspective, understanding, value, attitude, technique or skill. Landy and Trumbo define training as:

> 'Planned activities on the part of an organisation to increase job knowledge and skills, or to modify the attitudes and social behaviour of its members in ways consistent with the goals of the organisation and the requirements of the job'
> (Landy and Trumbo, 1976, p 222).

Training presupposes that what is behaviourally required can be treated as a problem to be solved by systematically following a predetermined path. As Warren argues, the only valid result of training 'is a measurable increase or improvement in a person's contribution to the organisational goals' (Warren, 1969, p 2).

'Development', on the other hand, is seen to prepare people to perform work beyond that which currently engages them and to accept responsibilities 'greater than they now have' (McGehee and Thayer, 1961, p 12). Brown and Moberg follow this line in defining development as 'involving the acquisition of broader knowledge and skills' (Brown and Moberg, 1980, p 397). To this, Warren adds the element of individual growth as an essential distinguishing feature of development (Warren, 1969).

Training and development in this broader sense rest on a perception that a person learns both to be and to do largely through experience, which may be actual, simulated, or vicarious (such as hearing or reading about the experience of others) (Stokes, 1966, pp 74–5). The human being is largely a product of such learning, and an appreciation of how he or she learns is a requisite of any training activity (see above, pp 77–88).

The general perception of this process is one which emphasises that the individual will learn effectively if three main conditions are met (or if they are created for the purpose):

1 The individual is motivated to learn something new to understand or cope with some general or special aspect of his or her environment.

2 The individual understands something of the relationship between what is to be learned and some acceptable goal which he or she possesses or of which he or she has been persuaded of the relevance to the achievement of these goals.

3 The individual has the capacity and ability to learn what is required for the purpose. This in turn depends on the individual having learned early how, generally, to cope and how to learn from that coping experience (Gagne, 1970).

Motivation, understanding and capacity form the tripod on which all effective learning rests.

Learning occurs as the individual interacts with his or her 'experience'. From this interaction the individual may autonomously develop perspectives, views, attitudes, and behaviour patterns. But he or she is likely to do so comparatively slowly and without conformity to standard 'solutions', unless there is something more. Learning is rarely 'just a matter of experience', skill-acquisition infrequently 'just a matter of practice making perfect', and perspective-formation simply an effect of 'trial and error'.

According to conditioning theory, learning is likely to occur if the experience is repeated and successful achievement reinforces the individual in the specific response (Skinner, 1965).

Seen from another viewpoint, this occurs when (or because) the learner (consciously or unconsciously) uses a closed loop control construct to help him or her organise the information produced by the experience so that a kind of rational learning occurs (Stammers and Patrick, 1975; Duncan and Kelly, 1983; Kolb, Rubin and McIntyre, 1974; Eckstrand, 1964).

In yet a third conception, which forms the rationale for 'discovery learning' (Belbin, 1969), learning is thought to occur as a result of the individual using deductive or inductive reasoning and active experimentation to find solutions to the problems he or she faces (Jackson, 1984).

Human agency is commonly involved in general socialisation or specific training to speed up the learning process and to establish standard or acceptable outcomes. This ensures repetition of experiences, injection of reinforcement, and encouragement of some reactions in preference to others, and provision of perspectives to assist organisation and assimilation (Kolb, Rubin and McIntyre, 1974, p 28). Good training deliberately structures such purposive intervention by others.

Training for Work

The traditionally held mode of training people for work relied on the dissemination of appropriate dispositions and skills through occupationally based institutions. Before the industrial revolution, the guilds (and the professions) assumed responsibility for training, and in the early industrial period employers were able to draw on the product of this system. This system was extremely slow to break down, and vestiges still remain in apprenticeships and professional training. Although a public education system was necessarily developed to provide a very broad and general preparation of people for work, it has not yet provided a substitute for the guild system.

Nevertheless, this early approach allowed many industrial organisations to avoid making their own provision for training. Industry's early strategies of control of the labour contribution assumed that the required knowledge, attitudes, skills, and behaviour patterns would be inculcated 'elsewhere', not within the employing organisation. As industry developed, apprenticeships and traineeships would be facilitated by the larger organisations, and training would be acquired independently by the ambitious and upwardly aspiring workers from the technical colleges; the organisation which chose to avoid making its own provision could probably survive by recruiting from the pool of trained labour thus formed. They were probably helped in this by the progressive simplification of work tasks and the associated reduction in the levels of skill required of workers.

This tradition of avoidance continues in what has come to be identified as the secondary sector, where it is expressed in a continued reluctance to train employees (see MSC, 1980; DE, 1972; NEDO, 1975) despite the persistence of skill shortages throughout the post-war period and into the present period of extremely high unemployment (see *Financial Times*, 12 May, 1986, p 1). If these enterprises provide any training at all, it is confined to 'induction training' (intended to introduce the individual to the undertaking and its ways).

The main development from this early approach left this and any other type of training which might be required to the supervisor. The kind of 'instruction' which is included in the idea of training became, in this context, little different from the 'instructions' which the foreman was expected to give to his section members. With the growth of Training Within Industry (TWI) at the time of the Second World War, some steps were taken to bring training 'instruction' more in line with the then emerging theories of learning.

The quality of instruction at this supervisory level was subsequently improved, but no radically new approach to, nor significant long-run increase in the amount of training provided within industry were introduced. As long as the educational system produced generally competent and broadly compliant citizens capable of picking up the skills of semi-skilled jobs, and the economic circumstances reinforced such values in the adult workers, no greater sophistication in training than that which could be provided by the generalist supervisor seemed to be called for.

This strategy of 'supervision' has had a particular impact on public sector organisations. These were often large enough to justify the development of sizeable functional departments, which might 'take over' some of the more purely instructional tasks of the supervisors. In some cases, the numbers involved were sufficient to justify the development of large training departments (or schools) staffed by specialist functionaries for each of the various craft and professional groups (as is most clear in the NHS). The training was (and is) consequently more directed towards the preservation of occupational standards than towards the development of organisationally relevant dispositions and skills.

Development Strategies

This system has been radically changed by new technologies. These have, in the context of the decline of the apprenticeship system and the failure of the educational system to fill much of the resultant gap, made these earlier selection/supervision strategies irrelevant and inadequate methods of securing the necessary labour contribution. The search for a more adequate response has created two new scenarios.

The first response to the problem was to recruit untrained labour and to train it in organisation-specific skills, replace the supervisor by specialist training staff, and move the training process from the actual workplace into the 'training department'. Many primary sector organisations now provide domestic training programmes to satisfy their more organisationally specific needs for trained and committed manpower.

The second response has been an extension of this. The same reliance on green labour recruitment is to be found, but instead of creating a separate function and process of training off the job, some attempt is made, however inadequately as yet, to integrate the individual's development with the on-going experience of the organisation. It usually concerns itself with much more than mere skill acquisition and development, although this broader remit may apply only to the 'core' workers. This figures in the literature, in association with suggestions that the particular enterprise aims to turn itself into a learning organisation (or in Schein's (1970) phrase, an institution which learns), capable of generating 'mission-relevant' experience which also allows the staff to learn and develop themselves beyond the point they have already reached in their growth as people.

One consequence of this development has been to make training more of a partnership between 'trainer' and 'trainee': trainees have more 'say' in defining the ends and means of the training pro-gramme, and their needs and wishes are taken more fully into account. A much wider set of objectives is, as a result, established for the training. The adoption of this approach thus completes the process of domesticating the training programme, effectively taking it out of the public domain and making it a full charge on the employing organisation.

This (technological) stimulus to organisational development has probably done more than the two main pieces of legislation on industrial training (the Industrial Training Act, 1964, and the Employment and Training Act, 1974) to make training a major strategy of control. It has, however, had its impact mainly on the core workers in the primary sector undertaking of private industry and left those in the secondary sector and in the public sector of the economy largely untouched. The NHS, for example, is still groping rather painfully towards a new philosophy of staff training and development that is more attuned to the new technologies which now permeate it. But attempts through competitive tendering to establish a core-periphery dichotomy have not been without pain, nor as yet, have they proceeded far.

The appearance and growth of the dichotomy has had the effect of recreating the need for individuals outside the core to secure their training and development 'for themselves'. One strategy which the educationally qualified can and do adopt is to secure initial accep-tance for training from a primary sector organisation, and having benefitted from the training provided, move on, possibly into the peripheral area. Another is to use the facilities for part-time study, for example, 'at the Tech', to haul oneself up by one's own boot-straps, in the hope that this will provide a passport into the core worker area. But many will be relegated permanently to peripheral worker status and have little opportunity to move from it. The public systems, whether of income supplementation or of training, will remain the only means of support available.

This tendency to polarise the sources of individual development is manifest in two opposing concepts of the training process, one self-directed and the other trainer-directed.

Self-directed Learning

The traditional predisposition of industry to leave training to be developed 'elsewhere' now manifests itself in a vogue for self-directed learning. This allows the individual to undertake learning for himself/herself, with a minimum of intervention from trainers. It still depends on some formal structuring of the learning and response processes, but this is more 'distant' from the trainee. It depends on the learner having already 'learned to learn', and it is this which allows direct intervention by the trainer to be reduced.

It manifests itself in two main forms:

1 Programmed instruction, developing largely from the work of Skinner (with its heyday in the 1960's), focused largely on the possibility of learning from a programmed text or machine, where, as in learning mathematics, language, or accountancy principles, there are clearly established rules about what is to be learned and the sequence in which this is best accomplished.

2 Professional self-learning, developing largely from the theories of Gagne on the development of intellectual skills or 'cognitive strategies', in which experience is deliberately used as a source of learning, regardless of the manner in which that experience presents itself, but conceived as a source of practice in applying new combinations of rules to the task of solving problems.

Both rely on the individual having been conditioned or socialised adequately to make use of the structured experience. Both risk the creation of a problem of communicating cognitions without emotional content (Drucker, 1980).

The development of new electronic technologies has assisted in the organisation both of instructional material and of the feedback of knowledge of the results of learning activity without the direct intervention of trainers. Although people may transcend the limits of their already learned perspectives, without such assistance, the paucity of external reinforcement and help with the organisation of responses to new material will tend to inhibit the learning process.

These approaches tend to give insuficient attention to reinforcement and 'response organisation'. A presumption must always exist that the self-directed learner will interpret his or her experience in the ways which are most congruent with what he or she already knows, and by this token, which are comfortable for him or her. Individuals will also tend to give themselves reinforcement in the form of intrinsic rewards which will probably be based on their own assessment of 'how well they are doing whatever it is they ought to be doing'.

This tendency to self-delusion is evident in a number of studies. Burns's early studies of managers' estimates of how they spent their time revealed that the estimates were consistent with what they saw as appropriate to their job titles and roles: production managers estimated that they spent most of their time on production problems, accountants on accounting problems, etc. Observer-recorded distributions of their time revealed, however, that they spent much more time on activities such as handling personnel problems than they had estimated (Burns, 1954). Similarly, Raia's study of Management by Objectives in action revealed an initial tendency for individuals to frame their future plans in rather idealised terms which only became 'more realistic' as time passed and as externally evaluated experience helped to 'break the mould' (Raia, 1965).

Formal Training

Formal training entails the deliberate and structured presentation of experiences, which may be considered helpful in aiding individuals to change their knowledge, understanding, attitudes or behaviours. In industry formal training is used for any of a variety of specific purposes.

1 *Induction* in which context it is used to complement and complete the selection and placement process by providing a systematic approach to the introduction of the new entrant to the organisation. In essence, what is intended by this use of training is the familiarisation of the individual with the physical and cultural situation in which he or she will be expected to operate. It aims to provide the individual with the information required to cope with the situation. It may, depending on basic strategy, take it as axiomatic that the individual is already competent to carry out the work tasks, while in other cases, it may be linked with post-entry job training. But in either case, the new entrant will need some intro-duction to the structures, rules, and procedures of the employing undertaking to enable him or her to cope.

2 *Skill acquisition*, where the aim in using it is to implant and develop new skills and abilities. Not all organisations can or want to recruit people who are already trained in required skills. A mature engineering or printing craftsman might present himself to an employer as fully trained, as a result of early apprenticeship (itself a form of skill training); a semi-skilled machine operator is less likely to be similarly endowed. With the progressive 'de-skilling' of work, more and more undertakings will actively seek employees in the latter category, and will undertake to provide the kind and degree of training necessary.

3 *Skill development*, where it is employed to 'update' a person's knowledge or skills at any stage in his or her career, and whenever changes occur in the work environment to make this necessary. With an increasing rate of technological change, the need for updating is also appearing more frequently. Short courses, which provide information on the 'new thing' and offer the opportunity to learn and practise new skills or new applications of old ones, therefore appear more often. Changing market situations may also call for changes in frames of reference and attitudes, and some undertakings are willing to attempt to bring about these changes through training programmes, particularly ones directed at managers.

4 *Increasing motivation*, entailing its use deliberately to increase the individual's willingness to work to the required patterns and standards. This rests on the belief that people are likely to work more effectively if they understand not only what they are expected to do, but also why they are expected to do it in this way. The inculcation of work-related values and norms is possible in training, although there are frequently expressed doubts about the likelihood of success attending training ventures of this sort; there are those who would argue that 'attitude change' is something which is better not attempted through training.

5 *Attitude change*, which is probably the most difficult objective to achieve through training, although it is sometimes attempted in conjunction with team-building and motivation development. In the primary sector organisation the high level of investment in the training of core workers is likely to force attention to be paid to the perspectives and attitudes which these workers adopt or develop in relation to the organisation and their work within it. Where the secondary sector organisation can use the strategy of selection as the method of recruiting appropriate work attitudes, this is not so readily or so cheaply available to the primary sector organisation. The task of changing attitudes has therefore to be tackled.

6   *Team-building*   Nevertheless, training may have some smaller or larger part to play in developing new climates, structure, and styles of management. These usually require new tasks to be learned, even if they also require new understandings and motivations before these tasks can be effectively performed. In team-building, training may help realise objectives, without itself being capable of delivering the whole result. It can help to create new awareness while at the same time transferring new skills of a social or interactive kind. Where the training is provided in a sufficiently supportive group context (see below, pp 450–59) it may also contribute to the development of appropriate motivations.

The extent to which undertakings become involved in these activities varies considerably, but where they do, the approach made depends on a number of common principles.

Basic principles

Formal training activity rests on the belief that there are correct and incorrect, or desired and undesired, ways of responding to situations, and that the trainer will stimulate and encourage the trainee to adopt the correct modes and avoid the incorrect ones. This need not imply that there is only one correct way, but it does imply that those offering training are in a position to arbitrate between the correct and the incorrect ones. The more complex the response to be learned, the more necessary is it that something more than mere experience is available to the learner. For this reason, Stokes (1966, pp 101–17) recognises the relevance of 'discipline' to training, and in fact, defines discipline as:

> 'a conscious effort to influence conduct towards the
> achievement of desired results and toward the prevention
> of undesired results'
> (Stokes, 1966, p 105).

In this sense, successful training interventions depend on the adoption and formal application of a number of principles derived from our understanding of the learning process.

1   Establishing what it is that the individual needs to learn to cope with some defined situation or problem, and developing the plan of training in a way which emphasises the integrity and the patterned nature of the attitudes, knowledge, skill and behaviour which the trainee must acquire to cope successfully with it.

2 Basing training upon a knowledge of how human learning in general occurs, upon what the trainee already knows or has learned (including what he or she has already learned about how to learn) and upon what the trainee is motivated to learn, recognising the necessity for negotiating with the trainee where training should start and finish.

3 Locating the trainee centrally in the learning/training process in order to recognise that while training entails transfer of knowledge (about) and 'know-how' from one or more others (who possess them) to the trainee (who does not), effective training cannot occur if the individual is treated as an empty bucket to be filled.

4 Managing the individual's learning process in a systematic manner on the basis of a partnership between the trainer and the trainee, with each contributing means and goals, thereby developing adequate confidence in the strategy and motivation to learn, rather than on the basis of just the trainer's goals (which reduces the trainee's interests to the status of instrumentalities).

5 Incorporating into the process of intervening all the elements of stimulus and reinforcement, which learning theory suggests are contributory to successful learning. Otherwise, as Seymour says of learning in the employment context, the learner is likely to 'give up the struggle and swell the labour turnover figures' (Seymour, 1949, p 170).

These principles apply generally but have traditionally allowed authority to take a more dominant role, particularly in the context of routine skill training.

As these are currently conceived and applied, however, it is recognised that they provide a necessary core structure but need to be interpreted in the light of the circumstances of their application. In effect, this is a recognition of Peters and Waterman's general principle of 'tight-loose' in the training context (see above, p 209). Training (and indeed self-directed learning) requires a basically systematic approach and structure, but a flexible application to accommodate individual (trainee) differences.

A Systematic Approach

The 'systematic' approach advocated is based on the notion of 'system' associated with the construct of an open or closed feedback control loop, with which all training decisions and actions can be

Figure 14

A systems approach to training

Main Steps in Training set in a Closed Loop Model

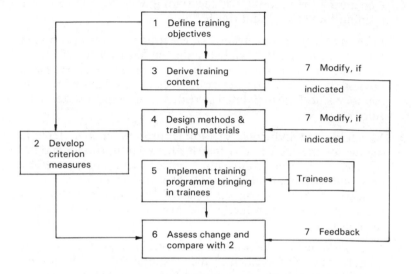

Based on: G A Eckstrand, 'Current Status of the Technology of Training' (AMRL Document Technical Report, 64–86, 1964), p 3.

See also: R Stammers and J Patrick, *The Psychology of Training* (Methuen, 1975) p 19.

M L Blum and J C Naylor, *Industrial Psychology: Its Theoretical and Social Foundations (Harper and Row, 1965) p 253.*

linked. Figure 14 shows one example. This model may be explicit but is often merely implicit in the way in which steps in the planning and implementation process are depicted. In either case, it serves to direct attention to the kinds of action required to mount a training initiative, each of which may be associated with relevant diagnostic questions (Young and Findlater, 1972, pp 7–8).

The first three actions are necessary to establish whether training is needed, what it might accomplish, and how success would be recognised if it were to be undertaken:

1   Definition of the current situation in terms of measurable differences between what is desired and what is being achieved.

2   Articulation of objectives to be achieved to improve the

situation by reducing the gap identified in (1), each objective being expressed in terms of contribution to this reduction.

3 Establishment of the criteria and the criterion measures which will eventually indicate whether and/or to what extent the proposed action has realised the objectives set in this way. Systematic attention to these issues will prevent the generation of expectations of training which cannot be met. In the course of giving this attention, it needs to be recognised that:

(i) It cannot be assumed that all performance problems faced by an organisation are responsive to training solutions, although there are those who regard training as a solution to almost any problem.

Training is not always the best response to problems. Changes in structures, organisations, and policies may be more pertinent solutions. A lack of profitability may be due to the production and marketing of the wrong products, the employment of inefficient methods of production organisation and work methods, or the failure to provide adequate structures of intrinsic and extrinsic incentives. Where everyone is fully skilled but disinclined to use those skills in working, the problem is not one which can be remedied by skills training. The requirement is some boost in motivation or morale, which may not be achieved by training. It may be necessary to adopt a non-training solution to the attitudinal/motivational problem.

(ii) Training may not be technically feasible if:

(a) the tasks may not be sufficiently well understood to permit their inherent rationality to be articulated as a basis for training;

(b) the inherent rationality cannot be presented in an acceptable fashion within a training programme with a reasonable expectation that it will result in some perceptible change in behaviour;

(c) the cost of achieving this state is unjustified in terms of the returns likely to be achieved by the changed behaviour.

Much managerial work is so unstructured that it does not meet these requirements. Consequently, management is frequently treated as something which has to be learned by experience of doing. It acquires something of the cast of an amateur activity, although as the DE (Hayes) Committee argued, it may be that 'the era of the amateur is coming to an end, and that "practical common sense" needs to be supported by thorough familiarity with a growing body of specialised knowledge and skill' (Dept of Employment, (Hayes Committee Report) 1972, p 5).

Whether training can help has therefore to be established in each situation. The model outlined above highlights the need to analyse the situation and the problem before embarking on training (although this is not always done). Consequently, as Donaldson and Scannel (1978, pp 13–23) say, the first design step involves, 'diagnosing problems to define the role of training'. Kenney, Donnelly, and Reid (1979, p 8) similarly make their first element 'identifying what training is needed'; and Singer (1977, p 13) makes a similar point.

PLANNING THE TRAINING PROGRAMME

Where the initial analysis suggests a need to train to reduce the problems identified, the next major step is to devise a training strategy. A strategy of industrial training is essentially 'concerned with preparing, creating, and using facilities so as to secure the training initiative and ultimate success' (Finnigan, 1970, p 11). Like any other plan, it requires a statement to be made now about the action to be taken by identified personnel at some future time.

The Assessment of Training Needs

Where the conditions are deemed to be such that training can help, it is then necessary to determine what it is that training can help with. This focuses on the assessment of training needs and the definition of training objectives. (These will be considered, for the sake of brevity, in the context of training for purposes of implanting or developing skills and abilities.)

The assessment of training needs is based on a systematic attempt to:

> 'determine the gap between the present results of the way people learn their jobs, and the desirable results if the learning process were to be improved. [The training needs analysis] will indicate ... the type of training which is most appropriate for a specific operation, and whether systematising training can make an economic contribution towards the solution of an operating or production problem'
> (Singer and Ramsden, 1969, p 16).

These authors suggest that in order to carry out such an analysis, some investigation (which need not be long-drawn-out or complicated) will be needed 'to set objectives for training and to establish that the cost of systematising training will be repaid' and thus generally to provide a basis for improving training, and ultimately behaviours (Singer and Ramsden, 1969, p 18; see also, Annett and Duncan, 1967, p 212).

In the context of training for skill, this calls for information on the kind and range of activities and tasks which people are required to carry out, the existing performance levels of those engaged in them, the length and cost of existing training under existing arrangements, and the difficulties which the present performers (or those who supervise them) experience in the course of learning the tasks and associated skills (Singer and Ramsden, 1969, pp 18–26). This information will have to be collated and related to practice in other areas such as recruitment, production scheduling and control, and manpower planning in the ordinary situation.

Training Objectives and Criteria

Training objectives flow from the analysis of need and are defined prior to embarking on a training exercise. They provide 'a basis for the planning of instruction, for the conduct of teaching ...' (Gagne, 1970, p 74) and they provide a definition of 'the domains of performance which [the evaluator] will attempt to assess or measure' (ibid). Objectives provide both the trainer and the trainee with a basis for evaluating what may be achieved, at what level of attainment, and under what assumed operating conditions.

The establishment of the Industrial Training Boards provided a major stimulus to the systematic derivation of such objectives by linking this element of the systematic approach to the levy-grant system. Consequently, most training programmes will now base themselves on assessment of the purposes of any task, the manner in which subtasks contribute to their goal, and the demands they make on the worker (Warr, 1971). The problem of integrating the definition of objectives with on-going processes of training in practice has, however, proved more difficult; it is accepted that prior definition is a 'good thing' to do, but it is less well recognised that it is pointless to do it unless the plans are implemented with these objectives clearly in focus.

To serve these ends effectively it is necessary to define the characteristics of the objectives precisely.

The first choice in definition has to be made from among the different types of learning (Williams, 1976, p 15). These attempts at classification usually rest on the natural kinds of change which it is desired to produce in the trainee. Bloom *et al* divide what they call the domain of training into the cognitive, the affective, and the psychomotor domains, indicating the direction of aimed at effect (Bloom *et al*, 1956). Others have additionally distinguished perceptual (Moore, 1967) and social or interactive categories (Bales, 1951; Rackham and Morgan, 1977). An alternative approach focuses on position on the continuum of knowledge-understanding-application-and-transfer at which the training is directed (Boydell, 1973). This is sometimes used to draw a broad distinction between education (designed to cover the first two and possibly the third) and training (designed to embrace at least the last two).

These indicate something of the kind of training approach which will be necessary if the objectives are to be realised.

Any statement of objectives must also indicate three things:

1 The *Attainment* aimed at, which will be expressed in terms of what a learner will be expected to be able to *do* at the end of the training exercise.

2 The *Conditions* which will be taken as normal for the person who is required to perform to this standard.

3 The *Criterion* by which attainment will be measured or assessed in order to be regarded as acceptable (Mager, 1975, p 21).

In other words, what will the trainee be expected to do, under what conditions, and to what standard measured on what basis?

In the context of skill development, training often aims to produce a capacity to perform a task in the one best way. This rests on the assumption that there is one outcome of thinking, feeling, or behaviour which is 'right' in a particular context (or at worst, a small number of them which might prove equally satisfactory). Stokes suggests that the 'right way of doing the job should always be the basis of skill instruction. When alternative methods are available, be sure you are using the best at a given time' (Stokes, 1966, p 25). This assumption derives from the formalistic rationality that pervades much of our thinking about behaviour in formal settings and which is best illustrated by the approach and objectives of the industrial engineer in defining work tasks. It implies that a particular relationship of causality is to be found, and once found, is to be applied as a standard to guide behaviours towards defined ends.

The establishment of criteria and, more pertinently, of measurement of results, is not necessarily easy. Hinrichs divides skills into three categories: motor skills, cognitive skills, and interpersonal skills (Hinrichs, 1976, p 833), and suggests that through this range, there is a movement from skills which have visible and measurable outputs to skills which have largely invisible and unmeasurable outputs.

Design of Training Content

The content of training will differ according to the type of training being considered. Once the objective of training is defined, the next question concerns what is to be communicated to the trainee and in what sequence in order to achieve this objective. The identification and presentation of the task or tasks to be learned by the trainee are central to the design of training content in the context of training for skilled performance. The task of the training designer is to 'select and sequence a series of learning experiences which will produce the desired behaviour' (Eckstrand, 1964, p 2).

Gagne has presented a set of principles which govern the determination of training content (and which also indicate the way in which the notion of the 'one best way' permeates thinking in this area):

(a) identifying the component tasks of a final performance;

(b) ensuring that each of these component tasks is fully achieved; and

(c) arranging the total learning situation in a sequence which will insure the optimal mediational effects from one component to another (Gagne, 1962, p 88).

The implication of this for training is that it is necessary first to establish what is the task and its component parts and then examine the extent of their mediation of a final performance (in the sense that final performance would not occur without their successful achievement on the way).

Job analysis is held to be a necessary precursor to training on the grounds that:

(a) 'unless the skills involved in any industrial operation are analysed and comprehended, there can be no assurance that they will, by training, be transferred from an experienced operator to a learner'; and

(b) 'however complete the analysis may be, it will not by itself enable the learner to acquire the skill' (Seymour, 1949, p 172).

Other proponents of job or skills analysis (see above pp 258−61) assert that these components are hierarchical in form. Stammers and Patrick state that:

> 'The acquisition of skill may be viewed as the progressive organisation of units of activity into a hierarchical structure'
> (Stammers and Patrick, 1975, p 43).

Annett and Duncan's hierarchical task analysis entails breaking down jobs into operations as the basic units of analysis. An 'operation' is defined as 'any unit of behaviour, no matter how long or short its duration and not matter how simple or complex its structure, which can be defined in terms of its objective' (Annett and Duncan, 1967).

They are in turn broken down further into suboperations until further breakdown becomes unjustifiable on cost-benefit grounds. But this is made possible only because objectives tend to be capable of identification in the form of a nested hierarchy.

> 'The conception of skilled activity as being hierarchically organised and controlled at each level by the feedback loop attached to each TOTE has important implications for training. If task performance is unacceptable, task analysis may proceed most economically from the higher levels until the source of the problem is identified. Poor performance may be a consequence of an inappropriate or ineffective plan, ineffective feedback for the test phase of a TOTE, or incorrect sequencing of sub-operations in the task'
> (Stammers and Patrick, 1975, pp 41–2).

In the subordinate unit, for example, the test element involves a comparison of the actual position of the hammer and its desired position in order to address the nail in the hammering operation. A discrepancy at this test stage leads to an operation to lift the hammer to the desired position. The same kind of sequencing may be established in relation to the striking operation itself. These two subunits may then be regarded as falling into a necessary sequence (for example, the strike subunit cannot precede the lift subunit) and hence, from the definition, into a 'plan' (Stammers and Patrick, 1975).

Matching Capacity to Learn

The associated step of establishing the manner in which content is to be presented to the trainees in order to accord with their capacities for taking it in (which Singer and Ramsden put at the head of their check-list of the conditions which influence the content of training) is equally important. This focuses on the analysis of human need and capacity to learn, just as the earlier step focuses on job analysis.

The capacity of trainees to learn will vary considerably, according to their general and special aptitudes, the amount and kind of formal learning undertaken previously, and their motivation to learn what is being offered. As a general principle, the learner's capacity is best accommodated by a process which involves feeding the learner 'digestible bits' of the total sequence which has to be mastered. Singer and Ramsden refer to this as a process of synthesis, where,

> 'Synthesis is the recombining of the identified facts, in such a way that the learning process is optimised by feeding new information to the learner in easily digested portions, rather than in asking him to spend consider- able time and effort in breaking up the total task, *by himself*, into digestible bits'
> (Singer and Ramsden, 1969, p 52).

The emphasis is on the concept of easily digestible bits, which serves to highlight the probability that digestibility will vary both with the nature and complexity of the task and with the capacity of the learner. This is usually considered in the literature in terms of 'part' versus 'whole task' learning and is sometimes reduced to the proposition that the 'best learning sequence is one which progresses from simple to complex' (Stokes 1966, pp 24–5) where the mastery of a part is probably simpler than mastery of the whole.

Naylor uses the concept of a hierarchical organisation of subtasks to examine the implications of 'task complexity' and 'task organisation' for the approach made to training (Naylor, 1962; see also above, pp 258–61). Any specific task or subtask may be more or less difficult to carry out, and the degree of difficulty is what provides Naylor with his measure of 'task complexity'. Tasks or subtasks may also be more or less interrelated and interdependent or mutually influential, and the degree to which this is present provides the measure of 'task organisation'.

Naylor suggests that where a total task is found to be difficult to perform, this may be for one of three possible reasons:

(a) the subtasks themselves may be difficult;

(b) the subtasks may be so interrelated that they make the whole difficult; or

(c) the difficulty overall may be a product of the measures of complexity and organisation.

Applying his concepts to the research findings on part- versus whole-job training published since 1930, Naylor attempts to relate them to the efficacy of the training being examined. He produces a matrix in which the dimensions of task complexity and task organisation are related to the approach made to training. This enables him to demonstrate a relationship which he expressed in two propositions:

1 In training for tasks with relatively high organisation, whole task training appeared to become more efficient than part-task methods as task complexity increased; and

2 In training for tasks with relatively low organisation, part methods appeared to become more efficient than whole task methods as task complexity increased.

The general conclusion is that the degree of interdependence or inter-relatedness between the subtasks influences the superiority of one approach over the other. This was supported in later studies by Naylor (Briggs, Naylor and Fuchs, 1962; Naylor and Briggs, 1963) and by studies by Bilodeau (1954, 1955, 1957).

Another approach which promises to permit a closer association of training method with individual capacities is that which recognises that people develop different 'learning styles' as a result of their make-up, their experience, and the demands of their situation on them (Johnson, 1972; Kolb, Rubin and McIntyre, 1974; Honey and Mumford, 1982; 1983; Pask, 1976). In the original conception, four styles were derived from a 2×2 matrix which set abstract conceptualisation and concrete experience on one dimension and reflective observation and experimentation on the other. Kolb, Rubin, and McIntyre identified four main learning styles which appeared to be associated with members of different professions:

1 The *convergers*, who combine abstract conceptualisation and active experimentation, and who include many engineers;

2 The *divergers*, who combine concrete experience with reflective observation, as do many personnel managers;

3 The *assimilators*, who combine abstract conceptualisation with reflective observation, and who include many researchers; and

4 The *accommodators*, who combine concrete experience and experimentation and who are found widely amongst marketing people.

Some attempt has been made to use this type of categorisation to select people with particular styles to participate in training programmes which emphasise different methods and styles of presenting material to the trainees (Honey and Mumford, 1982 and 1983), but more detailed work is needed to increase the confidence with which it might be applied. What it does do, however, is suggest that, for example, some people may respond more readily to the serial presentation of material and others more readily to its holistic presentation, just because of the way they have learned to handle new material and learn from it.

This provides the foundation for recognising what has been referred to as 'the hidden curriculum' of training (Snyder, 1973) – one that does not figure in formal statements about training objectives and methods. This is the training agenda which is contributed by the trainee from within his or her own conception of 'need', including the 'need' to acquire something which will assimilate with what he or she already knows. Hinrichs depicts the training process as one dependent on two kinds of input and productive of two types of output.

(a)   Inputs take the form of 'signal inputs' (which derive from the training programme and involve both cognitive and experiential (practice) elements) and 'maintenance inputs' (which stem from and depend on the person's personality and motivation and the extent to which the environment is supportive of the person's perceptions and perspectives on which the signal inputs build).

(b)   Outputs are represented by 'formal achievements' (in the forms of what, cognitively and affectively, has been 'learned' and what changed behaviours have been effected) and by 'personal satisfaction' (in the form of a sense of increased competence in thinking, feeling, or behaving, or of personal growth or development) (Hinrichs, 1976, p 833).

This emphasises the notion of a partnership between the person as an input-output system and the organisation cast in similar terms, but treating the individual as part of its input. The recognition that the individual plays a similar and parallel part in the training process highlights the limited scope of formal training, however efficiently conceived, to influence cognitions, emotions, and behaviour, in that the individual's existing personality and motivation are at least as important in determining what emerges from the training process.

Training Methods

The third part of the plan will indicate the training methods to be employed in order to realise the objectives in the defined circumstances.

The methods of training to be adopted are likely to respond to the complexity of the matter to be learned and the capacity of the trainees for learning, but in addition, they are likely to be influenced by other constraining factors such as the time and physical and human resources available and the cost of using them (Singer and Ramsden, 1969, p 52).

Training facilities comprise a whole range of locations, technologies, and skills. The locational choices can generally be classified as either on the job or off the job, although there are some combinations which, for example, take those who normally work together off the job to engage in discussion of work-related tasks and problems.

On-the-job training may occur either in the work area under the control of either the supervisor or the specialist training officer. Either may comprise a formal 'course' or involve the trainee in projects or assignments (where 'a project is defined as an activity which involves, planning, scheming or designing [and] involvement in such an activity is [considered] good for training' (ibid, p 18). The facility may be used in the employer's time or in the employee's own time.

Off-the-job training may be provided under full-time supervision in an area away from the normal workplace and using a properly defined syllabus (Finnigan, 1970, p 16), or it may involve the use of external, educational, and training organisations, ranging from universities and colleges to industry and company staff colleges and consultant training facilities (ibid, p 21).

A good deal of personal development (itself a process of training) takes place on an individual basis, with the person privately pursuing programmes of study either in some educational establishment or through 'correspondence' (as in modern forms of distance learning which may also involve periods of study in institutions). Increasingly often, particularly with professional and managerial staff, such 'private' developmental activities may be stimulated by counselling in connection with performance appraisal and undertaken with some form of employer assistance.

In recent years, improvements in communications technologies have made many new supports to training available. These are often included under headings of 'audio-visual aids', or 'educational technology' and include various types of image projectors, cassettes, and videos by means of which the communications associated with face-to-face interaction can be augmented and improved. The print media remain available for training purposes, and usually serve to support and underpin the more transient oral communications processes which may be involved in normal presentations.

Specific Methods

A number of distinct methods of training delivery are available and many may be used internally or externally, according to the particular objectives sought, and the learning capacities and styles of those involved.

The method of training adopted will respect the purpose behind the intervention. Although there are many specific devices, they can be grouped according to main purpose served. Joyce and Weil (1972) group the twenty two models of teaching which they identified into four 'families', defined according to purpose:

1 *Information processing models* These models are based largely on the learning problems and processes involved in assembling and disseminating information which is intended to influence cognitive, intellectual, and scholarly thinking processes. The lecture is a simple example of the vehicle which might be used to communicate in this context.

2 *Personal models* These models are most intimately associated with the kind of learning that takes place in processes of creation and adaptation. Theories and models of how different people construe reality and potentials for change in that reality represent the theoretical underpinnings of these models. Brainstorming sessions provide an example of one pertinent vehicle for this kind of learning.

3 *Social interaction models* These models are most directly linked to the processes of social encounter, in which both small group interactions and the influences of broader settings may be explored as a source of learning and insight. Sensitivity exercises, role-plays, games and simulations are examples of the techniques which might be associated with such models.

4 *Behavioural models* These models are the ones most directly associated with processes of skill training, where definite behavioural patterns can be defined as the relevant goals of

training activity. The kind of training which is based on task and skills analyses, or which rests solidly upon stimulus-response and conditioning theories, provides the basis for a range of examples.

Specific training methods may be classified according to the extent to which they allow self-direction in learning (as with No 1 in the list below), the extent to which they emphasise the top-down approach (as with Nos 2 and 3 below), and the extent to which they allow 'discovery' (as in Nos 4−10 below). This classification is not, however, meant to imply that they cannot be used to support a different kind of training style or objective.

One list which is related mainly to the communication of information, conceptualisations, and generalisations comprises:

1 The programmed text or the structured questionnaire (in which the individual is assisted to assimilate information in a controlled way for himself or herself) and, involving the use of more modern technologies like the interaction video (which admits a similar kind of control).

2 The 'talk' or lecture (a structured talk to give information or explanations, which may be undertaken with or without other aids and/or questions from the audience).

3 The tutorial (which most usually features in work organisations in the form of individual coaching or counselling by a supervisor) or seminar (a sequence of interventions by a trainer in face-to-face situations, interspersed with controlled discussion).

4 The case study (a controlled discussion of issues presented in the form of situational description).

5 The incident process (a controlled discussion in which the discussant's initiative in seeking information plays a significant role).

6 The syndicate (an assisted group-learning process in which members contribute help to each other).

7 The T-group or sensitivity training (in which major emphasis is on the members of the group learning about themselves and their behaviour in the group context).

8 The role play (in which individual participants are to assume real-life roles and act through a series of events relevant to the training objectives).

9 Business games (in which participants learn by doing in a simulated real-life situation).

Another list which is more directly associated with the development of manual/motor/mechanical skills would include:

1 Sitting next to Nellie, as in traditional apprenticeship arrangements, by means of which the learner may receive some formal instruction (on a serial/part basis), some practice in the activities involved, and some opportunity simply to copy or emulate the skilled worker's behaviour ('modelling').

2 The instruction manual which sets out in print, with illustrations, the way in which a machine should be operated (of the kind often supplied with domestic durable machines and equipment).

3 The talk and demonstration associated with aids to practice, such as might be used to introduce a learner to safe working with a lathe.

4 The computer-assisted simulator by means of which an individual can go through the motions of controlling equipment and receiving audible or visual feedback of results without risking loss or damage to property or injury to the trainee (as in the case of the aircraft simulator).

5 The safety-rigged machine on which the individual is invited to work out (in accordance with the cognitive theories of learning) how to operate the real machine (such as is sometimes used for learning about repair of electrical circuits).

Each of these methods possesses its own distinguishing characteristics and has greater or lesser relevance to different types of training (manual, professional, managerial). The characteristics arc given by a combination of the relationship of dependence established between the trainer and trainee in the learning process and the medium or media employed in the communication process on which it is based. Some involve a simple direct trainer-to-trainee relationship which bears practically the whole burden of facilitating the learning, while some spread the burden by involving others, such as the members of the trainee group or outsiders. Some involve a single medium, such as the written or the spoken word, while others comprise a number of media.

These characteristics have a bearing on the kinds of objective which might be served by their use. Any one method might prove more or less effective in communicating facts, offering explanations, securing emotional commitment, effecting transfer of learning to the 'real' situation, or improving actual performance in complex situations. The lecture may, for example, suit the communication and explanation of facts and theories, (see pp 424–5 below); role play may secure greater emotional involvement and commitment and greater modification of actual behaviour (see pp 441–65 below). This is the main issue that is discussed in what follows. An attempt to indicate main relationships of method and objective is made on pp 323–5 below.

Making Choices

The choice to be made by the training manager or trainer in any particular case will tend to depend on consideration of cost and effectiveness. Generally, on-the-job training incurs a lower cost to both provider and receiver than off-the-job training, but because of the variety of methods which may be used in either locale, there is no such simple correlation with effectiveness.

A trainer or training manager, faced with making a choice, needs a knowledge of each of the methods (as well as of the 'problem' to be reduced) so that he can make an informed choice. His skill is called for in determining the fit of the particular method to the particular training objective within the constraints of time and money budgets available – because the different methods better match the different subtasks into which it may be divided (see above, pp 313–15).

The urgency of realising the objectives of training often leads organisations into ineffective strategies. Where, say, management is clear on the result to be achieved, there is a strong temptation to use some direct top-down method of communicating what is required (such as a 'talk' or a lecture). The mere informing or demonstration of what is required, however, rarely produces changes in perceptions, attitudes, predispositions or behaviour, unless the recipients are already aware of the 'need' and merely await the trigger or the legitimation of the necessary response. (A command to 'get out' might well produce an instant response if the building is already full of smoke!)

It is frequently asserted that Japanese management culture approaches the problem from the opposite standpoint, spending time to get the preparatory communications and understandings right before looking for a response. What we identify as a training process can be employed in this way, allowing learners in the situation to walk round the problem for some time before the ultimate 'decision' on action is called for. Time might be expended in this way within the training process to ensure that when the time is ripe, appropriate action can and will be taken.

A staff of trainers is required to mount training programmes, but the availability of such modern devices as interactive videos and closed circuit television can reduce the labour-intensity of training. It is, however, most unlikely that training could be mounted on the basis that an impersonal technology could bear all the onus. Consequently, the availability, and the cost, of staff to engage directly in training and/or to produce the audio- or video-cassettes is likely to remain an important constraint on the methods of training which can be adopted.

Implementation

A training strategy provides a guide to future action by named others, mainly training staff. It is tested in implementation, and the process of implementation therefore requires not only the execution of the plan decided on, but also the measurement of outcomes (or results) and the evaluation of the plan in conception and execution. In effect there are three stages:

1   Execution of the plan, by bringing the intended content of the training into contact with those whom it is intended shall be influenced in some way by it, using the methods and procedures chosen for the purpose at the planning stage.

2   Measurement against the criteria selected at the planning stage (Donaldson and Scannell, 1978, p 23) of the extent to which performance has moved in the direction of the desired goal, using such measuring instruments as have been chosen as relevant at stage 2.

3   Evaluation, by comparison of intended and actual (measured) outcomes, of whether the objectives have been (sufficiently) realised, whether the contents of the plan or the methods of its execution have produced the expected effects, and whether changes in objectives or methods are called for in consequence.

Carrying all of these into effect calls for the exercise of various communications and influence skills on the part of the trainers.

Execution

Execution of a training strategy may be conceived as requiring seven distinct steps which bring together the instructor and the trainee in a process of two-way communications and mutual influence (Mills, 1967, p 10).

1   *Object:*   Both instructor and trainee must know, understand,

and accept as appropriate what is to be achieved as a result of the exercise. All of these conditions must be met if the trainer and the trainee are to be motivated to achieve.

2　*Preparation:*　The trainer should assess in advance of embarking on the training intervention just what the learner has already learned, what he or she needs to learn in order to realise his or her goals in this situation, and what mode of learning the trainee adopts. Without this kind of preparation, the training is likely to be directed at the wrong target through an inappropriate medium and start and finish at the wrong point on the trainee's learning curve.

3　*Presentation:*　The actual presentation of the material to the trainees demands adoption of appropriate methods and techniques and the effective use of communications and influence skills in the process. How the material is presented will vary with the capacities and learning modes of the trainees and with the nature of the training objectives and material content relevant to them.

4　*Reception:*　The trainee must be generally receptive to the material being presented in the manner adopted, or little learning can occur. If care has been taken to match method and styles of presentation with the capacity of the trainee, it is then the trainee's attitude towards learning and his or her motivation to learn which will determine how effective the reception is in the particular case.

5　*Assimilation:*　Receptivity can be influenced by varying the modes and styles of presentation, and such variation is commonly advocated to assist the trainee to assimilate the material. In skill training, for example, one aid to the trainee's digestion of the material presented is guided practice in using whatever may be presented through other media; in management training, digestion of complex data or theories may be facilitated by guided discussion with others (trainers or trainee-peers).

6　*Assessment:*　Because training is purposive, it is necessary to assess attainment or achievement, by conducting examinations, using attainment tests or by assessing progress by some other systematic method appropriate to the type of training in consideration. Periodical assessments during the progress of the training can serve as a means of feeding back the results of understandings or practice and can reduce the trauma often associated with the final test of competence.

7   *Feedback:*   Because practice makes perfect only if the results or
    outcomes of that practice are fed back to the trainee with appro-
    priate reinforcement, it is necessary to indicate to the trainee
    where and when successes and mistakes occur.

Measurement and Evaluation

Training and development interventions, like any others, need to be
evaluated to inform those who own the problem about the consequences of their earlier decisions and the possible need to take
subsequent ones. Not only is feedback important for the trainee; it
is necessary to allow trainers to learn and to improve their performance.

Evaluation is based on either measurement or assessment of
results, where the results in turn are related to the objectives originally set and to the criteria established at that stage in the planning
process. In the context of training for improved knowledge, understanding, or skill, two forms of measurement of the consequences
may be considered.

The first is the easier to perform in that it involves a measurement
of the trainee's immediate response and may be effected through
examination (to establish the extent to which the candidate has
acquired the knowledge or understanding) or attainment test (to
establish whether the trainee has acquired the skill or ability).

The second is more difficult, because it concerns itself with
whether the trainee, having passed those tests, is able to apply the
knowledge, understanding, or skill acquired in the training context
in the wider context of work: this focuses on the problem of
transference of learning from the 'classroom' (or training section) to
the real situation which other considerations (such as environmental
conditions and pressures or human motivation to achieve) affect the
outcome.

Measurement in the first case relies on the results of the examination or test, and in the second on the assessments which are made
subsequently either by the trainee or, more probably, by the
supervisor.

Measurement of results where training is used with the intention
of changing motivations, attitudes, or dispositions to cooperate, is
much more difficult and rests ultimately on opinions as to whether
any improvements in these individual traits and dispositions have
become noticeable in an on-going situation.

Evaluation may similarly be conceived at two distinct levels. It
may be carried out in respect of the training process treated
separately: it will then be based on the amount of 'success'

achieved, as measured by the examinations and tests which can be conducted at the end of the training process, and in the light of the costs of staff time and other resources involved. It may be carried out in the wider context of the training contribution to the realisation of wider enterprise objectives, as measured by the assessments of the amount of behavioural change apparently effected by the training programme.

None of this is 'easy' and all of it will be fraught with difficulties of interpretation of the meaning of the data produced and the conclusions that ought to be drawn. The further down the line is the organisation towards the ideal of a 'learning environment', the easier it will be to establish that training activities are valuable in themselves, but the more exposed will be the function to suggestions for improvement. However easy or difficult this evaluation process proves to be, it is, necessarily, one which has to be gone through to establish the function and value of the training department or the hired in trainers and the processes in which they engage.

SUMMARY

Industry's traditional approach to the problem of producing adequately skilled labour has been generally abstentionist; only with the depletion of the stock of capital in the form of trained labour and developments in technology has industry been drawn into the training process.

Currently, the labour market orientations of undertakings vary across a wide spectrum, and over it very different approaches to the general and the specific (for example, skill) training problems are in evidence. At one extreme, reliance is still placed on the trained labour stock being maintained 'elsewhere', and at the other, considerable investment is made in not only formal training, but the structuring of the organisation's experiences to maximise the learning opportunities which it provides. Within this range, increasing reliance is being placed on self-directed learning and on formal (largely domestic to the enterprise) training.

Self-directed learning relies heavily on (a) the probability that learners have already learned how to learn with a minimum requirement for structured reinforcement and reward; and (b) the capacity of modern technology to facilitate learning at a distance from the usual structures and supports for the process. Formal training may be directed at a number of different kinds of 'problem', induction, skill acquisition and enhancement, motivational and attitudinal change, and team development, although the capacity of training to deliver may decrease across this range.

Formal training may be more or less structured and more or less authoritarian, although it remains an activity which implies a 'discipline'. By reference to theories of human learning, a number of principles have been developed for application, and these facilitate the development of a systematic approach in which individual learning needs are given due weight.

Formal training needs to be evaluated in the manner that any other managerial activity is monitored to feedback to the management the data on which organisational and managerial learning can be based and subsequent decisions improved.

Reading:

Annett and Duncan (1967).
Bass and Vaughan (1966).
Belbin (1972; 1979).
Bilodeau (1969).
Brewster and Connock (1980).
Briggs *et al* (1962).
Burgoyne *et al* (1978).
Eckstrand (1964).
Ellis (1965).
Gagne (1970).
Gentles (1969).
Gibbs (1954).
Honey and Mumford (1982).
Jenson (1960).
Kenney, Donnelly and Reid (1986).
Kenney and Reid (1986).
King (1964).
McGehee and Thayer (1961)
Naylor (1962).
Rackham and Morgan (1977).

12 Performance Evaluation

The strategy of incentive (or control through a managerial bureaucracy) depends on these three types of action:

1   The identification of the tasks to be performed, together with the criteria to be used to measure successful performance;

2   The evaluation of the performance given, by assessment either of results where these are measurable, or of input of relevant effort or behaviour where they are not; and

3   The determination of the amount of reward, remuneration, or 'reinforcement' to be given to improve, maintain, or advance the current level of performance.

All three demand an exercise of judgement and therefore are associated with attempts to control the manner of its exercise. In practice, the first two of these are usually developed together or in unison (and will be considered together in this chapter). The third depends on these being done, but can be implemented in a distinct and later operation (and will be considered separately in the next chapter).

Performance at work is always subject to evaluation as part of some strategy of labour control: the only question is how this is done. A first distinction may be drawn with respect to the sophistication involved at each of the three stages. A second relates to the allocation of responsibility for carrying them out. In the context of a selection strategy, the decisions are taken in a general way by the agent who effectively subcontracts the work; in the context of a supervisory strategy, the supervisor exercises a broad judgement in determining performance and remuneration against a generally defined objective; in the context of an incentive strategy, the three tasks tend to be maintained in some distinction.

At the present time, formal appraisal plans of greater or lesser sophistication are common. Long surveyed 306 British companies and public sector organisations in the first half of 1985 and found that 82 per cent of them employed such schemes. This proportion represented a small increase over that found in earlier surveys. As about a third of current schemes were less than three years old, the suggestion of the data was that new schemes were being introduced for the first time and old schemes being revised. The organisations using these schemes were not exclusively medium-sized and large ones, suggesting not only that the need for review and evaluation is universal but also that managements find themselves under pressure to introduce systematic controls over their attempts to measure and assess performance (Long, 1986, p i).

Purposes and Objectives

The assessment of performance against defined standards is identified by a variety of labels which are used interchangeably: performance measurement, evaluation, appraisal, assessment, review, monitoring, or data feedback. 'Performance assessment' in the context of this chapter embraces a multitude of techniques which are used to determine whether the amount and quality of the person's effort, contribution, or results meet the standards laid down in some prior analysis of the work and its purposes. It tries to answer the question whether the amount of work effort or contribution put out by the person concerned is adequate or satisfactory in relation to the established performance standards: is the person working hard or effectively enough at the assigned tasks?

Variations in situation and the nature of the problem to be tackled in different situations have resulted in a multiplicity of objectives being set up for such plans. The position has now been reached where any one plan may attempt to secure a variety of objectives drawn from the following list:

1   Establishing what actions are required of the individual in a job in order that the objectives for the section or department are realised.

2   Establishing the key or main results which the individual will be expected to achieve in the course of his or her work over a period of time.

3   Assessing the individual's levels of performance against some standard, to provide a basis for remuneration above the basic pay rate.

4   Identifying the individual's levels of performance to provide a basis for informing, counselling, training and developing them.

5   Identifying those persons whose performance suggests that they are promotable at some date in the future and those whose performance requires improvement to meet acceptable standards.

6   Establishing an inventory of actual and potential performances within the undertaking to provide a basis for manpower planning.

7   Monitoring the undertaking's initial selection procedures by providing an assessment of actual performances against recruiters' expectations.

8   Improving communication about actual work tasks between different levels of authority in the job hierarchy.

Not all of these are likely to be found within any one plan, but what allows them to be grouped together is that they all depend on the twin activities of defining standards of performance and appraising performance in relation to these.

Classes of Objective

These can be grouped together to suggest three broad aims. One is to improve the performance or increase its relevance in the present position (whether by instruction or incentive). A second is to prepare plans for future manning and development for key personnel. The third is concerned with improving communications along one or more axes of the organisation. When confined within a single plan these may prove uneasy bedfellows.

Individual plans are likely to give different emphasis to these categories of objective. The first aim is to be found in most plans, but, for example, Behaviourally-Anchored Rating Scales (BARS) and Management by Objectives (MBO) tend to stress effective communication more strongly than time study or performance assessment plans. There is also a tendency for these classes of objective to be found in association with different grades of staff. Plans directed at staff low in the hierarchy are less likely to serve the second purpose than those applied to top management. The third category of aim, that of improving communications about relevant work tasks, is likely to be found in all applications to some extent but may be a fortuitous result rather than a deliberate intention in some cases.

With the emergence of new attitudes towards managerial careers and of internal labour markets in secondary sector organisations, the objectives covered in item 4 are becoming more strongly emphasised in many plans. In developed bureaucratic organisations, the subsequently listed objectives also assume a different significance, each being relevant to control of what is presumed to be a stable working environment.

As plans with more limited objectives are developed to meet the conditions of more volatile environments and organisations, self-appraisal and self-development, linked to career preparation and progression, tend to replace the earlier 'top-down' plans. Long (1986, p iv) found that more schemes were becoming participative, involving self-appraisal. In this context, the role of the manager/supervisor is more deliberately that of helper and mentor, as distinct from that of assessor, and the assessment process becomes progressively distanced from the mentoring process. The kind of activities outlined in the example of a corporate development plan given on pp 351-3 below, are then introduced into this process to facilitate individual self-development.

STANDARD SETTING

Over time, a succession of methods have been devised and applied to meet the need for definition and measurement of the performance required in respect of different types and levels of job. Traditionally some form of job analysis or work study has been employed for this purpose. These methods have been used to establish the standards to which work must conform in quality and amount if the undertaking's objectives, as defined by management, are to be realised. Gradually, however, this somewhat authoritarian top-down approach has given way to one that is more participative, in which job holders exert greater influence on both the determination of the criteria and standards and the appraisal process itself. The main sequence has run broadly as follows:

1   Work study applied mainly to routine productive work in factory or office. This appeared with scientific management, which coupled method and motion analysis with time standards based on stop watch or micro-motion studies, to produce 'the one best method' of working and a standard of time for performing it; the recording of production in the same terms then became the basis for future assessments of performance as well as of pay.

2   Merit rating, by which the personalities and attitudes of
       employees were separately brought within the ambit of assess-
       ment as judgements were demanded of employees' approach
       and attitudes towards work, so that those who exhibited unco-
       operative behaviour could be denied reward, promotion, or
       even employment; this development responded in some degree
       to the 'alienation' of the worker occasioned by the application
       of the above methods of 'scientific management'.

3   Performance appraisal of the McGregor/Drucker type, in
       which attention was focused not on personality nor on
       attitudes so much as on actual performance; 'performance'
       here might be construed as that which was measurable by
       concrete 'results', but might equally be that which is recognis-
       able only as an input of 'behaviour' in the performance of the
       job; this responded to the revealed reluctance of managers and
       supervisors to evaluate subordinates' personalities and the
       indications of research studies that use of work-relevant
       behaviour was more likely to encourage ratings to be made.

4   The synthesis, which is currently discernible, is that which
       allows a variety of different methods and plans to be applied
       to fit different circumstances and different objectives; the
       main thrust of this development is that a single plan of
       appraisal is unlikely to prove satisfactory for dealing with
       different kinds and levels of performance or with the require-
       ments of different purposes (pay determination, promotion
       assessment, training need, etc).

All of these exemplify the basic need to attach appraisal to a
measurable criterion and standard.

Work Study and Performance

In the present context, the main purpose of work study and related
methods of analysis is to establish standard definitions of the work
tasks which people will be expected to perform; the main aim is to
remove the worker's discretion in deciding form and amount of performance. It focuses on those results which are most immediately
measurable, concentrating on the number of units of product
produced or the time needed or taken to produce them. It has great
appeal because it is apparently 'objective' in the sense that it
measures what the individual does by way of contributing to the
realisation of the objectives of the enterprise. To the extent that
work study succeeds in its aim, an assessment of performance can

be made by ensuring that it is recorded in the same terms as are used to define the standard – number of pieces produced in a datum period, time taken to produce one item, time saved in producing the piece, etc.

This method has been, and still is, applied to a limited number of classes of labour and types of work. A condition for its success is that the work should be sufficiently routine and repetitive of particular tasks to make it feasible to derive an average time from a sample of operators and operations. It must also be possible for the worker concerned voluntarily to vary his or her output in ways which are readily measurable. It can therefore be applied quite readily to routine manual work. The jobs of the salesman and routine white collar worker can be treated in a similar manner, even if the standards are slightly more complex (as, for example, with the Clerical Work Improvement Programme (CWIP)).

It becomes progressively more expensive and more difficult to derive standard times for indirect work, such as maintenance or administration, and for this reason it is rarely used in these jobs. The same conclusion applies to a good deal of administrative, professional, and managerial work. Where the individual contribution is difficult to measure, however, it may still be possible to link performance with output on a group basis, the standard now being set for the group not the individual (as, for example, with Group Capacity Assessment (GCA)).

Similar individual or group standards can be set at the top executive level, where the standards can be expressed in profit or value added terms. Individual standards might be set for the director or manager in charge of an enterprise or a division where his or her actions can directly influence profitability. Given the corporate responsibility of the Board of Directors, allocation of results to individual directors may not be possible, and in this case, too, attribution of a group performance standard may be possible as a basis for control.

This method of standard setting is necessarily limited to those kinds of job where results are identifiable and attributable to the individual worker or the coherent working group. There are clearly many types of job where these conditions are not met. In addition, the development of production technologies has two main consequences for the application of this approach: first, the need for the time standards disappears in many cases as the worker is not 'tied to time' in the work performed; and secondly, the work ceases to be repetitive and therefore measurable by these methods. There is also a growing awareness that excessive managerial reliance on this kind of indicator (simply the amount produced) results in a range of problems in the medium to longer term. As listed by Sayles (1964, pp 165-6), these related to the growth of concentration on immediate interests and issues, on quantity rather than quality, manifest results not latent causes or conditions, avoiding the solution of difficult problems, and (for those whose work is not directly associated with such results) a search for spurious 'results' on which to base appraisals.

Developing Standards Based on Input

Recognition of problems of this kind, especially in complex bureaucracies, has led to the developmentof a variety of methods of standard setting and appraisal that are based on input (rather than output) or on observable behaviours thought to represent relevant 'performance' (in the common usage of this term). These may identify those behaviours which are thought to form key areas to be attended to or key tasks to be accomplished, but may often be only tentatively linked to output in any very concrete sense.

The contribution which these inputs make to output, or results, may be difficult to demonstrate but they are believed by some to be contributory. The individual's extremely specialist service or advice is simply assumed to contribute to the realisation of sectional, departmental, or overall objectives. But just how it does so, or what impact it has, is difficult to demonstrate in any direct and immediate way. In this lie the origins of the effort to institute performance analyses and assessment plans of such an indirect type.

In this context, performance analysis is usually carried out in a more participative or interactive manner to reduce the possibility of making quite unwarranted assumptions about what is relevant. Those who know best what is involved, the workers themselves, are frequently invited to establish the criteria and standards in dialogue with their superordinates (who, from this point of view, represent the overall 'organisational' or managerial requirement).

The need to control performance in these circumstances has led to the development of a number of sophisticated methods of establishing definitions, if not standards, of input. Two commonly used ones are Behaviorally Anchored Rating Scales (BARS), sometimes known as Behavioral Observation Scales (BOS) and Management by Objectives (MBO), which can be used in other contexts than this, but which are capable of being employed as a participative method of fixing input requirements. These methods identify the key tasks or task objectives by involving the staff members jointly with their supervisors in the process of definition. The product of these exercises is an indication of what is to be done, at what level of 'quality', and in what amounts.

This approach to the derivation of measures against criteria and standards of input is usually applied to those jobs which fall between the top and bottom executive levels of enterprise. These are the highly specialist professional, technical, and administrative jobs, which provide some service or support to the line personnel, and which have little meaning otherwise. Here, the possibility of relying on output scarcely exists because neither the individual's nor the small group's contribution to it can be distinguished with any degree of accuracy. At best, it can be asserted that a measure of the individual's input is as relevant as is the rating of effort in applications of time study: both approaches appear to have that much in common.

Behaviourally Anchored Rating Scales

It was to deal with the difficulty of finding a basis for appraisal in the functional middle management areas (and also in some of the service areas of work associated with non-managers) that a number of plans for scaling and assessing work-relevant behaviours were developed. The twin needs – to clarify for workers what they were expected to do and to remunerate such people fairly and on a rationally defensible basis – have spawned several methods of measurement which rely on a pertinent theory and a broad measure of their input.

They rely on some possibly unarticulated theory about what causes what in the way of performance for their validity. This theory serves to indicate what kind of behavioural input is considered to be relevant to the tasks of the organisation, even though its impact on results cannot be measured in any precise way. Inevitably, such schemes are complex in conception and form (because they have to justify input without much benefit from measures of output) and comparatively costly (because a good deal of time has to be spent on validating them).

The important distinguishing characteristic of BARS/BOS is that they are focused on behaviour, on what a person in a job does (BOS) or is expected to do (BARS). They all attempt to identify behaviour that is related to specific facets or dimensions of work performance, each of these being regarded as relevant to the performance of the group or section as a whole. How many dimensions are indentified varies, but Fineman and Payne (1974) identify a British BARS plan which used seven: supervision of operators, scheduling and planning, technical trouble-shooting, handling staff, communications, administrative problems, and dealings with other departments.

BARS and BOS are similar to one another in many respects. For example, the *leadership* aspect of work performance may be associated with such observed behaviours as 'helping or training staff to improve their performance', 'informing staff of their precise job requirements', 'consulting staff about ways of improving the section's performance', 'contributing helpful ideas on ways in which staff can improve their performance', and 'offering praise for work well done'. The number of such behaviours associated with any one dimension of work performance is usually determined by a careful job analysis. In the case of BARS, however, these observations of behaviour would be expressed in terms of scales of expectation, possibly associated with frequency or intensity: for example, from 'frequently helps, consults, offers praise, etc.' to 'rarely helps, consults, etc'.

These plans are difficult to implement because the content of the steps to be taken is not simple. BARS is introduced by the following five sequential steps:

1   Using something like the repertory grid or critical incident approach, examples of both effective and ineffective work performance are secured from those who are familiar with or who have expert knowledge of the job in question.

2   These examples are grouped into performance dimensions by those who contribute them.

3   A second group of experts reallocate the examples in step 1 to the dimensions established by step 2 in an attempt to eliminate those examples of behaviour which might prove ambiguous or too vague for ready allocation.

4   The second group of experts then rates the performance examples on a seven point scale from most effective to least effective or from outstanding to unsatisfactory, and any examples which reveal low inter-rater reliability are thrown out.

5   Finally, one scale is established for each performance dimension which is to be used, and each scale point is anchored to a description of the expected behaviour which can be associated with that level of effectiveness. This rating scale provides a 'measured' basis for making comparative judgements about relative value or worth.

This constitutes a complex and time-consuming exercise, especially where an attempt is made to conduct an analysis of all the jobs in a job family or organisation (Latham and Wexley, 1981)

The features of time-cost and complexity in implementation are two of the main disadvantages associated with these plans. Another, which research has shown to be relevant, is the difficulty which appraisers often find in associating observed behaviours with the behavioural anchors in the scales which they are required to use. The scales represent a brave attempt to overcome the problems associated with non-measurability of results, but they obviously do not overcome the common problems of rating.

Nevertheless, advantages are claimed for these schemes. They do attempt to identify the behaviours which managers (appraisers) would normally observe in the course of everyday supervision (and do not, to make the distinction, rely on purely abstract notions of performance levels). This aspect ought to be helpful in assisting appraisers to find justification for, and behavioural illustration of, any rating they make. They also involve the appraisers themselves in the development of the scales, thus qualifying as 'high participation' schemes.

Management by Objectives

Management by Objectives (MBO) represented an advance on previous approaches to defining tasks and providing a basis for assessment. It is applied in two distinct phases, one concerned with the setting of objectives and the other with appraisal of performance. But it is arguable that the main 'advance' was made by developing a set of techniques for setting goals in a participative manner, not particularly because it improved the appraisal process *per se*. The main improvement in the appraisal phase was that the appraisal was based on targets agreed earlier (usually a year earlier) between the boss and the subordinate rather than on some whim or fancy of the boss.

Many of the early plans attempted to set numerical targets for all manner of tasks. They were necessarily on surer ground in their attempts to target improvement in, for example, production ('up five per cent') or safety ('accidents down ten per cent'); they developed 'contrivances' in their attempts to target 'improvements in industrial relations climate' or 'development of team spirit' in a comparably numerical manner.

This highlights the fundamental problem in all these schemes which focus on input behaviours. They may indentify key 'objectives' of 'using tact and diplomacy in dealing with customer complaints' or one of 'developing improved training programmes for staff in the department', but counting customer complaints or numbers of staff undergoing courses of training does not provide any real measure of progress. Such approaches run into similar difficulties in this targeting process as did the older merit rating plans which tried to assess add-ons to the basic objective of securing some kind of output.

Nevertheless, MBO avoids some of the problems associated with top-down review and appraisal by making each a joint responsibility of boss and subordinate, but does not necessarily alter the underlying principles on which appraisal is based. Its main thrust is towards improving boss-subordinate communications and many of the benefits claimed for it are related to this. MBO therefore is as much a style of managing as a simple plan of performance review and appraisal.

Targets for the subordinate are set in one episode of dialogue in which what is desirable, feasible, and acceptable is established, and some acceptance by the boss of the responsibilities carried for subordinate performance at that level is secured.

The targets set in this earlier dialogue provide a basis for review and appraisal, as both superordinate and subordinate can assess progress on the basis of the control data which, as a part of the plan, are regularly supplied to them. The appraisal process can therefore be continuous, but it is commonly only at the end of the datum period that the two parties meet to review performance against the agreed criteria. That final review is intended to feed back to the consideration of future goals but it is precisely this feature which is disputed by psychological studies of the appraisal process.

Evaluation

In an early piece of research Raia has shown that first targets tend to be unrealistic and unattainable but that subsequently more realism is introduced into them. An alternative interpretation of his findings, however, is that the parties to the exercise learn to manipulate the process to produce results which, in terms of the values of the culture, are more acceptable in that they avoid any implication of 'failure' (Raia, 1965).

The Purex Corporation plan examined by Raia had three main ingredients:

(a) goal-setting by the manager under the guidance of his immediate supervisor;

(b) monitoring and control of performance by the individual concerned on the basis of data supplied by the supervisor;

(c) periodic review against agreed goals by both individual and supervisor with the object of removing obstacles to improvement.

Using data from records and from interviews, Raia was able to show that:

> 'Productivity improved in most plants in the group as a result of the programme and the increases were maintained; attitudes towards the scheme and motivation to improve performance were high in all fifteen plants in the group; and most respondents perceived communication to have been improved, a conclusion borne out by observation; but commitment to the scheme was higher at higher levels of management than at lower ones; and the company's stated policy of encouraging individual growth at all levels had not permeated all levels at the time of the study'
> (Raia, 1965).

This may suggest that a philosophy and style of managing will secure some adherents more quickly and others more slowly, possibly because of individual differences. It also suggests that managers and their supervisors may generally be willing to give a run to any scheme which increases the openness of the managerial process, but unwilling to embrace this to an extent which might spell considerable risk in career terms: the take up in Raia's case was cautious and realistic (as distinct from optimistic), although positive.

ASSESSMENT

Regardless of the type of criterion used and the method of setting standards of performance adopted, the ultimate purpose is to provide an equitable and acceptable basis for making assessments of actual performance. This, in current jargon, is the 'bottom-line'. High participation plans may be adopted which have the incidental advantages of informing workers about what they are expected to do and of giving the impression that they have had some influence on determining the criteria and standards against which they and their performance will ultimately be judged, but at the end of the day, the supervisor or supervising manager is required to make a judgement.

To help managers judge and to place some control over the judgemental process, it is usual to provide them with some type of rating scale which will be used in relation to each and every factor that has to be rated. It is this which partly distinguishes the formal assessment from the informal one which most of us make every day. The traits or factors included in these plans will be looked at below, but whatever they are in the particular case, the assessors are invited to rate or scale them. Frequently raters report a failure to understand what is meant by them, even after specific training has been provided.

The scale supplied to control the distribution of ratings may be verbal ('good', 'average', 'poor') or numerical (a three, five or seven point scale with a similar meaning to the verbal categories). Sometimes these are left open (so that the rater can place anyone anywhere he or she thinks appropriate), or require a forced distribution (with defined proportions to be placed in each of the categories provided). Numerical scales are often taken to imply a degree of precision which few would accept as applicable to ratings of the traits or factors usually identified.

The making of such judgements in these ways seems to be resisted both by organised labour on behalf of those assessed and by the managers who are expected to carry out the appraisals (who avoid the responsibility of making them). This cannot mean that workers do not expect to be assessed or that managers do not expect to make assessments of people in the ordinary course of their work. Common observation suggests that both sets hold these expectations. What the workers appear to object to is assessment which affects their basic securities and what the managers appear to avoid is a formal and semi-public commitment to their judgements.

In his *Uneasy Look at Performance Appraisal* (1957) McGregor advocated basing appraisal on what people did in response to clearly specified objectives, and this, coupled with Drucker's advocacy of Management by Objectives (MBO), led to a growth of plans emphasising subordinate participation in objective setting and severing the link between appraisal and remuneration. In time these suggestions were supported by other studies.

Maier argued that the top-down, God-like approach to appraisal produced defensive reactions in subordinates, so that even where the appraiser's intention was to be fair and helpful, any positive reaction from the subordinate was blocked by the erection of defensive barriers. Maier, like McGregor and Drucker before him, therefore, advocated a more participative, problem-solving approach to the whole question of improving performance.

Meyer's work at the General Electric Company of America generally supported these conclusions, in that doing two things (such as appraising performance in order to secure improvements in it and simultaneously determining remuneration or assessing promotability) at once appeared to stultify any attempts to improve performance by a shared evaluation of its past level. He also argued for the separation of the appraisal process *per se* from the remuneration or promotion processes, on the grounds that the latter necessarily got in the way of securing improvements in performance. As a result of this work, Meyer advocated more frequent joint boss-subordinate sessions devoted to problem-solving and goal-setting but not concerned with summary evaluations of past performance or future salary improvements.

The most telling survey of this problem in Britain was that carried out by Rowe (1964). She analysed 1,440 completed appraisal forms in six companies and found that in spite of the fact that managers had received training in how to carry out appraisals:

1   Appraisers did not always complete appraisal forms when required to do so.

2   They did not always complete every section of the form which they were required to complete.

3   They did not always acknowledge their authorship.

4   The content of the conclusions they entered was often evasive.

These findings implied that the schemes were foundering, failing to meet the objectives set for them. This set of results, she suggested, supported the conclusion that managers' motivation to appraise, to discuss their appraisals with subordinates, and to initiate any follow-up action on the basis of them, was low in each case. These results would also be consistent with the view that managers did not understand the purpose and value of such schemes, and treated them somewhat off-handedly for this reason. They might also reflect on managers' ability to make such judgements as these, and knowing their own shortcomings managers might be reluctant to appraise for this reason.

In the light of the increasing interest in performance assessment as a basis for determining performance-related pay, these conclusions must be worrying. Apart from the technical problems (lack of understanding of the meaning of concepts and misinterpretation of the degree of precision built into the scales) there seem to be three major problems which call for solution if assessments are to be used in the manner proposed.

1   The selection of appropriate factors to be assessed.

2   The control or structuring of the judgemental process involved.

3   The selection of the type of judgement to be made.

The Factors to be Judged

The problem with 'factors' is essentially one of selecting those which are regarded as sufficiently unambiguous by the assessors and the people assessed. This problem divides into two:

(a)   whether judgements are to be made of people, or their 'dispositions' in the working environment (which is likely to become increasingly important in the context of high technology enterprises where, it is thought, dispositions affect performance more than in lower technological environments)?

(b)   which performance-related factors are to be included in the assessment in what combination?

Assessing Dispositions

Dispositions have always been regarded as important influences on performance in some contexts; from this point of view, the period in which semi-skilled workers (whose dispositions had little opportunity to influence their performance) were the dominant element in the workforce, is somewhat atypical. More certainly, personality traits were always considered to be important in managers and in many others who were considered to need to display leadership 'qualities'. These were often written into both person specifications and appraisal forms. Where the person specification indicates the need for a certain type of personality with a defined set of qualities and qualifications, there is a temptation to regard these as needing assessment as part of the annual appraisal.

The belief develops from early psychological theories of leadership. These suggested that leaders were endowed with certain identifiable traits or qualities of leadership, whether they were born with them or developed them during socialisation. Much effort was devoted to trying to discover just what these were, and this resulted in lists of personal qualities which at least looked relevant. Barnard (1938) and May Smith (1933) presented lists as follows:

Barnard	May Smith
Intelligence	Intelligence
Vitality and endurance	Good judgement
Decisiveness	Insight and imagination
Persuasiveness	Ability to accept responsibility
Responsibility	A sense of humour
	A well-balanced personality
	A sense of justice

These have proved extremely difficult to identify and measure. In any case, they may be necessary but not sufficient attributes of 'leaders'. Important leaders in history have been 'neurotic, insane, epileptic, humourless, narrow-minded and authoritarian' (Brown, 1954, pp 219-20), suggesting that negative or irrelevant qualities were nevertheless present.

This does not necessarily invalidate the view that there are traits of personality relevant to leadership, but it does suggest caution in applying the list as if the qualities were absolutes. A modern psychologist, for example, would be more inclined to advance a more tentative list, such as Cattell's suggestion that the following make some contribution to leadership: 'above average intelligence, emotional stability, conscientiousness, extroversion, venturesomeness, shrewdness, radicalism, self-control' (Cattell, 1965).

The modern view is that these are helpful criteria to be used selectively to eliminate those unlikely to succeed, but they do not guarantee the identification of those who will be successful. Success, it would now be held, is more likely to stem from carrying out the actions which are necessary to goal achievement and group maintenance (see above, pp 232-3). Nor is it easy to measure these traits, even when the full complement of the psychologist's tool-kit is used. In the hands of untrained supervisors who are enjoined to appraise on these dimensions in the context of merit rating schemes, the results are likely to be distinctly less than satisfactory.

Assessing Work Behaviours

Lists of this type, or traits drawn from them, did, nevertheless, enter into early merit rating schemes. Assessing them was just as fraught with difficulty, because they are both difficult to define and difficult to measure, as in any other context. But merit rating plans also introduced other factors, based on work behaviours, and supervisors were expected to rate on these in addition within the compass of the one scheme.

Merit rating is a method which posits standards of both personality (or character) traits and work behaviours considered necessary to work, and assesses the extent to which they are present or applied. Merit rating is based on the simple idea that the personal qualities and performance ought to be reflected in the remuneration which that person receives. It aims to reward the loyal, willing, or cooperative worker as well as the high performing worker on the basis of an assessment made by others on criteria of both types.

A typical merit rating plan asks the superordinate to rate subordinates on dimensions such as:

1	Industriousness	7	Knowledge of the job
2	Initiative	8	Productivity
3	Judgement	9	Accuracy
4	Personality	10	Effective use of time
5	Versatility	11	Safety and health
6	Cooperation	12	Overall job performance

These have been deliberately grouped in columns to illustrate the difference in what is being 'measured'.

Factors in the second column are mostly capable of being assessed on the basis of facts or events. The person in question has either produced a lot or a little in a given time; he or she has a clear or a crowded safety record; he or she has few or many faults or rejects. The factor can be related to aspects of the work which most regard as at least relevant to merit, even if some might dispute the locus of responsibility for them (as in the case of safety).

Factors in the first column are different in the sense that it is difficult to appreciate just what 'industriousness' or 'versatility' is supposed to mean in this context, even though we may all have a general idea of what is meant by these terms. It is difficult to relate them to facts or events associated with performance of work. Actual plans are likely to give more guidance to raters than this bold tabulation of titles implies. When this is done, the quality being rated may acquire greater clarity, but the fundamental problem remains. For example, cooperation may be extended to identify 'ability to work with others', initiative to 'willingness to accept responsibility', and safety to 'safety consciousness'. These extensions add further dimensions to the meaning intended, but do not establish how the qualities are to be interpreted in relevant job terms.

Merit rating is fraught with problems in application for two main reasons. The difficulties of interpreting the meaning of the factors listed are likely to lead raters either to reject the rating scheme outright or to substitute other (and undisclosed) factors for those presented in the plan. Because human qualities, in particular, are notoriously difficult to define and measure, raters tend to place everyone in the middle categories ('central tendency') or to carry out only the general or more acceptable parts of the rating process. Rowe, in particular, found that central tendency was very marked in the companies whose plans she examined, and was marginally greater in respect of personality ratings than in performance ratings (Rowe, 1964).

The rating scheme is also fraught because of the large number of factors which often have to be rated separately. A study by Bittner in the heyday of merit rating revealed that the rating forms used in eighteen US companies contained a total of '35 supposedly different traits'. The largest number on one form was nineteen and the smallest four, with an average of ten (Bittner, in Dooher and Marquis, 1950, p 25). Most plans also called for a final 'overall' rating of either merit or, possibly, promotability. Although it is not possible to establish this from the evidence of this study, it is likely that the number of factors in plans applied to routine manual work will be small and restricted to those most readily measured by work output (for example, factors 6 to 10 in the above list).

Control of the Judgemental Process

The basic 'control' imposed on these assessments is the rating form itself. This aims to control by restricting judgements to the factors listed, but, as we have just noted, it sometimes fails to do this as raters substitute other factors because they cannot interpret or understand those provided. It also aims to control by providing a scale which raters are expected to use, but again as we have just seen, this intention may be thwarted where the rater bunches all his or her assessments in the middle of the range on the scale – the so-called 'central tendency' – because he or she is unwilling to 'risk' more extreme judgements.

Other controls are attempted through training designed to warn against other unconscious distortions of judgement. One common one is that associated with the 'halo effect', by which is meant that judgements under one heading are allowed to carry over and colour (distort) judgements under quite different headings.

Levine and Butler (1952) provided evidence of the halo effect in their study of the rating made by the twenty-nine supervisors of 395 workers in a large manufacturing plant. The workers to be rated embraced a wide range of skills and were paid different hourly rates according to the level of their job in a nine-grade pay structure.

Within each grade, three separate hourly rates were applied and individuals were allocated to one of these according to the rating given at six-monthly intervals. Supervisors were asked to rate on five factors: accuracy, effective use of working time, output, application of job knowledge, and cooperation, and the scores on each were added to give the overall rating.

Levine and Butler were asked to examine the scheme because, contrary to intentions, the foremen tended to give consistently high ratings to those working in the higher job grades and consistently low ratings to those in the lower grades.

> 'This ... resulted in the workers in the lower grades receiving the lowest of their respective wage rates, while the more highly skilled workers consistently received the highest of their respective wage rates. Evidently, the foremen were not rating performance of the individual worker, but the grade of the job as well'
> (Levine and Butler, 1952, pp 29-33).

Table 15
An illustration of the halo effect in rating

Group	A	B	C
No. of foremen	9	9	11
No. of men supervised	120	123	152
Mean rating (low group)	1.7	1.7	1.8
Mean rating (high group)	2.0	2.0	2.4
Mean difference	0.35	0.33	0.63
Significance*	0.01	0.07	0.01

*The probability that a difference of this size or greater could have arisen simply through errors of random sampling.

The authors demonstrate this halo effect by statistical measurement of the mean difference between ratings of the top five and the bottom five labour grades. The table illustrates this for the three groups used in the experimental procedure. The importance of this halo effect is that it might affect all the other variables on which a rating is required.

Selection of the Judgement to be Made

The final problem in this sequence is that of determining just what judgement is to be made. At one level, this relates to the 'purpose' for which the exercise is being undertaken: the judgement might be one of sheer merit, merit expressed in terms of a pay lift, or promotability. At another, however, it is more pertinent to the actual process of judgement. This is concerned with the question of whether a single evaluation is required or whether a judgement is needed on all of the factors listed.

The multiplicity of factors included in these schemes can prove a source of confusion to those who are called on to do the rating, simply because they find it difficult to make the necessary discriminations. Research has established the probability that inter-correlations and covariances occur. Ash studied the rating made on the twelve factors listed in the table above, and concluded that the use of only three factors would produce an overall rating almost as good as that obtained by using twelve.

The first such factor he identified as 'ability to do the present job', comprising factors 5, 6, and 7, and suggested that, 'it seems a safe generalisation to state that ratings of this one factor or variable would be nearly as valuable in predicting work competence as are ratings on all twelve traits' (Ash, 1941, pp 481-6).

The second factor — knowledge of the job, versatility, and accuracy — is less statistically significant because it is not completely independent of the first factor. He refers to this factor as 'the knowledge and skill possessed by the worker over and above the requirements for the specific job'.

Factor three includes only one specific loading variable — health — and is relatively independent of the other two. There is doubt as to whether it can, however, be measured by supervisors, and reference to company records might yield a much truer rating on this factor.

Given these findings, Tiffin concludes (and Ash agrees) that,

'Since there is a marked tendency to rate men at about the same level on various traits — whatever these traits may be — a great deal of time and effort can be saved by having the ratings made on only one job trait at the outset. Furthermore, most production men will agree that job performance is the basic factor in determining any employee's value to the company, and that the various other things such as cooperation, personality, etc., are worth considering only in so far as they contribute to the job performance. Rating on this basic characteristic is, therefore, made the foundation of this system'
(Tiffin, 1950, p 18).

Nevertheless there is reason to suppose that if the rater were (simply for his or her own information) to carry out ratings on all the separate factors listed, and *then* concluded with a single overall judgement, this judgement might be more valid and reliable because of the preparation undertaken. The problem arises because the judges are too often asked not only to make the separate assessments, but to record them as well.

This runs counter to the suggestion that because raters are likely to base their several ratings either on some general impression (say, a 'good craftsman') or on some specific factor other than that presented (say, results or measurable output), they should be encouraged to make such 'snap judgements'.

Taken together, the findings of these studies have effected a gradual, but significant, shift in approach, resulting in plans which are more single-minded, more participative, and more systematically based than had been many of the earlier ones. These principles are particularly applicable to those situations in which a developmental strategy is followed as a means of controlling performance.

Particularising Objectives

In this context, it is becoming increasingly frequent to distinguish between approaches which are made to the performance problem according to the general level of performance which individuals offer. People differ in both their willingness and their capacity consistently to deliver performance of the kind and level demanded. Some will show themselves to be over-performers and some under-performers, and some will give the appearance of having developed satisfying criteria in deciding on their level of performance. Such variations in performance are to be expected and ought to be identified in *any* plan of appraisal. Such differences could be enduring, however, and different plans have been devised to handle such differences.

Cummings and Schwab (1973, Chapter 9) suggest a way out of the difficulties posed by this type of variability of performance. They offer three plans with different objectives (related to 'disposal' rather than approach to method) but with links between them that permit flexibility in application.

1   The *development action programme,* which places the emphasis on planning work: setting goals for the work, and encouraging self-control of performance on the basis of performance data fed back to the employee.

2   The *maintenance action programme,* which puts most weight

on the determination of acceptable goals and levels of performance and the establishment of means of identifying and correcting departures from them.

3   The *remedial action programme,* which stresses the discovery of ways short of dismissal of dealing with unacceptable performance, through joint boss-subordinate analysis of the causes and identification of means through which acceptable improvements can be found.

These provide ways of handling the different kinds (and levels) of performance. Where there is fundamentally no real problem about performance and where the individual has 'the helicopter quality' (capacity for lift-off), a scheme which involves joint approaches to goal setting and self-appraisal on the basis of regularly fed back data is likely to prove adequate.

Where the individual's performance is satisfactory, but where there is no great likelihood that the individual will develop beyond the present level of job, the need is for a joint problem-solving approach to establish the kind of programme which will maintain the individual's performance levels and thus secure such performance increments as the individual may aspire to. A programme of topping-up knowledge and skills to maintain position may be all that is required.

Where the individual's performance is below the standard demanded, it may be necessary to make clear what the management's assessment is and where management sees the deficiencies to be. As the individual faces imminent deselection, this needs to be communicated in clear terms. Where the intent is to try to prevent dismissal, this assessment may be followed up by counselling on the kind of remedial programme necessary to retrieve the situation. The likelihood that the individual will be demotivated by the communication of the appraisal result cannot in this case be avoided, as the individual needs to know the real position before he makes his choices about going or staying.

Appraisal Interviews and Counselling

In all of these situations, there is a need for action to be taken to ensure that performance is either maintained at a satisfactory level, or improved where it falls below the standard expected. Such action will ultimately involve decisions about the remuneration, training, and development, or deselection, as may be warranted by the performance and the policy of the undertaking. On the way to this action, however, it is usually necessary to involve the individuals in the associated information, consultation, or codecision processes. These focus on the 'appraisal interview' as setting and on 'counselling' as process.

The appraisal interview is frequently required as part of the performance appraisal process. In the past, appraisal was carried out by the supervisor as a prelude to determining the level of remuneration to be paid to the individual in the ensuing period, and the affected individual was simply informed of this outcome. This was evaluated as a process which was less efficient than it might have been, because the individual was given no indication of what he or she might do to secure a better assessment 'next time'. The appraisal interview was introduced to fill this gap. It developed, however, into an instrument through which, as in the selection process, 'two people ... make a decision' (Torrington, 1972, p 3). In this case, the decision is not only how good, bad, or indifferent the performance may have been, but also what caused it and what might be done to improve it. This development introduced counselling to the appraising process.

Surveys of practice suggest that the appraisal interview is approached with no more enthusiasm than the appraising process itself. Rowe found that:

> 'In three of the six schemes, an interview was an integral part of the procedure, although one of them provided space on the form for giving reasons for not holding an interview. In another scheme, interviews were considered desirable, but were not insisted upon because of the newness of the scheme. In another, interviews were only considered desirable where written reports were required, dependent upon the performance grade given, but were not insisted upon and space was provided for giving reasons for not holding an interview. In the sixth scheme, interviews were not an integral part of the procedure, and were only required if an unsatisfactory grade was given for performance; no space was provided on the form for an interview report'
> (Rowe, 1964).

Similarly, Randell *et al*, referring to Fisons, found that managers were able to make assessments and identify areas of weakness, but usually stopped at this point, partly because they felt diffident about trying to assess motivation and reasons why a particular performance was given, and partly because they had difficulty in handling areas of intelligence and individual goals. They also record that:

'Many managers reported that they were uncomfortable in the interview situation and unsure of what was expected of them. This lack of skill had been confirmed by the training department, where managers attending courses on selection interviewing were asking for help and advice on how to conduct performance review interviews'
(Randell, *et al,* 1974, p 64).

Industrial responses to problems of this kind include an increase in the inspection of action taken (through the supervisor's own performance appraisal), the provision of check-lists of possible causes and remedies (Table 16), the provision of training in methods and techniques of interviewing and counselling, and the development of a more supportive climate of participative management.

Table 16
Activity guide for self development

The purpose of this guide is to assist individuals to plan their own development and their supervisors to give advice on how individuals might act to improve their performance ratings.

Performance Characteristics (and pertinent development activities)

1. *Position Knowledge*
   — coaching or counselling by supervisor
   — special assignments in works areas where knowledge is available
   — job rotation through areas which would reduce individual's deficiencies of knowledge
   — special courses in appropriate fields
   — participation in activities of technical or professional associations
   — systematic reading in appropriate subjects
   — field trips or plant tours

2. *Analytical Ability and Judgement*
   — coaching or counselling by supervisor
   — provision of more opportunities to use analytical ability and judgement in work
   — special courses, involving problem-solving activities
   — special assignments requiring the use of these skills
   — case studies

3. *Planning*
   — coaching and counselling by supervisor
   — opportunity to do more planning
   — special courses in the subject
   — special assignments to work where planning is required
   — special courses and conferences on the subject

Table 16 *(continued)*

---

4. *Initiative and Acceptance of Responsibility*
   — opportunity to assume responsibility by acting up and to use initiative
   — special assignments requiring use of initiative with responsibility for own and others' performance
   — assumption of position of chairperson of committees inside or outside work
   — membership or official position in organisations
   — coaching or counselling by supervisor

---

5. *Dependability*
   — opportunity to perform with guidance, coaching, or counselling
   — special assignments to stimulating and challenging jobs which will stretch the individual

---

6. *Creative Thinking*
   — opportunity to develop this ability with guidance
   — special assignments to projects concerned with new ventures and methods calling for this ability
   — special courses which require creative thinking or provide guided practice in creative thinking
   — conference leadership
   — attendance at conferences of intellectual and professional bodies

---

7. *Delegation of Authority and Responsibility*
   — special courses in management techniques
   — emulation of practice found in supervision and management
   — encouragement from supervisor to delegate tasks
   — courses on human relations (industrial psychology), principles of supervision, conference leadership, oral communication
   — special assignments and projects requiring delegation of authority and responsibility

---

8. *Personnel Handling and Leadership*
   — opportunity to engage in on the job coaching and counselling
   — course of reading
   — special courses on human relations (industrial psychology), job training techniques, coaching/counselling, oral communication
   — participation in organisational activities outside work (management fraternals, conferences, clubs, technical and professional societies)

---

9. *Relationship with Others*
   — coaching or counselling by supervisor
   — special courses on human relations (industrial psychology), conference leadership, oral communication

---

10. *Attitude*
   — opportunities to take decisions affecting operations, etc
   — coaching and counselling by supervisor
   — supervisor-subordinate relationship
   — selected readings
   — opportunity to participate in company sponsored activities

---

Table 16 *(continued)*

11. Emotional Stability
— coaching and counselling by supervisor
— special courses in industrial psychology
— special assignments requiring performance under pressure and in difficult situations
12. Health
— check-up with company doctor
13. Self-Expression
— communication courses in quick reading, oral and written communications, conference leadership

Counselling

Counselling is now offered to individuals at the various important thresholds of their careers. It may be offered outside the employer undertaking by careers advisers. It may be provided by the employer, particularly by those in primary sector organisations, at all the main thresholds — selection, placement, annual assessment, promotion, and deselection. All of these thresholds are likely to involve roused emotions in the individual affected, and some of them — such as discharge for redundancy or for failing to meet the desired standards of performance — are likely to be extremely traumatic. In such circumstances, the basic communications problem is that of avoiding excessive emotional interference in the process of communicating useful and usable information (see Gwent Industrial Mission, 1986).

The counselling process within industry focuses on answering possible questions about what the individual is expected to do, what the individual may not be doing correctly or to required standard, what the individual might do (training, practice, experience) to improve below-standard performance, what the individual is doing well, and what future courses of action might consequently be considered to avoid over-dependence on weaknesses and to capitalise on strengths. Only with highly dependent personality types is this likely to be worth doing in any way other than by dialogue in a setting which is conceived as a partnership: acceptance of advice is hardly likely when it is delivered as a verdict from 'on high' without consultation or involvement of the person being advised. For this reason, counselling is advised as a highly participative exercise, preferably conducted by someone trained in the process, not as a purely *ad hoc* exercise fitted into a busy work programme by an over-worked executive.

Table 17
Supervisory and managerial development
A build-up of training and development programme
for supervisors and managers

	Performance appraisal	On-the-job training	Counselling by superior	Temporary replacement for superior	Job rotation	Reading
Informal development	Annual review of performance and development needs	Under the guidance of trained instructor	Periodic discussions of progress	During vacations, illnesses, and other absences. Experience is gained for future promotion	Exposure to different jobs in department in order to gain broad technical knowledge	Supervisory and management journals

	Basic supervisory course	Personnel practices	Advanced counselling	Salary administration	Visitation programme
Formal development within company	To give an understanding of the scope of the supervisor's job, supervisory responsibilities, and training in supervisory skills. Methods of instruction – conferences, films	Understanding of supervisor's role in personnel policies of company. Visits to personnel department for orientation	Development of skill in obtaining facts, identifying the problem, reaching a satisfactory decision in personal and job problem situations through use of instruction and case method	Understanding company salary policies and procedures	Knowledge of other department functions

	Administrative practices	Seminars- company development	Developmental reading	Performance appraisal
	A series of case discussions involving policy formulation and administration	Periodic meetings with senior officers to become acquainted with latest developments in the company	Understanding of reading process and development of reading skills	Practice in rating procedure and counselling

	Membership in organizations attendance at conventions	Courses at universities	Special management schools	Effective speaking	Industry courses and conferences
Development outside company working hours	Examples are: BIM, IPM; IWM; JCC. Will add technical knowledge	To further self-development, evening or extension courses at universities or correspondence courses may be suggested. Eventually Henley or business schools	Seminars in: operations research, increasing productivity in office operations, managing punched-card systems, selection of office supervisors, etc	Preparing for public speaking engagements, sometimes representing company	To give broad knowledge of the industry

This requirement is clearly more pertinent to the situation in which below-standard performance is involved. It is comparatively easy (but not completely trouble-free) to inform someone of their strengths and their high achievements; it is less easy to do so when the centre stage is occupied by weaknesses and low achievements. Even in the context of redundancy discharge, for example, where the 'fault' does not lie with the individual, intense emotions are usually aroused as the individual copes with the initial shock, and retreats into defensive reactions before being able to acknowledge the fact and eventually adapting to the new circumstances. In the case of proposed deselection for fault, the shock may be greater or lesser dependent on the individual's performance history, but the defensive retreat is likely to be deeper and the stages of acknowledgement and adaptation much longer delayed.

Mentoring

Mentoring (sometimes known also as coaching, counselling, or sponsorship) represents a special form of counselling. It requires the establishment of a particular type of relationship designed to assist potential high-fliers to cope with demanding situations and to further their growth and careers. At a managerial level, it applies essentially the same principles which provided the foundation for apprenticeships: an experienced senior person takes a less experienced and usually younger person under his or her wing and guides them through challenging tasks in a way which encourages their development. Mentoring was described in the Harvard Business Review in 1978 in the following terms:

> 'Young people shall be given their heads, to challenge the organisation to grow. These young people will also have an older person in the organisation to look after them in their early years to ensure that their careers get off to a good start. Out of these relationships it is hoped that the young people learn to take risks, accept a philosophical commitment to sharing and learn to relate to people in an intuitive, empathetic way'
> (Collins, 1978).

It thus combines a kind of career induction, task and vocational guidance, and an opportunity for informal performance appraisal.

Although it is not universally liked or accepted because of its potential for encouraging favouritism, it is generally regarded as having benefits for both mentor and protegé. The protegé acquires a role-model and is helped to find his or her way round the power-nexus of the organisation, to develop self-confidence in the process, and to acquire career guidance and advice 'on demand'. The mentor secures a source of potential job satisfaction from the challenge of grooming a youngster and a higher career profile for himself or herself to the extent that he or she becomes associated with the production of successful managers.

The mentoring process is generally regarded as worthwhile only if there is top management support for it, if the mentors are carefully selected for their ability to develop people, if the mentors and protegés are carefully matched to one another, and if the potential problems of favouritism are worked at to eliminate disturbing resentments among other managers. Where these conditions are met, it is claimed that mentoring can improve managerial talent, improve communication, and ensure the maintenance of core values of the organisational culture.

SUMMARY

All employment work is expected to conform in form and amount to some standard, but differences in the nature of work roles require different methods of defining them.

The methods vary according to whether the individual's (or cohesive group's) performance is measurable by results.

Where, as in many 'line' jobs, the standard can be based on results, they are likely to be set by a top-down method, such as work study at the shop floor level or management by objectives at higher levels.

Where, as in many 'indirect' roles, results are not identifiable, standards will be based (as in the case of BARS) on inputs (or behaviours) as a proxy for results, probably using a participative approach.

Appraisal or assessment of personal qualities, dispositions, or observable performance is usually required. This may be expected to serve a variety of purposes, some related to performance improvement, some to remuneration or promotion, and some to organisational concerns (such as communication or manpower planning).

Appraisals necessarily rely on prior performance analysis to determine the kind of performance which is required.

A formal plan is likely to be designed to control the judgement processes involved. This identifies the factors to be rated and scales to be used, and indicates the type of conclusion to be reached.

Research has indicated a number of problems associated with the exercise of these rating judgements, and training in the use of the control instrument is a minimum requirement.

Factors to be rated need careful selection, it being more difficult (because of problems of interpreting meaning) to assess personality traits and dispositions than actual work performances.

Appraisals are only relevant to certain types of job, particularly to those where the worker has considerable discretion to determine the nature of the performance. Two broad categories of work fall into this category: those at the upper end of the managerial and the manual hierarchies.

The subjects of the ratings are frequently suspicious of these plans and of the manner in which they are implemented: in unionised undertakings, merit rating schemes are usually rejected as being based on arbitrary judgements.

Managers and supervisors who have to do the ratings are also notoriously 'reluctant to appraise' and by their conduct help ensure that the plans do not work in practice as intended in theory.

In its developed form and conception, performance appraisal becomes a device applicable to an undertaking in which relationships are professional or highly personalised, but less appropriately to the mechanised organisation.

Reading:

Adams (1973).
American Management
  Association (1950).
Clutterbuck (1985).
Cummings and Schwab (1973).
Elliott (1955).
Finemann and Payne (1971).
Flannagan (1949).
Gill *et al* (1973)

Gill and Taylor (1976).
Humble (1967).
Latham and Wexley (1981).
Long (1986).
Raia (1965).
Randell *et al* (1974).
Stewart (1977; 1978; 1982).
Torrington (1972).

13 Remuneration and Reward

The third major strategy of labour control available to management is that which focuses on the provision of remuneration for services provided by employees. This is to express the end of payment in its simplest form: it provides a wage payment which is related to the effort expended or the contribution made by the worker. The fact that the worker wants payment, while the industrial undertaking wants human effort or contribution, puts the two parties in the position where they 'need each other' and can use what is offered as 'an incentive' to the other to come across. The worker offers effort or skilled contribution to persuade the potential employer to offer employment; the employer offers remuneration as a means of persuading the worker to come into employment and to contribute as required once in it.

Because remuneration is extremely important to those who give it and those who get it, the whole process of remunerating and rewarding effort is contained within an elaborate system or structure of rules, found both in law and conventions. The 'wages system' is such a structure, still heavily relied on to effect a distribution of wealth through the population, although it is supplemented by a system of transfer payments for those not engaged in employment work. Remuneration (or 'consideration' in the lawyer's language) is a fundamental element in the identification and maintenance of the employment contract. Elaborate rules and rituals surround its determination and allocation, whether these take the form of collective bargaining or job evaluation.

The remuneration system is intended to secure one or both of two distinct ends, both of which allow remuneration (and indeed any other non-monetary awards) to be regarded as 'incentives' to induce action:

1 The attraction of workers into employment generally and into particular employments; inducing the non-employed into employment and those willing to be employed into employment with particular organisations which require labour service, and into remaining there.

2 The inducement of performance and increased performance from those who are in employment by linking reward to performance levels attained – the field of 'incentives'. In this context, the reward may be regarded as paying for extra contribution or as reinforcing desired behaviours.

Both depend on the existence of 'the wages system', which in the manner suggested by modern motivation theory (see above, pp 62–77), channels energies associated with securing a material standard of living into employment work. They also depend, as the pull-theories of motivation suggest, on other types or forms of 'consideration' than simply money, and the total benefits package conditionally offered by management to employees is therefore more complex than the notion of a wage or salary would imply.

Composition of the Reward Package

The package comprises two main types of reward (or benefit): financial and non-financial. Financial rewards are particularly important because they may be used flexibly for a variety of purposes. They may be further divided into those which are tied directly to productive performance and those which are not. An alternative classification divides the benefits into material (financial and non-financial) and non-material (mainly social and psychological rewards), with broadly similar implications for deciding on policy and approach. Three distinct classes of benefit can for present purposes be identified.

1 *Direct financial benefit* This focuses on two elements of remuneration which are directly related to performance:

(a) the basic rate of wage or salary which is usually paid for time spent in working to at least the minimum acceptable standard;

(b) any additional bonus which is paid for individual or group performance above this standard and based on the quality or quantity of individual(s) input or output.

These may be supplemented by additional payments for work in abnormal conditions, or 'fudge payments' (sometimes necessary to supplement rates which are too low to attract labour of the calibre required) and either permanent or occasional premia for inconvenient hours of work.

2   *Indirect financial benefit* This consists of those regular or intermittent payments (not related directly to performance) made for a variety of contributions (such as suggestions for improvement of production) or employee loyalty or commitment (such as high base rates, guaranteed annual wages, or pensions, sickness and hospitalisation schemes, company cars, or educational support plans.)

3   *Non-financial benefit* As a category this identifies a variety of plans and schemes which increase the morale of employees by giving increased job interest, recognition, opportunity for achievement, and social esteem. Among plans of this kind which have no financial implications are such experiments as job enlargement, job enrichment, quality circles, employee development programmes, non-financial suggestion schemes, and various 'participation' arrangements.

There is, however, nothing automatic either about their availability (supply) or about the attraction of different forms of reward to individuals (demand). Some may be made available by some organisations but not by others. Some may be attractive to some persons but not to others. The correlates of such differences are therefore of some importance in predicting the incentive conditions in different situations.

THE REMUNERATION STRUCTURE

Pay as Mobiliser

Pay and other perceived benefits serve the first purpose of attracting people into employment, both generally in influencing the decision to become part of the employed labour force and specifically in influencing decisions to join or leave particular undertakings offering employment. This is because most individuals must engage in some kind of employment activity and must do so in some firm or department of government or other undertaking to secure a share of the wealth generated in a society. An individual has to make some kind of choice of which activity in which workplace, no matter how restricted this choice may be by what is immediately available.

This necessity for choice offers to management the possibility of using pay (or other consideration) as an incentive to join and to stay with a particular undertaking. From this point of view, remuneration (for example) can be manipulated within limits to provide a greater or a lesser attraction to individuals. For the organisation, pay performs the first role of attracting employees from the labour market and of retaining their services against competing offers from elsewhere. It is this which makes the 'going or market rate' such a significant factor in managerial decisions about pay levels, and in negotiations about the appropriate levels of pay to be set.

There are two questions to be considered in relation to pay when it is looked at in this way. The first is the question about the *level* of pay: where the pay level is to be fixed in relation to factors such as the relative supply of and demand for labour, the profitability of the undertaking or the productivity of workers, the desired standard or the experienced cost of living, and the perceptions of what is a correct level for one group in comparison with what is received by another group. These factors figure prominently in any discussions of whether changes are required in amounts of pay offered and demanded (as a result in perceived changes in any of these variables) and if so what the amount of change should be. There is a presumption here that the structure of differential pay may be correct, and all that may be needed is a lifting or lowering of the whole structure relative to such things as changes in relative earnings, cost of living, increased prosperity, etc.

The second question concerns the internal relativities of this structure. Not everyone is paid the same amount of money for working, so there must, it is supposed, be some factor or set of factors which influence just how much difference there should be. Some of the factors already mentioned may act differentially (as do supply and demand forces, and profitability and productivity) resulting in changes for some groups and not others. But there may be other influences at work.

Market Factors

There is a widely held belief that pay rates for different jobs and therefore the 'structure of pay' for the job family (essentially, the group of jobs which constitute a career system), are (or *ought* to be) determined by the interaction of supply and demand. This will establish what is at least 'market fair' and will make it possible for the market to be cleared (all those seeking work will find work at the market rate). According to this view, it matters little how much influence particular decision-makers (managers or negotiators within the collective bargaining institution) may think they have on the rates of pay; the market will establish its own levels by driving those who depart from them out of business for one reason or the other.

This may, however, be little more than a ritual genuflection to the principles of pure competition, something which cannot obtain in practice given all the frictions and imperfections of the labour market. Only over the very long term is it likely to have any meaning, and in the long run, the particular influences of variations in supply and demand will tend to iron out, so that they will in any case be less significant. In the recent 'big bang' in the City of London, deregulation led to spectacular changes in levels and forms of remuneration (referred to in graphic terms such as 'golden helloes' and 'golden handcuffs') as the financial institutions were suddenly and temporarily exposed to labour scarcity and international competition for their services.

To describe wages and salaries as market rates at all is to adopt a convention which can give a wrong impression of the basis on which they are established. The number of rigidities which exist in the labour market, together with the degree of ignorance as to alternatives, make it unlikely that interaction will be the actual 'cause' of the rate in individualised labour markets. There is more reason to suppose that rates — even in the circumstances of the 'big bang' — are *decided* on either in the light of what management thinks it must pay to stay in the business or in the light of what it thinks it must pay to secure agreement and acceptance by the workforce.

The influence of 'the market rate' is also likely to be different according to the type of labour market relationship the undertaking develops. The growth of the so-called 'internal labour market' (Doeringer and Piore, 1971) in a large number of firms (who recruit green labour and develop and deploy it to their many job openings) reduces the extent to which there is an open 'market' for any but the new entrants. At this level of recruitment, the market rate is considered important, and consequently, the 'going-rates' for 16 year olds, 18 year olds, graduates and the like are often published to guide these decisions.

Thereafter, the rate of remuneration *per se* often assumes lesser importance in the total labour cost package for the employer. In these circumstances, the total cost is likely to be influenced by the level of investment in employee training and development and in the existence of accumulated fringe benefits and other rights which are not themselves cash benefits — for example, the right to more favourable treatment because of seniority, or the right to draw a pension of a given size in due course.

The concept of the market rate is more likely to be important to the firm which operates in the 'external labour market' and draws in such labour as it requires from outside the organisation. In principle, such firms might be expected to take labour from the market at whatever is the 'going-rate' determined by the interaction of supply and demand. There are many temporary examples of this being the case – where, for example, the introduction of computers led to sudden demands for computer programmers and systems analysts. But even in these circumstances, there is some doubt about the longer term significance of market interaction as a cause. Studies reviewed by Nolan (see Bain, 1983, pp 296-9) suggest that the 'equalisation' tendency is little in evidence, and although a distinction cannot be made between primary and secondary sector organisations, there must be a strong presumption that variations in rates within a single labour market must apply equally to the latter. Some other factor seems to be influential.

Remuneration Surveys

The remuneration survey remains a main method used to identify the pay rates which will prove sufficient to attract (mobilise) workers (of whatever designation) from the external market. Where the aim is to recruit established occupational categories (professional or non-professional, skilled or unskilled), a survey of the rates paid to these classes of worker will usually prove sufficient for the purpose. Similar purposes are served by such surveys in connection with hiring untrained staff at the entry port in the primary sector organisation.

The personnel specialist has frequently carried out such surveys informally through contacts in other organisations which employ the same skill categories. Professional associations and craft unions also have often carried out similar but more formal surveys. Such surveys often provided all the data which the management needed to determine its own strategy.

The more formally conducted survey remains a useful device where the undertaking has this task, but two qualifications may be stated.

1   Its usefulness is reduced in periods of rapid inflation because the time taken to update the information renders it less useful as a basis for current strategies than it might otherwise be in more stable conditions (Carvalho, 1971, pp 217-18).

2   With the extension of the boundaries of labour markets, particularly but not exclusively for managerial and professional

staffs, surveys may now increasingly need to take account of international rates.

With the development of organisation-specific skills and internal labour markets, such surveys have become more difficult to make. It now becomes more difficult to ensure that pay-rate data refer to the *same* level and type of skill as those under consideration in the recruiting organisation. This effectively places many undertakings in the position of the monopsonistic employer for whose labour categories there is no ready comparator. This has been the position in a number of nationalised industries and national services: few miners are employed outside the National Coal Board and few doctors and nurses outside the National Health Service. Finding acceptable comparators becomes a more complicated process.

The first response to this problem was to improve and formalise the survey techniques used (Elliott, 1960; Roy, 1960). The problem was defined as one of getting the definitions and mix of the skill categories 'right' for the purpose. Roy, commenting on the problem related to professional and technical staff, argued that 'one is never sure that the cross-section or the sample conforms to the sample of technical and scientific staff in one's own company' (Roy, 1960). His suggested solution was to have companies supply data on all their scientific staff in the form of a scatter chart to avoid the self-selection problem associated with surveys by professional institutes.

Such comparisons are also made even more complicated because 'fringe' benefits added to the basic rates have tended to proliferate in the primary sector. These include items such as 'company cars' (which may or may not be allocated on the basis of need in relation to job performance), health insurance and hospitalisation provisions (which may be presented as a full benefit or associated with co-insurance and/or payment of first amount and a proportion of the rest of any cost), education and pension schemes. Profit-sharing and gain-sharing schemes and share distribution schemes are 'fringe benefits' of a rather special kind, often confined to senior staff grades.

Many of them crept into the compensation package in reaction to incomes policies and changing modes and levels of taxation. Once introduced, they generated a 'fashion' as both management and trade unions saw opportunities to spread these more generally as apparently advantageous elements in any compensation package. This seems to be particularly true of the recently introduced 'golden' payments in the City and various proposals such as profit-related or regionally determined payments intended to meet new conditions. Consequently, many of them remain 'reactive' and not deliberately integrated with the undertaking's medium to long-term strategies.

The problems of deciding the exact composition and structure of the pay package (which have existed for a long time in connection with professional and executive compensation) also now appear among manual and routine clerical jobs, where divisions between core and periphery personnel are introduced in high technology undertakings. On the other hand, the differences between white collar and blue collar packages are narrowing with harmonisation of conditions of these groups.

All of the additions are costs to the employer, although they are not always seen simply as additional pay by the recipients. This fact allows the compensation package to be managed strategically to minimise the cost to the employer and maximise the advantage to the employees. For employees, the level of fringe benefits may be of lesser significance in attracting them into employment than in holding them.

A Method of Determining Rates

Some undertakings still retain sizeable workforces of a more stable kind than those associated with the big banks and other commercial activities. For them, surveys of going rates remain pertinent. Lupton and Bowey (1973a and 1973b) attempted to provide management with a more systematic basis for making such surveys intended for use in connection with recruitment, pay bargaining, or job evaluation (Lupton and Bowey, 1973, p 50) to meet some of the purely technical difficulties involved: it is based on a systematic evaluation of the characteristics of different jobs and their reward composition. The authors see the need for four choices to be made in relation to the job and pay data:

(a) which jobs are to be compared?

(b) what weights are to be applied to their component factors?

(c) what limits are to be set to the 'secondary weighting' of these factors?

(d) what rule is to be applied in comparing earnings, and particularly, the irregular elements of pay?

Their approach uses certain weights and formulae which they offer only as illustrations, acknowledging that these might be varied according to circumstances (Lupton and Bowey, 1973a, p 122).

Comparison of jobs needs, they suggest, should, be based on a systematic assessment and comparison of the job demands (such as skill, responsibility, mental and physical effort) and working conditions. Each of these can be broken down into subfactors to permit closer and more precise comparison between outside and inside jobs. Each such factor and subfactor can also be weighted to acknowledge the fact that they are assigned different importance by managers and workers alike. Care has to be taken that wide differences in weightings of particular but unimportant factors are reduced to prevent their distorting the outcome of the comparison.

Once this is done, the external comparator jobs are given a plus or minus score by reference to the internal job (which is rated at zero for the purpose). The pluses and minuses are all treated as positive, however, for purposes of producing an overall 'measure' of difference from the home-based job (which will, of course, have a total of zero). This allows a judgement to be made as to which outside jobs are closest to the home jobs and which are most different. This helps to ensure, 'that in comparing the pay of a benchmark job and a comparison job, one knows the extent to which one is comparing like with like' (Lupton and Bowey, 1973a, p 64).

To compare jobs in terms of pay, the pay itself must also be broken down into its component parts, if only to avoid difficulties arising from variable earnings from week to week or month to month. Average earnings are therefore divided into 'the part that is guaranteed (for example, base rate or job rate), the part that is regular although not guaranteed (for example, the pay for regular overtime), and the part that is sporadic and unreliable (such as very high bonus earnings or irregular and unpredictable overtime)'. From these data they derive a figure for 'compounded earnings' by applying a suggested formula which accommodates the irregularities of the third element: sporadic pay is defined as the amount of the third element which can be relied on for five weeks out of six, reduced by an amount equal to two thirds of the deviation of sporadic pay, and this is added to the first two elements.

This more systematic approach to comparisons thus attempts to avoid some of the technical problems of comparison and offers an approach which is readily associated with that used in job evaluation (where a similar concern with 'job demands' is demonstrated, see below, pp 370-80). It provides a more defensible approach to the establishment of the terms and conditions of employment which are likely to prove 'comparable' in the external labour market. It allows a conscious decision to be made to 'pay above (or below) the rates' in the market. But the substantive outcome will be a set of figures for pay which can be written into the advertisement or further particulars of any job that is put on offer in the knowledge that it bears some deliberately defined relationship to 'market rates'.

Collective Bargaining

A second perspective of the problem of fixing rates is that which regards collective bargaining as the main source (a fuller discussion of this subject is given in Thomason, 1984). In this model, trade unions are regarded as producing the same effect as the labour cartel, even if they are not, in fact, in the position of a cartel which 'sells' labour. This view allows them to be set alongside the 'buyers' of labour — the employers — in a framework of 'bilateral monopoly'; a single seller (the union) confronts a single buyer (the employer) in a situation in which they bargain with one another to determine the price at which labour effort, power, or contribution will be bought and sold. The outcome of this bargaining is embodied in the (voluntary) collective agreement, which, *inter alia,* lists the rates and certain other conditions (such as hours and fringe benefits) which will be accepted as binding on the relationship by workers and employer alike.

This does not strictly take away from individual workers or their employers the right to establish the actual terms of the contract. It implies that the terms in collective agreement will be the ones on which they will agree. If the trade union has been successful in recruiting the loyalty or solidarity of the workers in scope, it is likely that they will contract in these terms and accept no others. If it has not had this success, or if the circumstances change (with increases in the scarcity of a class of worker, or in unemployment, for example), workers may attempt to secure different (better or worse) terms to secure what they perceive to be in their own immediate interest.

What collective bargaining does do is substitute bargaining by the more powerful union for bargaining by the less powerful individual worker. Because the union can (usually) secure the concerted withdrawal of labour from the employer, the latter's opportunity to substitute one worker for another is denied him. Playing off the need of one worker against that of another is no longer a strategy which the employer can deploy in the face of a solidarist demand for a district or national rate to establish the wage he wishes to pay.

This apparent substitution of a 'price list' agreed prior to actually establishing the individual contract, is, however, no more likely to provide an adequate explanation of the process than is the market forces argument. This approach to pay-fixing also recognises that rates of remuneration are *decided* (not impersonally determined). In this case, the decision is a joint one, taken by union *and* employer on the basis of their perspectives of and preferences for fairness.

In the nature of the bargaining process, however, with the parties seeking to discover what, in those circumstances, the rate of remuneration ought to be, there is no need to rely on a survey of rates elsewhere to inform the decision about what they ought to be in the particular instance. Although 'objective facts' may be assembled and disseminated in argument within the framework of negotiation, the final compromise decision will be one which is (emotionally) acceptable to the parties. This idea is extended by Behrend to embrace both individual and collective bargaining. She suggests that what the bargainers actually attempt is the discovery (or uncovering) of the parties' beliefs or views of what is a fair relationship between effort and reward (Behrend, 1957).

Temporary variations in the relative power of the two parties (arising from full or empty order books, surplus or shortage of a particular class of labour, etc) may lead to temporary fluctuations in the pay structure, just as variations in supply and demand may do so. The tendency of the parties to bargaining to protect such 'improvements' as they may have secured by earlier negotiations from challenge, may help to ensure that what began as a temporary adjustment will continue for some time. The effect of this may then be to produce a pay structure as inconsistent with the real properties of the situation as that produced by short-run fluctuations of supply and demand. These 'anomalies', as they are often called, tend to produce an administrative response in the form of job evaluation.

Traditional Conceptions

In different ways both collective bargaining and job evaluation tend to rely on there being some underlying social belief in what constitutes 'proper' reward. Collective bargaining may be said to look towards the establishment of such consensus, and the use of it to inform pay decisions; job evaluation comparably looks towards discovering by systematic analysis what 'factors' contribute to the relative worth of jobs in what proportions.

Studies made of pay rates over very long periods tend to support the view that factors other than those of the market are important in establishing stability. The suggestion is that there are traditional views and values which will somehow assert themselves in the long run, no matter what instabilities are introduced by market forces. The observed tendency for the rates of skilled and unskilled workers to move in some kind of unison over centuries implies that there are possibly fundamental conceptions of what constitutes a right relationship, which triumph (in the long term) over the short-term market fluctuations.

Some sociologists have attempted to indentify these, and have suggested that concepts such as the following have a general and long term influence on rates of remuneration:

(a)   white collar work is superior to manual work and deserves higher remuneration

(b)   clean work is preferable to and should be rewarded more highly than dirty work

(c)   work which requires investment in training ought to command higher remuneration than that which demands little investment of this kind

(d)   work which is associated with a need to decide is more worthy than work which is more routine

(e)   work which involves the worker in assumption of responsibility for action ought to be accorded higher status than work which is performed at the behest of another (Caplow, 1964).

While it is accepted that fluctuations in supply and demand may temporarily interfere with the structure which reflects these influences, it is seen to have some capacity for asserting itself in the longer term. Between these two concepts, therefore, views differ as to what exerts the strongest and longest lasting influence on the structure.

In summary, it may be suggested that remuneration at any moment in time will find a place for all three of these influences – market, power, and tradition. The pay package will contain elements which derive from all three in variable proportions, just as it contains material and non-material elements which were sedimented there under different conditions (of incomes policy or income tax). The manager therefore needs to be able to define which circumstances are pressuring the wage and salary structure at any one time and in any one location.

The way in which the undertaking attempts to establish pay structures is likely to reflect which view of the sources of differentials is taken. It might do so by surveying current market rates and establishing its rates on the basis of the findings. It might do so by relying on collective bargaining, while attempting to maintain its own relative power to compel agreement on its own terms. It might do so by attempting to uncover the traditional distribution rules which affect the long term differentials, as attempted in job evaluation.

Job Evaluation

Recently many managements, faced with what they often consider to be anomalous and inappropriate pay structures, have adopted *job evaluation* as a preferred method of determining relative pay values. This produces an administered system of decision-taking that is based on the assumption that there are discoverable distribution rules which systematically relate job worth to job demand as is implied in the theory of 'traditional' influences on pay structure. On this assumption, job evaluation is described as 'an attempt to determine and compare the demands which the normal performance of particular jobs makes on normal workers, without taking account of the individual abilities or performance of the workers concerned' (ILO, 1960, p 8). In this case, everything depends on the assumption being correct and the evaluators succeeding in uncovering the underlying rationality.

The term 'job evaluation' refers to a group of methods and techniques of controlling the exercise of human judgement in determining the relative worth of different occupations or jobs — usually ones within a job family or within an organisation. The individual methods differ in the way they set about structuring the exercise of judgement (Thomason, 1980, pp 138-52), but they all focus exclusively on *the job done,* not on the nature or performance of the particular person doing it. They all attempt to provide a systematic approach to comparing and ranking job demands and/or job worth and use these as a basis for determining pay differentials.

Job evaluation aims to establish, on the basis of human judgement, whether any one job in a group (or job family) should be ranked or paid more, less, or the same as the other jobs which fall within the set of jobs in question. The various techniques usually establish in one exercise of judgement what is the appropriate rank order of the jobs in question, and in a separate exercise, what differential money value should be placed on them. Plans of job evaluation are usually distinguished by the way in which they approach the achievement of the rank order, and secondly, by the sequencing of the two operations of rank ordering and assigning money value.

Types of Plan

There are four main types of plan which attempt to structure judgements in different ways. Two are focused on the whole job — invoice clerk, fitter, packer, nurse, or whatever — and two are analytical in the sense that they require jobs to be broken down into component elements of mental and physical demands, responsibility, training and experience required, and so on. In addition, there are many other plans, some of them developed and used by consultant organisations, which combine some of these four basic types in different ways and/or refine some of the basic techniques. Here we focus on the four basics, all of which require the preparation of appropriate job descriptions.

1   *Ranking or grading* is usually regarded as the simplest and cheapest plan and is popular for this reason in those organisations where it is possible to use it. It is most useful where those who are called on to rank the jobs are very familiar with them and what is involved in performing them. The judges are required to place the job as a whole in a rank order of difficulty, 'job demand', or worth.

One recent innovation in this area has been the adoption of the device of the 'method of paired comparisons' by which every job in the set is compared with every other job and the rater is asked to say whether one is more, less, or the same as every other in turn on some defined criterion, like worth, or difficulty, or demand. These judgements can then be assigned arbitrary weights, of 1, 0, or -1 for more, same, or less, and each job's total score is worked out to provide the basis for a rank order. It is one way of increasing the control of the raters' judgements, compared with the open method of simply ranking by shuffling around those which fall closest to one another in the rater's mind (Thomason, 1980, pp 67-76).

2   *Job classification* is also a whole job type of plan; it is fairly simple, comparatively inexpensive, and dependent on it being possible for the evaluators to reach a consensus on the relative worth, or difficulty, or demand of *some* jobs, which then become the 'key' or 'bench-mark' jobs against which all others are compared. In this type of plan, it is usual to decide in advance that there are to be, say, six pay grades, and then to look for those jobs which everyone would agree should fall into each of them. When these jobs have been found, an attempt is made to establish why they fall into that particular grade. Job descriptions are then written for all the other jobs, taking those features of the bench-mark jobs into account. These jobs are then compared with the bench-mark jobs, and on the basis of the comparison, slotted into those categories where they seem most clearly to belong. At the end is a rank order expressed in terms of location in the classes initially established (Thomason, 1980, pp 62-7).

3   *Points systems* are numerous, increasingly popular, but comparatively expensive because they call for more detailed action and a greater degree of technical expertise. They require jobs to be rated and ranked separately on a number of factors which are considered to be the most important in determining the differences between jobs and which are reflected in differential pay.

A first decision in these plans is *what factors* are important and which ones are to be used. Plans vary tremendously in the number of factors identified, but usually these plans identify, at least: education and training, skill or experience, mental demands, physical demands, responsibility (which may be divided into types of responsibility for people, safety, money, etc.), and physical working conditions. Job descriptions are written to indicate the extent to which these factors are present in any job.

The second step is to decide what weight these factors should have in establishing the overall ranking. This is usually accomplished by assigning a variable number of points to the different factors to reflect the weighting. The weighting itself may be done by hunch, or by consensus hunch, or by using the weights others have used, or by employing computers to compare whole job ranking with factor rankings. It is important to recognise that the weighting given will largely determine the extent to which the final rank order will correlate with existing rankings as expressed in pay differentials. Because acceptability of the results of a job evaluation is an important factor in determining its 'success', the outcome of job evaluation cannot be too far removed from what already exists in the way of pay differentials.

The third step is to rank all the jobs on all the factors separately, assigning appropriate numbers of points to reflect the rater's judgements. These points are then added for all the jobs, and a rank order, in points, emerges. Once again, we have established whether any given job is above or below or at the same level, as any of all the other jobs (Thomason, 1980, pp 76-8), but, of course, the numbers of points themselves do not indicate the precise degree of difference.

4   *Factor comparison* is relatively little used in its 'pure' form because it is more complex, expensive, and difficult to comprehend. It formed the original basis for some schemes, like that of Hay-MSL (Thomason, 1980, pp 86-92). In its pure form, it is similar to points systems in that it breaks down jobs into factors and assigns them weights; it adds up the values assigned to secure a rank order. It is different, however, in that it uses money rather than points for the purpose, and, more-

over, establishes the money appropriate to the factor by establishing at the outset what part of the worth of any and every job is attributable to that factor. Because it uses monetary values in this way, the ultimate rank order is in fact a cash order, which is not the case with ranking or points systems (Thomason, 1980, pp 78-81).

These separate plans require different degrees of care and skill to apply them. They usually get what is required in this way, but not always. Sometimes, for example, the training and 'practice' which raters require may be skimped. More generally, however, the cheaper and more readily comprehensible plans based on whole job evaluations will be adopted unless there are compelling reasons for applying complex schemes. This means that more reliance is placed on existing perspectives and familiarity with the jobs concerned, and there is less need to provide separate and detailed training in rating. These short-cuts may be blocked off by the requirements of equal pay legislation, for reasons returned to below (pp 378-80).

Assignment of Money Value

The basic ranking or ordering of jobs is achieved by applying the methods just outlined, but this aligns the order with money value in only the second and the fourth general types of plan. The question of how much money is to be assigned to these rankings is one which has to be answered separately from the question of rank order as such. In job classification and factor comparison, the question is answered at the beginning, and in ranking and points systems, at the end of the ranking exercise.

The assignment of money value starts with the existing pay structure, particularly with the range of differentials from the minimum hiring rate to the top rate paid in the job family. Some of the existing rates in between may be anomalous because the job requirements have changed since the differential rates were first established. New jobs may be difficult to allocate to a rate because of this lack of system or coherence in the existing allocation. Job evaluation is often undertaken to get rid of these anomalies and/or to provide a basis for determining where new jobs should be fitted in. But fitted into what?

The simplest way of appreciating this is to visualise a plot that all job rates and (say) points score on a graph (as shown in Figure 15a). This will give a sausage-shaped scatter-plot of jobs. A line of best fit, or average relationship, can be placed over this sausage, and that line can be taken as the basis for the new structure of pay rates. (It

Figure 15a

Relationship of existing pay rates and the rank order of jobs given by scores in points in an evaluation

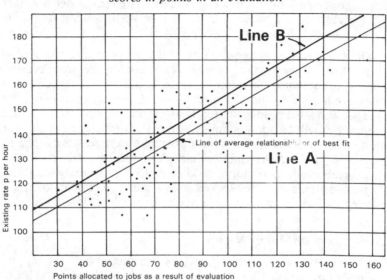

Points allocated to jobs as a result of evaluation

is only a basis because the employer may have to pay 5-10 per cent more on the existing rates to get the scheme in (as in line B in Figure 15a above), and because he will probably want to produce a limited number of pay grades (Figure 16) in place of the infinite variety of rates which a simple reading from the graph would give.) It is this straight line (or smooth curve, if the intention is to provide a variable differential) which provides the rationale for the new structure and removes the 'anomalies' by placing every job at the appropriate rate 'on the line' (Thomason, 1980, pp 21-8).

In implementing this conclusion, there is no problem about moving those below the line to the (higher) rates indicated by the graph. Those above (even when the extra 5-10 per cent increase has been awarded) are not going to take kindly to a reduction in their pay rates, and so usually, for those already in post, the existing pay rates are usually carried forward as 'personal rates' (identified as 'red circling'). These rates apart, however, the structure of pay for everyone else in the future will be rationalised on a systematic basis, which is usually what is sought by this kind of exercise. Importantly, however, the rationality is based on the *job* or the *tasks* performed and not on the conditions in which it is performed or the verve

Figure 15b

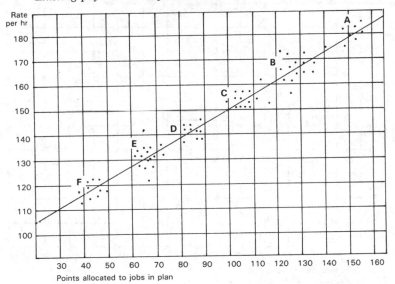

Existing pay rates and job evaluated points showing clustering

Six clusters are shown, suggesting that a grading including six rates might be feasible

displayed by the individual performer. These can be rewarded quite separately by special payments (heat money, unsocial hours payments, etc) or by incentives or bonuses based on merit rating or performance appraisals.

A job evaluation plan is likely to produce a pay (differential) structure which is not wildly different from that already existing for two main reasons. The first is that job evaluation is attempting to uncover the existing assumptions on which differential pay is based and to use these to produce a systematic structure: pay is, for example, thought to be a response to factors such as education or responsibility, rather than simply the exercise of muscle-power. The second reason is that the outcome must be acceptable to those concerned: acceptable to the employer as an affordable cost and to the worker or his or her representatives as a 'fair' structure of differentials. To propose to pay unskilled workers vastly more than skilled, for example, would hardly prove acceptable, given the attitudes which people hold about what is proper or fair remuneration. For this kind of reason, it has to be said that an

Figure 16

A graded structure with five grades

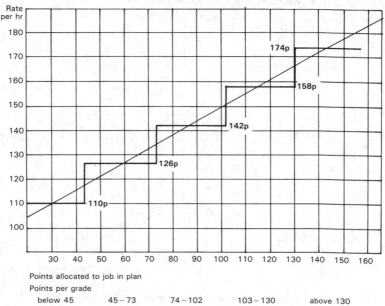

Points allocated to job in plan

Points per grade

| below 45 | 45 – 73 | 74 – 102 | 103 – 130 | above 130 |

important and ultimate criterion of judging the validity of job evaluation is its acceptability to those mainly concerned.

Challenges

Job evaluation has its limitations (in particular, those which stem from a dependence on a minimum requirement of stability in job structure), but it is essentially an honestly conceived method of trying to work out what, in a changing environment, the differential rates of pay of people at work ought to be. It must rely on the exercise of human judgement in the ranking and rating processes, and judgement tends to depend on what people have learned as the criteria of judgement. Although the various plans attempt to control this exercise in the interests of a kind of validity and objectivity, the exercise of shifting values, perspectives, beliefs and attitudes by some form of training presents a formidable task.

Two major challenges are being offered to job evaluation at the present time, however, one stemming from market volatility and the other from judicial challenges (under the equal pay legislation).

Market Volatility

The problem of market volatility is not in principle new. It presents itself with particular force currently because of the scale of the novelty introduced at various points.

The industrial application of computers in the 1960s simultaneously introduced some (apparently) new tasks and skills which did not appear to have much anchorage or association with those already in existence. Finding new rates for new skills was therefore a major undertaking and one which was made more difficult by the pressures of market forces.

The more recent deregulation of the City institutions produced a similar problem, but for quite different reasons: in this case the novelty was introduced by exposing what had hitherto been a stable and comparatively localised labour market to the pressures of an international market, again within conditions of scarcity somewhat artificially created by the change.

In neither of these situations, nor probably in any which stem from similar types of change, is there likely to be any mechanism of *systematic* decision-taking which can immediately assist in the solution of the problem of fixing rates. Job evaluation methods as such are unlikely to serve the purpose, partly because they can never cope adequately with sudden changes in market pressure and partly because they are rarely capable of dealing with jobs which are, or place themselves, outside some notional job family or career-related group of jobs.

It has always been problematical whether job evaluation plans ought to be extended through long hierarchies (including in one plan, for example, both manual and white collar, or manual and managerial staffs). It has also been the case that the remuneration of those personnel who were required to work as expatriates for a shorter or longer period of time has been fixed on different bases from that of compatriots who remained on home postings. Where workers in a localised national context are brought into a new relationship with workers in an international context (where the underlying norms relating to pay may well be quite different), the long-standing problem of determining relative pay for members of different job families and job market is exacerbated.

Idiosyncratic and *ad hoc* decisions are likely to be taken in order to allow operations to be started quickly: the effect is likely to be some kind of self-perpetuating escalation of rates in the circumstances of real or assumed scarcity. Even where rates are negotiated for new jobs in these circumstances, there is no reason to suppose that the compromise decisions will be any more 'measured' than they are when taken unilaterally by a management obsessed with the need to 'get moving'.

Only when a sufficient degree of stability is reintroduced (as the undertaking moves, for example, to a new phase in the product or organisational life-cycle) is a more systematic method of determining differentials likely to become relevant and to be used to sort out 'the anomalies'. Thus job evaluation may have limited application in highly volatile situations, but, as we have seen, not all situations display so much that the method has to be abandoned entirely.

Equal Pay Decisions

Job evaluation provides a basis for determining whether the work performed by a member of one sex ought to be paid the same as that performed by a member of the opposite sex (Equal Pay Act, 1971, s 1 (2) (b)). The regulations governing equal pay for work of equal value provide, *inter alia,* for 'experts' appointed by industrial tribunals to advise on claims of this type to carry out evaluations of the jobs identified in them (SI, 1983). On the face of it, the objectives of the equal pay legislation are quite consistent with those of job evaluation – namely, the removal of rate anomalies which arise from considerations other than the demands of the jobs themselves on the people doing them.

Several cases decided under this legislation have now advanced a number of criteria which have to be satisfied by job evaluation plans to conform to the requirements of the law. These state that job evaluation findings may be taken as conclusive proof of equality or inequality provided that they derive from:

(a)   A 'valid' study, in the sense of a study which 'objectively' assesses the jobs in question and prevents any extraneous subjective judgement from interfering with the conclusions (Eaton Ltd *v* Nuttall [1977] 3 All ER, 1131; [1977] ICR, 272, EAT). The problem here is that the law may expect more of schemes which depend on subjective human judgement than human judgement can meet.

(b)   A study which is 'impartial in intention and effect', which means that the study must not be designed to establish or result in separate rates for women or 'women's work' (Pepperell, 1948) or be applied to a separate job family in a manner which produces this effect (Waddington *v* Leicester Council for Voluntary Services, [1977] 2 All ER, 633; [1977] ICR 266; Pointon *v* University of Sussex, [1979] IRLR, 119, CA; British

Leyland Ltd *v* Powell [1978] IRLR, 57, EAT). This is an acceptable requirement, but it will require the careful selection of factors in points evaluation schemes against criteria which are only arguably to do with gender. Avoidance of those with gender connotations would probably eliminate many of them, and the solution must therefore be one which aims for balance.

(c) A study which meets the above criteria, whether or not it has been implemented and whether or not it is considered to be satisfactory by one party or another (Green *v* Broxtowe District Council [1977] 1 All ER, 694; [1977] ICR 141, EAT; O'Brien *v* Sim-Chem Ltd, [1980] 3 All ER, 132; [1980] IRLR, 373, HL); the decision in Arnold *v* Beecham Group Ltd, ([1982] IRLR, 307; [1982] ICR, 744, EAT) took the opposite view on this latter question, asserting that it was for the parties to establish the scheme's validity. This goes to the heart of the requirement that a job evaluation scheme must prove acceptable to those to whom it is applied; it implies that acceptability must be determined on criteria other than those with a gender implication.

(d) A plan which is correctly applied in accordance with the principles which are built into it to ensure that subjective judgement is controlled. This extends to applying conventions about red circling personal rates of those whose rates are indicated for reduction as a result of the study; where women's rates are brought up but the higher rates of men already in the jobs are maintained on a person basis, this is held to produce an unacceptable effect (Snoxall and Davies *v* Vauxhall Motors Ltd, [1978] QB 11; [1977] 3 All ER, 770, EAT). This requirement is unexceptionable but it focuses attention on the capacities of the plan being employed and the people applying it.

The general effect of these will probably be to nudge employers in the direction of factor or points plans of job evaluation to reduce the scope for conscious or unconscious bias to enter into judgements.

If when lawyers use these terms as criteria for the assessment of claims they assign them a similar meaning to that given by experts in job evaluation, they may find job evaluation a useful and willing support for their attempts to apply anti-discrimination laws. If they assign them other meanings of a more legalistic nature, then they are likely to render the devices useless to management as well as to law. In due course, when the tribunals apply the same rigid standards to the evaluations of their own appointed experts, they are likely to come to a more accommodating definition of them. In the mean-time, those introducing job evaluation schemes or reviewing existing schemes, will need to run a very careful gender template over them to avoid running foul of a very new law.

Fringe Benefits

Basic pay is supplemented by a variety of fringe benefits, whose origins lie either in management attempts to bind workers to the organisation or in attempts (by management, or trade unions, or both) to circumvent the constraints of fiscal and incomes policies imposed by government.

In the first category fall the various types of reward which are unrelated to performance but are associated with service or seniority. Among these are the schemes which provide cheap loans or 'company cars' to non-essential users, and hospitalisation and pension benefits, where these are made available after a period of qualifying service. Their effect is to provide the individual employee with either immediate or deferred gratifications which would be forfeited in the event of movement out of the employment. These are frequently justified as being comparatively cheap methods of purchasing employee loyalty: they tend to cost the employer less than the valuation which the employee places on the benefit received, even if this is undervalued *(PA Personal Services' Survey of Executive Pay and Fringe Benefits,* 1987*)*.

Government policies can and do affect such schemes, as is currently being demonstrated in the area of pensions. Governments have recently sought to encourage occupational pension schemes to take away dependence on State-provided pensions. Since 1978, when the opportunity to contract out of the State scheme was provided, most large private employers and practically the whole of the public sector have contracted out in favour of company plans. The current proposal to allow individuals to contract out of company schemes and to arrange for a personal pension scheme promises to change the existing pattern yet again. The general effect has been to reduce the degree to which the offer of pensions can be made a part of the policy for employee retention.

In the second category fall the provision of 'company cars' and some other 'benefits in kind' (rather than cash). These provisions generally respond to and reflect the comparatively high rates of taxation at certain levels of income, or offer a means of providing extra benefit when incomes policies restricted awards of cash to comparatively small additions to basic pay. Because these benefits tend to be pitched at a level higher of expenditure than the individual would voluntarily embark on, they tend to be widely sought as status symbols. A recent survey by (Brussels-based) Executive Compensation Service showed that company cars tend to be more prevalent among top executives in Britain than in other European countries, and that the average value of top executive pensions, insurance, and medical benefits, forms a higher proportion of basic salary than their continental counterparts.

The non-financial fringe benefits tend to fall into the first of these categories. Such devices as canteen facilities and sports and social clubs have in the past been provided as a way of encouraging identification with the employing organisation. They serve the purpose where they are not universally provided, but they often also tend to be destructive of employee initiatives where the benevolent paternalist attempts to meet all employee 'needs' without involvement of the employees in the planning and provision process. With the growth of high technology and the development of motivation theories of the Herzberg-type, emphasis is passing to the challenge and the interest of the work itself as sources of motivation to remain in particular employments.

SUMMARY

Remuneration of employees is recognised in law as a crucial element in the employment relationship, as it is by both parties, albeit for different reasons. For the employer, remuneration is a cost, albeit only a part of the total investment in human assets; for employees it is the basis of their living standards. Remuneration is itself complex, being made up of a number of different direct and indirect elements, and in addition, there are a variable number of non-pecuniary benefits which may enter into the total reward package which the worker secures from working.

Remuneration serves two main purposes, mobilisation of labour into employments and motivation of employees to work to established standards. As a mobiliser, it requires a conscious decision about how much will effect the movement required, and such decisions may be informed by the results of more or less sophisticated surveys.

Such decisions may be 'dictated' in some circumstances by market forces (movements in supply and demand) or taken by management either unilaterally on the basis of what can be afforded, or jointly with the trade union representatives on the basis of power bargaining, with the intention of producing an acceptable and fair rate.

A Textbook of Human Resource Management

Pay structures are always under pressures of these kinds and are therefore in a constant state of change. Attempts in stable environments to reduce the anomalies, in order to maintain a stable labour force or to satisfy criteria of fairness in relation to differentials, focus on plans of job evaluation. These rely on the deliberate exercise of human judgement to produce equitable 'rates of pay' which meet fundamental acceptability criteria. The way in which this judgement is controlled provides the basis for classifying plans into their four basic classes and into categories of hybrid plan advanced by consultant organisations.

The conventional approaches to job evaluation, and indeed to collective bargaining, are currently subject to challenge, in some circumstances of enterprise, from greater product and labour market volatility, and generally from those changes in social policy which are exemplified in equal pay legislation. The general effects are likely to be a more contingent approach to the use of such plans, on the one hand, and to their more careful selection and application, on the other.

INCENTIVATION

Pay As Motivator

Most people who engage in paid work are remunerated for spending a certain amount of time on it. During that time they are expected, as a condition of their continuation in employment, to perform a certain minimum amount of work and to make a minimum contribution to the realisation of the objectives of the enterprise. The basic salary paid in work may be said to act as an 'incentive' to achieve and maintain this standard performance, as well as a potential mobiliser of labour.

But pay also serves the more direct purpose of stimulating the contribution (or more simply the effort) which people make to the realisation of the undertaking's objectives. The term 'incentive' is used to identify the second purpose of remuneration. An incentive is defined as:

'Any available benefit which is sufficiently attractive to a person to lead him or her to decide to expend effort in obtaining it.'

Contribution to objectives is effected by structuring the effort in appropriate ways. In the terms of expectancy theory, a benefit of this kind which is offered regularly for performance resulting from expenditure of effort, will serve as a stimulus to behave in ways which are consistent with the terms in which it is offered. Such offers of a benefit can, in consequence, assist management to secure the kinds of conforming behaviour calculated to contribute most directly to the realisation of objectives.

The term 'incentive' is usually employed in industry to refer not to the basic wage or salary (potent though these may be as incentives in themselves) but to *extra* benefits offered for extra effort or contribution. To get people to do more or to contribute more, it may be necessary to tap motivation by offering appropriate incentives over basic wages or salaries. The narrow meaning of the term incentive focuses our attention on that element of remuneration or other benefit (not necessarily material) which is tied to the extra performance in some systematic fashion.

This encouragement of extra contribution is but one of the possible objectives for an incentive plan. It might be aimed at increasing staff loyalty to the enterprise or more simply at enhancing otherwise low rates of basic pay, or both at the same time. Setting the objective to be realised is a first consideration when introducing incentive plans. If the objective is to supplement low pay or to increase loyalty, the bonus plan is probably better described as a reward scheme rather than as an incentive scheme, as the latter demands that its payment is linked (and linkable in the mind of the individual) with the giving of extra performance.

Wage and Salary Systems

This aspect of remuneration is usually associated with the idea of a wage or salary system (as distinct from the wage or salary structure which is linked more with the arrangement of differentials in payment). Definitions of wage and salary systems usually highlight these requirements of additional performance or additional loyalty (associated with the attraction of the career structure which such incentives may engender). For example, the National Board for Prices and Incomes suggests that, in part, a salary system,

> 'should facilitate the deployment of employees in such a way as will conduce to the maximum efficiency of the undertaking . . . be adequately related to the attainment and continuance of high performance by individuals . . . and seek to achieve all these aims at the least cost to the undertaking'
> (NBPI, 1969, pp 7-8).

Similarly, Bowley suggests that a salary *policy,* the animating spirit of the system, should be designed to help to:

> 'encourage staff to make full use of their abilities and develop their potential; and to strive to achieve the objectives of their jobs and of the company; facilitate movement of staff across departmental, divisional, or sectional boundaries, and achieve these aims at minimum cost – a drift into overpayment must be avoided' (Bowley, 1972).

Neither of these statements alludes much to the concept of fairness as this might be construed by the workers themselves.

It is simply assumed that a payment system which proves sufficiently attractive to employees to bring about these results must (as is indicated in the expectancy model of motivation) be regarded as equitable.

There are, however, references to efficiency and economy, a reflection of the fact that from the point of view of the employing organisation all wage and salary payments (whether basic or 'additional') are a cost of production. From that same point of view, they can only be afforded if the value added by those who draw the wages or salaries is sufficient to yield a surplus of value over cost. One of the frequent criticisms of British industry in recent years has been that this ratio of labour cost to added value has been too high to secure a competitive advantage over international competitors (see, for example, *National Institute Quarterly Economic Review,* No 120, 1987). This has been used to justify the closing down of the 'heavy', nineteenth century industries and the encouragement of 'high-tech' or sunrise industries (where high wage costs can be more easily met from the value added). Wage and salary systems, and the extent to which they incorporate 'additional' benefits, are strongly influenced by these considerations.

This same kind of consideration has tended to discriminate between public service and private production sectors of the economy. In the terms already used above, the latter was the more able to measure results and to link payments to them; the former was unable to make such measures and loath to attach payment to performance measured on any other criterion. Consequently, pay in the public service sector has been linked to service and seniority, not performance; in so far as performance was taken into account at all, it contributed to decisions to promote staff to higher grades. Otherwise pay increases flowed from the passage of time.

Another way of recognising this type of constraint is to take account of the kinds as well as amounts of benefit which different kinds of enterprise have available to them for distribution. Generally speaking, private enterprise organisations are likely to have available cash, which can, in the absence of prior claims, be made available through wages and salaries; within this category, however, some organisations (such as stars and cash-cows) are likely to be better placed than others (such as the wildcats – who face prior claims – and dogs). Public sector organisations (being dependent for their cash on deliberate decisions of politicians whose election may be affected by their taxation policy) are usually less well placed from this point of view, and have to place much more emphasis on non-material benefits, such as security of employment, status symbols (such as public honours), kudos and social esteem, and a sense of community or personal service.

Fortunately, different people are oriented towards different kinds of reward from employment, some seeking material rewards, some rewarding work, some security, some fame (rather than fortune) and so on. Consequently, organisations which are limited in the kinds of benefit they can offer are usually able to find some employees who are directly attracted to the mix of material and non-material rewards on offer. It is, however, probable that as the culture becomes more materialistic, the task of securing employees willing to forgo material benefits at the level offered elsewhere will become progressively more difficult.

For this reason, the mix of incentives offered is likely to vary between different types of organisation – business, commonweal, professional or mutual benefit (to use Blau and Scott's (1963) categories). As we noted above, the mix may also vary because of the influence of government policies in respect of taxation and incomes, although this influence is often general, affecting all categories (or all categories other than those which come directly under government control). Thus profit-sharing and payment by results schemes have been used for a long time in private industry, but the former has had a fillip recently because of changes in government policy: on the other hand, the introduction of performance-related pay is a very recent development in the public sector.

Payment by Results

Payment by Results (PBR) schemes form one special type of incentive scheme which can be applied where the underlying conditions (essentially that material benefits are available and results are measurable) are right. They vary the amount of extra payment (whether in cash or kind) which may be made either to individuals or a small coherent group of them, according to the *results* that they achieve in their work.

Two conditions (in addition to availability of cash) must be present before a PBR system can be introduced with any degree of confidence that it will work:

1   Results must be identifiable and measurable: the individual's or the group's performance must be both identifiable and measurable in a way which allows variations in these results to be related directly and constantly to the payment available.

2   Results must be attributable to the effort and/or performance of the person or persons concerned, and be capable of being monitored both by them and by the organisation; otherwise the system will die if variations in pay are not seen by all concerned to be related to variations in the effort or performance of the persons in receipt of them.

The relationship of the payment made to the results achieved varies, but two distinct categories can be distinguished:

1   those in which the performer receives the whole benefit of the price of the results achieved;

2   those in which performer shares the benefit of the increased production with the employer.

The payments may also be made to individuals either on the basis of their own individual performance or on the basis of the performance of the group or team within which they work.

Individual PBR Schemes

Individual PBR schemes are applied to two categories of worker who have identifiable and measurable results which can be associated directly with the additional remuneration. The semi-skilled worker engaged in routine repetitive production tasks can be rewarded for the 'pieces produced' or the time taken to produce them. Workers at the bottom of other functional hierarchies (like salesmen or R & D scientists) can also be paid for production. Equally, the very top managers of an enterprise who carry functional responsibility for key activities can be rewarded (with shares of profit or deferred stock options) for their contributions to the profits (usually profit before tax) or the returns (on capital employed or on total assets) of the enterprise (IDS Top Pay Unit, June, 1987).

Full Benefit Plans

The plans which apply to workers at the bottom of the hierarchy take a variety of forms. Some plans offer the worker the whole benefit of any increased results, where 'whole benefit' is defined as the labour value of extra production. Among these are:

(a) Piece work, where a labour price is fixed for each 'piece' or unit of production produced and paid for each piece produced regardless of the number produced. This seems to be a basically 'fair' scheme, but it does cause a great deal of administrative work in a period of inflation as the 'prices per piece' have to be adjusted to accommodate inflation-induced changes in wage rates.

(b) Standard Hour Plans, in which this difficulty is removed by fixing the price in terms of time (rather than pieces), have all the advantages of piece work, but it is usually considered less easy for the worker to calculate his or her earnings as he has to multiply his production time expressed as a percentage of the standard time by the hourly rate.

(c) The Taylor Differential Piece Rate Plan, which originally offered two piece rates – one applying below standard performance and a much higher one from the standard onwards. This proved attractive to fast workers, but not to others, and is not now much used.

(d) The Merrick Multiple Piece Rate Plan was similar to this, but used three different rates, one for learners, one for average employees, and a higher one again for those who performed above standard.

In all of these cases, the individual is encouraged to contribute at a higher level than most likely apply on datal rates, in order to secure extra remuneration.

In recent years, accommodating some of the dissatisfaction of labour with time-studied rates of payment and some of the requirements of new technologies, measured day work has been introduced as a replacement for these types of plan. Work is defined by the methods of industrial engineering and basic rates are fixed by methods of job evaluation. That base rate is usually guaranteed, regardless of how the worker performs. The operator's level of performance is measured and recorded for a period (usually one to three months) and expressed as a percentage of the defined standard. He or she is then offered a guaranteed earnings rate for the next datum period which is based on his (percentage efficiency of performance) × (base rate). At the end of that period, a further calculation is made on the basis of performance during it, and a new offer is made.

An alternative to this is the Premium Pay Plan (PPP) which provides a stepped or graduated form of measured day work — individuals can choose their preferred level of work performance from a range offered to give them the rate of pay they want (or consider worth the effort).

Shared Benefit Plans

Other plans offer incentives on the basis that the gains made will be shared with the employer. Unlike the above plans, however, these generally offer a guaranteed base rate, even if the performance falls below the time studied standard. It follows that the 'incentive effect' of these plans will be lower than in the above cases. Chief among these are:

(a)   *The Halsey Plan* expresses standards in terms of time and originally offered the worker one third of the labour value for performance above standard, but may now offer half.

(b)   *The Bedaux Point System* is similar to the Halsey Plan, but the standard is expressed in terms of 'B's, each B being 'composed of relative proportions of work and rest as indicated by the whole job'. A normal operator was expected to achieve 60 Bs for each hour worked and was awarded three quarters of the Bs achieved above the standard.

(c)   *The Rowan Plan* provided for a share which was based on the ratio of time saved to the standard time, and in the nature of the scheme no operative could earn 200 per cent of standard.

(d)   *The Emerson Plan* is similar to the Halsey Plan, but it offered a small incentive at two-thirds of the standard which increased up to the level of the standard itself. Above the standard, extra results were rewarded at a constant rate of standard rate plus 20 per cent.

All of these plans tend to be regarded with suspicion by labour as they all provide for the employer to draw off some part of the value of the extra production achieved. Management can, however, justify doing so, as in the case of the Bedaux System, by claiming that direct workers must make a contribution to indirect expense and administrative overheads.

Any such plan of payment by results will work in appropriate circumstances provided that the amount of incentive is 'right' (anything up to 20 per cent in many schemes). The problem is to establish in advance whether any one particular plan can be expected to work in the particular situation. Adequate rewards depend on cash being available for the purpose as well as on a judgement about the amount to be produced without disruption of other considerations, such as quality or line balance.

At the top levels of the management hierarchy, the condition that results are both measurable and attributable to individuals is often present, and individual PBR schemes can be, and are, applied. In this case, however, the results are usually expressed in terms of profit or returns (but sometimes in terms of turnover) and the extra remuneration is made either in the form of a profit share (which obviously involves sharing the extra profit with the enterprise but allows immediate gratification), or of stock option schemes which allow purchase of stock on favourable terms (in which case the stock itself provides a further 'incentive' but defers gratification until some future date when the stock is sold). In recent years, some schemes of this type have secured the newspaper headlines because of the very large sums involved.

At this level, similar considerations to those encountered in shop floor schemes arise. It is possible for senior management to 'manipulate' the 'results' to maximise return (switching profits from one year to another, for example). It is also possible to go for quantity at the expense of quality, this usually taking the form of putting emphasis on short-run profit gains at the expense of necessary investment in the future. An important consideration is whether such incentive or merit payments should be incorporated in basic remuneration or whether they should remain for all time a variable amount dependent entirely on the results attained in the preceding period. Such schemes also raise the question of whether there should be a ceiling to bonus earnings, and whether there should be stepped percentages, although there is no 'right' answer to either.

Group PBR Schemes

Different approaches to the provision of incentive are necessary where there is no readily available yardstick of the individual's contribution to the objectives of the enterprise. This is but one of a number of factors which might make it undesirable to offer PBR schemes to the large army of middle managers and professional and technical workers whose contributions are often interdependent, not independent, and difficult to measure. Two expedients are adopted – group incentive schemes and incentives related to quality of individual performance.

There are circumstances in which it is difficult or impossible to measure the individual's contribution to results, although those achieved by the working group are measurable, whether this group is the small team of office staff or the employees of an establishment or undertaking as a whole. An incentive may therefore be offered to the members of the group as a whole on the basis of the group's measured output.

To do this, however, it must be possible to identify the group with responsibility for making a measurable contribution and with a degree of coherence which enables it to act 'like an individual' in contributing to these outcomes. In other words, for these schemes to work the group has to be relatively independent in its activities and sufficently cohesive to avoid jealousies and feelings of unfairness (which serve as major disincentives).

Plans which are related to objectively measurable outcomes of group performance are of two broad types. Some are based on the value of any extra production; some on reductions in the cost of production. They may be coupled with profit-sharing, or, as in many domestic plans in Britain, they are usually based on the concept of added value (Cox, 1979; Engineering Employers' Federation, 1972; 1976, p 18; Bowey, 1982, pp 329-33). All of these are 'uncertain' in their consequences because the value of any production may vary in response to factors unconnected with performance within the undertaking. Management may, however, argue for them on the grounds that they force people to recognise some of the underlying economic realities surrounding work.

There are many attempts to contrive such schemes in areas of indirect expense and administration. One example is the Clerical Work Improvement Programme (CWIP) in the clerical area. Another is the annual Christmas bonus for the general administrative staff. In both cases the incentive effect is difficult to establish empirically. They may serve other purposes, such as inculcating desirable work habits but they are really different in kind from the schemes devised for the top and bottom positions.

Group incentive schemes can also be applied at the senior levels of direction and management, where it is considered that (for example) profit-sharing based on individual contributions is either difficult to distinguish or potentially unfair to those not in central line management positions who make a significant but not readily measurable contribution to the profit or turnover 'results'. This is frequently handled by taking what results from the group's total contribution and dividing it according to the basic salary level of the individuals concerned.

Payment for Relevant Performances

Group schemes are frequently justified by the argument that many people, whose results are not readily identifiable or measurable, contribute to the attainments of those whose results are. Even in the individual PBR schemes, which require a sharing of results (and earned payments) with the undertaking, this justification is frequently found. In group schemes the justification is usually more directly related to the impossibility of measuring any individual results.

This has led to the alternative approach of paying for individual or group performance treated as input rather than output (Bowey, 1982, p 203). In this case, bonus is offered and paid either for more assiduous application of the individual's qualities or qualifications to the task in hand, or for improvements in individual performance of defined tasks which, not being directly associated with results, are nevertheless arguably relevant to objectives. The incentive may, in fact, be offered in return for possession and use of personal qualities and qualifications (and based on old style *merit rating*); or for skilled behaviours believed to be contributory to enterprise goals (performance review, based on key or priority tasks). In effect, however, such approaches tend to relegate the bonus payments to the category of 'rewards', not incentives, at least to the extent that it is no easier for the individual to work out the impact on results than it is for the organisation.

Where relevant and acceptable performance is used as a basis for bonus payment, the major problem is to establish as a matter of judgement what that performance is. When applied at managerial and professional levels, this is usually accomplished by the superordinate or by the superordinate and the post-holder jointly (as in MBO). There are in fact two questions to be answered in sequence:

(a)   what behaviour or performance is material to the achievement of results?

(b)   how much improvement has there been in that performance over a particular period?

In professional organisations such as the NHS or universities, there is often a fundamental difficulty in establishing relevant objectives and criteria. The managers are likely to emphasise resource-use efficiency, and the professionals the effectiveness of the service provided to the client (Cochrane, 1972). The manager will necessarily seek to economise the use of resources, consistent with providing some satisfactory service; the professional will aim to provide the best service to the client, independently of the resource implications.

Reconciliation of these two different sets of criteria is difficult to achieve and frequently prevents the development of effective performance-related pay systems. Once there *is* agreement, however, subjective judgements are put under control by the use of defined judgemental categories and rating scales (of greater or lesser sophistication) to standardise the ratings of different judges and prevent abuse and ultimate rejection.

Undertaking-wide Schemes

The same principle of allowing 'indirect' workers or 'administrative' managers to share in gains lies behind other more general bonus (or reward) schemes, now often referred to as 'gainsharing plans' to distinguish them from 'profit-sharing plans'. These share some pool of money (which may be regarded as taken from 'profits') among all employees usually in proportion to their basic rates of pay.

Undertaking-wide plans (such as the Priestman, Scanlon, and Rucker Plans) are based on very widely defined groups (whole firms or factories) (More and Ross, 1978). These are claimed to increase individual commitment to productivity or profitability, or, at very least, to the reduction or solution of production problems. They claim that it is this increase in commitment as much as anything which is rewarded in the bonuses paid for performance. In each, employees receive a guaranteed basic remuneration for their basic performance. In addition, they (as a group) are paid an extra bonus which, in the different plans, is calculated on a different basis.

In the *Scanlon Plan,* the extra bonus is based on the reduction achieved in the total labour cost of production (Bowey, 1982, p 323).

In the *Rucker Plan,* the extra bonus is based on the ratio of labour cost to total sales value (Bowey, 1982, pp 323-4). Both establish a fixed relationship between performance and remuneration above the base line, set on the basis of a figure representing the ratio of labour cost to sales value. It is the possibility that sales value may itself vary that reduces the predictability of the remuneration attracted by a given performance.

In the *Priestman Plan,* the bonus is based on the increase in production achieved over and above the target set. The method of calculating the base-line or standard is comparatively easy where there is only one product involved. It is much more complex where there is more than one. Once the standard is set, however, a direct relationship is then established between performance and extra remuneration.

Experience of these named plans in Britain is not extensive. Lockyer has claimed that, 'as yet there is too little experience with [the Scanlon Plan in particular] outside the US to judge its value in different employee/employer climates' (Lockyer, 1974, p 377; see also Butteris, 1975, pp 34-5 and 60-4; and Bowey, 1982, pp 249-64 and 321-47).

Experience in Britain with the value added concept has been unfortunate. There was an initial supposition that it would serve to indicate the limits of any claimed pay increase; in fact, the question of division of the added value between wages and profits remains to be settled in argument. Too high an expectation initially led to disillusion when that expectation was not realised.

Profit-sharing

As a consequence of this unhappy experience, there has been a tendency in Britain to rely on straightforward plans for profit-sharing. 'Profit-sharing' has been defined as:

> 'any procedure under which an employer pays to all employees, in addition to good regular rates of pay, special current or deferred sums based not only upon individual or group performance, but on the prosperity of the business as a whole '
> (American Council of Profit Sharing Industries, 1949, p 3).

This type of incentive scheme suffers from the same disadvantages as any input-related plan, but because it embraces all employees (and therefore an 'entity' of a kind), the difficulties are often not so obvious or immediate.

Such plans may involve immediate cash payments, deferred payments, or a combination of the two. They are usually tailor-made to suit the circumstances of the particular undertaking and have particular appeal where the intention is to recruit employee loyalty and develop labour force stability as a protection of training investment.

1   *Cash Plans* involve the periodic distribution of cash bonuses to employees out of the profits of the undertaking. The period

over which the calculation is made and the frequency of pay-out affects the relevance of the payment to the trend of performance by the undertaking, and the amount of actual cash distributed. A short period may result in strongly fluctuating payments because of the exigencies of sales. Consequently the recipients may not see that the payments are relevant to their work performance. A long period (such as a year with the payments made as a Christmas bonus, for example) may result in little incentive effect because of the distance between performance and reward, even though the amounts involved may be sizeable.

2 *Deferred Plans* involve the investment of a share of the profits of the undertaking in the name of the employee so that they become available after a defined period of time, or on retirement or other separation. The incentive effect is likely to be smaller than in the previous case, because the distance is even greater, and the plan is likely to have more appeal to the employee who seeks stable employment with one employer.

3 *Combined Plans* link together features of these two kinds of plan in some way. One not unusual form of linkage is to divide the available profit to be distributed between the two types of scheme, applying one third to immediate cash payment, one third to a reserve for distribution in poor profit-performance periods, and one third to deferred payments on retirement or separation.

Under any of these plans, one of three main procedures is usually adopted to put the allocation into effect:

1 Equal-share allocation to all embraced by the plan, on the principle that everyone contributes to profit and separate contributions cannot be worked out. Differential remuneration, it may be argued, is already taken care of in the basic rates.

2 Share according to the level of regular remuneration, on the principle that those who have been paid more in the datum period have probably contributed more to the profits than those who have been paid less. This is by far the most common method used.

3 Points systems, where employees are allocated points for seniority, pay level, attendance and time-keeping, quality of performance or cooperativeness (or some combination of these or similar factors) on the principle that profit-sharing

then rewards aspects of contribution not readily remunerated by other methods. This method is relatively popular, in spite of the burden of administrative work which it creates.

There is no empirical evidence by reference to which the idea might be tested, but it may, speculatively, be suggested that these are likely to prove differentially congenial to undertakings with different types of organisational structure and operating in different types of labour market.

Share option schemes provide another type of incentive plan with much wider objectives. These enable employees to purchase the shares of their company on favourable terms. They are more broadly conceived than those associated with the directorate and senior functional management. The intention here is to provide employees with a 'share of the action', as a long-term investment in the product of their own efforts and an encouragement of support for the private enterprise system. This kind of scheme therefore has long-term ideological or political associations, and may prove more appropriate and acceptable in those undertakings which have slimmed down their core workforce to a small size and which have, for whatever reason, found it necessary or desirable to allocate high discretion to their members (whether they are called workers or managers). In recent years such schemes have received more favourable treatment at the hands of the Inland Revenue.

Evaluation

The traditional belief or theory of incentives is that the offer of more money for the contribution of more performance secures such extra contribution directly, largely as a matter of paying for extra service. It implies a direct correlation and even direct causality. This underlies the traditional concept of payment by results (PBR) schemes: the demand for a 25 per cent increase in effort or contribution is backed up by the offer of a 25 per cent increase in rewards (Carroll, 1954) or something like 15 per cent more than people are presently getting (White, in Bowey, 1982, p 250). People offered that opportunity to earn are expected to respond with 25 per cent more effort.

The underlying idea is that of expectancy theory: that people calculate the terms and conditions under which it becomes worthwhile to contribute extra effort to give extra performance, and if those are met, as in the offer of an incentive payment, the extra effort and performance will be forthcoming. This places the emphasis on a general conception of bonuses as a reward for working, or for working at identifiable rates or levels of effort.

This simple relationship has been challenged recently by those who consider that the effects of incentives are mediated through a process of learning new work habits under the influence of the new reward conditions (which *reinforce* the desired behaviours). This provides some justification for those schemes which based 'extra' payments on input, rather than measured results of an 'objective' kind. It also supports the belief that the non-incentive payment systems of the kind associated with bureaucratic structures (increments related to seniority rather than merit or performance) will tend not to draw out extra performance (although this may be achieved in other ways by other methods of non-financial incentive organisation, such as career development).

Rothe (1961) surveyed the evidence of the effects of incentives on performance and concluded this with the statement that:

> '... while financial incentives do seem to result in greater productivity, their precise influence is impossible to determine. Productivity is clearly affected also by such factors as the size of the work group, the inherent nature of the task, the organisation of the work, the nature of the incentive system itself, and perhaps the length of time involved ...'
> (Rothe, in Fleischman, 1961, p 254).

This leads him to suggest that what may happen with the introduction of an incentive scheme is that the employees' work behaviours change, as they learn new habits of working under the guidance of the new effort-performance-remuneration condition.

Less focused evidence suggests that whatever payment systems operate in British manufacturing industry, they do not succeed in drawing out a level of performance (or level of productivity) which facilitates international competition. This is associated with the apparent paradox that wages and, more significantly, labour costs are well below those in most other industrialised countries, while unit labour costs are comparatively high because labour productivity is extremely low. The major consequence is that British manufacturing industry secures no competitive advantage from the low wage costs and is vulnerable to international competition in both domestic and overseas markets. There is no evidence to suggest that other sectors of industry are necessarily better placed in this regard, and every reason to suppose that they are not.

When therefore the question is asked, what can be done to improve competitiveness? other questions about the efficacy of the incentives used have to be answered first. This was the aim of

Rothe's survey, but the answers he came up with related to criteria which derived from his six stage model of motivated learning. This suggests that the learning of new and relevant work habits is facilitated where certain conditions are met, that:

1   the learner is motivated – that is, where he or she is in a state where he or she needs or wants something;

2   the immediate environment contains an available incentive which is related to that motivation;

3   the learner intends to learn some new way of coping with the immediate situation to secure the desired object;

4   the learner understands what it is he or she is supposed to be learning in order to secure his or her end;

5   the reward is made available invariably on completion of the required action; and . . .

6   . . . immediately it has been completed, and failure to complete the action invariably denies him or her the desired reward.

The six criteria derived from this model (which are then applied to test the efficacy of various forms of extra payment as in Table 18) are:

1   the presence of a motive (even if only that of willingness to learn);

2   understanding of what is to be learned;

3   appropriateness of the incentive to the intention;

4   relationship to some specific behaviour;

5   immediacy of reward for behaviour; and

6   certainty of reward for behaviour.

Rothe asserts that the first and second of these are likely to be present in *all* payment systems used as incentives. Application of the other main forms of 'extra' payment results in variable efficacy.

General increases and increases based on changes in the cost of living or length of service meet none of these four criteria. Productivity increases and increases negotiated with the unions may meet one or two of them. Profit-sharing, when applied to the run of the employees, meets only two of them, but is generally remote; only when it is applied to the senior management (who have a measurable responsibility for profit) is it likely to meet more criteria. Depending on the circumstances, merit increases might meet all four criteria, but this is by no means certain.

Table 18
The productivity effects of incentives

TYPE OF INCENTIVE	Conditions required for increasing productivity			
	3	4	5	6
General increases	No	No	No	No
Cost of living increases	No	No	No	No
Length of service increases	No	No	No	No
Negotiated increases	Possibly	No	No	No
Productivity increases	Possibly	Possibly	No	No
Profit-sharing plans	Possibly	Possibly	No	No
Merit increases	Possibly	Possibly	Possibly	Possibly
Bonuses and commissions	Yes	Yes	Possibly	Yes
Individual incentive schemes	Yes	Yes	Yes	Yes
Group incentive schemes	Yes	Yes	Yes	Yes

Source: Rothe, H F: *Does Higher Pay Bring Higher Productivity?* in Fleishman, E A: *Studies in Personnel and Industrial Psychology* (Dorsey Press, 1961 edn), p 257.

Note: The numbers at the head of the columns refer to the criteria listed in the text above.

The increases in remuneration which do meet the criteria are those assoicated with bonuses and commissions (of the sort applied to salesmen, for example), individual incentive plans, and group incentive plans. In all of these cases, the criteria advanced previously are also met: the persons concerned can influence the outcomes; they can monitor their performance against objective criteria; and they can compare their own assessments with those of others.

SUMMARY

Although there is a range of incentive systems available, all of which 'work' in particular circumstances, there is no guarantee that any of them will do so in all circumstances, defined with reference to the perceived needs of employees and the objectives and technology of the organisation. (Checklists for decision are offered in Bowey, 1982, pp 253 254, and 256-7.)

To the extent that they provide what the individual regards as 'valuable objects' they may vary in what they aim to achieve by offering payments or rewards in kind, and increasingly forms of remuneration and reward are tailor-made to the circumstances in which they are to be applied.

Financial incentives may take the form of direct payments by results or indirect payments according to assessed inputs, some other bonus linked to increases in production, added value, or profit, deferred remuneration through deferred stock option plans, annual (merit) increases based on results achieved, or superordinate or peer assessment of performance.

Non-cash incentives may take an infinite variety of forms, but the main ones are those which offer free or cheap finance, transport, health care, education or holidays. These remain a cost to the employer, but they may be regarded as costing less than the equivalent wage or salary cost to provide the same level of effect.

What that effect is, is disputed. Such schemes are usually introduced on the assumption that they reward service rendered; there is a contrary view which sees the remuneration which they offer as a means of reinforcing desired behaviours.

Reading:

Armstrong and Murlis (1980).
Blackaby (1980).
Bowey (1982).
Bowey and Lupton (1973).
Bowley (1973).
Currie and Faraday (1971).
EEF (1976).
Harper (1987), pp 323-402.
IDS Top Pay Unit (June, 1987).
Livy (1975).
Mcgaw (1982).
More and Ross (1978).
NBPI (1969).
OME (1973).
Thomason (1980a).
Vroom (1964).

14 Communication

Communication is the life blood of any system of human action; without it, no purposive or coherent activity can take place. This is widely attested in the literature on organisations and systems. Buckley, for instance, treats information exchange within human organisations as the more advanced equivalent of energy exchange in simpler cybernetic systems (Buckley, 1967, pp 46–50). In general systems theory, 'information and communications among individuals might be singled out from the general complex of inter-relationships for special treatment' (Boulding, 1956) because they are so important.

This communication is ultimately achieved through interaction among people (or between people and machines), but this interaction is neither random nor accidental. It is contained within structures of organisation, which, *inter alia,* channel interpersonal communications. Hanika defines social organisations 'as a set of roles tied into a system by their channels of communication' (Hanika, 1965, p 1). Organisations are designed to try to ensure, by prior structuring, that the information needed by a person for decision and action is channelled to him or her in the form and the amounts, and at the time, required. The 'technical' (as distinct from the semantic) issues which arise (Shannon and Weaver, 1949, pp 95–6) are focused mainly on the channels of communication and their capacity to carry messages.

Communication is initiated, and ultimately received by, human beings. They are, themselves, channels of communication with finite capacities, but they are also initiators and receivers. Their skills in both constructing and transmitting messages, and in receiving and assimilating them, affect the efficiency of the communication. The fact of individual differences, not only in their capacity as channels, but also in their capacity to construct and interpret symbols and the messages they convey, places the whole communications process in a context of uncertainty; it is not possible to make simple and universal assumptions about people in the communication process.

Criteria of Successful Communication

Most communication attempts are embarked on with the objective of producing some effect on the 'other' (the recipient). Usually the originator hopes or intends to bring about some change in the recipient at one (or more) of three levels – those of understanding, acquiescence, and action. The assessment of whether communication is successful or not usually relies on criteria related to these three factors in the intention. The extent to which the thinking, feeling, or behaviour of the individual is changed as a result of the communications/influence attempt becomes the measure of the degree of success.

The change at the level of understanding is one which alters the ideas (or images) which the recipient holds about some aspect of the reality around him or her. Ideally, the originator may intend that the recipient will substitute the originator's ideas for those which he or she held previously. For this to be successful the recipient must understand clearly the ideas which are presented to him in some form. This is more than understanding the language or the words which the recipient hears: it involves the recipient in seeing what the originator *means* by what he is heard to say. It does not follow that the recipient will accept that meaning (or the idea), but in the total sequence of effective communication, understanding must precede acceptance; without such understanding no other part of the response can occur.

The change at the level of acquiescence depends much more securely on the emotions of the recipient (rather than simply on his or her reason). This part of the response is almost entirely under the control of the recipient because it depends on his motivation or will to 'go along with' whatever he or she appreciates as the idea being conveyed to him or her. The recipient will decide whether to acquiesce in an instruction to act or to accept the factual information or interpretation of the situation which is being conveyed. The originator may use his or her skill to ensure that what is being conveyed is as clear as possible and is couched in terms which are as acceptable emotionally as possible, but the final decision reflects the recipient's act of will.

The third stage, of action, is not strictly a part of the communications process but it does serve that process by providing data on the effectiveness of the communication. Where 'action' of the intended kind can be identified and measured in some way (whether by scholastic examination or by observation of behaviour, for example) the communicator acquires a feedback of information which enables him or her to assess the effectiveness of the communication. It is not always possible to secure an immediate feedback in any of these ways, and often the effects of communications can only be assessed in the longer term and as a result of observing changes in patterns of thinking, feeling, or behaving over a period of time.

Effective communication in organisations consequently depends on both structures designed and skills applied by man. In this chapter we look in turn at these two aspects – channel capacity and human capacity to transmit and receive messages.

COMMUNICATION CHANNELS

One of the first requirements of communication is a medium or a channel which links the two 'ends' of the communication process (however these are defined and whether human or not). This central structure of the channel or medium possesses certain technical features which lend themselves to technical analysis and which are associated with technical problems which are independent of how the ends are defined: not all communications problems are of immediate human origin.

The engineer's technical definition highlights the sources of these problems. Clevenger and Mathews take the view that communication occurs when,

> 'an information *Source* manipulates the output of a *Transmitter* in such a way that a *Signal* is emitted into a *Channel* through which it passes to activate a *Receiver* which, in turn, makes some function of the signal available to a *Destination*.'
> (Clevenger and Mathews, 1971, pp 176–7).

The process can be depicted as forming a closed loop model of control (Figure 17) whose elements can be associated directly with the concepts used in Spence's more socially linked definitions (introduced below, pp 416–18).

Using the terms of the engineer's definition, people will form both the sources and destinations and the transmitters and receivers of communications. In an engineering concept these transmitters and receivers are sensibly separated from the sources and destinations, respectively, although in the context of interpersonal communication the two are usually found in the 'same person.'

Figure 17
Model of a two-way flow of communications between persons

	Projects signal through medium or channel	
Encodes message into signal		Decodes message from signal
Formulates idea		Comprehends idea
Conceives idea		Assimilates idea
SOURCE or PROJECTOR (of idea)		DESTINATION or RECEPTOR (of idea)
DESTINATION or RECEPTOR (of response)		SOURCE or PROJECTOR (of response)
Assimilates response		Conceives response
Comprehends response		Formulates response
Decodes reply from signal	Projects signal through medium or channel	Encodes reply into signal

The source is the human originator of the 'idea' to be communicated and the destination the human mind into which it is intended that it shall be implanted. The active role of the transmitter (as person) is to encode the information in the idea to render it suitable for transmission through the channel or medium available. Suitability here is defined by conformity to the kind of signals that the channel or medium can handle. The task of the human receiver is then to translate the symbols back into a form which conveys meaning to the destination.

Communications between these two 'nodes', transmitter and receiver, will make use of those media which can be linked to human senses of hearing, sight, touch, smell, and taste. These connect with the human being's mechanisms (sensory devices) which enable him or her to receive signals (Welford, 1960, p 38). Human beings can, in other words, only communicate by using sounds, images, shapes and textures, odours and flavours as media. Most communication makes use of sound waves (as with speech), literal images (as in writing), or pictorial images (as in drawings).

Modern technology may be employed to support and supplement these. Sounds and images may be transmitted in the form of signals through 'a pair of wires, a coaxial cable, a band of radio frequencies, a beam of light, etc' (Shannon and Weaver, 1949, p 5). In more everyday terms, these are identified with, for example, telephones, radio and television, telex, electronic mail systems, and even Morse or semaphore codes. The purely technical aspects of communication come into their own in these contexts, but some of the engineering solutions to these problems may also illuminate the problems of interpersonal communication.

Human Beings as Channels

The human being may be regarded not merely as the initiator and receiver of information but also as a communication channel (Welford, 1960, p 38), or 'conduit through which communication flows' (Pascale and Athos, 1982, p 109). Industry relies crucially on this human channel of communication: the human capacity to decide and act depends on our capacity as a communication channel, which is in principle limited in the same way as any other. Some roles, such as that of the supervisor, are particularly dependent on this phenomenon, in that they act very much as communications filters and amplifiers.

A person forms a crucial channel by virtue of two characteristics. Firstly, the human being's capacity to transmit and receive signals through the human sensory organs enables communication to take place. In human speech, the vibrations (signals) generated by the vocal tract of the transmitter are conveyed to the ear-drums of the receiver through the medium of a band-width of acoustic energies. The human being's same receptors enable him or her to pick up other signals sent along these same bands of acoustic energies as in the use of bells or buzzers, or along telephone wires, or radio waves.

Secondly, man may be regarded as a 'communication channel', not merely because he possesses appropriate sensory devices, but because his brain enables him to code and decode these signals and give meaning to them. He can link these signals with past experience or what already exists in the mind, to produce thoughts, feelings, and action. Giving meaning to signals given or given off by the human or physical environment relies on the individual's operating system, itself partly the product of endowment, but mainly acquired by learning. This entails, in Gagne's model, learning:

(a)   to recognize signals and respond to them in a diffuse way, rather like Pavlov's dogs;

(b)   to link stimulus and response in a more precise manner, so that in Skinner's words what is learned is a discriminant operant (Skinner, 1938);

(c)   to make connections between two or more stimulus-response connections, which is referred to as chaining;

(d)   to make verbal associations, in the sense of coping with chains which are verbal and depend on the existence of a repertoire of language;

(e)   to discriminate between signals in the sense of recognising which signals call for which kind of response – which names to give to persons or things;

(f)   to conceptualise, which is the opposite process of placing different stimuli in categories or classes – males, plants, animals, colours, friends, enemies, etc;

(g)   rules, which link together different concepts in a 'chaining' process, such that relationships can be established – if a person is an enemy, then he will offer aggression;

(h)   to solve problems, using all the previous elements, and particularly by combining rules in novel and appropriate ways to yield a solution to the perceived problem – because there is a relationship between a light switch and the ceiling light, if I press the switch I will no longer be in darkness.

With all of these capacities in place, the individual is able to 'operate' within the surrounding physical and social world. This includes being able to send and receive meanings from others who have been similarly socialised. The capacity of the mind based on this operating system thus forms the crucial part of this 'channel', because it is here that interpretation on the basis of learned 'program' and assimilation takes place.

Channel Problems

In the centre of the communications process are (in the technical language of the engineer) the signals which are passing along channels (or through some medium). The technical problems encountered in this part of the process are associated with:

(a)   the availability of channels which will accept the kinds of signals intended to be passed; and

(b)   the capacity of the channel to carry the signals faithfully between projector and receptor.

It is assumed here that the human transmitters and receivers have the capacity to code and encode. Solutions to these problems are usually structural, relating to the nature and capacities of the channels used.

Availability of Channels

Channels are a necessary prerequisite for communication to take place, being central to the transmission of signals or messages. Channels are the media 'used to transmit the signal from the transmitter to the receiver' (Shannon and Weaver, 1949, p 5). Such media may take many forms, but interpersonal communication requires that they link up with the human sensory organs or devices, through sight, sound, touch, smell, or taste. Some of the main media are therefore the printed word, the picture, the spoken word, the bell or buzzer, the telephone, radio or television.

A woman without access to a telephone cannot readily speak to her mother if she lives 500 miles away. She may write a letter or send a message via a third party, but if direct face to face communication is necessary, one or other party will have to make a journey. The problem of availability usually takes this form. Some channels (media) are likely to be available, but not necessarily the one(s) which are most convenient or (potentially) most effective.

In the context of work organisations, many direct and indirect channels of communication exist. Both face to face and technologically assisted communications are used to satisfy the communications demands of the modern organisation. But, at base, most of the communication which occurs there depends on the human being regarded as a complex channel in his or her own right. This depends partly on the existence of a wide variety of sensory devices which can be used to reinforce messages and partly on the human being's capacity to process, or make sense of, information communicated in a variety of forms from a variety of sources. Any person occupying a role in any organisation will necessarily have to function in this way, picking up messages, processing them to make sense of them, and passing out messages to reduce uncertainty for others.

The supervisor at the interface of management and operating systems provides a typical, but not unique, example; all functional specialists must communicate. Reliance on a single human being, such as the traditional supervisor, as a communications channel in complex organisations makes the role a potentially powerful one. But it also creates a potential problem in so far as this channel, in common with all others (Shannon and Weaver, 1949, p 107), will have a limited capacity for handling signals with speed and accuracy. It is restricted in its capacity both by the capacity of the human sense organs to 'pick up' and transmit signals and by the capacity of the mind to assign meaning to essentially meaningless signals.

Channel Capacity

The engineer measures the capacity of a channel by reference to the amount of uncertainty (or the number of choices) which is (are) removed by the information communicated. The concept of 'information' as employed in a measurement context, is to be understood to embrace both cognitive and affective components of meaning and message, and not just the former. Measurement is expressed in 'units of information'. The unit used in the context of 'artificial' or 'machine' communication is the 'binary digit' of information (or 'bit', for short). A 'bit' is the logarithm to the base '2' of the number of choices which the information resolves (Stammers and Patrick, 1975, pp 26−7).

This way of measuring capacity, and of identifying 'overload' on the channel can be applied more generally, and in particular to the human channel. There are always several different ways of construing and evaluating situations and of acting on them, and choice is rarely 'dictated' by the situation itself. The communication of a decision-premise (choice) can reduce uncertainty for the recipient by making the selection for another person and communicating this − as is done in 'instruction'. The communication answers the question which the individual must otherwise answer for himself or herself. The communication reduces the choice of answers to any question to one. If a question asks, for example, whether a switch is 'on' or 'off', and these are the only possible choices, one bit of information will dispel all doubt, and resolve the only choice open, such that $\log2\text{-}2 = 1$, referred to as unit information.

In any operating system, 'greater freedom of choice, greater uncertainty, and greater information' go hand in hand (Shannon and Weaver, 1949, pp 108−9). If there are many equally possible answers to a question, there will be considerable uncertainty as to what the answer might be, and, comparably, considerable reduction of uncertainty attendant on the information being made available. This is because the amount of information communicated is measured by the uncertainty which it removes. If the question asks for the key of a piece of music, there are 7 basic choices, A-G, and the selection of one of these, say C, will convey more information than in the previous case, $\log2\text{-}7 = 3$ bits.

Cause of Overload

Any channel can suffer from overload, which will detract from its efficiency. A normal person cannot listen to several people talking at once, nor read two books simultaneously. Where such events occur, the receptor will not be able to pick up the signals in a discriminating way, let alone go through the other processes which Spence (1969, p 118) identifies. Beyond mere reception, mental capacities will impose restrictions on amounts and rates of communication.

This load is 'mental' in that the process depends on the speed at which the mechanisms of the brain can take up the signals, interpret them, and act on them, not merely on the capacity of the sense organs or physical functions of the body (ibid; see also; Pew, 1966; Stammers and Patrick, 1975, pp 38 – 44). Consequently, when this load becomes overload, stress (or strain) is likely to be experienced and mistakes made (see Kasl, in Cooper and Payne, 1978).

The important general point, however, is that capacity is related to time: the amount to be communicated in a given period of time is the factor associated with overload. Consequently, one solution to the problem is the one which Japanese management is said to have adopted: that the time over which the communication occurs is extended to match the projected capacity of the human channel to handle the information and emotions associated with a proposed change of thinking, feeling, or action.

The load placed on the human 'channel' will generally prove to be greater, the greater the number of signals received in a given period of time, the finer the discrimination to be made to recognise them, the more complex the concepts associated with them, the greater the number of linkages which have to be made, and the larger the number of rules which have to be applied (Welford, 1960, p 58).

Applied to the position of the supervisor, through which passes a considerable volume of complex and detailed information, this provides one basis for the conclusion that the incumbents of this role are often 'overloaded' and subject to stress in work (Dubin, 1962; Kasl, 1978).

Noise

Apart from overload, however, these same communications nodes may have their efficiency reduced by noise in the system. Even if the (human) transmitters and receivers work 'perfectly', the message may not be conveyed because something occurs during transmission through the channel. It can be interfered with or otherwise distorted for reasons which are inherently technical and contained in the transmission process itself. This interference limits the amount of information and the rate at which it can be passed along the channel.

The noise problem may arise because of the physical circumstances of the workplace. Communication by word of mouth (using sound waves) in a weaving shed may prove to be difficult, and is often overcome by relying on mime or writing (using light waves). The problem arises from the presence of 'noise' in both the everyday sense and the technical communication sense. Anything which alters or distorts signals in a way that makes receipt (or decoding) difficult or impossible, is referred to as 'noise'. Noise can be so strong that the channel ceases to be available, although speech communication may be augmented by earphones or replaced by written communication in the noisy workshop.

Noise may be introduced in quite a different way. A number of people spread along the length of a long chain of command will each function as a filter and amplifier of any signals (or messages) which are passed along it (or up and down it). In the process of filtering and amplifying, distortions of the original message will tend to occur, so that the signal received at the destination is quite different from what was transmitted from the source. The classic example of this is provided by the First World War story of passing the message: 'Send me reinforcements, I'm going to advance' along the communications trench, only to find that at the other end, it became, 'Lend me three-and-fourpence, I'm going to a dance.'

The problem of communicating effectively with workers on night shifts, in subsidiary units or on out-stations, or with out workers is essentially similar. Channels of communication exist but they are not particularly convenient because they are usually restricted to short and intermittent communication episodes (whatever the medium used). Where such short and infrequent messages are in competition with many other messages deriving from other sources, this in itself introduces noise into the transmission. But written records and hand-over instructions may be supplemented by direct or indirect speech to reach shift-workers or out-workers (multiple-channelling).

Although on the face of it a different kind of problem, the difficulties often encountered by management in communicating directly with workers are essentially the same. These difficulties sometimes arise because the custom has grown up that direct communication to workers is through the shop stewards. This immediately admits the possibility that the signals will be distorted because of a simple filtering/amplifying effect of the kind already noted. It may be exacerbated as meaning is deliberately filtered out to serve some other end from that which originally prompted the message.

Emotion as Noise

Human emotions frequently create a problem of 'noise' when they interfere with the transmission of 'objective' fact or information which is intended to be factual and non-emotional. This is not to suggest that all emotional associations of communications are noisy in this sense. Sometimes communication must be concerned with emotions, and many attempts at influence are directed towards changing the emotions (aspirations, wishes, motivational bases, etc) of another; in such cases, the emotions are central to the purposes of the communication.

Occasions arise, however, where two people dislike one another, have no respect for one another, or do not trust one another, and in consequence cannot communicate effectively with one another. These emotions get in the way of and hinder communication which may be intended to be emotion-free. The classic story of the management which offered a pay increase before the union representatives had presented their claim, only to find that the union members spent a great deal of time trying to spot the trick or the strings attached, illustrates the way in which a communication can fail to achieve its objective because of a fundamental lack of trust. What this factor does, in the language of the engineer, is to introduce noise into the transmission of the coded signal.

The development of communications technology based on computers and peripherals has, however, created a new problem in this area. The machine can now communicate 'pure information' to anyone located at a terminal in a 'pure' form (free from channel distortion or channel noise). Information and its transmission become more 'impersonal'. This solves one major communications problem: it allows information to be communicated without the distortion that otherwise arises because, in particular, human emotions and biases interfere with the construction of the message or with its transmission, although interpretation remains a problem which has to be tackled.

This at one and the same time makes it more difficult to communicate the personal wishes, emotions, feelings, understandings and aspirations which have hitherto made up the fabric of organisational behaviour. As Drucker expresses this:

> 'We now have the problem of establishing the necessary minimum of communications so that we understand each other, and can know each other's needs, goals, perceptions, and ways of doing things. Information does not supply this. Only direct contact, whether by voice or written word, can communicate.'
> (Drucker, 1980, p 70).

In other words, the same process which 'permits' workers to work at the connected terminal at home, not only cuts them off from human contact with fellow workers in the rather obvious sense, but cuts them off more effectively because the terminal will feed information, not communications in the full-blooded sense indicated by Jaques's definition (below, p 414). Paradoxically, now that the problem of transmitting information effectively is resolved, it may be necessary to take more deliberate steps to communicate the sum total of feelings and wishes to hold the organisational system together.

Multiple Channelling

The solutions usually attempted to these problems tend to rely on the construction of an adequate number of channels and the allocation to managers, by virtue of their appointment to positions of authority, of access to them. In fact, one perspective of authority allocation in industry regards this process as one of ensuring that managers have access to channels. This is manifest in the granting of a 'command' or a department to a manager as his 'responsibility'. This aims to legitimate his or her right to communicate to the people within the command on a range of issues pertinent to the management of that operation. This process produces the 'channels' of the typical 'management organisation chart'.

It also tries to establish, through the legitimation of management 'style' within the organisation, which modes of communication are to be used to effect influence. These range from simple instruction (the 'commanding' of the classic management text) through persuasion and suggestion to joint or shared decision (Simon, 1953, pp 126–8). Each of these modes can, from the present standpoint, be regarded as a distinct channel of communication. Each may be used for a limited range of purposes (as in the division of subject matter associated with negotiation and consultation in many organisations).

Management may find that reliance on the ordinary hierarchical channels of communication do not prove effective in terms of shop floor responses by way of thought, feeling, or behaviour. On investigation it may be found that reliance on the first line manager or supervisor as the only filter/amplifier between management and workers results in overload of this (supervisor) channel. Institution of a joint consultative system, a house journal, or quality circles or briefing groups as additional channels may allow greater 'redundancy' in communicating the message which management wants to convey.

Multichannelling is, in principle, a solution to these problems of channel availability and 'noise', and it is also likely to improve effectiveness of communication if 'redundancy' (communication of the same message in a number of different forms) is deliberately built into them. The risk of 'overload' exists, but 'redundancy' offers an antidote to this. The development of multiple channels also threatens to increase costs because time spent in communication is time lost to direct productive activity. Such cost calculations tend, however, to discount the *consequential* cost of inadequate communication, and to rely only on costs of *prior* involvement in communications activity. It is widely asserted that the Japanese management practice of ensuring effective communication, prior to action being required, pays off in lower subsequent costs and contributes in no small measure to their success. This provides an example of a different style of legitimation of management's authority and responsibility to communicate from that which is reputedly adopted generally in Britain.

The remedies for overload are to be found partly in the development of such additional channels. These may be used to segregate communications by subject matter, as in the case where functional specialists are used to communicate about their 'specialty', or they may be used to carry the same message in a different form through different media to reinforce it by 'redundancy'. The new technology problem may also spawn solutions of the same general type, with special face to face communication meetings set up to ensure that emotions are deliberately engaged.

The training process provides many examples of the first of these. Where an instructor is teaching a person to file a piece of metal, reliance on oral instruction might quickly overload that channel. Therefore, other additional channels are opened up: the instructor will show the trainee a piece of metal and the finished product, will possibly show pictures of the operation, and probably demonstrate the filing operations (so that the person can see what is involved): the trainee will be offered an opportunity to practise (so that he can feel what is involved).

Similarly, in some of the new organisational developments, such as the project and matrix types of organisation, the attempt is made to get away from the classic principle of 'one man – one boss' (Dale, 1952, p 155) and replace it with multiple channels with different contents. In the typical matrix organisation, for example, one set of official channels is linked to career (pay and rations) matters and the other to work-task (project) matters. The 'task' and 'people' managers are given authority to communicate through a defined domain on a restricted range of subjects.

The development of consultative channels of communication between senior management and workers in addition to the 'normal chain of command' provides an example of the second. Here the aim is not, particularly, to channel new or specialist messages but to communicate the same ideas as are generally communicated through the chain of command by first-line managers. The development of such channels as are identified with briefing groups, quality circles, consultative machinery, and off-the-job team building exercises tends to reduce the exclusiveness of the chain of command as the main means of communication. Long chains of authority or communication become shortened and multipled within a flatter, less obviously hierarchical, structure.

Communication is, therefore, not always successful in reducing uncertainty, and there may be a number of purely technical reasons for this. Problems of channel availability, noise within existing channels, limits on channel capacity (and particularly on the capacity of the human being as a channel) arise in all organisational settings. Solutions may be found in multiplying the channels (for example, reducing exclusive reliance on pay as a motivator), reducing noise (for example, in avoiding interference from competing messages from different sources), and improving capacity (for example, by training in semantic and other communication skills).

There are other reasons for communications failures than those which are associated with the technical and structural features of the process. In particular, some of these need to be examined by reference to the semantic and task/skill 'levels' of analysis (Shannon and Weaver, 1949, pp 95–6) which are taken up below (pp 418–28).

EFFECTIVE INTERPERSONAL COMMUNICATION

The prominence given to communication in all theories of organisation or system operation suggests that the skills of communicating are fundamental to all other managerial skills. Such skills are needed by *everyone* within organisations and not by managers alone: anyone who must cooperate must also communicate effectively. Such communication is, essentially, of a deliberate and direct kind: the originator intends to produce an effect on another and acts in a way which he or she thinks will produce that effect. Although it may not always succeed completely in achieving its intention, the degree of success attained will reflect the originator's skill as a communicator.

Human beings are not the only beings who communicate (as the dawn chorus in spring will illustrate), nor are inanimate objects incapable of communicating signals and messages of a sort (witness the many messages which poets have drawn from 'nature'). One very important variation on this latter theme, which is relevant to industrial activity, is the 'communication' effected by 'the system': this system may well have been created by people, but individuals are scarcely to be identified as the sources or transmitters of the messages received from it. Although this is important for the support or lack of it which the system gives to deliberate and specific human communications, for present purposes, attention will be directed mainly to interpersonal communications, where people are fairly readily identifiable at each end of the process.

This is not the only way in which non-personalised communication takes place. It may occur and produce an effect without the originator having any intention that it should do either. Neither occurrence nor its effects may even be noticed by the originator. Goffman (1959, p 1) talks of indirect communication taking place when 'impressions' are given off, quite unintentionally, by a person in the presence of another. A person listening to another talking may *look* interested or uninterested, whether he is or not. A speaker may form an impression of the other's interest which may or may not be intended. A person's facial expression may communicate one message, say of dislike, when at the same time the words being uttered purport to convey the opposite emotion. Thus a person may give off an impression which is not intended and not even noticed by him or her.

Nor is it only the person who gives off such impressions. The status symbols with which a communicator or a recipient is surrounded – the bigger office, the larger carpet, the fancy title, etc, – also give 'messages', sometimes by intent and sometimes by accident. These tend to form a symbolic language which indicate something of the possessor's status, worthiness, esteem, power and importance. These may be used 'deliberately' in communication, but they will usually have an effect on thinking, feeling, or conduct, whether they are used deliberately or not.

Nevertheless, the communication that occurs between individuals, not some impersonal process inhering in the system concept as such, is arguably the most important type which occurs in industry. 'Interpersonal communication is a basic fact of organisational life' and a 'central process in the act of organising' (Baskin and Aronoff, 1979, p 1). Interpersonal communication in this sense comprises 'the sum total of directly and indirectly, consciously and unconsciously, transmitted feelings, attitudes and wishes' (Jaques, 1951, p 301).

Emotions as well as facts form a significant component of inter-personal communication. Ability to communicate either may be developed with practice and through training. But effective training, here as elsewhere, will depend on analysis of the objectives and tasks involved and identification of the skills associated with them.

Representation of the Communication Process

This likelihood that skill in communication will be universally taken for granted gets in the way of giving greater conceptual precision to the process. It seems that communication is adequately identified by saying simply that it is no more than a matter of 'who . . . says what . . . in what way . . . to whom . . . with what effect?' (Lasswell, 1969, p 1). This, however, implies that communication is no more than direct face to face communication between persons, under-taken with some purpose in mind.

There is more to communication than that: persons may not be involved as senders, as 'messages' can be read into purely physical configurations such as those of clouds or landscapes; speech (saying something) may not be involved as messages may be conveyed by lamps, buzzers, bells, colour combinations and so on. An attempt to identify the essential elements of *any* process of communication is therefore difficult because of the variety of forms which has to be accommodated.

It is also complicated because the analysis of communication may be undertaken at different levels for different reasons, such as the technical, the semantic, and the effectiveness levels each of which highlights different kinds of problem. As a first approximation, however, *interpersonal* communication may be represented as em-bracing two persons in a two-way process of interaction in which ideas are formulated and transmitted by each in turn to the other in order to bring about some change in the other's thinking, feeling, or behaviour.

Baskin and Aronoff's definition of it as 'the exchange of messages between persons for the purpose of constructing common meanings' (Baskin and Aronoff, 1979, p 4), where 'anything that can be sensed by human receptors is a message, if it elicits meaning in another person' (ibid), and where meanings are mediated by individual needs, perceptions, and values (op cit, p 7), has ap-propriate emphasis.

For purposes of analysis and solution of 'problems' associated with it, the process may be depicted diagrammatically (as on p 403, above) in a way that adverts to both the technical and the semantic levels of analysis. The one uses the language of 'source', 'destination', 'signal' and 'channel'; the other the concepts of 'projector', 'receptor', 'medium', 'message' and 'meaning', as employed in Spence's eight stage description of the process of interpersonal communication:

> 'A *communicator* (projector) conceives an *idea* to which he gives a *form* and encodes into a *message* which he then projects through some *medium* to a *receptor* who *decodes* it, *comprehends* (or applies meaning to) it, *assimilates* it and uses it as a basis for response.'
> (Spence, 1969, p 118).

Both help to identify the main and subtasks involved.

Stages in Interpersonal Communication

The social scientist's conception of the process helps to identify the stages (or subtasks) involved in communication and the 'human' problems (as distinct from the technical ones) associated with it. These focus mainly on questions of content and meaning, rather than those of process-capacity and structure.

Spence employs the concept of 'an idea' to indicate the content of what is being communicated, although it is possible to describe this in a variety of ways, information, instructions, thoughts, feelings, values, etc. An 'idea' in this context is a mental image of some aspect of experience of life, a spiritual representation of some physical emotion. The image may be of things or events, which together are described generically as 'referents' of the physical reality to distinguish them from the idea or thought activated through one of the senses (Spence, 1969, pp 84–5). However abstract the ideas and thoughts related to objects and events become, they remain anchored in sensuously appreciated reality.

The idea must first be grasped or imagined, and this Spence refers to as the first stage, the *inception* of the idea. At this stage it may simply conjure up an image of its referent – that is a concrete object such as a hammer or an assembly line, or an abstract concept or principle such as freedom or obedience. Although it is not possible to identify the referent except by giving it a name, the inception stage does not necessarily involve conception of the referent in terms of the symbols or signs which are conventionally employed to identify it.

This takes place at the second stage, *formulation,* where the person whose mind conjures up the idea moulds it into a form which he or she can understand. This understanding may make use of symbols or signs which function as a 'code' into which ideas, thoughts, or images are translated to render them into some form which is communicable. In human communication, this relies on language, particularly the language which is normally used by the individual in thinking out ideas and in communicating them to other people within the same culture group.

The third stage is that of *projection* in which the moulded idea is passed into that physical process by which language can be expressed — vocal or written articulation. This is the stage of speaking or writing and is essentially a physical or 'technical' process through which the aural or visible signals and signs are produced. This stage may therefore be associated with the process of 'coding' the messages which will move through some medium or channel from projector to receptor.

The fourth stage is that of *reception* of the coded message by the receptor. At this point in the sequence, the message has passed along the channel or through the medium, and is seen or heard. At this stage, the message consists of sounds (produced by speaking) or signs (produced by writing). It is meaningless to the receptor until the sounds or signs are decoded. Consequently, reception involves a process of decoding, so that the message can be understood in 'signal' terms. What are the 'words' that are being uttered in speech or writing?

This decoding does not by itself produce 'understanding' of the meaning of the message. This is a process which initially occurs at the stage of *interpretation*. Interpretation involves assigning to the coded signals a meaning — that is, a mental construction of what the receptor interprets as the meaning intended by the projector. The classic misinterpretation of the First World War message illustrates how this assigning process can lead to errors. What the receptor interprets the meaning to be may not, and frequently does not, correspond to that which was intended.

Interpretation is necessary to *understanding,* but not the whole of this process. Once a meaning has been attached by the receptor, it is 'taken into his or her mind' and becomes a part of his or her experience of the world. Understanding, however, requires that this 'new element' be linked with the 'old elements' already there in the mind. It has to be associated with already learned programmes which permit sense to be made of experience, including in this case, the 'new' idea which has been received. Many people, for example, confronted with some of the messages emanating from government departments, find them incomprehensible, simply because they cannot link them to meanings which already repose in the mind. The sixth stage is therefore one which involves the development of comprehension.

The seventh stage, *assimilation,* involves consolidation of the understood meaning within the mental constructs of the receptor. Whether he or she accepts or rejects what the projector is trying to get across, he or she must first evaluate it from the point of view of whether it will fit, or prove congruent with what is already there in the way of ideas and constructs. Assimilation thus implies a process of judging the acceptability of the messages received and understood. This is a necessary prelude to the individual making any kind of reaction or response to that idea or message.

Reaction is then the final stage in communication. It is not necessarily to be understood as a physical or motor reaction – that the receptor must physically do something. It is sufficient that the individual reveals a shift in his or her thinking or feeling, and this revelation may come via some oral or written reply, although it may be inferred from a behavioural reaction, such as carrying out an order or a suggestion. This provides the 'feedback' of data which enables the projector to test whether his or her communication has been successful.

The Semantic Problem

However efficient the transmission system, communication will fail if the intended meaning of the message is not communicated. The successful transmission of information is not to be equated with the successful communication of 'meaning' (Shannon and Weaver, 1949, p 99). Examination of this problem must focus on the roles of the transmitter and receiver as interpreters of meaning and on the nature and composition of the messages which are conveyed. The problem to be solved is how the meaning intended at the initiation of the communication can be interpreted 'correctly' at the destination.

The concepts of source and destination are rather impersonal in their implication. Having served their purposes of distancing certain roles from those of the ends of the transmission process, we may now discard them by recognising that in much of the communication with which we are concerned, the source and the transmitter on the one hand, and the destination and the receiver on the other, may be treated as persons. The focus of our attention will, in other words, be on the people at each end of the communication process and on the messages (as distinct from the signals of the earlier discussion) they construct and interpret.

When analysis is concentrated on the semantic aspects of communication, some of these elements are retained but are likely to be identified by different concepts which admit the human sources (projectors) and destinations (receptors) and place more emphasis on human processes of cognition and affect.

This recognises that *human* communication is mediated by perceptions and perspectives or expectations, themselves the creatures of communications. As Spence suggests (1969, p 102), all natural language moves on both intellectual and emotional planes. Human communication is not simply concerned with the transmission of information, conceived as 'facts' or 'descriptions', and with the clear reception of appropriate 'meanings' at this level. What is communicated between people in the guise of fact or description is affected by the way people (whether senders or receivers) already think, feel, and act.

The messages which carry the 'information' will exist in smybolic form, commonly that of language. In the context of impressions given off by things, these symbols may be of length, breadth, height, or weight, or any other symbols of dimension and quality. In the context of information deliberately constructed by persons, however, the symbols will normally be words used with specific meanings accepted within the culture group concerned. Thus in human communication, the normal basis for constructing messages will be that of language.

Not all communications are deliberately 'sent' by one person to another, however, nor are all communications transmitted in a verbal (oral or written) form. Some communications are effected by means of colours, lights, bells or buzzers: red for danger, flashing light for emergencies, telephone bell to arouse attention, or buzzer to mark the end of a work period. All of these involve a predetermined code, and they only work if the recipient is aware of the code. This, however, is also true, in a special sense, of verbal communication. An injunction to 'stop' demands, for its effectiveness, a command of the English language. Rituals and status symbols also rely on an understanding of the code involved for their effectiveness.

In this context information is not to be thought of as merely concerned with 'objective' facts or descriptions. It may be this, but it is important to human interaction because the kind of information we are concerned with here is that which answers some question or which resolves some choice between alternatives. The information, 'that animal is a cow', answers the question 'What is that animal?' and it removes all the other options or choices that might exist – that it is a man, a monkey, a cat, etc., etc. Information need not be assumed to be 'factual' in the sense that 'it is a fact that that animal is a cow'; it is sufficient for the purpose that, whether factually or speculatively, it resolves the question and removes some options. In other words, its importance lies in its capacity for removing uncertainties and resolving choices which would otherwise exist.

But language is not so certain and unchanging in its meaning that all uncertainty is removed from messages simply by constructing them on this basis. The words used to construct messages may be used to convey meaning according to:

(a)   what the words are thought to denote or connote;

(b)   the linguistic context in which they are uttered;

(c)   the manner in which they are uttered
      (Clevenger and Mathews, 1971, pp 33–46).

(a)   *What the words denote or connote*

Words identify something: nouns identify persons or things and verbs identify actions. What is identified is what the word denotes. The word 'cow' identifies (denotes) the red and white quadruped in the field which gives milk; the word 'wage' usually identifies (denotes) what workers receive as a return for engaging in employment work. The word 'run' identifies (denotes) movement over the surface of the earth at a rate faster than walking; the word 'measures' identifies (denotes) activities which are dedicated to establishing with some precision how big or little something is.

But words are not always free from ambiguity, which may be increased by the context in which they are used. Words like aggressive, creative, with flair, numerate, initiative, etc., which are often used in job advertisements, illustrate this aspect. On the face of it, they merely identify a 'quality' – an apparent fact – which is sought in those who apply for the job. But further reflection on them will indicate that they also imply a standard which may be in the mind of the writer, but may convey quite a different meaning to the reader: how aggressive is 'aggressive' and how much 'flair' would be regarded as qualifying? Uncertainty of this kind could deter the reader from applying for the job.

Words frequently also imply something which is wider in meaning than the dead-pan definition indicates. This is not an additional or alternative meaning or definition: rather, it is a kind of 'aura' which is over and above the definition. The word 'cow' carries with it connotations of stupidity (and not just because of Alf Garnett's use of the two words in juxtaposition). The word 'wage' connotes, *inter alia,* that the workers in question are manual rather than white collar workers. What words connote can provide meanings beyond what might be intended if attention is paid only to dictionary definition. The words dame, lady, woman, and female all refer to human beings of one sex: but if they are substituted in the sentence, 'that person is a . . . .', they might well convey different meanings to the recipient of the message, because of their connotations.

(b)   *The linguistic context in which words are uttered*
Britain and America have often been described as two nations kept apart by a common language. The serious aspect of this is that although the official language of both societies is English, the same word may denote something different in the two contexts (one can think of the words 'purse' or 'knocking up') and more probably will connote something distinct (try the word 'dame' in the previous paragraph). Such differences are often much more local: if a Scots person asks an English person 'where are you staying?', the reply might not give the information the questioner expects.

All societies and cultures have a linguistic context in which communication may be less hazardous than where boundaries are crossed. The following story of the lady ordering coal from the merchant shortly after Britain joined the Common Market illustrates the problem. 'Would you deliver me a ton of coal, s'il vous plaît?' 'Certainly, madam, how would you like it delivered, à la carte or cul de sac?' Management excursions to foreign countries, where the language is very different, frequently lead to difficulties of this kind, sometimes much more serious in their consequences.

(c)   *The manner in which they are uttered*
The tone of voice used to communicate can very often 'give off' (in Goffman's term) meaning which is not necessarily carried in the words themselves. 'Will you close the door?' can be said in a number of different tones to indicate politeness, sympathy, interest, annoyance, anger, and probably many other emotions. The manner of uttering words or messages is, in other words, likely to enable the communicator to convey emotion as well as information (or purely factual meanings).

It is possible to use words to convey emotions – 'You annoy me' or 'I like you' – and this may prove to be the only way to do so when communication is in writing. In oral communication, however, emotions can often as easily or more easily be conveyed by tone of voice. The hearer will draw emotional meaning as well as factual meaning.

Social Structuring of Meaning

The meanings transmitted and received, on the other hand, are also likely to be influenced by three other factors which describe the situation rather than the symbolism involved:

(a)   the nature of the source;

(b)   the nature of the destination; and

(c)   the social context in which they are conveyed.

(a)   *The nature of the source*
The nature of the source can influence meaning simply because of the possible contrast between what that source has acquired as a set of meanings of words and what the recipient has acquired. Neither transmitter nor receiver of messages can entirely free him/herself from the linguistic context in which he or she was socialised. This will tend to leave each with views about what words denote and connote, and each will tend to attach these meanings to words which are used in particular social contexts. Not only does the word 'dame' have different meanings in different cultural contexts, but the hearer will tend to attach a different meaning according to whether he or she hears it uttered by a Briton or an American. The difficulties arise when such words are used by people from other cultures and the hearer is not sure whether they learned British English or American English.

The 'source' may, however, choose to do a double-take in this respect. Not only has he or she a knowledge of the denotations and connotations of words he or she normally uses, but a similar know-ledge of the words his or her listener normally uses. The source/transmitter can, therefore, code messages in a way which uses words to denote and connote what the listener would normally expect them to mean. The obvious example is the person speaking a foreign language to nationals of the country concerned. In more local contexts, as for example, between a manager and a worker, this kind of double-take can often produce confusion where words have different meanings in the two − management and worker − contexts. If a worker referred to a workmate as a clown, this might be interpreted as an accolade; if a manager did so, it might be taken as a term of abuse.

The possibilities for manipulating the symbols are considerable. It should not be assumed that all sources are involved in simple, honest communication, when the intention is to bring about changes in the hearer. Much that is not fair in other contexts may be fair in com-munications when the aim is to produce some change in thinking, feeling, or behaviour. The intentions of the communicators in selecting some information and emotions for communication in preference to others, and in choosing one set of symbols to convey the meaning rather than others, are often important determinants of what is attempted. That intention in turn is likely to reflect (at least in broad terms) the interest of the source, not that of destination.

(b) *The nature of the destination*
At the other end of the process, similar considerations arise in connection with interpretation of the meaning of the symbols derived from the signals. All the factors which can be identified as affecting the source's ability to communicate can be adduced, *mutatis mutandis,* in relation to the destination. The receiver has a perception of meanings within a linguistic tradition, has learned to code and decode within that tradition, and can be as selective in 'receiving' messages and meanings as the transmitter can be in 'sending' them. The problems of receipt are the problems of despatch considered from the opposite standpoint.

It is, however, generally in the nature of industrial organisation that managerial learning of language will have been influenced by grammar and syntax, and (even if now only very indirectly) by classic conceptions of language, than that of the workers. The manager's language is more likely to be cosmopolitan and the worker's local – even if such social distinctions have had less appeal and force since the era of The Beatles. One consequence of this is that the manager's more likely use of a mannered language is likely to be wrecked on the shoals of some local dialects. What applies at the level of 'pure language' can also apply at the level of meaning (see Jones and Lakin, 1978, which recounts the confrontation of a 'southern' management style with a 'northern' worker style).

(c) *The social context in which the messages are conveyed*
These differences may be diminished or exacerbated by the context in which the communication occurs. Communication in a small group is commonly couched in well understood terms: communication between members of different groups or classes is commonly couched in less well understood terms. It is as if the boundaries of any social grouping refract the meanings which pass over them in either direction. For this reason, it is generally argued that the development of subgroups within organisations (whether 'departmental' or 'informal' groups) tends to erect barriers to free communication within them.

Such barriers are then supported by any attempt to maintain either physical or social distance. Failure to bring sources and destinations together in 'real' experiences is likely to avoid opportunities to reduce the barriers. Success in maintaining social distance between the members of one group and another is likely to ensure that they become higher.

The solution to this kind of problem is likely to emphasise some element of greater sharing of experiences and perceptions. This may take the form of a deliberately more participative style on the part of management, the greater harmonisation of 'conditions', or the removal of physical barriers (such as those between 'office' and 'shop' work stations).

Constructing Messages

The construction of messages by the source is generally thought to have a bearing on whether the recipient is likely to act on their receipt in the manner intended. The underlying thought here is that communication is usually undertaken to bring about some change in the other, and some messages have properties which are more likely to bring about this result than others.

Cartwright (in March, 1965, p 19) has listed eight such properties whose relevance has been demonstrated in research.

1   The extent to which the message contains rational argument as distinct from emotional appeal.

2   The extent to which it relies on positive rather than negative appeals, providing opportunities for the recipient rather than embargoes.

3   The extent to which it uses two-sided arguments as opposed to one-sided arguments.

4   The extent to which it takes up moderate positions, as distinct from extreme ones. There is no way that a person can be persuaded to accept redundancy (although there may be additional incentives which can sweeten it).

5   The extent to which it explicitly draws attention to the conclusions to be drawn from the factual matters or the arguments expressed.

6   The clarity and logicality of the sequence of arguments.

7   The extent to which it makes use of attention-arousing devices and techniques.

8   The extent to which it makes use of redundancy or repetition of points for the sake of effect.

As in the case of coding and decoding signals, the coding and decoding of messages may require 'a code book' but it is usually one which is socialised into the individual and which has become part of his operating system for use within his 'system'.

This use of the concept of information, however, is not to be interpreted as meaning, simply, that communication is concerned only with 'factual' information. Used in this context, it applies to the communication, for example, feelings, as much as to the communication of cognitions. The successful communication of feelings can be as contributory to the reduction or removal of uncertainties as that of factual information. For example, in the learning process, the expression of praise for successful attainment can 'tell the learner where he or she stands' and thus remove some of the doubts which might otherwise inhibit assimilation. Thus it might be said that communication is associated with all three aspects of human cognition, emotion, and action.

The second covers not only 'failure' to communicate at all, but also that associated with the production of an outcome which was not intended. The originator of a communication is usually better placed than the recipient to control what happens – simply because he or she can work out what he or she wants to do and how he or she should do it while the recipient must wait for the communication to be transmitted before he or she can establish any kind of response. But the recipient also has a vital part to play in the process and the originator's control can never therefore be absolute: the latter is always dependent on processes which go on within, and which are therefore under the control of the recipient.

Barriers to Communication of Meaning

A number of barriers to the communication of meaning exist – and are often of a kind which cannot be broken down, for example, simply by managerial action. Many of these barriers exist in the differences in the ways in which people in the two nodes have been socialised. In effect, this means that they have learned to give different meanings to words, messages, events, etc., so that the communication of any one will tend to result in the interpretation of a different meaning from that intended by the sender.

This kind of barrier can be further strengthened by the presence of 'social distance', a term used to indicate how far apart, currently, are those who occupy two nodes. The distance between a manager, having his or her being within a subculture defined as 'management', and a worker, having his or her being within a subculture defined as, for example, working class, can be great. The consequences of this for successful communication or meaning are similar to those arising from differential socialisation, of which, indeed, it forms a special part. It keeps people within systems of meaning which reinforce existing frames of reference, and avoids a meeting of minds on what may be meant by those outside the subculture.

These may be regarded as special and rather general cases of the individual's group affiliation, influencing frames of reference and therefore the kinds of interpretation which he or she makes of any phenomena which impinge on his or her consciousness. It is reasonably well established that communication across any group boundary tends to result in 'refraction' of meaning – simply because interpretation of a given message within the group will tend to be different from interpretation outside it or within some other group. Such 'groups' abound in any sphere of life, not least within the context of work.

As all of these possibilities of group formation tend to be present in most work situations, the opportunites for refraction or distortion of meanings in communication are considerable. Some of them are consequences of the so-called 'informal system' and some of them respond to the organisation of the formal system, but all can have the same effect on communication. They constitute 'channels' of communication which link intra-cultural nodes and which are often outside the control of managers seeking to communicate.

Barriers to Assimilating Messages

Communication is often made less effective than it might otherwise be because people who ought to perform the role of receptor do not do so. This applies to everybody, but it can be, and often is, a particular problem for managers. They do not hear, and more certainly do not listen out for communications which might not only facilitate effective decision-making but might also improve effective transmission of messages. This is the problem usually referred to as the problem of not listening enough.

The reasons for the problem are, in the main:

1   The managerial culture is one which emphasises managerial initiative and initiation of action for others. This suggests that what managers are there to do is decide and communicate that decision in such a way that others act on it. Elaborate models are put forward to explain how managers arrive at the decisions about what should be done (by themselves and others) but rarely do they find much place for listening to what those who operate within the system think might be the way forward. The image of the macho (or Rambo) manager does

not find much of a place for appearing to respond to what others suggest ought to be the decision.

2   The manager's pattern of work is often such that he or she finds little time to do much more than gather the data thought necessary to decide, take the decision, and communicate it as many times as it may take to get the message across. The whole emphasis is placed on devising the appropriate messages and transmitting them to those who 'need to know'. This takes up so much time that little time is left for listening to what others think or feel about the proposals or about what ought to be done in the circumstances.

Thus at the cultural and the practical levels, the manager's situation tends to militate against him or her being an effective receptor of communications. Because this is the case, many of those communications which are so often seen as the lifeblood of organisations simply fail.

This is particularly serious where it is necessary or desirable (which is most of the time) for the manager to secure feedback to enable him or her to check the effectiveness of what is being communicated. A basic failure to listen may be exacerbated by the existence of the same cultural imperative in the receptors: they may remain silent rather than admit failure to understand, or they may assert an understanding which they (know they) do not have of what has been said to them. The one results in no feedback and the other in a feedback of false information, and either might have drastic consequences if the originator then worked on the assumption that his or her communication exercise had been effective.

A rather special case of this general problem of not listening is associated with the process of selective perception. This is a process through which we all go, if only to reduce to manageable proportions the welter of information which continually bombards our eyes and ears. As we simply cannot take in all that we see and hear (the capacity of the channel is never large enough) we adopt the defence mechanism of taking in only that bit of the bombardment which most readily fits our existing perceptions and perspectives and which appears most readily to 'make sense' to us. Thus even when subordinates do communicate back to the manager, he or she may hear only or mainly what he or she wants to hear, thinks he or she ought to be hearing, or which accords most readily with his or her prejudices and biases. Thus even when the manager is listening, the messages assimilated may be distorted ones.

To reduce these problems, it may be necessary for the manager to work hard on improving his or her listening capacity and his or her listening skills. This is not merely a question of telling oneself, 'I must listen more'. It may involve asking questions which draw out information and providing a supportive context in which people will feel comfortable in communicating, for example, to a more senior manager who is seen to be 'distant' by virtue of the given position in the organisation.

Reaction as a Measure of Effectiveness

The effectiveness of communication is to be measured by the effect it has on the receptor (who may also, in a two-way flow, be the projector when looked at from the alternative standpoint). Effectiveness can only be determined by the reaction of the receptor, whether in terms of his or her thinking, feeling, or concrete behaviour. In order to produce such changes, the communication will have to meet the technical and semantic criteria, but it will also have to prove 'persuasive' at the assimilation stage if a reaction is to be produced at the final stage. No matter how accurately the signals are transmitted, and no matter how clearly the intended meanings are understood by receptors, communication does not always result in changes in the thinking, feeling, or action of those to whom the communications are addressed.

This 'emotional' component in the communication process is given even more prominence in the approaches to communication which concentrate on the problems of 'effectiveness'. Whether the individual assimilates the 'message' received in such a way that he or she changes his or her thinking, feeling, or behaviour, not only depends on these prior cognitive and emotive states, but also, and more significantly, on motivation to change in one of these ways.

In order to render it likely that communications will be persuasive at this stage, certain conditions have to be met. These focus mainly on perceived status and legitimacy in the communications activities of the communicator and on the amount of trust which the receptor is prepared to place on the projector.

There is a clear sense in which 'persuasion' in this sense is aimed at bringing about the changes by altering the way in which the individual recipient orders his or her thinking or preferences, or willingness to act in the ways indicated, so that, in fact, he or she changes because of conviction. This is certainly one way in which influence can be construed, but in the context of management, it has to be acknowledged that changes may be brought about by other methods, by coercion, or by manipulating utilities. This is done on the basis that the influencer has the power (and authority) to restrict the individual's freedom or to offer different amounts of incentive in order to effect compliance with his wishes. But in the case of 'pure' persuasion the end is pursued by means which involve the manipulation of symbols in order to alter the convictions of the recipient.

SUMMARY

Effective communication is vital for the efficient operation and long-term survival of any organisation.
A consideration of the technical and social aspects of the communications process highlights:

(a)   the structural problems associated with channel availability and capacity and the problem of noise, and those associated with the development of new impersonal processes of transmitting information, devoid of emotional content; and

(b)   the human/social problems associated with differential socialisation, maintenance of experiential and social differences, and the resultant detraction from communication ability.

There are (partial) solutions to these problems in:

(a)   the reduction of the desired rate (amount per unit of time) of communication, the multiplication of channels available, and the deliberate increase in redundancy in communication;

(b)   the reduction of artificial (office/works; staff/manuals) barriers to communication, the communising of actual work experiences, and the deliberate training of communicators in coding and communicating skills.

Effective communication is likely to depend on appropriate answers to the questions:

1   Are there enough channels available to management and to individual managers?

2   Are existing channels, including the individual employees viewed as channels, overloaded?

3   Does management, do managers, spend enough time on communicating new ideas, assessments, requirements for action?

4   Do learning opportunities available to members of the organisation need to be increased to improve communication (in terms of both time taken and effectiveness)?

5   Are there unnecessary or unacceptable barriers to effective communication which can be reduced by reorganisation or change of management/supervisory styles?

6   Is enough use made of the various media – speech, writing, videos, payment systems, public reports, etc., – to support improved communications?

7   Is communication as effective as training might make it?

Reading:

Bartlett (1983).
Cartwright in March (1965).
CBI (1975).
Clevenger and Mathews (1971).
Collard (1981).
Dewar (1980).

Drucker (1980).
Dubin (1962).
Gibson *et al* (1976).
Hutchins (1981).
Irvine (1970).
Shannon and Weaver (1949).
Spence (1969).

15 Changing Perspectives and Attitudes

Criticism of managers' or workers' attitudes to work is widespread. The recurrent theme in the criticisms is that existing attitudes are wrong in principle, inappropriate to the situation, or impediments to industrial and social progress. As a result, the way in which people see their situation and their motivation to tackle its problems are also inappropriate and unhelpful. This association with motivation gives the clue to the commonest reason for the criticism – that the critic usually wants to see a change in *behaviour or conduct*. Short-term expedients intended to compel or encourage a change of behaviour having proved ineffectual, attention is switched to the possibility of changing 'underlying' traits which support current behaviours.

These traits are identified by reference to human perspectives, attitudes, and behavioural predispositions. All of these seem to mediate between the critic's intention and the behaviour of the criticised. But Brewster and Connock (1980, p 110) make the point that those who suggest that attitudes should be changed usually mean that behaviour, not attitude, should be changed. If, however, attitudes can be changed by exhortation, persuasion, or even training (Kilcourse, 1977, p 32), behaviour might be made more consonant with the critic's perception of the situational need.

Not everyone believes that changing perceptions and attitudes is possible (Lowry, 1984). The rather easy assertions that attitudes can be changed rest on the assumption that 'an attitude' exists as an independent entity, which may be replaced by another such entity as a consequence of the exertion of some appropriate kind of influence. Where, for example, the existence of a negative attitude towards new technology is detected, the thought is that this may be changed into a more positive one by increasing either the person's knowledge or awareness of it, or its attractiveness to that person

431

in terms of his or her goals and preferences.

Many of these popular proposals for changing attitudes may be faulted on two grounds. First, that attitudes have properties of their own which are not sufficiently acknowledged. Secondly, that attitudes do not have the quality of independence, but must mesh with the individual's perceived needs and values. Thirdly, that attitudes, along with associated perspectives and behaviours, being anchored in group experiences, are not capable of changing without accommodating those groups in the change process.

The development of a strategy for changing attitudes *in order to bring about changes in behaviour* demands attention to all three.

ATTITUDES AND THEIR PROPERTIES

Management has an interest in developing employee attitudes appropriate to 'the real properties' of the field of work, and, like the young husband who thinks he can change his wife's attitudes, often talks blandly about changing them.

Attitudes are not, however, so simple in their composition as some statements about them imply. Prohansky and Seidenberg assert that, 'an attitude is a *complex* tendency of the person to respond consistently in a favourable or unfavourable way to social objects in his environment' (Prohansky and Seidenberg, 1969, p 97, *italics added).* The clue to the complexity which they identify is contained in their later statement that 'attitudes are structured psychological tendencies consisting of *cognitive, affective* and *behavioural* components,' *each of which* 'may be examined in terms of its *content* and *structure'* (ibid). Comprehension of the concept of attitude, therefore, seems to call for its appreciation at different levels and in different areas.

Content

There can be wide variations in the content of an attitude (independently of the object to which the attitude relates), and these will affect the probability of influence on behaviour:

1   The cognitive element of an attitude towards some issue or object, sometimes treated as synonymous with 'opinion', highlights the person's perception and definition of and beliefs about it. Workers may perceive a management proposal to change an established working practice in different ways and may also reveal distinct beliefs about the meaning and import

that should be associated with it. Keenoy's 'laggers' tale' well illustrates the variety of possible meanings which may be attached to a single set of events (Keenoy, 1985, pp 1–26).

2   The affective component of an attitude places the emphasis on the feelings which the individual has towards the object or issue. This is not merely a matter of whether the individual holds favourable or unfavourable attitudes. Two people may have an unfavourable attitude towards something, but one may feel that it is threatening in some way while the other may feel that it is unworthy of much attention because of its triviality.

3   The behavioural aspect of an attitude stresses the predisposition of the person to react to the issue or object in a specific way. Sometimes, attitudes are defined in ways which suggest that it is only the behavioural aspect which is in contention. Yoder (1662, p 1) defines it as a 'reactive predisposition that tends to shape overt behaviour'. The existence of a strong positive attitude towards a proposed change might predispose the holder to support it and work for it; a negative attitude might be associated with a predisposition to reject it and to work against it. But action is likely to depend also on the person possessing action beliefs about what can and should be done in respect of the object or issue in question. Without these cognitive supports for action, action may not follow.

It is clear in this that the element of 'predisposition' in the definition is *not necessarily* linked to action in the sense of concrete behaviour (as 'behaviour' is a separate and distinguishable element). Because of these differences in composition, the predisposition may be to think or to feel, but not necessarily to act. Thus changing attitudes in order to change behaviour (so often presented as a rationale for attitudinal change) may be unnecessary or unproductive or both (see below, pp 441 *et seq*).

It is also clear that the individual's perceptions of the object and its situation form a particular part of the process of attitude formation. How the individual perceives is something which is itself affected by the frames of reference – values, beliefs, theories, etc. – which the individual already possesses. There is therefore an element of circularity in the process: the attitude is partly a product of existing frames of reference which themselves are partly a product of existing attitudes. To talk of changing attitudes is, in this sense, to talk also of changing perceptions.

Structure

There may also be wide variations in *structure,* where this term is used to indicate something of the context or anchorage of the particular attitude.

1   In the cognitive area, the same attitude may be held by two people, one of whom has an extensive knowledge of and a complex set of beliefs about the object and the other only a very superficial knowledge of it and very limited beliefs or theories about it. For example, a shop steward may hold a negative attitude towards a management proposal to alter the time standard on a job, and this may be based on detailed knowledge acquired in a number of negotiating sessions and a complex set of beliefs based on a lifetime of experience in negotiating bonuses. One of the steward's least active members may also have a similar negative attitude even though he has merely heard a rumour about it on the grapevine and may in any case have little understanding of how such bonus systems work.

2   In the affective area, some attitudes may be nested in a variety of specific emotional reactions, while others may reflect only vague feelings of like or dislike. One may react to a proposal to change because that person dislikes the idea that he or she will have to work out new ways of coping with the situation, fears the threat which change is perceived to pose to basic securities, and dislikes being required to change by someone else. Another may react in the same fashion simply because they dislike change.

3   In the behavioural area, some attitudes may strongly predispose the individual to act in specific ways while others may do so only rather weakly. The person may be led to resist some change with all the forces at his or her command, or to complain about it vocally but go along with it (behaviourally) once the vocal protest has been uttered.

This structural dimension, therefore, does not suggest any simple homogeneity in the concept.

Whether the attitude is positive or negative, or for or against any specific object or issue, the content may still vary through a wide range of possibility in each of these component areas. We cannot be sure that the various components are consistently related to one another. A person may hold a negative belief about something, but it does not necessarily follow that he or she will also dislike it and be disposed to make a negative behavioural response to it. This lack of correlation means that easy assumptions are unlikely to be useful.

The Attitude and the Person

An attitude is not something which is merely absorbed or 'taken over whole' by the person revealing it. The person selects attitudes which fit with his or her perceived needs and values. Whatever may be presented in the way of experience, including the 'experience' of possible attitudes to hold, is not absorbed as by a piece of blotting paper. It is more likely to be considered in terms of its relevance to what already exists in the form of values, beliefs, theories, perceptions of need, and frames of reference. In other words, man 'as scientist' (in Kelly's term) will exercise his capacity to select from the environment those elements which most readily accord with his self image and meet his needs as he attempts to cope with his environment.

This may make attitude formation a function of motives in the person: attitudes develop and will be maintained where 'they satisfy the basic motive patterns of the person' (Proshansky and Seidenberg, 1969, p 104). These motive *patterns* are likely to represent the product of what the individual thinks he or she needs to live or to live well and the enduring perspectives which the individual has developed as a result of experience about the chances of the environment meeting them.

These form the basis of concept of orientation, usually defined as composed of 'wants' and 'expectations'. Goldthorpe *et al*, in their Luton study, suggested that it was not possible to understand workers' comments about job satisfaction, without establishing what 'meaning' the workers gave to their work, in terms of what they wanted from it and expected to get from it (Goldthorpe *et al*, 1968, p 8). This concept therefore places emphasis on the cognitive ('meaning' or expectation) and affective (evaluation of satisfaction from the job) aspects of attitude.

This may also indicate something of the source of the strength of the attitude. Where the attitude in question is consonant with orientations which have, in the past, consistently 'paid off' (in whatever terms) for the individual, it is likely to be held strongly and firmly. The 'pay off', in other words, serves to *reinforce* the attitude, and the individual is only likely to be predisposed to change it if the pay-off conditions are changed significantly. A small or obscure change in those conditions might not produce any change of attitude.

The Attitude and the Group

The association of attitude with the *individual* is usually taken as supporting the desirability of bringing about behavioural change by changing attitudes. If attitudes are considered to be developed autonomously by and in the individual simply as a result of sampling and construing experience, however, there is a danger that the most potent factor guaranteeing their longevity will be missed. This factor is the influence of the 'group' on the stability of individual perceptions and attitudes. The thought here is that the various small groups in which the individual has membership or to which the individual makes reference, help to hold such perspectives and attitudes in place. In other words both membership and reference groups may play an important part in mediating between per-ceptions of need and perceptions of what is satisfactory. Although the selection of attitudes to hold is for the individual to make, the selection is likely to be influenced by the kinds of pressures which desired group membership generates.

Demonstrating the role of the group in this respect is difficult because each individual could be regarded as responding to the same external situation in the same way, without, that is, the group as such having any mediating role. Workers' attitudes could be the same because they react to the same managerially structured terms and conditions of employment, not because their work groups play any part in producing consensus. Similar attitudes may arise because of the operation of the 'birds of a feather principle'; people who already hold the same attitudes associate with others who already hold them.

What is fairly clear is that any attitude adopted may have to accord with the individual's perception of need, including (importantly) the need to develop a coherent integrated image of the self. There is, however, persuasive evidence that such coherence and integration is at least underpinned by what membership or reference groups consider to be coherent and integrated. Not everyone is affected by groups to the same degree: the early categorisation of people by Riesman (1952) into tradition-directed, inner-directed, and other-directed, and the later categorisation by McClelland (1961), suggest that the different categories reveal different degrees of orientation to, or reliance on, group values and norms.

There is reason to suppose that some people at least depend on group support for their attitudinal positions, and that change is only likely to be brought about in them if the altered perspectives can be made to accord with the group consensus. For this reason, the individual's membership and reference groups are likely to claim acknowledgement in any programme of attitude change (Lewin, 1947). Thus is posed the duality: that the individual is the source of change and the group the source of stability. Only by weakening the group's support for stability is the individual likely to be 'freed' to change.

Group Properties

A group is commonly defined by reference to frequencies and intensities of 'interaction', underpinned by perceptions, the group seen as providing the main opportunities for inter-personal communication and co-operation. Sprott defines the social group in a fashion which is similar to that of Homan's classic on *The Human Group* (1951, p 84), as

> 'a plurality of persons who interact with one another in a given context more often than they interact with anyone else'
> (Sprott, 1958, p 9).

Other interactionists have coupled the simple fact of interaction with perception of the others, singly and collectively, in order to avoid confusion with the accidental part of (for example) a football crowd or an audience.

Sprott's restriction to 'context' is important, because people may have simultaneous membership of a number of small groups. A group of workers with many group affiliations outside work may form a voluntary group mainly because the formal organisation throws them together with a common goal. Most of the men in the Bank Wiring observation room at the Hawthorne plant of the Western Electric Company, for example, formed themselves into two cliques which broadly reflected the formal division of labour (Roethlisberger and Dickson, 1939). Social and psychological bonds, quite separate from other bonds which develop outside work, often arise out of the contacts necessitated by performance of work tasks.

A group is thus seen to define itself by reference to intensity of members' interaction, by their perceptions of a psychological unity, and by their propensity for acting in a unitary manner in relation to the environment.

Such groups (and others which do not form in quite the same way) are thought to serve purposes which have much to do with the wants, wishes, and aspirations of those who comprise the membership. People become members of groups because membership is perceived as satisfying need. Whether or not man is naturally gregarious, membership of the group, any group, will potentially provide the person with benefits or advantages which social isolation must necessarily deny. The benefits provided for the individual by group affiliation are thought to be those of the following:

1   *Social identity* The individual will frequently refer to some sets of friends or acquaintances as 'our crowd' or 'our bunch' (as Warner and Lunt (1941) found in Yankee City). This may indicate the individual's identification (in the Freundian sense) with a group of people whose better known public image the individual would like other people to associate with himself or herself. The individual's identity (or self-knowledge) is anchored in the group.

2   *Perspectives of social reality* Given that the world does not define itself and that the way the world works is not self-evident, the group may provide the individual with perspectives of the social reality or frames of reference which enable him or her to make sense of the environment.

    'Experiments dealing with memory and group pressure on the individual show that what exists as "reality" for the individual is to a high degree determined by what is socially accepted as reality ... "Reality" ... is not an absolute. It differs with the group to which the individual belongs' (Lewin and Grabbe, 1945, quoted in Katz and Lazarsfeld, 1955, p 54; see also, Asch, 1951; Sherif, 1936 and 1958).

    This emphasises the function of the group in exchanging information among members.

3   *Friendship and social esteem* Individuals may find friendship (be chosen as friends) and social esteem (be considered worthy) in groups. For this benefit, they are expected to pay with conformity to the group's norms of behaviour (as Newcomb and Stouffer demonstrated in their studies of college girls and American soldiers, respectively) (Swanson, Newcomb, and Hartley, 1952; reprinted in Proshansky and Seidenberg, 1969, pp 215–25; Stouffer, 1949).

4   *Emotional support* Although people may be the product of learning within groups, any one individual comes to any one group with some set of values, perspectives, and emotions already in place. The group may, for this person, provide a congenial or comfortable social context within which he or she may feel supported in the expression or display of already held

values, perspectives, and attitudes. This may provide a potent source of mutual attraction between member and group.

5 *Action to achieve goals* Some things which the individual may want to achieve may not be realisable without the assistance of others. A person who wants to become proficient in choral singing could scarcely realise this ambition in a hermit's cave. The group can therefore assist the individual to achieve such ambitions.

These are not mutually exclusive functions, and a number of them may be served by any one episode of interaction within a single group.

The Group in its Environment

These functions provide the ends towards which 'groups' as groups will orient themselves and raise questions about their compatibility with the ends of any formal organisation within which the groups may be located. The resultant 'group' tasks are carried out through the interaction of group members, who may then be regarded as performing a set of distinctly group tasks, rather than merely activities which satisfy their own immediate needs.

The way in which these tasks are described is consistent with the manner in which the tasks of the larger organisation are described. They are usually presented under two headings which refer to the goal achievement and the group maintenance functions:

Goal Related	*Process Related*
Providing meanings	Disseminating information
Providing support	Expressing emotions
Providing assistance	Fostering cooperation

The particular content of these tasks and the ends to which they are oriented may be consistent with or opposed to those of the wider social structures which contain them. Their ways of regarding the world may be supportive to or inhibiting of successful adjustment of the surrounding formal organisation to its environment. Their standards of behaviour may respect or reject those of the wider society. Their structures may facilitate or hinder integration with the social system. In general terms the group may be supportive or competitive with the encapsulating organisation, and for this reason cannot be ignored as a factor in influencing perspectives, attitudes, and behaviours.

Similarities and Differences

The property of mutual attractiveness, however, serves to reduce the uniqueness of any particular group. People's attitudes will both reflect the inferences which they draw from their experiences of the systems within which they work and be underpinned by their group and class affiliations. Broad similarities of experience, such as of work or of dealing with employers, or of dealing with workers, tend to produce similar responses. Classes of people tend, in consequence, to adopt perspectives, attitudes, and modes of behaviour which are common or very similar.

This is exemplified in recent studies of orientations to work (referred to above, p 435). The surveys revealed differences in orientations to work between broad categories of people which themselves contained individuals whose individual orientations were very similar. It does not follow that these categories demonstrated the properties of cohesive, face-to-face groups.

They represent groupings which would normally be associated with 'political' perspectives, rather than with political associations. This is the more clearly seen in the studies by Popitz, *et al* (1969) of the views which workers in Germany took of their 'work reality'. They focussed on the views taken by workers of the structure of their work-society and of the way in which this structure might best be coped or lived with. Their conclusions were expressed in terms of class images, with the two such images most in evidence being those of the benign hierarchical structure and the class divided society.

The studies by Goldthorpe *et al* (1968) are more closely focused on work and the workplace and on the view of workers on how this more limited situation might be coped with. These researchers classify the meanings ascribed by workers to their work into three overlapping 'orientations to work', which they call instrumental, solidaristic, and bureaucratic (Goldthorpe *et al,* 1968, pp 37–42; Daniel, 1969; 1971). Different *groups* of workers, they found, displayed different orientations which reduced the significance of individual differences within those groups and allowed those who confronted different 'work experiences' to express similar attitudes about them and to behave in ways apparently incongruent with those attitudes.

An instrumental orientation is displayed where the workers see the job as a means to some other end, such as 'living', and work does not attract deep personal commitment. A solidaristic orientation is displayed where people experience work as a group activity, and derive a good deal of emotional reward from involvement in its relationships. This group could be the enterprise or the class, or trade union, or simply the working group. A bureaucratic orientation is revealed where the individual sees work as a career based on service to an enterprise which will steadily increase his or her rewards for the service rendered (Beynon and Blackburn, 1972).

The point of this type of categorisation is to suggest that the way people will be predisposed to act will reflect this kind of ordering of priorities in relation to work. The instrumentalist will *calculate* whether a given action is economically worthwhile, while the solidarist will *assess* the effects of an action on the continuity of emotional gains, and the bureaucrat *evaluate* an action in terms of its implications for service *and* reward (Goldthorpe *et al,* 1968, pp 36–42).

The implication is that different orientations can coexist with attitudes and behaviours which might otherwise appear to be indicative of incongruent predispositions. The worker who regards his or her work as boring and may believe that it could be made more challenging, does not necessarily express dissatisfaction with his job, nor refuse to perform it, *because* he is prepared to do it for other satisfactions such as those associated with spending his pay (in the case of the worker with an instrumental orientation). It is, therefore, not a question of preserving sanity and self-conception by sublimating feelings of distaste for the work as such, but one of accepting the perceptions and beliefs as concomitants of instrumental satisfactions.

In the face of such similarity of perspective, attitude, or orientation, the small group may appear to have little relevance. But it is generally thought that these are held in place or reinforced through the small group affiliations, just as are those which are more deliberately given off or deliberately communicated by management. Therefore, any attempt to change them is likely to require that influence be exerted on and through the sustaining group.

If, therefore, the group is seen to be a guardian of attitudinal and perceptual stability, a knowledge of the group's properties, both in general and in particular, becomes a significant requirement for those who seek to influence people.

CHANGING ATTITUDES

Although attitudes are thought to be strongly entrenched in the mental set of the person, they cannot be impervious to change, even though the group structures will serve to prevent this occurring. An attitude may, for similar reasons, be 'an enduring system' (Freedman, Carlsmith and Sears, 1970) which gives it its predictability but it is also 'a mental and neural state of readiness organised through experience' (Allport, 1935, p 798). Consequently, because they are acquired (learned) through past experience, further experience, possibly experience which is deliberately structured, they may be changed over future time.

Influence and Reinforcement

Where a change in behaviour is sought as a result of changing attitudes, changes may need to be made in both of the other components and in the action component simultaneously. Success in this endeavour depends on there being a rather simple and consistent relationship between a person's attitudes and behaviour. This is not borne out by the research reported in this area. Only *some* attitudes reveal a high potential for predisposing behaviour. Where, for example, a person holds very extreme positive or negative attitudes towards an object or issue, the behavioural tendencies may be consistent with them; where they are less extreme, the relationship may not hold (Bettelheim and Janowitz, 1950).

Beyond this, the potential of the attitude for influencing actual behaviour is likely to depend on which of the components of attitude (see above pp 432–3) are structurally dominant. Where the cognitive component is dominant, this 'intellectualised attitude' may have little influence on behaviour. Similarly, a person may reveal strong liking or disliking for something, but 'know' little about it and have a very ill developed action orientation towards it. In this case, the attitude is largely affective. Only where the behavioural component is strong (the person perceiving action as something relevant to him or her) and supported by action beliefs in the cognitive area is the behaviour of the person likely to reflect what an attitude implies (Katz and Stotland, 1959).

The implication of this is that quite different kinds of intervention are required to bring about a change in attitude but that only some of these can be expected to influence behaviour. Greater information about an object or issue might well change the intellectualised attitude, but might not result in any behavioural change. Action to change feelings about the object or issue might be successful in changing the affective component, but again need not produce a change of behaviour. Action to change behaviour would need to concentrate on perceptions of the relevance of such action for the individual and on the action beliefs which the individual holds. But this might in any case be attempted directly (for example, by requiring or coaxing a change in behaviour by fiat or incentive), without necessarily modifying the cognitive and affective components of attitude.

Changes in the predisposition to *perceive* and to *think* about the world in particular ways may be brought about by education or training in which the cognitive and perceptive components of attitude are subjected to challenge by information and (logical) argument. The underlying thought here is that instruction or 'sound training imparts not only a way of doing, but also a way of thinking, so that a trained man confronted with a situation acts wisely and quickly' (Mills, 1967, p 4). This is to emphasise that rational informational aspects of communication.

Changes in the attitudinal predisposition to like or dislike an object may also be wrought by rational argument, focused on its desirable and undesirable qualities. The aim will be to indicate favourable or unfavourable aspects of the object which the individual may not have been aware of and to demonstrate how these will accord with the individual's perceived needs and existing perspectives of what is good and bad. No less than in respect of the other components, however, change in this one will demand that group standards of liking, etc, be involved.

There may, however, be some tendency for management to see this problem in terms of discipline, rather than in terms of group standards and processes. This comes through in Stokes's suggestion that the basis of skill instruction is, 'the right way of doing the job' (Stokes, 1966, p 25) linked with the need to inculcate a discipline (a 'conscious effort to influence conduct towards the achievement of desired and towards the prevention of undesired results' (ibid, p 105), to facilitate the development of attitudes which will predispose the individual to perform the job in 'the right way'.

Conditions Conducive to Change

Certain conditions of the structure of attitudes are likely to be more conducive to *autonomous* change in attitudes than others. They are likely to focus on the degrees of differentiation and of organisation of the attitudinal components:

1   Where the attitudinal components are not consistently related (or aligned) with one another, there may be a presumption that such alignment will be appealing to the individual, and attempts to bring about greater consistency may be easier to effect. An isolated attitude (not integrated with others) may be more open (and therefore easier) to change than one which is nested in a coherent cluster, especially where the attempt is to make an isolated negative attitude align with the other positive attitudes.

2   Where the attempt to effect change is aimed at *increasing* the
       strength of positive or negative attitudes (a change in the same
       direction as the existing attitude), it may prove easier than
       where the attempt is to decrease their strength (a change in the
       opposite direction to the existing attitude). The strength of the
       underlying values with which the attitude is associated will be
       positively correlated with the ease of making a same-direction
       change and negatively correlated with an opposite-direction
       change.

3   Where the individual's group affiliation is based on a calcu-
       lative involvement rather than a moral one. If the attraction of
       conformity to the group is based on the rewards and penalties
       available, change may be easier to bring about than where it
       exists because group affiliation satisfies some very deep-seated
       need. This is likely to be important in the context of work
       groups, as, important though they may be from some points of
       view, they may commonly be of lesser significance to the
       individual members than their extra-work groups (Dubin,
       1956).

4   Where the extent of the existing overburden or underpinning
       of reinforcement is limited, or alternatively where these are
       replaced by stronger forces tending in the opposite direction.
       It is also likely to be difficult to bring about changes deliber-
       ately without making appropriate changes in the reinforcing
       processes.

These may *allow* changes to take place readily as a result of new or
changed 'experience', but as with all learning from experience, this
is likely to be slow and patchy in its results. For this reason, it is
usual to see it as necessary to introduce some element of structuring
(or reinforcement of learning from experience).

   The actual processes of effecting changes in attitudes are, therefore, comparable with those applicable in training directed towards
changing skill or performance, even though many would argue that
training, as such, is not an appropriate vehicle for effecting
attitudinal change (Brewster and Connock, 1980, p 109). Certain
common principles can be recognised:

1   There may be a need to motivate (mobilise the energies of) the
       individual to accept the need for change.

2   There may be a need to introduce changes into the individual's
       situation to encourage the perception of need to change at the
       level of the individual.

3   There may be something (attitude or practice) to unfreeze or unlearn before a change can be introduced.

4   There may be a need to construct the messages concerning the change in a way comprehensible to the individual.

5   There may be a need to provide the individual with opportunity to 'test' the new practice or attitude in some real situation as part of the learning process and to facilitate movement from one position to another.

6   There may be a need to review how the situation in which the new practice or attitude is introduced impinges upon it and reinforces or weakens the relevance of the desired attitude.

These remain relevant to a process of change whether change is deliberately structured or left to inference from new experience, which is itself deliberately structured.

Changing the Environment

Attempts to dissociate attitude change from training may simply respond to the perception that attitudes, being comparatively deep-seated, are less amenable to change than are skills which have possibly less anchorage in the personality. This leads to the conclusion that attitudes are best changed by providing an environment which reinforces the attitudes which are desired.

> 'If we wish to change attitudes ... we must start by changing the pressures on people, altering the controls, and thus changing the way the individual has to behave. This may eventually lead to a change of attitude. It cannot be achieved the other way round'
> (Brewster and Connock, 1980, p 110).

This 'environment' may, in the hands of different commentators on the issue, be wide or narrow. For example, the payment system as a whole may be regarded as a major element in the reinforcing process for all workers. The search for 'more cooperative' attitudes on the part of workers by way of more participative management, consultation, briefing groups, quality circles, or anything else which delivers exhortation to them, is unlikely to be aided by a payment system which is based on hourly rates paid in arrear and dependent for continuation on a week's notice.

Changing attitudes by structuring experiences is only possible where there is a range of options open to 'the system' to change its approaches and practices. This in turn is likely to reflect the nature of the market relationship, the technology available and affordable, and the cultural constraints imposed on the enterprise. These often make attitudes irrelevant to actual work/task activities, although there are many emergent situations in which this is no longer true. In high technology contexts, attitudes become important for this reason and also because they are associated with more nebulous requirements such as loyalty, cooperation, acceptance of responsibility and self-direction.

To change these attitudes, it may be necessary for management to ensure that what is experienced at the interfaces of worker and enterprise (for example, *around the actual job* and in the treatment accorded by the 'system' to the employee) is supportive of the attitudes regarded as desirable. This proposition relies on the view that attitudes are the product of reactions to repeated and reinforced experience and that those of cooperation, etc., may more readily develop from experiences of 'cooperation' etc., offered by management in the name of the organisation. The instances of such offered cooperation are many, including those associated with job and work group structuring, the relationship effected between remuneration and effort or contribution, and the treatment accorded when individual and 'system' are brought into critical interaction as in the cases of disciplinary and grievance activities. All of these have their 'own' objectives and intentions, but they necessarily 'give off' messages which are likely to be assimilated into attitudes through the informal group structures.

Deliberately Engineered Changes

Not all changes in attitude are left to be brought about autonomously by the individual as a result of assimilating what is 'given off' by the manner in which experience is structured. There is always a pressure on those who face problems of coordination and control to bring about changes deliberately to facilitate the development of cooperative behaviours.

Attempts to change attitudes are usually made with one or other of three aims associated with the three components of an attitude: the cognitive, the affective (or feeling), and the action components (Freedman, Carlsmith and Sears, 1970). The aim, then, is to bring about some change in the thinking, feeling, or behaviour of another (Cartwright, in March, 1965, pp 1–47). The aim may be to change the way in which the person thinks about some thing or some issue. Alternatively, it may be to change the way that the individual feels about it. In these two cases, however, the attempt to influence is usually made in the hope that the individual will also become pre-disposed to act differently in relation to the object or issue.

Successful attempts to change attitudes may be seen as depending on knowledge and understanding of three influential factors:

(a)   the structural properties of the attitude itself;

(b)   the culture of the pertinent groups to which the individual is affiliated;

(c)   the functional bases of the attitude.

Consequently, anyone attempting deliberately to change the attitudes of another must rest the influence attempt on an appreciation of how the person currently perceives the environment, and himself or herself in relation to it, together with an understanding of how a given attitude might relate to that environment. The influencer might believe that one attitude might be in the individual's best interest in the environment in which he or she operates, but successful influence might still depend on subjecting that belief to critical examination before the influence attempt is made. The attitude supporting moderation of wage demands may seem to government or employers as being in the worker's best interests in the long run, but the individual may well not see it that way and refuse steadfastly to adopt it no matter what influences are brought to bear.

Methods of Influence

A variety of methods of interpersonal influence may be drawn on to bring about changes in either behaviour, or attitude, or both. Which is used may well reflect the objectives pursued and the circumstances in which this occurs, and will therefore vary from one situation to another.

Simon's consideration of the manner in which the work organisation 'fits the individual's behaviour into an overall pattern' hinges on the view that human decisions are based on certain value and factual premises, some of which are amenable to influence by the organisation. He identifies a number of *modes of influence:* authority, communication, training, efficiency and identification (organisational loyalty) (Simon, 1945, p 123), which differ in the way and the extent to which they affect the relevant value and factual premises, either alone or (more probably) in combination.

'When the individual decides upon a particular course of action, some of the premises upon which this decision

is based may have been imposed upon him by the exercise of the organisation's authority over him, some may have been the result of his training, others of his desire for efficiency, still others of his organisational loyalty, and so forth'
(ibid).

It is possible to assert the existence of influence in organisations where the assumption holds that individual members set themselves 'a general rule which permits the communicated decision of another to guide [their] own choices (that is, to serve as a premise of those choices) without deliberation on [their part] on the expediency of those premises' (Simon, 1945, p 125).

This leads Simon to make a distinction between authority and influence. In an authority relationship, the subordinate 'holds in abeyance his own critical faculties for choosing between alternatives and uses the formal criterion of the receipt of a command or signal as his basis for choice' (op. cit. p 127). In other relationships in which the critical faculties remain in use, recommendation, persuasion, or suggestion may be employed to alter the evidential bases on which the individual will make his or her own choice as to course of action, but that choice will be made on the basis of personal conviction. It is in this sense that it is obviously easier to influence behaviour by issuing a command, always providing that it is possible to rely on the other's abdication of choice within the authority relationship.

Where this assumption does not hold, then influence must depend on the would-be influencer being possessed of a resource which can be deployed to secure a change in the way in which the other perceives and evaluates the problem which calls for some kind of action. This is commonly expressed in terms of possession or control of one or more of four kinds of resource and deployment of that resource through four modes of influence, giving different types of compliance response on the part of the other (Cartwright, in March, 1965, pp 5−7; Etzioni, 1961, pp 12−14):

Resource:	*Mode:*	*Type of Compliance:*
Physical power	Coercion	Alienative
Utilities	Remunerative	Calculative
Information	Normative	Moral

In this model, the individual who has control over the individual in physical terms (such that he can confine him or even kill him) can physically coerce him to bring about a desired pattern of behaviour, but cannot thereby count on his willing compliance. A person able to command material resources which have value (utility) for the other may secure compliance by offering remuneration for desired behaviours, but in this case the most likely response will be one which is described as 'calculative' − the other will comply as long as it remains worth it. The possession of information and ideas can be deployed argumentatively, suggestively, or persuasively to change the other's standards or norms and to bring about compliance by virtue of (moral) conviction.

Change by Command, Selection, and Delegation

The quickest way to effect a change of behaviour is that which makes use of some form of authority to 'coerce' the other. This may be more or less subtle in its operation, but where the authority of a supervisor is accepted as legitimate, the individual might be brought to change his or her behaviour more directly and economically through command or instruction, or by some other direct use of that authority.

The first, and most direct, method is that which allows the supervisor (or anyone in authority) to require certain behaviours as a condition of continued employment or remuneration. The individual is then presented with a simple − if harsh − choice: either to comply or to quit. If compliance is forthcoming, then the questions of whether attitudes have any bearing on conduct or whether they have changed appropriately, do not arise. The real objective of changing behaviour in this limited framework has been realised. This may have other unwanted spin-offs, affecting 'co-operation', 'loyalty', or some other such quality which the organisation deems important, but the immediate goal has been achieved.

Similarly, in the circumstance where the enterprise has a relatively high labour turnover, the process of selection may be used to recruit the kinds of attitude which are considered to be desirable. This involves a similar use of authority to offer or deny employment opportunities to individuals on the basis of the displayed attitudes. These may be ascertained by careful interviewing or by means of a validated attitude test, and offers to those who are otherwise suitable may be determined on the basis of the results obtained. Where the rate of turnover is sufficiently high this method can produce a reasonably quick result.

This method has been used effectively where plants are being started up or relocated on greenfield sites. The recruitment literature may emphasise certain desirable attitudes and the selection process used as in the previous example.

This approach is less likely to be used in on-going work situations which do not meet these conditions. In those circumstances, however, the processes of delegation, job rotation, and promotion can be used with similar aims. The delegation of authority and trust to a subordinate to act on behalf of a boss is sometimes conceived as a way of 'maturing' the individual by forcing him or her to face up to new responsibilities; the extra authority and trust then serve as potential rewards for, or reinforcers of, conforming behaviours *and* attitudes.

In principle, job rotation can be employed in the same manner, in the expectation that changing responsibilities may result in a similar modification of behaviours and attitudes. This may be possible in spite of the fact that no advancement or promotion is involved in the rotation process. Where there is some element of promotion, the possibility of this being taken as a reward or reinforcer is so much more likely, and the individual's calculation of the utilities more likely to lead to behavioural change.

Thus through this range, there is a movement from influence based on simple coercion to influence based on manipulation of utilities. These are likely to be applicable, however, only in circumstances where authority is accepted by the workers concerned and the existence of alienative or calculative responses are acceptable to management.

Change through Interaction

Where the necessary conditions do not hold, a more subtle approach may be necessary. This may involve the deliberate restructuring of the environment – as a matter of 'policy' – of the kinds referred to above. Alternatively, it may focus on the use of training and development processes to bring about change. Changing attitudes through training, however, is more likely to require a less authoritarian process than is often employed in training. The 'trainer' is more likely to function as a 'resource person' capable of structuring experiences uncovered or discovered by the 'trainee' in the course of interacting with the environment (Lewin, 1947 and 1953).

Lewin's work focused on attempts to bring about change in conduct (whether in the food-serving habits of American housewives, or in productive behaviour of American workers) where that conduct could be regarded as anchored in attitudes which themselves reflected social standards of thinking, feeling, and behaviour. Much of the work involved comparing the immediate and longer-term consequences of using methods of 'individual instruction', 'lecture', and 'group decision'. The results showed that the latter method produced most and the most permanent effects on attitude and behaviour.

Lewin's findings agree with those of researchers who have looked carefully at the process of influence based on communication to the individual (construed as a communications channel in his or her own right). Katz and Lazarsfeld's study (1955) of the way in which mass media messages are effectively communicated, led them to conclude that this involves a two-stage communications process in which the individual's group memberships play a crucial part at the second stage. In the first stage the message is received by the individual, but this results in no assimilation of the information or action on it. In the second stage, the meaning and import is evaluated and validated within some group and results in assimilation and action *on terms determined with the group's interaction.*

The principles which emerge from Lewin's work may be summarised as:

1   That the object of the change attempt should be regarded as a process, not a 'thing'; a revealed attitude is an indication of the point reached in the individual's progress in developing perspectives and direction-sets relevant to the world in which he or she lives.

2   That this object, while it is a product of the working of the individual's mind, is, nevertheless, held in place and reinforced by the operation of forces in the individual's environment (and is potentially liable to change if those forces serve to reinforce other attitudinal responses). Many of these 'forces' have a 'social' character, in that they are processes through which group standards are implanted in the minds of group members.

3   That a situation of 'no change' constitutes, in Lewin's terminology, 'a quasi-stationary equilibrium', in which (as with a river) there is constant movement in a set direction over a period of time, and 'change' can be represented as a change in either velocity or direction.

4   That in a situation of 'no change' the forces which tend in one direction at one velocity are balanced by those which tend in an opposite direction at a different velocity, and 'change' can be represented as one outcome of a change in the strength of one set of forces or another (an alternative outcome of this might be increased tension or conflict).

5   That there are, in principle, two alternative approaches to effecting change: in one the strength of the forces tending in the desired direction may be increased; in the other the strength of forces opposed to the desired change may be reduced. The first would tend to increase tension and the second to reduce it.

6   That it is easier to change attitudes (or other 'standards') within a 'group' context than within a simple dyadic context (of changer and changed) because group standards can be erected and the strength of the forces holding them in place reduced, allowing the individual freedom to respond in a conventional (experientially learned) way to the social pressures which he or she then experiences.

7   That the process of bringing about change (in attitude or anything else which has a social underpinning) will involve the three subprocesses of *unfreezing* existing perceptions and direction-sets (possibly by stirring up the individual's emotions), *moving* the individual to a new position (in the sense of communicating effectively the dimensions of that new position), and *freezing* the new perceptions and direction-sets in place with the aid of group processes.

8   That transference of the new attitudes to the on-going processes of the individual will be facilitated if the operation of the immediately surrounding social system is such that the application of the new attitude to on-going affairs results in its reinforcement.

These are supported and supplemented by the insights provided by the communications studies. These suggest that direct communication to the individual is rarely likely to prove effective, and that the group is a significant mediator in this process. The person who would effect change must therefore be able to answer such questions as: Who are the opinion leaders or influentials (in Katz and Lazarsfeld's terms) within the group who will play major parts in the process of generating a new consensus? How do these people link into the structure and with which members are they in contact? The answers have to be found to ensure that channels with appropriate capacity are available to the would-be influencer.

These conclusions and principles are now usually incorporated into the various behavioural modification and management development methods used to bring about changes among those who are usually higher rather than lower in industrial hierarchies. It is arguable that they could be incorporated into methods of changing attitudes of lower order participants, but this is often not done for reasons of cost; it is only in relatively high-tech situations that such exercises are considered to be worth their cost.

Similarly, the relevance of the group to this process is often acknowledged in practice, even if the theoretical underpinning is not articulated in so doing. Industrial organisations make a good deal of use of groups to facilitate communications and influence. These are often structured – that is, integrated into the formal organisation – in different ways as attempts are made to accommodate different forms of authority relationship and different perceptions of member need.

Training Applications

These principles can be applied through formal programmes of communication, training, and development. It is not unusual for some such changes in attitude to develop in the course of training, even where attitudinal change is not deliberately intended as a significant outcome. But reliance on training programmes to bring about changes in attitude is probably sterile for the reason mentioned above – that attitudes are formed under the influence of generalised experiences over life and of influential people within local structures of interpersonal relations who are accepted as opinion leaders.

People are unlikely to change attitudes simply because some instructor suggests that they ought to do so. They are more likely to respond to repeatedly presented experiences which are reinforced in the messages they give off than to simple exhortations. Where deliberate attempts are made to effect change, it may prove necessary to review and change the experiences offered, and to avoid glib solutions such as those implied in specialised training programmes.

Such deliberate attempts need to be supported (reinforced) by the presentation of appropriate inferences and conclusions, and in this training may assume a supportive role. Such training needs to follow the principles which have developed from research studies of the problem of attitude change. These tend to emphasise the need to start with the structural properties of the attitude in question and to recognise the necessity of involving the group as the source of attitudinal anchorage.

It is even more likely, however, that changes in attitude will be wrought by structuring experiences which are presented to people 'in the ordinary course' of their (working) lives. This means that in order to change attitudes, industry needs to consider the development of policies and strategies which construe the work environment as an essentially learning situation. What the industrial system 'gives off' by way of impression is likely to be as significant in forming attitudes as what it intentionally provides in the form of communication, instruction, training, remuneration (as reinforcement) or other conditions. The organisation itself is the message which is likely to prove at least as influential as the verbalised ones put out in its name. The way it is organised and the policies and practices in which it engages impinge more directly and more constantly on the individual's experience than the intermittent pronouncements of its representatives.

The Command Group

The command group — that group which develops from the manner in which the undertaking structures the supervisory process — is a prime example. This, in fact, and whatever the intention, functions primarily to channel management's communications downwards. There may exist the hope (even the intention) that the group will also function to channel workers' thoughts, feelings, and (particularly) grievances upwards, but usually this does not happen because the structure of authority gets in its way. The idea that the supervisor functions even-handedly as a filter and amplifier (filtering information as it passes up from the shop floor and amplifying management's instructions as they pass downwards) is a convenient, but not necessarily realistic one, especially where trade unions or staff associations are recognised.

It is extremely unusual for the supervisor to be chosen by the workers supervised; normally, he or she is appointed to the position by external authority. This tends to place the supervisor in a marginal position in relation to both systems, those of management and workers. Some organisations have in the past tried to circumvent this by appointing as supervisors (some of) those who were elected as shop-stewards or other kinds of representative. This has a limited effect as a device for appointing acceptable shop-floor group leaders, because the appointee quickly distances himself or herself from the group as he or she responds to norms and instructions which derive from management.

The problem is that the supervisor is expected to operate as a *general-purpose* group leader, whose multiple purposes hinder the performance of any particular function (such as ensuring upward communication). The solution to this has traditionally been that of appointing specialist functionaries to 'assist' the supervisor in the technical aspects of the work. This in turn often creates a condition of role conflict, the supervisor being bombarded with competing claims for his or her attention. Role ambiguities and conflicts tend to detract from the supervisor's ability to function as an effective node of communication and influence.

Two ways out of the difficulty are currently tried. The first involves the creation of new and additional channels of communication which may or may not involve the supervisor directly, with the object of exerting influence on the perspectives, attitudes, and behaviours of the people supervised. The second makes more deliberate use of group properties to ensure that the necessary decisions are taken and, as a consequence, to dispense with the need for a formally appointed supervisor. In each category several different approaches are to be found, some being more and some less holistic in their concern with the problem of changing structures to change perspectives and attitudes.

The Briefing Group

A first deliberate utilisation of the group concept for managerial purposes is that which uses this phenomenon for communication of information and explanation. The Industrial Society has used the term 'briefing group' to identify its employment for this purpose. A 'briefing group' is essentially a created device for allowing face to face communication, not merely of information about strategies and policies (and changes in them), but of explanation of the reasons for them as well. It usually comprises a group of about 15 people who represent some departmental or task association, led by a supervisor (whether that supervisor is a managerial supervisor of managers or a first-line type of supervisor of white collar or manual employees).

The rationale of the briefing group is that while information about strategy and policy changes will normally move through an organisation quickly enough on the grapevine, this will usually attribute incorrect motivations or reasons for them and result in little positive appreciation of or commitment to the purposes to which they relate. To reduce these problems, management needs consciously and deliberately to plan the dissemination of both the information and the relevant considerations which led to the decisions involved. This planning demands attention to:

(a) the preparation of a brief but accurate and comprehensive statement of any change and the reasons for it;

(b) the full briefing by written and oral communication of the supervisors (at whatever level) on any proposed change and the reasons for it;

(c)   the organisation of briefing groups in which the supervisors will communicate information and explanation to those within their units or sections.

Each of these three elements requires specific planning and informed execution.

1   The brief which sets out the facts and the explanations may be presented in the form of a *management bulletin* addressed to each individual manager or supervisor who will be expected to act on it. It will be brief and confined to matters affecting personnel, which are new, and for that reason, immediate and urgent. It will be addressed to either managers or managers and supervisors according to the assessment of whether it can be passed to all of these in written form without further face to face explanation. It will end with an indication of who is take what action on it, and particularly on when and how the information is to be communicated.

2   Where important changes in strategy or policy have been decided on by management (whether unilaterally or in negotiation with trade union representatives), a written statement of the outcomes and the reasons for them may not be sufficient. It may be necessary for each manager to convene a briefing group of all his or her immediate subordinates, so that the matter can be discussed in a face to face setting and questions used as the stimuli for more detailed explanations by management. This approach was often used in the productivity bargaining era of the 1960s to communicate effectively about proposed changes, when it was often referred to as a set of cascading discussions (Thomason, 1971, pp 41 – 5).

3   The final step involves the supervisors in communication of the information and explanations to their immediate subordinates in the context of briefing groups. These must draw in all employees, whether on day work or shift-work, in groups which are small enough (certainly under 20 members) to allow free exchange. They will occur within a limited time of the issue of a bulletin, but not become a regularly scheduled meeting whether there is anything to communicate or not. They should be run by the supervisor and should be limited in duration to something under half an hour (probably just after a lunch break or at the beginning or end of a shift). They should deal with one matter or issue which is of importance to the people who make up the briefing group, but not be allowed to

become a forum for airing other grievances not related to the matter in hand.

As with so many other management processes, these devices work effectively where there is a tradition of using them to communicate important information. They acquire their own momentum, and that is the dynamic of the new structure which is relied on, tacitly, to effect changes in attitudes. Where it is necessary to start them from scratch, some training may be necessary to provide the necessary degree of self-confidence in the group leaders and the necessary skill in communicating.

Some effort may need to be devoted to convincing the managers and supervisors that this approach to communication is not likely to lead to the expenditure of more time and effort, but to a reduction of time spent in explanations on a more haphazard and intermittent basis in the ordinary course of the job. The first exercises need to be carried out in relation to something which is important but not excessively controversial (such as safety or some matter agreed with workers' representatives).

Project Groups and Working Parties

Project groups and working parties are similar to these and to one another in the sense that they both involve the creation of 'working' groups for purposes of improving communications. The first two are, however, usually allowed a limited life, during which they are expected to realise certain ends and to do so in a disciplined way, following some formal set of rules and procedures. Project groups, in particular, may be associated with matrix organisations, within which the general overview of people problems (pay, careers, etc) is separated from the supervision of these people's work activities. This is not, however, a necessary condition for the use of such groups.

The theory behind the inception of the project group is that attributed to Miller and Rice (1967), who explore the relationship between the task group (akin to the formal group identified in the Hawthorne researches (Roethlisberger and Dickson, 1939) and the work group identified by Bion (1961)) and the sentient group (akin to the informal and the basic groups, respectively). Two main relationships are possible:

(a)   The task and sentient groups may be identical, a situation which had previously been advanced as indicating the 'right' form of organisation (Rice, 1958; Trist *et al*, 1963).

(b)   the task and sentient groups may not overlap, with the latter
       being set within wider or narrower boundaries than the
       former.

The later work of Miller and Rice (1967) argued that the first of
these might be appropriate to operation within stable environments
or enterprise systems, but that the second was more appropriate to
(and functional for) unstable conditions.

Miller and Rice (1967) proposed that the *project* type organisation
is both universally applicable (they present examples from construction, marketing, airlines, research, etc) and particularly relevant to the condition where the enterprise is faced with the need to
achieve greater operating flexibility or to cope with technological or
market change (Miller and Rice, 1967, p 257). It also provides 'the
most appropriate basis for a general theory of organisation' (Miller
and Rice, 1967, p 129).

In a project organisation, typically, the group is brought together
to perform some particular task and is then disbanded when the task
is completed (ibid, p 129). But the need for a sentient group to which
the individual members will feel able to commit themselves has to be
met in this situation, they argue. This may be achieved by creating
a wider group of employees with similar or complementary interests
(a group of flying crew members, salesmen, or research scientists,
etc). The potential for attracting commitment may, in these circumstances, be increased where the individuals have shared craft or
professional standing. This provides the rationale for the 'people'
group, where the shorter-term tasks provide the basis for the 'task'
or 'project' groups.

Project groups that are, however, more akin to *ad hoc* working
parties which deal with specific problems for a limited period, are
also prevalent. In this context, they need not (although they may) be
led by a separate supervisor (as in the matrix organisation). They
often then have something in common with the quality circle, being
limited in their focus and concerned to resolve specific problems.

Training

Akin to these uses of the group in communication is its use in the
training context where it is often employed more deliberately to
bring about changes in perspectives and attitudes. The use of the
seminar and the group discussion of incidents or cases which make
use of the knowledge and understanding of others in the development of those of the trainee, is widespread. This approach relies on
the capacity of a group to share definitions of reality and frames of

reference for individual members, provided it is seen as a source of satisfaction.

A further use of this method relies on the group's function in providing emotional support to the individual in what may be a stressful situation (as learning of new ideas and perspectives often is). Where the group does provide support, transfer of learning is likely to be facilitated beyond the level which would be attained simply on the basis of the tutor-trainee relationship. The full development of this idea is to be found in sensitivity or T-group training (of which there are many specific variants).

A T-group is composed of a small number of people who are brought together in a group without a formal agenda, task, or structure. The object is to allow the *process* of group interaction to rise to the surface of members' consciousness, without being complicated by the considerations or demands of interactional *content*. This enables participants to identify and explore the affective (or 'feeling') level of consciousness without becoming bogged down in considerations of the cognitive (or 'informational') level (Cooper, 1972, p 9).

Individual members in effect develop a greater consciousness of the human and interactional problems that have to be resolved by any group which seeks any degree of permanence. These problems are those which concern:

1   The identity or character of the individual member which pressures the individual to consider what kind of a person he or she is, in his or her own perceptions and as perceived by others in the group.

2   The receptiveness of the individual member to others, which leads the individual to consider how much of the self is to be exposed to other members, and how much intimacy the individual can accept and respond to in others.

3   The tolerance of the individual member for absence of social structure, which raises questions about the needs of the member(s) for leadership, role definition, or rules in their interactions with others.

4   The awareness of the individual member of the effect on others of his or her normal behaviour, which focuses on the kinds and amounts of emotional response which he or she generates.

All of these can, as here, be expressed as impacts on the individual, but they also imply impacts on the group structures and processes *per se*.

The use of the small group in these ways allows the individual's capacities for human relations to be enhanced (although it cannot, of course, guarantee it). The emphasis is usually on one or more of the following outcomes:

1   The development of sensitivity, defined as ability to recognise what is occurring in a group at any particular time.

2   The development of a diagnostic ability, defined as ability to assess the kind of action (or reaction) which in the situation might lead to one or other outcome.

3   The development of an ability to intervene successfully to change the situation in the interests of improving goal achievement or the functioning of the group itself.

These are the activities which any would-be leader or manager must engage in to effect change in a given situation.

This approach is often used to change attitudes and behaviours which are related directly to people. The individual develops a heightened awareness of the impact of others on the self and the impact of self on others. This is facilitated by the interpretations of group dynamics which the 'resource person' provides when asked by the group members.

The Representative Group

The obverse of the briefing group and training group is the representative group which is adopted and used to ensure equally effective upward communication of the aspirations and attitudes of employees. In any normal situation the first-line supervisor will be made aware of these thoughts and feelings among his or her subordinates. They may be passed up the hierarchical chain of command, but management is often not able to gauge the strength of these views on this basis. The establishment of a method of face to face meeting between senior managers and employees at *diverse* levels below them can often provide a more sure basis for assessment than any process of reporting through the chain of command.

Where trade unions are recognised in the undertaking for purposes of representing their member-employees, the ordinary grievance and negotiating procedures may provide the basis for representative group meetings. Similarly, it has been claimed of the autonomous working group that the team captain is a representative, not an executive head, and is for this reason better placed to communicate upwards (Buchanan, 1979, p 101). Where trade unions are not recognised, however, managements may need to create this kind of meeting to ensure that they do receive information at its full strength. This is a role which the representative is usually well able to perform, although even in unionised undertakings managements may need to provide a regular opportunity for this kind of communication if it is to serve any management need. Where it is convened only when a grievance comes up, the level of emotion may negate the whole of management's purpose, even if it serves those of the grieving employees.

The role of the representative group is not to be confused with that of the briefing group. The representative group can be treated in the same way as a briefing group to reach the 'influentials' and possibly also to bolster their status and authority, but not used as a briefing group. The latter is designed to communicate management's main messages. The former is designed to communicate the workers' messages. There may be some temptation to use the representatives as a short-cut method of communication to the shop floor. This is likely to produce distortion, where the representatives do communicate to their constituents, and management has no control over the process. It is, however, just as likely not to happen at all. Placing workers' representatives in the position where they appear to be acting as management's spokespersons is to ensure role conflict for them. The stress which this is known to create may be a deterrent or a reason for distortion as they couple the communication with interpretation according to the perspectives and frames of reference of the worker group.

Supplementary Groups

The idea of utilising the working group for managerial purposes is based on a recognition that any group has a capacity for developing disciplined cooperation in the performance of some common task. The autonomous working group generalises the ideas which inform the development of the more specialised project groups, working parties, and quality circles. All of these make use of the same set of group properties, but differ in the extent to which they subordinate the free or voluntary element of group development to the realisation of external objectives. It is in this context that the idea of dispensing with the externally imposed leader arises.

Quality Circles

Quality circles (QCs) offer a currently fashionable example of the process of opening up new channels of communication. They do not extend as far as the autonomous working group in devolving decisions to the group, but they are a kind of half-way house. They have been described as:

> 'small groups of employees who normally work together, meeting regularly to agree ways of improving quality, productivity and other aspects of their day-to-day working arrangements'
> (Collard, 1981, p 27).

They are usually composed of between five and ten voluntarily participating employees, led by a supervisor or someone selected from within the working group. They usually meet regularly to discuss problems of quality and quantity of output and working arrangements relevant thereto. But they take on a number of different forms, according to the situations in which they exist.

They represent an alternative approach to bringing back together the planning and execution processes which were sundered by the application of the principles of 'scientific management'. Unlike job enlargement or job enrichment, this approach does not aim to increase the discretion of the worker in the *actual performance of the job*. Rather, it aims to provide the worker with an additional opportunity to engage in planning activity outside the immediate contours of the job — although the hope and belief is that to do so will be to produce an effect in terms of quality in the performance of the individual's job.

In the Japanese context (from which much current practice derives) quality circles form part of the philosophy and style of management, and serve as a counterweight to those aspects of them which follow the tenets of scientific management. There, they:

(a)   form an integral part of the management philosophy and approach, not something added on to the existing structure, in the hope that it may achieve something worthwhile;

(b)   are endowed with authority to implement any changes which may be agreed after consideration of the problem; and

(c)   are integrated with other policies which 'protect' the integrity of those individuals who participate (thus there is a tendency for work to be organised within small groups, for people to be job rotated to produce all-round capability, for the social distance between management and workers to be minimised, and for employment to be offered in the larger organisations on a life-time basis).

In terms reminiscent of McGregor's philosophy, management is enjoined to recognise that:

(i)   people do have something to contribute which is no less significant than what managers may contribute; and

(ii) they will be willing to do so provided the right structure is developed to facilitate it.

If quality circles are seen as little more than devices for increasing employee loyalty and commitment to the existing management and its objectives, they are likely to fail. Britain does not have a life-time employment concept which offers protection of the person's integrity in work and therefore even greater efforts are likely to be needed to provide a protected environment for this kind of activity. If it is seen, rather, as a means of allocating more authority to the worker in relation to his or her work, then the levels of commitment may well be raised.

They are, in one sense, no more than a particular 'branded' method of communication, ranking alongside production committees, briefing groups, discussion groups (as used in the context of productivity bargaining, for example), working parties, etc., all of which in their time have been developed as ways of improving communication in order to improve work performance. Nevertheless, they do have their own distinguishing characteristics and serve some communications purposes more readily than they do others.

Autonomous Working Groups

Autonomous working groups carry forward the idea of supplanting the supervisor, by allowing the group autonomy to take those decisions which might otherwise fall to the supervisor to take. In practice, this does not not always follow from the introduction of such groups, but it is a logical consequence. Autonomous working groups, however, are not always feasible (because of technological constraints) nor always economically desirable (because of comparative cost factors). They are not, therefore, to be seen as universal panaceas for all problems of failure to change workers' perspectives of, and attitudes to, work.

Rice's early experiments with organisational forms in conditions of technological change in the Indian textile industry, led him to present the conditions under which the contrived coincidence of task and sentient boundaries might prove effective. In 'relatively stable technologies', he suggested (1958), it was necessary that:

1   The group should experience its collective task as a complete or whole one.

2   The group must be able to regulate its own activities on the basis of input/output data available to it.

3   The group must be of a small enough size to permit internal regulation and the provision of satisfactory internal relationships.

4   The members' status and skill differences should not be so great as to emphasise affiliations external to the group at the expense of internal affiliation and commitment.

5   The group should not be unique, with the consequence that anyone disaffected could not leave without severing the employment relationship as a whole.

This set of conditions becomes the basis on which the autonomous working group is erected.

The autonomous working group is not applicable in all situations. Frequently, the technology does not permit the meeting of the necessary conditions, and work will continue to be allocated to individuals by a formal supervisor. Where it is possible, however, it is regarded as bestowing a number of advantages, both for the individual member and for the management.

1   The individual is able to acquire work which is meaningful because the group's association with the whole task gives more immediate meaning than do the formal processes of allocation through the ordinary chain of command.

2   The individual is more readily assured of affiliation and social support in the work situation, simply because he or she is part of a team.

3   The individual may be enabled to develp a better identity or self-concept.

4   The individual may experience a greater feeling of economic and social security.

5   The group may assume responsibility for actions which would otherwise fall to the supervisor or manager as in the selection of members, the organisation and allocation of work, and the development of a disciplinary code.

6   The group working concept may allow the development of greater flexibility in coping with work tasks.

7   The autonomous working group may facilitate communication between management and workers, as the group's commitment to the fulfilment of tasks is raised.

8   Performance levels may be increased, as set up times are reduced, rates of application to work during the working period are increased, errors are more quickly noted and rectified, and quality is improved.

9   With the development of team spirit, the incidence of withdrawal behaviours (lateness, absenteeism, idling or labour turnover) may fall.

These are not necessarily all found together in any one application, but they have all been claimed in some.

This kind of development does not always commend itself to organised labour, who see it as a means of incorporating the individual, through his or her group, into the managerial organisation. Individual workers may also resist the development of such methods of organisation because they fear the tyranny of the group more than they fear the tyranny of the supervisor or the bureaucracy. It may also be resisted or resented by supervisors, who may see this greater autonomy as a threat to their roles and positions. As it also cannot be developed in all working situations, it therefore cannot be regarded as a panacea for all managerial *or* all social ills in the work situation.

It has been applied quite extensively, particularly in Scandinavian countries, but it has made little progress in Britain, although some experiments have been carried out. In Britain, more reliance has been placed on processes of job enlargement and job enrichment, which retain the element of individual allocation of tasks, a practice which may reflect something of the difference in underlying cultural values.

SUMMARY

It may be the case that perspectives and attitudes of managers and workers have become incongruent with the real properties of the situation. Changing them appears to be a task whose completion could only result in benefit.

Changing attitudes is not a task which can be entered on lightly, because attitudes have properties which render them difficult to change, and because the social structure functions to hold them in place. Attempts to bring about change depend on a knowledge of both.

Changing the environmental supports for incongruent attitudes may call for different policies related to 'treatment' of employees, so that new messages are given off by their experience, and for a degree of restructuring of the social organisation which holds workers (and their attitudes) in place. Each of these currently manifests itself in a number of different ways.

Changing attitudes by more deliberate and direct means is an exercise which appears to be fraught with problems. There are doubts whether 'training and development' methods can succeed, and there is good reason to suppose that they will not succeed unless they are supported by changes in methods and approaches adopted by line management in the course of work.

If it is desired that attitudes shall be changed, therefore, industry is likely to face major tasks of measuring its communications performance *in toto* against the set of attitudes which that performance generates or maintains, and of making such changes in structure, policy, or practice as such assessment may indicate.

Reading:

Allport (1935).　　　　　　　Lewin (1967).
Buchanan (1979).　　　　　　Triandis (1971).
Joyce and Woods (1980).

16 Organisational Development

The task of creating an appropriate organisational context for successful action brings together a package of management skills. A context is necessary to facilitate cooperation in support of the ends of the enterprise; the package of skills is necessary to ensure that the many facets are developed in unison both with the external environment and one another. The skills are those of creating or developing those relationships between people (in their work roles) which will ensure both that efficient performance is given and that the demands on those giving it are tolerable and acceptable to them. This division between goal achievement and group maintenance relates to the subtasks generally associated with leadership in any context, although they may be given different labels (see above pp 232–3).

This perspective establishes the instrumentality of organisation, but not necessarily that of individual human beings. The organisation is an instrument of the two purposes of realising the ends which depend on successfully coping with the demands of the external environment, and of realising the 'maintenance' goals of the stakeholders who throw in their lot with it. The fact that the interests of the different categories of stakeholder – shareholder, supplier, customer, community and worker – are not identical, makes the achievement of successful cooperation more difficult than it might be in other circumstances. The current organisational problem is that of adjusting the structures and processes of the instrument to meet the volatile demands of both the internal and external environments. But the realisation of the twin purposes in the context of potential conflict is a measure of the managerial task as of any other leadership role.

The dynamic of such organisations is people-powered interaction, both across the boundary between organisational system and external environment, and between stakeholders within that boundary. Neither of these 'sets' of interaction is independent of the other: what happens over the boundary affects what happens within it, and *vice versa*. The construct of the figure-of-eight communication and control loops links the external and the internal environments through the central managerial nerve centre or 'brain'.

Ensuring that the dynamic is maintained becomes a prime function of those within an organisation who constitute the 'brain'. It is realistic to regard this brain as composed of the management, although there is no reason in principle why it should be so restricted. Management can muster the organisation's resources of power to influence the thinking, feeling, and behaviour of those associated in some way with it whether *internally* (such as workers or managers) or *externally* (such as customers), where it is appropriate to do so. How those resources are deployed in marketing or production decisions is a matter of judgement; that they are available to management for deployment is a matter of fact.

ACHIEVING ORGANISATION – ENVIRONMENT FIT

In a comparatively stable environment, the evolution of a satisfactory organisational structure tends to occur relatively slowly without doing great damage to the enterprise. Changes are made iteratively as new ideas emerge from a measured reflection on experience. A broad central concept of organisation gradually develops, and because it is copied from previous exemplars and because it changes only marginally and slowly, it appears to be universal in its applicability. This helps to explain the universality and permanence of the 'bureaucracy', taken over from governmental and military forms of organisation, and modified slowly and partially to meet the needs of expanding industry.

This slow change helped to create the impression that organisation was to be equated with the drawing of a management organisation chart in the course of which the main problem was to ensure that the relationship of line and staff personnel was 'properly' depicted (Urwick, 1949). The map of the territory was virtually standard in form; only the names of the innocent population were different. The presence of line and staff relationship problems was virtually dictated by the scale of enterprise and the capacity of managers to cope with the numbers of employees; only the labels of the specialist functionaries needed to be inserted. Once such a chart was drawn, the enterprise was, it was supposed, 'organised'.

Managers have, for some time, recognised that such forms of organisation depend on environmental stability (Peters and Waterman, 1982, p 9). The insight is now being absorbed into management literature (Woodward, 1958; Burns and Stalker, 1961). Where such stability was absent, it was not merely the names and the titles that needed alteration, but the way in which the internal structure was developed to match the demands of the environment. Woodward's researches in Essex revealed that managements follow different rules of organising according to their market relationship. Burns and Stalker's studies suggested, similarly, that the mechanistic form of bureaucratic organisation suffered a sea-change in volatile environments. This insight in turn spawned the view that managements might adjust organisations to their changing circumstances and by so doing reveal the existence of a limited number of structures patterned to identifiable environmental positions (Lippitt, 1969).

As this realisation has grown in recent years, the definition of what constitutes the relevant 'environment' to be taken into account has also changed. The concept itself is not new: it has been recognised as an essential element in characterisations of system functioning for many years. But the tendency to treat organisations (and their human populations) as instruments has tended to restrict attention to the external environment as the 'given' in any decision-making about required adaptations and accommodations.

Only comparatively recently has the health, or state of readiness to act, of the 'internal environment' been recognised as an important and mutable variable. This recognition awaited a realisation that the economic power of the large-scale organisation was often such that changes could be made in the external environment and that the demands which it made on the organisational instrument could be structured by such devices as product advertising and promotion or political lobbying. This made the external environment less of a 'given', and opened up the possibility that it could be modified to suit the capability of the organisation.

Such recognition also reflected a growing awareness that the human instruments of production are now less compliant, and less accepting of traditional forms of authority, than has been true in the past. Being less amenable to simple discipline, it became desirable to find ways of attacking the external environment to match the capacity for action which could be generated inside the enterprise. The basis for conceiving management's role as one of a 'directing brain' at the cross-over point in the control figure of eight was thus put in place (see Figure 1, p 14).

Organisational Development Strategies

The process which has come to be identified as 'Organisational Development' (OD) has been advanced (mainly by academics and consultant organisations) to refer to the process of developing organisational responses to the internal and external environments, when the basic condition of environmental stability is no longer present. This usually treats the problem as one of facilitating management learning about how best, organisationally and stylistically, to cope with environmental changes. It has been defined as:

> 'a complex educational strategy designed to increase organisational effectiveness and health through planned intervention by a consultant (or other change agent) using theory and techniques of applied behavioural science'
> (Beach, 1975, p 426).

It is focused on the 'people variables' of organisation as distinct from the financial or technological variables. The educational (or learning) component is therefore directed towards changing the dimensions of values, norms, attitudes, relationships, and socio-emotional climate. Without necessarily seeking to change any or all of these variables, it aims to allow the members of the brain (whoever they may be in the particular case) to learn about ways of structuring the relationships for greater effect, based on an understanding of the requirements of the situation and the 'solution' apposite to them.

It is, however, concerned with control of the labour process as much as with mere 'human relations' processes. Emphasis is placed on effectiveness, which is here focused on the criterion of long-term performance of the organisation as a whole. In a profit-oriented enterprise, that emphasis will be on whether in the long run the organisation will still be producing the goods which its customers need and demand and will show themselves ready to provide cash in sufficient quantities to meet the demands of stakeholders within the organisation. In a service organisation, the emphasis will be on long-term capacity to go on delivering the demanded service at a cost which the clients or the common purse will be willing to meet.

Effectiveness in this context is thus associated with long-term capacity to go on meeting the needs of the citizen-customer and the other stakeholders (stockholders, workers, managers, creditors, etc). The way in which managers are encouraged to think about controlling the situation is by way of developing a feedback loop to provide the necessary intelligence as a basis of decision-taking and a feed-out loop to ensure that relevant responses can be brought to bear on the problem (Figure 1). Application of this model, then, inevitably leads to the recognition that action may be necessary to change the substantive (as distinct from the essentially processual) aspects of the situation. Examples of this outcome are to be found in attempts to redesign jobs and work roles or to modify the specifications of the kinds of person required to perform them.

Organizational Development and the Concept of Organisational Health

Achievement to the end of producing relevant responses will depend on what the various stakeholders are willing (as well as able) to do and go on doing. It is for this reason that OD is concerned with the *health* of the organisation, with the underlying assumption that an unhealthy organization, like an unhealthy person, cannot be effective. Bennis (1966), one of the early exponents of this approach, adopted Marie Jahoda's criteria of the healthy individual and applied them to organisations, thus treating them *as if* they were persons in their own right. On this basis, a healthy individual and a healthy organisation need to satisfy three criteria:

1 active mastery of the environment;

2 awareness of own identity; and

3 realistic perception of the world and of the self in relation to it (Bennis, 1966, pp 52–5).

If these three criteria are satisfied, not only will each be 'healthy' but each will also have the capacity to be effective, capable of coping effectively with the environment (although that is not 'automatic', even for the healthy individual or organisation).

The original thrust of many of the OD interventions was towards effecting learning in the area of management. The assumption was that because management was, effectively and congruently with Taylor's conception, the 'brain' of the organisation, it was by changing management's perceptions, theories, and motivations that changes would be made in the organisation's responses to changing environments. The approach developed thus emphasised a form of top-down direction and continued the idea that change was something which could only be effected through individuals – the sources of change in thinking, feeling, and behaviour. The function of the group, as the source of stability, was acknowledged only to the extent of using group influences on the dissemination of meanings to facilitate this kind of change.

Changes in attitudes of non-managers and changes in the demands made on non-managerial workers as a result of technological innovation have, however, pushed the approach to OD in the direction of encouraging changes in perceptions, theories, and motivation at this other level, too. This has manifest itself in calls for effecting changes in 'attitude' by training and propaganda, but this has not generally commended itself as a method of securing the desired end. Consequently, much of the burden of this activity has been borne by attempts to redesign jobs and harmonise employee conditions, an approach which is based on the widely prevalent view that workers' responses to their work environment are largely conditioned by the work-tasks they are required to perform: where these are simple and fragmented, for example, the extent to which they can command the worker's commitment must be limited (Kasl, in Cooper and Payne, 1978)

This perspective implies that action to increase commitment, particularly in high technology situations, should be concentrated on enlarging or enriching jobs (for example, by vertical job loading or by donating more discretion or autonomy to the work group) (Buchanan, 1979). Because the focus can be directed towards these variables, OD is not simply concerned with *changing* the people variables to achieve some improved state or structure. In fact, *change* need not be a prime or necessary focus, except in the sense that an OD approach will lead to change if deficiencies on any of the criteria are found.

Bennis (1966) did give OD just such a focus on change. But what he called 'planned organisational change' was directed towards improving both individual and organisational health by developing each in relation to the three criteria offered by Marie Jahoda. His orientation of OD to change stemmed from his diagnosis that many modern organisations were currently conceived and structured in ways that denied them opportunities to become healthy. It then followed that only if organisations changed could the criteria be met.

But it need not be set up 'to bring about change', expressed as a deliberate substantive aim. Argyris, one of the early advocates of the OD approach, specifically rejects the need for it to be focused on change as an end in itself. He points out that, in order to be healthy, individual human beings require a degree of stability both in themselves and in their environments. The pursuit of change could therefore lead to ill health or un-health at both the individual and the organisational levels. Whether change should occur is therefore left to the client to decide, after review.

This, again, was initially conceived and expressed in terms of management-as-client: decisions about whether to go for change were for management to take – after a managerial review. But progressively, this same principle has been applied to decisions in respect of work restructuring, where workers are increasingly allowed to function as the 'client-organisation' within the meaning of this approach. There are many who advocate the desirability of job restructuring on a variety of grounds (economic, political, social and psychological) and the advocacy is often 'aimed at' the management as those who have traditionally defined work tasks for workers. But many recent experiments in this area have either indicated that the workers have decided views about the desirability of making these apparently beneficial changes or accepted that it is really (if beneficial consequences are to flow) for the workers themselves to decide whether to adopt the changes.

Objectives

The fundamental objective of OD is to 'achieve a sense of commitment, self-direction, and self-control' among all within the ambit of the programme. It seeks to create the condition in which people will accept ownership of the organisation's problems and realise that there are mechanisms through which they can ensure that their actions to deal with them are protected and supported.

More particular objectives falling within this broad statement can be identified, although not all of them need be present in any one scheme:

1   Secure a decentralisation of decision-taking, moving away from highly centralised decision and control systems to ones which emphasise decision close to the point of action.

2   Achievement of a climate of cooperation in place of the common power struggles and destructive competition amongst managers or between managers and workers.

3   Achievement of a system in which disagreements and conflicts are brought into the open and dealt with realistically, rather than one in which they remain bottled up until a major disruption has to occur to clear the blockages.

4   Changes in the ways in which people conduct themselves or in which they carry out their work, making them more responsive to the real needs of the situation – for example, where technological changes indicate a new way of working.

5 Increase the openness of communication, between individuals, groups, divisions, and departments, so that real issues can be confronted in place of the shadow-boxing which often characterises organised activity.

6 Modification of organisational structures and procedures where the existing ones appear to impede progress or performance.

7 Improve the capacity of people caught up in the enterprise to deal with work problems and work situations, thus contributing to their development as persons.

It is to be expected, on *a priori* grounds, that not all organisations will find this approach with these objectives necessary or desirable. Some will find that they have no stomach for it at all. This approach, however, is likely to commend itself more particularly to high technology undertakings rather than to smoke-stack industries (where the pressures to secure a more committed work-force are probably less and less easy to achieve), and to large-scale undertakings rather than to small-scale ones (where less elaborate measures may suffice to produce the same kinds of consequence). Nor is there any reason why workers will necessarily embrace this approach.

Principles

OD (or Organisational Development) arose out of a particular kind of management training approach, that found in the National Training Laboratory's development of T-groups, or sensitivity training. This, when applied to small groups of managers 'off-the-job' was usually found to be non-transferable to their conduct in these home organisations. It was the movement of sensitivity training into the organisation that spawned what became OD (and, indeed, sensitivity training remains an element in the OD approach).

To this, however, there needs to be added the contribution from mainstream social science thinking, which emphasises the necessity for management action to be based on realistic theories about what human beings can or cannot achieve in the way of results. Social science theories are built into the approach where they become statements of belief about what leads to what.

Because of its provenance, the exponents of OD have been careful to articulate the values which should govern the conduct of those who engage in it and their relations to the clients and client-systems. Most main writers on the subject articulate a set of such values: the following list is taken from Beach (1975), who suggests that the OD professional would accept the following propositions:

1   Man is basically good, responsible, helpful, trustworthy and capable of self-control – pretty much what McGregor (1960) built into his Theory Y assumptions about the nature of man.

2   Man has a need for confirmation and support in what he is doing – pretty much the same kind of thing that Herzberg referred to as motivators in his motivation-hygiene theory.

3   Man is capable of growing and developing both in terms of his capacity and his personality under the right conditions.

4   Health is improved if the people concerned in organisation accept that the differences among mankind are opportunities for development, not aberrations to be reduced or removed.

5   Health is improved if people learn how to express their opinions, feelings, and emotions in an open but controlled way, and do so without feeling that this detracts from their approach to work and to others caught up in it.

6   Health is improved if people express themselves honestly and openly, and avoid, as far as possible, being obtuse and political in their dealings with colleagues.

7   Effectiveness and health are improved if, in the performance of work tasks, due attention is given to the attitudes and aspirations of others and to the capacity of the existing relationships to carry the work forward.

8   Effectiveness and health are improved by deliberate policies and practices of generating cooperation and reducing the element of competition between people at work.

9   Effectiveness and health are facilitated if disagreements and conflicts are confronted, rather than ignored or suppressed.

These principles are intended to ensure that the 'human context' of organisation is maintained in good health; however, they link most directly to a conception of organisation which is heavily dependent on the 'human relations' perspective, and other views call for incorporation in the approach.

Focus of Action

These 'additional' elements in the perspective of organisations have been incorporated in the McKinsey model, developed by Peters and

Waterman (1982, p 10). This model recognises that:

(a)   a broad distinction can be made between hard (formal) and soft (informal) organisation but, while this is useful for understanding, it need not imply that the one is manageable and the other not;

(b)   three hard elements of structure, strategy, and systems are interconnected both with one another and with the soft elements of shared values (culture), staff, style, and skills (or strengths), all of which demand management attention (these make up the McKinsey 7-S framework).

     As a diagnostic tool, the McKinsey 7-S framework provides a focus for action in the context of organisational development.

Traditionally, management has concentrated on the 'hard' elements: the definition of objectives and strategies (developed in relation to the 'market', often taken as a given); the development of a structure of authority and power to create and apply rules (reflecting culturally supported conceptions of authority); and the organisation of systemic channels of communication between decision nodes (often taking over from other professional specialities the conceptions of 'system' employed therein).

These 'hard' elements have recently been reviewed, and the realisation has dawned that they are less hard than has been assumed. A volatile external environment, coupled with a more direct relationship between worker and end-product, has forced it on our attention that objectives and strategies are not only more fluid, but subject to greater influence by the worker in charge of complex 'automatic' production systems. For similar reasons, and particularly that people in charge of complex plant cannot be docile cogs, the structure of authority has been made flatter than is customary. The channels of communication to 'management' are now not only facilitated by modern technology, but they can be and are more often channelled through work-stations to provide information to those who need it most immediately.

The 'soft' elements (culture, style, staff, and skills) have only more recently been forced on management's attention. The immediate stimulus for this may appear to have been the 'findings' of academic researchers (such as the seminal Hawthorne studies), but the underlying reason for their consideration is as likely to have been the changing relationship of enterprise to environments (such as the growth in international market competitiveness or the rate of substitution of capital for labour). The insights and models of the thinkers may assist management thinking about their problems, but they do not, by themselves, ensure take-up.

Once taken up, however, they call for serious consideration along with the hard elements. The way in which these are directed to management's attention is most clearly seen by taking as an example the small, high-tech, production unit which has emerged in recent years. The main need in such complex production units with few staff is to extend the culture or values which might previously have been shared by management to embrace the other staff members; these same staff, at all 'levels', may need to become multi-skilled to cope with the manifold tasks which are now to be allocated among few people; the foundations of the managing style are likely to change as the need to develop commitment to the new partnership develops; this in turn will call for a more respectful and trusting conception of man.

The focus of organisational development is therefore increasingly on this wide range of factors, some hard, some soft, which together make up the weft and warp of enterprise in a modern economy.

Key Roles in the OD Approach

The traditional OD approach has, however, tended to take over the top-down concepts associated with earlier approaches to training. This may now be changing. Because the OD approach is usually conceived as an educational strategy linked to the dissemination of social scientific insight and theory, it tends to emphasise the need for an 'external' stimulant to the whole process. This stimulant is commonly spoken of as a 'change-agent', and may take the form of a consultant brought in from outside the organisation or a personnel specialist operating within the organisation.

This is not necessarily the same thing as saying that the whole approach is conceived as a top-down one: much depends on the view taken of the client and the values which the change-agent brings to bear in the relationship. Clearly, it could be top-down, if it treated the change-agent as something concerned to do things for or to the client-system. But to be consistent with the values already listed, it could emphasise more the need for a partnership between agent and client-system as a whole, and this is the direction in which such interventions are now tending.

In the more general expositions of the approach it is usual to identify four factors:

1   *The change-agent,* who may be a person, a group, or an organisation, who is professional in his approach to the client

(that is, accepting the values already listed), and who stimulates, guides, and stabilises the developmental activities within the client system.

2   *The client-system,* which may be an organisation but is conceived as an assemblage of individuals who comprise the clients of the 'professional' change-agent. It is emphasised that the OD professional is not in the position of regarding, say, the head of the organisation, or the executive who called in the change-agent, as the main or sole client.

3   *The catalyst of change* or the person or group within the system who, in true catalytic fashion, speeds up, maintains, or slows down the rate of change within the client system, without himself undergoing change. The commonest catalyst is the person who brings the change-agent and client-system together, and to see him as catalyst helps to avoid confusing him with the client.

4   *The pacemaker,* who may take the same forms as the change-agent, and who functions to stimulate and control the change process itself, deriving power and authority to do so from a source other than the client-system itself. An internally appointed trainer and developer, required by, say, the Managing Director, to assist the change-agent, might provide an example.

The change-agent and the client-system are commonly regarded as the more important contributors to the change or developmental process, with the catalysts and pace-makers performing secondary roles in the process. The change-agent and the pace-maker positions are, on the other hand, usually occupied by persons external to the client system (particularly in the sense that they draw their authority from outside), where the catalyst does not. In all cases, however, as Reddin (1985, p 87) makes clear, there is a need to provide some degree of protection for those who adopt any of these kinds of role from attack during the change process. Reddin suggests that they be given explicit and distinct authority to act, so that they are insulated from the day to day political pressures of organisations.

Process

Traditionally, OD has been a process of stimulating and facilitating learning on the part of the members of the client-system, so that they will be better able and more willing to take those decisions which are necessary to give – in Bennis's words – 'mastery of the internal and external environments', a better sense of identity and a realistic conception of what is relevant and necessary to individual and organisational health in the circumstances.

Because it has a learning focus, there is clearly a close link between OD and training (and particularly management development (MD)). Training as traditionally conceived, however, is often an authoritarian process through which useful techniques and devices are identified by someone in authority and communicated to those who will be expected to employ them, with controls being used to check on how well the recipients have mastered and applied them. It tends, therefore, to have a rather narrow and short-term focus.

Within the context of OD, however, problem-solving and decision-taking are conceived as generalised abilities which can be improved, not only by formal training but also and more effectively by guided practice in problem-solving and decision-taking in actual or closely simulated situations. To be realistic the problems to be solved must be located in a social and political context, which as nearly as possible replicates the actual situation within which the problem solvers and decision-takers will work. This implies that off-the-job sessions will most probably involve the 'team' normally concerned with problem-solving, and that on-the-job sessions will take place within the actual management structure. Realism also means that the constraints which the actual situation imposes on solutions and decisions must be built into the learning process: everyone can think up ideal solutions to abstract problems, but work usually denies these relevance or legitimacy.

For these reasons, OD tends to have a much broader focus and orientation than management development, although some methods are common to both. A case in point is sensitivity training – such as that associated with Blake's or Reddin's grids. In the context of management training, sensitivity training is usually provided for individual managers because someone has decided that they need to be made more aware of their behavioural impact on other people so that they can accomplish their given jobs better. The criteria are usually individual, immediate, or short-term and current-job oriented.

In the context of OD, on the other hand, any management training would be introduced only if it appeared to the consultant that it could help the client system to resolve some of its problems of relationships, and then it would be carried out in the context of the appropriate working groups. In the extreme case, it might also be necessary to extend the definition of 'management' to embrace non-managers who nevertheless take management-type decisions in the course of their work. A typical example of this is provided by the doctors who work in NHS hospitals; in carrying out diagnoses and in determining treatments, they dispose resources which are nominally allocated by general managers. Training for purposes of developing the organisation's capacity for action would necessarily embrace such non-managers. The criteria applied to this extended form of training are then more likely to be group-related, longer-term, and oriented towards general problem-solving.

Organisational Training Approaches

The traditional conception of, and approach to, securing organisational development, has relied on training lower level participants in the skills considered to be necessary to serve the organisation's given objectives. This reflected a 'top-down' view consistent with the tenets of scientific management (particularly that which states that it is the responsibility of the manager to define jobs and ensure that people are capable of performing them). As Sayles has suggested, the parallel development of scientific management and new technologies challenged management to find, by meticulous analysis, 'the right combination of inanimate tools and animate motions' (1964, p 9) and 'to ensure, through training, that the workers produced [the appropriate] habitual conditioned responses' (ibid).

In Sayles's view, both Taylor (in his enuciation of the principles of scientific management focused on manual work) and Weber (in his exposition of the principles of bureaucratic organisation applied to administrative work) and their disciples, defined the manager's task as something involving three steps:

1　Analyse the work to be performed.

2　Develop from this a series of job descriptions incorporating an appropriate degree of specialisation, so that the requisite tools could be provided and employees with adequate abilities could be recruited and trained for the positions.

3　Appraise the performance of employees, their ability to follow the content and motions of the job descriptions and the rules of the organisation. Those who succeeded should be given increased remuneration, responsibility and assurance of tenure (Sayles, 1964, p 10).

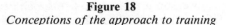

Figure 18

Conceptions of the approach to training

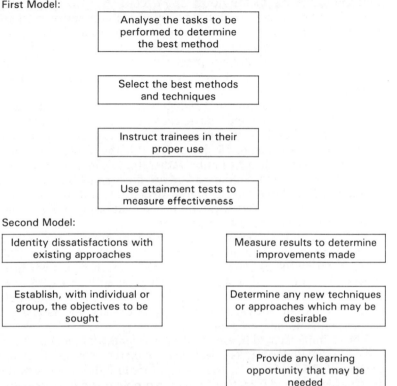

First Model:

> Analyse the tasks to be
> performed to determine
> the best method

> Select the best methods
> and techniques

> Instruct trainees in their
> proper use

> Use attainment tests to
> measure effectiveness

Second Model:

> Identify dissatisfactions with
> existing approaches

> Measure results to determine
> improvements made

> Establish, with individual or
> group, the objectives to be
> sought

> Determine any new techniques
> or approaches which may be
> desirable

> Provide any learning
> opportunity that may be
> needed

This led to training being structured (the first model in Figure 18): the manager defines the routines to be learned and provides training, and then uses some fairly conventional assessment procedure to measure how well the trainees have grasped them.

This approach usually throws up problems of motivation and of learning transfer. The willingness of the trainees to learn the best method may be low and may affect the efficiency of training. In addition, however effective the training may be in the classroom, successful trainees find it difficult to transfer the skills and techniques they have mastered to their work situations.

This consequence has often led to the decision either to provide training close to the job itself, or to simulate 'real situations' in the training vestibule to reduce the 'distance' that learning has to be transferred. It has also often led to a more systematic approach, supported by more sophisticated controls being adopted to the design of the training process. These may help to reduce some of the inherent problems in top-down approaches, but the element of control, although now structured around the concept of a closed (feedback) loop, remains linked to the management and is not extended to the trainee. These changes are therefore limited in their effects in so far as they prepare people to cope with the here and now and do not help them to learn how to deal with different or changing conditions.

More recent conceptions of training (such as those associated with MBO, Quality Circles, and 'participative management' have therefore sought to bring the trainee more directly into the decision and control processes. Figure 18 shows that it is the trainee's dissatisfaction which is made the stimulus rather than a simple managerial/ supervisory decision (although *their* dissatisfactions are not excluded). The closed loop model is carried forward, but it is now used to facilitate 'self-control' by the individual or group rather than control from above or by the trainer.

A more complex process of establishing the necessary directions of change is used to facilitate learning. Anyone may have ideas about the way 'things ought to be changed', but these are worthless unless they are tested against the reality in order to determine feasibility and likely outcomes. Providing a means for testing these and for developing the participants' perceptions and understandings is the significant new element.

This is implemented in a manner which replicates the manner in which individual projects (designed to increase experience) are conceived. The object is to establish a procedure through which the person is given guidance in defining the problem and in systematic- ally searching for possible solutions to it and testing out their probable effects, before making up his or her mind on what should be done about the problem. This ensures that any 'ideas' which the individual or the small group may have are treated with respect, but not accepted as a matter of course. The person or persons concerned are encouraged to work through the ideas to the point where (a) they are convinced about what, if anything, ought to be done, and (b) they have enough evidence to enable them to convince others as to its correctness.

Development and Participation

The need for change and development within complex organisations is frequently encountered but achieving it is usually difficult when approached on a simple top-down basis. People, it is said, tend to resist change when they do not see the immediate need for it, when they do not understand it, when it threatens some of the basic securities which people think they possess. In addition, where they perceive themselves to have no real power to make changes, they are unlikely to engage their efforts in the process of bringing it about.

It is likely to proceed more smoothly – if initially also more slowly – if those who will be required to work within and with the changed structures or methods, etc., are involved from the start. Through involvement, the people concerned are more likely to approach the change with better appreciation of need, greater understanding, and improved perceptions of the new securities which it will bring. This is what is offered by this disciplined approach to using 'dissatisfaction' as a stimulus to learning.

Managers are often suspicious of such delegation (or participation) because of a lack of trust and confidence in the wills and abilities of subordinates. Greater involvement of subordinates is often perceived by them as threatening their securities, and there is some suggestion that anxiety and stress may be suffered by managers in the face of movements in this direction. One approach to the solution of this kind of problem is that which introduces a standing practice and procedure which can be invoked as and when needed. As it can be invoked for relatively small and unthreatening changes, it enables managers to develop a greater appreciation of others' motivation and capability in advance of any major change being required.

This approach requires top managerial legitimation, subordinate involvement, and responsible decision taking (ensuring that decisions are reached within the same kinds of limits as would apply to any responsible manager acting within his or her authority). This latter process requires a degree of structuring to ensure a realistic outcome, and this may be attempted by setting up a procedure for people to follow in working out practicable solutions to new problems. This may continue to be used as a guide to activity even when projects are integrated into more advanced approaches to development. One such procedure is outlined in Table 19.

MANAGEMENT DEVELOPMENT

Organisational development is scarcely possible without simultaneous management development. But management training may be a necessary, but not sufficient, element in the process. Organisations have no independent being, but exist only through the people (agents) who have power and authority to act for them.

Table 19
An approach to development

An approach to 'development' of problem-solving capacity which incorporates managerial legitimation, emotional involvement in the constrained search and choice processes, and opportunities for learning about the reality of economic processes.

A. *Legitimation*

Management adopting this approach and policy must be prepared to:

1 Select projects which it is prepared to delegate to learners.

2 Find within the organisation and appoint (that is, endow with necessary authority) a leader,
— with authority to authorise expenditures of time and money on any development project
— with time to ensure the project is properly planned and controlled
— with sufficient knowledge and experience to assist in choosing objectives and strategies.

3 Assemble a project (task) group
— with skill sufficient to secure and use necessary information
— with time to devote to the necessary processes of definition and search involved in decision-taking
— with authority to act in respect of proposals.

4 Allocate specialists and resources to assist
— to supply and analyse the information needed by the group
— to supply theories and prepare models for group analysis
— to keep records of deliberations and prepare reports.

B *Learner Involvement*

The approach relies on the mobilisation of energies resulting from dissatisfaction with what is. Management must therefore encourage the leader and project group to

1 Involve human emotions in
— expressing dissatisfaction and uncovering causes of it, in order to define the problem
— deciding on the project's most desirable aims, expressing them in quantitative terms if possible
— preparing the (project) task group to think creatively about the problem.

2 Review the objectives by
— checking that any objective sought is emotionally worthwhile and realisable in terms of available resources
— relating the objectives to wider issues and concerns in organisations
— expressing the objectives in terms of real things rather than in complex concepts.

3 Utilise existing knowledge, theories, and models to facilitate inter-personal and inter-group communication by
— adopting a systematic ('rational') approach to the resolution of the problem, recognising the same constraints as any manager would in tackling the issue
— using simplified charts, diagrams, existing records, performance data, and procedure analyses
— attending consciously to the needs of the group as a social system in the process of solving the problem.

Table 19 *(continued)*

4   Recognise that the problem is *owned* by some manager, whose discretion to deal with it is constrained and whose constraints become constraints on the project group's discretion, in order to avoid disappointment of over-expectations.

C   *Planning and Control*
The group's approach will be required to conform to a basic managerial problem-solving pattern, involving

— planning and preparation of budgets of the amount of time and other resources warranted by the problem.

— checking on the availability of any resources required.

— securing prior commitment of necessary resources.

— progressing the decision process by defining the problem, reviewing possible solutions, assessing each against aims and budgets, and selecting the preferred alternative.

— making use of expert assistance to assist in working through the problem and its solutions, to evaluate the thoroughness of the planning and the proposed action programme, and to check the feasibility of the chosen plan.

— evaluating the group's own progress on the basis of recorded information on achievements and the group's own performance as an operating system, with the information being fed back to facilitate group learning, and attention being given specifically to the group's own learning curve.

— reco rding and reporting the plan to indicate who and what will be expected to change, and how, what materials from where will be required, at what cost, and on what criteria and measures will the success of the plan be assessed.

— presenting the proposal to those with responsibility for the problem, or likely to be affected by the proposed solution.

These agents are usually the managers and they largely determine what kinds of change, and how much of it, will occur within organisations. Non-managers are not without authority and power, but such as they have is usually less, unless it is derived from key (decision-making) roles in relation to the production or marketing system.

Management development is, essentially, a process of training. The traditional top-down conception of training is, however, difficult to apply to these roles for three main reasons:

(a)   The work tasks are relatively unstructured and difficult to rationalise as to the specific behaviours required; much will depend on the manager's sense of priority and capacity for self-organisation.

(b)   The personality of the manager is generally considered to have an important influence on job performance (because intellect and emotion are intimately involved), much more so than in the case of more structured work roles.

(c)   The centre cannot readily predetermine training content, because it can have only a relatively limited and superficial knowledge of what is involved in carrying out the specialist tasks (again the example of the doctor's tasks is pertinent).

Constrained in this way, the task of identifying training content is difficult to accomplish by the approaches and methods which are applied to, say, routine manual work.

Management development is therefore conceived as a complex package of approaches and techniques which seek to bring about changes in the thinking, feeling, and behaviour of managers by tackling problems of change in values, attitudes, perspectives, interests and theories, as well as skills or abilities. The whole panoply of social science is brought to bear on the problem, and this is revealed most clearly in the conception of 'Grid Training'.

Evolution of Approaches

On the way to developing this complex package approach, however, management development has been approached in a more piecemeal fashion.

First, managers were treated like the craftsmen in the early days of the industrial revolution who were hired on the basis that, at the time of appointment, they possessed the qualities, qualifications, and skills specified as required by the role incumbent. The person hired as works manager, or personnel manager, or accountant, was hired as being one equipped by prior and external training, with all that was required to perform the role. As Burns and Stalker have shown (in their discussion of mechanistic management systems), there are situations in which this approach may be apposite.

The pressures on management groups, however, may require that the work of this team be brought under closer control. The need is to develop a management cadre in which the *application* of cosmopolitan knowledge to local circumstances is more closely monitored, usually through some system of performance review and appraisal.

The need for management training was then often flagged up by performance appraisals, which could and did show up the weaknesses or deficiencies of managers in actually performing their roles. The requirement might be for some technical up-dating, or for development of human relations skills. The solution might be a formal course on, say, computer applications in the office, or a course of sensitivity training. Whatever the general skills possessed, they were made more situation-specific by these devices.

In this process, steps could be, and were, taken to draw out a more 'organic' approach to the objective of solving the undertaking's problems, so that, for example, Burns and Stalker's conception of the 'contributive nature' of knowldege and skill could be introduced into the organisation confronted with a more volatile environment. However much these might improve the *individual's* capacity to perform as an individual, they usually did little to draw the individual into the structure of values which characterised the specific undertaking.

Secondly, more formalised approaches to the task of team-building subsequently developed. At the simplest level, these focused on the device of the committee or working party, which, in tackling real problems facing the organisation, carried along the members of the management team in a structure of values and frames of reference which were applied to the solution of these problems. Individuals brought into the structure learned the 'right' way of doing things in the undertaking from such participation.

The next phase in this development focused on removing the managers from the hurly-burly of day to day management, with its fluctuating pressures and constant interruptions, and placing them in an off the job setting (conference centre or hotel) for a period (say, a weekend) where they were expected to deal exclusively with one (or a small number of) problem(s) facing the undertaking, freed from more disruptive requirements (noise). These team-building sessions were intended to serve the same ends as the immersion of the manager in committees and working parties, but were believed to have greater efficacy because the 'noise' present in work situations was reduced. The extent to which the insights of the social sciences were used to improve the efficiency of the approach could, however, vary greatly.

Grid Training

The next phase in the development of this approach to management development was to put together the local requirements and the more cosmopolitan concepts of how commitment might be developed. One major example of this development is the device of 'grid training'.

This approach builds on these main insights offered by the social scientists.

1   The distinction between achievement and maintenance

functions in the natural system concept of organisations, and in concepts of the leadership role and function.

2   The Theory X and Theory Y assumptions of the nature of man, as advanced by McGregor.

3   The model of compliance relationships advanced by Etzioni. It also attempts to bring together the advantages of off-the-job training with the perceived need to keep the training (learning) process focused on real issues of attaining production ends, and maintaining a healthy and efficient organisation. Because one part of the 'reality' consists of operating within a team situation – that is within a set of relationships which might prove as instrumental as the individual skills in realising objectives – the move to combine team training with skill training was an obvious next step. It is this which also brings the concepts of OD and MD together, the one being focused on the team and the other on the individual's capability and contribution.

The objective of the 'grid approach' to management development is to secure greater manager commitment to the aims and methods of the enterprise in which the manager is engaged. To secure this end, grid training makes use of all the theories of individual and group learning, as exemplified in syndicates and T-groups. It is an assumption in these approaches that *task* concerns are more likely to be present in managers, and the greater emphasis in development, therefore, needs to be on *people* concerns. It is this latter concern which justifies the utilisation of the methods of training in group dynamics and interpersonal skills. The relatively unstructured situational approach of the T-group is, however, abandoned in favour of greater structure to secure greater managerial commitment to enterprise objectives of a 'real' kind.

The best known examples of the use of so-called managerial grids in management development are those advanced by Blake and Reddin. Both have comparable theoretical bases in the social sciences, although ostensibly they have different forms.

Blake's Grid

Blake's grid is the creation of Dr Robert R Blake, formerly a faculty member of the psychology department of the University of Texas. He is currently a consultant, trading as Scientific Methods Inc, of Austin, Texas, and makes available his Grid Training as an indivisible six-phase package to any mangement group which may be interested in his particular brand of management development. He is a prolific writer on group dynamics, T-group training, and management training – and his writings figure as essential reading for those who go through the grid training exercise.

The starting point for both is the simple premise that an enterprise is both an instrument of production (whether of goods or services) and a social organism based on a necessary cooperation, even if it is also characterised by a necessary conflict. Consequently, organisations are seen to have two interlaced objectives:

(a) the development of a satisfactory relationship with the external environment (customers, for example) by pursuing effectively its substantive objectives (production or service) and

(b) the creation and maintenance of a healthy, functioning organisation, or of an inside climate which will support the effective pursuit of the substantive objectives.

As a preparation for grid training managers may be asked to read literature which highlights this particular duality of organisational purpose.

On this simple premise Blake has erected a graphic model of the managerial concerns which stem from it. The horizontal axis measures the amount of the manager's concern for production – the substantive tasks of the organisation; the vertical axis measures the amount of his concern for people – the relational tasks of the organisation.

Each concern is graded through nine intervals, so that the graph presents a matrix with 81 coordinates. In practice, only five areas of the graph are separately identified and used for purposes of 'placing' managers – the four corner areas and the middle one. These may be identified in words or numbers, 'low-low' or 1.1, 'low-high' or 1.9, 'high-low' 9.1, 'intermediate' or 5.5, and 'high-high' or 9.9. In each case, the first word or number indicates the extent of the manager's concern for people, and the second the extent of the manager's concern for production. A three-point scale on each axis would serve this purpose just as well (Figure 19).

The grid thus forms a tacit invitation to the manager to locate himself on it. More than this, as 'balance' tends to be a valued condition in our culture, there is an invitation to give equal weight to the two concerns, and as there is also a high value on achievement, the invitation extends to the manager to work towards the position at the top-right-hand corner, the 9.9 position. Blake denies that this is intended by the grid approach, as there are many other

Figure 19

Main dimensions of Blake's and Reddin's Grids

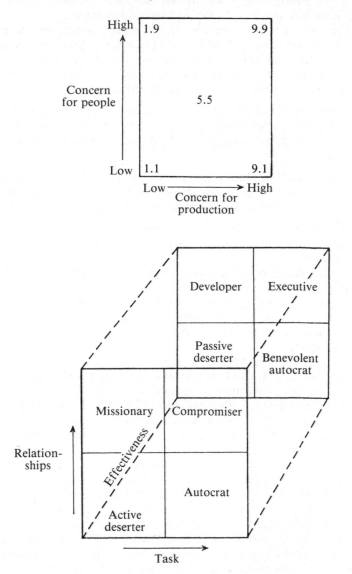

positions which might prove right or acceptable under some circumstances, but while this may be true of the intention, there is unlikely to be any escape from the pressures of the surrounding culture and, in consequence, from the unintended consequence. It is this which provides the stimulus to *development*.

Reddin's Grid

Reddin's three-dimensional grid is an extension of this same basic idea. Reddin, an academic from the University of New Brunswick, is critical of the central 'human relations' approaches of both McGregor and Blake, arguing that their concepts ignore the important question of *effectiveness* in human action. He therefore adds a third dimension of effectiveness to the two-dimensional grid offered by Blake.

Reddin has criticised the extreme simplicity of Blake's two-dimensional model along with McGregor's reliance on the assumption that attention to relationships will produce optimal performance. McGregor sees the pure relationship orientation in his Theory Y assumptions as likely to lead to optimal performance. Blake, in turn, moves beyond this in suggesting that optimality is only likely to be associated with a *combination* of concerns with production and relationships (his 9.9 style). Reddin moves one stage beyond this in advancing 'effectiveness' as a third dimension, so that any of Blake's first four positions on either of his 'concerns' may be seen as more or less effective. For Reddin, it is possible for those with, for example, a high concern for relationships and a lower concern for production to be effective or ineffective, although the optimal performance is still likely to be associated with a balanced concern, provided that it is effective.

Reddin thus continues to rely to an extent on the ideas of both McGregor and Blake, but argues that the assumptions of the one and the concerns of the other must be recast as orientations (as being more behavioural and less intellectual) and linked with a new dimension of effectiveness. Reddin's orientations are then to 'task' and 'relationships', either of which can be implemented effectively or ineffectively, according to their import for what he calls 'long-run production' – his criterion of effectiveness (Reddin, 1964, p 14).

The three-dimensional Grid makes most use of two planes, one of ineffectiveness and the other of effectiveness. On each such plane, four main 'positions' (or combinations of orientations) are depicted, each described in terms of a North American stereotype of leadership style – active and passive deserters, missionary, autocrat, compromiser, developer, benevolent autocrat, and executive. Where in Blake's grid it is the 9.9 position which is held out as the acme of performance and style, in Reddin's grid it is the 'executive' which fills this role. This 'position' becomes the preferred goal of all self-respecting managers who undergo the training exercise. This occurs in spite of Reddin's demonstration that different kinds of situation tend to throw up different styles of management, and his assertion that this is not necessarily an error (Reddin, 1985, pp 70−9).

The greater emphasis on 'effectiveness' in Reddin's grid makes it more relevant to the process of organisational development and team building. As Reddin argues, MBO is a useful tool for developing effectiveness, provided that it is used as a process of developing individual objectives within the context of the team, rather than as a device for setting objectives on a one-for-one basis between manager and subordinate. Managers who are conversant with Reddin's grid as a result of immersion are prepared for the approach to team building which uses the effectiveness concept in preparatory work and during the team building process and programme itself.

Management by (Group) Objectives usually involves a training session of two or three days away from the job, and is preceded by something like 15 to 20 hours of preparatory work by all the participants. The sessions may be run for any team at any level in the organisation, sometimes for the top team, and sometimes for more specialist teams. In each case, however, the 'team' involves the boss and his or her entire group of subordinates.

The object of the sessional meeting is to:

(a)   decide the team's actual role in the organisation and how it might best contribute to overall effectiveness;

(b)   explore the job of each team member and agree on the method by which the member's effectiveness should be judged;

(c)   decide on an optimal team organisation;

(d)   decide on how the team will make decisions in the future;

(e)   decide on key specific team objectives to be accomplished in the next six to twelve months;

(f)   agree on any other objectives which team members might suggest.

To prepare for this exercise − to ensure that it is, itself, likely to be effective − participants are asked to work out ideas and answers in advance for discussion in the session. This helps to ensure that discussion can actually start. The pre-work tasks, some of which are restricted to senior team sessions, are listed as:

1   *Introduction and objectives,* designed to indicate what the participant may expect to happen in the training session.

2   *Team members' effectiveness areas,* designed to invite the individuals to state in three or four words what effectiveness areas they could or do set objectives for, what the objectives are, and by what criteria they measure success in them.

3   *Unit effectiveness areas,* designed to ask the same kind of questions for the unit, concentrating on the criteria and criterion measures applicable.

4   *Optimal team organisation,* designed to ask for thoughts on how the organisation of the team might be improved, assuming that the required competence is available or capable of being provided by training.

5   *Team improvement objectives,* designed to ask the participants to consider what specific problems would have been solved if the team worked at a high level of effectiveness over the next year, and usually produces 30 or 40 suggestions from which the top priority areas can be agreed in the session.

6   *Team members' effectiveness,* designed to ask for suggestions as to what might be done personally by top members, other team members, and by the individual himself (or herself), to improve his effectiveness without impairing the effectiveness of the other persons.

7   *Team effectiveness evaluation,* designed to ask each participant to assess the effectiveness of the team over the preceding six months on such scales as creativity, data collection, setting objectives, planning, introducing change, implementation, productivity and evaluation.

8   *Team meeting improvements,* aim to secure ideas on whether the formality, frequency and effectiveness of the team's meetings might be improved.

9   *Team decision making,* designed to focus on the relevance of the distribution of power to decide within the team to the requirements of decision-taking in its situation.

10   *Job rotation plan,* the first of three top member questions which seeks to ascertain whether a plan of job rotation for some members of the team is desirable as likely to contribute to effectiveness.

11   *Committee structure plan,* a second such question which

invites consideration of whether more or fewer committees might increase effectiveness.

12 *Project team plan,* the third question which asks whether project groups or working parties do or could assist in achieving the objectives of the team.

13 *Senior manager review,* which prepares participants for the final evaluation session in the three-day meeting in which the manager more senior than the top member(s) of the team invites the team to say what it has achieved in the three-day event, and offers a senior management commentary on its feasibility as a plan for the future. As this more senior manager will already have participated in a similar process, he or she will probably be more open to suggestions than might otherwise be the case.

Reddin claims that something like 9 out of 10 of these sessions proves successful in increasing awareness and effectiveness.

SUMMARY

What OD seeks to achieve might be described as greater *flexibility* in thinking, feeling, and behaving, so that these different aspirations and goals may be provided with some opportunity for realisation. This flexibility may make it possible and desirable that some changes should be made, but it stops short at saying that flexibility is to be achieved so that the organisation is able to make changes if changes should prove necessary; it does not require that changes must be made in any event.

Where undertakings find themselves in the position of having to be continuously innovative, these various approaches come together. As they do so, however, they suggest new ways of construing 'messages' which have been expressed in earlier approaches. Instead of top-down approaches to the definition of tasks and other requirements, emphasis is placed on a partnership in decision-taking. Instead of a training approach, a learning facility is provided. Instead of putting training into the vestibule or the country house or hotel, it is facilitated as learning on and through the job itself (with the job becoming the essential part of the contribution which some team member makes to the overall task). Instead of a bureaucratic structure, a natural system of cooperation is aimed at, and in time, achieved.

This is not to suggest that these approaches are mutually exclusive.

Probably one of the main contributions of Peters and Waterman has been to establish that successful undertakings may need to achieve tight (disciplined and proceduralised) structures and loose (creative and experimental) structures simultaneously. For different purposes, therefore, both top-down and partnership, training and learning environments may need to be created. The demand on the diagnostician is to decide which is the more relevant to the immediate circumstances.

Reading:

Alderfer (1977).
Argyris and Schon (1978).
Bennis (1966; 1969).
Blake and Mouton (1964).
Likert (1967).
Lippitt (1969).
Miner (1973).
Reddin (1970).

Part C:
Challenges in Human Resource Management

This book has been concerned with the art of managing human resources or people. As an art, management depends on the exercise of judgements in relation to concrete events, facts, and situations. The data on which judgements are made and actions decided tend to be specific, ephemeral and uncertain in their implications. The data will vary in their specificity, ephemerality, and uncertainty with the kind of task involved: designing a new product is likely to throw up information of a different order from that found in the context of scheduling next week's production or disciplining an employee. They may also vary on these dimensions according to their situation, including the nature of the industry, the product, and its markets (or the service and its clients), but this relationship has not so far been much researched, although some broad insights have been offered on this score.

The book has focused on the principles and theories, which guide managerial judgements and influence processes in relation to people. It has tried to indicate both the limits of socially acceptable action and the means, methods, and techniques which have been found to produce desired effects. These are necessarily expressed in generalisations which, as such, cannot apply to every situation or accommodate every degree of uncertainty present in them. Faced with situational variety, it remains for the manager to judge what is relevant and useful. It is this which makes management an art, rather than a science.

Statements of principles and theories about how society attempts to control conduct, how markets operate, how people tick, or how enterprise is organised (as discussed in the first part of the book) seek to equip those who have choices to make and decisions to take with a basic understanding on which they can build. They are not deterministic and they do not remove from the manager the need to assess the nature of the immediate situation which confronts him or her.

In comparable fashion, statements (such as many of those in the second part of the book) of 'scientific' theories of causality (of the '. . . if *this* is done, then *that* has some probability of being achieved' variety) do not guarantee that if one action is taken the results will be assured. Such theories are embraced either as aids to judging, or as guides to decisions, not as replacements of them. The individual must still assess whether, and if so, how such theories can be applied to the concrete situation.

The generalisations of the management textbook can never take the place of on-the-spot judgements − that is, in relation to the idiosyncracies of the immediate situation. They may offer some guidance and comfort to the manager involved in the making of choices or decisions, or in trying to influence the thinking, feeling, and behaviour of others to achieve concrete ends. But they offer less on both counts if the situation itself changes, either for reasons beyond the control of the manager or because he or she has moved into a new position. This remains the area where the textbook can give little guidance − or comfort − but it can offer some.

A Changing Situation

The broader dimensions of the situation which management has encountered in the past few years have changed significantly, although not all managements have met with the same type or degree of change.

The changed conditions of international competition, changed levels of human resource availability, and changed physical techno-logies, rather than any significant developments in principle and theory, have led to the application of different methods and techniques from those used previously.

Since 1979 British society has been shaken out of its economic lethargy and forced to confront the realities of its trading position in the world. The values of the collectivism prevalent in the 1960s and 1970s have been placed in a kind of suspended animation. Those of individualism as an animating philosophy in economic affairs have been resurrected, although they must now relate to an institutional structure characterised by large and powerful, often multinational, business undertakings.

A number of more immediate consequences for institutions and individual behaviours have been added to these. The extent of legal regulation of business behaviour has been reduced significantly and more reductions in controls over self-interested behaviours are proposed. In the human resource area, these are likely to free more employers from the constraints on discipline and dismissal, and delay the development of a more appropriate structure of enterprise. The freedoms previously granted by law to trade unions are likely to be further restricted reducing capacity for protest. Participation rights for trade unions or workers are likely to be left to management to grant or not as they choose. Put together, these do require managers to work to different values.

Whether this new approach will benefit society as a whole will continue to be debated by the politicians. The gamble is that it will provide adequate incentives for a new race of entrepreneurs to increase the country's wealth and secure general acceptance by tapping the folk memory of a former golden age (when the country was prosperous). Only if it succeeds is there likely to be sufficient cash in the national kitty to take care of those who fail through misfortune. Only if it succeeds quickly enough is the demand for protection in those industries faced with international competition, and of those workers faced with a new sweated labour condition, likely to prove resistable.

What it does do, however, is create situations that differ from one another in their susceptibility to control by various known methods and techniques. It is likely to increase the sheer *variety* of methods found in any cross section of industry, as the separate parts respond to quite different situational elements. Three of these elements are likely to prove important in the context of human resource management – changed markets, changed technologies, and changed 'human resources' (defined particularly by their capacities and their motivation).

Market Changes

Changes in government industrial policy have occurred in the context of a world trade recession which has simultaneously subjected British industry to market pressures. One effect of this has been to create more (BCG-type) 'dogs' and to reduce cash availability within undertakings as prices have become more competitive.

The tighter financial strait-jacket which recession has imposed on most of manufacturing industry has stimulated managerial consideration of the need for new market strategies. But monetary control, like budgetary control, is a comparatively blunt instrument. It signals that something needs to be done, but does little to indicate what it might be. A first response is usually to cut costs, and, labour costs being comparatively easy to cut, shedding labour becomes the main means by which a first adjustment to new circumstances is made. Internal labour markets are converted into external ones, with the attendant loss of investment in human assets.

In many instances, particularly in the traditional industries, undertakings have been faced with the immediate necessity of reducing their unit labour costs by significant amounts – of the order of 50 per cent – in order to meet the competition in domestic or world markets. This has led management to require immediate productivity improvements of a sizeable order, not small annual improvements over some years, as a condition of continued operation, with redundancy as the alternative option, frequently adopted as the initial response. The figures recently produced on comparative unit labour costs in British and competitor nations' manufacturing industries, indicate that there remains a sizeable gap still to be closed on this dimension (National Institute Economic Review, No 120, 1987). A first source of cost reductions is the opportunity to make employees redundant, at a time when techno-logical improvement is not markedly increasing the amount of new employment available.

The effect is likely to continue the trend towards greater depen-dence on services than on manufacturing, which, as entry costs in respect of manufacturing are unlikely to fall, will also be fostered by the new entrepreneurialism (Rajan, 1987). As a consequence, manufacturing is likely to be concentrated in fewer business under-takings, even if into dispersed plants to reduce the relative costs of transport to markets.

Whether this stimulus will lead to more widespread developments of long-term corporate strategies based on the real properties of the market, is another open question. In so far as this happens, the effect is likely to be a more streamlined matching of production capacities to market conditions, along the lines indicated by Porter's characterisation of strategic options open to those not in a market leadership position (Porter, 1985).

Technological Developments

The second main option open to management in these conditions is to seek price reductions in the product or service being offered by introducing new technologies. These may be mechanical techno-logies which effect a substitution of capital for labour and either lead to redundancy or increased labour flexibility (ACAS, 1987; Daniel, 1987). Redundancy sacrifices any investment in the human assets of the undertaking; labour flexibility tends to increase it (as the undertaking bears the cost of developing new skills). They may also be organisational technologies which may be based on a 'slimmed-down' workforce or associated with the need to accommodate greater flexibility amongst multi-skilled managers and non-managers alike.

Technological development bears a cost, and in recession conditions finding the finance to support it is often a difficult or impossible task. It becomes easier only if the financial institutions are willing to invest on a longish term promise of substantial gain, and this is an area in which Britain may be at a disadvantage compared with some major competitors. The response is often, therefore, one of attempting to pull the undertaking up by its own bootstraps, and this is only possible under certain limited conditions of enterprise control.

Nevertheless, undertakings and industries do make the change-over and find themselves more closely involved in high-tech operations, which offer a number of challenges and opportunities for restructuring the working environment. These are frequently identified as requirements and opportunities for greater flexibility – of working (time) patterns, skill-utilisation, conditions of employment (as with harmonisation), and organisational relationships. But the introduction of new systems, such as CAM and CAD, based on chip technology, usually imposes a necessary period of learning about how to cope with the new element in the production system, and the role of 'training' is thereby extended.

This same requirement of flexibility tends to reflect itself in the growth of more organic systems of organisation, replacing the more staid bureaucratic structures, appropriate to more stable past environments but ill suited to the more volatile current ones. The new structures emphasise open communications (which may be assisted by new communications technologies) through less rigidly structured role-relationships, and the contributory nature of the role of the multi-skilled worker. Authority acquires a new meaning in these circumstances, becoming more firmly based on qualifications and track record, and less firmly linked to 'position' within some authority structure. One effect, particularly in the context of significant technological changes, is a reduction in the average age of the workforce as more recently qualified personnel are brought in to handle the new systems in a more open fashion.

Human Capacity and Attitude

It has been suggested that people's attitudes have changed in the direction of a 'new' or greater realism in economic affairs. Support for this is found in voting patterns in recent elections, the results of strike ballots, and the decline in union membership. Daniel's recent

(1987) survey of industry's experience with the introduction of new technology, suggests, *inter alia,* that changes are less difficult to secure than had been widely supposed. This could betoken a major long-term shift in perspectives but could be no more than a simple pragmatic adjustment to altered circumstances. Daniel's study allows both that the changes might be fully accepted and that the rather peremptory approach to their introduction, in many cases, might lead to later rejection when circumstances change. In either event, the changes may be significant for human resource management, if the conditions which either initiated the change or supported it are maintained.

A similar conclusion might be reached about changes in motivation: people are likely to make the best they can of their circumstances, even if they may seek to change these in the longer run. This can be illustrated from the responses made to opportunities to work shorter or flexible hours. These are likely to attract both those who would prefer full-time regular work but see no chance of securing it, and those who would not 'want' to work 'full-time' because of 'their circumstances', even if it were on offer to them. The perceived necessity for others to hold on to the jobs they already have, in the face of widespread redundancy, might also result in changed predispositions to perform to higher standards and to cooperate in changed working practices. In both cases, however, the change may be 'circumstantial' not fundamental.

Changes in human resource capacities may, however, prove more significant. The denial of work and training opportunities to large numbers of young people, and the dismissal of many older workers to premature retirement, have together reduced the present and likely future stock of available skills. The failure, as yet, to produce any very effective national training scheme for young people promises that the future supply may be deficient in quantity and quality. The period during which the economy can eat into the capital stock of skill is likely to prove extremely short.

Such schemes as have been tried so far have depended largely on central government initiatives. As government spokesmen are so prone to argue, however, government is not able to provide the training or experience needed without the help of industry itself. Industry has participated in YOPS and YTS and other such ventures, but as yet there has been no very real attempt by industry to take on board the problem of young person training. The control of training by occupational groups themselves (for example, through apprenticeship or professional qualifications) has been significantly reduced in many areas, but employing organisations (other than a few associated with new technologies) have not yet fully accepted the need for them to assume control. This, too, could prove to be a temporary phenomenon, but a more fundamental change is likely to await industry's experience of severe problems of recruitment.

Impact on the Management of Human Resource

Such changes in industrial policies, markets, and technologies have produced responses in the approach made by industry to human resource management. Indeed, the very concept of human resource management is itself seen by some as one response, implying a need to move away from a soft, welfare-linked conception of personnel management and towards a harder, business-oriented approach to the management of the labour resource.

This is considered to be immediately manifest in the readier use of the redundancy option in the undertakings most severely affected and in pressures to secure major reductions in unit labour costs in others. These have produced little that is novel in the way of methods or techniques, but many renamed and relaunched services have been gathered together to suggest that something new has been developed. How these changes in market structures, technologies, and attitudes will affect the management of human resources over the longer term is more difficult to forecast, partly because the stimuli themselves are not universally found in industry and partly because much of the response already made has been traditional.

Where changes have been made at the leading edge of the new management realism, they have produced new definitions of the problem in at least eight main areas of human resource management (other than that of redundancy itself), and these may prove significant for the future development of approach and method:

1   *The first affects industry's demand for new types of skill*
The usual form taken by this changed demand is for more extensive skills, applicable to a wider range of work tasks, with consequences for greater flexibility in working practices. Both managers and workers in the high-tech areas are expected to be multi-skilled. As work tasks of the core and peripheral workers are defined, the core becomes composed of multi-skilled personnel and the periphery of single skilled specialists often providing the 'expert' back-up to the generalists. In other working situations, many of the artificial job demarcations have been removed. Where these were upheld by agreement with the unions, they have often been negotiated out of existence.

2   *The second affects patterns of working hours, these being linked to extensions of plant operating periods*
A much wider variety of working patterns gets away from the fixed-hour working day, working week, working year concepts, and for some people their range of choice in working patterns has been increased. In high-tech undertakings, this may be associated with different patterns applied to core and peripheral workers; in other organisations, it may be linked with variations in customer-initiated work loads during the working week or during the year (as in the seasonal industries). (Connock, October 1985, p 36).

3   *The third affects the undertaking's training strategy*
Recession has drawn many undertakings back from the more corporatist type of strategy in which undertaking-specific skills are developed 'in-house', although some continue with it. Those others who have reduced their generally limited involvement in training activities are necessarily living on previously accumulated capital, but the shortening of planning horizons may lead them to regard this as an acceptable price to pay in recession conditions. Government-funded schemes, such as YTS, have been developed to fill some of the gaps, but these remain a pale imitation of schemes which have for years been run in competitor economies. In spite of acceptance of the desirability of reducing government expenditures, pressure continues to be applied to have the government fund training activities, albeit with more industrial direction, as a public service.

4   *A fourth and related impact has been on the recruitment and selection function.*
On the face of it, a period of high unemployment ought to make for easier recruitment and selection (in the sense of meeting industry's requirements) at a lower *per capita* cost. This occurs when the need remains for comparatively unskilled or generally skilled labour, because many undertakings are now able to capitalise on the stock of skill accumulated in the preceding period. But it does not happen in all cases, and the demand for specifically skilled labour – at both managerial and non-managerial levels – remains unmet from the existing supply. Thus trends already visible suggest that some strategic action to improve the skill stock is urgently required, whether this is achieved through a public education and training service or by industry itself.

5   *Remuneration practice has been affected in a rather patchy manner*
Wage and salary rates generally have continued to rise at levels

above the rate of inflation in the economy. This appears to be because both individual bargaining (for example, in relation to professional and managerial jobs, and in the service sector particularly) and collective bargaining (on behalf of the organised workers remaining in employment) have succeeded in securing a share of the cost savings from either technological change or redundancy for the workers concerned.

The composition and structure of the pay packet have, however, changed markedly in some widely reported cases in the financial and economic services sectors and among senior management positions where performance-related pay has been developed extensively. In some of these cases, and particularly those applying to junior staff, the developments are at least partly a response to cost-push factors in the booming south-eastern part of the country. In many other work situations, where such cost pressures are less apparent, the composition of the pay packet has changed much less dramatically in this direction of greater dependence of pay on delivered performance.

6   *Another significant impact has been on the approach to communication within organisations*
There is a widely held view that further improvements in communication are necessary and desirable, particularly in the context of advanced technology, in order to improve human judgement at all levels. A recent survey of managerial opinions on communications within their organisations revealed that company-employee communication was thought to be deteriorating, and in spite of the reporting requirements of the Employment Act, 1982, showed little positive development (only about a fifth stating that this had brought about specific improvement). It also recorded that communications remained heavily dependent on notice boards and written circulars (although almost three quarters now made use of briefing groups and a half of videos) (Vista Communications, 1987).

Nevertheless, in some organisations developments in communications technology, allowing workers direct access to terminals, have made it more possible for 'data' or 'pure information' to be disseminated widely throughout the working groups. There may, however, be a danger in communicating pure information in this way, because this fails to encourage feelings of loyalty to others within the undertaking or the working group. It may therefore be necessary to supplement this with direct interpersonal communication, 'contaminated' though this may be, in order to foster affective ties among employees. Some of these responses are essentially 'organisational', in the sense of scheduling meetings to consider data so that the wishes, aspirations, and evaluations of others are communicated along with the 'pure information'.

7   *These same technical developments, coupled with policies on recognition of representative bodies, have also had an impact on the achievement of organisation-wide loyalty and commitment to goals*

The evidence suggests that at least some undertakings are moving in the direction of breaking down traditional barriers to communication, whether these be occupational demarcations (for example, process *v* maintenance), or grade distinctions (for example, staff *v* manual workers). Anecdotal evidence also suggests that some organisations are deliberately reducing their reliance on union organisations as a source of recruiting commitment or of discipline. Withdrawal of union negotiating rights and a substitution of alternative channels of communication is increasingly frequently reported. Such changes, where they occur, tend to produce looser organisational structures. But these changes are not universal: the aforementioned Vista Communications study found that two thirds of the organisations still relied heavily on union representatives as a communication channel to the workforce.

8   *The final impact of note is that on the specialist personnel management function itself*

This is separate from the impact on the function which arises from the separate effects of changes in specific areas of activity. The increasing prevalence of the market as a source of problem-definition, and the greater availability of relatively unskilled labour has tended to draw authority back to line management. Progress towards legislative deregulation and the curbing of trade union power has tended to encourage the slimming down of specialist personnel departments as the perceived need for specialist competence in this area is reduced.

Although all these changes do not necessarily appear in the same undertaking, where they have occurred, their effect has been to alter the numerical and authority relationships between personnel specialists and line management in favour of the latter. Consistently, activity within the slimmed-down and decentralised personnel departments has often polarised between the routinely administrative and the more creatively corporate tasks as the departmental managerial link between the two has been removed. The consequential threat in this is that the occupation will cease to contain within itself a specialist career path leading from the basic routine tasks to the corporate policy-making concerns, as managerial careers become more spiralist.

Implications

The greater emphasis on an orientation to business or service mission, both defined more directly in efficiency terms, can be expected to ensure that the undertaking's relationship with customers or clients will in future have a more marked effect on the kind of human resource approach which it adopts. It is also likely that this same orientation will demand greater emphasis on human resource 'strategy' than on personnel 'policy' (where the one indicates a plan of action directed at concrete results, and the other a set of guiding principles on how the agents of the undertaking will approach the resolution of its problems).

The basic orientation is likely, as a consequence, to imply that the way in which the human resource question is approached will vary from one category of market/client situation to another. There is a strong suggestion in the existing literature than not all situations are alike, but may nevertheless be classified into a small number of categories (Blau and Scott, 1963; BCG, 1970; Porter 1985; etc). There is also a strong suggestion that both the organisation and the substantive content of the managerial response to the human resource question varies fairly systematically from one category to another (Woodward, 1958; Thomason, 1985). This observation applies to the variable incidence of emphasis on strategy or policy, and is, for this reason, most likely to affect the extent to which the core methods of the personnel specialist are relied on in any given situation.

This implies that more so in the future than in the past, the practice of human resource management will have a leading edge which both pushes the frontiers forward and attracts publicity for so doing, and a fuzzy wake, which meets minimum requirements of law and convention and makes some use of more developed techniques where it can, without aiming to lead in their use.

It leads to the suggestion that some undertakings will require their managers to be creative and to provide opportunities for development; others will have less need of this and may, in any event, be less well provided with cash resources to permit it to happen. The requirement for human resource management and for personnel management specialists will vary in consequence.

At the leading edge human resource management will focus more creatively than in the past on eight types of task:

(a)   analysing and diagnosing the trends in markets and resource capacity and selecting winning strategies appropriate to them, taking account of the real properties of both external and internal environments;

(b)   introducing new physical and organisational technologies which match corporate objectives or the market-mission, and allow the human resource strengths of the organisation (where it has some) to be deployed to greatest effect;

(c)   establishing flexibility in working and employment patterns to support the economically dictated operational needs, not only to meet the undertaking's strategic needs but also to provide a wider range of choice to workers;

(d)   securing worker commitment in the absence of conventional organisational regimentation and simple monetary incentives, by developing core values and methods of encouragement and reinforcement which respect the holistic conception of the human being;

(e)   coping with computer-assisted coordination of diffused and dispersed contributions from peripheral workers supporting a small entrepreneurial core of multi-skilled 'professionals', in an imaginative way which makes use of modern communications technologies but acknowledges that people thrive on more than raw data;

(f)   determining, by full consideration of the existing cultural values, the core values which will animate the activities of the members of the undertaking in their dealings with outsiders and with one another;

(g)   creating an open and humane structure of relationships which will sustain these values as the strategies are pursued effectively;

(h)   creating opportunities for members of the organisation to learn through their work tasks and interactions more about how to cope with the situation and about how to work in a co-operative environment.

Many of these will necessarily confront and challenge existing cultural values and traditional practices.

In the fuzzy wake, on the other hand, human resource management will focus more on control of labour resource allocation and involve specialists as advisers to and supports for the line management in resolving problems associated with the labour process.

The specialist service is likely to continue to focus on fire-fighting and trouble shooting, and to be based on a lower level of sophistication. It will tend to emphasise the collection and collation of data and information (on labour availability, rates of remuneration, etc,) for use by line management in reaching the decisions with which it is charged. Utilisation of electronic means of collating and distributing data will help to facilitate the withdrawal of authority to the line managers. Human resource strategies and policies will tend to be minimal and espoused rather than explicit.

For the rest, conventional solutions to problems (defintion of duties, organisation of authority, structure of communication, dealing with organised labour, etc,) will tend to remain based on the exercise of personal authority. This will serve to reduce the likelihood of developing complex bureaucratic structures to sustain a highly sophisticated and 'impersonal' approach to the human resource question. It will also more directly match the limited availability of resources to be applied to this function. Inevitably, more reliance will be placed on external agencies (for the training of workers or managers, negotiations with unions, handling grievances and complaints) to avoid the need to maintain such expensive bureaucratic structures within the undertaking itself.

The art of human resource management is, therefore, one based on the ability to exercise judgement of what in terms of human resource strategy is appropriate to what, in terms of both economic and social situations, confronts the undertaking. The day of the specialist who humps around a repertoire of specific 'personnel' methods and techniques for universal application is probably numbered, and certainly he is unlikely to secure a foothold in the leading edge undertaking: the only chapmen in personnel management in future will be independent consultants who subcontract for specific tasks in this type of undertaking. What the specialist needs to possess is an aptitude and an ability to make judgements, a knowledge of principles which might inform the development of methods and techniques, and a skill in persuading others, in management or out of it, to adopt practices which are likely to pay off for both organisation and individuals.

Bibliography

Note: references commencing pp refer to pages in the publication quoted.
References commencing ... refer to the pages in this text.

A

ABEGGLEN, J C: *The Japanese Factory,* Free Press, 1958
ABELL, D: 'Industrial Relations and Safety Representation' in *Personnel Review*, 8 (3), 1979, pp 30-3 ... 152
ABELL, P (ed): *Organizations as Bargaining and Influence Systems,* Heinemann, 1975
ACTON SOCIETY TRUST: *Size and Morale,* Acton Society Trust, 1953 and 1957 ... 4
ACTON SOCIETY TRUST: *Management Succession,* Acton Society Trust, 1956
ADAMS, R: 'Performance Appraisal and Counselling' in Torrington, D P and Sutton, D F (eds): *Handbook of Management Development,* Gower, 1973, pp 219-60 ... 257
ADVISORY CONCILIATION and ARBITRATION SERVICE: *Industrial Relations Handbook,* HMSO, 1980
ACAS: Annual Reports, HMSO/ACAS, 1975 onwards
ACAS: *Code of Industrial Relations Practice,* HMSO, 1972
ACAS: *Code of Practice No. 1, Disciplinary Practice and Procedures in Employment,* ACAS, 1977 ... 131
ACAS: *Code of Practice No. 2, Disclosure of Information to Trade Unions for Collective Bargaining Purposes,* ACAS, 1977
ACAS: *Code of Practice No. 3, Time Off for Trade Union Duties and Activities,* ACAS, 1977 ... 153
ACAS: *Redundancy Arrangements,* ACAS, 1987 ... 275, 501
AHAMAD, B and BLAUG, M (eds): *The Practice of Manpower Planning,* Elsevier, 1973
AJIFERUKE, M, and BODDEWYN, J: 'Culture and Other Variables in Comparative Management Studies' in *Academy of Management Journal,* 13, 1970, pp 153-63 ... 117
ALBRIGHT, L E, GLENNON, J R and SMITH, W J: *The Use of Psychological Tests in Industry,* Muksgaard, Copenhagen, 1963
ALBROW, M C: *Bureaucracy,* Macmillan, 1970
ALDERFER, C P: 'Job Enlargement and the Organisational Context' in *Personnel Psychology,* 22, 1969, pp 418-26 ... 43, 495

510

ALDERFER, C P: *Existence Relatedness and Growth, Human Needs in Organizational Settings,* Free Press, 1972 ... 65, 66, 88

ALDERFER, C P: 'An Empirical Test of a new Theory of Human Needs' in *Organisational Behaviour and Human Performance,* 4, 1969, pp 142-75

ALDERFER, C: 'Organisational Development' in *Annual Review of Psychology,* 28, 1977, pp 197-223

ALDERFER, C and MCCORD, C: 'Personal and Situational Factors in the Recruitment Interview' in *Journal of Applied Psychology,* 54 (4), 1970, pp 377-85 ... 297

ALLEN, D: 'A Review of Process Theories of Decision-Making' in *Management Education and Development,* 8 (2), 1977, pp 79-94 ... 23

ALLEN, G C: *The Structure of British Industry,* Longmans, 1961

ALLEN, G C: *Monopoly and Restrictive Practices,* Allen and Unwin, 1968

ALLEN, G C: *British Industry and Economic Policy,* Macmillan, 1979 ... 23, 135

ALLPORT, F H: 'Attitudes' in Murchison, G (ed), *Handbook of Social Psychology,* Clark U P, 1935 ... 442, 466

ALLPORT, G W: *Personality,* Constable, 1937 ... 7, 88

ALLPORT, G W, VERNON, P E and LINDZAY, G: *Study of Values,* Houghton-Mifflin, 3rd edn., 1960 ... 60

AMERICAN COUNCIL of PROFIT-SHARING INDUSTRIES: *Profit-sharing Manual,* ACPSI, 1949 ... 393

AMERICAN MANAGEMENT ASSOCIATION: *Rating Employee and Supervisory Performance,* AMA, 1950 ... 357

AMY, R: 'Pensions After 1988: Sizing up the Options' in *Personnel Management,* December, 1986, pp 42-5

ANASTASI, A: *Individual Differences,* Wiley, 1965

ANASTASI, A: *Psychological Testing,* Macmillan, 1961, 5th edn, 1982 ... 50-59, 88

ANDREWS, K R: *The Effectiveness of University Management Development Programmes,* Graduate Division, Harvard University, 1966 ... 77

ANDREWS, K R: 'Towards Professionalism in Business Management' in *Harvard Business Review,* March-April, 1969, pp 49-60

ANGEL, J: *How to Prepare Yourself for an Industrial Tribunal,* IPM, 1980 ... 131

ANNETT, J: 'Training in Theory and Practice' in Warr, 1978, q.v. pp 59-75

ANNETT, J: *The Role of Knowledge of Results in Learning: A Survey Report No. 342-3,* US Naval Training Devices Center, 1961

ANNETT, J and DUNCAN, K D: 'New Media and Methods' in Robinson, J and Barnes, N (eds): *Industrial Training,* BBC, 1968 ... 86

ANNETT, J and DUNCAN, K D: 'Task Analysis and Training Design' in *Occupational Psychology,* 41, 1967, pp 211-21 ... 311

ANNETT, J, DUNCAN, K D, STAMMERS, R B and GRAY, M J: *Task Analysis,*

DE Training Information Paper No. 6, HMSO, 1971; MSC, 1979 … 327

ANNETT, J and KAY, H: 'Skilled Performance' in *Occupational Psychology*, 30, 1956, pp 112-17

ANSOFF, H I: *Corporate Strategy,* Penguin, 1975 … 2

ANSOFF, H I and STEWART, J M: 'Strategies for a Technology Based Business' in *Harvard Business Review*, 45, 1967, pp 72-83

ANSTEY, E: *Staff Reporting and Staff Development,* Allen and Unwin, 1961

ANSTEY, E and MERCER, E O: *Interviewing for Selection of Staff,* Allen and Unwin, 1956

ANSTEY, E, FLETCHER, C and WALKER, J: *Staff Appraisal and Development,* Allen and Unwin, 1966

ANTHONY, P D: *The Conduct of Industrial Relations,* IPM, 1977 … 18

ANTHONY, P D and CRICHTON, A: *Industrial Relations and the Personnel Specialists,* Batsford, 1969

ARBOSE, J R: 'Quality Control Circles: The West Adopts a Japanese Concept' in *International Management*, 38 (12), December, 1980, pp 31-9

ARENSBERG, C M and MCGREGOR, D: 'Determinants of Morale in an Industrial Company' in *Applied Psychology*, 1, 1942, pp 12-34

ARGYLE, M: 'The Concepts of Role and Status' in *Sociological Review*, 44 (3), 1952, pp 39-49

ARGYRIS, C: *Executive Leadership,* Harper and Bros, 1953 … 93

ARGYRIS, C: *Strategy, Change and Defensive Routines,* Ballinger, 1955

ARGYRIS, C: *Personality and Organisation,* Harper, 1957

ARGYRIS, C: *Understanding Organisational Behaviour,* Tavistock, 1960

ARGYRIS, C: *Interpersonal Competence and Organisational Effectiveness,* Tavistock, 1962

ARGYRIS, C: *Integrating the Individual and the Organization,* Wiley, 1964 … 472

ARGYRIS, C: 'Organisational Leadership in Participative Management' in Huneryager, S G and Heckman, I L, 1967, q.v. pp

ARGYRIS, C: 'The Incompleteness of Social Psychological Theory' in *American Psychologist*, 24, 1969, pp 893-908

ARGYRIS, C: *Reasoning, Learning and Action: Individual and Organisation,* Jossey Bass, 1982

ARGYRIS, C: 'Dangers in Applying Results from Experimental Social Psychology' in *American Psychologist*, 30, 1975, pp 469-85

ARGYRIS, C: 'Theories of Action that Inhibit Individual Learning' in *American Psychologist*, 31, 1975, pp 638-54

ARGYRIS, C and SCHON, D A: *Theory in Practice,* Jossey Bass, 1974 … 11, 13, 15, 16, 23, 286, 495

ARGYRIS, C and SCHON, D A: *Organisational Learning: A Theory of Action Perspective,* Addison-Wesley, 1978

ARMSTRONG, M: *A Handbook of Personnel Management Practice,* Kogan Page, revised edn, 1984

ARMSTRONG, M and MURLIS, H: *A Handbook of Salary Administration,* Kogan Page, 1980 ... 399

ARMSTRONG, P J, GOODMAN, J F B, and HYMAN, J D: *Ideology and Shop Floor Industrial Relations,* Croom Helm, 1981 ... 114

ARMSTRONG, SIR W: *Personnel Management in the Civil Service,* HMSO, 1971

ARVEY, R D and CAMPION, J E: 'The Employment Interview: A Summary and Review of Recent Research' in *Journal of Applied Psychology,* 35 (2), Summer, 1982, pp 281-322 ... 297

ASCH, S E: 'Effects of Group Pressure upon the Modification and Distortion of Judgements' in Guetzkow, H (ed), *Groups, Leadership, and Men,* Carnegie Press, 1951, and in Cartwright and Zander, 1953, q.v. pp 151-62 ... 438

ASCH, S E: *Social Psychology,* Prentice Hall, 1952

ASH, P: 'The Reliability of Job Evaluation Ratings' in *Journal of Applied Psychology,* 32, 1948, pp 313-20, and in Karn and Gilmer, 1952, q.v. pp 151-62 ... 347

ATKINSON, J W: 'Motivational Determinants of Risk-Taking Behaviour' in *Psychological Review,* 64, 1957, pp 359-72

B

BADGER, A: *Man in Employment,* Arthur Barker, 1958

BAILEY, C T: *The Measurement of Job Performance,* Gower, 1983

BAILEY, J: *Job Design and Work Organisation,* Prentice Hall, 1983 ... 111

BAIN, G S (ed): *Industrial Relations in Britain,* Blackwell, 1983 ... 156, 363

BALDAMUS, W: *Efficiency and Effort,* Tavistock, 1961 ... 32, 45, 178

BALDAMUS, W: 'Type of Work and Motivation' in *British Journal of Sociology,* 2, 1952, pp 44-58

BALES, R F: *Interaction Process Analysis,* Addison-Wesley Press, 1951 ... 312

BALES, R F and STRODTBECK, F L: 'Phases in Group Problem-solving', in Cartwright and Zander, 1953, q.v. pp 386-400

BALFOUR, C: *Participation in Industry,* Croom Helm, 1973a

BALFOUR: C: *Unions and the Law,* Saxon House, 1973b

BALL, J M and SKEOCH, N K: *Inter-plant Comparisons of Productivity and Earnings,* Dept of Employment Working Paper, No. 3, Unit for Manpower Studies, Dept of Employment, May, 1981

BARBER, D: *The Practice of Personnel Management,* IPM, 1979

BARBER, J W: *Industrial Training Handbook,* Iliffe Books, 1968

BARKER, R G, 'The Social Inter-relations of Strangers and Acquaintances' in *Sociometry,* 5, 1942, pp 169-79

BARNARD, C I: *The Functions of the Executive,* Harvard U P, 1938 ... 23, 342

BARNARD, C I: 'The Functions and Pathologies of Status Systems in Formal Organizations' in Whyte, W F (ed), *Industry and Society,* McGraw Hill, 1946, pp 207-43

BARRON, and MORRIS: *Sexual Division and the Dual Labour Market,* Barker and Allen, 1976 ... 171, 178

BARTHOLOMEW, D J (ed): *Manpower Planning: Selected Readings,* Penguin, 1976 ... 269, 275

BARTHOLOMEW, D J, HOPES, R F A and SMITH, A R: 'Manpower Planning in the Face of Uncertainty' in *Personnel Review*, 5 (3), Summer, 1976, pp 5-17, and in Smith (1980), q.v. pp 126-53 ... 275

BARTHOLOMEW, D J and MORRIS, B R (eds): *Aspects of Manpower Planning,* English Universities Press, 1971

BARTLETT, J B: *Success and Failure in Quality Circles,* Employment Relations Resource Centre, Cambridge, 1983 ... 430

BASKIN, O W and ARONOFF, C: *Interpersonal Communication in Organisations,* Scott Foreman, 1979 ... 188, 414, 415

BASNETT, D: 'Disclosure of Information – A Union View' in Kessler and Weekes, 1971, q.v. pp 115-23

BASS, B M: *Leadership, Psychology and Organizational Behaviour,* Harper, 1960

BASS, B M and VAUGHAN, J A: *Training in Industry – The Management of Learning,* Tavistock, 1966 ... 8, 79, 81, 327

BASSETT, P: *Strike Free, New Industrial Relations in Britain,* Macmillan, 1986

BEACH, D S: *Personnel Management of People at Work,* Macmillan, 3rd edn, 1975 ... 218, 470, 475

BEDAWY, K M: 'Design and Content of Management Education: American Style' in *Management International Review*, 18 (3), March, 1978, pp 75-82

BEENSTOCK, M and IMMANUEL: H: 'The Market Approach to Pay Comparability' in *National Westminster Bank Review*, November, 1979, pp 26-41

BEER, M: 'Performance Appraisal, Dilemmas and Possibilities' in *Organisational Dynamics*, 9, 1981, pp 24-36

BEER, M, RUH, R, DAWSON, J A, MCCAN, B B, and KAVANAGH, M J: 'A Performance Measurement System: Research, Design, Introduction and Evaluation' in *Personnel Psychology*, 31, 1978, pp 505-35

BEESLEY, M and HUGHES, M D: *Corporate Social Responsibility: A Reassessment,* Croom Helm, 1978

BEHREND, H: 'The Field of Industrial Relations' in *British Journal of Industrial Relations*, I, 1963, pp 383-94

BEHREND, H: 'The Effort Bargain' in *Industrial and Labour Relations Review*, 10 (4), 1957, pp 503-15 ... 32, 45, 74, 178, 368

BEHREND, H: 'A New Approach to the Analysis of Absence from Work' in *Industrial Relations Journal*, 5 (4), Winter, 1974-5, pp 4-21 ... 275

BEHREND, H and POCOCK, S: 'Absence and the Individual' in *International Labour Review*, 114 (3), November/December, 1976, pp 311-27 ... 275

BELBIN, E: *Training the Adult Worker,* Problems of Progress in Industry, No. 15, HMSO, 1964

BELBIN, E and BELBIN, R M: *Problems in Adult Retraining,* Heinemann, 1972 ... 327

BELBIN, R M: *The Discovery Method in Training,* HMSO, 1969 ... 327

BELL, D J: *Planning Corporate Manpower,* Longmans, 1974 ... 252, 265, 269, 271, 275

BENNIS, W G: *Changing Organizations,* McGraw Hill, 1966 ... 471, 472, 479, 495

BENNIS, W G: *Organizational Development,* Addison-Wesley, 1969 ... 495

BENNIS, W G, BENNE, K D and CHIN, R: *The Planning of Change,* Holt, Rinehart and Winston, 1961, 2nd edn, 1969

BENNIS, W G, BERKOWITZ, N, AFFINITO, M, and MALONE, M: 'Authority, Power and the Ability to Influence' in *Human Relations*, 11, 1958, pp 143-55

BERGER, C J and CUMMINGS, L L: 'Organisational Structure, Attitudes and Behaviour' in Staw and Cummings, 1979, q.v. pp 169-208

BERGER, S and PIORE, M: *Dualism and Discontinuity in Industrial Societies*, Cambridge UP, 1980 ... 171

BERNARDIN, H J and BUCKLEY, M R: 'A Consideration of Strategies in Rater Training' in *Academy of Management Review*, 6, 1981, pp 205-12

BETTELHEIM, B and JANOWITZ, M: *The Dynamics of Prejudice,* Harper and Row, 1950 ... 442

BEVERSTOCK, A G: *Industrial Training Practices,* Classic Publications, 1969

BEYNON, H and BLACKBURN, R M: *Perceptions of Work: Variations Within a Factory,* Cambridge UP, 1972 ... 45, 441

BILODEAU, E A and BILODEAU, I McD: 'Variable Frequency of Knowledge of Results and the Learning of a Simple Skill' in *Journal of Experimental Psychology*, 55, 1958, pp 379-83 ... 316, 327

BILODEAU, E A and BILODEAU, I McD: *Principles of Skill Acquisition,* Academic Press, 1969 ... 316, 327

BILODEAU, I McD: 'Information Feedback' in Bilodeau, E A (ed): *Acquisition of Skill*, Academic Press, 1966 ... 316, 327

BINDRA, D and STEWART: J, *Motivation,* Penguin, 1971

BION, W R: *Experiences in Groups,* Tavistock Publications, 1961 ... 457

BITTNER, R: 'Developing an Employee Merit Rating Procedure' in *Personnel Psychology*, 2, 1948, pp 403-32, and in Dooher and Marquis, 1950, q.v. pp 20-34 ... 345

BLACKABY, F: *The Future of Pay Bargaining,* Heinemann, 1980 ... 399

BLACKABY, F: *De-Industrialization,* Heinemann, 1978

BLACKBURN, R M: *Union Character and Social Class,* Batsford, 1967 ... 136, 156

BLACKBURN, R M and MANN, N: *The Working Class in the Labour Market,* Macmillan, 1979 ... 175

BLACKLER, F and BROWN, C: *Job Redesign and Management Control,* Saxon House, 1978 ... 45

BLAIR, J: 'Three Studies in Improving Clerical Work' in *Personnel Management*, February, 1974, pp 34-7 ... 45

BLAKE, R R and MOUTON, J S: *The Managerial Grid,* Gulf Publishing Company, 1964 ... 479, 488-91, 495

BLAKE, R R and MOUTON, J S: 'Using Line Instructors for Organisation Development' in *Training and Development International*, 20, 1966, pp 28-35

BLAKE, R, and MOUTON, J: 'Loyalty of Representatives to In-Group Positions during Inter-Group Conflict', in *Sociometry*, 24, 1961, pp 177-84

BLAKE, R, and MOUTON, J: 'The Inter-Group Dynamics of Win-Lose Conflict and Problem-Solving Collaboration in Union-Management Relations' in Sherif, M (ed): *Inter-Group Relations and Leadership,* Wiley, 1962, pp 95-140

BLAU, P: *The Dynamics of Bureaucracy,* University of Chicago Press, 1955 ... 194

BLAU, P and SCOTT W R: *Formal Organizations,* Routledge and Kegan Paul, 1963 ... 72, 207, 285, 507

BLOOD, J W: *The Personnel Job in a Changing World,* AMA, 1964

BLOOM, B S et al: *Taxonomy of Educational Objectives,* Handbook I, Cognitive Domain, David MacKay, 1956 ... 312

BLOOMFIELD, M and WILLITTS, J H: *Personnel and Employment Problems in Industrial Management,* American Academy of Political and Social Science, 1916 ... 236

BLUM, F H: *Work and Community,* Routledge and Kegan Paul, 1968 ... 220

BLUM, M L and NAYLOR, J C: *Industrial Psychology,* Harper and Row, 1968 ... 308

BOARD of TRADE: *The Conduct of Company Directors,* HMSO, 1977

BODDEWYN, J (ed): *Comparative Management: Teaching, Training and Research,* New York Graduate School of Business Administration, 1970

BOELLA, M J: *Personnel Management in the Hotel and Catering Industry,* Barrie and Jenkins, 1974

BOSEMAN, G F G and JONES, R E: 'Market Conditions, Decentralization and Organizational Effectiveness', in *Human Relations*, 27, 1974, pp 665-76

BOSTON CONSULTING GROUP: *Perspectives of Experience,* BCG, 1970 ... 72, 73, 163, 164, 176, 178, 195-6, 226, 499, 507

BOSWORTH, D and EVANS, G: 'Manpower Forecasting Techniques' in *Personnel Review,* 2 (4), Autumn, 1973, pp 4-16 ... 267

BOULDING, K: 'General Systems Theory — The Skeleton of a Science' in *Management Science*, 2, 1956, pp 197-208 ... 15, 180, 186, 400

BOWEY, A: *Handbook of Salary and Wage Systems,* Gower, 1982

BOWEY, A and LUPTON, T: *Job and Pay Comparisons,* Gower, 1973 ... 390, 391, 392, 393, 398, 399

BOWLEY, A L: *Wages and Incomes since 1860,* Cambridge U P, 1937 ... 365, 366, 399

BOWLEY, A: *Salary Structures for Management Careers,* IPM, 1973 ... 383, 399

BOYDELL, T H: *A Guide to Job Analysis,* BACIE, 1970 ... 45

BOYDELL, T H: *Experiential Learning,* University of Manchester Monograph No. 5, 1976

BOYDELL, T H: *Identification of Training Needs,* BACIE, 1971 ... 312

BOYDELL, T H: 'What's it all about?' in *Industrial Training International,* 8 (7), July, 1973, p 195

BRADFORD, UNIVERSITY of *Developing Industrial Relations Policies,* University of Bradford Management Centre, 1970

BRADLEY, J and HILL, S: 'After Japan: The Quality Circle Transplant and Productive Efficiency' in *British Journal of Industrial Relations*, 21 (3), November, 1983, pp 291-311

BRAITHWAITE, R and POLLOCK, J: 'Analysing Response to Recruitment Advertising' in *Personnel Management*, December, 1974, pp 25-7 ... 287

BRAITHWAITE, R and SCHOFIELD, P: *How to Recruit,* BIM, 1979 ... 297

BRAMHAM, J: *Practical Manpower Planning,* IPM, 1975

BRAMMEL, D: 'Interpersonal Attraction, Hostility and Perception', in Mills, J, *Experimental Social Psychology,* 1969, pp 3-120

BRANDT, F S: *The Process of Negotiation,* Industrial and Commercial Techniques Limited, London, November, 1973 ... 211

BRANNEN, P: *Authority and Participation in Industry,* Batsford, 1983

BRAVERMAN, H: *Labour and Monopoly Capital: The Degradation of Work in the Twentieth Century,* Monthly Review Press, 1974

BRECH, E F L: *The Principles and Practice of Management,* Longmans, 1953, 3rd edn, 1975 ... 2, 71, 234, 263-4, 444, 445

BREWSTER, C, and CONNOCK, S L: 'IR Training — A Focus on Policy' in *Personnel Management*, August, 1977, pp 28-35

BREWSTER, C and CONNOCK, S L: *Industrial Relations Training,* Kogan Page, 1980 ... 327, 431

BREWSTER, C and CONNOCK, S: *Industrial Relations: Cost Effective Strategies,* Hutchinson, 1985 ... 229

BREWSTER, C, GILL, C G and RICHBELL, S: 'Developing an Analytical Approach to IR Policy' in *Personnel Review,* 10, (2), 1981, pp 3-10 ... 213

BRIDGE, J, *Economics in Personnel Management,* IPM, 1981 ... 160, 167, 178

BRIDGES, A: 'Assessment Centres: Their Uses in Industry in Great Britain', UMIST Department of Management Sciences, 1984 ... 297

BRIGGS, G E, NAYLOR, J C and FUCHS, A H: *Whole versus Part Training as a Function of Task Dimensions,* US Naval Training Devices Centre, Report No. 950-52, 1962 ... 316, 327

BRIGGS, J H and MURRAY, R: *Responsibility of Industry in the Field of Health,* Foundation for Business Responsibilities, 1975

BRIM, O G and WHEELER, S: *Socialisation after Childhood: Two Essays,* Wiley, 1966 ... 8, 79, 88, 111

BRITISH INSTITUTE of MANAGEMENT: *Merit Rating — A Practical Guide,* BIM, 1964

BIM: *The Cost of Labour Turnover,* Management Publications, 1959 ... 275

BIM: *Absence from Work — Incidence and Cost Control,* Management Publications, 1961 ... 275

BIM, *Job Evaluation,* BIM, 1961

BIM: *Academics in Industry,* BIM Notes No. 10 (4), August, 1969

BIM: *Industrial Relations Training for Managers,* BIM, September, 1971

BIM: *The Board of Directors: A Survey of its Structure, Composition, and Role,* BIM Management Survey Report No. 10, 1972

BIM: *Employee Participation, A Management View,* BIM, 1975

BROSNAN, P: 'The Ability to Predict Worker Performance' in *Human Relations,* 28 (6), 1976, pp 519-41

BROWN, J A C: *The Social Psychology of Industry,* Penguin, 1954 ... 343

BROWN, W: *Some Problems of a Factory,* IPM, 1951 ... 158

BROWN, W: *Exploration in Management,* Penguin, 1960, 2nd edn, 1971 ... 213

BROWN, W: *Piecework Abandoned,* Heinemann, 1962

BROWN, W D and MOBURG, D J: *Organisation Theory and Management,* Wiley, 1980 ... 298

BROWNING, K W: 'Management Succession Planning' in *Personnel Management,* XLV (365), September, 1963, pp 107-10 ... 275

BRUNER, J S: *Towards a Theory of Instruction,* Belknap Press, 1966

BRYANT, D J: 'Recent Developments in Manpower Research' in *Personnel Review,* 1(3), Summer, 1972, pp 14-31

BRYANT, D J: 'A Survey of the Development of Manpower Planning Policies' in *British Journal of Industrial Relations,* III (3), November, 1965, pp 279-90 ... 264

BUCHANAN, D: *The Development of Job Design Theories and Techniques,* Gower, 1979 ... 45, 460, 466, 472

BUCHANAN, D A and BODDY, D: *Organisations in the Computer Age*, Gower, 1983

BUCKINGHAM, G L, JEFFREY, R G and THRONE, B A: *Job Enrichment and Organisational Change*, Gower, 1975

BUCKLEY, W: *Sociology and Modern Systems Theory*, Prentice Hall, 1967 ... 15, 186, 400

BULLOCK, Lord: *Report of the Committee of Inquiry on Industrial Democracy*, HMSO, 1977 ... 153

BULMER, M, (ed): *Working Class Images of Society*, Routledge and Kegan Paul, 1975

BURGESS, L L: *Top Executive Pay Package*, Free Press, 1963

BURGOYNE, J, BOYDELL, T H and PEDLER, M J: *Self-Development: Theory and Application for the Practitioner*, ATM, 1978

BURGOYNE, J G and SINGH, R: 'Evaluation of Training and Education' in *Journal of European Industrial Training*, 1 (1), 1977, pp 17-21 ... 327

BURGOYNE, A and STUART, R: *Management Development: Context and Strategy*, Gower Press, 1978 ... 327

BURGOYNE, J and STUART, R. 'Implicit Learning Theories as Determinants of the Effect of Management Development Programmes' in *Personnel Review*, 6 (2), Spring, 1977, pp 5-14

BURGOYNE, J et al: *A Manager's Guide to Self-Development*, McGraw Hill, 1978 ... 327

BURKE, W W: 'A Comparison of MD and OD' in *Journal of Applied Behavioural Science*, 7 (5), 1971, pp 569-79

BURKITT, B and BOWERS, D: *Trade Unions and the Economy*, Macmillan, 1979 ... 178

BURNS, T: 'The Directions of Activity and Communications in a Departmental Executive Group' in *Human Relations*, 7, 1954, pp 73-97 ... 304

BURNS, T: 'Research, Development and Production: Problems of Conflict and Co-operation' in I R E *Transactions on Engineering Management*, March, 1961

BURNS, T: 'Industry in a New Age', in *New Society*, 1 (18), 31 January, 1963, pp 17-20

BURNS, T: 'Management in Action' in *Operational Research Quarterly*, 8, 1957, pp 45-60

BURNS, T and STALKER, J M: *The Management of Innovation*, Tavistock, 1961 ... 173, 194, 196, 207, 469, 487

BURNS, T: 'The Sociology of Industry' in Welford, A T (ed), *Society*, Routledge and Kegan Paul, 1962, pp 188-218 ... 18, 87

BURNS, T: *The BBC*, Macmillan, 1977 ... 194

BUTTERIS, M: *Job Enrichment and Employee Participation — A Study*, IPM, 1971

BUTTERIS, M: *Techniques and Developments in Management – A Selection,* IPM, 1975 ... 393

BYHAM, B: 'Assessment Center for Spotting Future Managers in *Harvard Business Review,* 48, 1979, pp 150-60

BYHAM, B: 'Assessing Employees without Resorting to a Centre', in *Personnel Management,* October, 1984, pp 56-7 ... 293, 294, 297

C

CABLE, J and FITZROY, F R: 'Productive Efficiency, Incentives and Employee Participation: Some Preliminary Results for West Germany', in *Kyklos,* 33 (1), 1980, pp 100-121

CABOT, H and KAHL, J A: *Human Relations,* Vol. 1, *Concepts,* Harvard UP, 1953

CAIRNES, J E: *Some Leading Principles of Political Economy Newly Expounded,* Harper and Bros, 1874, pp 70-3 ... 49

CAMERON, S, ORCHIN, K and WHITE, G C: *Improving Satisfaction at Work by Job Re-design,* Work Research Unit Report No. 1, 1974 ... 43

CAMPBELL, J P: 'Personnel Training and Development' in *Annual Review of Psychology,* 22, 1971, pp 565-602

CAMPBELL, J P, DUNNETTE, M D, LAWLER, E E, and WEICK, K E: *Managerial Behaviour, Performance and Effectiveness,* McGraw Hill, 1970

CAPLOW, T: *The Sociology of Work,* McGraw Hill, 1964 ... 369

CARBY, C: *Job Redesign in Practice,* IPM, 1976

CARROLL, P: *Time Study for Cost Control,* McGraw Hill, 1954 ... 395

CARROLL, S J and SCHNEIDER, C E: *Performance Appraisal and Review Systems,* Scott, Foresman and Co, 1982

CARR-SAUNDERS, A M and WILSON, P A: *The Professions,* Cass, 1933, 2nd edn, 1964 ... 139, 141

CARTER, L, HAYTHORN, W, SHRIVER, B, and LANZETTA, J: 'The Behaviour of Leaders and Other Group Members' in *Journal of Abnormal and Social Psychology,* 46, 1950, pp 589-95, and in Cartwright and Zander, 1953, q.v. pp 551-60 ... 232

CARTWRIGHT, D: 'Influence, Leadership and Control' in March, J G, *Handbook of Organizations,* Rand-McNally, 1965, pp 1-47 ... 82, 424, 430, 446, 448

CARTWRIGHT, D (ed): *Studies in Social Power,* Institute for Social Research, University of Michigan, 1959

CARTWRIGHT, D, and ZANDER, A: *Group Dynamics: Research and Theory,* Row Peterson, 1953 ... 282, 283

CARVALHO, G E: 'Managing a Dynamic Compensation System' in *Management and Personnel Quarterly,* 3, 1965, pp 3-10, and in MacFarland, 1971, q.v. pp 213-33 ... 363

CATELL, R B, EBER, H W and TATSUOKA, M M: *Handbook for Sixteen Personality Factors Questionnaire,* Institute for Personality and Ability Study, Champaign, Ill, 1970
CATTELL, R B: *Personality,* McGraw Hill, 1950 ... 7
CATTELL, R B: *Introduction to Personality Study,* McGraw Hill, 1950
CATTELL, R B, (ed): *Handbook of Multivariate Experimental Psychology,* Rand McNally, 1965 ... 343
CEMACH, H P: *Work Study in the Office,* Maclaren, 1969 ... 45
CENTRAL TRAINING COUNCIL: *Training for Commerce and the Office,* HMSO, 1966
CENTRAL TRAINING COUNCIL: *Training of Training Officers: A Pattern for the Future,* HMSO, 1968
CHADWICK-JONES, J K: *Automation and Behaviour,* Wiley, 1969
CHADWICK-JONES, J K, BROWN, C A, and NICHOLSON, N: 'Absence from Work: Its meaning, measurement and control' in *International Review of Applied Psychology,* 22 (2), 1973, pp 137-55
CHASE, S: *The Proper Study of Mankind: An Inquiry into the Science of Human Relations,* Phoenix House, 1950
CHERRY, C: *On Human Communication,* Chapman and Hall, 1957
CHILD, J (ed): *Man and Organization,* Allen and Unwin, 1973
CHILD, J: 'Culture, Contingency and Capitalism in the Cross National Study of Organizations' in Cummings, L L, and Staw, B M (eds), *Research in Organizational Behaviour,* JAI Press, 1981, pp 303-56
CHILD, J: 'Organizational Structure, Environment and Performance: The Role of Strategic Choice' in *Sociology* 6 (1), January, 1972, pp 1-22, and in Salaman and Thompson, 1973, q.v. pp 91-107
CHILD, J: 'The Industrial Supervisor' in Esland, G, et al (eds), *People and Work,* Holmes/McDougal, Edinburgh, 1975
CHRISTAL, R E: *Factor Analytic Study of Visual Memory,* Psychometric Monographs, No. 13, 1958 ... 51
CLAYTON, E H: 'A Proprietary Right in Employment' in *Journal of Business Law,* 1967, pp 139-43 ... 131
CLEGG, C W et al: 'Managers' Attitudes towards Industrial Democracy' in *Industrial Relations Journal,* 9 (3), Autumn, 1978, pp 4-17
CLEGG, H A: *The Changing System of Industrial Relations in Great Britain,* Blackwell, 1979 ... 214
CLEMENTS, R V: *Managers: A Study of their Careers in Industry,* Allen and Unwin, 1958
CLEVENGER, T and MATHEWS, J: *The Speech Communication Process,* Scott Foresman, 1971 ... 400, 420, 430
CLIFTON, R and TATTON-BROWN, C: *Impact of Employment Legislation in Small Firms,* DE Research Paper No. 6, 1979
CLUTTERBUCK, D: *Everyone Needs a Mentor,* IPM, 1985 ... 357
COCH, L and FRENCH, J R P: 'Overcoming Resistance to Change' in

522   *A Textbook of Human Resource Management*

Human Relations (1), 1948, pp 512-32, also in Cartwright and Zander, 1953, q.v. pp 257-79, and in Maccoby, Newcomb and Hartley, 1958, q.v. pp 233-50

COCHRANE, A L: *Effectiveness and Efficiency,* Nuffield Provincial Hospitals Trust, 1972 ... 392

COHEN, K J and CYERT, R M: *Theory of the Firm,* Prentice Hall, 1965 ... 160

COHEN, M D, MARCH, J G and OLSEN, J P: 'A Garbage Can Model of Organisational Choice' in *Administrative Science Quarterly,* 17 (1), March, 1972, pp 1-25

COLLARD, R: 'The Quality Circle in Context' in *Personnel Management,* 13 (9), September, 1981, pp 26-30 ... 107, 430, 462

COLLIN, A: 'Notes on Some Typologies of Management Development' in *Personnel Review,* 8 (4), Autumn, 1979, pp 10-14

COLLINGRIDGE, J M and RITCHIE, M: *Personnel Management: Problems of the Smaller Firm,* IPM, 1970

COLLINS, E G C: 'Everybody who Makes it has a Mentor', in *Harvard Business Review,* July-August 1978, pp 89-101 ... 355

COLLINS, H: 'Capitalist Discipline and Corporatist Control' in *Industrial Law Journal,* 11, 1982, pp 78-93 and pp 170-7

COMMISSION ON INDUSTRIAL RELATIONS: *Facilities Afforded to Shop Stewards,* Report No. 17, Cmnd 4668, HMSO, May, 1972 ... 131

CIR: *Disclosure of Information,* Report No. 31, HMSO, 1972

CIR: *Industrial Relations Training,* Report No. 33 and Report No. 33A, Statistical Supplement, HMSO, 1972/1973

CIR, *Worker Participation and Collective Bargaining in Europe,* Study No. 4, HMSO, 1974

CIR: *Trade Union Recognition — CIR Experience,* Study No. 5, HMSO, 1974

CIR: *Ballots and Union Recognition: A Guide for Employers* HMSO, 1974

CONFEDERATION OF BRITISH INDUSTRY: *The Provision of Information to Employees: Guidelines for Action,* CBI, 1975 ... 430

CONFERENCE BOARD INC: *Boards of Directors: Perspectives and Practices in Nine Countries,* Conference Board Report No. 728, 1977

CONNOCK, S: 'Workforce Flexibility: Juggling Time and Task' in *Personnel Management,* October, 1985, pp 36-8 ... 92, 275, 504

COOPER, C L (ed): *Theories of Group Processes,* Wiley, 1975 ... 459

COOPER, C L: *The Stress Check,* Prentice Hall, 1980

COOPER, C L and PAYNE, R L: *Stress at Work,* Wiley, 1978 ... 39, 45, 275, 408, 472

COOPER, R: *Job Motivation and Job Design,* IPM, 1977

COPEMAN, G: *Employee Share Ownership and Industrial Stability,* IPM, 1975

COPEMAN, G: 'Profit-Sharing in Perspective' in *Personnel Management,* 11, (1), January, 1979, pp 36-9

CORLETT, E N and MORCOMBE, V J: 'Straightening Out Learning Curves' in *Personnel Management*, 2 (6), June, 1970, pp 14-19

COSIJN, E: 'European Patterns in Working Time' in *Personnel Management*, September, 1985, pp 33-6

COWAN, L D: 'Developing and Implementing Personnel Policies' in University of Bradford Management Centre, 1970, pp 18-21 ... 216, 229

COWAN, L D: *Personnel Management and Banking,* Institute of Bankers, 1983

COX, B: *Value Added,* Heinemann, 1979 ... 390

COX, J: 'Introducing Quality Circles — Training's Key Role,' in *Journal of European Industrial Training*, 5 (7), 1981, pp 17-22 ... 216

CRAIG, C, GARNSEY, E and RUBERY, J: *Payment Structures and Smaller Firms: Women's Employment in Segmented Labour Markets,* DE Research Paper No. 48, 1984 ... 173, 178

CRAIG, C, RUBERY, J, TARLING, R, and WILKINSON, F: *Labour Market Structure, Industrial Organisation and Low Pay,* Cambridge U P, 1982

CRAIG, R L and BITTEL, L R: *Training and Development Handbook,* McGraw Hill, 1967

CRICHTON, A: *Personnel Management in Context,* Batsford, 1968 ... 19, 237

CRICHTON, A and COLLINS, R G: 'Personnel Specialists — A Count by Employers' in *British Journal of Industrial Relations*, IV (2), July, 1966, pp 137-53

CRONBACK, L J and GLESER, G C: *Psychological Tests and Personnel Decisions,* University of Illinois, 1965

CROSBY, P B: *Quality is Free: The Art of Making Quality Certain,* McGraw Hill, 1979

CRYSTALS, G S: *Financial Motivation for Executives,* AMA, 1970

CUMING, M W: *The Theory and Practice of Personnel Management,* Heinemann, 1975

CUMING, M W: *Hospital Staff Management,* Heinemann, 1971

CUMMINGS, L L and SCHWAB, D P: *Performance in Organisations: Determinants and Appraisal,* Scott Foresman, 1973 ... 348-9, 357

CUMMINGS, T G, MALLOY, E S, and GLEN, R: 'A Methodological Critique of Fifty-eight Selected Work Experiments' in *Human Relations*, 30 (8), pp 675-708

CUNNISON, S: *Wages and Work Allocation,* Tavistock, 1966

CURNOW, B: 'The Creative Approach to Pay', in *Personnel Management*, October, 1986, pp 70-5

CURRIE, R M: *The Measurement of Work,* Pitman, 1972

CURRIE, R M and FARADAY, J E: *Financial Incentives Based on Work Measurement,* BIM, rev. edn, 1971 ... 399

CUTHBERT, N H and HAWKINS, K H: *Company Industrial Relations Policies,* Longman, 1973

CUTHBERT, N H and PATERSON, J M: 'Job Evaluation: Some Recent Thinking and Its Place in an Investigation' in *Personnel Management,* September, 1966, pp 152-62

CYERT, R M and MARCH, J C: *A Behavioural Theory of the Firm,* Prentice Hall, 1963

D

DALE, B G and BALL, T S: *A Study of Quality Circles in UK Manufacturing Organisations,* Occasional Paper No. 8306, Department of Management Studies, UMIST, 1983

DALE, E: *Planning and Developing the Company Organization Structure,* AMA, 1952 ... 412

DALTON, M: *Men who Manage,* Wiley, 1958, 1970

DANIEL, W W, 'Industrial Behaviour and Orientation to Work — A Critique' in *Journal of Management Studies,* 6, 1969, pp 366-75

DANIEL, W W: 'Productivity Bargaining and Orientation to Work: A Rejoinder to Goldthorpe' in *Journal of Management Studies*, 8, 1971, pp 329-35 ... 440

DANIEL, W W and MILLWARD, N: *Workplace Industrial Relations in Britain,* Heinemann, 1983 ... 151

DANIEL, W W and STILGOE, E: *The Impact of Employment Protection Laws,* Policy Studies Institute, 1978

DANIEL, W W: *Workplace Industrial Relations and Technical Change,* Policy Studies Institute/Francis Pinter, 1987 ... 207, 500, 501-2

DAVENPORT, H J: 'Non-Competing Groups' in *Quarterly Journal of Economics*, 40, 1926, pp 52-81 ... 173

DAVIES, K: 'The Case for Participative Management' in Huneryager, S G and Heckman, I L, *Human Relations in Management,* Arnold, 1967

DAVIS, L E: 'The Design of Jobs' in *Industrial Relations*, 6 (1), 1966, pp 21-45 ... 35

DAVIS, L E and CHERNS, A B: *The Quality of Working Life*, Vol. 1 and Vol. 2, Collier-Macmillan, 1975 ... 41

DAVIS, L E and TAYLOR, J C (eds): *Design of Jobs,* Penguin, 1972 ... 42

DAVIS, S M: 'Executive Age and Corporate Performance' in *Harvard Business Review*, March/April, 1979, pp 6-7

DEUTSCHER, I: 'Towards Avoiding the Goal-trap in Evaluation Research' in Abt, CC (ed), *The Evaluation of Social Programmes,* Russell Sage, 1976, pp 249-68

DEVERELL, C S: *Personnel Management: Human Relations in Industry,* Gee, 1968

DEWAR, D L: *The Quality Circle Handbook,* Quality Circle Institute, 1980 ... 430

DODD, A E and RICE, J O (eds): *How to Train Workers for War Industries,* Harper and Bros, 1942 ... 259

DOERINGER, P: 'Determinants of the Structure of Industrial Type Internal Labour Markets' in *Industrial and Labour Relations Review*, 20, (2), January, 1967, pp 206-20

DOERINGER, P and PIORE, M: *Internal Labour Markets and Manpower Analysis,* Lexington, 1971 ... 171, 178, 362

DOLLARD, J, DOOB, W, MILLER, N E, MOWER, O H and SHEARS, R R: *Frustration and Aggression,* Yale UP, 1939

DONALD, B: *Manpower for Hospitals,* Institute of Hospital Administrators, 1966

DONALDSON L and SCANNEL, E E: *Human Resources Development: The New Trainer's Guide,* Addison-Wesley, 1978 ... 310, 323

DONOVAN, LORD: *Royal Commission on Trade Unions and Employers' Associations,* Report, HMSO, 1968 ... 145, 214, 225, 234

DOOHER, M J and MARQUIS, V: *Rating Employee and Supervisory Performance: A Manual of Merit Rating,* AMA, 1950

DORE, R P: *British Factory — Japanese Factory: The Origins of National Diversity in Industrial Relations,* Allen and Unwin, 1973

DOULTON, J and HAY, D: *Managerial and Professional Staff Grading,* Allen and Unwin, 1962

DOYLE, F P: 'Organising the Enterprise', in Marceau, L (ed): *Dealing with a Union,* AMA, 1969, pp 21-34 ... 165

DRENTH, P J D and KOOPMAN, P L: 'Experiences in Werkoverleg in the Netherlands: Implications for Quality Circles', paper to the Annual Colloquium of the Industrial Democracy in Europe International Research Group, March, 1982, Free University of Amsterdam, 1982

DROUGHT, N E: 'The Operations Committee: An Experience in Group Dynamics', in *Personnel Psychology,* 20, 1967, pp 153-63

DRUCKER, P F: *The Practice of Management,* Mercury Books, 1961 ... 11, 12, 19, 235, 238

DRUCKER, P F: *Managing For Results,* Heinemann, 1964 ... 332, 340

DRUCKER, P F: *Managing in Turbulent Times,* Heinemann, 1980 ... 303, 410, 430

DUBIN, R: 'Industrial Workers' Worlds' in *Social Problems,* III, January, 1956, pp 131-42 ... 58, 59, 77, 444

DUBIN, R: 'Business Behaviour Behaviourally-Viewed' in Strother, G B (ed): *Social Science Approaches to Business Behaviour,* Dorsey Press, 1962 ... 408, 430

DULEWICZ, V: 'The Application of Assessment Centres' in *Personnel Management,* 14 (9), September, 1982, pp 32-5

DUNCAN, C P, 'Recent Research on Human Problem-Solving' in *Psychological Bulletin,* 46, 1959, pp 397-429

DUNCAN, K D and KELLY, C J: *Task Analysis, Learning and the Nature of Transfer,* MSC, 1983 ... 299

DUNCAN, R and WEISS, C V: 'Organisational Learning: Implications for Organisational Design' in Staw and Cummings, 1979, q.v. pp 75-123

DUNKERLEY, D: *The Study of Organizations,* Routledge and Kegan Paul, 1975 ... 207

DUNKERLEY, D: *The Foreman,* Routledge and Kegan Paul, 1975

DUNNETTE, M D: *Personnel Selection and Placement,* Tavistock, 1976

DUNNETTE, M D and BASS, B M: 'Behavioural Scientists and Personnel Management' in *Industrial Relations,* 2 (3), 1963, pp 115-30 ... 291

DUNNING, J H: *Japanese Participation in Britisn Industry,* Croom Helm, 1986 ... 95

DYER, L D: 'Job Search Success of Middle-Aged Managers and Engineers' in *Industrial and Labour Relations Review,* 26, (3), 1973, pp 969-79

DYER, W G: *Team Building: Issues and Alternatives,* Addison-Wesley, 1977

E

ECKSTRAND, G A: *Current Status of the Technology of Training,* Wright-Patterson A F B Aerospace Medical Laboratories, Report AMRLL – TDR – 64–86, 1964 ... 299, 308, 313, 327

EDELSTEIN, J D and WARNER, M: *Comparative Union Democracy,* Allen and Unwin, 1975

EDWARDS, C and HARPER, D G: 'Bargaining at the Trade Union and Management Interface' in Abell, 1975, q.v. pp 41–71 ... 175

EDWARDS, J et al: *Manpower Planning,* Wiley, 1983

EDWARDS, P: 'Myth of the Macho Manager' in *Personnel Management,* April, 1985, pp 32–5

EDWARDS, R: *Contested Terrain: The Transformation of the Workplace in the Twentieth Century,* Basic Books, 1979

EDWARDS, R and PAUL, S: *Job Evaluation,* Association of Professional, Executive, Clerical and Computer Staff, 1977

EISNER, E W: 'Educational Objectives: help or hindrance?' in *The School Review,* 75, 1967, pp 250–60

ELBOURNE, E T: *Fundamentals of Industrial Administration,* MacDonald and Evans, 1934 ... 236

ELGOOD C, ASSOCIATES: 'Experiential Learning' in *Industrial and Commercial Training,* December, 1976, pp 478–81

ELLIOTT, A G P: *Staff Grading,* BIM, 1960 ... 364

ELLIOTT, A G P: *Revising a Merit Rating Scheme,* IPM, 1955 ... 357

ELLIOTT, J: *Conflict or Cooperation,* Kogan Page, 1978

ELLIS, C D: 'Danger Ahead for Pension Funds' in *Harvard Business Review,* May–June, 1971, pp 50–56

ELLIS, H C: *The Transfer of Learning,* Macmillan, 1965 ... 327

EMERY, F E: *Systems Thinking,* Penguin, 1969

EMERY, F E: *Characteristics of Socio-Technical Systems,* Tavistock, 1959 ... 180, 199, 200, 203, 207

EMERY, F E and TRIST, E L: 'Socio-Technical Systems' in *Management Sciences: Models and Techniques,* Pergamon Press, 1960 ... 180, 207

EMERY, F E and THORSUD, E: *Form and Content in Industrial Democracy,* Tavistock, 1969

EMPLOYMENT, DEPT. OF: *Company Manpower Planning,* Manpower Paper No. 1, HMSO, 1968

EMPLOYMENT, DEPT. OF: *Industrial Relations Procedures,* Manpower Paper No. 14, HMSO, 1975

EMPLOYMENT, DEPT. OF: *Code of Industrial Relations Practice,* DE, 1972; reissued by ACAS

EMPLOYMENT, DEPT. OF: *Code of Practice on Picketing,* HMSO, 1980

EMPLOYMENT, DEPT. OF: *Code of Practice on Closed Shop Agreements and Arrangements,* HMSO, 1983

EMPLOYMENT, DEPT. OF: *Training for the Future,* DE, 1972 ... 380

EMPLOYMENT, DEPT. OF: *Training for the Management of Human Resources,* The Hayes Report, HMSO, 1972 ... 1, 238, 239, 309, 310

EMPLOYMENT, DEPT. OF: *Trade Union Immunities,* HMSO, 1980

EMPLOYMENT, DEPT. OF: *Democracy in Trade Unions,* HMSO, 1983

ENGINEERING EMPLOYERS' FEDERATION: *Business Performance and Industrial Relations,* EEF, 1972, reprinted 1976 ... 390, 399

ENGINEERING INDUSTRY TRAINING BOARD: *Training for Engineering Craftsmen: the Module System,* EITB, 1968

EQUAL OPPORTUNITIES COMMISSION: *Equal Pay for Work of Equal Value: A Guide to the Amended Equal Pay Act,* EOC, undated ... 131

ETZIONI, A: *A Comparative Analysis of Complex Organizations,* Free Press, 1961; 1975 ... 448

ETZIONI, A: *Modern Organizations,* Prentice Hall, 1964

ETZIONI, A: *A Sociological Reader on Complex Organizations,* Holt, Rinehart and Winston, 2nd edn, 1969

ETZIONI, A: *The Active Society: A Theory of Social and Political Processes,* Collier-Macmillan, 1968

EVANS, A: *Computerizing Personnel Systems,* IPM, 1986

EVANS, G J and LINDLEY, RM: 'The Use of RAS and Related Models in Manpower Forecasting', Research Paper No. 22, Centre for Industrial Economic and Business Research, University of Warwick, 1972

EVERETT, J E, STENING, B W, and LONGTON, P A: 'Some Evidence for an International Management Culture' in *Journal of Management Studies,* 19 (2), 1982, pp 153–62

EWING, D W: 'The Knowledge of the Executive' in *Harvard Business Review,* 42 (2), March – April, 1964, pp 91–100

EYSENCK, H J: *Structure of Personality,* Methuen, 1960 ... 7

F

FAGEN, R E and HALL, A D: 'Definition of Systems' in *General Systems*, 1, 1956, pp 18–28

FALK, R and CLARK, I: 'Planning for Growth', in *Management Today*, June, 1966, pp 85–8 and 151

FARMER, R N and RICHMAN, B M: 'A model for research in Comparative Management' in *California Management Review*, Winter, 1964, pp 55–68 ... 100, 101, 102, 111

FARMER, R N and RICHMAN, B M: *Comparative Management and Economic Progress*, Richard D Irwin, 1968

FARRER, J H: *Company Law*, Butterworths, 1985

FAYOL, H: *General and Industrial Administration*, Durod, Paris, 1915

FIELDS, A: *Method Study*, Cassells, 1969

FINEMAN, S and PAYNE, R: 'Applications of Behavioural Rating Scales: Some Reliability and Validity Findings' in *Industrial Relations Journal*, 5, 1974, pp 38–44 ... 335, 357

FINNIGAN, J: *Industrial Training Management*, Business Books, 1970 ... 310

FISCHER, F E: 'The Personnel Function in Tomorrow's Company' in MacFarland, D E: *Personnel Management*, Penguin, 1971

FISHER, M R: *The Economic Analysis of Labour*, Weidenfeld and Nicholson, 1971

FITZGERALD, T H: 'Why Motivation Theory Doesn't Work' in *Harvard Business Review*, July–August, 1971, pp 37–44

FLANAGAN, J C: 'Critical Requirements: A New Approach to Employee Evaluation' in *Personnel Psychology*, 2, 1949, pp 419–25 ... 357

FLANAGAN, J C: 'The Critical Incident Technique' in *Psychological Bulletin*, 51, 1954, pp 327–58

FLANDERS, A: *Industrial Relations: What's Wrong with the System?*, IPM, 1965; and in *Management and Unions*, 1975, pp 86–99 ... 214

FLEISHMAN, E A: *Studies in Personnel and Industrial Psychology*, Dorsey, 1961 ... 396

FLETCHER, C and WILLIAMS, R: *Performance Appraisal and Career Development*, Hutchinson, 1985

FLETCHER, E: 'The Road to Joint Control' in *Management Today*, April, 1970, pp 90–93 and p 162

FLORENCE, P S: *The Logic of British and American Industry*, Routledge and Kegan Paul, 1953, 2nd edn, 1961

FOGARTY, M P: *Personality and Group Relations in Industry*, Longman, 1956

FOGARTY, M P: *The Rules of Work*, Chapman, 1961

FOGARTY, M P: *The Just Wage*, Chapman, 1961

FOGARTY, M P: 'An Independent Comment' in *Personnel Management*, XLV (363), March, 1963, pp 23–5

FOGARTY, M P: *Company and Corporation – One Law?*, Chapman, 1965

FOLLETT, M P: see Metcalf and Urwick, 1941

FORBES, A F, MORGAN, R W and ROWNTREE J A: 'Manpower Planning Models in Use in the Civil Service Department' in *Personnel Review*, 4 (3), Summer, 1975, pp 23–35; and in Smith, 1980, q.v. pp 89–111

FORD, R N: *Motivation through the Work itself,* American Management Association, 1969 ... 43

FOSTER, K E: 'A Perspective on Executive Compensation' in *Compensation Review*, 3, 1980, pp 47–54

FOULKES, D: *Law for Managers,* Butterworths, 1971

FOURACRE, S and WRIGHT, A: 'New Factors in Job Evaluation' in *Personnel Managment*, May, 1986, pp 40–43

FOWLER, A: *Personnel Management in Local Government,* IPM, 1980

FOX, A: *Industrial Sociology and Industrial Relations,* RCTUEA, Research Paper, No. 3; HMSO, 1966b; and in Flanders, 1969, q.v. pp 390–409 ... 227

FOX, A: 'Management's Frame of Reference' in Flanders, 1969, q.v. pp 390–409

FOX, A: *Beyond Contract: Power Work and Trust Relations,* Allen and Unwin, 1974a ... 131, 173

FOX, A: *Man-Mismanagement,* Hutchinson, 1974b

FOX, A: 'Corporatism and Industrial Democracy' in SSRC: *Industrial Democracy: International Views,* SSRC, 1978

FOX, H W: 'A Framework for Functional Co-ordination' in *Atlanta Economic Review*, 23 (6), 1973, pp 8–11

FOY, N: *The Missing Links: British Management Education in the 1980s,* Oxford Centre for Management Studies/Foundation for Management Education, 1978

FOY, N: 'Management Education – Current Action and Future Needs' in *Journal of European Industrial Training,* 3 (2), 1979, pp 1–28

FRASER, J M: *Introduction to Personnel Management,* Nelson, 1971 ... 262, 290

FRASER, J M: *Employment Interviewing,* MacDonald and Evans, 4th edn., 1966

FRASER, W H: *Trade Unions and Society: The Struggle for Acceptance, 1850–80,* Allen and Unwin, 1974

FREEDMAN, J L, CARLSMITH, J L and SEARS, D O: *Social Psychology,* Prentice Hall, 1970 ... 441, 446

FREEDMAN, R D, COOPER, C L, and STUMPF, S A: *Management Education,* Wiley, 1982

FRENCH, J E: *The Description of Aptitude and Achievement Tests in Terms of Rotated Factors,* Psychometric Monographs, No. 5, 1951 ... 51

FRENCH, W: *The Personnel Management Process,* Houghton-Mifflin, 1974

FRENCH, W and BELL, C H: *Organisational Development,* Prentice Hall, 1973, 2nd edn., 1978

FRIEDMAN, M: 'The Social Responsibility of the Business Enterprise is to Increase its Profits' in *Issues in Business and Society*, 1977, p 168

FRIEDMAN, M: *Capitalism and Freedom,* Phoenix Books, 1963 ... 194

FRIEDMAN, M G: '10 Steps to Objective Appraisals' in *Personnel Journal,* June, 1986, pp 66–71

FROST, P J, MOORE, L F, LOUIS, M R, LUNDBERG, C C, and MARTIN, J: *Organisational Culture*, Sage, 1985 ... 111

FULTON, Lord: *The Civil Service, Vol. 1, Report of the Committee,* HMSO, 1968, Cmnd 3638 ... 184

G

GADALLA, I E and COOPER, R: 'Towards an Epistemology of Management' in *Social Science Information*, 17 (3), 1978, pp 349–83

GAGNE, R M: 'Military Training and Principles of Learning' in *American Psychologist*, 17, 1962, pp 83–91; and in Yukl and Wexley, 1970, pp 451–61 ... 313

GAGNE, R M: *The Conditions of Learning,* Holt, Rinehart and Winston, 1970 ... 8, 299, 311, 327, 404-5

GAGNE, R M and BRIGGS, L J: *Principles of Instructional Design,* Holt, Rinehart and Winston, 1974

GARDELL, B: 'Alienation and Mental Health in the Modern Industrial Environment' in Levi, L (ed): *Society, Stress and Disease*, Vol. 1, Oxford U P, 1971, pp 148–80 ... 34

GARDINER, G: *The Operating Executive and the Personnel Department,* AMA, Personnel Series No. 121, 1948

GARDNER, W and TAYLOR, P: *Health at Work,* Associated Business Programmes, 1975 ... 88

GARNETT, J: *The Work Challenge,* Industrial Society, 1973

GARNETT, J: *The Manager's Responsibility for Communication,* Industrial Society, Notes for Managers No. 2, 1964

GENDERS, J E and URWIN, N J: *Wages and Salaries,* IPM, 1962

GENNARD, J: *Financing Strikers,* Macmillan, 1977

GENNARD, J, DUNN, S, and WRIGHT, M: 'The Extent of the Closed Shop Arrangements in British Industry' in *Employment Gazette*, January, 1980, pp 16–22 ... 151

GENTLES, E M: *Training the Operator – A Practical Guide,* IPM, 1969 ... 327

GEORGE, C S: *The History of Management Thought,* Prentice Hall, 1972

GEORGE, J: 'Appraisal in the Public Sector: Dispensing with the Big Stick' in *Personnel Management*, May, 1986, pp 32–5

GHISELLI, E E: 'The Validity of Aptitude Tests in Personnel Selection' in *Personnel Psychology*, 26, 1973, pp 461–77

GIBBS, C B: 'The Continuous Regulation of Skilled Response by Kinaesthetic Feedback' in *British Journal of Psychology*, 45, 1954, pp 24–39 ... 327

GIBSON, J L, IVANCEVITCH, J M, and DONNELLY, J H: *Organizations: Behaviour, Structure, Processes,* Irwin Dorsey, 2nd edn, 1976 ... 430

GILES, W J and ROBINSON, D F: *Human Asset Accounting,* IPM, 1972

GILL, D, UNGERSON, B and THAKUR, M: *Performance Appraisal in Perspective – A Survey of Current Practice,* IPM, 1973 ... 357

GILL, R W T and TAYLOR, D S: 'Training Managers to Handle Discipline and Grievance Interviews' in *Journal of Education and Training*, May, 1976, pp 217–27 ... 357

GILLING-SMITH, D: *The Manager's Guide to Pensions,* IPM, 1974

GLASER, R (ed): *The Nature of Reinforcement,* Academic Press, 1971

GLASER, W: 'Cross National Studies of Organizations' in *International Studies of Management and Organization*, 5, 1975, pp 68–90

GLUECK, W F and JAUCH, L R: *Business Policy and Strategic Management,* McGraw Hill, 1984 ... 165

GOFFMAN, E: *The Presentation of Self in Everyday Life,* Doubleday, 1959 ... 4, 414

GOFFMAN, E: *Encounters,* Bobbs-Merrill, 1961

GOLDSMITH, M and MACKAY, A: *The Science of Science,* Penguin, 1966

GOLDSTEIN, I L: *Training: Programme Development and Evaluation,* Brooks/Cole, Monterey, 1974

GOLDSTEIN, I L: 'Training in Work Organisations' in *Annual Review of Psychology*, 31, 1980, pp 229–72

GOLDTHORPE, J H, LOCKWOOD, D, BECHOFER, F and PLATT, J: *The Affluent Worker: Industrial Attitudes and Behaviour,* Cambridge UP, 1968 ... 33, 62, 64, 88, 110, 435, 440, 441

GOODMAN, M J: *Industrial Tribunals' Procedure,* Oyez Publishing, 1976

GOODMAN, P S: 'Why Productivity Programmes Fail' in *National Productivity Review*, 1 (4), 1982, pp 369–80

GORE, W J (ed): *Administrative Decision-Making: A Reader,* Free Press, 1962

GORER, G: *Exploring English Character,* Cresset Press, 1955 ... 84, 109

GOSPEL, H F and LITTLER, C F: *Managerial Strategies and Industrial Relations,* Heinemann, 1983

GOTTSCHALL, D: 'Quality Circles – Problems an der Basis losen' in *Manager Magazine*, 12, 1980, pp 50–57

GOULDER, A W: *Patterns of Industrial Bureaucracy*, Routledge and Kegan Paul, 1955b ... 241

GOWER, L C B: *Principles of Modern Company Law,* Stevens, 4th edn, 1979 ... 149

GOWLER, D: 'Determinants of the Supply of Labour to the Firm' in *Journal of Management Studies*, 6 (1), February, 1969, pp 73–95

GOWLER, D: 'Values, Contracts and Job Satisfaction' in *Personnel Review*, 3 (4), Autumn, 1974, pp 4–14 ... 116, 131

GOWLER, D and LEGGE, K: *Managerial Stress,* Gower, 1975

GOYDER, G: *The Responsible Worker,* Hutchinson, 1975

GRANICK, D: *Managerial Comparisons in Four Developed Countries,* MIT Press, 1972

GRANT, J V and SMITH, A: *Personnel Administration and Industrial Relations,* Longman, 1969

GREENLAW, P and SMITH, R D: *Personnel Management: A Management Science Approach,* International Textbook Company, 1970

GREGSON, D and RUFFLE, K: 'Rationalising Rewards at Rogertstone' in *Personnel Management*, 12 (10), October, 1980, pp 62–64

GRINOLD, R C and MARSHALL, K T: *Manpower Planning Models,* North Holland, 1977

GUEST, D and FATCHETT, D: *Worker Participation: Individual Control and Performance,* IPM, 1974

GUEST, D and KNIGHT, K: *Putting Participation into Practice,* Gower, 1979

GUEST, R H: *Organisation Change — The Effect of Successful Leadership,* Tavistock Publications, 1962

GUILFORD, J P and HOEPFNER, R: *The Analysis of Intelligence,* McGraw Hill, 1971

GUILFORD, J P and ZIMMERMAN, W S: 'Fourteen Dimensions of Temperament' in *Psychological Monographs*, 70, 1956

GUION, R M: *Personal Testing,* McGraw Hill, 1965

GULOWSEN, J: *Selfstyrte Arbeidsgrupper,* Tanum, Oslo, 1971

GWENT INDUSTRIAL MISSION: *Redundant? A Personal Survival Kit,* People and Work Unit, Newport, Gwent, 1986 ... 353

H

HAAS, E: 'Breakthrough Manufacturing' in *Harvard Business Review*, 87 (2), March – April, 1987, pp 75–81 ... 121

HACKMAN, J R and LAWLER, E E: 'Employee Reactions to Job Characteristics' in *Journal of Applied Psychology*, 55 (3), 1971, pp 259–86 ... 43, 44

HACKMAN, J R, LAWLER, E E, and PORTER, L W: *Perspectives of Behaviour in Organizations,* McGraw Hill, 1977

HACKMAN, J R and OLDHAM, G R: 'Motivation Through the Design of Work: Test of a Theory' in *Organisational Behaviour and Human Performance*, 16, 1976, pp 250–79

HACKMAN, J R and OLDHAM, G R: *Work Redesign,* 1980

HACKMAN, R C: *The Motivated Working Adult,* AMA, 1969 ... 68

HACKMAN, J R: 'Coming Demise of Job Enrichment' in Cass, E L and Zimmer, T G (eds): *Man and Work in Society,* Van Nostrand, 1975, pp 97–115

HACKMAN, J R, OLDHAM, G, JANSON, R, and PURDY, K: 'A New Strategy for Job Enrichment' in *California Management Review*, 17 (4), Summer, 1975, pp 57−71 ... 43, 45, 88

HADDEN, T: *Company Law and Capitalism,* Weidenfeld and Nicholson, 1972, 2nd edn, 1977

HAGUE, H: *Executive Self-Development,* Macmillan, 1974

HAGUE, H: *Management Training for Real,* IPM, 1973

HALEY, SIR W: 'The Look of Management' in *The Manager*, 32 (11), November, 1964, pp 25−30

HALL, D T and NOUGAIN, K E: 'An Examination of Maslow's Need Hierarchy in an Organizational Setting' in *Organization Behaviour and Human Performance*, (3), 1968, pp 12−35 ... 88

HALL, M: 'Towards a Manpower Grid' in *Personnel Management*, June, 1965, pp 72−8

HAMBLIN, A C: *Evaluation and Control of Training,* McGraw Hill, 1974

HAMBRICK, D C, MACMILLAN, I C and DAY, D L: 'Strategic Attributes and Performance in the Four Cells of the BCG Matrix: A PIMS-based Analysis of Industrial-Product Businesses' in *Academy of Management Journal*, 25 (3), 1982, pp 510−31 ... 163

HAMBRICK, D C, MACMILLAN, I C and DAY, D L: 'The Product Portfolio and Profitability − A PIMS-based Analysis of Industrial-Product Businesses' in *Academy of Management Journal*, 25 (4), 1982, pp 733−55

HANDY, C: 'The Changing Shape of Work and Life' in *Policy Studies Institute Journal*, 1982, pp 189−98

HANDY, C: *The Future of Work: A Guide to a Changing Society,* Blackwell, 1984

HANDY, C: *Understanding Organisations,* Penguin, 1986

HANIKA, F de P: *New Thinking in Management,* Hutchinson, 1965 ... 400

HANSON, C G: *Trade Unions: A Century of Privilege,* Institute of Economic Affairs, Occasional Paper No. 38, 1973 ... 151

HARBISON, F and MYERS, C A: *Management in the Industrial World,* McGraw Hill, 1959 ... 11

HARPER, S (ed): *Personnel Management Handbook,* Gower, 1987 ... 399

HARRIS, P R and MORAN P T: *Managing Cultural Differences,* Gulf Publishing Company, 1983 ... 88, 94, 95

HARRISON, R: *Redundancy in Western Europe,* IPM, 1975

HARRISON, R: 'Self-Directed Learning' in *Management Education and Development*, April, 1975, pp 19−36

HARVEY, B and MURRAY, R: *Industrial Health Technology,* Butterworth, 1968

HARVEY, D: 'The Japanese Way to Industrial Harmony' in *The Director*, 30, January, 1978, pp 42−4

HARVEY, J: *Elementary Economics,* Macmillan, 3rd edn, 1971

HAWES, W R and BROOKES, C C P: 'Change and Renewal: Joint Consultation in Industry' in *Employment Gazette*, April, 1980, pp 353–61

HAWKINS, K: 'Company Bargaining: Problems and Prospects' in *British Journal of Industrial Relations*, IX (2), July 1971, pp 198-213 ... 205, 216

HAYES, J J and MAIER, N R F: *Creative Management*, Wiley, 1962

HAYES, K J: 'Genes, Drives and Intellect' in *Psychological Reports*, 10, 1962, pp 299–342 ... 57

HAYNES, M G: 'Developing an Appraisal Program' in *Personnel Journal*, 57 (1), 1978, pp 14–19

HEALD, G (ed): *Approaches to the Study of Organizational Behaviour*, Tavistock, 1970

HEALTH and SAFETY COMMISSION: *Code of Practice: Time off for Training of Safety Representatives*, H & SC, No. 9, 1978a ... 153

HEALTH and SAFETY COMMISSION: *Safety Representatives and Safety Committees*, H & SC, 1978b ... 152

HEINRICH, H W: *Industrial Accident Prevention: A Scientific Approach*, McGraw Hill, 4th edn., 1959

HEKEMIAN, J S and JONES, C H: 'Put People on Your Balance Sheet' in *Harvard Business Review*, January–February, 1967, pp 105–13

HELLER, F: 'An Evaluation of the Personnel Management Function' in MacFarland, D E, 1971, q.v. pp 30–43

HENEMAN, H G and SCHWAB, D P: 'An Evaluation of Research on Expectancy Theory Predictions of Employee Performance' in *Psychological Bulletin*, 78, 1972, pp 1–9

HEPPLE, B A and O'HIGGINS, P: *Employment Law*, Sweet and Maxwell, 3rd edn, 1979 ... 131, 156

HERBST, P G: *Socio-Technical Unit Design*, Tavistock Institute of Human Relations, 1966 ... 204, 207

HERRIOTT, P: 'Graduate Recruitment: Getting it Right' in *Employment Gazette*, February, 1987

HERZBERG, F: *Work and the Nature of Man*, Staples, 1966 ... 67, 88, 110

HERZBERG, F: 'One More Time: How do you Motivate Employees?' in *Harvard Business Review*, 46 (1), 1968, pp 53–62 ... 37, 39, 40, 41, 42, 43, 45, 88

HERZBERG, F: 'The Wise Old Turk' in *Harvard Business Review*, 52 (5), 1974, pp 70–80

HESSELING, P: *Strategy of Evaluation Research in the Field of Supervisory and Managerial Training*, Van Gorcum, 1966

HILL, J M M: 'A Consideration of Labour Turnover as a Resultant of a Quasi-Stationary Process' in *Human Relations*, 4 (3), August, 1951, pp 255–64 ... 275

HILL, L, and HOOK, C: *Management at the Bargaining Table*, McGraw Hill, 1945 ... 227

HILL, P: *Towards a New Philosophy of Management,* Gower, 1971 ... 180, 204, 206, 207

HILL, S: *Competition and Control at Work,* Heinemann, 1981 ... 20

HINRICHS, J R: 'Personnel Training' in Dunnette, M D (ed): *Handbook of Industrial and Organisational Psychology,* Rand-McNally, 1976, pp 829–60 ... 313, 317

HINTON, B L: 'An Empirical Investigation of the Herzberg Methodology and Two Factor Theory', in *Organization Behaviour and Human Performance,* (3), 1968, pp 286–309

HOFER, C S: 'Towards a Contingency Theory of Business Strategy' in *Academy of Management Journal,* 18 (4), December, 1975, pp 784–810

HOFSTEDE, G: 'Nationality and Espoused Values of Managers' in *Journal of Applied Psychology,* 61 (2), 1976, p 146–55 ... 165

HOFSTEDE, G: 'Culture and Organisation – A Literature Review Study' in *Journal of Enterprise Management,* 1, 1978, pp 127–35

HOFSTEDE, G: *Culture's Consequences,* Sage, 1980

HOGARTH, R M: *Evaluating Management Education,* Wiley, 1979

HOLDING, D H: *Principles of Training,* Pergamon, 1965

HOMANS, G C: *The Human Group,* Routledge and Kegan Paul, 1951 ... 4, 203, 437

HOMANS, G C: *Social Behaviour,* Routledge and Kegan Paul, 1961

HONEY, P: 'On the Trail of the Personnel Professional' in *Personnel Management,* April, 1976, pp 33–5

HONEY, P: *Face to Face,* IPM, 1976

HONEY, P and MUMFORD, A: *Manual of Learning Styles,* Honey, 1982 ... 316, 317

HONEY, P and MUMFORD, A: *Using Your Learning Styles,* Honey, 1983 ... 317, 327

HOPKINS, R R: *A Handbook of Industrial Welfare,* Pitman, 1955

HOPKINS, T K: *The Exercise of Influence in Small Groups,* Bedminster Press, 1964

HOPPOCK, R: *Job Satisfaction,* Harper and Bros, 1935

HOVLAND, C I and JANIS, I L (eds): *Personality and Persuadability,* Yale U P, 1959

HOVLAND, C I and MANDELL, W: 'An Experimental Comparison of Conclusion Drawing by the Communicator and the Audience' in *Journal of Abnormal and Social Psychology,* 47, 1952, pp 581–3

HOVLAND, C I and WEISS, W: 'The Influence of Cause Credibility on Communication Effectiveness' in *Public Opinion Quarterly,* 15, 1952, pp 635–50

HOWELLS, R and BARRETT, B: *The Manager's Guide to the Health and Safety at Work Act,* IPM, 1976; 2nd edn, 1982 ... 156

HUGHES, C L: *Goal Setting: Key to Individual and Organizational Effectiveness,* AMA, 1965

HUGHES, C L: 'Why Goal Oriented Performance Reviews Succeed and Fail' in *Personnel Journal*, June, 1966, pp 335–41

HULIN, C L and BLOOD, M R: 'Job Enlargement, Individual Differences and Worker Responses' in *Psychological Bulletin*, 69 (1), pp 41–55 ... 43, 44, 96, 109

HULL, C L: *Principles of Behaviour,* Appleton-Century-Crofts, 1943

HUMBLE, J W: *Improving Management Performance,* BIM, 1965

HUMBLE, J W: *Management by Objectives,* Industrial Educational and Research Foundation, 1967 ... 357

HUMBLE, J W: *Management by Objectives in Action,* McGraw Hill, 1970

HUMBLE, J W: *The Experienced Manager,* McGraw Hill, 1973

HUMBLE, J W: *Improving Business Results: The Definitive Work on Management by Objectives,* McGraw Hill, 1967

HUNERYAGER, S C and HECKMAN, I L (eds): *Human Relations in Management,* Edward Arnold, 1967

HUNT, D: 'Mentorship: A Career Training and Development Tool' in *Academy of Management Review*, 8 (3), 1983, pp 475–85

HUNT, R G and LICHTMAN, G M: 'Counselling of Employees by Work Supervisors: Concepts, Attitudes and Practices in a White Collar Organisation' in *Journal of Counselling Psychology*, 16 (1), 1969, pp 81–6

HUNTER, J E and HUNTER, R F: 'Validity and Utility of Alternative Predictors of Job Performance' in *Psychological Bulletin*, 96, 1984, pp 72–98

HUNTER, J E and SCHMIDT, F L: 'The Economic Benefits of Personnel Selection Using Psychological Ability Tests' in *Industrial Relations*, 1982, pp 293–308

HUSBAND, T M: *Work Analysis and Pay Structure,* McGraw Hill, 1975

HUSBAND, R M: 'Payment Structures Made to Measure' in *Personnel Management*, April, 1975, pp 27–9 and p 39

HUTCHINS, D: 'How Quality goes Round in Circles' in *Management Today*, January, 1981, pp 27–32 ... 430

HYMAN, H H: 'The Value Systems of Different Classes: A Social-Psychological Contribution to the Analysis of Stratification' in Bendix, R and Lipset, S M (eds): *Class, Status and Power,* Free Press, 1953, pp 426–42

HYMAN, R and BROUGH, I: *Social Values and Industrial Relations,* Blackwell, 1975 ... 74

I

IMAIZUMI, M: *Quality Control Circle Activities in Japan and Western Countries,* Paper to the Asia Quality Circles Conference, November, 1981 (Hong Kong Industrial Relations Association, 1981)

INBUCON: Survey of Executive Salaries and Fringe Benefits in the UK, INBUCON, annually

INCOMES DATA SERVICES: 'Performance Appraisal of Manual Workers', IDS Study No. 390, July, 1987

INCOMES DATA SERVICES, Top Pay Unit: *Executive Bonus Schemes,* IDS/IPM, July 1987 ... 399

INDIK, B P: 'Some Effects of Organizational Size on Member Attitudes and Behaviour' in *Human Relations*, 16, 1963, pp 369–84

INDIK, B P: 'Organization Size and Member Participation: Some Empirical Tests of Alternative Explanations' in *Human Relations*, 18, 1965, pp 339–49

INDUSTRIAL DEMOCRACY IN EUROPE (IDE): *Industrial Democracy in Europe,* Oxford UP, 1981

INDUSTRIAL SOCIETY: *Design of Personnel Systems and Records,* Goulet, 1969

INDUSTRIAL SOCIETY: *Guide to the Health and Safety at Work Act,* Industrial Society, 1974

INDUSTRIAL SOCIETY: *Practical Policies for Participation,* Industrial Society, 1974

INGHAM, G K: 'Organizational Size, Orientation to Work and Industrial Behaviour' in *Sociology*, 1 (3), September, 1967, pp 239–58

INGHAM, G K: 'Plant Size and Political Attitudes and Behaviour' in *Sociological Review*, 17 (2), July, 1969, pp 235–49

INSTITUTE OF PERSONNEL MANAGEMENT: 'Statement on Personnel Management and Personnel Policies' in *Personnel Management*, March, 1963, pp 11–15

IPM: *Practical Participation and Involvement,* IPM, 1981

IPM: *Code on Recruitment Practice,* IPM, 1978

INTERNATIONAL LABOUR ORGANISATION: *Job Evaluation,* ILO, 1960 ... 370

IRON AND STEEL INDUSTRY TRAINING BOARD: *Identification of Training Needs,* ISITB, 1975

IRVINE, A: *Improving Industrial Communications,* Industrial Society/ Gower, 1970 ... 430

ISHIKAWA, K (ed): *Quality Control Circle Activities,* Union of Japanese Scientists and Engineers (JUSE), 1968

J

JAAP, T and WATSON, J A: 'A Conceptual Approach to Training' in *Personnel Management*, September, 1970, pp 30–33

JACKSON, J M: 'The Normative Regulation of Authoritative Behaviour' in University of Kansas *Comparative Studies of Mental Hospital Organization,* University of Kansas, 1962

JACKSON, K F: *The Art of Solving Problems,* Bulmershe College of HE, 1984 ... 299

JACKSON, P: *Local Government*, Butterworth, 1976

JAFFE, A J and FROOMKIN, J: *Technology and Jobs,* Praeger, 1968

JAFFE, A J and STEWARD, C D: *Manpower Resources and Utilisation,* Chapman and Hall, 1951

JAHODA, *Current Concepts of Positive Mental Health,* Basic Books, 1958 ... 471

JAMES, R: 'Is there a case for Local Authority Policy Planning?' in *Public Administration,* 51, Summer, 1973, pp 147–63

JANSON, R: 'A Job Enrichment Trial in Data Processing, in an Insurance Organisation' in Davis and Cherns, 1975, Vol. 2, q.v. pp 300–14 ... 43

JAQUES, E: *The Changing Culture of a Factory,* Tavistock, 1951 ... 24, 414

JAQUES, E: *Measurement of Responsibility,* Harvard U P, 1956

JAQUES, E: *Equitable Payment,* Heinemann, 1961

JAQUES, E: *Time Span Handbook,* Heinemann, 1964

JAQUES, E: *Progression Handbook,* Heinemann, 1968

JARMAN, L C: 'The Nature of Management Development' in Torrington, D P and Sutton, D F: *Handbook of Management Development,* Gower, 1973

JENKINS, Lord: *Report of the Company Law Committee,* Cmnd 1749, HMSO, June, 1962

JENNER, R: 'Analysing Cultural Stereotypes in Multinational Business: United States and Australia', in *Journal of Management Studies,* 19 (3), 1982, pp 309–25

JENSEN, G E: *Dynamics of Instructional Groups,* National Society for the Study of Education, Yearbook, 1960 ... 327

JOHNSON, D M: *The Psychology of Thinking,* Harper and Row, 1972 ... 247, 316

JONES, G, BELL, D, CENTER, A and COLEMAN, D: *Perspectives in Manpower Planning,* IPM, 1967

JONES, G N: *Planned Organizational Change,* Routledge and Kegan Paul, 1969

JONES, J K C, BROWN, C A and NICHOLSON, N: 'Absence from Work: Its Meaning, Measurement and Control' in *International Review of Applied Psychology,* 22 (2), 1973, pp 137–55

JONES, K: *The Human Face of Change – Social Responsibility and Rationalization at British Steel,* IPM, 1974

JONES, P: 'Incomes Policy and the Public Sector' in *Personnel Management,* 10 (2), February, 1978, pp 38–43

JONES, R M and LAKIN, C: *The Carpetmakers,* McGraw-Hill, 1978 ... 423

JONES, R M: *Absenteeism,* Manpower Paper No. 4, HMSO, 1971

JOYCE, B and WEIL, M: *Models of Teaching,* Prentice-Hall, 1972 ... 319

JOYCE, L: 'Developments in Evaluation Research' in *Journal of Occupational Behaviour,* 1 (1), 1980, pp 181–90

JOYCE, P and WOODS, A: 'Joint Consultation in Britain: Towards an Explanation', in *Employee Relations,* 6 (2), 1984, pp 2-8 ... 466

JURAN, J M: 'Product Quality: A Prescription for the West' in *Management Review,* June – July, 1981

K

KAHN, R L and KATZ, D: 'Leadership Practices in Relation to Productivity and Morale' in Cartwright and Zander, 1953, q.v. pp 612 – 28

KAHN-FREUND, O: *Labour and the Law,* Stevens, 1972, rev edn, 1977 ... 123, 131

KARN, H W and GILMER, B v H: *Readings in Industrial and Business Psychology,* McGraw Hill, 1952, 2nd edn, 1962

KASL, S V: 'Epidemiological Contributions to the Study of Work Stress' in Cooper and Payne 1978, q.v. pp 3 – 50 ... 44, 182, 408

KAST, F E and ROSENZWEIG, J E: 'General Systems Theory: Applications for Organization and Management' in *Academy of Management Journal,* December, 1972, pp 447 – 65

KATZ, D: 'Consistent Reactive Participation of Group Members and Reduction of Intergroup Conflict' in *Journal of Conflict Resolution,* 5 March, 1959, pp 28 – 40

KATZ, E and LAZARSFELD, P F: *Personal Influence,* Free Press, 1955 ... 438, 451, 452

KATZ, R L: 'The Executive Skills' in *Harvard Business Review,* September – October, 1974, pp 90 – 102

KAY, H, DODD, B and SIME, M: *Teaching Machines and Programmed Instruction,* Penguin, 1968

KEENAN, A: 'Some Relationships between Interviewers' Personal Feelings about Candidates and the General Evaluation of Them' in *Journal of Occupational Psychology,* 50, 1977, pp 275 – 83 ... 297

KEENAN, A: 'The Selection Interview: Candidates' Reactions and Interviewers' Judgements' in *British Journal of Clinical Psychology,* 17, 1978, pp 201 – 21

KEENAN, A: 'Interviewing for Graduate Recruitment' in *Personnel Management,* February, 1978, pp 31 – 5

KEENAN, A: 'Where Application Forms Mislead' in *Personnel Management,* February, 1983, pp 40 – 43

KEENOY, T: *Invitation to Industrial Relations,* Blackwell, 1985 ... 433

KELLEY, H H: 'Communication in Experimentally Created Hierarchies' in *Human Relations,* 4, 1951, pp 39 – 56; and in Cartwright and Zander, 1953, q.v. pp 443 – 61

KELLEY, H H: 'A Classroom Study of the Dilemmas in Interpersonal Negotiations' in Archibald, K (ed): *Strategic Interaction and Conflict,* Institute of International Studies, University of California, 1966, pp 49 – 73

A Textbook of Human Resource Management

KELLY, G A: *A Theory of Personality: The Psychology of Personal Constructs,* Norton, 1963 ... 57

KELLY, R W: *Hiring the Worker,* Engineering Magazine Company, New York, 1918

KENNEDY, G; BENSON, J and McMILLAN, J: *Managing Negotiations,* Business Books, 1980; 3rd edn, 1987

KENNEY, J, DONNELLY, E and REID, M: *Manpower Training and Development,* IPM, 2nd edn, 1979 ... 310, 327

KENNEY, J and REID, M: *Training Interventions,* IPM, 1986 ... 57, 327

KENNEY, T P: 'Stating the Case for Welfare' in *Personnel Management,* September, 1975, pp 18–21 and p 35

KIESLER, S: *Interpersonal Processes in Groups and Organisations,* AHM Publishing Company, 1978 ... 47

KILCOURSE, T: 'IR Training: What the Line Manager Needs to Know?' in *Personnel Management,* May, 1977, pp 32–5 ... 431

KIMBERLEY, J R, MILES, R H et al: *The Organizational Life Cycle,* Jossey Bass, 1980

KING, D: *Training Within the Organization,* Tavistock, 1964 ... 8, 327

KING, P: *Performance Planning and Appraisal,* McGraw Hill, 1984

KINGSLEY, R and M: *An Industrial Day Nursery: the Personnel Manager's Guide,* IPM, 1969

KLEIN, L: *New Forms of Work Organisation,* Cambridge UP, 1976

KLUCKHOHN, C: *Culture and Behaviour: Collected Essays,* Free Press, 1962 ... 66, 111

KLUCKHOHN, F R: 'Dominant and Variant Cultural Value Orientations' in Cabot, H and Kahl, J A (eds): *Human Relations, Vol. 1, Concepts,* Harvard UP, 1953, pp 88–98 ... 93, 94, 111

KLUCKHOLN, F R and STRODTBECK, F L: *Variations in Value Orientations,* Row Peterson, 1961

KNIGHT, I B: *Company Organization and Worker Participation,* HMSO, 1979

KNIVETON, B: 'Industrial Negotiating: Some Training Implications' in *Industrial Relations Journal,* V (3), Autumn, 1974, pp 27–37

KNIVETON, B: 'Negotiation Training and Social Psychology' in *Industrial Relations Journal,* 6 (4), 1975/6, pp 59–72

KNIVETON, B and TOWERS, B: *Training for Negotiation,* Business Books, 1978

KOLB, D A, RUBIN, I M, and McINTYRE, J M: *Organisational Psychology: An Experimental Approach,* Prentice Hall, 1974 ... 299, 300, 316

KOONTZ, H: 'A Model for Analysing the Universality and Transferability of Management' in *Academy of Management Journal,* 12 (4), December 1969, pp 415–29

KOONTZ, H and O'DONNELL, C: *Management: A Book of Readings,* McGraw Hill, 1968 ... 234, 243

KOONTZ, H, and O'DONNELL, C: *Management: A Systems and Contingency Analysis of Managerial Functions,* McGraw Hill, 1976

KOONTZ, H, O'DONNELL, C, and WEIHRICH, H, *Management,* McGraw Hill, 1980, 7th edn

KORACH, M: 'The Science of Industry' in Goldsmith and MacKay, 1966, q.v. pp 226–43 ... 179, 207

KORNHAUSER, A: *The Mental Health of the Industrial Worker: A Detroit Study,* Wiley, 1965 ... 34, 44

KOTTER, J P: 'What Efficient General Managers Really Do' in *Harvard Business Review,* November – December, 1982, pp 156–67 ... 13

KOTTER, J P: 'Power, Dependence and Effective Management' in *Harvard Business Review,* Nov – Dec. 1956, pp 25–9

KOTTER, J P and SCHLESINGER, L A: 'Choosing Strategies for Change' in *Harvard Business Review,* March – April, 1979, pp 106–14

KRAM, K: *Mentoring at Work,* Scott, Foresman 1985

KROEBER, A L, and KLUCKHOHN, C: *Culture: A Critical Review of Concepts and Definitions,* Vintage Books, 1952 ... 92

KROEBER, A L, and PARSONS, T: 'The Concepts of Culture and Social Systems' in *American Sociological Review,* 23, 1958, pp 582–3

KRUISINGA, H J (ed): *The Balance Between Centralization and Decentralization in Managerial Control,* Stenfert Kroese NV, Leiden, 1954 ... 197

L

LABOUR, MINISTRY OF: *Training Within Industry,* HMSO, 1962 ... 257

LABOUR, MINISTRY OF : *Dismissal procedures,* HMSO, 1967

LABOUR, MINISTRY OF: *Glossary of Training Terms,* HMSO, 1967; 1971; see also MSC, 1981

LANDY, F J and TRUMBO, D A: *Psychology of Work Behaviour,* Dorsey Press, 1965; 1976 ... 67, 74, 298

LANG, D: 'Project Control Comes to Personnel' in *Personnel Management,* May, 1974, pp 27–30

LARKCOM, J (ed): *Personnel Management Handbook,* Business Publications, 1967

LASSWELL, H D: 'Communication as an Emerging Discipline' in *Audio-Visual Communication Review,* 6, 1958, pp 245–54 ... 415

LASSWELL, H D and KAPLAN, A: *Power and Society,* Yale U P, 1950

LASSWELL, H D et al: *Propaganda and Promotional Activities,* University of Chicago Press, 1969

LATHAM, G P et al: 'The Situational Interview' in *Journal of Applied Psychology,* 1980, pp 422–7

LATHAM, G P and WEXLEY, K N: *Increasing Productivity through Performance Appraisal,* Addison-Wesley, 1981 ... 336, 357

LAWLER, E E: *Pay and Organizational Effectiveness,* McGraw Hill, 1971

LAWLER, E E: 'A Causal Correlation Analysis of the Relationship between Expectancy Attitudes and Job Performance' in *Journal of Applied Psychology*, 52, 1968, pp 462–8

LAWLER, E E, HACKMAN, J R and KAUFMAN, S: 'Effects of Job Design: A Field Experiment' in *Journal of Applied Social Psychology*, 3, 1973, pp 49–62 ... 43

LAWLER, E E and SUTTLE, J L: 'A Causal Correlational Test of the Need Hierarchy Concept' in *Organizational Behaviour and Human Performance*, 7, 1972, pp 265–87

LAWRENCE, P R and LORSCH, J W: *Organization and Environment*, Harvard U P, 1967

LAWRENCE, J (ed): *Company Manpower Planning in Perspective*, IPM/IMS, 1975 ... 251, 264, 267, 269

LAWRENCE, J: 'Manpower and Personnel Models in Britain' in *Personnel Review*, 2 (3), Summer, 1973, pp 4–26; and in Smith, 1980, q.v. pp 18–46

LAWSCHE, C H: *Principles of Personnel Testing*, McGraw Hill, 1948

LEAVITT, H J: 'Applied Organisational Change in Industry' in *March* 1965, q.v. pp 1144–70

LEAVITT, H J: *Managerial Psychology*, Chicago U P, 3rd edn, 1972

LEGGATT, T W: *The Training of British Managers*, NEDO, 1972

LEGGE, K: *Power, Innovation and Problem-Solving in Personnel Management*, McGraw-Hill, 1978

LEIGHTON, P E and DUMVILLE, S L: 'From Status to Contract – Some Effects of the Contract of Employment Act, 1972' in *Industrial Law Journal*, 6, 1977, pp 133–48

LEMON, N: *Attitudes and their Measurement*, Batsford, 1963; 1968

LESSEM, R: *The Roots of Excellence*, Fontana, 1985 ... 105, 111, 133

LEVINE, R A: *Culture, Behaviour and Personality*, Hutchinson, 1973 ... 88

LEVINE, J and BUTLER, J: 'Lecture vs Group Decision in Changing Behaviour' in *Journal of Applied Psychology*, 36, 1952, pp 29–33; and in Cartwright and Zander, 1953, q.v. pp 280–86 ... 345-6

LEVINE, S: 'Occupation and Personality: Relationship between the Social Factors of the Job and Human Orientation' in *Personnel and Guidance Journal*, 41, 1963

LEVINGER, G: 'The Development of Perceptions and Behaviour in Newly-formed Social Power Relationships' in Cartwright, D (ed): *Studies in Social Power*, University of Michigan, 1959, pp 83–98

LEVINSON, H M: 'Management by Whose Objectives?' in *Harvard Business Review*, July/August, 1970, pp 125–34

LEVITT, T: 'The Changing Character of Capitalism' in *Harvard Business Review*, September – October, 1956

LEVITT, T: 'Exploit the Product Life Cycle' in *Harvard Business Review*, 43, November – December, 1965, pp 81–94 ... 163

LEWIN, K: *Principles of Topological Psychology*, McGraw Hill, 1936

LEWIN, K: *Field Theory in Social Science,* Harper, 1951

LEWIN, K: 'Studies in Group Decision' in Cartwright and Zander, 1953, q.v. pp 287–301; and in Maccoby, Newcomb and Hartley, 1958, q.v. pp 197–211 ... 437, 450, 451

LEWIN, K: *Resolving Social Conflicts,* Harper and Row, 1967 ... 466

LEWIS, C: 'What's New In Selection?' in *Personnel Management,* January, 1984, pp 14–16 ... 287, 297

LEWIS, R, and STEWART, R: *The Boss,* Phoenix House, 1958 ... 11

LIEBERT, R M and SPIEGLER, M D: *Personality: An Introduction to Theory and Research,* Dorsey, 1970

LIKERT, R: 'Measuring Organisational Performance' in *Harvard Business Review,* 36 (2), March–April, 1958, pp 41–50

LIKERT, R: *New Patterns of Management,* McGraw Hill, 1961 ... 45, 233, 248

LIKERT, R: *The Human Organization,* McGraw Hill, 1967 ... 495

LINDBLOM, C E: 'The Science of Muddling Through' in *Public Administration Review,* 19, 1959, pp 79–88

LINDBLOM, C E: *The Intelligence of Democracy,* Macmillan, 1965

LINDBLOM, C E: *The Policy Making Process,* Prentice Hall, 1968

LINTON, R: *The Study of Man,* Appleton-Century-Crofts, 1936; 1964

LINTON, R: *The Cultural Background to Personality,* Routledge and Kegan Paul, 1945 ... 90

LINTON, R: *Science of Man in the World Crisis,* Columbia, 1945

LINTON, R: *Most of the World,* Columbia, 1949

LIONBERGER, H F: *Adoption of New Ideas and Practices,* Iowa State University Press, 1960

LIPPITT, G L: *Organisational Renewal,* Appleton-Century-Crofts, 1969 ... 190, 469, 495

LITTLE, A and WARR, P: 'Who's Afraid of Job Enrichment?', in *Personnel Management,* 3 (2), 1971, pp 34-7 ... 43

LIVY, B: *Job Evaluation,* Allen and Unwin, 1975 ... 399

LLEWELLYN, W G: *Executive Compensation in Large Industrial Corporations,* National Bureau of Economic Research, 1968

LOCKE, E W: *Fundamentals of Personnel Management,* IPM, 1943

LOCKYER, G: *Factory and Production Management,* Pitman, 1974 ... 31, 393

LONG, P: *Performance Appraisal Revisited,* IPM, 1986 ... 329, 331, 357

LORIN, B C and CARSTEVENS, E R: *Coaching, Learning and Action,* AMA, 1971

LORSCHE, J W, BAUGHMAN, J, REESE, J and MINTZBERG, H: *Understanding Management,* Harper and Bros, 1978

LOVERIDGE, R and MOK, A: *Theories of Labour Market Segmentation,* Academic Press, 1981 ... 171, 172, 178

LOWRY, P: 'A Matter of Attitudes: Penetrating the Platitudes' in *Personnel Management,* 13 (10), October, 1981, pp 46–7 ... 431

LUCIUS, M J: *Personnel Management,* Irwin-Dorsey, 1975

LUPTON, T: *Industrial Behaviour and Personnel Management,* IPM, 1964

LUPTON, T: *Management and the Social Sciences,* Penguin, 1971

LUPTON, T (ed): *Payment Systems,* Penguin, 1972

LUPTON, T and BOWEY, A: *Job and Pay Comparisons,* Gower, 1973 ... 365

LYMAN, E L: 'Occupational Differences in the Values Attached to Work' in *American Journal of Sociology,* 61, 1955, pp 138 – 44

LYNCH, B: 'Graphology: Towards a Hand-picked Workforce' in *Personnel Management,* March, 1985, pp 14 – 18

LYNCH, J U: *Making Manpower Effective,* Pan, 1968

LYNCH, P: 'Are Careers Obsolete?' in *Personnel Management,* 1 (9), August, 1968, pp 30 – 33

LYNTON, P R and PAREEK, U: *Training for Development,* Dorsey, 1962

LYONS, T P: *Personnel Function in a Changing Environment,* Pitman, 2nd edn, 1985

LYTLE, C W: *Job Evaluation Methods,* Ronald Press, 1946

LYTLE, C W: *Wage Incentive Methods,* Ronald Press, 1942

M

MACCOBY, E E, NEWCOMB, T M, and HARTLEY, E L: *Readings in Social Psychology,* Henry Holt, 1947; 1958

MACKAY, L: 'The Macho Manager: It's No Myth' in *Personnel Management,* January, 1986, pp 25 – 7

MACKENZIE-DAVEY, D, et al: *Attitude Surveys in Industry,* IPM, 1970

MADDEN, J M: 'A Review of Some Literature on Judgement with Implications for Job Evaluation' in USAF Technical Note, No. 60 – 212, 1960

MAGER, R F: *Preparing Instructional Objectives,* Fearon Publishers, 1961 ... 312

MAHLER, W R: 'Let's get More Scientific in Rating Employees' in Dooher and Marquis, 1950, q.v. pp 49 – 59

MAIER, N P: *Psychology in Industrial Organisations,* Houghton-Mifflin, 4th edn, 1973 ... 340

MAKIN, P and ROBERTSON, I: 'Selecting the Best Selection Techniques' in *Personnel Management,* November, 1986, p 38 – 40 ... 288, 291, 293, 297

MANGHAM, I: 'Uncovering the Company Unconscious' in *Management Today,* March, 1968, pp 109 – 12

MANGHAM, I: *The Politics of Organisational Change,* Associated Business Publishers, 1978

MANN, J: *Changing Human Behaviour,* Scribner's Sons, 1965 ... 248

MANN, M: *Consciousness and Action among the Western Working Class,* Macmillan, 1973

MANPOWER SERVICES COMMISSION: *People at Work: Auditing Management Development,* MSC, 1979

MSC: *Outlook on Training: Review of the Employment and Training Act, 1973,* MSC, 1980 ... 300

MSC: *Annual Report, 1974–5,* MSC, 1975

MANSFIELD, R and POOLE, M: *International Perspectives on Management and Organisation,* Gower, 1981

MANSFIELD, R, POOLE, M, BLYTON, P, and FROST, P: *The British Manager in Profile,* British Institute of Management, 1981

MANSFIELD COOPER, W and WOOD, J C: *Outlines of Industrial Law,* Butterworth, 1974

MANT, A: *The Rise and Fall of the British Manager,* Macmillan, 1977

MANT, A: *The Experienced Manager,* BIM, 1969

MARCEAU, L (ed): *Dealing with a Union,* American Management Association, 1969

MARCH, J G (ed): *Handbook of Organisations,* Rand McNally, 1965 ... 424, 446, 448

MARCH, J G and SIMON, H A: *Organisations,* Wiley, 1958

MARCHINGTON, M: *Responses to Participation at Work,* Gower, 1980

MARGERISON, C: *Managing Effective Work Groups,* McGraw Hill, 1973

MARGERISON, C: 'Action Research and Action Learning in Management Education' in *Journal of European Industrial Training,* 2 (6), 1978, pp 22–5

MARGUILES, C J and RAIA, A P: *Organisational Development,* McGraw Hill, 1972

MARKS, W: *Induction – Acclimatising People to Work,* IPM, 1974

MARKS, W: *Preparing an Employee Handbook,* IPM, 1972; revised edn, 1978

MARKWELL, D S and ROBERTS, T J: *Organisation of Management Development Programmes,* Gower Press, 1969

MARPLES, D: *The Decisions of Engineering Design,* Institute of Engineering Designers, 1961

MARRIOTT, R: *Incentive Payment Systems,* Staples Press, 1968

MARSH, A I: *Employee Relations Policy and Decision-Making,* CBI/Gower, 1982

MARSH, A I: 'The Managerial Grid' in *Industrial Welfare,* October, 1965, pp 256–9

MARSH, A I, GILLIES, J and RUSH, M: *The Training of Managers in Industrial Relations,* Training Services Agency, MSC, August, 1976

MARSH, A I: 'Tailoring IR Training to the Manager and his Needs' in *Personnel Management,* August, 1977, pp 26–7 and p 35

MARTIN, P and NICHOLS, J: *Creating a Committed Workforce,* IPM, 1987 ... 466

MASLOW, A H: 'A Theory of Human Motivation' in *Psychological Review,* 50, 1943, pp 370–96 ... 88

546 *A Textbook of Human Resource Management*

MASLOW, A H: *Motivation and Personality,* Harper and Row, 1954; 1970 ... 8, 57, 67

MAYFIELD, E: 'The Selection Interview: A Re-evaluation of Published Research' in *Personnel Psychology,* 17, 1964, pp 239–60; and in Fleishmann, 1967, q.v. pp 23–39 ... 291

MAYMAN, D: 'What Price People?' in *Personnel Management,* December, 1974, pp 35–7

MAYO, E: *The Human Problems of an Industrial Civilisation,* Macmillan, 1933

MAYO, E: *The Social Problems of an Industrial Civilisation,* Harvard Business School, 1949; Routledge and Kegan Paul reprint, 1975

McBEATH, G and RANDS, D N: *Salary Administration,* Business Books, 1969

MC CARTHY, W E J: *Trade Unions,* Penguin, 1972 ... 156, 157

McCARTHY, W E J: *The Closed Shop in Britain,* Blackwell, 1964 ... 151

McCLELLAND, D C: *Personality,* Dryden, 1951 ... 58, 69, 88

McCLELLAND, D C: *The Achieving Society,* Van Nostrand, 1961 ... 436

McCLELLAND, D C and WINTER, D C: *Motivating Economic Achievement,* Free Press, 1969

McCONNELL, C R (ed): *Perspectives on Wage Determination: A Book of Readings,* McGraw Hill, 1970

McCORMICK, B: *Wages,* Penguin, 1969

McCORMICK, E J: *Job Analysis: Methods and Implications,* AMACOM, 1979 ... 28, 297

McDOUGALL, C: 'How Well do you Reward your Managers?' in *Personnel Management,* March, 1973, pp 38–43 ... 63, 64, 73, 88

McFARLAND, D E: *Personnel Management Theory and Practice,* Macmillan, 1968

McFARLAND, D E: *Personnel Management,* Penguin, 1971

McGEHEE, W and THAYER, P W: *Training in Business and Industry,* Wiley, 1961 ... 298, 327

McGREGOR, D: 'An Uneasy Look at Performance Appraisal' in *Harvard Business Review,* 35 (3), 1959, pp 89–94 ... 332, 340, 491

McGREGOR, D: *The Human Side of Enterprise,* McGraw Hill, 1960 ... 23, 83, 96, 462, 488

McGREGOR, D: *The Professional Manager,* McGraw Hill, 1967

McIVER, R M and PAGE, C H: *Society – An Introductory Analysis,* Macmillan, 1953

McKINLAY, J B: *Processing People,* Holt, Rinehart and Winston, 1975 ... 18, 87

MEADE, J P de C and GREIG, F W: *Supervisory Training: A New Approach for Management,* HMSO, 1966

MEGAW, Sir JOHN: *Inquiry into Civil Service Pay,* Cmnd 8590, HMSO, 1983 ... 73, 399

MEGGINSON, D F and BOYDELL, T H: *A Guide to Management Coaching,* BACIE, 1978

MEGGINSON, L C: *Personnel – A Behavioural Approach to Administration,* Irwin, 1972 ... 231

MERRIE, A H: 'Evaluation of Manual and Non-Manual Jobs' in *Personnel Management,* XXX (198), July – August, 1948, pp 174 – 81

MERTON, R: *Social Theory and Social Structure,* Free Press, 1949 ... 194

METCALF, H C and URWICK, L: *Dynamic Administration,* Pitman, 1941

MEYER, H H: 'Split Roles in Performance Appraisal' in *Harvard Business Review,* 43, January – February, 1965, pp 123 – 9 ... 340

MEYER, H H: 'The Validity of the In-Basket Test as Measure of Managerial Performance' in *Personnel Psychology,* 23 (3), Autumn, 1970, pp 297 – 308

MILLARD, G: *Personnel Management in Hospitals,* IPM, 1972

MILLER, D C, and FORM, W H: *Industrial Sociology,* Harper and Bros., 1951 ... 6, 8, 46, 73, 87

MILLER, E J and RICE, A K: *Systems of Organization: The Control of Task and Sentient Boundaries,* Tavistock, 1967 ... 207, 457, 458

MILLER, F B: *Personnel Research Contributions by US Universities,* New York State School of Industrial and Labour Relations, 1960 ... 85

MILLER, G A, GALANTER, G E and PRIBAM, K H: *Plans and the Structure of Behaviour,* Holt, Rinehart and Winston, 1960

MILLER, K: *Psychological Testing,* Gower, 1975

MILLERSON, G: *The Qualifying Associations,* Routledge and Kegan Paul, 1964 ... 139, 156

MILLS, H R: *Teaching and Training,* Macmillan, 1967 ... 223, 443

MILLWARD, G E: *Organisation and Methods,* Macmillan, 1959 ... 28, 45

MINER, B and CRANE D P: 'Motivation to Manage and the Manifestation of a Managerial Orientation in Career Planning' in *Academy of Management Journal,* 24 (3), 1981, pp 623 – 33

MINER, J B: 'The OD-MD Conflict' in *Business Horizons,* 16 (6), 1973, pp 31 – 6 ... 495

MINER, J B and MINER, M G: *Personnel and Industrial Relations,* Macmillan, 3rd edn, 1977 ... 88, 262

MINTZBERG, H: *The Nature of Managerial Work,* Harper and Row, 1973

MINTZBERG, H B: 'The Manager's Job: Folklore and Fact' in *Harvard Business Review,* July/August, 1975, pp 49 – 61

MINTZBERG, H B: *Power in and Around Organizations,* Prentice Hall, 1983

MITCHELL, E: *The Employer's Guide to the Law on Health, Safety and Welfare at Work,* Business Books, 1974

MITCHELL, F, SAMS, I, TWEEDIE, D, and WHITE, P: 'Disclosure of Information: Some Evidence from Case Studies' in *Industrial Relations Journal,* 11 (5), November/December 1980, pp 53 – 62

MITCHELL, G D (ed): *A Dictionary of Sociology,* Routledge and Kegan Paul, 1969 ... 92

MONOHAN, C J and MUCHINSKY, P M: 'Three Decades of Personnel Selection Research: A State of the Art Analysis and Evaluation' in *Journal of Occupational Psychology,* 56, 1983, pp ... 291

MOODY, C: 'The Perils of Portable Pensions' in *Personnel Management,* December, 1984, pp 34–6

MOODY, D: 'Absence Minded' in *Personnel Management,* November, 1971, p 28

MOORE, M R: *A Proposed Taxonomy of the Perceptual Domain and Some Suggested Applications,* Educational Testing Service, 1967 ... 312

MORE, B E and ROSS, T L: *Scanlon Way to Improve Productivity: A Practical Guide,* Wiley, 1978 ... 392, 399

MORLEY, I, and STEPHENSON, G: *The Social Psychology of Bargaining,* Allen and Unwin, 1977

MORRIS, J W: *Principles and Practice of Job Evaluation,* Heinemann, 1973

MORRISON, R F, OWENS, W A, GLENNON, J R and ALBRIGHT, L E: 'Factored Life History Antecedents of Industrial Research Performance' in *Journal of Applied Psychology,* 46 (4), 1962, pp 281–4

MOSS, A: 'A Company Approach to Industry Manpower Forecasting' in *Personnel Review,* 3 (2), Spring, 1974, pp 8–24

MOXON, G R: *The Functions of a Personnel Department,* IPM, 1966 ... 237

MUKHERJEE, S: *Changing Manpower Needs,* PEP, 1970

MUMFORD, A: *The Manager and Training,* Pitman, 1971

MUMFORD, A: 'What's New in Management Development?' in *Personnel Management,* May, 1985, pp 30–32

MUMFORD, E: *Computers, Planning and Personnel Management,* IPM, 1969

MUMFORD, E: 'Job Satisfaction: A Method of Analysis' in *Personnel Review,* 1 (3), Summer, 1972, pp 48–57 ... 115-16

MUMFORD, L: *The Myth of the Machine,* Secker and Warburg, 1966

MURRAY, H A: *Explorations in Personality,* Oxford UP, 1938

MURRAY, H A (ed): *Myth and Mythmaking,* Beacon, 1968

MYERS, C S: *Industrial Psychology in Great Britain,* Jonathan Cape, 1933

MYERS, M S: *Managing Without Unions,* Addison-Wesley Press, 1976

N

National Advisory Council on Education for Industry and Commerce: *Report of the Committee on Technical Courses and Examinations,* The Hazlegrave Report, HMSO, 1969

National Board for Prices and Incomes: *Payment By Results,* Report No. 65, HMSO, 1968

NBPI: *Job Evaluation,* Reports Nos. 83 and 83S, HMSO, 1968
NBPI: *Salary Structures,* Report No. 132, HMSO, 1969 ... 383, 399
NBPI: *General Problems of Low Pay,* NBPI Report No. 169, Cmnd 4648, April, 1971
National Economic Development Office, Management Education, Training and Development Committee: *Management Training in Industrial Relations,* NEDO, 1975... 300
NEDO: *Productivity: A Handbook of Advisory Services,* NEDO, 1967
National Institute of Industrial Psychology: *Statistical Records about People at Work,* NIIP, July, 1964
NAYLOR, J C: 'Parameters Affecting the Relative Efficiency of Part and Whole Practice Methods: A Review of the Literature', US Navy Training Development Centre Technical Report, No 950–51, 1962 ... 315, 316, 327
NAYLOR, J C and BRIGGS, G E: 'Effects of Task Complexity and Task Organisation on the Relative Efficiency of Part and Whole Training Methods' in *Journal of Experimental Psychology,* 65, 1963, pp 217–24; and in Yukl and Wexley, 1971, q.v. pp 443–50 ... 316
NAYLOR, R and TORRINGTON, D: *Administration of Personnel Policies,* Gower, 1974
NEWCOMB, T M: *Social Psychology,* Tavistock, 1952 ... 56, 61
NEWCOMB, T M: 'Attitude Development as a Function of Reference Groups: The Bennington Study' in Maccoby, Newcomb, and Hartley, 1958, q.v. pp 265–75
NEWELL, A and SIMON, H A: 'Heuristic Problem-Solving' in *Operations Research,* 6, Jan/Feb, 1958, pp 1–10; and May/June, 1958, pp 449–50
NEWSHAM, D B: *The Challenge of Change to the Adult Trainee,* HMSO, 1969
NEWSTROM, J W, REIF, W E, and MONCZKA, R M: *A Contingency Approach to Management: Readings,* McGraw Hill, 1975
NICHOLS, D: *Three Varieties of Pluralism,* Macmillan, 1974
NICHOLSON, N: 'Absence from Work and Job Satisfaction' in *Journal of Applied Psychology,* 61, 1976, pp 728–37
NICHOLSON, N: 'Absence Behaviour and Attendance Motivation' in *Journal of Management Studies,* 14, 1977, pp 231–52
NIEBEL, B W: *Motion and Time Study,* Irwin, 1972 ... 27, 29, 30, 32, 45, 262
NIVEN, M M: *Personnel Management, 1913–63,* IPM, 1967 ... 235, 284
NOLAN, P: 'The Firm and Labour Market Behaviour' in Bain, G (ed): *Industrial Relations in Britain,* Blackwell, 1983 ... 168, 173, 178, 363
NORSTEDT, J P and AGUREN, S: *The Saab-Scania Report,* Swedish Employers' Confederation, 1972
NORTHCOTT, C H: *Personnel Management, Principles and Practice,* Pitman, 1955 ... 237, 251, 284

NORTON, M: *The Corporate Donor's Handbook,* The Directory of Social Change, Radius Works, Back Lane, London, NW3 1HL, 1987

O

ODIORNE, GS: *Personnel Policy: Incomes and Practices,* Merrill, 1963 ... 231

Office of Manpower Economics: *Measured Daywork,* OME/HMSO, 1973 ... 399

Office of Population Censuses and Surveys, Social Survey Division: *Workplace Industrial Relations, 1972,* by S Parker, HMSO, 1974

O'HIGGINS, P: *Workers' Rights,* Hutchinson, Arrow Books, 1976 ... 120

OLDFIELD, F E: *New Look Industrial Relations,* Mason Reed, 1966

OLDFIELD, R C: *The Psychology of the Interview,* Methuen, 1941

OLDHAM, G R and HACKMAN, J R: 'Work Design in the Organisational Context' in Staw and Cummings, 1980, q.v. pp 247–78

OLSEN, K: 'Suggestions Schemes, Seventies Style' in *Personnel Management,* April, 1976, pp 36–9

OPSAHL, R L and DUNNETT, M D: 'The Role of Financial Compensation in Industrial Motivation', in *Psychological Bulletin*, 66, 1966, pp 94–118 ... 88

Organization for Economic Cooperation and Development, OECD: *The Requirements of Automated Jobs,* OECD, 1965

OECD: *Job Re-design and Occupational Training for Older Workers,* OECD, 1965

ORTH, C D, BAILEY, J C and WOLEK, F W: *Administering Research and Development,* Richard D Irwin, 1964 ... 73

ORTH, C and JACOBS, F: 'Women in Management: Pattern for Change' in *Harvard Business Review*, July–August, 1971, pp 139–47

ORZACK, L H: 'Work as a Central Life Interest of Professionals' in *Social Problems*, 7, 1959, pp 125–32

OUCHI, W G: *Theory Z: How American Business can Meet the Japanese Challenge,* Avon Books, 1981 ... 63, 95, 97, 98, 99, 110, 112, 211

P

PAHL, R E and WINKLER, J T: 'Corporatism in Britain: Why Protecting Industry Need Not Mean More Bureaucracy' in *The Times*, 26 March, 1976

PAINE, F T, DEUTSCH, D R and SMITH, R A: 'Relationship between Family Backgrounds and Work Values' in *Journal of Applied Psychology*, 51 (4), 1967, pp 320–23

PALMER, C J and McCORMICK, E J: 'A Factor Analysis of Job Activities' in *Journal of Applied Psychology*, 45 (5), 1961, pp 289–94

PALMER, R: 'A Participative Approach to Attitude Surveys' in *Personnel Management*, 9 (12), December, 1977, pp 26–7 and p 37

PANITCH, L: 'The Development of Corporatism in Liberal Democracies' in *Comparative Political Studies*, 10 (1), 1977, pp 61–90

PANITCH, L: 'Recent Theorisations on Corporatism: Reflections on a Growth Industry' in *British Journal of Sociology*, 31, 1980, pp 159–87

PAOLILLO, J G P: 'Managers' Self-Assessment of Managerial Roles: The Influence of Hierarchical Level' in *Journal of Management*, 7 (1), 1981, pp 43–52

Paper and Paper Products, ITB: *An Approach to IR Training within a Company,* PPPITB, 1973

PARSONS, T: 'Suggestions for a Sociological Approach to the Theory of Organisations' in Etzioni, A: *Complex Organisations: A Sociological Reader,* Holt, Rinehart and Winston, 1964, pp 32–46 ... 188, 189

PASCALE, R T and ATHOS, A G: *The Art of Japanese Management,* Penguin, 1982 ... 91, 95, 98, 110, 112, 404

PASK, G: 'Styles and Strategies of Learning' in *British Journal of Educational Psychology,* 1976, pp 4–6 ... 316

PATERSON, T T: *Job Evaluation,* Business Books, 1972

PATTEN, T H: *Manpower Planning, and the Development of Human Resources,* Interscience, 1971 ... 271

PAUL, W J and ROBERTSON, K B: *Learning From Job Enrichment,* ICI, 1970 ... 39

PAVLOV, I P: *Conditioned Reflexes,* Oxford UP, 1927

PAYNE, R and COOPER, G L (eds): *Groups at Work,* Wiley, 1981

PEN, J: *The Wage Rate under Collective Bargaining,* Harvard U P, 1959 ... 168, 210, 211

PEPPERELL, E M: 'Why and How we Introduced a Job Evaluation System' in *Personnel Management*, XXX (295), January–February, 1948, pp 16–22

PETERS, T J and WATERMAN, R H: *In Search of Excellence,* Harper and Row, 1982 ... 110, 112, 197, 208, 209, 210, 219, 229 307, 469, 475-6

PETTIGREW, A: *The Politics of Organizational Decision-Making,* Tavistock, 1973

PETTMAN, B O: 'Some Factors Influencing Labour Turnover: A Review of Research Literature' in *Industrial Relations Journal*, 4 (3), Autumn, 1973, pp 43–61

PEW, R W: 'Acquisition of Hierarchical Control over the Temporal Organisation of a Skill' in *Journal of Experimental Psychology*, 71, 1966, pp 764–71

PHELPS-BROWN, E H with BROWNE, M: *A Century of Pay,* Macmillan, 1964

PHELPS-BROWN, E H and HART, P E: 'The Share of Wages in the National Income' in *Economic Journal*, 62 (246), 1952, pp 276–83

PHILLIPS, M H: 'Merit Rating for Skilled and Semi-Skilled Workers' in *Personnel Management*, June, 1962, pp 120–28

PIGORS, P and MYERS, C A: *Management of Human Resources,* McGraw Hill, 1973

PIGORS, P and MYERS, C A: *Personnel Administration,* McGraw Hill, 1973
PILDITCH, J: *Communications by Design: A Study in Corporate Identity,* McGraw Hill, 1970
PILKINGTON, Sir A: 'Science and Technology' in *RSA Journal,* CXXIV (5241), August, 1976, pp 523–36
PLATT, J W: 'Education for Business' in *Board of Trade Journal,* 27 August, 1965
PLUMBLEY, P R: *Recruitment and Selection,* IPM, 1968; 4th edn, 1983 ... 256, 258, 286, 287, 289, 290, 292, 294, 297
PLUNKETT, L C and HALE, G A: *The Proactive Manager,* Wiley, 1982
POLLARD, H R: *Developments in Management Thought,* Edward Arnold, 1965
POLLARD, S: *The Genesis of Modern Management,* Edward Arnold, 1965 ... 20, 180
POOLE, M: *Towards a New Industrial Democracy,* Routledge and Kegan Paul, 1986 ... 156
POPITZ, H, BAHRDT, H P, JUERES, E A and KESTING, A: 'The Worker's Image of Society' in Burns, T, 1969, q.v. pp 281–324 ... 440
PORTER, L W: 'Job Attitudes in Management: Perceived Deficiencies in Need Fulfilment as a Function of Job Level' in *Journal of Applied Psychology,* 46, 1962, pp 375–84 ... 110, 133, 196
PORTER, L W: 'A Study of Perceived Need Satisfactions in Bottom and Middle Management Jobs', in *Journal of Applied Psychology,* 45, 1961, pp 1–10
PORTER, L W: 'Job Attitudes in Management: Perceived Importance of Needs as a Function of Job Level', in *Journal of Applied Psychology,* 47, 1963a, pp 141–8
PORTER, L W: 'Job Attitudes in Management: Perceived Deficiencies in Need Fulfilment as a Function of the Size of Company' in *Journal of Applied Psychology,* 47 (6), 1963, pp 386–97
PORTER, L W and LAWLER, E E: 'Properties of Organization Structure in Relation to Job Attitudes and Job Behaviour' in *Psychological Bulletin,* 64, 1965, pp 23–51 ... 67
PORTER, L W and LAWLER, E E: *Managerial Attitudes and Performance,* Irwin-Dorsey, 1968
PORTER, L W, LAWLER, E E, and HACKMAN, J R: *Behaviour in Organizations,* McGraw Hill, 1975 ... 69
PORTER, M E: *Competitive Strategy,* Free Press, 1980
PORTER, M E: *Competitive Advantage,* Free Press, 1985 ... 23, 161, 162, 178, 226, 500, 507
POWELL, L S: *Communication and Learning,* Pitman, 1969
PRANDY, K: *Professional Employees,* Faber and Faber, 1965 ... 156
PRATTEN, C F: *Labour Productivity Differentials Within International Companies,* Cambridge U P, 1976a

PRATTEN, C F: *A Comparison of the Performance of Swedish and UK Companies,* Cambridge U P, 1976b
PRENTICE, D D: 'A Company and Its Employees: The Companies Act, 1980' in *Industrial Law Journal,* 10 (1), March, 1981, pp 1−9
PRICE, N: 'Personnel: Human Resources Management' in Brech, 1975, q.v. pp 555−655 ... 238, 251
PRIESTLEY: *Royal Commission on the Civil Service, 1953−5,* Cmnd 9613, HMSO, 1955
PROHANSKY, H and SEIDENBERG, B: *Basic Studies in Social Psychology,* Holt, Rinehart and Winston, 1969 ... 432, 435, 438
PRYOR, R: 'A Fresh Approach to Performance Appraisal' in *Personnel Management,* June, 1985, pp 38−9
PUGH, D S (ed): *Organization Theory,* Penguin, 1971
PURCELL, J: 'Employee Relations Autonomy Within a Corporate Culture' in *Personnel Management,* February, 1986, pp 38−41
PURCELL, J and Smith, N (eds): *The Control of Work,* Macmillan, 1979
PURKISS, C J: 'Manpower Planning Literature: Manpower Demand' in *DE Gazette,* November, 1976, pp 1−4

R
RACKHAM, N and HONEY, P: *Developing Interactive Skills,* Wellens, 1971
RACKHAM, N and MORGAN, T: *Behaviour Analysis in Training,* McGraw Hill, 1977 ... 312, 327
RAIA, A P: *Managing by Objectives,* Scott Foresman, 1974
RAIA, A P: 'Goal Setting and Self-Control' in *Journal of Management Studies,* February, 1965, pp 34−53 ... 304, 338-9, 357
RAIMON, R L: 'The Indeterminateness of Wages of Semi-skilled Workers', in *Industrial and Labour Relations Review,* 6, January, 1963, pp 180-94 ... 178
RAJAN, A: *Services: The Second Industrial Revolution,* Institute of Manpower Studies Report to the Occupational Services Group, Butterworths, 1987
RANDALL, P E: *Introduction to Work Study and Organization and Methods,* Butterworths, 1969
RANDELL, G A et al: *Staff Appraisal,* IPM, 1972, 2nd edn, 1974 ... 350-51, 357
RAUDSEPP, E: *Managing Creative Scientists and Engineers,* Macmillan, 1963 ... 247
RAY, M E: *Practical Recruitment Advertising,* IPM, 1974 ... 283, 287, 297
REDDIN, W J: *Managerial Effectiveness,* McGraw Hill, 1970 ... 478, 495
REDDIN, W J: 'The Tri-dimensional Grid' in *Training Director's Journal,* July, 1964 ... 479, 491-4
REDDIN, W J: 'The Blake Approach and the Grid' in *Training Director's Journal,* December, 1963 ... 491

REDDIN, W J: *The Best of Bill Reddin,* IPM, 1985 ... 478

REDGRAVE'S FACTORIES ACTS, eds: Thompson, J and Rogers, H R, Butterworths, 1966

REES, W D: *The Skills of Management,* Croom Helm, 1984

REEVES, J W and WILSON, V W: *Studying Work,* National Institute for Industrial Psychology, 1951

REIF, W E and LUTHANS, F: 'Does Job-Enrichment Really Pay off?' in *California Management Review,* 15, Fall, 1972, pp 30–37 ... 43

RENOLD, G C: *Joint Consultation over Thirty Years,* Allen and Unwin, 1950 ... 284

RENOLD, Sir C: *The Organizational Structure of Large Undertakings: Management Problems,* BIM, 1950

REVANS, R W: 'The Education of Managers: The Theory of Practice' in *Universities Quarterly,* 16 (4), September, 1962, pp 340–55

REVANS, R W: *Developing Effective Managers,* Longmans, 1971

REVANS, R W: *Action Learning,* Blond and Briggs, 1980

REYNOLDS, H and TRAMEL, M E: *Executive Time Management,* Gower, 1981

REYNOLDS, L: 'Wage Differences in Local Labor Markets' in *American Economic Review,* 36, 1946, pp 366–75 ... 178

RICE, A K: *Productivity and Social Organization: The Ahmedabad Experiment,* Tavistock, 1958 ... 200, 457, 463

RICE, A K: *The Enterprise and Its Environment,* Tavistock, 1963

RICE, A K and TRIST, E L: 'Institutional and Sub-Institutional Determinants of Social Change in Labour Turnover' in *Human Relations,* 5 (4), 1950, pp 347–71

RICE, A K et al: 'The Representation of Labour Turnover as a Social Process' in *Human Relations,* 3 (4), 1950, pp 349–72

RICE, G H and BISHOPRICK, D W: *Conceptual Models of Organizations,* Appleton-Century Crofts, 1971

RICHARDSON, F L W and WALKER, C R: *Human Relations in an Expanding Company,* Labour and Management Centre, Yale University, 1948 ... 37

RICHBELL, S: 'Participation and Perceptions of Control' in *Personnel Review,* 5 (2), Spring, 1976, pp 13–19

RIDEOUT, R W: 'The Contract of Employment' in *Current Legal Problems,* 19, 1966, p 111–27

RIDEOUT, R W: *Principles of Labour Law,* Sweet and Maxwell, 3rd edn, 1979 ... 121, 131

RIDEOUT, R W: *Industrial Tribunal Law,* McGraw Hill, 1980

RIESMAN, D: *The Lonely Crowd,* Doubleday, 1952 ... 58, 69, 94, 436

RITZER, G and TRICE, H M: *An Occupation in Conflict: A Study of the Personnel Manager,* Cornell, 1969

ROBENS, Lord: *Safety and Health at Work: Report of the Committee,* HMSO, 1979

ROBERTSON, I T and MAKIN, P J: 'Management Selection in Britain: A Survey and Critique' in *Journal of Occupational Psychology*, 1986, pp 45–57

ROBINSON, D: *Local Labour Markets and Wage Structures,* Gower, 1970

ROBINSON, J and BARNES, N: *New Media and Methods of Industrial Training,* BBC, 1968

ROBINSON, O and WALLACE, J: *Pay and Employment in Retailing,* Saxon House, 1976

ROCHE, G R: 'Probing Opinions: Much Ado about Mentors' in *Harvard Business Review*, January – February, 1979, pp 14–28

RODGER, A: *The Seven Point Plan,* NIIP, 1952 ... 262, 290

ROETHLISBERGER, F J: *Man-in-Organisation,* Harvard U P, 1968 ... 188

ROETHLISBERGER, F J and DICKSON, W F: *Management and the Worker,* Harvard U P, 1939 ... 195, 437, 457

ROFF, H E and WATSON, T E: *Job Analysis,* IPM, 1961 ... 45

ROGERS, C R: *Client-Centred Therapy,* Constable, 1951

ROGERS, C R: *On Becoming a Person,* Houghton Mifflin, 1961

ROGERS, C R and STEVENS, B: *Person to Person: The Problem of Being Human,* Real People Press, 1967

ROGERS, T G P and WILLIAMS, P: *The Recruitment and Training of Graduates,* IPM, 1970

ROMAN, P M and TRICE, H M: 'Psychiatric Impairment among Middle Americans' in *Social Psychiatry*, (7), 1972, pp 157–66 ... 35

ROMAN, P M and TRICE, H M: *Spirits and Demons at Work: Alcoholism and Other Drugs on the Job,* New York State School of Industrial and Labour Relations, 1978

RONCAGLIA, A: *Petty: The Origins of Political Economy,* UCCP, 1985 ... 158

RONISZOWSKI, A J: *The Selection and Use of Teaching Aids,* International Textbook Company, 1968

RONKEN, H O and LAWRENCE, P R: *Administering Changes,* Harvard U P, 1952

ROSE, A M: *Human Behaviour and Social Processes,* Routledge and Kegan Paul, 1962

ROSS, J: 'Predicting Practical Skill in Engineering Apprentices' in *Occupational Psychology*, 36 (1 and 2), 1962, pp 69–74

ROSS, M G and HENDRY, C E: *New Understandings of Leadership,* Association Press, 1957

ROTHE, H F: 'Does Higher Pay Bring Higher Productivity?' in *Personnel*, 37, 1960, pp 20–38; and in Fleishman, 1961, q.v. pp 251–9 ... 396-8

ROTHWELL, S: *Labour Turnover: Its Costs, Causes and Control,* Gower, 1980

ROWE, J C F: *Wages in Theory and Practice,* Macmillan, 1929

ROWE, K H: 'An Appraisal of Appraisals' in *Journal of Management Studies*, 1 (1), March, 1964, pp 1–25 ... 341, 345, 350

ROWNTREE, J A and STEWART, P A: 'Estimating Manpower Needs – II Statistical Methods' in *Manpower Planning in the Civil Service,* HMSO, 1976, pp 36–53

ROY, A S: *Staff Grading,* BIM, 1960 ... 364

ROY, D: 'Efficiency and the Fix' in *American Journal of Sociology*, LX (3), November, 1954, pp 255–66

RUBENSTEIN, A H and HABERSTROH, C J (eds): *Some Theories of Organization,* Irwin-Dorsey, 1960

RUBNER, A: *The Ensnared Shareholder,* Penguin, 1966

S

SAMUEL, P J: *Labour Turnover: Towards a Solution,* IPM, 1971

SAMUELS, H: *Industrial Law,* Pitman, 1967

SANFORD, A C, HUNT, G T and BRACEY, H J: *Communication Behaviour in Organisations,* Merrill, 1976

SAUNDERS, N F T: *Factory Organisation and Management,* Pitman, 3rd edn., 1952

SAVAGE, N: *The Companies Act, 1980: A New Business Code,* McGraw Hill, 1980 ... 149

SAYLES, L: *Managerial Behaviour,* McGraw Hill, 1964 ... 13, 232, 333-4, 480

SAYLES, L R and STRAUSS, G: *Personnel: Human Problems of Management,* Prentice Hall, 2nd edn, 1967

SCHAFFER, R H: *Managing by Total Objectives,* AMA, 1964

SCHEIN, E H: *Organizational Psychology,* Prentice Hall, 1970; 3rd edn, 1980 ... 110, 302

SCHEIN, E H: 'The Individual, the Organization and the Career' in *Journal of Applied Behavioural Sciences,* 7, 1971, pp 401–16

SCHLECH, E C: *Managing for Results,* McGraw Hill, 1961

SCHMITT, N and COYLE, B W: 'Applicant Decisions in the Employment Interview' in *Journal of Applied Psychology*, 61, 1976, pp 184–92

SCHMITTHOFF, C: 'Employee Participation and the Theory of Enterprise' in *Journal of Business Law,* 1975, pp 265–72 ... 149

SCHNEIDER, A et al: *Organizational Communications,* McGraw Hill, 1973

SCHRAMM, W L (ed): *The Science of Human Communication,* Basic Books, 1963

SCHULSTER, J R, CLARK, B and ROGERS, M: 'Testing Portions of the Porter-Lawler Model regarding the Motivational Role of Pay' in *Journal of Applied Psychology,* 55, 1971, pp 187–95

SCHULTZ, T: *Investment in Human Capital,* Free Press, 1971

SCHUMACHER, C: 'Personnel's Part in Productivity Growth' in *Personnel Management*, 13 (7), July, 1981, pp 26–30 ... 149

SCOTT, Sir BERNARD, Chairman: *Report of the Inquiry into the Value of Pensions,* Cmnd 8147, HMSO, February, 1981 ... 73

SCOTT, W E and CUMMINGS, L L (eds): *Readings in Organisational Behaviour and Human Performance,* Irwin-Dorsey, 1973

SCOTT, W H et al: *Technical Change and Industrial Relations,* Liverpool U P, 1956 ... 202

SELEKMAN, B J: *A Moral Philosophy for Management,* McGraw Hill, 1959

Selwyn's Law of Employment, Butterworths, 1976

SELZNICK, P: 'Foundations of the Theory of Organization' in *American Sociological Review,* 13, 1948, pp 25–35; and in Etzioni, 1969, q.v. pp 19–32 ... 188, 190

SELZNICK, P: *Leadership in Administration,* Harper and Row, 1957 ... 104-5

SELZNICK, P: *TVA and the Grass Roots,* Harper, 1966 ... 196

SELZNICK, P: 'An Approach to a Theory of Bureaucracy' in *American Sociological Review,* VIII (1), 1943, pp 47–54; and in Coser, L and Rosenberg, M (eds): *Sociological Theory – A Reader,* Collier-Macmillan, 1969, pp 459–72 ... 189, 190

SEYMOUR, W D: *Industrial Skills,* Pitman, 1966

SEYMOUR, W D: 'Recent Developments in Operative Training' in *Personnel Management,* July – August, 1949, pp 169–80 ... 259, 307, 313

SEYMOUR, W D: *Skills Analysis Training,* Pitman, 1968

SHACKLE, G L S: 'The Nature of the Bargaining Process' in Dunlop, J T (ed): *The Theory of Wage Determination,* Macmillan, 1957, pp 292–314

SHACKLE, G L S: *Expectation, Enterprise and Profit: The Theory of the Firm,* Allen and Unwin, 1970 ... 212-13

SHAFRITZ, J M, Hyde, A C, and Rosenbloom, D H: *Personnel Management in Government,* Marcel Dekker, 1981

SHANNON, C E and WEAVER, W: *The Mathematical Theory of Communication,* University of Illinois Press, 1949 ... 249, 400, 406, 407, 413, 418, 430

SHEPARD, R J: *Men at Work: Applications of Ergonomics to Performance and Design,* C C Thomas, 1974 ... 43

SHERIF, M: 'Group Influences Upon the Formation of Norms and Attitudes' in Maccoby, Newcomb and Hartley 1958, q.v pp 219–32 ... 438

SHERIF, M: *The Psychology of Social Norms,* Harper and Bros, 1936

SHERIF, M and SHERIF, C: *Social Psychology,* Harper and Row, 1969

SHONE, K J and PATERSON, R G: *Analysis of Controls and Design of Production Planning Control Systems,* Sawell Publications, 1963 ... 15, 186

SIDNEY, E and BROWN, M: *The Skills of Interviewing,* Tavistock, 1961

SILBERBERG, H: 'Gratuitous Payments for the Benefit of the Company' in the *Journal of Business Law*, 1968, pp 213–28

SILVERMAN, D: *The Theory of Organizations*, Heinemann, 1970

SIMITIS, S: 'Workers' Participation in the Enterprise – Transcending Company Law' in *Modern Law Review*, 38, 1975, pp 1–22

SIMON, H A: *Administrative Behaviour*, Macmillan, 1953 ... 411, 447, 448

SIMON, H A: *Models of Man: Social and Rational*, Wiley, 1957

SIMON, H A: 'Theories of Decision-Making in Economics and Behavioural Science' in *American Economic Review*, XLIX, June, 1959, pp 253–83

SIMON, H A: *The Shape of Automation*, Harper and Row, 1965

SINGER, E J: *Training in Industry and Commerce*, IPM, 1977–8 ... 310

SINGER, E J and MacDONALD, I D: *Is Apprenticeship Outdated?*, IPM, 1970

SINGER, E J and RAMSDEN, J: *The Practical Approach to Skills Analysis*, McGraw Hill, 1969 ... 260, 318

SINGER, E J and RAMSDEN, J: *Human Resources*, McGraw Hill, 1972 ... 310, 311, 315

SINGLETON, W T: 'Acquisition of Skill: The Theory Behind Training Design' in Robinson and Barnes, 1968, q.v

SKINNER, B F: *Behaviour in Organisations: An Experimental Analysis*, Appleton-Century, 1938

SKINNER, B F: *Science and Human Behaviour*, Macmillan, 1953; 1965 ... 57, 83, 299, 303, 404

SKINNER, B F: 'The Science of Learning and the Art of Teaching' in *Harvard Educational Review*, 24, 1954, pp 86–97

SLATER, P E: 'Social Bases of Personality' in Smelser, N J (ed): *Sociology*, Wiley, 1967, pp 658–600

SMELSER, N: *Sociology: An Introduction*, Wiley, 1967

SMILES, S: *Lives of the Engineers*, Murray, 1862

SMILES, S: *Self-Help*, Murray, 1908

SMITH, A R (ed): *Models of Manpower Systems*, English U P, 1970

SMITH, A R: 'Developments in Manpower Planning' in *Personnel Review*, 1 (1), Autumn, 1971, pp 44–5

SMITH, A R (ed): *Manpower Planning in the Civil Service*, Civil Service Studies No. 3, HMSO, 1976 ... 265, 275

SMITH, A R (ed): *Corporate Manpower Planning*, Gower, 1980 ... 275

SMITH, B and DELF, G A J: 'Strategies for Promoting Self-Development' in *Industrial and Commercial Training*, November, 1978, pp 494–501

SMITH, I G: *The Measurement of Productivity*, Gower Press, 1973

SMITH, I G: *The Management of Remuneration: Paying for Effectiveness*, IPM, 1983

SMITH, I G: 'Matching the Incentive to the Performer' in *Personnel Management*, January, 1984, pp 27–30

SMITH, M: *An Introduction to Industrial Psychology*, Cassell, 1933 ... 342

SMITH, W J, ALBRIGHT, L E, and GLENNON, J R: 'The Prediction of Research Competence and Creativity from Personal History' in *Journal of Applied Psychology*, 45 (1), 1961, pp 59–62

SNYDER, B R: *Hidden Curriculum,* MIT Press, 1973 ... 317

SORGE, A and WARNER, M: 'The Societal Context of Industrial Relations in Britain and West Germany' in *Industrial Relations Journal*, 11, 1980a, pp 41–50 ... 112

SORGE, A and WARNER, M: 'Manpower Training, Manufacturing and Workplace Industrial Relations' in *British Journal of Industrial Relations*, 18, 1980b, pp 318–33

SPENCE, A C: *Management Communication: Its Process and Practice,* Macmillan, 1969 ... 46, 57, 216-17, 228, 229, 407

SPICER, E H: *Human Problems in Technological Change,* Russell Sage, 1952 ... 93, 106

SPROTT, W J H: *Human Groups,* Pelican, 1958 ... 437

STAINER, G: *Manpower Planning,* Heinemann, 1971 ... 267, 275

STAMMERS, R and PATRICK, J: *The Psychology of Training,* Methuen, 1975 ... 80, 299, 308, 314, 407, 408

STAW, B L and CUMMINGS, L L (eds): *Research in Organisational Behaviour,* Jai Press, Vol. 1, 1979; Vol. 2, 1980

STEELE, M, MILLER, K and GENNARD, J: 'The Trade Union Act, 1984: Political Fund Ballots' in *British Journal of Industrial Relations*, XXIV (3), November, 1986, pp 443–67

STEERS, C E B: *Clarifying Objectives in Supervisory Training,* BACIE, 1966

STEERS, R N and PORTER, H W: *Motivation and Work Behaviour,* McGraw Hill, 1977 ... 9, 58, 61, 65, 88

STEWART, A: *Practical Performance Appraisal,* Gower, 1977

STEWART, A: *Managing the Manager's Growth,* Gower, 1978

STEWART, A: *Tomorrow's Managers Today,* IPM, 2nd edn, 1981

STEWART, A: *Managing the Poor Performer,* Gower, 1982

STEWART A: 'Stress at Work', in Harper, S: *Personnel Management Handbook,* Gower, 1987, pp 252-74 ... 277, 292, 297

STEWART, A and V: 'Selection and Appraisal: The Pick of Recent Research' in *Personnel Management*, 8 (1), January, 1976, pp 20–24

STINCHCOMBE, A L: 'Bureaucratic and Craft Administration of Production' in *Administrative Science Quarterly*, September, 1959, pp 168–87

STINCHCOMBE, A L: 'Formal Organizations' in Smelser, N J: *Sociology* Wiley, 1967, pp 151–202 ... 74, 75

STOKES, P M: *Total Job Training: A Manual for the Working Manager,* AMA, 1966 ... 298, 306, 315, 443

STONE, C H and KENDALL, W E: *Effective Personnel Selection Procedures,* Staples Press, 1957

STOUFFER, S A et al: *The American Soldier,* Princeton U P, 1949 ... 438

STRASSMANN, P A: *Information Payoff: The Transformation of Work in the Electronic Age,* Free Press, 1985

STRAUSS, A: *Negotiations,* Jossey Bass, 1978

STRAUSS and SAYLES, see Sayles and Strauss

STRAUSS, G: 'Is There a Blue-collar Revolt against Work?' in O'Toole, J (ed): *Work and the Quality of Life,* MIT Press, 1974, pp 40−69 ... 44

SULLIVAN, G R: 'The Relationship between the Board of Directors and the General Meeting in Limited Companies' in *Law Quarterly Review*, 93, October, 1977, pp 569−80

SUPER, D E and CRITES, J O: *Appraising Vocational Fitness,* Harper, 1962... 60

SUTER, E and LONG, P: *Cashless Pay and Deductions,* IPM, 1987 ... 127

SWANNACK, A R and SAMUEL P J: 'The Added Value of Men and Materials' in *Personnel Management*, February, 1974, pp 26−9 and p 41

SWANNACK, A R: 'Small Firm Salary Structures' in *Personnel Management*, January, 1974, pp 31−4

SWANSON, G E, NEWCOMB, T M, and HARTLEY, E L (eds): *Readings in Social Psychology,* Henry Holt, 2nd edn, 1952 ... 438

SWEDISH EMPLOYERS' CONFEDERATION: *Job Reform in Sweden,* SEF, 1975

SYKES, A J M: 'A Study in Changing the Attitudes and Stereotypes of Industrial Workers' in *Human Relations*, 17 (2), May, 1964, pp 143−54

SZAKATS, A: 'Compulsory Unionism: Strength or Weakness? − The New Zealand System Compared with Union Security Agreements in GB and USA' in *Alberta Law Review*, X (2), 1972, pp 313−43 ... 151

T

TAFT, R: 'The Ability to Judge People' in Whisler, T L and Harper, S F (eds): *Performance Appraisal,* Holt, Rinehart and Winston, 1962, pp 28−52 ... 251

TAGIURI, R: 'Value Orientations of Managers and Scientists' in Orth et al, 1964, q.v. pp 63−71

TALBOT, J R and ELLIS, C D: *Analysis and Costing of Company Training,* Gower, 1969

TANNENBAUM, R: 'The Manager Concept: A Rational Synthesis' in *Journal of Business*, 22 (4), October, 1949, pp 225−41; and in Tannenbaum, R, Weschler, I R, and Massarik, F: *Leadership and Organization,* McGraw Hill, 1961, pp 243−64 ... 12, 13, 23

TAVERNIER, G: *Industrial Training Systems and Records,* Gower, 1971

TAYLOR, F W: *Shop Management,* Harper and Bros, 1910 ... 107, 480

TAYLOR, F W: *Scientific Management,* Harper and Bros, 1947 ... 10, 15

TAYLOR, G W, SMITH, W R, GHISELIN, B and ELLISON, R: *Explorations in the Measurement and Prediction of Contributions of One Sample of*

Scientists', Report No. ASD-TR-61-96, Personnel Laboratory, ASD, Lackland AFB, Texas, 1961

TAYLOR, P: *Absenteeism – the English Sickness,* Industrial Society, July, 1970

TAYLOR, P J: *Absenteeism – Causes and Control,* Industrial Society Notes for Managers No. 15, 1973

TEEVAN, R C and BIRNEY, R C (eds): *Theories of Motivation in Personality and Social Psychology,* Van Nostrand, 1964

TERRY, M: 'The Inevitable Growth of Informality' in *British Journal of Industrial Relations,* XV (1), 1977, pp 76–88

THACKERAY, J: 'The New Organisation Man' in *Management Today,* September, 1981, pp 74–7 and p 168

THELEN, H A and WITHALL, J: 'Three Frames of Reference: The Description of Climate' in *Human Relations,* II (2), 1979, pp 159–76

THIBAUT, J: 'An Experimental Study of the Cohesiveness of Under-privileged Groups' in *Human Relations,* 3, 1950, pp 251–78; and in Cartwright and Zander, 1953, q.v. pp 102–20 ... 50

THOMAS, B, MOXON, J, and JONES, J A G: 'A Cost-benefit Analysis of Industrial Training' in *British Journal of Industrial Relations,* VII (2), 1969, pp 231–64

THOMAS, J: 'Group Capacity Assessment' in *DATA Journal,* May, 1967, pp 9–10

THOMAS, K: *Attitudes and Behaviour,* Penguin, 1971

THOMAS, R E: *The Government of Business,* Phillip Allen, 1976

THOMAS, R E: *Business Policy,* Phillip Allen, 1977 ... 211

THOMASON, G F: 'Managerial Work Roles and Relationships' in *Journal of Management Studies,* 3 (8), October, 1966, pp 270–84; and 4 (1), February, 1967, pp 17–30 ... 248

THOMASON, G F: *Experiments in Participation,* IPM, 1971 ... 456

THOMASON, G F: *The Management of Industrial Relations,* UCCP, 1971

THOMASON, G F: *The Management of Research and Development,* Batsford, 1970

THOMASON, G F: *Improving the Quality of Organization,* IPM, 1973

THOMASON, G F: *The Individual, the Trade Union and the State: Some Contemporary Issues,* Irish Association for Industrial Relations, 1978

THOMASON, G F: *Job Evaluation: Objectives and Methods,* IPM, 1980a ... 370, 371, 373, 374, 399

THOMASON, G F: 'Corporate Control of the Professional Association' in Poole, M J F and Mansfield, R (eds): *Managerial Roles and Industrial Relations,* Gower, 1980b, pp 26–37

THOMASON, G F: *A Textbook of Industrial Relations Management,* IPM, 1984 ... 120, 123, 125, 128, 136, 140, 507

THOMPSON, J and ROGERS, H R, (eds): *Redgrave's Factories, Truck and Shops Acts,* Butterworth, 19th (edn), 1956

THOMPSON, J D (ed): *Approaches to Organisational Design,* University of Pittsburgh Press, 1966

THOMSON, F: 'Briefing Groups and the Seven Deadly Sins' in *Personnel Management,* February, 1983, pp 32–5

THORNDIKE, R L: *Personnel Selection: Tests and Measurement Techniques,* Wiley, 1949

THURLEY, K: 'Personnel Managers in the UK – A Case for Urgent Treatment' in *Personnel Management,* 13 (8), August, 1981, pp 24–9

THURLEY, K E, GRAVES, D and HULT, M: 'An Evaluation Strategy for Management Development' in *Training Research Bulletin,* 6 (2), ATT ITB, Staines, 1975

THURLEY, K and HAMBLIN, A C: *The Supervisor and His Job,* HMSO, 1963

THURLEY, K and WIRDENIUS, H: *Approaches to Supervisory Development,* IPM, 1973

THURLEY, K and WOOD, S J (eds): *Industrial Relations and Management Strategy,* Cambridge U P, 1983

THURSTONE, L L: *Primary Mental Abilities,* University of Chicago Press, 1938 ... 51

THURSTONE, L L: *A Factoral Study of Perception,* Psychometric Monographs, No. 4, 1944 ... 51

THURSTONE, L L and CHAVE, E J: *The Measurement of Attitudes,* University of Chicago Press, 1929

TIFFIN, J: 'Merit Rating: Its Validity and Techniques' in Dooher and Marquis 1950, q.v. pp 11–19 ... 347

TIFFIN, J and MCCORMICK, E J: *Industrial Psychology,* Prentice Hall, 1965

TIFFIN, J and ROGERS, H B: 'The Selection and Training of Inspectors' in *Personnel,* 18 (1), 1943, pp 3–20 ... 259

TOFFLER, A: *The Adaptive Corporation,* Pan, 1985 ... 207

TORRINGTON, D: *Face to Face,* Gower, 1972 ... 290, 350, 357

TORRINGTON, D and CHAPMAN, J: *Personnel Management,* Prentice Hall, 1979 ... 9

TORRINGTON, D and HALL, L: *Personnel Management: A New Approach,* Prentice Hall, 1987 ... 251

TORRINGTON, D and MACKAY, L: 'Will Consultants Take Over the Personnel Function?' in *Personnel Management,* February, 1986, pp 34–7 ... 251

TOSI, H L and CARROLL, S: 'Some Factors Affecting the Success of Management by Objectives' in *Journal of Management Studies,* 7 (2), May, 1970, pp 209–23

TOULSON, N: *Managing Pension Schemes,* Gower, 1986

TRADES UNION CONGRESS: *Automation and Technological Change,* TUC, 1965

TUC: *Costs and Profits: Financial Information for Trade Unionists,* TUC, 1970

TUC: *Industrial Democracy,* TUC, 1974
TUC: *Job Evaluation and Merit Rating,* TUC, 1974
TUC: *Guide to the Bullock Report on Industrial Democracy,* TUC, February, 1977
TUC: *Paid Release for Union Training,* TUC, 1977
TUC: *TUC Handbook on Safety and Health at Work,* TUC, 1978 ... 153
TRAINING SERVICES AGENCY: *A Five Year Plan,* HMSO, 1974
TREITEL, G H: *The Law of Contract,* Stevens, 1975 edn ... 122, 131
TRIANDIS, H C: *Attitudes and Attitude Change,* Wiley, 1971 ... 466
TRIST, E L and BAMFORTH, K W: 'Some Social and Psychological Consequences of the Longwall Method of Coal-Getting' in *Human Relations,* 4 (1), 1951, pp 3–38 ... 180, 198, 200, 201, 202
TRIST, E L, HIGGIN, G W, MURRAY, H and POLLOCK, A B: *Organizational Choice,* Tavistock, 1963 ... 24, 457
TURNER, A N and LAWRENCE, P R: *Industrial Jobs and the Worker,* Harvard University Division of Research, Graduate School of Business Administration, 1965 ... 34, 44, 96, 109
TURNER, H: *Trade Union Growth, Structure and Policy,* Allen and Unwin, 1962 ... 156, 174
TYLER, R W, GAGNE, R M, and SCRIVEN, M: *Perspectives of Curriculum Evaluation,* Rand, 1967
TYSON, S: 'Is this the Very Model of a Modern Personnel Manager?' in *Personnel Management,* May, 1985, pp 23–5

U
ULRICH, L and TRUMBO, D: 'The Selection Interview since 1949' in *Psychological Bulletin,* 63 (2), 1965, pp 100–116 ... 291, 297
UNDY, R and MARTIN, R: *Ballots and Trade Union Democracy,* Blackwell, 1984
UNGERSON, B (ed): *Recruitment Handbook,* Gower Press, 1970
URWICK, L: *The Elements of Administration,* Harper and Bros, 1943
URWICK, L: *Problems of Growth in Industrial Undertakings,* BIM, 1949 ... 468
URWICK, L: *Personnel Management in Perspective,* IPM, 1959
URWICK, L and BRECK, E F L: *The Making of Scientific Management,* Vols. I, II, and II, Management Publications, 1945–8 ... 107

V
VAN BEEK, H G: 'The Influence of Assembly Line Organization on Output, Quality and Morale' in *Occupational Psychology,* 38, 1964, pp 161–72 ... 38
VERNON, H M, WYATT, S and OGDEN, A D: *On the Extent and Effects of Variety in Repetitive Work,* Industrial Fatigue Research Board, Report No 26, 1924 ... 33

VERNON, P E: *Personality Assessment: A Critical Survey,* Methuen, 1964
VERNON, P E: *Intelligence and Attainment Tests,* London U P, 1960
VERNON-HARCOURT, T: *Rewarding Top Management,* Gower, 1980
VETTER, E W: *Manpower Planning for High Talent Personnel,* University of Michigan, 1967
VICKERS, Sir G: *The Art of Judgement,* Chapman and Hall, 1965
VICKERS, Sir G: *Towards a Sociology of Management,* Chapman and Hall, 1967 ... 244-6, 247, 251
VICKERS, Sir G: *Value Systems and Social Progress,* Tavistock, 1968
VISTA COMMUNICATIONS: *Second Annual Survey of Communications,* Vista Communications, 15a, George Street, Croydon, CR0 1LA, 1987 ... 505, 506
VITELES, M S: *Industrial Psychology,* Norton, 1932 ... 259
VOLLMER, H M and MILLS, D L (eds): *Professionalization,* Prentice Hall, 1966
VON BERTALANFFY, L: 'The Theory of Open Systems in Physics and Biology' in *Science,* 3, 1950, pp 23−9 ... 180
VROOM, V H: *Work and Motivation,* Wiley, 1964 ... 66, 399
VROOM, V H: 'Industrial Social Psychology' in Lindzey, G and Aronson, E (eds): *Handbook of Social Psychology,* Addison-Wesley, 2nd edn, 1969 ... 43
VROOM, V H and DECI, E L: *Management and Motivation,* Penguin, 1970

W

WAGNER, R: 'The Employment Interview: A Critical Summary' in *Personnel Psychology,* 2, 1949, pp 17−46 ... 291
WAINWRIGHT, D: *Race and Employment,* IPM, 1970
WALKER, C R and GUEST, R H: *The Man on the Assembly Line,* Harvard UP, 1952 ... 37, 202
WALKER, J W: 'Individual Career Planning: Managerial Help for Subordinates' in *Business Horizons,* February, 1973, pp 65−72
WALL, T D and LISCHERON, J A: *Worker Participation,* McGraw Hill, 1977
WALLUM, P: 'Financial Incentives for Top Executives' in *Personnel Management,* April, 1983, pp 32−5
WALSH, K et al: *The UK Labour Market: IMS Guide to Information,* IMS, 1980
WALSH, P B: 'Enrichment in the Office' in *Personnel Management,* 1 (6), October, 1969, pp 42−4
WALTON, C B: *Corporate Social Responsibilities,* Wadsworth, 1967
WARNER, M (ed): *The Sociology of the Workplace,* Allen and Unwin, 1973
WARNER, M: 'Thoughts on Industrial Democracy and Self-Management' in *Human Relations,* 28, 1976, pp 401−10

WARNER, W L and LUNT, P S: *The Social Life of a Modern Community,* Yale U P, 1941 ... 438
WARR, P (ed): *Psychology at Work,* Penguin, 1971; 2nd edn, 1978 ... 311
WARR, P B and BIRD, M W: *Identifying Supervisory Training Needs,* Training Information Paper No. 2, HMSO, 1968
WARR, P B, BIRD, M W and RACKHAM, N: *Evaluation of Management Training,* Gower, 1970
WARR, P and WALL, T: *Work and Well-being,* Penguin, 1975
WARREN, M W: *Training for Results,* Addison Wesley, 1969 ... 298
WARREN, N and JAHODA, M: *Attitudes,* Penguin, 1969
WATERS, L K and ROACH, D: 'Relationships between Job Attitudes and two forms of Withdrawal from the Work Situation' in *Journal of Applied Psychology,* 55, 1971, pp 92–4
WATERS, L K and ROACH, D: 'Job Attitudes as Predictors of Termination and Absenteeism: Consistency over Time and Across Organisations' in *Journal of Applied Psychology,* 57, 1973, pp 341–2
WATES, J: 'Reporting on Employee Involvement' in *Personnel Management,* March, 1983, pp 32–5
WATSON, T J: *The Personnel Managers,* Routledge and Kegan Paul, 1977
WEBBER, R: *Culture and Management,* Irwin, 1969
WEBER, M: *The Theory of Economic and Social Organisation,* Free Press, 1947; 1964 ... 21, 192-4, 480
WEDDERBURN, K: *The Worker and the Law,* Penguin, 1971 ... 146, 156
WEEKES, B, MELLISH, M, DICKENS, I and LLOYD, J: *Industrial Relations and the Limits of Law,* Blackwell, 1975 ... 156
WEINSHALL, T D (ed): *Culture and Management,* Penguin, 1977 ... 112
WEIR, D: *Men and Work in Modern Britain,* Fontana, 1973
WELFORD, A T: *Ergonomics of Automation,* HMSO/DSIR, 1960 ... 403, 404, 408
WELLENS, J: *The Training Revolution,* Evans Bros, 1963
WELLMAN, G: 'Practical Obstacles to Effective Manpower Planning' in *Personnel Review,* 1 (3), Summer, 1972, pp 32–42
WENSLEY, R: 'PIMS and BCG: New Horizons or False Dawn?' in *Strategic Management Journal,* 3, 1982, pp 147–58
WEXLEY, K N and YUKL, G A (eds): *Organizational Behaviour and Industrial Psychology,* OUP, 1975
WEXLEY, K N and LATHAM, G P: *Developing and Training Human Resources in Organisations,* Scott-Foresman, 1981
WHEELER, H N: 'Punishment Theory and Industrial Discipline' in *Industrial Relations,* 15 (2), May, 1976, pp 235–43
WHELAN, C T: 'Orientations to Work: Some Theoretical and Methodological Problems' in *British Journal of Industrial Relations,* XIV (2), 1976, pp 142–58

WHISLER, T L and HARPER, S F: *Performance Appraisal,* Holt Rinehart and Winston, 1962

WHITE, G: 'Has the Private Health Perk Reached its Peak?' in *Personnel Management,* August, 1983, pp 34–40

WHITE, M: 'Incentive Bonus Schemes for Managers' in Bowey, A (ed): *Handbook of Salary and Wage Systems,* Gower, 1982, pp 249–64 ... 395

WHITE, M: *Motivating Managers Financially,* IPM, 1973

WHITE, M: 'What's New in Pay' in *Personnel Management,* February, 1985, pp 20–23

WHITEHEAD, F E: 'Trends in Certified Sickness Absence' in *Social Trends,* (2), 1971, pp 13–23

WHITELAW, M: *The Evaluation of Management Training,* IPM, 1972

WHITMORE, D A: *Measurement and Control of Indirect Work,* Heinemann, 1971

WHYTE, W F et al: *Money and Motivation,* Harper and Bros, 1955

WHYTE, W H: *The Organisation Man,* Cape, 1957; Penguin, 1960

WILD, R: *Work Organization,* Wiley, 1975

WILENSKY, H: 'The Professionalization of Everyone?' in *American Journal of Sociology,* 70, 1964, pp 137–58

WILKES, J (ed): *The Future of Work,* Allen and Unwin, 1981

WILLE, E: *The Computer in Personnel Work,* IPM, 1966

WILLIAMS, A (ed): *Using Personnel Research,* Gower, 1983

WILLIAMS, Sir B R: 'Pyramids of Disillusion' in *Management Decision,* Winter, 1967, pp 25–9

WILLIAMS, G L: 'The Validity of Methods of Evaluating Learning' in *Journal of European Industrial Training,* 5 (1), 1976, pp 12–20 ... 311

WILLIAMS, L K, WHYTE, W F and GREEN, C S: 'Do Cultural Differences Affect Workers' Attitudes?' in *Industrial Relations,* 5 (3), May, 1966, pp 105–17

WILLIAMS, R: *The City and the Country,* Granada, 1975

WILLIAMS, R: *Culture and Society, 1780–1950,* Penguin, 1977

WILLS, G: *Technological Forecasting,* Penguin, 1972

WILSON, B: 'The Added Value of Pay' in *Management Today,* November, 1977, pp 101–4

WILSON, N A B (ed): *Manpower Research,* English Universities Press, 1969

WINKLER, J T: 'The Ghost at the Bargaining Table: Directors and Industrial Relations', in *British Journal of Industrial Relations,* XII (2), 1974, pp 191–212 ... 234

WINKLER, J T: 'Corporatism' in *Archives Européens de Sociologie,* 17 (1), 1976, pp 100–136

WINKLER, J T: 'The Corporate Economy: Theory and Administration' in Scase, R (ed): *Class Cleavage and Control,* Allen and Unwin, 1977, pp 43–58

WITHNALL, A: 'The Aims and Methods of the Education and Training of Shop Stewards: A Case Study' in *Industrial Relations Journal*, 2 (1), 1971a, pp 35–53

WITHNALL, A: 'The Challenge from Below: An Analysis of the Role of the Shop Steward in Industrial Relations' in *Industrial Relations Journal*, 2 (3), 1971b, pp 52–60

WITHNALL, A: 'Education and Training for Shop Stewards: A Re-assessment' in *Industrial Relations Journal*, 3 (1), Spring, 1972, pp 40–50

WOLF, M G: 'Need Gratification Theory: A Theoretical Reformulation of Job Satisfaction and Job Motivation' in *Journal of Applied Psychology*, 54 (1), 1970, pp 87–94

WOOD, D; 'The Uses and Abuses of Personnel Consultants' in *Personnel Management*, October, 1983, pp 40–44

WOOD, D A: *Test Construction,* Merrill, 1960

WOODWARD, J: *Management and Technology,* HMSO, 1958 ... 19, 73, 184, 196, 202, 207, 248, 507

WOODWARD, J: *Industrial Organization: Theory and Practice,* Oxford UP, 1965 ... 202, 469

WOODWARD, J: *Industrial Organization: Behaviour and Control,* Oxford UP, 1970 ... 202, 469

WORTMAN, M S: *Creative Personnel Management,* Allwyn, 1967

WRAY, S: 'Marginal Men in Industry: The Foreman' in *American Journal of Sociology*, LIV, 1949, pp 298–301

WRIGHT, A: *Contracts of Service,* BIM Management Survey Report No. 48, 1980

WRIGHT, O R: 'Summary of Research on the Selection Interview since 1964' in *Personnel Psychology*, 22 (4), 1969, pp 391–413 ... 297

WRIGHT, V: 'Does Profit-sharing Improve Performance?' in *Personnel Management*, November, 1986, pp 46–50

WYATT, S, FRASER, J A, and STOCK, F G L: *The Comparative Effects of Variety and Uniformity in Work* Industrial Fatigue Research Board, Report No. 52, 1928

WYATT, S, FRASER, J A, and STOCK, F G L: *The Effects of Monotony in Work: A Preliminary Inquiry,* Industrial Fatigue Research Board, Report No. 56, 1929 ... 33

Y

YODER, D: *Personnel Management and Industrial Relations,* Prentice Hall, 1962 ... 433

YORKE, D: *Personnel Management and Industrial Relations,* Prentice Hall, 6th edn, 1970

YORKE, D and DOOLEY, C: 'Checking Manpower Costs' in *Personnel Management*, 2 (6), June, 1970, pp 34–5

YOUNG, A: 'Models for Planning Recruitment and Promotion of Staff' in *British Journal of Industrial Relations*, III (3), 1965, pp 301 – 10

YOUNG, A F: *Social Services in British Industry*, Routledge and Kegan Paul, 1968

YOUNG, D E and FINDLATER, J E: 'Training and Industrial Relations' in *Industrial Relations Journal*, 2 (1), 1972, pp 3 – 22 ... 308

YUKL, G A and WEXLEY, K N: *Readings in Organizational and Industrial Psychology,* Oxford U P, 1971

Z

ZERGA, J E: 'Job Analysis: A Resumé and Bibliography' in *Journal of Applied Psychology*, 27, 1943, pp 249 – 67

Index